Robert E. Lee

Robert E. Lee

A Biography by

EMORY M. THOMAS

W · W · NORTON & COMPANY

NEW YORK · LONDON

Frontispiece: **Alfred Waud sketch of Robert E. Lee riding away from the McLean House at Appomattox on April 9, 1865, following his surrender. Behind Lee is his aide Charles Marshall, who drafted General Orders #9, the General's farewell to his army.**
Library of Congress / Museum of the Confederacy.

THE TEXT OF THIS BOOK is composed in Galliard with the display set in Garamond. Composition and manufacturing by The Haddon Craftsmen. Cartography by James D. Ingram and Xueling Hu, Cartographic Services Laboratory, University of Georgia. Book design by Marjorie J. Flock.

Library of Congress Cataloging-in-Publication Data

Thomas, Emory M., 1939–
    Robert E. Lee—a biography / Emory M. Thomas.
        p.   cm.
    Includes bibliographical references and index.
    1. Lee, Robert E. (Robert Edward), 1807–1870.   2. Generals—United States—Biography.   3. Generals—Confederate States of America—Biography.   4. Confederate States of America.   Army—Biography.
    I. Title.
E467.1.L4T48   1995
973.7'3'092—dc20
[B]   95-10522

ISBN 0-393-03730-4

W. W. Norton & Company, Inc., 500 Fifth Avenue, New York, N.Y. 10110
    W. W. Norton & Company Ltd., 10 Coptic Street, London WC1A 1PU

For
Laura Leonardy Thomas
Janice Marie Thomas
Marshall Emory Thomas

And two who have gone before
Thomas Lawrence Connelly
James Robert Crumrine

Pax Nunc

Contents

10   Contents

Maps

Preface

I GREW UP IN RICHMOND, VIRGINIA. That explains a lot about this book.
Every weekday morning my family (and I then assumed everyone else's family in Richmond) sat at the breakfast table and listened to fifteen minutes of commentary on the news of the day by Douglas Southall Freeman. Only when Dr. Freeman had concluded his remarks at 8:15 A.M. did I leave the house for Ginter Park Elementary School or Chandler Junior High School. I never met Freeman; but later in life I did meet Inez Freeman, and she was kind enough to inscribe and give me a copy of *The Last Parade,* her late husband's paean to the final reunion of the Army of Northern Virginia. During our initial meeting, some of the first words my graduate mentor Frank E. Vandiver said to me were, "Douglas Freeman is god."

Soon after meeting Vandiver, I met a fellow graduate student at Rice University named Thomas Lawrence Connelly and began a dialogue that lasted almost thirty years. Connelly devoted a large measure of his considerable brilliance to an assault upon Freeman's *R. E. Lee: A Biography* and Freeman's image of Robert E. Lee as noble soul and military genius. Yet I once heard Connelly say in public, "*R. E. Lee* is the finest biography in the English language."

Freeman's four-volume study won a Pulitzer Prize in 1934 and has been "the definitive Lee" ever since. In the final chapter of the final volume Freeman wrote, "Robert Lee was one of the small company of great men in whom there is no inconsistency to be explained, no enigma to be solved. What he seemed, he was—a wholly human gentleman, the essential elements of whose positive character were two and only two, simplicity and spirituality." So Freeman concluded his work: "There is no mystery in the coffin there in front of the windows that look to the sunrise." For a long, long time Lee, essentially Freeman's "Lee," has been an American hero. This same Lee has been the patron saint of the American South.

But always a few unbelievers doubted Lee's sanctity—Allen Tate, T. Harry Williams, and more. At last in 1977 Tom Connelly published *The Marble Man: Robert E. Lee and His Image in American Society.* Connelly argued that Lee's

image was contrived and that Lee himself endured a life "replete with frustration, self doubt, and a feeling of failure. . . . He was actually a troubled man,
convinced that he had failed as a prewar career officer, parent, and moral
individual."

So the revisionist critique of Lee began in earnest and continues even now.
Allen T. Nolan in 1991 flattered Connelly with imitation (albeit pale) in *Lee
Considered: General Robert E. Lee and Civil War History*. In 1993 Ted Turner
released *Gettysburg,* the motion picture based upon Michael Shaara's Pulitzer
Prize-winning novel *The Killer Angels* (1975). In film and fiction, as in more
formal history, revision of Lee persists. The principal exception that proves the
rule is a first novel by M. A. Harper, *For the Love of Robert E. Lee,* which I
consider the finest portrait of Lee that now exists in American fiction.

The biography that follows this preface is neither classical in the Freeman
sense nor revisionist after the Connelly model. I can best describe my work as
"post-revisionist"—informed by the extensive corpus of secondary writings
about Lee, but resting for the most part upon my research in primary materials
by or about Lee. The "Lee" that emerges here is sui generis.

One constant remains, however. Lee continues to be a consequential
human being for me as he was for Freeman, Connelly, Shaara, and the rest.
Lee performed important acts; he was a person of substance. Lee was also
significant as a person; his experience offers ample lessons about the human
condition. And Lee has been influential as symbol; he is still an American icon
and the ultimate icon in the American South.

Because of the enduring potence of Lee's deeds, person, and persona, I am
well aware that the portrait of Lee in these pages may offend equally those who
revere and those who revile the man. I can plead only effort and honesty in
defense of my understanding.

I conclude that Lee was a great human being, perhaps as great as Freeman
believed, but not great in the ways that Freeman described. Afflicted with
many, though surely not all, of the frustrations and frailties that Connelly and
others discerned, Lee was great in his response to his tribulations and to his life
in general. He redeemed many moments and brought grace to otherwise grim
circumstances. Lee was a great person, not so much because of what he did
(although his accomplishments were extraordinary); he was great because of
the way he lived, because of what he was.

DURING THE LONG PERIOD DEVOTED to research and writing this biography,
I have had help from many people and institutions. My confederates, accom-
plices, and friends were in no way co-conspirators in my interpretations or
analyses.

Michael P. Musick of the Military Reference Branch of the National Archives was enormously helpful. I only regret not having enough lives to spend
several of them following Michael's many suggestions. At the Virginia Historical Society, Charles F. Bryan, Jr., Frances S. Pollard, Howson Cole, and

Nelson D. Lankford were ever helpful, and the Society was kind enough to grant me an Andrew W. Mellon Research Fellowship to aid my work. Elizabeth Lux, Guy Swanson, Robin Reed, and Cory Hudgins were gracious and generous at The Museum of the Confederacy. At the Valentine Museum nearby, Jane Webb Smith assisted my work in manuscripts and photographs the Valentine holds. C. Vaughn Stanley was twice helpful—once at Stratford Hall with manuscript materials and later in his current position as Special Collections/Reference Librarian at Washington and Lee University. Virginia Smyers presided over the rich Lee Collections at Washington and Lee during my earlier sojourn there. Judy Hynson opened to me the fine photograph collection at Stratford Hall most recently. Robert K. Krick, chief historian at the Fredericksburg and Spotsylvania National Military Park, allowed me to rummage through his files and collections, once more demonstrating the way research materials should be shared in that "best of all possible worlds." At the Special Collections Division/Academy Archives of the United States Military Academy, West Point, Alan Aimone allowed me to work "after hours" and sent me copies of materials from this fine resource. Wilbur E. Meneray at Special Collections, Howard Tilton Memorial Library, Tulane University was a delightful host and also sent me copies of manuscript items.

I must also thank those professionals at the Missouri Historical Society (especially Martha Clevenger), the Henry E. Huntington Library, the Manuscript Department, William R. Perkins Library, Duke University, the Louis Round Wilson Library, University of North Carolina at Chapel Hill, the Manuscript Division, Alderman Library, University of Virginia, and the Archives at the Virginia State Library (especially Petie Bogen-Garrett). Eleanor Lee Templeman of The Society of Lees of Virginia was thoughtful enough to write to me. And Jon Kukla of the Historic New Orleans Collection, Kemper and Leila Williams Foundation, offered a wonderful, witty letter linking Lee to Edgar Allan Poe.

Joan E. Winter of the Family Institute of Virginia contributed method and insight, because she is extremely bright and interested in people. My friend Walker Blanton at Jacksonville University connected me with Jack Milne and two Lee letters I would not have seen otherwise. Dan P. Camp of Carrollton, Georgia, allowed me to read a soldier's diary he owns.

At the University of Georgia, I have received support of various sorts. Department of History heads Lester Stephens, John Morrow, and David Roberts assisted me with those two vital commodities, travel and time. Bonnie Cary "processed" every word of this tome, throughout drafts and revisions; but for her, this book would exist only on ink-laden legal pads. My colleagues Jean D. Friedman and Edward J. Larson listened to my ideas and fed back their own. Nancy Heaton did her best to match my travel and research needs with university regulations and smiled all the while.

Several "generations" of graduate students have furnished research assistance and clever minds to fuel my work. They include Lesley Gordon-Burr, Jennifer Lund Smith, Brian S. Wills, Russell Duncan, Jonathan Bryant, Glenn

Eskew, Beth Hale-Levit, David McGee, and David Dillard at the University of Georgia and Jennifer Gross at the University of Richmond.

During the course of my research, the Reverend Don Raby Edwards asked me to offer remarks at St. Stephen's Church, Richmond, Virginia, about the spiritual dimension of Lee. From this request evolved my conclusions about Lee and God, and assisting this evolution were a number of wonderful Episcopalians. These include the Right Reverend Bennett J. Sims, the Right Reverend Peter J. Lee, the Right Reverend Francis Campbell Gray, Pat and Bob Crumrine, the Reverend B. Madison Currin, Eleanor Currin, and John F. Woolverton.

Raby Edwards contributed more than his invitation to speak at St. Stephen's Church. He and Jane Edwards are great friends, kind enough to listen to Lee stories and respond to my ideas. In this category I must also name Tammy and Bran Parker, Sid Gates, Elizabeth and Sheffield Hale, Betsy Fleet, Marshall Collins, Lori Sullivan Crumrine, Patti and Kip Campbell, Virginia Shadron, Diana Varlay, Mary Hugh and Jay Weidler, Martha and Walter Perrin, Teresa Weidler, Berkley Cone, the Reverend Churchill Gibson, the Reverend Frank Wade, Mary Wade, Steven Wade, and many more whom I shall be mortified to recall later.

I completed the text of this biography while holding the Douglas Southall Freeman Professorship of History at the University of Richmond. I shall be forever grateful to Mary Freeman McClenahan, who is Dr. Freeman's daughter and oversees the endowment that supports this visiting chair. And at the university Susan and John Gordon, Harrison Daniel, Ernie Bolt, Carol and Bob Kenzer, colleagues, students, and staff were all delightful people. Their enthusiasm for my project was most welcome.

Patricia Haile, Postmaster at Manquin, Virginia, seemed almost as excited as I was to mail the manuscript to New York. At W. W. Norton, Jim Mairs displayed the patience and keen judgment of the very fine editor he is.

My sons/chums, Emory Thomas, Jr., and the Reverend John T. Thomas, both married while I was working on this book. And Emory and Laura Leonardy Thomas adopted a small son. These events inspired some of the dedication of this work.

My first wife, Frances Taliaferro Thomas, worked for money and worthy causes, chaired a city Preservation Commission, wrote and published *A Portrait of Historic Athens and Clarke County* (University of Georgia Press, 1992), and partially renovated two houses during the period I labored with Lee. Nevertheless she read chapters in draft, offered wise counsel, and remained moderately sane. I thank her for help, friendship, and fun.

Emory M. Thomas

Foreword

ROBERT EDWARD LEE was to the manor born; he was even in the manor, Stratford Hall, born. But at age two, he left the manor and returned only as a guest. Indeed, Lee spent much of his life as a houseguest and never owned a home in which he lived.

Lee suffered all of his life from a birth defect: he was the son of Light Horse Harry Lee. Lee never knew his father, who was seldom at home, left his family when Robert was six, and died when Robert was eleven. Yet Light Horse Harry conditioned his son's life. Lee's father was a source of shame for the family, and Lee's pious mother did her best to ensure that young Robert did not emulate his father's infamy.

Robert Lee became a righteous young man. He assumed male responsibilities for the household while still an adolescent. He endured the discipline and rigor of West Point without incurring a single demerit. He embarked upon a career as an engineer officer and pursued public works within a military establishment that most often rewarded diligence ahead of brilliance.

Lee married Mary Custis, a woman ostensibly as pious as his mother, who possessed the status, wealth, and stability Lee's mother never enjoyed. But Mary Custis proved a liability. She was spoiled and helpless when she married Lee, and she became more so when confronted with the obligations of being spouse, adult, and parent. Never robust, Mary in time developed arthritis which rendered her an invalid in form as well as fact.

Further frustrations plagued Lee. He was often anxious about his seven children, none of whom seemed able to escape his shadow and lead fulfilling lives. When his father-in-law died in 1857, Lee only inherited more problems than he could solve. When he transferred out of the Engineer Corps to command cavalry in Texas, Lee discovered duty even more monotonous than constructing islands for the Engineers.

He was a brave soldier who never recoiled from combat; but he usually withdrew from personal conflict. Lee's characteristic response to conflict was to walk away from it and hope that it would go away. From Texas where he had returned to duty, Lee wrote his daughter Agnes, "It is better too I hope for all that I am here. You know I was very much in the way of everybody and my tastes and pursuits did not coincide with the rest of the household. Now I hope everybody is happier." In other circumstances, Lee's reluctance to confront superiors and subordinates had consequences that affected victory and defeat on his battlefields.

Certainly Lee achieved successes, even attained triumphs, during his life. But his triumphs always seemed tainted. He knew he could move the Mississippi River back to St. Louis and blast navigable channels through the Des Moines and Rock Island Rapids; but the powers that were withdrew necessary funds before he completed his tasks. Lee performed brilliantly in the Mexican War; on several occasions he made the difference between victory and defeat. However, he held no command in Mexico. He served as a member of Winfield Scott's staff, and in the aftermath of victory, saw his mentor recalled in disgrace, the victim of domestic political intrigue.

Lee achieved victories in command of the Army of Northern Virginia fighting for the continued existence of the Confederate States of America. But Lee's career as a Confederate included more than a year without any bona fide command—a year in which he presided over defeat in western (now West) Virginia and retreat from the coast in South Carolina, Georgia, and Florida, and tried to advise a stubborn president amid reverses that appeared unremitting. And Lee's Confederate experience also included those long months in the trenches around Petersburg in a grinding war of attrition that Lee knew he would likely lose. Lee's claim to fame as a Confederate came from conducting a war against substantial odds; but he eventually lost that war and surrendered his army.

In the wake of defeat, Lee accepted the leadership of an obscure, struggling college. He then spent himself and his prestige to make his college match his vision of higher education. But once more his achievements were incomplete, and he knew he would die before his exalted hopes came to fruition.

Through it all—the frustrations, triumphs tainted, and larger failures— Lee endured. He maintained self-control, followed rules, and repressed his desire to break free from the various shackles—social, moral, professional, and cultural—that constrained him. He once wrote, "I am fond of independence," and then explained that this fondness "prompts me to come up strictly to the requirements of law & regulations." Lee wished neither to "seek or receive indulgence from any one." The sins of his father would never afflict Robert Lee.

Lee's independence was essentially internal, however. He was a shy person who avoided crowds and people he did not know well. He had an extensive public career yet never made a speech longer than a few pro forma sentences. It is interesting to note that none of the people who should have known Lee best—his wife, children, or staff—ever felt that they understood him. He was an enigma. Lee lived inside himself, under control.

Lee also believed that self-control separated human beings from beasts and established a hierarchy among races and classes of people. Restraint was a badge of superiority; consequently Lee aspired to self-mastery. Because he accepted, even venerated, the various rules, regulations, and conventions that bound him, though he knew or sensed his need to be free, Lee's life was tragic.

He believed that "the great duty of life" was "the promotion of the happiness & welfare of our fellow men." Conversely, he believed that evil sprang from selfishness. So Lee spent much of his life in pursuit of his duty to other people in the attempt to deny himself. And in these ethical endeavors did Lee most reveal himself: he found freedom principally in the course of doing his duty.

He displayed his creative spirit as an engineer in his capacity to redirect the Mississippi. In Mexico he discovered ways to overcome supposedly impossible obstacles and thus transform adversity into advantage for the American invaders. During the Confederate War, Lee defined audacity and won victories in apparently impossible circumstances. And as president of Washington College, he abolished rules and reformed ancient curricula in his quest for practical enlightenment. Perhaps because his personal life was so toilsome, Lee seemed to make his work his play. He acted out a paradox: duty set him free.

Nor was Lee's private repression as absolute as it appeared. He appeared to accept evangelical Christianity and seemed obsessed with sin and judgment. Yet when an African American dared to receive communion at St. Paul's Church, Richmond, during Reconstruction, Lee it was who joined the black man at the communion rail and so redeemed the moment. Lee was faithful and dutiful to his wife throughout his married life. But he maintained a lively, witty, and sometimes sensuous correspondence with a series of clever young women to the end of his life. Lee was lavish in the sermons and strictures he heaped upon his children. Yet he believed that children "should be governed by *love,* not *fear. . . ,* " and he often expressed his love for his children in deeds, even as he wrote or spoke moralizing platitudes.

One way or another Lee found outlets for his creative energies and mitigation for his many frustrations. In so doing he made peace with himself and his acute degree of the universal human tension between freedom and control. Some of Lee's compensations—his risqué wit and clever correspondence with young women who may or may not have understood what they read, for example—seem pitiful now. But *then* Lee seemed satisfied, and most of the time he acted out the paternal counsel he once offered his oldest son, Custis, then at West Point. "Shake off those gloomy feelings," Lee wrote. "Drive them away. . . . All is bright if you will think it so. All is happy if you will make it so. . . . Live in the world you inhabit. Look upon things as they are. Take them as you find them. Make the best of them. Turn them to your advantage."

Late in life Lee wrote what may have been the most revealing phrase he ever used about himself. He confessed that he was "always wanting [lacking] something." Frustrated by his heritage, marriage, family, and profession; doomed to command smaller battalions when God, as usual, favored larger battalions; and compelled to struggle through his declining years amid the corporate shame and ruin that flowed from defeat, Lee surely lacked many things. In such circumstances he might have withdrawn from life, or exploded in the faces of those who made incessant demands of him, or waxed sour on life in general. He did none of the above. Lee learned to accept reality flawed and to make the best of whatever was. He resisted the temptation to take himself seriously and developed a comic vision of life—the opposite of tragic vision—alive to the absurdities of the human condition.

Lee, the enigma, seldom if ever revealed himself while he lived. To understand him, it is necessary to look behind his words and see, for example, the true nature of the lighthouse keeper Lee encountered during his surveying mission in 1835. It is also important to peer beyond Lee's words and recall what he did as well as what he said. Sometimes the existential Lee contradicted the verbal Lee.

There is a third caveat to understanding Lee. In addition to looking behind and beyond his words, it is well to remember that Lee was once possessed of flesh and blood. This is important because so many have made so much of Lee during the years since he lived that legend, image, and myth have supplanted reality. Lee has become a hero essentially smaller than life.

People usually venerate as a hero someone who exemplifies (or who they believe exemplifies) virtues which they admire or to which they aspire. Heroism thus reveals more about the society that admires than about the hero. Lee has been several sorts of American hero, and within the American South he has attained the status of demigod. Over time Lee has been a Christ figure, a symbol of national reconciliation, an exalted expression of bourgeois values, and much, much more. In life Lee was both more and less than his legend.

The time has come—indeed, the time is long overdue—to review and rethink Lee alive. History needs Robert E. Lee whole.

Robert E. Lee

Prologue: Advent

THE DAY OF THE WEDDING was sultry and hot as only Tidewater Virginia can be sultry and hot in the middle of June. Twenty-four years later and 850 miles removed, the groom still recalled the tropical heat of the day and place.[1]

The groom was Henry Lee, III, called "Light Horse Harry" to honor his exploits as a cavalry commander during the American Revolutionary War. A graduate of Princeton, once a member of the Virginia House of Delegates, then Virginia delegate to the Continental Congress, Lee was Governor of Virginia on his wedding day, June 18, 1793.[2]

The bride was Ann Hill Carter, called Nancy by her father Charles Carter, who loved her dearly, though she had twenty living siblings. She was twenty years old and thoroughly smitten with Harry Lee.

The wedding took place at Shirley, a plantation since the seventeenth century and the home of Carters since the 1720s. The Great House was (and still is) on the north bank of the James River, about 25 miles southeast of Richmond. Several thousand of the 25,000 acres Charles Carter owned surrounded the Great House at Shirley, and hundreds of African American slaves toiled there to produce the wealth which kept the Carters comfortable and prominent. Atop the roof of the Great House was (and still is) a finial carved in the shape of a pineapple, traditional symbol of welcome. For the Carters and their guests, Shirley was a happy and privileged place. Ann Carter was a young woman accustomed to fine things and many friends in her extensive and extended family.

In the Great Hall of the Great House, relatives and friends gathered with the principals and an Episcopalian cleric for the marriage ceremony in the evening. The heat of the day persisted, however, and the fashionable clothing appropriate to the occasion doubtless rendered the event an ordeal for many in attendance.[3]

But sweat was sweet that night at Shirley. A dashing governor married an accomplished Carter—a union of fame and fortune. On the surface and at the time, the prospects of Ann Carter and Harry Lee appeared propitious indeed.

The *Virginia Gazette* (published in Richmond) proclaimed: "On Tuesday evening . . . was married at Shirley, Governor Lee, to the amiable and accomplished Miss Ann Carter, daughter of Charles Carter. Esq.—An event which
promises the most auspicious fortune to the wedded pair, and which must give
the highest satisfaction to their numerous and respectable relatives."[4]

Ill omens there were, however, and most of them concerned Harry Lee.
The governor was thirty-seven, seventeen years older than his bride. Portraits
of Lee during his adult life portray him steadily stouter, and by 1793 he was
beginning to appear somehow delicate and dissolute at once. This was Lee's
second wedding; his first wife, "the divine Matilda," had died in 1790. At the
Governor's Mansion at Richmond were Lee's three children from his first
marriage.

As a widower Lee had been anxious to remarry and wrote about the de-
lights of "every sweet nymph." Lee also wanted further fame. He had resigned
from the Continental Army in 1782, before the Revolutionary War ended, for
reasons still obscure, but likely related to envy of some of his brother officers
and slights real or imagined from his superiors. Lee hoped in 1792 his old
commander and idol George Washington would give him charge of the new
United States Army. When Washington passed over him, Lee seriously sought
a command in the army of Revolutionary France. Friends dissuaded him,
however, and Washington pointed out the obvious: how could Lee enlist in
the cause of France while he was Governor of Virginia? In May of 1793 Lee
wrote Alexander Hamilton, "I mean now to become a farmer and get a wife as
soon as possible."

The woman Lee most wanted to "get" for his wife was not Ann Carter but
her cousin and one of her best friends, Maria Farley. But Maria Farley rejected
Lee's attentions and his proposal of marriage. Ann Carter reportedly told her
friend, "O stop, stop Maria—you do not know what you are throwing away."

On the rebound Lee then focused his attention upon Ann Carter. She
responded, and very soon Governor Lee was asking Charles Carter for his
daughter's hand in marriage.[5]

Carter was less than pleased; most probably he was appalled. He no doubt
knew something of Lee's avid courtship of Maria Farley and likely believed his
daughter's professed love for Lee was in the nature of passing fancy. Charles
Carter knew with greater confidence Harry Lee's reputation for imprudence
and impropriety in his personal affairs.

Like many of his contemporaries, Lee speculated in land; unlike most of
his contemporaries, Lee consistently lost money in his speculations. Too often
he responded to failed financial expectations with still greater speculation.
Moreover, Lee developed a very casual attitude about his debts; he kept forgetting them, or he paid them with paper or promises that proved worthless.
Both Lee's father and his hero and father figure George Washington were
poorer but wiser for trusting Light Horse Harry. When Washington as President considered Lee for command of the United States Army, he noted that
he had military ability but "lacks economy."

Lee's father Henry Lee, II, died in 1787, but Harry inherited none of his personal property and only some of his lesser lands. Although Harry was Henry's oldest son, the father made his second son, Charles, executor of his estate. Harry Lee did get control of his first wife, Matilda's, magnificent plantation, Stratford; he sold off parcels of the place at an alarming rate to finance his speculative ventures and cover his debts. Accordingly Matilda, while on her deathbed, arranged to leave Stratford in trust to her children and bequeath to her husband only the right to live on the estate. However, Lee used his influence with the Stratford trustees (his brother and brother-in-law) to enable him to sell still more acres of Matilda's plantation.

The best story circulating about Lee's scruples involved his visit to a neighbor with a request to borrow a horse. The neighbor not only lent Lee a horse; he also sent a servant with him on a second horse, so that Lee would not have to go to the trouble of returning the borrowed horse himself. After several weeks the slave returned on foot and in disheveled condition. He told the neighbor that Lee had sold both horses. "Why didn't you come home?" the neighbor asked. " 'Cause General Lee sold me, too." The story may or may not be true. That people told it reveals what Lee's neighbors thought of his integrity.[6]

Charles Carter cared a great deal about his daughter and about the reputation of his family. Carters were righteous folk, staunch Protestant Episcopalians, a clan known for honesty and respectability. Carters were also wealthy; Charles Carter was a grandson of Robert "King" Carter, who once owned 300,000 acres and 1,000 slaves. And Carters had never married Lees, a circumstance dating to a feud between "King" Carter and Harry Lee's great-uncle Thomas Lee.

Gossip, stories probably apocryphal, vague feelings about family traits, and ancient feuds offered Charles Carter no firm grounds for objection to the marriage his daughter so ardently desired. So Carter seized upon Harry Lee's flirtation with France; he would not permit his daughter to marry a man about to launch a second military career in Europe. Lee, however, protested that he no longer had any intention of fighting for France. Then Carter had little choice but to embrace Lee as his son-in-law and bless the marriage.[7]

Wedding festivities at Shirley probably lasted several days after the ceremony itself. Eventually, though, Ann Lee and the Governor traveled to Richmond to begin their life together.

Waiting for the newlyweds were Harry Lee's three children: Philip, who was nine; Lucy Grymes, eight; and Henry, six. Philip soon died—no one now knows when or how. Lucy likely resented her stepmother; she never mentioned her in correspondence and would later act out rebellion against her family and childhood. Henry (IV) was not a problem . . . yet. Virginia's Governor's Mansion in 1793 was much a misnomer. It was an unpainted frame house with two stories and four rooms furnished with fairly plain furniture. In such circumstances and surroundings, "Nancy" Carter became Ann Lee.[8]

A friend and admirer later estimated that the bride was happy for all of two weeks. She "became his [Lee's] delighted wife, but to find in the short space of a fortnight that her affections were trampled on by a heartless and depraved profligate. I am right as to time. One fortnight was her dream of happiness from which she awoke to a life of misery."[9]

This statement is hyperbole, but only in degree. Ann Lee did not have an easy time as the wife of Light Horse Harry. Lee's fortunes seemed to begin a rapid decline about the time of his second marriage. The timing was mere coincidence. Ann Lee did not abet her husband's downfall; she tried as best she could to abort the process.

When he learned that Lee had given up his notion of fighting for France and intended marriage a second time instead, President Washington wrote to Lee, "We are told that you have exchanged the rugged and dangerous field of Mars for the soft and pleasurable bed of Venus. . . ." and thereby added his blessing to the wedding. But in September 1794, Governor Lee took advantage of his constitutional prerogative as commander in chief of the Virginia Militia and rode off in search of a "rugged and dangerous field of Mars." The occasion was the "Whiskey Rebellion" in western Pennsylvania. Lee led an expedition of 15,000 militia troops to root out the rebels and in so doing assert the will and strength of the national government to enforce its laws. As it happened, Lee made a long march and found no rebels; he encountered some rugged fields, but none especially dangerous. He did garner the rank and title of general, and he acted out the policy of Washington's administration regarding challenges to the power of the Federal government.

When Lee returned from his extended mission in Pennsylvania, he discovered that many Virginians resented his eagerness to do the bidding of the administration and abandon his duties as governor. In his absence Lee's constituents had declared the office of governor vacant and elected another in his stead.[10]

Ann and the young Henry were ill when Harry left home, and so they retreated to Shirley. Ann was pregnant and remained at Shirley until the baby came—a son, born April 2, 1795, named Algernon Sidney Lee after the English Protestant rebel/martyr from the seventeenth century. Eventually (1795–96), Ann, Harry, Henry, Lucy Grymes, and Algernon Sidney Lee moved to Stratford. There Algernon Sidney died on August 9, 1796.[11]

Although completed in the same year—1738—Shirley and Stratford were (and are) very different houses. Shirley is more open to the out of doors: two-story porches front and rear, many windows (including those set in the mansard roof on the third floor), front and rear doors carefully aligned to catch breezes and frame the rising and setting sun at the spring and fall equinoxes, all echo the welcome-symbol pineapple finial at the center of the roof. Shirley is more graceful, too, exemplified by the three-story carved walnut stairway which rises through the center of the house with no visible supports. Shirley had been home for Ann Lee. And to the degree that buildings possess a transcendent capacity to reflect human traits and values, Shirley communicated hospitality, romance, and fun.[12]

Stratford "says" some of the same things that Shirley does. Windows containing thirty-two panes each surround the formal rooms and the huge Great Hall on the second floor. The exterior stairs front and rear are wider at the bottom than the top and thus tend to draw the visitor into the house. Inside, rooms are bright and airy, and set into the twin clusters of four chimneys each are platforms which offer spectacular views of the surrounding landscape and the Potomac River. But the house is a massive, brick block "H" whose exterior appears sturdy in the extreme, practical for certain, yet forbidding and more like a fortress than a home. In an aesthetic sense, Harry Lee's home was indeed his castle as well. The exterior doors beyond those beckoning stairs appear small in the great scale of the house and consequently seem designed to exclude more people than they admit. Ironically, both a granddaughter and a cousin/brother-in-law of Harry Lee met their deaths in falls from the steps leading to the Great Hall. Harry Lee's first wife Matilda first saw him returning from the Revolutionary War to seek his fortune and her hand from one of those observation platforms among the chimneys. She was impressed by her suntanned swain and curious about Lee's white orderly, George Weldon, who insisted upon kissing the colonel's hand.[13]

Ann Lee, however, did not spend much time in the formal rooms or Great Hall upstairs. Nor did she often sit on the observation platforms on the roof. Her husband's debts forced him to sell or dismiss the servants necessary to maintain Stratford in style or comfort. The Lees could not afford to entertain, and eventually Ann and the children had to restrict themselves to a few rooms on the ground floor because they lacked the resources to heat or furnish the rest.

Harry Lee's orderly remained at Stratford, and his son Henry Weldon was supposed to manage the plantation, despite the fact that Henry could neither read nor write. Tenants actually did most of the farming at Stratford during Harry Lee's tenure there, paying their rent in produce and crops. However, the number of acres and tenants shrank constantly. In 1775, the plantation included 6,595 acres; by the time of Matilda's death, it included about 4,000 acres. Ten years later, Stratford contained 2,000 acres.

As his material fortunes declined, Lee continued to display to the world a bold facade. He continued to plunge into reckless speculations and continued to lose his gambles. He was away from home a lot. Stratford was in Westmoreland County on the Virginia "Northern Neck," the peninsula between the Potomac and Rappahannock Rivers. The region had been the home of important people and great families; however, it was isolated, very rural, and except by water, not really "on the way" to anywhere. Ann and the children were often alone. She once phrased her plight that at Stratford she was "the world forgetting, by the world forgot."[14]

In 1799 Lee ran for election to Congress, and owing largely to the active support of former President Washington, who rode to Montross (the seat of Westmoreland County) to cast his vote, Lee won. So Ann, Lucy Grymes, Henry, and Ann's second son Charles Carter, born November 8, 1798, accompanied Lee to Philadelphia, which was then the seat of the national government. There Lee made his eloquent pronouncement in eulogy for his commander and benefactor George Washington—"first in war, first in peace, and first in the hearts of his countrymen." Otherwise, what became Harry Lee's last public service was essentially undistinguished.[15]

In spite of some lapses when desire for fame or personal gain overcame his principles, Harry Lee was, heart and soul, a Federalist. He believed in government by the rich, the well-born, and the able, because he considered himself one of that number. He supported an energetic national government, capable of directing the new nation's fledgling economy. He favored a broad interpretation of the Constitution, which made the Federal government strong at the expense of the member states. And he favored England over France, should the Old World draw the New World into its ancient quarrels.[16]

When he was much a "lame duck" member of Congress in 1801, Lee voted for Aaron Burr for President. The rival Republicans had nominated Thomas Jefferson for President and Burr for Vice President in 1800. However, the way the Constitution prescribed for the electoral college to function at that time (lacking the Twelfth Amendment, which requires electors to vote for President and Vice President separately) produced a tie between Jefferson and Burr. Since neither candidate had a majority, the House of Representatives had to choose the President. By the time House members voted, founding Federalist Alexander Hamilton was instructing fellow Federalists to vote for Jefferson. Lee was alone among Virginia representatives to defy the party scion and reject a fellow Virginian in favor of Burr. Some speculated that Lee hoped to secure patronage favors from Burr; others suggested that Lee was merely venting his otherwise-minded nature and his hatred of Jefferson.[17]

Meanwhile, at Stratford Ann Lee gave birth to a daughter, Ann Kinloch, on June 19, 1800. And Harry Lee continued to wheel, deal, and sell his family's land. In 1801, Lee paid taxes on about 2,000 acres; one year later, he paid taxes on only 236 acres. By 1802 Ann was again pregnant; but she and the children accompanied Harry on an extended trip to Philadelphia and New York. She planned to return to Stratford by the time the baby came. However, Harry tarried, and Ann went into labor in Camden, New Jersey. She had to depend upon the hospitality of strangers, in this case a family named Smith in Camden. When Ann's baby boy arrived on September 2, 1802, she named him Sidney Smith, calling him Smith in gratitude to her hosts.[18]

Finally back at Stratford with her family, Ann's health failed. She referred in a letter written in 1803 to "dropsy," which was the common term for edema, swelling caused by a disorder of the kidneys or heart. However imprecise this diagnosis, it was the best Ann Lee could do. She did write about her infirmity: "I am much of an invalid" (May 3, 1804); "being much indisposed" (January 1805); and "being so often an invalid" (October 1, 1805).[19]

Lucy Grymes Lee fled the family in the summer of 1803; she married her stepmother's younger brother, Bernard Moore Carter, thus becoming her own aunt. She referred to her new husband as "such a fool!" and threatened to burn his plantation house if forced to live there. Eventually Lucy Carter moved to Philadelphia and lived alone.[20]

Also in 1803 Ann's father Charles Carter revised his will in order to leave his daughter a trust fund which her husband could not invade. Carter was the third relative (after Harry's father and first wife) to make specific provisions in a will to protect an estate from Light Horse Harry Lee.

Still Harry hoped for more prosperous times, while he installed a chain across the doorway at Stratford to forestall his creditors. In the spring of 1806 Ann realized she was once more pregnant. During the summer she visited Shirley, but her homecoming was devastating; she arrived shortly after her father died. The family mourned Charles Carter's death. Then it became time for Ann to return to Stratford. She had no carriage, however, and still had none after she all but begged Harry to send some conveyance for her. At last someone secured an open carriage, and Ann returned home in late November or December to Stratford with her children. By this time Carter was eight, Ann six, and Smith four. The rigorous trip in frigid weather made their mother ill, and she feared for herself and her unborn child.

On January 11, 1807, Ann wrote her friend Elizabeth, who was married to one of Harry's brothers and who was also pregnant. "You have my best wishes for your success my dear," Ann said, "and *truest assurances,* that I do not envy your *prospects,* nor wish to *share in them.* "[21]

Eight days after she confided such candor, Ann Lee again underwent childbirth. Still sick with a terrible cold in her chest, Ann surely huddled near a fireplace while the raw wind blew outside; the Northern Neck was brutally cold as only the Northern Neck can be in mid-January. Harry may or may not have been with her. The baby born on January 19, 1807, was a boy, and Ann named him after two of her favorite brothers—Robert Edward Lee.

1

"Robert Was Always Good"

ROBERT EDWARD LEE was the less-than-longed-for fifth child of a mother in uncertain health and reduced financial straits struggling essentially alone to maintain the facade of family in a home that was never hers. The infant's father was a war hero in a war that had been over for a quarter century. He was desperately in debt, in flight from his creditors, and apparently oblivious to the realities of his fading fame and absent integrity. Robert had an inauspicious advent, and during his early childhood his family circumstances got worse.

Harry Lee's life became still less stable. During the spring of 1807 his sister-in-law Mildred Carter died and became the fourth relative to make special provisions in a will to exclude him from undue access to the estate. She left almost all of her property to "my dear sister [Ann] Lee during her life free from the control of her husband General Lee."[1]

In June, the British warship *Leopard* fired upon the U.S. ship *Chesapeake*, inflicting damage and casualties and seizing four alleged British deserters from the American crew. The incident provoked American ill-will toward Great Britain and prompted President Thomas Jefferson to confront the crisis with economic sanctions (an embargo). Lee leaped upon the excuse to vent frenzy upon Jefferson and the Republican Party. In the autumn of 1808 Lee wrote a vicious diatribe against the President, *A Cursory Sketch of the Motives and proceedings of the Party Which Sways the Affairs of the Union* . . . Published in 1809, Lee's pamphlet brayed: "Bonaparte rules by the sabre and by the bayonet; the miserable French are his slaves. Jefferson rules by exiling from the public councils of the state and nation truth, honour and intelligence. . . . We are reaching with quick steps the French condition. . . ."[2]

When young Robert was two years old, his father's creditors finally brought "Light Horse" to bay. On April 24, 1809, Harry Lee took up residence in the Westmoreland County Jail in Montross, Virginia, imprisoned for his debts. Confined at night to a twelve- by fifteen-foot cell, Lee was able to go about the courthouse green during the day. In this same courthouse, Lee had been a "Gentleman Justice," and to this place had ridden former President

Calmly he looked on either life and here
Saw nothing to regret, and there to fear.

These are brave words, and Harry likely did believe them. For all his obvious flaws, he was certainly no coward.

Harry had many maxims and much advice for his son Carter, too. It all seems sound, if only the counsel had come from someone other than Harry Lee. Because it did come from Harry Lee, the advice sounds at least ironic; at most like that of Polonius in *Hamlet*—do as I say, not as I do or have done. "Avoid debt," Harry preached, "the sink of mental power and the subversion of independence, which draws into debasement every virtue, in appearance certainly, if not in reality." To Carter, Harry Lee held up Frederick the Great, who "early habituated himself to keep his wants within his means, and this habit became confirmed as he grew up, and adhered to him till his death." Still lacking "means" himself, Harry the father wrote his son, "If any debts hang on you, tell me the amount, and I will enable you to deliver yourself from a state abhorrent to a noble mind and sure to degrade the most chosen." Surely Harry wrote from experience; but just as surely he never made good his good intentions to send his son money.[12]

Robert knew nothing of his father's letters to his older brother until much later in his life. He was too young at the beginning of Harry Lee's self-imposed exile to remember much about his father. And Harry did not know much about Robert, except that he had once been a happy, good boy. To Carter, the father wrote, "Robert was always good, and will be confirmed in his happy turn of mind by his everwatchful and affectionate mother. Does he strengthen his native tendency?" This was Light Horse Harry Lee's sole mention of Robert and the earliest written reference to the boy which now survives—"always good . . . happy turn of mind."[13]

Speculation and some fragments of family lore are only clues to Robert's childhood. He learned the Episcopal catechism before he learned to read, and he said it to the Rector of Christ Church, Alexandria, future Bishop of Virginia. The catechism and other early lessons Robert learned from his mother. Ann Lee taught piety; her life was a lesson in loyalty. Robert left his mother to attend schools at Eastern View in Fauquier County where Carter boys studied, at Shirley, perhaps, and in Alexandria.

The house on Oronoco Street was certainly home for a time. But Ann Lee moved about. In the spring of 1816, she wrote Carter, "I expect to live in Mr. Charles Lee's [Harry's brother] house and only wait Mrs. Alexander's removal from it, to take possession: which she says will be next week." That summer she instructed Carter to write to her at Fauquier Court House.[14]

Robert grew accustomed to going about and getting along with members of his extended family. He grew accustomed also to being a houseguest and learned early to live without the stability of a permanent home. Paradoxically, however, Robert was a reserved, shy young man, and he never relished crowds

George Washington in 1799 to cast his vote and throw his decisive weight for Lee's election to Congress. Now "Light Horse" Harry was an object of derision at the scene of his past triumphs. Not only was Harry a debtor in Westmoreland County; he served time in the Spotsylvania County Jail as well.[3]

Harry did not despair. He made use of his enforced leisure to write his war memoirs, which he planned to publish and sell in order to recover his solvency. And while he labored away on his memoirs, Lee did not hesitate to write to President James Madison from "Spots. C. House" to ask for a federal judgeship for his youngest brother Edmund Jennings Lee. Whatever is the Protestant Christian equivalent of *chutzpah,* Harry Lee possessed it in abundance.[4]

While her husband was in jail, Ann Lee seemed to gather strength and will. When her widower brother-in-law Carter Berkeley offered her and her children refuge with him and his children at his plantation, Ann declined with genuine thanks. "Mr. Lee in all his letters, requests I will remain here till his arrival— that the negroes may also remain, and that I should not take any step towards fixing myself elsewhere. . . ," she wrote, and added, "I gave him a positive promise . . . that I would do so, reserving to myself the right of choosing my place of residence afterwards. . . ." She concluded, "I feel an unconquerable inclination to fix myself permanently, be it in ever so humble a manner, and must indulge myself, in at least making the attempt."[5]

Not only was Ann aware that continuing to live at Stratford was impractical; she also knew that by the terms of Matilda Lee's will, Matilda's son Henry, now over twenty-one years old, owned what was left of the place. So, while adhering to her promise to stay at Stratford during Harry's incarceration, Ann cast about for a new home for herself and her children.

Harry did not complete his military memoirs in prison. He finally confessed his absolute insolvency, and what then served as a bankruptcy law offered him release from jail. Set free on March 20, 1810, Harry returned to Stratford with his manuscript, which he had had to pledge to his brother Richard to satisfy some of his debt. While Harry continued to write, Ann continued her quest for some permanent residence. With or without Harry Lee's consultation, she decided to move to Alexandria, a town of 7,500 inhabitants across the Potomac River from Washington, D.C., where her children would benefit from schools and their extended family of several Lee relatives who lived there.

Some time during the summer of 1810, Ann, Harry, and their four children left Stratford and moved into a small house at 611 Cameron Street in Alexandria. Henry (IV) remained behind, master of what remained of his mother's plantation. The place did not prosper, but Henry did win election to represent Westmoreland County in the Virginia General Assembly.[6]

Family legend has little three-year-old Robert returning one last time to his mother's room where he was born and spent much time (at the southeast corner of the ground floor) to bid goodbye to the two angels represented in iron at the back of the fireplace.[7]

One of the last things Harry Lee did before leaving Stratford (or one of the first things he did after settling in Alexandria) was to conceive with Ann their sixth child. Catherine Mildred (called Mildred) arrived February 27, 1811.

By this time the family (Ann, Harry, Carter, Ann, Smith, Robert, and Mildred) had moved again, to the townhouse owned by William Fitzhugh, a distant relative, at 607 Oronoco Street. The move of only a few blocks placed the Lees still very much in the center of town and within what was almost a compound of homes owned by Lee family members.[8]

Harry Lee filled much of his time in Alexandria writing his memoirs and playing the role of military hero. He may have become something of a bore to his friends and acquaintances. Finally, in the fall of 1811, Lee completed his work, and in 1812 *Memoirs of the War in the Southern Department of the United States* appeared in print. The book did offer a more or less accurate narrative of the Revolutionary War in the South along with some anti-Jefferson cant. It did not sell well, however.[9]

Americans had a contemporary war with England to confront that year. Fresh from his chronicle of the last war with England, Harry Lee was ambivalent about the War of 1812. Lee the good Federalist deplored Anglo-American enmity; Lee the good patriot cared deeply for his country, no matter who the enemy was or which party was attempting to prosecute the conflict.

On June 18, 1812, President James Madison received from Congress a declaration of war upon Great Britain. On July 28, Light Horse Harry Lee became an ironic casualty of that war.

Lee went to Baltimore for reasons still obscure and while there he contacted a friend, Alexander C. Hanson, who edited a fiercely partisan Federalist newspaper, the Baltimore *Federal Republican.* Hanson had written and published some bitter rhetoric in condemnation of the war and the Madison administration. The editor's editorials provoked a patriotic fury among some of his fellow Baltimoreans, who destroyed Hanson's printing press and wrecked his office. Hanson then adjourned to Georgetown, printed another edition of the *Federal Republican,* brought his paper back to Baltimore, and circulated more anti-war, anti-Republican prose. This time the enraged patriots assembled before Hanson's home/office with firearms on the night of July 27.

Inside the house were Hanson, twenty-one of his friends, and Light Horse Harry Lee. The old revolutionary took command. He barricaded the house and issued weapons and orders to his garrison.

Outside Hanson's house the crowd became a mob. Exchanges of gunfire left one member of the mob dead and another wounded; Hanson and his friends were still unscathed.

Then Maryland Militia troops appeared in the street and negotiations began. The solution which seemed best at the time was to place Hanson and his comrades in protective custody. So Harry Lee once more moved into a jail—this time in defense of his friend, his politics, and civil liberties.

On July 28, members of the anti-Hanson mob whipped themselves and

others into another frenzy. Meanwhile the Maryland militiamen dispersed, and only the jailer stood between the mob and its intended victims. At dark the mob broke into the building. Lee ordered his cohorts to kill each other and so spare themselves death at the hands of the mob. But the men demurred and chose to take their chances at surviving.

The mob made short work of breaking into the large cell. The victims fought for their lives, and indeed about half of the Hanson band were able to escape serious injury. The "patriots" killed one man outright and beat eleven others severely. Harry Lee was one of eight men believed dead and piled on top of each other outside the jail. And when the beatings stopped, mutilations began.

Finally some local physicians came to the scene and secured permission to carry off the dead. At first they were convinced that Lee would soon die and reported his death as fact. Miraculously Lee endured. Eleven days later, he could speak. And late in the summer Lee was able to leave Baltimore and return to his family in Alexandria. He was mangled, however, and he never completely recovered.[10]

For some time Lee had sought to leave the country for the sake of his health, physical and fiscal. Now he intensified his efforts, and early in the summer of 1813 he managed to secure passage to the Barbados. One of his political enemies, Secretary of State James Monroe, made it possible for Light Horse Harry to emigrate to the empire of Lee's former and present enemies.

Robert was six years old when his father boarded a ship at Alexandria and sailed away down the Potomac. Harry Lee maintained the fiction that this was a temporary separation from his family; when his health and "prospects" improved he would return from his sojourn south, gather his family, and live in a style he had only pretended in the past. When he thought about it, Robert probably believed some of his father's pipe dream, which became part of the Lee family lore.[11]

Hindsight confirms that Lee never returned. He wandered from island to island seeking health and some way to wealth. He wrote letters to his wife; but his letters to Carter, oldest son of his second family, are his most revealing. In them he displayed the breadth of his mind and learning; he discoursed on Socrates, John Locke, Francis Bacon, Tacitus, Xenophon, Caesar, Polybius, Homer, Sophocles, Virgil, Lucretius, Marcus Aurelius, Shakespeare, Isaac Newton, Hannibal, Roger Bacon, John Milton, and many more thinkers, writers, and poets from ancient times to his own. Only a man of significant learning could have paraded so many sages before his son.

Harry Lee's favorite poet was Alexander Pope. In his journal he copied some lines from Pope which he thought described his wife:

> So unaffected, so composed a mind,
> So firm, yet soft, so strong, yet so refined,
> Heaven as its purest gold, by tortures toy'd.

Himself Lee saw in a couplet again from Pope:

or strangers very much. His shyness led some people to think him aloof, however "correct" his behavior. Still others would later confuse Robert's reserve with a sense of presence, a dignity of destiny. With warm friends and close family, he was warm and close; yet the houseguest syndrome persisted in Robert and sent enigmatic signals to those who did not know him well.[15]

When Robert was eight years old, in 1815, his oldest full brother Carter left the fatherless family to attend Harvard College. Carter was Ann and Harry Lee's first son, after all, and consequently the chief repository of the family's advantages and hopes.

The principal source of income for Ann Lee and her children was the trust fund established by her father Charles Carter in his will. Most of this money was in the form of stock in the Bank of Virginia, which yielded $1,210 annually, and this sum represented over half of Ann's income. In 1816, however, the Bank of Virginia joined generally hard economic times and reduced its dividend drastically.

Ann had to write Carter at Harvard and ask him to reduce his expenses as much as possible. She informed him that she could not afford for him to come home for the summer vacation in 1816 and also admitted that she had had to "trespass" upon Carter's college fund in order to survive.

"Previous to the war [1812]," she explained, "the dividend was $1,440 annually; since that period, $1,210—It is now $605." Ann insisted, "I am lessening my expense in every way—have sent off two of the servants, Sebrey and William, and when I leave home, shall hire out Louis—I fear the next sacrifice must be the horses. . . ."

The mother made a game of deciding what would compose dinner. As she wrote to Carter,

We have very seldom more than one dish on the table, of meat, to the great discomfort of my young Ladies and Gentlemen, whom you know have various tastes—It requires a length of time every night, to determine what shall be brought next morning from market—As there is to be but one dish, all cannot be pleased: Ann [now sixteen] prefers fowls, but they are so high, that they are sparingly dealt in; and if brought to table, scarcely, a back, falls to Smith [now almost fourteen] and Robert's [now nine] share, so that they rather not be tantalized with the sight of them; and generally urge the purchase of veal; while Mildred [now five] is as solicitous, that whortleberries or cherries should compose our dinner.

These were straitened circumstances, but hardly dire straits; the Lees were not prosperous, but neither were they hungry.[16]

However much Ann Lee and her four remaining children visited within the Lee and Carter families, they seldom seem to have returned to Stratford to visit Ann's stepson and the children's half brother, Henry Lee, IV. Henry served in the War of 1812 as a staff officer with the rank of major and returned to his estate to find it dilapidated indeed. In 1817, though, Henry's prospects improved when he married very well. His bride was Ann McCarty, who was an orphan and quite wealthy. This latest Ann Lee brought considerable charm and ample cash to Stratford, and for a time these Lees lived again in style. Ann McCarty Lee also brought her younger sister Elizabeth ("Betsy") McCarty to live at Stratford, and the Westmoreland County Court made Henry Lee Betsy's guardian.

In 1818 Ann and Henry rejoiced in the birth of a daughter, and at least this branch of the fragmented Lee family seemed secure once more. But Henry Lee, IV, continued out of touch with his namesake in the West Indies and his stepmother and half siblings in Virginia. If surviving letters are any index, Harry Lee seems to have focused his attention upon Carter. And none of Henry's newfound wealth found its way to Alexandria to help his father's second family.[17]

Meanwhile Harry Lee's health remained precarious, and during the late winter of 1818 he decided to return home to die. He spoke of recovering his health and making another new start at age sixty-two; but he probably did not believe this bravado. Lee blamed his pain upon the Baltimore mob. He suffered in his lower abdomen—bladder, intestines—maybe a tumor, maybe some connection with the kicks and beating he had endured in 1812.

Lee left Nassau in early March 1818. However, his pain became so intense that he had to go ashore at Cumberland Island, Georgia, and seek refuge at Dungeness, the home of his Revolutionary comrade Nathanael Greene. Greene was dead; but his daughter Louisa and her husband James Shaw took Lee into their home and did what they could to make him comfortable. They summoned a surgeon, William Barnwell, from the U.S. Navy ship *John Adams* which was at nearby St. Marys. Barnwell, however, could offer little help and less hope for Lee.

Harry Lee spent the last two weeks of his life at Dungeness, growing each day more feeble. His pain became so intense that he bellowed and abused those who tried to care for him. On March 24 he finally became silent, and at about six o'clock on the evening of March 25, 1818, Light Horse Harry Lee died.[18]

The Shaws continued their hospitality and buried Lee in the family cemetery at Dungeness. Officers and men from the *John Adams* rendered military honors at the burial on March 26, and letters informed family members in Virginia.[19]

Robert was barely eleven years old when he learned that his father had died. He saw his father's grave for the first time in 1862, forty-four years later. Sigmund Freud once said that the most important day in a man's life is the day his father dies. This may be true; but in the life of Robert Lee, the death of his father requires some interpreting and analysis.

When did Light Horse Harry Lee die for his son Robert? Did he "die" that day in May 1813 when he left his family? Did he "die" when Robert learned the sad news from Cumberland Island in the spring of 1818? Or did Harry Lee "die" some time later in Robert's life, when the son reflected upon the life of his father and decided what sort of man he had been?

In one way or another, Robert attempted throughout his life to come to terms with his father's memory. In 1832, Robert had to read his half brother Henry's vicious *Observations on Writings of Thomas Jefferson* in which Henry sought to laud Light Horse Harry at the expense of Jefferson. In 1837, at age thirty, Robert conducted some research on his geneology and undertook to reproduce the Lee coat of arms. In 1862, he spent a few moments at his father's grave. And near the end of his life, in 1868, Robert edited a new edition of his father's *Memoirs* which printed the series of letters to Carter from the West Indies and included a biographical sketch.[20]

In his introductory "life" of his father, Robert avoided unpleasantnesses and repeated the old family euphemisms. Light Horse Harry suffers no financial distress in his son's biographical sketch, spends no time in jail, and moves to Alexandria "for the purpose of educating his children." Only his father's mysterious resignation from the Continental Army provoked serious questions. By this time Harry Lee's son knew more than he wanted to know about petty jealousy and envy within an officer corps. So Robert Lee invented excuses for his father. He was "enfeebled by ill health." He "must have known what Burke has impressed upon mankind, that it is 'in the nature and constitution of things for calumny to accompany triumph.'" Therefore General Lee concluded of Lieutenant Colonel Lee, "It is probable that some domestic trouble was mingled with those already mentioned, and that the disease of his body was aggravated by care and anxiety of mind."[21]

What Robert Lee really wanted to do at this late stage of his life was to write his own memoirs. Instead, he re-edited his father's memoirs. Of course there were reasons for this: many of his reports and wartime papers were scattered or lost; his brother Carter urged him to undertake the task he did; and he did not wish to reopen very fresh wounds by writing what others might perceive to be apologia. Nevertheless, within two years of his own death, Robert Lee was still trying to lay his father to rest.

During the last year of his life, Robert went for the second and final time to visit Harry Lee's grave. No one can know how much he knew about his father's failures or when he knew what. Robert had to know more than he wrote; his relationship with his father remained unresolved. Harry Lee never did "die" for his son Robert.

What Robert Lee was likely trying to do was to make this enigmatic man who conditioned so much of his life live and reveal himself. As it was, Robert could only learn essentially negative lessons from Harry Lee. The father continued to remind the son that fortune is fickle, that fame and failure can cohabit, and that the stability of family and status is fragile indeed.

2

"How Can I Live Without Robert?"

ANN HILL CARTER LEE is much a mystery. She left very little of herself for historians to ponder. Only one portrait which may or may not be hers survives, and the woman in it, wearing a miniature of George Washington on her left breast and holding a spray of spring flowers, looks nothing so much as she does mysterious. A dress which was hers preserved in Richmond suggests that she was about five feet, six inches tall and of medium build. A mere handful of letters are extant. But she did leave one revealing legacy of herself—her son Robert.[1]

All of his life, Robert Lee knew his father only at a great distance. He continued to learn about his father; but learning about and knowing are not the same thing. The constant parent in Robert's youth was Ann Lee, his mother. He knew her well and responded directly to her influence and example throughout his life.

When the fatherless Lee family learned of Harry Lee's death in 1818, Robert was most likely in the process of attending school at Eastern View in Fauquier County, Virginia. Boys in the Carter family, Ann Lee's relatives, usually studied with a schoolmaster there; the girls usually went to Shirley, Ann Lee's childhood home.

Whenever Robert, his older brother Smith, and oldest brother Carter were at home in Alexandria, they spent time caring for their mother. Ann Lee was often unwell. She probably suffered from tuberculosis; the disease ebbed and flowed during her forties and early fifties and eventually killed her. The boys' sister Ann was sickly herself, and their younger sister Mildred (born in 1811) was too young to help very much.[2]

Carter, the perceived scholar in the family, was at Harvard. In 1818 he won the Bowdoin Prize, given for "the advancement of useful and polite literature," for an extended essay on Milton's *Paradise Lost*. He also won the Boylston Prize for oratory. Carter took his bachelor's degree from Harvard in 1819 and soon began a practice of law in New York City.[3]

Smith remained at home until he was almost eighteen. Then in 1820 with the aid of his father's one-time associate, long-time political enemy, and benefactor President James Monroe, Smith secured a midshipman's commission in the Navy and went to sea.

By the time Smith left home, Robert had ceased his studies at Eastern View and entered Alexandria Academy. Schoolmaster William B. Leary was a good teacher; and Alexandria Academy was free for local boys after January 1821, perhaps free for Robert before then.

At age thirteen Robert became the oldest male in his immediate family still at home. In addition to his studies and adolescent play, he "carried the keys"— an expression used to identify the person in authority within a household. Robert probably did some of the marketing, had charge of the stored food, and directed the work of the several slaves who served the family.

He also became the family nurse and cared for his mother and sisters when they were ill. Family legend has Robert insisting that his mother go for after-noon drives in her carriage and that she do so in good cheer. If the day was cold, Robert supposedly crammed paper into the cracks of the carriage with his knife.[4]

When she felt able, Ann Lee continued to visit friends and relatives, and when not in school Robert accompanied his mother and sisters. They proba-bly went most often to Ravensworth, the plantation home of William Henry Fitzhugh, in whose Alexandria townhouse the Lees lived. He was one of Ann Lee's Carter cousins and related to Lees as well. Fitzhugh's young wife Anna Maria was especially solicitous, and the large (22,000 acres) estate offered a retreat for Ann Lee and her children.[5]

Ann and her children also went to Arlington, the home of William Fitzhugh's sister Mary. Mary had married George Washington Parke Custis, Martha Washington's grandson and the adopted son of George Washington after he married Martha. The Custises had only one child who survived in-fancy; Mary Anne Randolph Custis was very close to Robert's age. Upon this daughter did her parents shower attention and advantages. At Arlington, Rob-ert saw an incredibly close-knit family. Parke Custis never achieved very much, though he dabbled at painting, planting, poetry, sheep breeding, and more. He never had to achieve very much, because he was the "child of Mount Vernon," the great Washington's heir, possessed of family connections and sufficient wealth to indulge himself, his family, and friends. Mrs. Custis was gracious and warm at once. Robert could not help being impressed by his visits to Arlington.[6]

Ann Lee must have taken her children to visit Stratford, although the family correspondence which survives does not mention any such visit. Later in his life, Robert described his birthplace in sufficient detail to imply first-hand knowledge of the house and grounds. Since he never lived there after age three, and Stratford passed out of the Lee family when he was fifteen, he had to have been there with his mother at some time or times to visit his half brother Henry.[7]

Henry and his wealthy wife Ann and her sister Betsy lived well at Stratford for a time. But in the summer of 1820 Ann and Henry's two-year-old daughter died as a result of a fall down the front steps of the house. Ann was inconsolable. She "took to her bed," and then began taking morphine in serious quantity with dangerous regularity.

While his wife was often in an altered state of consciousness, Henry Lee shared his grief over his dead child and his concern for his wife with his sister-in-law and ward Betsy McCarty. Then Henry and Betsy shared more than grief and concern. There may have been a child, stillborn, aborted, or murdered. Rumor persists. For certain there was adultery for which Betsy felt remorse and which Henry admitted rather freely.

In 1821, Betsy petitioned the Westmoreland County Court to undo what the court had done in 1817 when it granted her request to make Henry Lee her guardian. She asked to return to the care of her stepfather, Richard Stuart. The court complied and observed that "Henry Lee hath been guilty of a flagrant abuse of his trust in the guardianship of his ward Betsy McCarty."

For his part, Henry submitted to the court order but managed to ensnarl the property committed to his care as Betsy's guardian in ways that required years and courts to resolve. The morality of the matter seemed to concern Henry very little; the ethics of the situation not at all.[8]

He did protest the wisdom of a Virginia law which defined sexual intercourse between a man and his sister-in-law or a woman and her brother-in-law as incest. In a letter written later, Henry confessed, "I *am* fully sensible of the enormity of my sin. . . . It was an act of adultery. . . ." But then he began to mitigate. The law in Virginia, Henry offered, promoted an artificial familiarity, so that a man "associates with the sister of his wife, with all the unguarded intimacy which he would observe toward his own sister and there being no blood connection, no barrier of instinct between them, is liable to be surprised into adultery. . . ." Having demonstrated to his own satisfaction, at least, that an antiquated law lay at the root of his indiscretions, Henry raised a variant of the everybody-is-doing-it defense and cited Thomas Jefferson to prove his point.[9]

In 1821 Henry Lee's conduct provoked ample gossip and local scandal; Robert, who was then fourteen, must have known about the affair. Quite likely his mother used her stepson's shame as an example for all her children of the prevalence and consequences of sin in the world.

Then in June of 1822 Henry Lee lost the farm, quite literally. Unable to restore money belonging to Betsy which he had spent while acting as her guardian, Henry had to sell Stratford to pay his debt. The once-great estate passed out of the Lee family forever.

Henry reconciled with his wife Ann, and the two lived in Washington during Robert's youth. Unfortunately, Ann continued to be dependent upon morphine, although very few people were aware of her addiction. Henry attempted to support them both with various writing projects. He even placed his pen at the service of Andrew Jackson during the presidential election campaign of 1828. From a Lee perspective this was heinous apostasy—the first-born son of Light Horse Harry Lee, fallen from Federalist grace, in league with a Democrat.

Robert likely knew very little about his half brother's life beyond the essential facts of the scandal and sale of Stratford. Carter seems to have kept in touch with Ann and Henry, and Carter then relayed news of "Black Horse Harry" to members of his family. Home, mother, sisters, and school probably provided Robert all the concerns an adolescent boy could manage.[10]

At Alexandria Academy, Robert displayed an aptitude for mathematics. He mastered arithmetic and then learned algebra and geometry. Precision appealed to him, and his mind accommodated the abstract reasoning involved.

William B. Leary, Robert's teacher, offered a classical education to his pupils. In addition to mathematics Leary emphasized Greek and Latin literature, and among other authors Robert read Homer and Longinus in Greek and Tacitus and Cicero in Latin. It is impossible to know exactly the impact of these lessons; however, these four writers shared an emphasis upon noble traditions and traditional virtues. Homer essentially defined heroic conduct in his epic tales of gods and Greeks; Longinus wrote a critical literary treatise *On the Sublime* in which he emphasized with examples elevated thought and denigrated pretension. Tacitus was a historian whose descriptions of Britons and Germans emphasize the love of freedom and the practice of integrity. Cicero, Roman statesman and orator, was eloquent in his attacks upon corruption and treachery—*O tempora, O mores!* (O these times, O what customs!). And like the other classical writers Robert read, Cicero spoke and wrote from a posture of selfless service to others and of the celebration of faithfulness.[11]

With his acquisition of classical learning, Robert entered the select fraternity of gentlemen in nineteenth-century America. His capacity to sprinkle his speech with words which were not English, to quote Latin mottoes appropriately, and to understand allusions to classical history and mythology marked him as a member of a social elite. Robert's education befit his birth; Lees and Carters were supposed to have read the *Iliad* and to know what happened at Cannae. When Robert entered the company of important people, he spoke and understood their language.[12]

As he entered his later teens, Robert and his family—immediate and extended—gave serious thought to his future. He possessed a name, social graces, manners, and the requisite education for a gentleman. But he was without wealth or any clear way to acquire wealth. Consequently, as younger sons and young men of Robert's circumstance usually did, he considered a profession. He probably thought about teaching, law, medicine, the church, and the military.

The cost of further education had to be a factor in Robert's decision; if his profession required more schooling, he would have to find a patron to pay for it. He had likely seen quite enough of doctors from witnessing those who attended his mother and sister; indeed he avoided physicians throughout his life whenever he could do so. He was a practicing Christian, but he had never felt called to be confirmed in the Episcopal Church and thus was an unlikely candidate for holy orders. He never believed that he could become an effective teacher, perhaps because he was shy, and besides, teaching was a very marginal profession in the nineteenth century. Robert's public reticence probably precluded much consideration of law. Carter was the lawyer in the family, and if his example counted for anything, the law was less than lucrative for Lees.

By process of elimination, if nothing else, Robert seemed destined to become a soldier. Light Horse Harry needed a successor on the field of Mars. And if Robert could secure an appointment to the United States Military Academy, then his education would be free. His obligation would be five years, and that included his four years at West Point. The Academy taught engineering, maybe not yet the best engineering in the country, but definitely good enough. If Robert found Army life distasteful, he would have an alternate career.[13]

Soon after Robert's seventeenth birthday (February 1824) he and his family made the decision to try to win for him an appointment to West Point. It was likely a shared decision, and no one can know how enthusiastic Robert was or was not at the time. Once they made the decision, family members closed ranks and began in earnest the campaign for Robert's appointment as a cadet.

The authority to appoint young men to the Academy lay essentially in the hands of the Secretary of War, who recommended candidates to the President. From quite chaotic beginnings the Military Academy had become a very respectable institution and would soon be even better. Families and sons were besieging the Secretary of War with applications, and very soon (in self-defense) the Secretary established the rule of admitting young men by congressional district. In 1824, however, Secretary of War John C. Calhoun could appoint cadets as he chose and use his appointments to spread the loaves and fishes of patronage.[14]

Someone arranged for Robert to meet Calhoun in early February 1824, and apply in person for an appointment to West Point. William H. Fitzhugh of Ravensworth in whose Alexandria home the Lees lived composed a letter of introduction (February 7, 1824) to Calhoun for Robert. Fitzhugh wrote of Robert's "amiable disposition, & his correct and gentlemanly habits," of Light Horse Harry's service in the Revolution, and especially of Ann Lee, "one of the finest women the State of Virginia ever produced."[15]

The meeting between Robert E. Lee and John C. Calhoun in February 1824 was at the very least ironic. At forty-one, Calhoun was a veteran of Washington politics. He had represented his upcountry South Carolina district in Congress (1811–17) and well served the Monroe administration as Secretary of War (1817–25). Later in 1824 he would win election as Vice President of the United States. Eventually as senator from South Carolina, Calhoun became the principal voice of Southern sectional interests in national councils, and his brilliance as a political theorist shone long after his death in 1850. When Southerners seceded from the Union in 1860–61, they acted out Calhoun's interpretation of the United States Constitution. Lee, of course, would lead an army which attempted to secure independence for the Southern nation. And in the wake of Lee's surrender at Appomattox someone observed, "The whole South is the grave of John C. Calhoun."

Soon after Robert's interview with Calhoun, William B. Leary wrote to the

Secretary to verify his student's academic qualifications. Robert S. Garnett, who represented Westmoreland County in Congress and who was Calhoun's close political ally, also recommended Robert (February 16, 1824) and praised his "excellent disposition." Another Virginia congressman, C. F. Mercer, wrote on Robert's behalf, and someone, possibly half brother Henry, secured the signatures of Virginia Congressman George Tucker, Virginia Senator James Barbour, Kentucky Senator Richard M. Johnson, Louisiana Senator Henry Johnson, Alabama Senator William Kelly, and Mississippi Senator David Holmes at the bottom of Mercer's letter. Carter Lee wrote (February 28, 1824) Calhoun a letter to accompany another letter from Robert and testified that "his disposition is amiable." Finally Henry Lee offered (March 6, 1824) his endorsement, one more reminder of his father's conspicuous public service, and thus the debt the country owed Light Horse Harry's youngest son.[16]

Of the six letters sent to Calhoun to plead Robert's case, three mentioned his disposition; two stated that it was "amiable," and the third described it as "excellent." Either Robert's genial nature was a dominent personal trait, or his referees coordinated the language in their recommendations.

As it happened, Robert needed all the help the family could muster. Competition for the approximately one hundred appointments was keen, and the Secretary of War rejected no less than twenty-five applications from Virginia in 1824. Calhoun, however, did appoint Robert on March 11, 1824. But the press for appointments was so heavy that Calhoun agreed to admit Robert to West Point in July 1825, a year beyond the date he expected and almost four months beyond Calhoun's tenure as Secretary of War. Still, Robert got his wish, and Calhoun made the most of his patronage opportunities.

In what became the earliest Robert E. Lee letter now known to exist, Robert accepted the appointment. The letter, written on April Fools' Day 1824, was an inauspicious beginning for an academic career. The body of Robert's missive contained only two sentences and a misspelled word ("honnoured").[17]

Entering cadets still had to pass an academic examination soon after their arrival at West Point and a series of stiffer examinations the following January which usually reduced the class by a fourth. Thus in February 1825, Robert at eighteen began a course of final academic preparation for West Point. He had not attended school for some time, and a new schoolmaster in Alexandria, Benjamin Hallowell, had earned high praise in the community. So Robert worked with Hallowell, whose home on Oronoco Street was only a few blocks away.

Much later, Hallowell recalled: "He was a most exemplary pupil in every respect. He was never behind time in his studies; never failed in a single recitation; was perfectly observant of the rules and regulations of the institution; was gentlemanly, unobtrusive, and respectful in all his deportment to teacher and his fellow students." Hallowell may have helped Robert with spelling; but the teacher remembered best Robert's lessons in geometry. "His specialty was *finishing up,"* Hallowell wrote. "He imparted a finish and a neatness, as he proceeded to everything he undertook. One of the branches of Mathematics he studied with me was Conic Sections, in which some of the diagrams are very complicated. He drew the diagrams on a slate; and although he well knew that the one he was drawing would have to be removed to make room for another, he drew each one with as much accuracy and finish lettering and all, as if it were to be engraved and printed."[18]

Hallowell's most vivid memory of Robert Lee as a student sustains at least two interpretations. Robert's insistence upon *"finishing up"* may have simply indicated disciplined attention to his work, conscientious concern of an eighteen-year-old that he perform as well as he could at all times.

"Finishing up," though, may have been for Robert an act more profound than fastidious. His great care with each transitory conic section may have been an existential statement. Robert became absorbed in each problem as though there were no other. He was lost in the here and now of the present task, committed to making the best of the moment. So Robert filled his slate for the sake of the process, engaged in the doing of it. Then, having resolved this issue, having wrung from this problem all that he could, he wiped his slate clean.

In the spring of 1825 Robert finished up with Benjamin Hallowell and prepared to leave home likely forever. Cadets at the Military Academy could leave the post only once during four years; they were eligible for an eight-week furlough after two years if they earned this respite. And then the War Department might send Robert anywhere for his initial duty post. This leavetaking was a significant passage in young Robert's life.[19]

Ann Lee responded very much like a mother. "How can I live without Robert?" she reportedly exclaimed. "He is both son and daughter to me." Yet Ann must have also felt proud of her accomplishments as her last son left home. She had launched three young men into the great world. Her daughter Ann Kinloch married the following year, and Mildred, now fourteen, remained to help her.[20]

Ann Lee had made the best of an unfortunate marriage and raised her children in circumstances usually "comfortable," if hardly splendid or always secure. She had managed to educate them and expose them to life among the Virginia gentry. Never wealthy, she still had black slaves to serve her, and she usually traveled in her own carriage behind her own horses. Her children possessed little in the way of monetary legacy; but they had family name, social connections, and proper training for successful lives.

When Robert was ready to leave his mother, she must have known that he would carry with him her enduring influence. For if Robert was, as she insisted, "both son and daughter to me," then she had been both mother and father to him. If Robert learned generally negative lessons from the memory of his father, his mother taught him positive precepts to offset Light Horse Harry. Ann Lee likely taught some lessons directly and told Robert and the rest of her children exactly what they should and should not do. She probably taught by example as well. But whether in response to his mother's lectures or her life, Robert learned habits of mind and action he retained all his life.

Harry Lee had been glib in his learning and insistent in his conversation. Robert seemed shy and quiet. His father had relished attention and had nursed his fame all the more as it faded. Robert was reticent and self-effacing, insistent that deeds speak for him instead of words. Harry had been often out of control and more proud than prudent. For Robert, self-control was nearly an obsession and prudence governed passion. It requires no genius to speculate about the source of Robert's stable behavior; his father's fate reinforced his mother's maxims.

Moving and sustaining Ann Lee as wife, mother, and person was her religious faith. She may have harkened to the call of the Second Great Awakening which roused the country and especially the South about 1800. Her faith may have been a mild form of rebellion against her husband's skepticism. Whatever the source, Ann Lee was a committed evangelical Christian. She was, with cause, aware of the sinful nature of human beings and hoped for her redemption in a personal relationship with Jesus, the risen Christ. Her response to God was emotional, not rational, and she marked her life with discipline, morality, and missionary zeal.

Ann Lee expressed the essentials of her faith in a letter she wrote to Carter at Harvard in 1816. Much of her missive concerns "money matters"; but at the conclusion she delivers the more important message. "All your friends enquire after you with much interest," she wrote, "They say they have formed high hopes of your character—Disappoint them not I entreat you—Let your ambition be to realize their expectations." Then she expressed her concern "lest you should become a socinion"—that is, a disciple of Faustus and Laelius Socinus, sixteenth-century Italian theologians who rejected the doctrines of the Trinity, the divinity of Christ, and original sin. She felt guilty for allowing her son to attend a college where such hearsay existed. "Oh! pray fervently for faith in Jesus Christ," she exhorted. "He is the only rock of your salvation, and the only security for your resurrection from the grave!"[21]

Before he could read, Robert learned his catechism from his mother and said the words to William Meade, Rector of Christ Church in Alexandria. With the words came the fundamentals of evangelical Protestantism. Robert knew about sin and redemption; his mother saw to that. Yet he never joined the church as a youth or young man. He would wait until he was forty-six years old to seek confirmation and then he did so with two of his daughters, perhaps in response to their zeal more than his own. Quite possibly Robert felt unworthy of his mother's faith, beneath her high standards of belief and conduct. He never had any "born again" experience that he shared with anyone else.

Young Robert was a religious person, though. He attended church, said sincere prayers, and grew in spiritual depth and sophistication. Certainly he believed in sin; he knew that he was sometimes guilty, and he knew that evil infected people in the world. If the church had never taught about original sin, Robert Lee would have invented it. For Robert, sin was at base an absorbtion with self; the ultimate evil was selfishness. Conversely, virtue consisted in serving others, giving instead of taking. As a young man he adopted a practical ethic: he placed the needs of other people before his own. He refined this practice, but he never abandoned it. And in so doing, he emulated his mother.[22]

When Robert left his mother, he carried within himself eighteen years of experiences blended mysteriously with genes and happenstance. He lived at Stratford, Alexandria, Ravensworth, Arlington, Shirley, Eastern View, and more. He knew about fame and infamy. He sought family, stability, and control, because he knew about their opposites. He liked mathematics and read classical classics. He seemed shy but managed his household from age thirteen and was often a houseguest. He associated with people of wealth and status; but he possessed manners without a manor. He was quite conscious of sin, morality, discipline, and prudence. He was a good Episcopalian who remained unchurched. He pursued an ethic of selflessness. His catechism, his family, and his experience taught him the frailty of the human condition; he expected people to fall short of perfection. He could lose himself in making the best of a moment—existential exercises with conic sections. Young Robert was not the simple fellow he often appeared to be.

He was going further from home than he had ever been to a place he knew only by word of mouth. Very little in his life prepared him for the regimen of a West Point cadet. For the past five years of his life—all of his adolescence—Robert had lived with females, his mother and sisters. Now he would live for four years with males.

3

The "Marble Model"

To reach West Point Robert Lee had to reach New York City. Then, as did most travelers to the Point, Lee boarded a steamboat and churned 37 miles up the Hudson River. The physical setting of the school is spectacular. West Point is indeed a point of land on the west side of the Hudson. The river is wide and mighty, and the land rises (190 feet) from the banks and then flattens to form a more or less level plain. It is and certainly was when Lee arrived a lush, serene-looking place. Lee may have seen prints depicting West Point before he went there in June of 1825. But no representation of the site does justice to the beauty there.[1]

The United States Military Academy contrasted severely with its setting. The Academy consisted of four fairly stark, stone buildings with stucco facades set upon the plain. North and South Barracks, four and three stories respectively, housed the cadets. The two-story Academy building contained a chapel, library, classrooms, and laboratories. The messhall, also two stories, served as well as a small hotel for visitors. In the vicinity were other structures, professors' homes, old Fort Clinton, North's Tavern, and more. But cadets seldom if ever legally left the confines of the school. West Point was a military monastery, a single-sex community of vigorous study, rigid discipline, and Spartan living.[2]

Very much the "abbot" of this martial order was Brevet Lieutenant Colonel Sylvanus Thayer, Superintendent of the Military Academy. Lee encountered Thayer when he reported to him upon arrival and again at his preliminary examination by the Academic Board. The Superintendent was forty years old in 1825. He had grown up in modest circumstances in Braintree, Massachusetts, and graduated from Dartmouth before entering the Military Academy in 1807. Thayer graduated in just one year, served in Paris studying the operation of the Ecole Polytechnique, then considered the best school of military engineering in the world.

Thayer's return to the United States coincided with a crisis at West Point (the disastrous administration of Superintendent Alden Partridge), and in 1817 President James Madison made Thayer the new Superintendent. Thayer then began to install the system of discipline and education which would characterize the institution for the remainder of the nineteenth century and in some respects survives there still.

West Point was the special province of the Corps of Engineers; the chief of the corps in Washington supervised the operation of the Academy and the Superintendent was an engineer officer. Consequently West Point became very much an engineering school, with a prescribed curriculum emphasizing mathematics and science. In time Thayer assembled an outstanding faculty that made the school prestigious and extended Thayer's influence long after he left the Academy in 1833. Thayer's system also prevailed in the Academic Board, a governing body composed of the Superintendent, Commandant of Cadets, and heads of the various academic departments. This body determined the curriculum, conducted examinations, ranked the cadets in order of merit, and recommended the branch of service for each graduate.

Thayer required each instructor to grade each of his students every day and submit weekly reports. After their first term Thayer divided cadet classes into sections according to performance; department heads usually taught the best section, and each section progressed at a speed corresponding to the abilities of the students. Finally, Thayer set 200 demerits in one year as the limit beyond which a cadet became liable for dismissal, and was himself ever vigilant in the capture of miscreants. A bachelor, Thayer devoted his time and energy almost totally to West Point, and this included spying on cadets and investigating malicious gossip, as well as offering his charges superior technical training.[3]

With Thayer in charge, the Academic Board examined each of the 107 entering cadets orally. Lee passed this test without difficulty; however, twenty of his contemporaries did not. In fact, over half of each entering class failed to graduate for one reason or another. In Lee's class (1829), forty-six men survived and graduated, and this was the largest number of graduates West Point had produced to that time. Attrition tended to be greatest in the first year (fourth class); the total number of cadets at the Academy at any one time varied considerably, but probably averaged 225 to 250.

During the remainder of the summer of 1825 Lee and his fellow "plebes" (fourth classmen) joined the rising first classmen (seniors) and third classmen (sophomores) at Camp Adams (in honor of President John Quincy Adams), a community of tents on the plain where all but the rising second classmen on furlough spent the summer. At summer camp plebes endured a thorough orientation and learned the rudiments of infantry drill.[4]

Like every cadet, Lee had an account established at the Academy against which he charged his expenses and into which went $16 per month pay and $12 per month subsistence allowance. To secure his share of the necessities to wash himself and his quarters—mirror, wash basin and stand, pitcher, pail, broom, and scrub brush—and to buy his uniform, Lee and his classmates incurred instant debt.

The uniform was gray pants, vest, and coat; the fatigue jacket and pants were blue. For summer wear Lee purchased four pairs of white duck pants and doubtless wondered how he would keep them clean while while living in a tent. Less practical than white pants, however, was the standard hat worn by cadets. It was black leather, seven inches high and topped with a pompom. It was also heavy, hot, and expensive. High-top black shoes and a black stock completed Lee's costume for the next four years of his life.[5]

Institutional cooking has always been by definition bland and bad. Mr. Cozzens who operated the messhall at West Point apparently reached real depths in the quality of his food, care in its preparation, and variety of his menu. Boiled meat (beef, veal or pork), boiled potatoes, bread and butter composed breakfast; boiled meat, boiled potatoes, bread and butter was dinner (midday); bread and butter or occasionally cornbread and molasses was supper. Alterations there were in this monotonous fare; but Cozzens's menu repeated itself each week. Quite often the butter was rancid, or the molasses was sour, and cadets could expect little surprises in their food. Cockroaches and smaller insects inhabited soups and sugar, and once a cadet discovered a nest of three small mice in his bowl of bread pudding.

Fortunately the daily schedule at the Academy allowed precious little time for cadets to eat. Lee and his classmates had to bolt their food so fast they had little opportunity to contemplate its quality.[6]

During that first summer in camp Lee learned the regulations that would govern his life at West Point. Forbidden to cadets were alcohol, tobacco, visitors, playing cards, novels, plays, and places beyond the plain. With the permission of the Superintendent, Lee might subscribe to one magazine. Bathing in the river required permission. Otherwise cleaniness came only from his wash basin in water pumped from a well and carried to his tent (or room during the academic year).

A system of demerits which reduced a cadet's conduct ranking in his class and associated punishments such as extra tours of guard duty or confinement during recreation periods reinforced the rules of West Point. Some offenses, such as drinking alcohol or fighting, warranted trial by court-martial and dismissal; otherwise Thayer and the faculty assessed from 1 to 10 demerits for offenses ranked within eight categories. A cadet late for roll call received only 1 or 2 demerits for an eighth-grade offense. Ten demerits was the price of leaving the Academy grounds without permission and other first-grade offenses.[7]

Cadet Lee survived four years at West Point without incurring a single demerit. If he were ever late to class or if his shoes were ever unblacked, no one in authority caught him. Such a record was rare but not unheard of. In fact, five other members of the class of 1829 were equally unscathed. A survey conducted in 1831 revealed that one hundred fifty cadets then enrolled had received less than 50 demerits, eighty-eight cadets less than 100, thirty-four cadets less than 150 demerits, and sixteen had received between 150 and 200. Lee adhered to rules and regulations; he remained in control of himself. West Point prescribed obedience and punished initiative. Lee proved to himself and others that he could adapt to such an environment and thrive in a small world of schedules and standards.[8]

The lockstep life in a military monastery, however, only challenged some cadets. Like Jefferson Davis, they slipped off to Benny Havens's tavern in nearby Highland Falls to eat and drink. Like William T. Sherman, they made "hash" in their rooms from a stolen chicken and whatever other edibles they could scavenge. They smuggled liquor, tobacco, prostitutes, and anything else illegal into the Military Academy. And some young men, like Edgar Allan Poe who enrolled in 1830, simply disappeared one day and never returned.

Most of those cadets who survived to graduate from West Point underwent an intense experience in male bonding with their classmates. Adversity drew them together, and out of their common circumstance they derived strength from each other.[9]

Lee made lasting friendships and clearly enjoyed the camaraderie he experienced at West Point. Two of his close friends were Joseph E. Johnston and Jack Mackay. Johnston was a fellow Virginian with whom Lee would remain in contact for the rest of his life. Mackay was from Savannah, Georgia, and Lee "adopted" the Mackay family during his first duty assignment at Cockspur Island, just downriver from Savannah. He remained in touch with Jack Mackay until the latter's death in 1848. Most of his life Lee preferred the company of women to men. However, most of his life he worked exclusively with men, and with male friends maintained relationships much like those he experienced with his fellow cadets at West Point.[10]

Cadet summer camp corresponded with a burgeoning social season at West Point. The site and the cadets were magnets which attracted not only military notables and their families but also fashionable families from the region and beyond. Especially did prominent parents with daughters enjoy the daily parades and weekly dances that relieved the summer routine somewhat for cadets.[11]

Plebe Lee likely saw little of the social set during that first summer of 1825, and at the end of August the cadets broke camp and marched to the barracks; the academic year began in earnest on September 1. In North Barracks four men lived in a room; in South Barracks three men shared space. Heat came from coal-burning fireplaces; light from candles or whale-oil lamps. In these rooms cadets placed their wash basins and stands; already in place were straight-backed chairs, tables, mattresses (rolled during the day, spread upon the floor for sleeping at night). Nothing else—any decoration was forbidden. Privacy was out of the question.[12]

A gun sounded reveille each day at dawn (5:30 A.M.). The cadets dressed quickly, fell into formation for roll call, and then returned to their rooms to clean them. From six to seven cadets studied, and then marched to breakfast. A half-hour of recreation followed breakfast (7:30–8:00) and then classes from 8:00 until 1:00 P.M. Dinner (lunch) was from 1:00 to 2:00 P.M., followed by more classes and study periods until 4:00. If weather permitted, the cadets drilled for two hours, from four until six; in winter this period was for study and recreation. Supper was at 6:00 P.M. Then more study from 7:00 until 9:30;

a half-hour of recreation, and taps at 10:00 P.M. This schedule relaxed a bit on Sunday afternoons and all day on Christmas Day and New Year's Day.[13]

Letters from cadets to friends and families complained of the lack of time to write them and spoke to the monotony of a regimen which left letterwriters little "news" to relate. Lee wrote letters while at West Point; however, none are now available. Still, the life of a cadet was so prescribed and monitored that Lee's letters, if extant, would probably reveal little beyond the public record and circumstances that applied to every cadet then at West Point.

During Lee's first (fourth class) year, he took courses in mathematics (Algebra, geometry, trigonometry, and analytical geometry) and French (Lesage, *Gil Blas*), finished the academic year ranked third in his class, and earned an appointment as cadet staff sergeant. In his second (third class) year, Lee took more mathematics (analytical and descriptive geometry, differential and integral calculus, and surveying), more French (*Gil Blas* and Voltaire, *Histoire de Charles XII*), and he also took courses in drawing (human figure). Lee ranked second in his class in June 1827, retained his cadet staff sergeant appointment, and earned his furlough.[14]

On June 30, 1827, Lee left West Point on furlough for the first time in two years. He visited his mother, now living in Georgetown with Mildred and Carter, who had migrated there from New York. Ann Lee was unwell. Her tuberculosis had advanced; but she roused herself to travel with her children that summer. Robert's sister Ann Kinloch had married William Lewis Marshall the previous June. His brother Smith was on leave from the Navy and joined the family in a series of visits to relatives.

Carter had experienced indifferent success with his practice of law—he enjoyed literature and good living too much. He was certainly the main attraction during that summer's socializing with his mother, sister, and brothers.

Together, the reunited Lees visited Kinloch in Fauquier County, the home of Ann Lee's cousin Edward Carter Turner. Also visiting at Kinloch that summer was Mary Custis from Arlington. Cadet Lee impressed her, and she began to think of him as someone quite special.

Too soon the summer ended, and Lee had to return to the Academy. He arrived on August 28, in time to march to the barracks for another academic year.[15]

During Lee's third (second class) year at West Point the curriculum prescribed courses in chemistry, "natural philosophy" or physics (mechanics, acoustics, optics, and astronomy), and drawing (landscape and topography). Lee ranked number two in his class in June 1828, and won the prize of promotion to cadet adjutant, the highest rank in the corps.

In his final (first class) year, Lee continued his work in chemistry, took a catch-all course in geography, history, ethics, and law, and undertook the heart and soul of an Academy education, military engineering. The latter course included field fortification, permanent fortification, artillery, grand tactics, and civil and military architecture.[16]

In his final exams before the Academic Board and a Board of Visitors, Lee earned a maximum score in artillery and tactics and outstanding scores on other subjects. For class rankings the various academic subjects over the four-year curriculum had weighted values. Engineering, for example, counted for 300 out of 2,000 total points, while French, drawing, and chemistry rated 100 points each. Mathematics, sciences, and engineering consumed over 70 percent of classroom hours in the curriculum and counted for 55 percent of the score on which class rank depended.[17]

Lee's scores placed him second in the class of 1829. First in the final class ranking, as he had been first in class ranking for each of the three previous years, was Charles Mason of New York. West Point, however, was the zenith of Mason's public career. He served one year as an instructor at the Academy, resigned his commission, settled in Burlington, Iowa, and became a prominent "solid" citizen.[18]

In the Thayer system, education meant the acquisition of information and the capacity to manipulate facts and numbers using appropriate formulae. Classes at West Point were "recitations," and the term well described the classroom process. Cadets answered questions about the contents of their textbooks, and the accuracy of their responses determined their grade for the day. In courses in science and mathematics, the instructor called several cadets to the blackboards that lined the classroom and assigned them problems to solve. After questions and critiques, the instructor dismissed the first group and called more cadets to the blackboards. The process continued until all cadets in the section had taken a turn.[19]

Then and since, critics of the system—many of whom were the cadets who endured it—have observed that the Thayer regimen emphasized memorization at the expense of understanding, rewarded rote at the expense of enlightenment, and suppressed independent thinking in favor of doctrine and dogma. These critics are correct. But in the educational context of Thayer's time, the system was innovative and effective. The traditional, classical education offered in American colleges did not address the science and technology which increasingly preoccupied American thought and life. So obsessed with piety and platitudes was much of what passed for higher education in the United States that proponents of Thayer's system might with justification have said *tu quoque* (you, too) to those who found excessive degrees of memorizing, rote, doctrine, and dogma at West Point.[20]

Within the limits of its goals, Thayer's system worked. The Military Academy attracted faculty who became authorities and authors of superior texts in their fields and produced graduates who excelled in military and civil pursuits. Whatever Thayer's graduates did or did not achieve after graduation, while they were cadets at West Point they learned to master the material in their courses and pursue perfection. During the course of the final examinations in 1833, the president of the Board of Visitors that year, Joel R. Poinsett, said to someone at dinner that the cadets had performed so well it seemed they must have known the questions the examiners intended to ask. Thayer learned of Poinsett's comment and took it literally as an affront to the integrity of his examinations instead of as a compliment. He reassembled the board and the class, submitted course outlines from the faculty to the board, and insisted that members of the board interrogate each cadet on any topic contained in the course outlines. Poinsett protested; Thayer insisted; and the cadets again performed flawlessly. Thayer's system produced men who knew with precision the substance of Thayer's curriculum.[21]

Precious little in that curriculum strayed very far from science and technology. Even courses in strategy and tactics seemed all but afterthoughts. Cadets studied French in order to read French texts on mathematics and engineering, which Thayer considered the best in the world. Lee never learned much conversational French; nor did he learn much about French culture. French phrases appear occasionally in his writing, but seldom in reports of his speaking. *Gil Blas* is picaresque satire; but Lesage enforces stern moral standards even when his hero strays from them. So while Lee was learning to read French, he was reinforcing his (and Thayer's) commitment to hard work and righteous living.[22]

Cadets learned to draw so that they might present designs and data graphically, not for the sake of artistic expression. Lee's instructor was Thomas Gimbrede, who did inject some humor and humanism into his course. Gimbrede began his first session with his students by insisting that each of them could learn to draw. "There are only two lines in drawing," he stressed, "the straight line and the curve line. Every one can draw a straight line and every one can draw a curve line—therefore every one can draw."[23]

The omnibus course on geography, history, ethics, and law taught to first classmen (seniors) by the chaplain was as close as Lee came to social science or humanities in the Academy curriculum. Chaplain Thomas Warner taught the course during Lee's tenure and presided at the mandatory chapel services on Sundays. The course took up only 3 percent of Lee's total time at West Point.[24]

Lee did supplement his technical training with selections from the Military Academy library. Available to cadets for only two hours on Saturday afternoons, the library permitted them to borrow books and periodicals only until the following Monday, unless they were using the materials for a course. Lee checked out no novels. He read a new edition of his father's *Memoirs of the War in the Southern Department,* the *Works* of Alexander Hamilton, and Rousseau's *Confessions* (in French), as well as volumes on navigation, astronomy, travel, and geometry. He read some periodicals—*North American Review, Edinburgh Review,* and *Retrospective Review.* This was pretty ponderous reading, but it did offer some relief from equations and theorems.[25]

After his first year at the Academy, Lee's background and performance in mathematics earned him an appointment as acting assistant professor and an extra $10 per month. He taught and tutored cadets with less preparation and ability in mathematics than he possessed.[26]

Someone certainly gave Lee good advice when he or she suggested during the spring before he reported to West Point that he study with Benjamin Hallowell. Lee encountered conic sections, one of the topics he had studied with Hallowell, during the fall term of his second year (third class) at the Academy.[27]

Mathematics lay at the heart of the curriculum and contributed to courses in science and engineering as well. Indeed, an analysis of the records of cadets who left the Military Academy because of academic deficiencies reveals that failure in mathematics accounted for 43.1 percent of the total and mathematics in combination with one or more other subjects for 35 percent. Lee's firm grounding in mathematics served him well and doubtless reinforced his confidence and capacity in other subjects, too.[28]

As Lee prepared to graduate, he received the balance which remained in his account book: $103.58. The $10 per month he earned while an acting assistant professor of mathematics made possible much of this positive balance. Nevertheless, Lee was an extremely frugal cadet; most young men at West Point never saw a positive balance in four years.[29]

Jefferson Davis, later Lee's commander in chief, was in the class of 1828 at the Academy, one year ahead of Lee. During Davis's fourth class year he wrote to his older brother asking for "some Cash," a request very much against Academy regulations. Davis devised an ingenious rationale for his plea: "The Yankee part of the Corps find their pay entirely sufficient some even more, but these are not such as I formed an acquaintance with on my arrival . . . nor are they such associates as I would . . . at present select." In other words, only Yankees can survive on the pay and allowance of a cadet; a Southern gentleman must have more; therefore please send money. Cadet Leonidas Polk, later an Episcopal bishop and Confederate general, informed his father, "exactly like nineteen twentieths of the corps, I am indebted to the aforesaid tailor, merchant, etc., the major part of my next month's pay. . . . Not even the rigid economy of the Yankees can withstand it." Lee's refund was rare indeed, an eloquent testimony to his mother's training and Lee's concern for his personal finances.[30]

Because of his outstanding performance, Lee earned a commission as brevet (temporary) second lieutenant in the Corps of Engineers. Like his classmates, he received a two-month furlough; the Corps of Engineers would decide his first duty assignment and send him orders during his leave.[31]

So for the second time Lee boarded the steamer, left West Point, and sailed down the Hudson toward home. His experience at the Military Academy had been good for him. He had enjoyed success and from his accomplishments gained confidence. He had likewise enjoyed the camaraderie of shared hardships with his fellow cadets and entered enduring friendships. He had acquired a profession and professional training in arms and engineering.

At West Point, Lee had matured—not least, physically. He did have tiny feet (size 4 1/2C); but he was tall for his time, five feet, eleven inches, and he was incredibly handsome. Lee adopted a military bearing and posture without becoming even slightly stiff, and he moved with grace and poise. His eyes were dark brown, sharp, and engaging; his black hair waved and was thick and full. Probably because they had little beyond themselves about which to talk in so closed a society, cadets at West Point were keen students of physical beauty and homeliness. In each class, members knew who was most and least handsome. About Lee someone recalled, "His limbs, beautiful and symmetrical, looked as though they had come from the turning lathe, his step was elastic as if he spurned the ground upon which he trod." Lee's classmates spoke of him as the "Marble Model."[32]

The monastic rule at the Academy had been demanding; Lee could be proud of himself for enduring unscarred. But in one sense life at West Point was easy. Cadets simply obeyed orders; Lee had made very few choices during four years of his life. Now he was free—free to relax for a time, but also free to choose. For the first time in four years, really for the first time ever, Robert Lee's life was his own.

4

"As Bold as a Sheep"

BREVET SECOND LIEUTENANT Robert Lee arrived "home"—Ravensworth this time—from his graduation at West Point to visit his mother on her deathbed. Ann Lee had seemed to rally during the spring of 1829; but by the time her son reached her in June, she was sinking steadily. The tuberculosis which most probably killed her was far advanced, and about all Robert or anyone else could do was make her as comfortable as possible and feign good cheer. On July 24, Ann Lee made her will, and in the morning of July 26 she died.[1]

She had lived fifty-six years, the last thirty-six of which were very much conditioned by her marriage to Light Horse Harry Lee. Certainly she had been steadfast in her trials, and at the time of her death all five of her surviving children were grown and somewhat settled. From the time her husband went to jail for debt, Ann had said, "I must have my own house . . . to fix myself permanently, be it in ever so humble a manner"; but this she was never able to manage. After her stepson Henry became twenty-one (in 1801) and inherited Stratford from his mother, Ann and her children lived in a succession of borrowed homes, and she died a houseguest at Ravensworth.[2]

In her will Ann Lee left her personal effects, a few slaves, and the trust funds (about $20,000) left to her by her father and sister to her daughters, Ann Lee Marshall and Mildred Lee. Her sons, Carter, Smith, and Robert, received some land (20,000 acres) in Patrick County, southwestern Virginia, and thirty slaves. Carter, who helped administer his mother's estate, most probably sold or had someone else sell some of the slaves and divided the proceeds with his brothers. The land only offered a quandary; it seemed worthless at the time, and with it Robert and his brothers inherited bills for back taxes. Eventually they decided to pay these taxes and thus retain the land.

Most probably Robert chose to invest his share of proceeds from the sale of his mother's slaves and "hire out" (rent) the women he owned as a result of the bequest. He never saw his land in southwestern Virginia; Carter later lived on the property and tried in various ways to make a living there.[3]

Now Lee was an orphan at age twenty-two and still a houseguest. Carter took up the task of finishing up his mother's affairs and closing her house in Georgetown; he was the eldest son and a lawyer. Robert remained at Ravensworth for only several days and then moved on with Mildred to Eastern View, home of his maternal aunt Elizabeth and his uncle Robert Randolph, and to Kinloch, where Marietta Turner who was Mildred's best friend lived. Lee informed his military superiors that he intended to spend August and September in the "interior of Virginia." He was reacquainting himself with his extended family and friends, whom he had not seen since his furlough summer two years earlier.[4]

One of his old friends was Mary Custis, and the summer his mother died Lee seemed to have developed some sort of relationship with Mary. Marietta Turner was Mary Custis's best friend as well as Mildred's, so Custis and Lee likely were summer guests at Kinloch together. The two had family ties to Ravensworth as well and probably plotted simultaneous visits there. In any event, by September Lee had secured permission to write to Mary Custis. And in a letter to him, she cautioned Lee to be discreet. Others, including her mother, regularly read her mail and especially her letters from men. The only logical reason for cautioning a correspondent to be discreet is concern or conviction that he or she might have something they didn't want revealed.[5]

While Lee was visiting family and friends and apparently courting Mary Custis, the Engineer Corps in Washington decided his immediate professional fate. On August 11, 1829, Brigadier General Charles Gratiot who commanded the Corps of Engineers signed an order directing Brevet Lieutenant Lee to Cockspur Island in the Savannah River. There Lee was to assist Major Samuel Babcock in preparing Cockspur Island, which lies about 12 miles down the Savannah River from the city of Savannah, for the construction of a massive fort. When erected the fort would control the mouth of the river and thus access to the port at Savannah.[6]

Lee had never been to Savannah; indeed, he had probably never been south of the James River in Virginia. However, Lee's good friend at West Point, Jack Mackay, had grown up in Savannah, and Mackay was assigned to an artillery command in his home city. So Lee took comfort in the fact that he would have at least one friend at his first post.[7]

He would have a slave, as well. Nat, the aged black house servant and coachman to Lee's mother, belonged to Mildred now by the terms of his mother's will. But Nat was old and ill, thus of no value to Mildred, and someone in the family decided that Nat might need a warmer climate. So Lee agreed to take Nat with him to Cockspur Island and assume responsibility for the old man.

To reach Savannah from Virginia, Lee and Nat first had to travel north to New York, most likely by stagecoach. Then they embarked on a packet boat for Savannah. Lee's orders were to report to Major Babcock at Cockspur by "the middle of November," and Lee was nothing if not punctual, so he probably arrived early in November (1829).[8]

One of the first things Lee learned was that, thanks to the Mackays, he

would enjoy Savannah, then a community of about 7,500 people. Jack
Mackay's mother Elizabeth was a widow who had six children besides Jack.
Nevertheless, she "adopted" Lee and assigned him a room in her home on
Broughton Street whenever he came to Savannah. Four of Elizabeth Mackay's
children were daughters ranging in age between fourteen and twenty. And
because he was a friend of the Mackays, Lee made friends with many Savan-
nahians, most of whom were lively young women.[9]

The next lesson Lee learned was that Cockspur Island was not Savannah.
Named for a plant with long, nasty thorns, Cockspur was just barely an island.
In 1829 it was essentially marsh—roughly a mile long and about two thirds of a
mile wide—most of which flooded at high tide and all of which flooded during
storms. It was a good location for a fort, because once built the fort would
command Tybee Roads, the wide mouth of the Savannah between Tybee
Island to the south and Turtle and Daufuskie Islands (South Carolina) to the
north. Cockspur was a good location for a fort for everyone except those who
had to build the fort.

Lee was on hand for the very beginnings of what became Fort Pulaski. The
first task, however, was to create an island capable of supporting the future
fort, and this involved dikes and ditches. On the fringes of Cockspur Island
was some sand; most of the island was pure marsh mud—mud which seemed
to possess no bottom and which clung to boots, clothes, and skin with a
tenacity that defied baths and laundries. Legend, likely true, has Lee spending
considerable time in marsh mud and water up to his armpits during his duty on
Cockspur.

Work on the island was decidedly seasonal. The Corps of Engineers hired
white men and rented black men to labor in the late fall, winter, and spring.
Brutal, humid heat and voracious insects rendered work on Cockspur impossible during the summer and early autumn. And even during the working season, sand fleas in the region can provoke madness in otherwise sane persons.[10]

In addition to moving large amounts of marsh mud to create ditches and
dikes (Lee termed them "embankments"), Lee had to oversee setting up
houses for the workers and a wharf to permit the reception of supplies, building materials, and equipment. Actually Lee's superior Major Babcock was responsible for doing all of this; but according to Lee, Babcock was content to
stay away while Lee did the work and then appear in time to marvel at how well
his project was progressing.

Babcock took up residency on Cockspur on May 1, 1830. In Lee's mind,
Babcock's only contribution to the work on the island before then was to
overrule Lee's plan to locate the wharf on one side of the island instead of the
other. About the wharf superior and subordinate had "issue joined," and Babcock, of course, prevailed.[11]

Because Babcock was so seldom on hand, Lee had to remain at Cockspur
to oversee the project for most of the working season of 1829–30. He wrote
Carter that he had been to Savannah only eleven times between November
1829 and May 8, 1830. When he did go to the city, Lee much enjoyed the

company of Jack Mackay's sisters, Margaret, Elizabeth Anne (Eliza), and Catherine. He also called upon Sarah and Phillipa Minis and gave Sarah pen-and-ink drawings of an alligator and a terrapin he did on Cockspur. During the winter Jack Mackay received orders to Alabama, "ordered up among the Indians" as Lee phrased it, so Lee's circle of special Savannah friends became almost exclusively young females. The circle narrowed some more when Margaret Mackay became engaged to one of Carter Lee's Harvard classmates, Ralph E. Elliott. Lee, who had been interested in Margaret, shifted his attention to Eliza, to whom he gave two pen-and-ink drawings of an alligator and a terrapin all but identical to those he gave Sarah Minis.[12]

In March 1830, probably about the time he began anticipating going to northern Virginia on his summer leave, Lee heard discouraging news from "home." His half brother Henry's adultery with his sister-in-law in 1820 became very public knowledge, and the Lee family suffered significant disgrace.

"Black Horse Harry" had long since reconciled with his wife Ann. After he lost Stratford, in 1822, Henry became a minor civil servant in Washington and eventually lent his pen to the political cause of Andrew Jackson. In 1828, soon after he wrote his letter to John C. Calhoun on behalf of Robert's candidacy for West Point, Henry learned that Stratford had changed hands again. The new owners were Betsy and Henry Storke, and Betsy Storke had once been Betsy McCarty, his partner in adultery. It was an odd case of inverse double standard. Betsy McCarty Storke lived at Stratford in social prominence for fifty years. Henry Lee continued his slide down the social scale.

Henry and Ann moved into Andrew Jackson's home, The Hermitage, outside Nashville while Henry worked on a campaign biography of Jackson for the presidential election of 1828. Henry never completed the biography. But Jackson won the election and still considered Henry Lee eligible for some spoils of patronage. The President offered Lee a post as United States consul in Algiers; Lee leapt at the boon and soon left the country for Morocco. Not the least reason Lee wanted to leave was Ann Lee's continued dependence upon morphine and his fear that her addiction would embarrass him. And, like his father, Henry set out for foreign lands only one step ahead of his creditors.

President Jackson submitted Henry Lee's name to the Senate for confirmation along with an especially questionable set of nominees for government posts abroad. Like Lee, most of the nominees were writers or editors, and many senators seriously wondered about their qualifications as diplomats. The debate never became public record; but Henry Lee's decade-old indiscretion got loudly proclaimed. The Senate refused to confirm some of Jackson's appointees. In Henry Lee's case the rejection was unanimous!

Gossip mills in Washington ground the Lees again. Henry Lee departed Algiers and with Ann sought refuge, first in Italy, then in Paris. He eventually embarked upon a biography of Napoleon; she remained addicted to morphine; and the two of them grew even more pitiable.[13]

Even knee-deep in marsh mud on Cockspur Island, Lee could not fail to hear the sad news from Washington. He could read the bare facts reported circumspectly in the *Daily Savannah Republican* and no doubt read between the lines as well. He kept abreast of his half brother's travels and travails via Carter, who corresponded with Henry. At this point neither half brother and very few besides Henry knew the extent of Ann's troubles. Henry had had endorsements from Chief Justice of the Supreme Court John Marshall and from some of the same senators who ultimately voted against his confirmation. This only served as an index of how damning was the day-long debate in executive session of the Senate. To a degree Henry's self-imposed exile must have seemed the best resolution possible for the family reputation.[14]

By the time Major Babcock suspended work on Cockspur and Lee was free to travel north for the summer, some of the scandal had subsided. Lee took Nat with him aboard the packet boat for New York.

When they reached the city they probably visited Carter, who had moved to 15 Pine Street in lower Manhattan and was once more practicing law in New York. Carter spent much of his young manhood and midlife attempting to settle down and like the law. Robert's letters to his older brother changed very subtly in tone over time. If Carter had ever been a mentor to his younger brother, roles gradually reversed; Robert eventually counseled Carter. At this point the two brothers seem to have been friends and equals.[15]

Lee and Nat soon headed south to Virginia and more serious visiting. Lee made the rounds among family and friends once more, but spent a considerable time at Arlington with Mary Custis.

The plantation encompassed 1,100 acres, then within the District of Columbia; and on a hill across the Potomac from the Capitol, Arlington House crowned the estate. Designed in Greek Revival style by the English architect George Hadfield, the house is imposing indeed. Construction on the south wing commenced in 1802 and continued in fits and starts until 1817, when the structure was finally complete. Arlington was a showplace, modeled after a Greek temple, named for the Custis family estate on Virginia's Eastern Shore, boasting massive Doric columns and a portico sixty feet wide, twenty-five feet deep. But behind the portico the house was smaller than it appeared, and the lives of the inhabitants much simpler than the grand facade implied.[16]

George Washington Parke Custis was Martha Washington's grandson by way of her earlier marriage. An orphan from infancy, Custis grew up at Mount Vernon with his grandmother, and George Washington had adopted him as his son. Washington, however, may well have regretted his beneficence toward Custis. Blessed with every advantage a young man could have in the United States, Custis seemed determined to squander his good fortune and the fortunes of others as well.

Custis enrolled in the College of New Jersey; the college authorities expelled him. He enrolled at St. John's College in Annapolis; he left without graduating. Young Custis had to answer in court an accusation that he stole two teaspoons from Gadsby's Tavern in Alexandria, and his adoptive father spoke of Custis's "almost uncontrollable disposition to indolence in everything that did not tend to his amusements."[17]

Martha Washington died in 1802, and then Custis no longer had reason or excuse to remain at Mount Vernon. Fortunately he had inherited 15,000 acres in four large tracts from which to choose to establish his home. Custis selected the plantation on the Potomac, changed its name from Mount Washington to Arlington, and settled into a cabin while work began on Arlington House.

In 1806, Custis married Mary Lee Fitzhugh, daughter of William Fitzhugh, sister of the William H. Fitzhugh who owned Ravensworth and was Ann Lee's counselor and benefactor. This Mary Custis was an accepting and giving person; Lee would call her "Mother" and mean the compliment.

Mr. Custis, Lee eventually called "Father," and he may have understood the irony in this address very well. Custis shared some of Light Horse Harry Lee's less admirable traits. The master of Arlington was never a planter, nor even a farmer. He gave other men charge of his productive land and slaves and lived on the money his tenants and managers paid him. He was a man of passing enthusiasms: he bred sheep and held contests for a time to encourage the development of American species; he painted massive canvasses; he composed poetry; he gave orations. Of all these activities, Custis was most successful with sheep. His paintings and poetry were bad. And his orations tended always to say the same thing: George Washington had been the greatest man in America's golden age, and subsequent Americans were apostates from the founding faith.

Custis was a Federalist long after the party ceased to function in national politics. He made Arlington House into a Washington memorabilia museum. Not at all physically imposing, Custis was quite short and possessed of a premature paunch. He was forever the "child of Mount Vernon."

Yet Custis could be charming, and he was essentially harmless to anyone who did not resent his unearned wealth or possess a low boredom threshold regarding the Father of Our Country. To the extent that any slaveholder could, Custis indulged his slaves and gave them freedom in his will. He certainly loved and pampered his daughter, and he and his wife helped define Virginia hospitality. Custis brought from Mount Vernon a large punch bowl painted inside to represent a ship—the hull at the bottom of the bowl and the mast extending up the side to the rim. When the Custises entertained, the men in attendance had to drink the full height of the mast from the potent bowl.[18]

The father Robert Lee never knew was famous for previous deeds, and before Robert was born Light Horse Harry Lee became more pose than anything else, a fiction his family perpetuated during his exile and after his death. The man Robert Lee called "Father" for twenty-six years, George Washington Parke Custis, claimed fame for the mere fact of his birth and the largess of his step-grandfather while he was still an infant. Custis, too, was principally posture, all but devoid of substance, sustained by wealth he possessed because he outlived his grandmother, and humored by friends and family too kind to speak a demeaning truth to his face.

Some time during that summer of 1830, Lee asked Mary Custis to marry him. She assented, presumably with enthusiasm, but deferred to her parents' opinions in accord with custom.[19] Her mother readily consented to the marriage; but her father withheld his consent. Most likely Custis simply did not want to lose his daughter. He also had to be concerned about a union with the Lee family and its scoundrels and recent scandal. Custis well knew that his daughter's beau was poor. The couple would be compelled to live on a lieutenant's salary, and Custis himself was often short of cash in spite of his lands and slaves; his potentially great wealth was less than liquid. Hence he knew that he could not much supplement the couple's income, even if Lee were willing to accept his help.

So Custis exercised his prerogative, and the marriage was in limbo when Lee had to return to Cockspur Island in November. Those who knew Custis, however, knew that he was certainly not adamant in his position. If Mary Custis wanted to marry Robert Lee, she most probably would do so. Her father was hardly a man of bold, independent commitment; nor was he a father capable of denying his daughter whatever she desired.[20]

With some flourish, Lee wrote his older brother, "I am engaged to Miss Mary C. Think of that. . . . That is, she & her mother have given their consent. But the Father has not yet made up his mind, though it is supposed will not object." Tentative plans for a wedding the following spring (1831) proceeded, while Custis was supposedly making up his mind.[21]

Lee lingered at Arlington into October of 1830 and then set out for New York via Baltimore, where he paid a visit to his sister Ann Marshall. He traveled alone this time; Nat followed him about a month later. Lee boarded the packet boat in New York on November 7 and arrived on Cockspur Island during the night of November 10.

Next morning he was not pleased. When he surveyed the remains of his hard work the previous season, Lee found that his buildings were still in good condition. But storms had wrecked the system of ditches and dykes he had designed and constructed, and destroyed the wharf. Lee took cold comfort in the fact that he had been right and Major Babcock wrong about the location of the wharf. What mattered now was the immense amount of work he would have to do all over again and the necessity of redesigning the system to withstand autumn gales in the future.

For the present, the only thing to do was wait for Major Babcock. Lee went to Savannah and spent a few days at the Mackays' home. Rumor had it that Mrs. Babcock had left the major and taken their youngest child with her. Still, no one knew anything about Babcock himself.

So Lee returned to Cockspur and began himself the work of repairing the embankments. On December 1, Babcock had still not arrived. Lee, however, had succeeded in rebuilding much of his embankment and was preparing to direct his laborers to redig the ditches which drained the work site.[22]

Georgia was cold that winter, and more storms than normal seemed to lash the coast. Nat, Lee's slave and charge, arrived on Christmas Day after a harrowing voyage of twenty-five days from New York. He was convinced that he had been at sea for five weeks, and his health suffered accordingly. He was quite weak and racked with coughing spasms. Lee was alarmed for Nat's life and cared for the old man as best he could. However, at some time during this winter, Nat died: one more link with Lee's youth was severed.

Again Lee enjoyed Savannah that winter. In addition to the friends he had made the previous year, he had relatives in town. His nephew Charles (son of half sister Lucy Carter) and Charles's bride had journeyed south for the sake of her health. They spent the winter in Savannah, and Charles at least was a source of some amusement. Lee wrote Carter, "You never saw a fellow take a thing more kindly than Sweet Charles does his marriage." He expanded, "There is not a party of any kind afloat, but what he is figuring away in his black *tights* & white silks, dancing and flirting with all the girls, while the madam is left at home to take care of her health." Of course Lee had good reason to observe the behavior of newly married couples so closely.

He attended dinner parties though he termed them "my abomination," and professed, "evening parties I can stand." When he returned to Cockspur soon after the first of the year, Lee hoped he would be "better pleased with the quiet and uniformity." The truth was Lee was shy and took pains to avoid large numbers of people and any number of people he did not know well.[23]

Eventually someone found Major Babcock, and his superiors in the Army had him arrested. Babcock resolved the issue of his protracted absence by resigning from the Army. In Babcock's place, the Engineer Corps assigned Lieutenant Joseph K. F. Mansfield to command the project on Cockspur Island. Mansfield would remain in charge for fifteen years, until 1846, only one year before Fort Pulaski was completed.[24]

Mansfield arrived in January 1831, and soon after concluded that Cockspur Island would not support the fort the Engineer Corps intended to build there. He began to redesign the proposed structure and asked for help. In April, Captain Richard Delafield came to consult, and Mansfield and Delafield continued the redesign. Lee served the pair as problem solver and sketch drawer.

Meanwhile the powers that be in the Engineer Corps decided to reassign Lee. With Mansfield on the job at Cockspur, Lee became a luxury there and one the Corps could not afford. Had he had the opportunity Lee would certainly have requested an assignment closer to Arlington, both for the sake of his impending marriage and of his and Mary Custis's ties with northern Virginia. Maybe Lee had someone powerful in Washington to speak a word or two in his behalf. At any rate he received orders to report for duty at Old Point, Virginia, at the tip of the peninsula formed by the York and James Rivers, and site of Fort Monroe. That fort was nearly complete; Lee would assist Captain Andrew Talcott with the outworks and the moat. In addition, Lee had charge of work on Fort Calhoun (later Fort Wool), which was then essentially a pile of stone a short way offshore.[25]

Some time in April Lee left Cockspur Island and started north by stagecoach. En route he visited Georgetown (South Carolina), Charleston, Fayetteville, Raleigh, and Richmond—none of which he had ever seen before.

He reported for duty at Fort Monroe on May 7, 1831, and almost immediately Talcott, his superior, left for Philadelphia. Policy in the Engineer Corps required at least one officer on duty whenever work took place, and here the work stopped in winter. Consequently Lee began to wonder when he would get married and whether he could secure leave from his new post to attend his own wedding. Lee lived in Talcott's quarters, learned his way around a new community, and watched the mail for news from Arlington.

As often happens with weddings, the various elements fell into place at nearly the last minute. June 30, a Thursday evening, was the date. Lee secured a furlough from late June until early August, and in the process of making these arrangements he became better acquainted with Talcott. The two young officers (Lee twenty-four, Talcott thirty-four) became in time very good friends; indeed, Talcott would prove one of Lee's best male friends.[26]

Meanwhile at Arlington very likely frenzy prevailed. Mr. Custis was $12,-000 in debt and the month following the wedding had to postpone paying off a note of only $65—he was, he said, "very short of cash at this time." Mrs. Custis was ill, some sort of stomach ailment which made a relative concerned that she might have "got into bilious habit." Mary Custis was having twelve attendants, six bridesmaids and six groomsmen; family members were planning to attend and remain for a few days; and Arlington House did not have rooms or room for this horde. The Custises borrowed cots, blankets, candlesticks, and other such necessities and planned for some of their guests to sleep three in a bed.[27]

At Old Point, Lee confessed to Carter, "I begin to feel quite *funny* when I count my days. . . ." He did not go to Arlington and compound the chaos there until "the *important* day." At least these were his bride's instructions. At last the wedding day dawned. Lee probably arrived at Arlington by boat; that had been his plan earlier in the month.[28]

At Arlington he found brother Smith, who was his best man. Most of his other groomsmen were junior officers serving at Fort Monroe. John P. Kennedy had been a classmate at West Point; James A. Chambers, Lee had met in Savannah. "Dick" Tilghman and James H. Prentiss, Lee likely knew less well than the others. Thomas Turner, like Smith, was a naval officer who was also a cousin from the Carter side of his family. Lee made few close male friends, and some of those he did make, his brother Carter and John Mackay, for example, were unable to attend the wedding. Talcott became a close friend, but only later. As a result Lee's groomsmen—Smith Lee and John Kennedy excepted—seem to have been groomsmen because they were available.

Mary Custis's bridesmaids included her friends from childhood Catherine Mason and Marietta Turner, and some of her cousins—Mary Goldsborough, Angela Lewis, Julia Calvert, and Britannia Peter. Other friends and relatives were also present and some had been for two or three days. The Custises presided with their usual grace, having somehow managed the logistics of sleeping and eating for their guests.[29]

Lee later wrote Talcott, "There was neither fainting nor fighting, nor anything uncommon which could be twisted into an adventure." Actually there was one adventure. To officiate at the ceremony, the Custises had asked the Reverend Reuel Keith, who had charge of Virginia Theological Seminary in Alexandria and who had also been Rector of Christ Church. As Keith was traveling the relatively short distance between Alexandria and Arlington, he encountered a summer rainstorm and arrived soaking wet. The only man with clothes to spare for Keith was Custis. But Keith was tall and thin, and Custis was short and chubby. Keith's vestments solved the problem. He wore Custis's clothes, but wore cassock and surplice over the misfits, and only those who had seen Keith unfrocked shared the joke.[30]

Lee recalled that Keith "had few words to say, though he dwelt upon them as if he had been reading my Death warrant. . . ." The groom confessed to feeling "as bold as a sheep." Lee then remembered that he had been "surprised at my want of Romance in so great a degree as not to feel more excitement than at the Black Board at West Point."

Then the wedding ceremony was over and the party commenced. The wedding party remained in residence from Thursday, June 30, until the following Tuesday, July 5, when most of them left. Some of the women stayed until the end of that week, when the Lees and Custises were finally alone.

Lee went into Washington on July 11, called upon General and Mrs. Gratiot, and gleaned the latest news and gossip from the Engineer Corps. Then the couple and Mrs. Custis visited Ravensworth, Kinloch, and maybe Eastern View.

In his letter to Talcott about the wedding, Lee engaged in a very mild form of barracks bravado regarding his new intimacy with Mary. He recounted the departure of the last of the wedding party, and then wrote, "I would tell you how the time passed, but fear I am too prejudiced to say anything more, but that it went *very* rapidly & still continues to do so." Near the close of the letter, Lee apologized for his haste and explained: "I actually could not find *time* before I left the District [Arlington] for anything except———."[31]

As Lee the young husband came to know his new wife, he confirmed that she was quite unlike him. The sole surviving child of doting parents, Mary Lee was accustomed to having her way. She tended to center her attention upon herself, and in confronting new situations her first concern was usually how the situation would affect her. She was disorganized in her personal life and notoriously late for just about every occasion. Nor was she especially pretty, in sharp contrast to her husband, who was extremely handsome and seemed important when he entered a room. Still she chided "Mr. Lee" as though he were her servant.

As a recent bride she suffered "an attack of the Fever & Ague" within two weeks of her wedding. It was a portent; later in her life Mary Lee would endure wretched health. Afflicted by various ailments at various times, arthritis became her constant nemesis in midlife and relegated her to a wheelchair by the time she was in her mid-fifties.

Mary Lee was, or wanted to be, intensely pious. Filled with evangelical Protestant Christian zeal, she did not take kindly to the fact that "Mr. Lee" remained unchurched. She was concerned for his soul's health and hoped that he would hear and respond to God's call in his life.[32]

In her health and religious zeal, Mary Custis must have reminded Lee of his mother, and her chiding may have seemed maternal to him as well. Otherwise, she seemed very little like Ann Lee, who had been self-reliant, precise, and generous to the point of sacrifice.

But Mary Custis possessed just about everything to which Ann Lee had aspired—a stable family, a proper home, and assured status. Two years after his mother's death, Lee made a safe and acceptable marriage. He was, as he said, "as bold as a sheep." He did not "marry his mother" or a woman anything like his mother. He did, however, marry his mother's unfulfilled dreams.

5

"Happy as a Clam in High Water"

NEWLYWEDS Mary and Robert Lee moved in August 1831 from the splendor of Arlington House into two rooms at Fort Monroe. These rooms formed a wing of the quarters occupied by Lieutenant Lee's immediate superior, Captain Andrew Talcott. The Lees were not houseguests, of course; but they did live for a while communally with the Talcott household.[1]

In time Talcott became very close to Lee. This was fortunate, because besides Talcott, the captain's household included his sister and brother-in-law, Abigail and Horace Hale, and their two daughters, Rebecca and Catherine (Kate). Actually Talcott and Horace Hale were not often at home, so the quarters were not as crowded as they might seem.[2]

The Lees contributed one of Mary's slaves, Cassy, to the living arrangement. Talcott, at least, and perhaps Hale too, had slaves either owned or rented to perform household chores. Slaves also did the cooking in a kitchen probably separate from the living quarters and carried meals on covered trays to the house.[3]

Very soon after Mary and Robert arrived at Fort Monroe, slaveholders in Virginia and throughout the South suffered a shock to their presumptions of domestic tranquility. In Southampton County, across Hampton Roads about 60 miles as the crow flies from Fort Monroe, Nat Turner and a band of black followers carried out the largest sustained slave revolt in American history. The rising began in the very early morning hours of August 22, 1831, and concluded the following day. During this period Turner and his men killed more than fifty-five white people and spread terror far beyond the borders of Southampton County. Because Nat Turner remained at large in hiding until October 30, fear persisted locally as alarm spread over the entire slaveholding South.

Federal troops from Fort Monroe joined Virginia Militia companies from far and wide to suppress the revolt. However, local militia managed to quell the rising long before the masses of soldiers and armed men arrived. Reverberations grew, though, as stories of the revolt spread, and trials and executions of the participants continued nearly until Christmas.[4]

Lee assured the Custises in a letter written August 31 that the revolt was very much over. He decried overreaction on the part of some of the militia and hysteria within the white community generally. But he did repeat tales which spread the conspiracy as far as Norfolk and so betrayed the nervous mood in southeastern Virginia.[5]

In the aftermath of events in Southampton County, five more companies joined the "Artillery School of Practice" at Fort Monroe. This influx increased the garrison strength to 680 men, a very mixed blessing for the Engineer Corps officers stationed there. Engineer officers were accustomed to lonely construction sites with few if any other officers on hand as companions. The concentration of artillerymen much enhanced social life at Fort Monroe, and one of the new arrivals was Joe Johnston, who had been one of Lee's closest friends at West Point.[6]

However, with the Artillery School and an enlarged garrison came the potential for friction between branches of the Army. In November, for example, Colonel Abram Eustis who commanded Fort Monroe responded to the continuing concerns over slave uprisings by banning all black people from the fort. "No negroes or persons of color of either sex, other than the servants of officers, and those employed in the Hospital and Quarter Masters Dept. are to be harboured or tolerated within the walls of the Fort." Eustis's order ignored the needs of the Engineers, whose work crews were black. Although most of the work that remained at Fort Monroe involved the moat and outworks, which were outside of the fort, the men needed access to the fort to secure water for themselves and the horses, and for the mortar used in construction. Too, Eustis had not considered the slaves belonging to the Engineer officers (Talcott and Lee) or to the clerks and draughtsman who were living within the fort. Or maybe he had considered these slaves and simply wanted to harass the Engineers and civilians who cluttered his post. At any rate, because Talcott was away, Lee protested the order to Eustis and to General Gratiot in Washington. Somehow, most likely by instructions to Eustis from his superiors, the situation got resolved and the construction continued at the fort. Tension between the artillery and Engineers persisted, however.[7]

His tour of duty at Fort Monroe also offered Lee an initiation into garrison life within a peacetime army. He became disillusioned by the behavior of many of his fellow officers. "I have seen minds formed for use and ornament," he wrote Jack Mackay, "degenerate into sluggishness and inactivity, requiring the stimulus of brandy and cards to rouse them to action." When a young lieutenant fresh from West Point was arrested for being too drunk to function on parade, Lee commented, "He is a fine looking young man. Graduated very well in 1832 and appears to be intelligent. But his propensity, it is impossible for me to understand."[8]

The engineering tasks at Fort Monroe were not especially challenging but the job required constant attention. Lee had to be alert to ensure that nothing went awry. Talcott was often absent.

During the three construction "seasons" of 1832, 1833, and 1834, workers completed most of the crude masonry work on the ditch (moat) and on the outworks beyond. Lee designed some buildings, wharves, and fortifications, prepared reports, kept the accounts, and contracted for labor and materials. He confronted an outbreak of cholera which interrupted work during the late summer and fall of 1832, and he endured the storms which periodically swept into Hampton Roads from the Atlantic to threaten work in progress.[9]

Also Lee's responsibility, indeed his alone, was the artificial island offshore in Hampton Roads. Eventually the rocks and sand there were supposed to support Fort Calhoun. But an attempt at building atop the stone already in place had proven premature. So Lee's task was to organize the dumping of more rock and sand until the "island" stopped sinking and the site would support a fort. As Engineer Corps funds permitted, Lee contracted with the captains of vessels to transport and offload stone and sand. In time the site became Fort Wool (instead of Calhoun); in Lee's time it was known simply "Rip Raps," because that was what it was—stone randomly placed in water as a foundation. The United States was still spending money on Fort Wool in 1861.[10]

Lee served at Fort Monroe/Rip Raps from August 1831 until November 1834. The assignment was a professional success of sorts; he proved that he could manage a quasi-independent project, and his superiors in the Engineer Corps appreciated his efficiency and dependability. Lee made professional and personal friends during his stay at Fort Monroe, and somehow he impressed people that he was destined for tasks more challenging than dumping stone and sand on top of previously dumped stone and sand in Hampton Roads. On May 17, 1832, the Army removed the "brevet" (temporary) from Lee's rank; his initiation period was over. He became a bona fide second lieutenant as of July 1, 1829.[11]

Possibly because of the routine nature of the work, certainly because of strained relations with Eustis and the politics of the military at peace, Lee grew frustrated and restless at Fort Monroe. In June 1834, he wrote to Talcott, "As much as I like the *location* of Old Point & as fond as I am of the company of some of the officers and some persons in the neighborhood & notwithstanding the great partiality I have for *my comd*g *off* (I mean *no flattery*) & my belief I shall not meet with such another—yet there are so many of the *désagremens* [vexations] connected with the duty that I should like to get another post." Later that summer, Lee wrote Carter in serious jest, "I suppose I must continue to work out my youth for little profit and less credit & when old be laid on the shelf."[12]

Far more important than Lee's professional life at Fort Monroe was his personal life. He had pursued the duties of an engineer before; before Fort Monroe he had never been married.

Mary Custis Lee seems to have adjusted rather well to reduced circumstances as the wife of a very junior officer. Yet a letter she wrote to her mother after about three or four weeks at Fort Monroe is quite revealing. She began with the assumption that her mother would "feel most anxious to know how my soul prospers" and launched a discussion of her religious life. She felt, she wrote, "an anxious desire to do something to show forth my gratitude to that all merciful Saviour who has done all for me but it is hard to find out what I can do." Having proclaimed herself anxious "to do something," Mary Lee then began a recitation of many things she had not done:

The only actively pious family here have not visited me . . . & the rest of the ladies seem not to be exerting themselves to improve the condition of the people here. . . .

There is a Sunday School . . . but I have not seen it nor do I know how it is conducted. . . .

I am much obliged to you for the books though I must confess I have not read the others yet. . . .

Mrs. Hale & I commenced the life of Luther, but like you she is so much interrupted between children & servants that we have not progressed far. . . .

There is a Mrs. Haliburton at the tavern who says she is a relation of mine but I have not seen her yet. . . .

I do not know how it is, but we do not seem to find a great deal of time for reading. . . .

Of course the Lees were still very much newlywed and doubtless spent intimate time together. But, as Mary wrote to her mother, "Robert has but little [time] for going about as his duties require his presence daily & keep him pretty well employed but this this you know is no misfortune." By the time she wrote, she had been at Fort Monroe at least three weeks, likely more. Robert Lee had assured Talcott that he could arrange the household items he had shipped "in five minutes after my arrival." Mary Lee assured her mother, "We are very well fixed up & have got about as much in our little room as it will hold." So the question remains about Mary Lee: how did she spend her time? She seems, in this letter at least, devoted to doing very little.[13]

Even when she lived in only two rooms, Mary was probably a poor housekeeper. Later, after the Lees had secured more spacious quarters at Fort Monroe, Robert Lee wrote of himself, "I don't know that I shall ever overcome my propensity for order & method but I will try." Despite his efforts, though, Robert Lee persisted in his insistence upon "order & method."[14] His best statement about the issue occurs in a letter he wrote from St. Louis a few years later.

We have not yet got fixed, and are but poorly accommodated at what is called the best Hotel in the City. The House is very crowded, and a dark *dirty* room is the only one we could procure. The dinner was very good indeed, well cooked and well served, but the table is too large and full, and contains too many guests both for the viands and servants. This part could be borne with, but the room is intolerable, and so soon as I close this letter I shall sally out in quest of another. I may be perhaps *over* scrupulous in this respect, but I can readily bear the *clean dirt* of the *earth,* and drink without a strain the mud of the Missouri, and if necessary could live in it and lie in it, though this *domestic* filth is revolting to my taste.[15]

From Fort Monroe, Robert Lee wrote about impending houseguests, "Tell the ladies that they are aware that Mrs. L. is somewhat addicted to *laziness* &

forgetfulness in her housekeeping. But they may be certain she does her best. Or in her mother's words, 'The spirit is willing but the flesh is weak.' "[16]

Lee periodically chided his wife about other issues as well. During the spring of 1832 Horace Hale died. At the time Mary Lee was away from Fort Monroe on a protracted visit to Arlington. "I am sorry," Robert Lee wrote, "it has so happened that you have not been with Mrs. Hale, when in the one case she needed your assistance & in the other your sympathy. I am sure you would have been delighted both to have nursed and relieved one so kind and good as she is. . . ." In the fall of 1833 Mary Lee was again at Arlington and in need of clothes. Robert Lee responded, "If you have need of any funds let me know it & get such frocks as will suit yourself, since my taste is so difficult, I will conform to yours." Lee was not a demanding husband; however mild these words may seem, from Robert Lee they were fairly stern rebukes.[17]

In that early letter to her mother, Mary interrupted a train of her thought to interject, "What . . . would I give for one stroll on the hills at Arlington this bright day." She did miss Arlington and thought of it as home no matter where she lived. And during her first few years of marriage, Mary Lee spent a lot of time at her childhood home.[18]

The Lees lived together at Fort Monroe from early August 1831 until about Christmas. They paid a visit to Shirley and then went to Arlington for the holidays. In January 1832, Robert Lee had to return to duty at Fort Monroe. Mary Lee, however, lingered at Arlington; she lingered for at least five more months and only returned to Fort Monroe some time after June 6, 1832. And when she returned, she brought her mother with her.

Mary Lee was pregnant that summer of 1832, and on September 16, 1832, gave birth to her first child, a boy, George Washington Custis Lee. There is no reason to believe that Mary Lee had too much difficulty with her pregnancy, or with childbirth. Both new parents seem to have been delighted with their healthy child.

But mother and son left Fort Monroe a month earlier than Robert Lee to go to Arlington for the Christmas season. During the first eighteen months they were married, the Lees spent at least a third of the time living apart from each other. And for various reasons this pattern persisted throughout their married life.[19]

While Mary Lee remained at Arlington during the first half of 1832, circumstances changed considerably at "The Tuileries" (Quarters No. 17) where the Lees and the Talcotts' extended family lived. Horace Hale, Talcott's brother-in-law, died; Talcott's sister Abigail and her two daughters moved out. Then on April 11 Talcott married Harriet Randolph Hackley of Norfolk and subsequently moved his bride into his quarters at Fort Monroe. Of course the Lee family expected to expand by one that fall, so in the summer of 1832 Mary and Robert Lee took over the top floor in the Engineer Corps half of The Tuileries, and the Talcotts lived on the floor beneath them.[20]

Lee explained his thoughts about their living arrangements to "Molly," his pet nickname for Mary. "You seem to think Molly you would prefer living as we are, but are you right in this. We ought not to give others the trouble of providing for us always, and besides as I can see how we might inconvenience & be a restraint upon them, I can also see how we can be more pleasantly situated by ourselves." He amplified the latter point, adding, "We may escape company that might not be agreeable (and I have had some examples this spring) & always have our friends when we choose. . . ."[21]

For the Lees, the move to more spacious space and independent living entailed the employment of more slaves. Robert Lee still owned at least four women, part of his mother's bequest to him, but did not think well enough of three of the women to have them serve in his household. "Letitia," he wrote Mary, "will have to be your Femme de Chambre & in the meantime you may do with all of them as you please if opportunity offers. But do not trouble yourself about them, as they are not worth it." Lee estimated, *"Two* good servants are as much as we should require. . . ." However, he seemed resigned to keeping more slaves, because "What they want in quality we must make up in quantity." If Mary were not able to settle upon suitable servants from among those people owned within the family, Robert Lee suggested that she hire someone "for 6 or 8 dollars a month."[22]

Then and later in his life, Lee may not have felt comfortable as a slave-holder. Some years later he wrote to his wife that "Slavery as an institution, is a moral & political evil in any Country." But he also wrote about African Americans: "The blacks are immeasurably better off here than in Africa, morally, socially & physically. The painful discipline they are undergoing, is necessary for their instruction as a race, & I hope will prepare & lead them to better things. How long their subjugation may be necessary is known & ordered by a wise Merciful Providence." He himself continued to own black people at least as late as 1846.[23]

When Mary Lee and her mother arrived at Fort Monroe in June 1832, they brought with them more furnishings for the Lees' expanded quarters and at least two slaves, owned or hired, to serve the household. The newlywed Talcotts moved into their quarters in The Tuileries about the same time, and Robert Lee began an extended mock love affair with Harriet Talcott.[24]

She was beautiful and apparently possessed a lively wit. Lee called her "my beautiful Talcott" and "Talcott, My Beauty," and often included messages to her in his letters to Andrew Talcott. On the occasion of the birth of the Talcotts' first child, a daughter, Lee proposed marriage on behalf of his son Custis and even claimed paternity of the new Talcott for himself: "The all accomplished & elegant Master Custis Lee begs to place in her hands, his happiness & life, being assured that as for her he was born, so for her will he live. His only misery can be her frown, his only delight, her smile. He hopes that her assent will not be withheld from his most ardent wishes, & that in their blissful union Fortune may be indemnified for her miscarriage of the Affaire du Coeur of the *Father* & *Mother."*[25]

Mary and Robert Lee were much unlike in lots of ways, and living together surely accentuated their differences. But Robert Lee loved his wife and bore (in usually good humor) what seemed to him her eccentricities. His father's negative example, if nothing else, must have fueled Lee's resolve to be a dutiful spouse. To his old friend Jack Mackay, Lee wrote in 1834, "I would not be unmarried for all you could offer me."[26]

But Mary and the satisfaction of self-control could not fulfill Robert Lee's zest for life. So he flirted with many women and formed special friendships with some of them. He was scrupulous about informing his wife of his flirtations and friendships. And he seems to have been very careful to keep his relationships with women only verbal, never physical. No evidence exists that Lee acted out any of his many fantasies. But fantasies he certainly had.

In April 1832, while he waited impatiently for Mary Lee's return to Fort Monroe, Robert Lee wrote his bride, "Let me tell you Mrs. Lee, no later than today, did I escort Miss G. to see Miss Kate! Think of that Mrs. Lee! . . . How I did strut-along. . . . Surely it was a sight for the Old Pointers to see. And I only wish you could have been of the number. How you would have triumphed in my happiness & Molly I would have been *happy."*[27]

To Mackay he wrote in the summer of 1834, "As for the Daughters of Eve in this country, they are formed in the very poetry of nature, and would make your lips water and fingers tingle. They are beginning to assemble to put their beautiful limbs in this salt water. . . ." And a few years later he confessed to Mackay to a preference "in favor of the pretty girls if there are any here, and I know there are, for I have met them in no place, in no garb, in no situation that I did not feel my heart open to them, like the flower to the sun." To Talcott he described some of the festivities following the wedding of his brother Smith: "My spirits were so buoyant last night when relieved from the eyes of my dame that my Sister Nanie [Smith's bride Nannie], was trying to pass me off as her *spouse,* but I was not going to have my sport spoiled in that way, undeceived the young ladies & they concluded I was *single,* & I have not had such soft looks & tender pressures of the [ha]nd for many years." Lee also wrote Talcott in 1833, *"Sally* is as blythe as a lark & admitted me (an innocent man) into her bed-chamber a few days after the frolick."[28]

Very early in his married life, Lee revealed the intimacy he still shared with Eliza Mackay, sister of his friend Jack and sometime companion in Savannah during his tour of duty on Cockspur Island. At Arlington in January 1832, the Lees received a late invitation to Eliza Mackay's wedding. Robert Lee responded on the day of the wedding: "But Miss E. how do you feel about this time? Say 12 o'clock of the day, as you see the shadows commence to fall towards the East and know that at *last* the sun will set." Interrupted then, Lee returned to his letter four days later; by this time Eliza Mackay was married. Lee inquired," . . . And how did you disport yourself My Child? Did you go off well like a torpedo cracker on Christmas morning. . . ." The metaphor is indeed graphic, and it requires no genius to relate the phrase to Eliza's wedding night.

This letter speaks to a rich relationship Robert Lee shared with Eliza Mackay. But because the invitation included her, Mary Lee appended her stiff, correct congratulations to Eliza, whom she had never met, and she surely read her husband's portion of the letter. Unless Mary Lee was incredibly naive, she surely understood the sexual reference in the "torpedo cracker" metaphor. So one letter may reveal the degree of intimate candor Robert Lee shared with not one but two women.[29]

At Fort Monroe, Mary and Robert Lee learned they could live together in general harmony. They also discovered that marriage had not quelled Robert Lee's fondness for the company and companionship of women. So they began a pattern of compensating and accommodating that not only endured but also grew throughout their married life. Robert Lee retained his self-control and remained faithful to Mary. However, he revealed some of his feelings about her in a letter he wrote from Fort Monroe to Talcott in July 1833. "Mrs. Custis & Mary," he said, "have gone up to Shirley which is as much to say that I am as happy as a clam in high water."[30]

All the while Lee was establishing his relationship with his wife, he was also attempting to complete work on Fort Monroe and to prepare the foundation for a fort at Rip Raps. Eustis and his garrison were no help. From time to time the intra-army enmity flared into open warfare. The great Fort Monroe sand skirmish of 1833 is a good example of the possibilities for pettiness within an army at peace.

At issue was sand from the beach near the wharf. Engineer workers used the sand for mixing mortar; Quartermaster crews used it for the surface of a road. Each of the work crews hauled sand in one-horse carts, and the drivers liked to position their carts in one way at one spot to load the sand.

On June 27, 1833, the Quartermaster drivers reported to their supervisor Captain Timothy Green that Ebenezer Shaw the overseer in the employ of the Engineers had forbidden them to load sand in the way to which they had become accustomed. Green told the men to return to the usual place and ignore Shaw. Shaw chased away the teamsters, who returned to Green. Then Green accompanied his men to the site and demanded access to the sand from Shaw.

Shaw refused and stood in the middle of the road blocking the way of the Quartermaster carts. Green ordered his drivers to run over Shaw if he did not move. Shaw then picked up a rock and said or implied that he intended to defend himself.

Cursing ensued. Finally Green and his men left the scene. But the captain soon thereafter filed formal charges against Shaw and demanded a trial by court-martial. Eustis as post commander prepared to assent to Green's demand for a court-martial and so informed Lee as Shaw's superior.

Lee took the position that as a civilian employed by the Engineer Department, Shaw was outside the bounds of military justice, and he sent copies of all the relevant correspondence to Chief of the Engineer Department General Charles Gratiot in Washington. Gratiot sustained Lee's position and referred the squabble to his superior with a recommendation that he order Eustis to cease any court-martial proceedings and "prevent in future any interference with the operations of the Engineer Department."[31]

So a major general in Washington who commanded the entire United States Army eventually brought peace in the great Fort Monroe sand skirmish of 1833. Lee informed Talcott, "If I had time I would make you laugh about this Green & Shaw affair, but must reserve that till you return. . . ."[32]

Although the Engineers won some skirmishes with the Artillery at Fort Monroe, the Artillery eventually won the war. Lee sensed some bureaucratic perfidy afoot on July 18, 1834, when Alexander Macomb, the major general commanding the Army, and John Forsyth, acting Secretary of War, arrived at Fort Monroe to inspect the state of construction. Talcott and Lee had already had their annual inspection, so clearly this visit boded ill. Then on July 24, Army Inspector General Colonel John E. Wool appeared and inspected some more.

A week after Wool's inspection the War Department ordered some alterations in assignments at Fort Monroe. The Artillery would henceforth complete the work on the fort. Only one Engineer officer would remain in the area; he would live at Rip Raps and continue the work there.[33]

Talcott and Lee were livid. Lee wrote Carter, "By this proceeding those in authority have thought proper to cast an insult upon the Engr. Dept & pointed censure upon the officers of Engrs charged with the work." Talcott demanded a court of inquiry to exonerate him of any implied misconduct. Lee informed Carter that if the Army failed to grant "reparation," then "I shall refuse to enter upon any other duty."[34]

In time Lee's anger cooled somewhat. The Army refused to grant Talcott's demand for a court of inquiry, but did offer him credit and compliments for his work on the fort. Talcott resigned from the Army in June 1836 to apply his skills in the private sector.[35]

Lee was the Engineer officer initially left in charge of the work at Rip Raps, and he dutifully took up his exile upon the barren, artificial island. From Rip Raps he responded in kind to what he still considered pettiness. In accord with the order of the War Department, he transferred all the property associated with Fort Monroe to the post quartermaster by August 31, 1834. Then he informed the Engineer Department that he could no longer employ laborers for any purpose. Denied the facilities of Fort Monroe, Lee reported, "We are now destitute of the means of supplying the Laborers with Bread, or the Sick with a Hospital & are without the necessary Houses & Storerooms for the Accommodation of Persons employed & the protection of Boats & other property." If the Army chose to expell the Engineers from Fort Monroe, the Army would have to reap the consequences of the choice. And Lee was more than willing to point out some of those consequences.[36]

Lieutenant Lee did not long languish at Rip Raps; General Gratiot shuffled some assignments and offered Lee a place in Washington as his assistant. Although Lee had reservations about "the duties of the office," he agreed to the transfer and assumed his new duties in November 1834.[37]

So Robert Lee returned to Arlington; Mary Lee and Custis had been there since August. In one sense Lee was returning "home" to northern Virginia. But the house to which he returned was not his. Mary Lee was at home. Robert Lee was still very much a houseguest.

6

"I Must Get Away from Here"

GEORGE WASHINGTON PARKE CUSTIS was one of those people Ann Lee had warned her son Robert to avoid. The contrast between Lee and his father-in-law was dramatic. Lee was tall, dark, handsome, diligent, self-controlled, and purposeful; Custis—short, fair, and fat—was dilatory, self-indulged, and aimless. But Custis had great wealth and Lee was poor.

Mediating and ameliorating the differences between the two men were their wives. Mary Lee adored her father and loved her husband; Mary Custis adored her son-in-law and loved her husband. So Parke Custis and Robert Lee endured each other, even though they probably never understood each other.[1]

Once someone in the Custis family proposed a plan which seems eminently logical. Mary Custis wrote her daughter in October 1831, not many months after her marriage, "David thinks as your Father is so literary a character that he would find it greatly to his advantage to withdraw Robert from his present profession and yield to him the management of affairs." Mrs. Custis responded, " . . . that would please me very well if Robert and Mr. Custis were of the same mind, but there did not seem any tendency to such a state of things at least in Mr. C——. Robert I could not answer for."[2]

While he was at Fort Monroe, Lee visited Smith Island in the Chesapeake Bay (just north of Tangier Island), which Custis owned. On his return he wrote, "My dear Father," and began his letter, "Supposing you may feel an interest in hearing something relative to Smiths [sic] Island, I take advantage of the first leisure day since my return to give you an account of my visit there. And also to submit to your better judgement my views of the means of turning it to profit." It would seem from this introduction that Lee's trip was his own idea and his counsel unsolicited. In his letter Lee described the island and its resources and made sensible recommendations about the wild cattle, sheep, and timber he observed there. He also said that he had intended visiting White House, another large Custis property; but his horse Boliver "took it in his head to die just as he would have been useful," so Lee was unable to undertake that trip.[3]

Custis may or may not have responded to his son-in-law's report. He did not take Lee's advice, however, and this letter is the only one extant in which Lee assumes any direct role in the "management of affairs" for his father-in-law.

About four years after Lee wrote his description and strategies about Smith Island, he gave Carter an acerbic account of Custis's activities, rare in its unveiled sarcasm. "The Major [an honorific title which doubtless galled Second Lieutenant Lee] is busy farming. His *corn* field is not yet enclosed or ploughed [on May 2!] but he is *rushing* on *all he knows.* 'Montgomerie' [a play about thirteenth-century Scotland] *failed.* The 'big Picture' has been exhibited in the Capitol, and attracted some animadversions from the Critics, which he says were levelled at his Politics!!"[4]

In contrast, some of Robert Lee's regard for his mother-in-law appears in a letter to Mary Lee concerning their transition to independent living and larger quarters at Fort Monroe. The Lees were corresponding during the spring of 1832 about what household items, furnishings, and slaves Mary should bring with her from Arlington. Robert Lee observed, "I know your dear mother will be for giving you everything she has, but you must recollect *one* thing & that is that they have been accustomed to comforts all their life, which now they could not dispense with and that we in the commencement ought to contract our wishes to their smallest compass & enlarge them as opportunity offers."[5]

Lee gave his mother-in-law credit for sharing his conviction as he later phrased it, that "the great duty of life" is "the promotion of the happiness & welfare of our fellow men." So he knew she would give her daughter *"every-thing,"* at the sacrifice of her own comfort. Maybe Mary Custis would indeed have given Mary Lee *"every*thing." The important fact is that Robert Lee believed she would, and thus believed that she and he shared an ethic of selflessness. So his words were high praise indeed. It may or may not have been significant that Lee did not suggest that Mr. Custis "will be for giving you *every*thing."[6]

Mary Lee more than shared her husband's good opinion of her mother and never seemed to undergo any sort of rebellion against her mother's authority. She had always depended upon her mother, and when she married Robert Lee, she simply added another person in her life upon whom she could depend to protect her from unpleasantness.

In her portion of the Lees' joint letter to Eliza Mackay Stiles congratulating her upon her marriage, Mary Lee wrote to this person she had never met, "I suppose you remain in Savannah near your Mother? What happiness! I am with mine now—the past and future disregarded." Beside invoking the blessing of "our beneficent Creator and Father," motherhood was the only substantive subject Mary Lee raised.[7]

When he went to work as assistant to the Chief of the Engineer Department (Corps) in Washington in November 1834, Lee hoped to rent a house in the city for himself, his wife, and two-year-old Custis. He was unsuccessful, however, and commuted to his office across the Potomac River.

But he did rent a room for himself at Mrs. Ulrich's boardinghouse so that he might remain in Washington when duty required or when the weather turned foul and streets and roads became streams of mud. In the "mess" or dinner company at Mrs. Ulrich's were Lee's old friend Joseph E. Johnston, other young officers, and a few consequential politicians, members of Congress and cabinet. Lee entertained at Mrs. Ulrich's house, and on one occasion he invited five fellow officers to dinner at 4:00 P.M. and added, "Those who can sleep three in a bed will find 'comfortable accommodations.'" During this period of his life Lee still served wine and stronger spirits to his guests. In time, however, he became concerned that his acquaintances might become addicted to alcohol and offered it to guests less and less.[8]

Washington was a very young village when Lee first went to the capital. People usually lived there because they worked in the government and so had to live there. And like the young officers Lee invited to his dinner, residents of Washington had to make their own fun. In fair weather Lee rode his horse down the hill from Arlington House, across the Long Bridge over the Potomac River, and up 14th Street to Pennsylvania Avenue. Offices of the War Department were then just west of the White House on 17th Street, between G Street and F Street (where the Executive Office Building would later stand). The offices of the Engineer Department, like most other government facilities, opened at 9:00 A.M. and closed at 3:00 P.M. Then, when his duties permitted, Lee remounted his horse and retraced his route back "home" to Arlington.[9]

In the beginning Lee probably found his new assignment somewhat exciting. He was a junior officer stationed among the powerful. He saw the great men of his time, living, breathing versions of people who were only names to the vast majority of Americans. Even when assigned to Fort Monroe, Lee had taken advantage of his visits to Arlington to cross the river and spend some time in the galleries of the houses of Congress listening to speeches and debates. In the midst of the Nullification Crisis during the winter of 1833, for example, Lee reported to Talcott, "The South has had to bear some hard kicks from all sides." He added, "John Randolph of R[oanoke] has arrived in W[ashington] & it is reported that he is to assemble the people in the House of R[epresentatives], deliver a speech from the chair Against Nullification, The Proclamation, Genl Jackson, Mr. Clay, Calhoun & Webster."[10]

Lee's superior Charles Gratiot was from St. Louis, one of the first graduates of West Point, an honored veteran of the War of 1812, and a capable Chief of the Engineer Department. General Gratiot obviously liked Lieutenant Lee; he had brought Lee to Washington, instead of allowing him to languish at Rip Raps, and Gratiot soon trusted Lee to manage the office while the general made his necessary visits and inspections of the various projects in which the Corps was engaged.[11]

Moreover, Lee had the great good fortune to begin his service in the Engineer Corps during an expansive period of public projects. In addition to constructing forts, the Engineers were involved in "internal improvements" of all sorts—building roads, improving harbors, dredging rivers, and such. Although Congress was less than reliable in its appropriations to fund these ventures, public money did flow, albeit in gushes and trickles, into these projects. For the moment, at least, Lee served a growth industry.

To Lee's dismay, however, Andrew Jackson and the Democrats possessed power and purse strings during Lee's first tenure in the capital. By birth, training, marriage, and experience, Lee was a Federalist. He believed in government by the rich, the well-born, and the able. He believed in government sufficiently strong to keep the vulgar mob in its place and to ensure its deference to its betters. He believed in order, in social hierarchy, and in *noblesse oblige.* The "best" people should have power and exercise authority for the good of the whole people. His profession and his church prescribed hierarchical relationships for soldiers and Christians in matters of power and episcopacy as extensions of the natural order in society.

Like his father, Robert Lee revered George Washington as model and hero, and he looked back upon Washington's time as a "golden age." Of course the Federalist era was long over by the mid-1830s. The so-called Second Party System in the American Republic had begun about the time that Lee entered West Point. Americans now tended to be Democrats or something else, and the many and varied expressions of opposition to Jackson and his party were forming a new coalition as the Whig Party. To the degree that Whigs were neo-Federalists, Lee was a Whig.[12]

Robert Lee believed that he was one of the political elect, the "best" people. He was not rich; but he was well-born and able, and he had followed the Lee family tradition of "marrying well." To make sure he was well-born, Lee would soon do a modest amount of genealogy in the course of securing an accurate representation of the Lee coat of arms. Robert Lee believed, whether accurately or not, that he was descended from Robert Bruce and other Old World notables.[13]

In 1832, his half brother Henry had reinforced the family political heritage with the publication of the extended pamphlet entitled *Observations on the Writings of Thomas Jefferson, With Particular Reference to the Attack They Contain on the Memory of the Late General Henry Lee.* A recently published compilation of Jefferson's correspondence included some letters containing slurs upon Light Horse Harry Lee's integrity and his capacity to tell the truth. Henry Lee seized the opportunity to laud his father and heap scorn upon Jefferson. Here is a sample of the vitriol:

Stuart, the celebrated portrait painter, used to say, I am told, that he could never take a likeness to satisfy himself until he had discovered to which of the lower animals the countenance to be portrayed bore a resemblance; nor can I distinguish the character of Mr. Jefferson's mind more expressively than by denominating it as of the chameleon order.[14]

Carter Lee embraced the attack upon Jefferson and published another edition of the tract in 1839. Robert Lee was more circumspect, but shared his brother's sentiments, if not their zeal. When Henry Lee's first volume on Napoleon appeared in 1835, Robert Lee complained that the work *"Squints towards Jacksonism.* " By this time Henry Lee had sold his political soul to Jackson; Robert Lee continued faithful to patriarchal polity.[15]

Somehow, Lee believed in original sin and progress at the same time. Human beings are corrupt and tainted; yet mysteriously these same beings are evolving toward perfection. Divine Providence makes it all happen. The Kingdom of God is indeed far off; but God is at work in the world, and in God's good time the Kingdom will come. "The truth is this," he wrote later in life, "The march of Providence is so slow and our desires so impatient; the work of progress is so immense and our means of aiding it so feeble; the life of humanity is so long, that of the individual so brief, that we often see only the ebb of the advancing wave and are thus discouraged. It is history that teaches us to hope."[16]

Ostensibly Robert Lee looked backward politically to the Founding Fathers, his own father, and Washington, the father of the country. Yet he looked also forward, toward Social Darwinism, a concept he never heard formulated. Although Charles Darwin (who was two years younger than Lee) would not publish *Origin of the Species* until 1848, Lee anticipated the conservative appropriation of the theory of evolution. He associated social class and human progress with an evolutionary transit from beastliness to beatitude. The common herd were common, because they were a herd—animals who walked upright. People emerged from the herd when they learned to suppress urges toward bestial behavior. They moved up the scale from simply upright to righteous as they developed increasing self-control and transformed their instincts from selfish to selfless.[17]

Lee might have believed with founding Federalist Alexander Hamilton that "the people is a great beast," but he was simply too refined to speak so harsh a truth. Indeed, Lee seldom spoke a political word; he seemed content to observe, absorb, and very rarely comment in private.

Robert Lee believed in politics, because he believed in power and control. During the Age of Jackson he likely suffered; but he suffered for the most part in silence. He was profoundly conservative in his politics. But Lee's conservative convictions did not grow out of disguised greed or spring from some anxious search for security, two common sources of the conservative tradition among Americans. No, Lee was a magnanimous, "progressive," humane conservative. His silence upon the great political issues of his time was the silence of superiority.

He had plenty of time to ponder the iniquities of Democratic and democratic politics because the work of the Engineer Department was incredibly dull. Much of it involved correspondence.

Your communication of the 19th ulto, remarking on the change made by the local Agent at Erie, in his accounts forwarded a few days before, was duly received; and the acknowledgement postponed until the examination of the Vouchers at this office. This having been done, I have now to inform you that the charge for Superintending of $2 per day, and 2½ per cent for disbursing has been reduced by the Department to conform to the statements furnished by you of the allowances to the several agents of works under your general superintendence which states [illegible name] at $75 per month, and 2½ per cent on disbursements; the charge for Office rent disallowed. . . . The Vouchers for disbursements made during the first quarter of this year by Mr. Hubbard, Agent on Account of the improvement at Ashtabula Creek, Ohio, have been examined in this Department and approved, and in conformity with regulations, paragraph 898, they are, herewith, transmitted to your Office.[18]

Day after day correspondence continued as reports, queries, estimates, clarifications, vouchers, complaints, requests, and public funds passed through the offices of the Engineer Department. Accounts had to balance; budgets required approval; and appropriations needed channels. However boring, the work was meticulous; it demanded constant attention to detail and the capacity to take "paragraph 898" quite seriously.

During this duty in Washington, Lee became increasingly aware of the dependence of the Army in general, and the Engineers Corps in particular, upon the fickle favor of patronage. In the cause of right and justice for himself and fellow Engineer officers, Lee compiled statistics and composed statements. One such statement he wrote during February 1836 Gratiot placed "in the hands of Mr. [Senator Thomas Hart] Benton, who happened to be in the office this mor^g. and he at least showed great patience in *listening* to our grievances." Lee planned to "have several copies made and place them in the hands of some of my acquaintances in the Senate & House, so that should the matter be brought up, if they choose they may speak the truth." Especially did Lee depend upon William C. Preston, who was a South Carolina senator. "His father and mine were old acquaintances and friends, and once laboured together. Why should not the Sons?" Gratiot was no fool. He had brought Lee to Washington to assist him in more than minding his office. And Lee seemed to relish his role as lobbyist for the Engineer Corps.[19]

In February 1835, Lee wrote his brother Carter, "I am obliged to spend the most of my time in W[ashington] am constantly occupied till near four & by the time dinner is over it is night. I then most generally go to A[rlington]." He had been on duty in Washington only about four months when he asked for reassignment. Lee told Gratiot that he was "unable to make ends meet"; his salary did not support the life he had to lead. It was, he stated, "impossible for me to hold the station in society at this place to which an officer is entitled."[20]

Someone wrote on Lee's plea "to receive early attention." But all Lee received for his lament was a clerk and a trip to the woods. James Eveleth had worked for Lee at Fort Monroe, and in July 1835 Eveleth rejoined him in Washington. Gratiot also assigned Lee to an expedition, led by Andrew Talcott, to survey the boundary between Ohio and Michigan during the summer of 1835.[21]

Mary Lee was once more pregnant—-expecting a child in July, in fact. Nevertheless, Robert Lee seemed eager to leave home and rejoin his friend Talcott on the expedition. He left in May, journeying to Albany, New York, where he and the rest of the party had to wait for their instruments to arrive before heading west. Then once they began to survey, Lee and the others encountered still more delays and constantly projected later returns home.[22]

Meanwhile, Robert Lee was cruising the Great Lakes and roaming what was then the northwestern American wilderness attempting to help Talcott distinguish Ohio from Michigan. He wrote from Turtle Island, Michigan, to the young lieutenant who was his temporary replacement in the Engineer Department in Washington: "Our present abode may have many beauties, but to me they are as yet undiscovered. . . . The country around savours marvellously of Bilious Fevers, and seems to be productive of nothing more plentifully than of *Moschitoes* [sic] & Snakes. Of the good people in this country, we have seen nothing." Lee also informed his friend that this summer excursion would consume some of the fall as well. "I hardly think I shall [?] be in Washington before *October*—and possibly not then."[23]

In this same letter to "Mon Ami" (Lieutenant George W. Cullum), Lee asked his friend, "Tell the Genl. that in my last communication I forgot to confess an act of indiscretion which I now beg leave to do through you." While on the Canadian side of Lake Erie, Lee and another lieutenant sought to use a lighthouse off Pelee Island as a survey point. Lee recounted the ensuing incident:

The door was locked & we could just not gain admittance, but after some time succeeded i[n] getting through the window i[n] rear when we discovered the keeper at the door. We were warm & excited, he irasible & full of venom. An altercation ensued which resulted in his death. We put him in charge of the men, gained the Top, attained our object, & in descending I discovered some glass lamp shades, which we stood much i[n] need of as all ours were broken. I therefore made bold to *borrow* two of his Majesty, for which liberty, as well as for that previously taken, I hope he will make our Apology to his Minister at W[ashington]. We have nothing to offer in our behalf, but *necessity* and as we found the Lt. House in a most neglected condition & shockingly dirty, & were told by the Capt. of the Cutter that there had been no Light in it for more than a year, I hope it will not be considered that we have lopped from the Government a useful member, but on the contrary—to have done it some service, as the situation may now be more efficiently filled & we would advise the New Minister to make choice of a better Subject than a d——d Canadian *Snake*.[24]

Lee's story of his "indiscretion" was a joke! Told in the mock heroic, Lee's experience at the lighthouse most likely corresponded to his narrative—except that the "keeper" of the lighthouse was literally a snake, a reptile. Lee was simply trying to liven his letter with a heroic tale of killing a snake in an abandoned lighthouse.[25]

When the surveying party arrived in Detroit, Lee received a disturbing letter from his wife. Mary Lee, no doubt anxious about her health, apparently implored her husband to come home at once. Robert Lee replied:

But why do you urge my *immediate* return, & tempt one in the strongest manner, to endeavour to get excused from the performance of a duty, imposed on me by my Profession for the pure gratification of my private feelings? Do you not think that those feelings are enough of themselves to contend with, without other aggravations; and that I rather require to be strengthened & encouraged to the *full* performance of what I am called on to execute, rather than excited to a dereliction, which even our affection could not palliate, or our judgement excuse?[26]

Lee chose to persevere in his duty and leave his wife's care to others.

The surveyors journeyed as far west as Michigan City on Lake Michigan before commencing their return east. In early October Lee reached Washington, found that his family was at Ravensworth, and learned that his wife was quite ill.

Mary Lee had recovered very quickly from the birth of her daughter, Mary, on July 12, 1835, and according to Robert Lee's analysis she had attempted to be too active too soon. She caught a cold, recovered somewhat, then developed a severe illness of some sort accompanied by "bilious symptoms." Then she experienced swelling and pain in her groin, most likely severely swollen lymph glands. Her physicians diagnosed this condition as "Rheumatic Diathesis" (a predisposition to rheumatism), ordered her to remain in bed, treated her with applications of moist heat, and drew blood by means of cupping and leeching.[27]

Lee moved his wife on her bed from Ravensworth to Arlington so that she would be closer to her doctors. Mary remained ill for quite some time. Her husband's letters to his friend Andrew Talcott and his brother Carter offer some chronicle of his wife's symptoms and ailments during the next several months.

On October 12, she was "very slowly getting better, still confined to her bed." On October 21, "the inflamation I told you of pointed & broke outwardly 2 days since. There has been a great discharge & a relief . . . but she is still as weak & helpless as ever & confined to her bed." On November 9, "I am happy to say that Mary is improving. The 2nd Imposthume [pustule?] . . . has been opened & by its discharge she has been much relieved in so much that when she moves a *soreness* is substituted for *acute pain.* . . . She is dreadfully reduced, & so weak that she *cannot stand,* but being relieved from constant & corroding pain is a great point gained." On November 18, Lee reported, "Mary gets better & better every day. She can now sit up & has lost all soreness, pain, etc., but is still very weak. Her appetite is famous and the Partridges, Buckwheat muffins, etc. disappear at breakfast, as fast as the Pheasants, chickens, etc. at dinner." As she continued to feel better, Mary began to care again about her appearance, and her husband wrote on November 25, "Her hair got in such a *snarl* while confined to her bed, that she on her first sitting up, took the scissors and cut it all off. It is now coming out so rapidly, that when I left today she talked of having it shaved off, and I expect on my return to find her bald."[28]

During the winter months of 1836, Lee announced, "We are not very well over the river. Mary is liable to cold and its effects, and I suppose will long be so." In June he wrote, "Mary's gen[eral] health I think has been improving

this Spring, though she is now laboring under an attack of the *Mumps.*" Mary
Lee's mumps, Lee later reported, "appeared to throw her all back again. . . .
She became extremely ill, affected with fever, which fell upon the brain, and
seemed to overthrow her whole nervous system. During this time she suffered
extremely, and what I then experienced could never be repeated."[29]

Lee took his wife that summer (1836) with their two children (Custis
three, Mary not quite one), Mrs. Custis, and four slaves to attend them in two
carriages to Warrenton Springs and other Virginia spas to test the healing
capacity of mineral waters. "I myself," Lee confided to Carter, "have more
confidence in the continuous journeys, diversifying the scene, amusing the
mind, and endeavoring to strength the body." Nevertheless Lee would continue to indulge his wife in the medical/social summer season at mountain
spas for the rest of his life. He enjoyed the company, while he hoped against
reason that the waters might help his wife.

About her condition in August of 1836, Lee concluded: "Her nervous
system is much shattered. She has almost a horror of crowded places, an
indisposition to make the least effort, and yet a restless anxiety which renders
her unhappy and dissatisfied."[30]

Mary Lee's health eventually improved. But she was never really well again.
She bore five more children; indeed, the Lees conceived their next child about
a month after Robert Lee wrote his gloomy conclusion quoted above. Still,
Mary Lee's health increasingly conditioned and constrained her. And in turn
her malaise continued to afflict Robert Lee.[31]

General Gratiot did what he could for his young assistant, and during the
fall of 1836 (September 21) Lee received a promotion to the rank of first
lieutenant. Nevertheless Lee fretted about his career while he worried about
his wife's health.[32]

To his friend Andrew Talcott, Lee poured forth his frustration over his
profession and himself. He wrote of his "talent for procrastination" and continued,

You ask what are my prospects in the Corps? Bad enough unless it is increased and
something done for us, and then perhaps they will be better. As to what I intend doing,
it is rather hard to answer. There is one thing certain. I must get away from here, nor
can I consent to stay any longer than the rising of Cong[ress]. I should have made a
desperate effort, last spring, but Mary's health was so bad, I could not have left her &
she could not have gone with me. I am waiting, looking and hoping for some good
opportunity to bid an affectionate farewell to my dear Uncle Sam. And I seem to think
that said opportunity is to drop in my lap like a ripe pear, for d——l [devil] a stir have I
made in the matter. And there again I am helped out by the talent I before mentioned I
possessed in so eminent a degree [proscrastination].[33]

At the very time that Lee seemed overwhelmed by personal and professional frustrations, opportunity did indeed drop into his lap like a ripe pear.
Gratiot found a new assignment for Lee. The good burghers of St. Louis had
become alarmed that the Mississippi River would shift its channel away from

the city and leave the port and associated commerce quite literally high and dry. Congress appropriated funds to finance an effort to redirect the river, and Gratiot selected Robert Lee to direct the project. The engineering challenge was fascinating; Lee was supposed to change the course of the "Father of Waters".[34]

To accomplish this feat Lee of course would have to go to St. Louis. He would have to leave Arlington and his in-laws, Washington and the pettiness of politics, and his wife and two small children. Robert Lee likely had very mixed feelings about his projected sojourn west. His dominent mood, however, seems ebullient as he contemplated the new assignment. To Talcott he wrote, "I shall leave my family in the care of my *eldest son* who will take them over the mountains somewhere this summer, and his GrMother along with them."[35]

Custis Lee was five years old. His father could write such cavalier prose because he was about to flee his frustrations. Flight in his case was fine, even noble, because Lee found escape in doing his duty.

7

"*They Wanted a Skillful Engineer ... and Sent Me*"

ILLIAM HENRY FITZHUGH LEE emerged on May 30, 1837. His father consistently addressed him as "Fitzhugh"; to other family and friends he was "Rooney." His mother recovered from the birth, while her mother and several slaves cared for him and his siblings, Custis (now five) and Mary (nearly two). When the infant was about two weeks old, his father First Lieutenant Robert Lee left for the Mississippi.[1]

Three tasks awaited Lee on the "Father of Waters." Congress had appropriated funds to improve navigation on the Mississippi above the mouth of the Ohio River and to improve (save) the river harbor at St. Louis. Lee's superior and Chief of the Engineer Department General Charles Gratiot was initially from St. Louis and likely told his young (thirty-yard-old) protégé what the assignment entailed.

Above St. Louis on the Mississippi were two significant sets of rapids, the sole obstacles to navigation for 1,200 miles above the mouth of the Ohio River. The Des Moines Rapids was an 11-mile section just above the mouth of the Des Moines River and the town of Keokuk, Iowa. The Rock River Rapids was a treacherous 15-mile stretch of the Mississippi above the mouth of the Rock River near the modern cities of Moline and Rock Island, Illinois, and Davenport, Iowa.

Two of Lee's tasks were to render the Des Moines Rapids and the Rock River Rapids navigable at all stages of the river for boats plying the upper Mississippi. These projects offered enormous long-term advantages to the expanding American West. They all but defined the country's commitment to "internal improvements."

Lee's third challenge was to alter the flow of the Mississippi in such a way as to reverse a process which threatened the St. Louis harbor. Just upstream from the city, almost in the center of the river, lay Bloody Island (so called to recall the many duels fought there). The river current was scouring Bloody Island

and depositing silt and sand on Duncan Island near the Missouri shore just below St. Louis. This action of river current, shifting sands and silt, and the resultant accretion of Duncan Island, if continued unabated, would surely seal the docks of St. Louis behind the advancing upstream (northern) end of Duncan Island. Already, steamboats had run aground on the sandbar extension of Duncan Island as far north as Olive Street (just upstream from the site of the Gateway Arch).[2]

Lee first traveled north from Arlington and Washington to Philadelphia, where he tried to buy the surveying instruments he would need for his mission on the Mississippi River. His traveling companion and assistant was Second Lieutenant Montgomery C. Meigs, only one year out of West Point. Born in Augusta, Georgia, Meigs had moved to Philadelphia as a boy and attended the University of Pennsylvania before his appointment to the Military Academy. Meigs and Lee worked well together, but Lee wrote very little about his junior companion. Much later Meigs wrote glowing, generous descriptions of Lee; but he did so only after he was old and Lee was dead.[3]

From Philadelphia, Lee and Meigs traveled on the Pennsylvania Canal to Pittsburgh and then boarded a steamboat to begin their passage down the Ohio River. At Louisville, Lee encountered his fellow Engineer officer Captain Henry M. Shreve, who had some experience on the Mississippi. Shreve had developed the "snag boat," a steam-powered craft designed to remove obstructions formed by logs, trees, and brush (snags) from river channels. He had just completed construction of a new steamboat which Lee immediately chartered for his project, along with two boats rigged to raise submerged rock and a lighter (open barge) in which to transport spoil. With Shreve's help, Lee also hired a crew for his boats and a gang of rivermen to perform the heavy labor he anticipated.[4]

Also at Louisville, Lee took on two charming young women as passengers for the long voyage down the Ohio. They were relatives of General Henry Atkinson's wife, and Lee agreed to escort them to Jefferson Barracks to visit the family. Robert Lee was careful and candid in his account to Mary: "Miss Vir[ginia] Bullet is young and sprightly, quite pleasing in manners and appearance and sings sweetly and uneffectedly. Her cousin Mrs. Miller is a handsome young widow scarcely over twenty I should think, of a good deal of conversation and reading and appears to be very amiable and of *proper* behavior." Lee went ashore at Jefferson Barracks (about ten miles below St. Louis) and escorted his passengers to the Atkinson quarters. Then he continued his trip to St. Louis, arriving on the morning of August 5, 1837.[5]

With Meigs, Lee took a room in what was supposed to be the best hotel in the city, but found the accommodations "intolerable"—crowded table at dinner and "a dark *dirty* room." He found a better hotel—*"excellently* kept though the building itself is bad"—and began to collect the instruments and equipment he would need to survey the river.

Impatience increased as preliminary chores consumed time and energy. To Andrew Talcott, Lee complained after ten days in St. Louis, "Instead of being nearly done with our examinations here we have not *commenced* them." He proclaimed, "They [Westerners] are the greatest people for promising and not fulfilling that I ever saw."

Lee's frustration over beginning his project encompassed the entire city. St. Louis, he wrote, "is the dearest [most expensive] and dirtiest place I was ever in. Our daily expenses about equals our daily pay." He did find "some very pretty girls" in the city, but called the entire region a "bloody humbug."[6]

Heat and drought combined to sour Lee still more. He had apparently arrived at the height of an infamous St. Louis summer. "It is *astonishingly* hot here," he wrote his wife, "thermometer 97° in the House." Soil ground fine by wind and water became powder, which "is now only ankle deep in the streets." Dust "put in motion by the slightest wind . . . penetrates every where."[7]

Finally the stray boats and most essential instruments arrived. After sixteen days in St. Louis, Lee was ready to start work. He decided to begin at the Rock River Rapids, about 350 miles upriver, to take advantage of the period before low water jeopardized the passage of boats and might compel a long, tiresome hike. He also wished to leave the August heat and dust in St. Louis. So with fourteen companions he started upriver.

The first significant decision Lee made during his expedition up the Mississippi was to change his plan. When the party reached the Des Moines Rapids, they discovered water too low to permit their steamboat to ascend farther, so Lee set to work surveying the lower set of rapids. For a time the men continued to live on the boat and to conduct their labors from a floating headquarters. Later Lee established an abandoned log cabin as a barrack for his "troops" and found lodging for himself and Meigs about a mile away.[8]

Lee reflected in a letter to Talcott, "How utterly had the *Hotels* seen by the Gen [Gratiot] disappeared, and to what miserable *Cabins* had the *fine Farm Houses* been changed!" He then explained that Meigs and he "took up our blankets and walked a short mile to the *City of Des Moines* [then so called], composed of the worst kind of a small log cabin which contained the Proprietor and the *entire population*. Here we were kindly received and accommodated with the softest *Puncheon* [rough board] in the floor."[9]

To Mary Lee, Robert Lee wrote that his host, "the Nabob of his section of country," was a "hard featured man of about *fifty*, a large talker, and has the title of *Doctor*, whether of Law, Medicine or Science, I have never learned but infer of all three." Married to his second wife—a girl fourteen years old—the man had expansive plans for a town, a bridge over the river, a mill, and a distillery. "His whole time and attention is devoted to his several projects, the most of which as the Major [Custis] would say are in *effigee*, and he tells me his several farms are all lying idle, while he buys his meat and bread, corresponds with the *company*, members of Congress, of the State Legislature and other influencial men."[10]

Lee was impressed with the potential he saw as he traveled. He found topsoil three and a half feet deep, land "you could cultivate with your feet." He wrote to Jack Mackay, "This is a beautiful country, and must one day be a great one." Lee was an engineer, not a naturalist. Nevertheless, his beautiful/great dichotomy reveals a rare depth of understanding about the fate of the environment in the face of orderly exploitation.

Similar sensitivity Lee displayed in some observations he shared with Carter about women in the West:

The *wimming* [women] alone show the only true heroism that is here exhibited. To see with what cheerfulness and even pleasure they leave everything behind and enter these forests. Subject themselves to every privation and drudgery; and . . . toil patiently and constantly. They are always ready to offer kindness and relief, are frugal and attentive while their rough consorts are careless unthrifty speculating *lazing* [sic] or worse.

The influence and example of Ann Carter Lee still lived in one of her sons.[11]

When not observing the land and the habits of strangers, Lee undertook and directed difficult work. He made an accurate map of the 11 miles of river and sounded the depth of the water at various intervals, within and across the channel(s). As he collected and recorded data, Lee pondered plans to blast a path through the rapids. Steamboats could run the Des Moines Rapids during all but the three months of lowest water. Lee's goal was to open the river year-round and to render the rapids easier to negotiate at all river stages.[12]

During the time Lee and his men were making their survey, the river was running about one or two feet above its lowest normal level. Steamboats bearing cargo had to offload their freight onto keelboats—large, shallow-draft vessels with boards protruding along the long axis of the hulls. Horses towed the keelboats to the head of the rapids, then transferred the cargo to other steamboats. This process was cumbersome and expensive; consequently most of the people Lee encountered on the upper Mississippi wished him well in his mission. But many were skeptical, too.

At the head of the Des Moines Rapids, Lee, Meigs, and their men found shelter with the small garrison of United States Army troops at Fort Des Moines. From this point, when finished with the survey of the Des Moines Rapids, Lee led his men 150 miles upriver to the Rock River Rapids. There he used the upper decks of a steamboat whose hull had crashed on the rocks as a base.

The work proceeded as before; however, these rapids did not present as much challenge as the set to the south. Soundings, sightings, and measurements still took time and energy, though, and the expedition took its toll. Lee reported to his brother Carter, "I have been quite well the whole time," but "some of the party were occasionally sick, and some of the men really quite so. Others deserted but we struggled along with the rest."[13]

Lee and his party returned to St. Louis on October 8, 1837. He entrusted three men "who were greatly reduced and about whom I was quite uneasy" to the Sisters of Charity. Then he rented the second story of a warehouse near the river and there began the work of producing finished maps and practical plans. Meigs helped. Also assisting in the drafting and analysis were J. S. Morehead, the captain of Lee's steamboat and a son-in-law of Captain Shreve, and Henry

I. Kayser, a German-born cartographer/surveyor from St. Louis. Kayser became one of Lee's good friends, and served then and later as Lee's contact in St. Louis.[14]

To address the pesky problem of the relationship of the river and the St. Louis harbor, Lee first directed a careful survey of the Mississippi from the mouth of the Missouri just north of St. Louis to some point south of the city. He was not the first "expert" to confront the situation. The city fathers had already borrowed $12,000 to pay John Goodfellow for hauling away sand from Duncan and Bloody Islands with wagons and teams of oxen. An engineer had built huge wooden boxes, positioned them across the channel between Bloody Island and the Illinois shore, and filled the boxes with sand to form a dam.

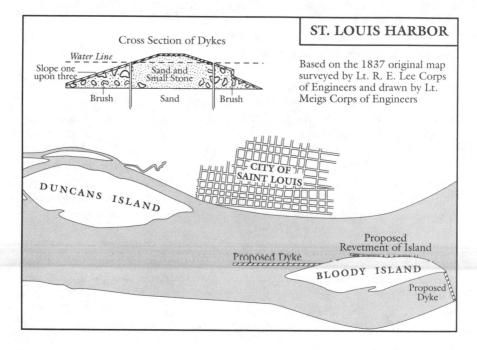

The Mississippi apparently had a mind and will of its own, however. The river found more sand to deposit on Duncan and Bloody Islands and did so faster than John Goodfellow's ox teams removed it. The river also made short work of the sand/box dam and seemed to like its channel on the Illinois side of Bloody Island. Young Lieutenant Lee confronted a worthy adversary indeed.[15]

Lee proposed to do three things: (1) construct a dam from the head of Bloody Island to the Illinois shore; (2) construct a dyke from the foot of Bloody Island at least 1,000 yards directly downstream; and (3) shield the western shore of Bloody Island from its head to its center with a stone revetment. The effect of his plan would be to throw the full current of the Mississippi into the western (Missouri) channel. The current, in turn, would then wash the sandbar and eventually Duncan Island downstream away from St. Louis.

Crucial to Lee's scheme was the construction of the dam and dyke. Lee proposed a structure similar to successful dams built on the Hudson River in New York. He had likely learned about these dams from his friend and former superior Andrew Talcott, who worked on the Hudson after he left Fort Monroe. Lee proposed to drive two parallel lines of piles into the riverbed twenty-five feet apart. Within each line, the piles would be five feet apart. Then he planned to create a very large snag (or "strainer" in the idiom of modern river speech). He planned to weave brush into each line of piles, slope each brushpile gently outward to the river bottom, and anchor the brush "by throwing stones promiscuously over, and distributing them as equally as possible." In the center, between the lines of piles, Lee planned to dump sand and gravel, and to cap the structure with a loose stone revetment one and a half to two feet thick.

The dam from Bloody Island to Illinois, as originally proposed, would be 594 yards (six football fields) long; the dyke, constructed in the same manner as the dam, would be at least 1,000 yards (over half a mile) long. And the reveted bank of Bloody Island would extend about a third of a mile. Lee estimated the cost at $158,554 and said in his report, "The erection of these works will be attended with great difficulty."

Lee's plan was a good one. He proposed to use indigenous materials and do the simplest construction possible. Because he respected the raw power of the Mississippi, Lee designed his dam and dyke to be as strong as possible. But he also proposed to work with, not against, the river. Indeed, he hoped to coax the Mississippi to do most of his work for him. Guided by Lee's dam and dyke, the river would deepen the harbor at St. Louis. The river would also contribute more brush and logs to Lee's structures. And the river would sweep away the bar from Duncan Island and in time all of the island as well. Lee's proposal was more strategy than solution.

The same was true of his proposals for the Des Moines Rapids. Henry Shreve, who had greater rank in the Engineer Corps and more experience with the Mississippi, proposed to carve an arbitrary, artificial channel through the Des Moines Rapids along the western bank. Lee proposed to follow the natural channel of the river and blast and remove only enough rock to achieve a relatively straight channel 200 feet wide and five feet deep at low water. Shreve's solution would have required (by Lee's estimate) removing more than a million cubic yards of rock and earth. Lee's strategy promised the same effect much faster and cheaper, because he estimated the need to remove only about 95,000 cubic yards (less than one tenth).

At the Rock River Rapids, Lee found a pretty well-defined channel which required blasting and removing rock in only a few places in order to achieve the depth desired. The great difficulty in running these rapids involved the sharp turns sometimes required and the necessity to "ferry" or navigate across the current from one side of the channel to the other.

Lee proposed blasting and removing rock to straighten the sharpest turns somewhat and to install buoys to mark the channel more clearly to permit safe passage in foul weather and faint light. Shreve had already written that no buoys could withstand chunks of ice carried by the current during seasons of cold and thaw. Lee respectfully acknowledged the opinion of his senior but nevertheless suggested the installation of buoys. He proposed to design buoys that offered the least possible resistance to rushing water, to secure these markers firmly in the riverbed, and to place the buoys so that ice would float above them in the current. As it happened, Lee's buoys failed the ice test during the winter of 1839–40, and he subsequently advised removing the buoys at the onset of winter and replacing them the following spring.[16]

Maps, proposals, and reports occupied Lee until December. He was confident enough of the clear wisdom of his plan to contract for the construction of a 115-foot (keel) steamboat and obligate the United States for $9,200 to pay for the craft. Then Lee had nothing more to do in St. Louis until the following spring when he could commence the actual work for which his plans called. So, with Meigs in tow, Lee headed home to Arlington.

Meigs did not return with Lee the following spring, and Lee did not again encounter him in any official capacity until over twenty years later, in 1861, when Meigs replaced Lee's old friend Joseph E. Johnston as Quartermaster General of the United States Army. By this time both Lee and Johnston had joined another army. Lee's riverboat captain and assistant J. S. Morehead also left the project when he resigned from the service during the winter of 1837. So Lee depended upon Henry Kayser as his principal assistant and his contact in St. Louis, and the relationship soon ripened into friendship. In December 1837, Lee believed he knew Kayser well enough to leave him in charge of the preparations for the spring of 1838. Kayser even kept watch over Lee's bank account in St. Louis and no doubt reconciled a discrepancy of $1.20 Lee detected between his own balance and Kayser's figure.[17]

Waiting for Lee at Arlington were his wife and three children. Mary Lee was well, as were Custis ("Boo" or "Mr. Boo"), Mary ("the little woman"), and Fitzhugh ("Rooney"). Robert Lee vowed not to return to St. Louis alone on his next trip. "Life is too short," he exclaimed to Jack Mackay, "for them [his children] and their mother to be in one place, and I in another."[18]

Christmas at Arlington, accounts to settle, reports and maps to shepherd through the printing process, and probably some family visiting occupied Lee over the winter. He divided his time between his family and his profession, while with Gratiot's blessing he made ready to return to St. Louis.

Kitty, a slave, made the trip with the family; but daughter Mary (not yet three) remained behind with the Custises. Robert, Mary, Custis and Rooney, along with Kitty, traveled first to Baltimore by train, in late March 1838 to visit Robert Lee's sister Ann and her husband William Lewis Marshall.

The Lees and Kitty tarried in Baltimore; Robert Lee wrote Kayser that he was "detained here ten days by the indisposition of both my children," but another factor in the delay was Lee's decision to have his portrait painted. William E. West, an American artist recently returned from artistic successes and financial failure in Europe, did the first ever portrait of Robert Lee. Posed in his dress uniform, Lee looks lively, wise, and extremely handsome. After some indecision (she preferred Sully), Mary Lee, too, agreed to sit for West. Her portrait is less than lovely; but then so was Mary Lee.[19]

From Baltimore the travelers again traveled away from their destination to Philadelphia. After some sightseeing they took the train from Harrisburg, where they boarded a canal boat for Pittsburgh, and then after a week of waiting there, a steamboat down the Ohio. It was a leisurely journey, with time in Cincinnati and Louisville en route. Robert Lee wrote, "Our journey was as pleasant as could be expected in a country of this sort. . . . The boys stood it manfully and indeed improved on it, and my Dame, taking advantage of frequent opportunities for a nap . . . defied the crowding, squeezing, and scrambling."

Finally, on May 1, 1838, the party arrived in St. Louis, and the first news to greet them was bad. Through Kayser, Robert Lee believed he had rented rooms for himself and his family; however, the arrangement had miscarried. Lee also believed that furniture he had purchased in Cincinnati was following him to St. Louis aboard another steamboat; however, the other boat blew up en route, and Lee lost his household goods.[20]

Finally, on June 1, the family were able to settle themselves in a portion of a house on the southeast corner of Vine and Main Streets (now in downtown St. Louis). The house was more properly a mansion; it belonged to William Clark, formerly Governor of Missouri (1813–21) and the Clark of the earlier Lewis and Clark expedition to the Pacific Ocean. Sharing the Clark home with the Lee family of four, plus Kitty, was the Beaumont family of five.

William Beaumont was a fifty-three-year-old Army surgeon who had made significant medical history. Beaumont was serving a frontier garrison on Mackinac Island (Michigan) on June 6, 1822, when a young soldier, Alexis St. Martin, accidentally blew a large hole in his upper abdomen with a shotgun. Beaumont responded to what seemed a hopeless case, cleaned the wound, and removed shot, wadding, and shirt fragments from St. Martin's stomach. The young man survived but retained a hole in his stomach. Beaumont later made use of this "window" to study the process of digestion in a living person. He even had St. Martin swallow various foods attached to silk threads and withdrew the food items after varying lengths of time in the stomach. In 1833 Beaumont published a work still cited in the literature of the subject, *Experiments and Observations on the Gastric Juice and the Physiology of Digestion.*[21]

William Beaumont's wife Deborah ("Debby") took charge of the cooking for the household, which often included Captain Ethan Allen Hitchcock, once Commandant of Cadets at West Point near the end of Lee's cadet tenure. The Lees and Beaumonts became friends as well as housemates. The Beaumont children included Sarah ("Tasy") sixteen, Lucretia ("Cush") eleven, and Israel, nine. Especially did Robert Lee find Tasy Beaumont delightful. On many evenings he sat beside her and turned pages while Tasy played the piano and Hitchcock the flute.[22]

Mary Lee seems to have adjusted fairly well to her new surroundings. But after describing a particularly bountiful corn field to her mother and the fertility of the soil, Mary added, "Rich as it is I would rather a thousand times live in Old Virginia or somewhere near it." She tired of her boys, too, and considered "trying Custis at school this fall." She wished for some of the slave children from Arlington "to amuse Rooney the time Kitty is washing; for I find it rather tiresome to nurse all day such an unsettled brat, tho' his father has come to the conclusion that there is not such another child in all Missouri & that he would not exchange him for the whole state."

During the summer, Mary Lee was ill: "rather low & weak," she said; "very bilious" and "affected by lassitude" was Robert Lee's description. She recovered by fall and became pregnant once more in September.[23]

Robert Lee spent a "season" of ambivalence in his professional life. He resented the politics of his position and the niggardliness of Congress. He knew he could perform the tasks assigned him; he knew the amount of money required. However, the Army told him to perform his tasks with only about a third of the funds necessary. In June 1838, Lee confessed to his old friend Jack Mackay, "I wish all were done and I was back again in Virginia. I volunteered my services last year to get rid of the office in Washington and the Gen'l at last agreed to my going. I was cognizant of so much iniquity in more ways than one, that I feared for my morality, at no time strong, and had been trying for two years to quit. I spent last winter in Washington partly on duty and partly not. Had a pleasant time with some friends in Virginia, and now here working for my country."[24]

And the work was frustrating. A combination of early cold in the fall, strange rises and falls in the level of the river, and the difficulty attending the job permitted Lee only twenty working days on the Des Moines Rapids and none on the Rock River Rapids. Meanwhile his work crews did construct a length of dyke from the head of Bloody Island. The dam from the head of Bloody Island to the Illinois shore remained only a line on a map, though, and Lee became convinced that he must change even that. He redrew the line to begin the structure farther up the Illinois shore and angle more gradually to the head of Bloody Island. He believed this new proposal would not cost more than his first, because the longer dam would not have to be as high.

Lee did have the satisfaction of knowing that his blast-and-remove method of altering the channel of the river through a rapid indeed worked. Moreover, his dyke at St. Louis began to have the effect he had predicted. Still, he did not complete his tasks, and he doubted that Congress would appropriate the money to permit him to carry his projects to conclusion.[25]

On July 7, 1838, the same army which had so frustrated and abused First Lieutenant Lee made him Captain Lee. Promotion in peacetime was rare, and Lee had advanced with less than two years as a first lieutenant.[26]

During that fall Lee settled accounts from the working season, crafted his report for the year, and redrafted his plans to show the revised axis of the dam between Bloody Island and the Illinois shore. When he had completed these chores, he could do no more until spring. But he had to remain in St. Louis with his family, because ice closed the river for travel and he considered an overland trip out of the question with Mary Lee pregnant and two young children involved. So for the first time since West Point, Lee would spend Christmas away from Virginia.[27]

With the Christmas season came the news that the same army which had recently promoted Captain Lee had dismissed General Gratiot in disgrace. Accused of fraud, using public funds for private gain, Gratiot was most probably the victim of someone's scheme to remove him from his post. Lee was devastated. "I was as little prepared for such an event, as I would have been for the annihilation of the City of Wash[ington] by an earthquake," he wrote to Talcott. "Nothing has distressed me so much for many years . . . I believe the news of his *death* would have been less painful to bear."

Lee attempted to aid his deposed chief. But Gratiot remained disgraced and tumbled from his position of power and influence to a clerkship in the general land office in Washington.[28]

Gratiot's fall from grace seemed part of a pattern in Lee's life. He seldom had the benefit of a strong male superior. His father had disappeared and then died; even his older brothers, Carter and Smith, were less than surrogate fathers. His first commanding officer, Samuel Babcock, was surely no role model. Andrew Talcott was an exception, but Talcott left the service. And now Lee's remaining mentor Gratiot was gone. Rarely could Lee depend upon the authority of "the old man" until he became "the old man" himself.

While Lee fretted about Gratiot and probed his own genealogy in St. Louis during the winter of 1838–39, in Washington the United States Congress confronted the consequences of the Panic of 1837, a sharp "bust" phase of the business cycle. For Lee the immediate result of these congressional deliberations was no new appropriation to fund his projects.

Gratiot's successor in command of the Engineer Corps, Colonel Joseph G. Totten, could do no more than act out the will of Congress. Of the $40,000 which remained available for improving navigation on the Mississippi and Missouri Rivers, Shreve got half ($20,000) to spend on the Missouri and Lee got the other half ($20,000) for his work. Lee calculated that after three months' labor on the rapids, "We shall be obliged to hang up our fiddle."[29]

Totten authorized Lee to use government property—boats, pile drivers, and such—at St. Louis. But no money remained in the appropriation to hire workers to operate the boats and equipment. If, however, the city of St. Louis were to make funds available to Lee, he could continue his harbor project.

All this Lee wrote in a letter to St. Louis Mayor John Fletcher Darby. Elected in 1835, Darby had followed Lee's work with great interest and thought well of the young engineer. Impressed with Lee's energy and devotion, Darby later recalled, "He had none of that . . . petty . . . planning and scheming which men of little minds . . . use to take care of their fame." Darby also wrote that Lee worked "most indefatigably, in that quiet, unobtrusive manner and with the modesty characteristic of the man." The mayor decided to try to raise the money to support the completion of Lee's labors, and called a mass meeting of citizens for the night of March 27, 1839, to approve the emergency appropriation by the city. Lee wrote, "I cannot venture to guess at the result."[30]

Indeed, many people in St. Louis did not share Darby's faith in this young engineer from the East. The popular newspaper *The Missouri Republican* was Lee's most persistent critic and spoke for numerous naysayers. Lee was able to ignore opposition as long as he had support and funds in Washington. Now his work depended upon the faith of those most vitally affected. Still, however, he remained silent on the subject.[31]

In fact the city government of St. Louis did advance Lee $15,000 to use for harbor improvements. With this money he was able to construct a temporary dam between Bloody Island and the Illinois shore during the summer of 1839. By this time Lee's strategy had begun to work. The current washed away the bar that threatened the harbor at St. Louis and then began to erase Duncan's Island. Before St. Louis, Lee reported, "there are now 15 feet water where it was formerly dry at the same stage of the river."[32]

Meanwhile, as soon as spring arrived, Lee secured a brief leave of absence to escort his wife and children back to Arlington. Mary was expecting their fourth child in June, and Lee anticipated spending much of that summer away from St. Louis. Perhaps the best statement of Mary Lee's mood occurred in a letter she wrote to Harriet Talcott in January 1839: "This is quite a large place and I have found some very fine & agreeable people but I am getting too old [she was thirty-one!] to form new friends and would rather be among those I know and love." She would not return to St. Louis.[33]

The Lees, and presumably Kitty, set out on May 1, 1839, by steamboat for Wheeling, Virginia, and then by stagecoach to Washington, making the trip in only eleven days. Robert Lee lingered in northern Virginia for a couple of weeks and then began his return to St. Louis.

From Louisville on June 4 he wrote to his wife, "You do not know how much I have missed you and the children, my dear Mary. To be alone in a crowd is very solitary. In the woods I feel sympathy with the trees and birds, in whose company I take delight, had no experience no pleasure in a strange crowd." Robert Lee was homesick.[34]

The year Lee had just spent with his family, or most of it, confirmed in his mind some ideas about children and parents. He worried about Mary as a mother and tried to encourage her to be constant and consistent in her parental attention.

> You must not let him [Rooney] run wild in my absence, and will have to exercise firm authority over all of them. This will not require severity, or even strictness but constant attention and an unwavering course. Mildness and forbearance, tempered by firmness and judgment, will strengthen their affection for you, while it will maintain your control over them.

Attention, affection, and control seem to have been Robert Lee's watchwords as a parent during this stage of his children's lives.[35]

Back on the Mississippi River Lee enjoyed a good season at the Des Moines

Rapids. His crews removed 2,000 tons of stone from the river and were able to "open a channel *four miles* long through the worst portion of the rapids." Lee lamented the limits imposed upon his project by underfunding. In his annual report he made repeated references to what would be possible with money to build more boats and hire more workers. In the end, however, he had to do the most and best he could with the limited resources available.

Lee also attended work on the harbor at St. Louis and once more made efficient use of finite resources. He was aware that his dam was less strong than he wanted; but time and treasure were short.

The best index of Lee's success at coaxing the current of the Mississippi back to the St. Louis shore was an injunction order issued by the judge of an Illinois court. A resident, maybe the only resident, of the Illinois "town" of Brooklyn which existed principally on paper watched the river leave the Brooklyn waterfront and petitioned the court to stop the process. On August 27, 1839, Lee had to cease his work (only begun August 12) and await a hearing projected for February 1840.[36]

During the late fall, Lee made an inspection tour of the Missouri River to record the achievements of Shreve's snag boats. Back in St. Louis, Lee next gave the government's entire inventory of river equipment—everything from a steamboat to a teapot—on loan to Kayser, who represented the city of St. Louis. Then Lee was free to return to his family, so long as he took the circuitous route via the lower Mississippi to inspect engineer activities on the Arkansas and Red Rivers. After what he described as a "hard journey," Lee reached Arlington very near the end of 1839.[37]

Waiting for him were Mary Lee and now four children. The baby was "Annie" Carter Lee, born June 18, only a few weeks after her father had had to journey west once more. Now she was more than six months old.[38]

The first thing Lee did was take leave from January to April 1840. Actually Lee's superior Colonel Totten did not exactly know what to do with Lee. Logic seemed to demand that Lee return to St. Louis and complete his work there; but that depended upon appropriations from Congress, and no one could predict what Congress would do, especially in an election year. So with Totten's blessing, Lee spent the rest of the winter at home.[39]

No sooner had Lee become reacquainted with his immediate family and his in-laws than he heard bad news about family more distant. His half brother Henry (Black Horse Harry) had died in 1837 in Paris; now Henry's widow Ann was destitute and dependant upon opium and laudanum. She wrote plaintive letters to Carter Lee informing him of her penury, but not her addiction. "Oh, if poor Mr. Lee could see me now," she wailed, "I am abandoned of heaven and earth." In January 1840, Carter shared his concern for Ann Lee with his brother Robert and informed him that their widowed half sister-in-law needed $900 to $1,200 per year in order to live in Paris.[40]

Robert Lee quickly responded that he, Smith, and Carter did not have that much money, certainly not every year for years. "I will tell you frankly what I think best," Robert Lee wrote back. "That Richd Stuart take his sister to his house, and her property into his hands and manage it for her benefit." Richard Stuart, who was Ann's half brother, seemed to be in a position to oversee her affairs, and Lee took it upon himself to write to Stuart and make his suggestion. But Stuart responded that if he became involved with Ann's distress, he would insist that she attempt in court to recover her property sold by her late husband. This of course would open an old family wound, and none of the Lees wanted that. So Robert and Carter Lee continued to correspond about Ann, but did very little more than hope their half sister-in-law would return to her family.

On August 22, 1840, Robert sent Carter a note worth $180 if the person who signed the note could raise the money. He had been unable to do so since March 1840 when the note had come due. "If he can pay it to you, you can send it to Mrs. Lee. It is all I can do," Robert wrote. But at this point Ann Lee was all but beyond help. She died in Paris on August 27.[41]

Lee worked in the Engineer Department office in Washington during the spring and early summer. He still awaited the will of Congress regarding internal improvements and western water; yet he canceled his subscription to the St. Louis newspaper and told Kayser, "Sell the Mules if possible, and *anything* else that you can get a fair price for."

At last in late July Congress adjourned without appropriating a cent to Lee's project. Totten ordered Lee to St. Louis again; but only to sell his equipment and close accounts on the entire venture.

En route west Lee decided to spend a few days at White Sulphur Springs resort. "I am not very well & I hope a little delay here may prevent greater detention hereafter & that thereby I may avoid more serious indisposition." Worse rationalizations have justified time at White Sulphur Springs. Lee took a room in "Bachelors Row" and collected gossip which he relayed to Mary Lee. His major complaint regarded the Hoffmans, who had constructed a cottage nearby. "I am compelled to witness their ridiculous pride, superciliousness & shallowness," he complained to Mary.

Lee also found Bettie and Mattie Mason in residence. "They with other though inferior Angels reside in *Paradise* Row. . . . [They] have numerous acquaintance & for all I know lovers, and enjoy all that is gay & agreeable that is going forward. I am today to have a seat at table by Miss Mattie, so that I shall enjoy my dinner more than I have done for some days."[42]

He liked young women. Back in January he had begun a correspondence with Mary Lee's approval with Tasy Beaumont, the teen-aged daughter in the Beaumont family with whom they had shared quarters in St. Louis. And from St. Louis Lee wrote a long letter to Bettie and Mattie Mason. A portion of it read:

What then must I tell them of? It shall be of belles & beaux of this new country & I will commence with what they all wish to come to, bride & bridegroom. A specimen of this species I have before me every day at dinner. He was a loafer about Natchez. She is very pretty, an heiress & just from the altar. She has not yet laid aside the manners she acquired in her belleship. Sits during dinner expanding her large eyes & pouting her pretty lips & has all the appearance of one that has not found matrimony what it is cracked up to be.

Lee was a keen observer. And his description of the disillusioned bride is very nearly titillating. His analysis of newlyweds continued:

The next in position and first in rank comes Genl. [Edmund Pendleton] & Mrs. [Myra Whitney] Gaines. . . . She declares that the Genl. has more than fulfilled every promise he ever made her & that he could not have believed that they could have again experienced in all their freshness the joys of wedded life. I am afraid at seventy [actually he was sixty-three] they will prove too exhausting to his veteran frame. He already appears to be sinking under them & her prospects are very good of again becoming a happy widow.

This is pretty candid commentary for two young "angels." Lee seemed to enjoy it, though, and it is possible that he needed such an outlet. He did not know many people in his professional or family circles who did "enjoy all that is gay & agreeable that is going forward."[43]

In St. Louis, Lee had to look over his unfinished work and dismantle the enterprise he had spent four years assembling. Kayser returned the equipment, steamboat, teapot, and the rest that Lee had loaned the city of St. Louis. Because Lee's dam and dyke were for the moment having the desired effect, the city seemed unwilling to complete the job. Lee sold everything he could sell, scuttled the smaller boats, and rendered a final accounting.

Kayser became city engineer at St. Louis; however, even though Lee insisted and Kayser well knew that "both piers [dam and dyke] . . . require to be finished," the municipal government would spend no money on the work until it required redoing.[44]

In mid-October 1840 Lee returned to Washington. There the scant supply of public money delayed any decision about his next assignment.

Robert Lee's four years on the Mississippi had been in one sense a bittersweet experience. He had planned, and worked, and proven that his plans would work, only to have to leave his projects incomplete and never see fruition for his skill and energy. But he had the satisfaction of knowing and proving his capacity to solve problems that had baffled others.

When Lee first steamed up the Mississippi from St. Louis in August 1837, he passed Hannibal, Missouri, where two-year-old Sam Clemens lived. After Lee was dead and Sam Clemens became Mark Twain, Twain wrote a book about *Life on the Mississippi* (1883), in which he waxed rhapsodic about population growth on the river above St. Louis: "There was this amazing region, bristling with great towns, projected day before yesterday, so to speak, and built next morning." Twain was young then (thirty-nine); but he was older than the human development along the upper Mississippi. Lee had not made all this growth possible; other engineers took up the work he began. Lee,

however, had begun the process of developing the upper Mississippi and opening the river to navigation.[45]

Brooklyn, Illinois, is still a small community across the river from St.
Louis. Yet St. Louis continued to be the great river port during the nineteenth
century because Lee moved the Mississippi to the Missouri shore. Very early in
his sojourn to St. Louis, Lee informed his friend Jack Mackay, "They wanted a
skillful engineer on the upper Miss. and Missouri, and sent me." Lee meant his
statement tongue-in-cheek, more mock-heroic bravado. But he understated.[46]

8

"You Are Right in My Interest in the Pretty Women"

AVING GUIDED THE Mississippi River away from Brooklyn, Illinois, Robert Lee's next assignment took him to the Brooklyn in New York. Lee's headquarters was Fort Hamilton, a stone rectangle named for Federalist patriarch Alexander Hamilton. Lee had charge of repairs and renovations of the four military installations at the Narrows between Upper and Lower New York bays—space now spanned by the Ver-razano Narrows Bridge.

On the Brooklyn side were Fort Hamilton on the mainland and Fort Lafayette located on an acre of reef just offshore. On the Staten Island side were Battery Hudson and Battery Morton. Lee elected to live and work at Fort Hamilton; he visited the other sites by boat. From his new post Lee had access to Manhattan by ferry and could look beyond Coney Island to the broad Ambrose Channel and the New Jersey shore.[1]

Before taking up his duties in New York, Lee visited some coastal fortifications in the Carolinas and made reports and drawings of his observations to Colonel Joseph Totten, who still commanded the Engineer Corps. While officially on duty in New York, Lee also served as a member of the Board of Visitors to West Point (1844), as assistant to Totten in Washington (1844), and as a member of the Board of Engineers for Atlantic Coast Defense (1845–48).[2]

The work at the Narrows was less than challenging professionally. The tasks did require energy and care for details; but here Lee confronted rotten gun platforms and leaking casemates—pretty routine problems with obvious solutions compared with the Mississippi River at St. Louis and rapids up-stream. Lee's assignment in Washington was likely as boring as it had been ten years earlier, and meetings of boards were mundane by design.[3]

Lee consorted, consulted, and constructed from late 1840 to 1846; however, the period was in many ways professionally profitless. Captain Lee did not much mature; but Robert Lee grew and developed significantly. Mary and

Robert Lee had three children during this time, and acquired a dog (Spec). But Robert Lee experienced increased frustration with his wife. He gave vent to his concerns and continued to seek emotionally fulfilling relationships beyond his marriage. These relationships, probably "innocent," tended to focus upon bright young women as Lee himself moved into midlife.[4]

The years from 1840 to 1846 were unexciting and unproductive at the surface; Lee neither achieved great engineering success nor found any measure of fame at this time. Beneath the surface, however, Robert Lee's was a life in ferment, and this period from 1840 to 1846 was important.[5]

Lee had some choice in his duty assignment after St. Louis. Within the Engineer Corps for officers of Lee's maturity and accomplishments, assignments were to some extent negotiable. As early as 1839 Lee had had the opportunity to return to West Point as an instructor. He declined as firmly and as tactfully as he could. "There is an *art* in imparting . . . knowledge, and in making a subject agreeable to those that learn," he wrote to a friend, "which I have never found that I possessed, and you know the Character of Cadets well enough to be convinced that it is no easy matter to make the labor of mind & body pleasant to them."[6]

There were lots of reasons not to go to West Point. Within the year Congress would engage in serious debate about abolishing the Military Academy. Faculty positions at the Point were often intensely political and inadvertent missteps might injure Lee's otherwise promising career. Maybe West Point still possessed for Lee some "ghosts," conscious or subconscious memories of unpleasant events during his cadetship. Most likely his reluctance to return to West Point lay simply in his preference for "some work of Construction."

Lee's assertion about teaching as an "art" and his assumption that education involved "making a subject agreeable" and rendering the "labor . . . pleasant" are interesting. He got no such notions from Sylvanus Thayer. Lee had thought about the matter and reached his own enlightened conclusions.[7]

He went alone to Fort Hamilton to survey his tasks and to secure housing for himself and his family. Mary was still recovering from the birth of her fifth child, Eleanor Agnes (called Agnes), born on February 27, 1841.[8] Lee wrote to his wife on April 18 about his impressions and their prospects. "Everyone says it is healthy. I am told . . . that the Sea breezes are very cool and refreshing." Looking west toward the water, "the scene is very animating & interesting. Vessels of all kinds are constantly passing, & the view is extensive." On the land side, Lee wrote of his surroundings (an area now comprising the neighborhoods of Bensonhurst, Bay Ridge, Sunset Park, and Borough Park), "The country in the neighborhood is fertile & well cultivated & there are quantities of handsome Country Seats in all directions." At the time Brooklyn was 12 square miles inhabited by 30,000 people.

The Lees would live outside the fort in quarters much in need of renovation. "A nice yankee wife," Lee suggested, "would soon have it in fine order." He proposed to "whitewash & clean it up but am afraid [I] can do but little with it before your arrival. . . ." He reported, "I have got myself a Bedstead, mattress etc. a dozen chairs, pitcher & basin. You can get everything you desire in New York, but they show you so many handsome things that it is dangerous to go in the stores."

For the moment Lee was boarding with a nice family; however, he much favored establishing their own kitchen when Mary arrived with the children. He informed her, "I receive poor encouragement about servants & everyone seems to attend to their own matters. They seem to be surprised at my inquiring for *help* & have a wife too & appear to have some misgivings as to whether you possess all your faculties."[9]

Between the lines of his letter, Robert Lee seemed to challenge his wife to do what he considered her duties as his spouse. But he surely knew that Mary Lee was neither housekeeper nor cook. When she did arrive at Fort Hamilton (after several delays) in June 1841, she depended upon servants to do the work in her new home.

Already Robert Lee was concerned about Mary as parent. "Our dear little boy [Rooney] seems to have among his friends the reputation of being hard to manage. . . ," he wrote from St. Louis; "You must assist me in my attempts, and we must endeavor to combine the mildness and forbearance of the mother with the sternness and, perhaps, unreasonableness of the father."[10]

To his mother-in-law, Robert Lee wrote of his wife, "It requires much earnestness to induce her to conform to what she is not herself impressed with the necessity of." He worried that her "discipline will be too lax, too inconstant, and too yielding." Consequently, Robert Lee implored Mrs. Custis "to *make* her [Mary Lee] do what is right."[11]

For her part, Mary Lee did not have an easy life as wife and mother. Her husband was often away from home, even when she and the children lived at his duty post. In addition, during this period Mary was often either pregnant or attempting to recover from childbirth. By February 1843, Mary Lee was once more pregnant. The sixth Lee child was a boy, Robert Edward Lee, Jr., born October 27, 1843. By May 1845, when "Rob" was still under two years old and Agnes barely four, Mary Lee was pregnant again. Her seventh and final child, Mildred Childe, arrived on February 10, 1846. At this point Mary and Robert Lee were both fast approaching forty, and their seven children ranged in age from thirteen to the new infant. Add in Mary Lee's defense, as well, her deteriorating health. She suffered from periodic colds and likely began to have symptoms of the arthritis which afflicted her during the 1850s and would render her an invalid during the 1860s.[12]

Robert Lee attempted to compensate for what he believed were Mary's shortcomings as parent. He read textbooks on child rearing, but complained, "What I want is to apply what I already know." He continued to chide his wife. "I am very glad that you are all well and enjoying yourself," he wrote. "I wish indeed that I was with you, for I fear your *vanity* has caused you to overburden yourself with children for the purpose of *exhibition*. I am sure nothing could have induced you to take that fine boy Rob but the pleasure of showing him, & if he is not 'too good' is he to blame?" Robert Lee was even so bold as to veto his wife's suggested name for the child who became Mildred. "It may be very *appropriate,*" he wrote of the name Mary Lee preferred, "but I do not think it very handsome . . . we must try to find a better." And so they did.[13]

Quite often Robert Lee suffered the frustration of trying to act out parenthood through his wife by mail. His family spent a significant amount of time at Arlington while Lee was at Fort Hamilton. Then he seemed to feel that he was losing contact with his children—and what was worse, he was losing control.

When opportunity or necessity presented itself, Lee was very much the concerned, involved parent. On one occasion at Fort Hamilton, he set out to New York City with young Rooney in tow. The lad had complained of pains in his legs that morning, but Lee believed the ailment imagined. When Rooney had difficulty walking about the city, his father attributed his troubles to new shoes. But then Lee realized that his son was indeed unwell, so he took the boy home and put him to bed. Later:

I gave him a dose of salts & at bed time steamed him in a tub of water as hot as he could bare [sic] it. Next day he was better with still some pain. The hot bath was repeated again at night, but the next night as I began to fear it was something of inflamatory rheumatism, I gave him a tepid bath & repeated it in the mor^{ng}. He began . . . to mend, but did not get out of bed for five days, except when lifted and during the first two or three days, even this was attended with great pain. What made it worse, too, was that poor Mary was suffering with her face & Mary Cole [servant] was occupied with the baby. So that he had me for chief nurse & except at night I could only make him flying visits. Perhaps however it was as well as he seemed to think my touch hurt him less than anyone else's.

Rooney recovered completely, in part because Robert Lee was such a sensitive, engaged parent.[14]

The Lee children seemed prone to illness and injury during their residence at Fort Hamilton. Little Annie somehow injured her eye with a pair of scissors, a mishap which Lee noted later in his will with a request that his executor see to any special needs she might have. And Rooney managed to slice off the ends of two of his fingers.[15]

He was eight years old at the time (November 24, 1845), and bored that day. Both parents were away, and the only activity around his home was some work at the barn. Rooney wandered into the barn, then climbed up to the loft and began playing with straw cutters. His hand must have slipped into the blades, because he cut off his left forefinger at the top of the fingernail and his left middle finger at the first joint. The pain and blood were extensive.

Jim, the servant in charge of the household, retrieved the severed finger ends and rushed Rooney to the hospital at the fort. But the doctor was in New York at the time, so Rooney's wounds went undressed for more than an hour. When the doctor returned, he attached the ends of Rooney's fingers, bandaged the wounds, and offered some hope that the flesh would knit. All the while, Rooney remained calm and brave.

Rooney's accident upset the Lee household considerably. Almost a week passed before Robert Lee took the time to write the news of Rooney's misfortune to Custis, who was away at school in Virginia. The father began his letter with a classic parental comment: "I am pleased with your progress so far & the last report sent me by Mr. Smith gave you a very good standing in all your studies. I was surprised to see that you were lower in Algebra than in any other. How was that for I thought you had some talent for mathematics." Never mind the multiple successes; think about this one imperfection. Students have read and heard words to this effect probably forever.

Then Lee recited the tale of Rooney's fingers. Very probably in keeping with the textbooks on child rearing at the time, Lee attempted to use the incident to teach a moral lesson to Custis, who was thirteen at the time. "I hope my dear son," he preached, "this may be a warning to you to meddle or interfere with nothing with which you have no concern & particularly to refrain from going where you have been prohibited or have not the permission of your parents or teacher." Rooney was never supposed to leave the yard or go to the barn without permission, and Jim had warned the boy not to touch the straw-cutting box. "Notwithstanding all this he did both & you see the fruits of disobedience. He may probably lose his fingers & be ruined for life.

"Do take warning," Lee added, "from the calamity that has befallen your brother. I am now watching by his bedside lest he should disturb his hand in his sleep. I still hope his hand may be restored." The father continued to write of Rooney's tendencies to be "heedless, obstinate, disobedient," but granted him "some very good qualities" and hoped he would "correct his evil ways."

Nor did Robert Lee abandon the issue when Rooney recovered. A few weeks later he had Rooney dictate a letter to Custis and announce the failure of the sewn finger-ends to knit with his fingers. The father wrote for his son and recorded Rooney's pleas that "neither of us will disobey our parents." For himself the father added, "See how two have been punished for their inattention & disobedience. One with the loss of an eye [Annie], another with the amputation of two fingers."[16]

In many ways these were dreadful letters, and Robert Lee's didactic zeal was at least excessive. In his outrageous emphasis upon the morality at stake, however, Lee was following the counsel of contemporary authorities on child rearing. And he probably resorted to hyperbole—"calamity," "fruits of disobedience," "ruined for life," "evil ways," "amputation"—to compensate for Mary Lee's likely silence on the subject.

Amid all the righteous rhetoric it is possible to overlook one extremely important sentence. "I am now watching by his bedside lest he should disturb his hand in his sleep." All the while Lee was writing down such doom, he was doing something very different. He sat with his son for many nights, acting out love even as he wrote of judgment.

This existential Robert Lee, whose actions were at odds with the prescribed things he wrote and said, calls to mind the final passage in a modern novel about a model parent: "He turned out the light and went into Jem's room. He would be there all night, and he would be there when Jem waked up in the morning." The "he" is Atticus Finch in Harper Lee's *To Kill a Mockingbird*.[17]

Robert Lee worked hard at being a good parent. He concentrated, too, upon being a good husband; he had to do so, because Mary Lee often frustrated her husband. From Fort Hamilton, he wrote to Tasy Beaumont in March 1843, "My beautiful Tasy; I have just returned from Washington where your charming letter followed me. I have brought it back with me to enjoy it. I wish you were here in person, for I am all alone. My good Dame not wishing to leave her mother so soon, even to follow such a spouse as I am."

About a mutual young friend in love Lee wrote, "Poor Alex K I pity him. Comfort him Tasy, for if the fire of his heart is so stimulating to the growth of his whiskers there is danger of his being suffocated. What would be the verdict of a jury in that case? Suicide? It is awful to think of. . . . I hope the sympathy between himself and Miss Louise is not so intimate as to produce the same effect on her, for I should hate her sweet face to be hid by such hairs unless they were . . . mine."

Later in the same letter Lee offered some verse he claimed was a translation from the bucolic Greek poet Theocritus inscribed upon a statue of Cupid:

> Mild he may be, and innocent to view,
> Yet who on earth can answer for him? You
> who touch the little god, mind what ye do.
> Although short be his arrow, slender his bow:
> The King Apollo's never wrought such woe.

This is clever stuff, ripe with double entendre, and the lines from Theocritus offer Freudian metaphors fully thirteen years before the birth of Sigmund Freud. Lee's correspondent may or may not have been equally clever.[18]

He confided to his friend Henry Kayser in 1845, "You are right in my interest in the pretty women, & it is strange I do not lose it with age. But I perceive no diminution."[19]

In September 1844, Lee commenced a correspondence with Martha Custis ("Markie") Williams, who was eighteen then; and he would continue to write to her for twenty-six years, until he was within weeks of his death. "Oh Markie, Markie," Lee wrote her, "When will you ripen." A year later he wrote, "Your good long letter my dearest Markie gave me infinite pleasure. I have thought upon it, slept upon it, dwelt upon it (pretty long you will say) & have not done with it yet." Markie was Mary Lee's first cousin and a cousin to Robert Lee as well. She grew up a short distance from Arlington across the Potomac at Tudor Place, and later she visited Arlington and shared a bedroom with Mary, the Lees' oldest daughter.[20]

Tasy Beaumont and Markie Williams offered Robert Lee the zest and excitement Mary Lee seemed to lack. This much is pretty clear. But also involved were at least two species of "control." Lee could maintain control of himself if he pursued apparently "impossible" relationship on paper, via the mails. And well he knew the dangers of losing control in matters marital. At the same time Lee the older man of experience could assert control in the lives and affairs of his young female friends. However much frustration he felt in his marriage to

Mary Lee, with younger women his opinions seemed to matter and his words found listeners and appreciative readers.

Robert Lee continued to love Mary and likely did nothing to jeopardize his marriage. Indeed, he took pains to inform and even involve his wife in his correspondence with young women. To a degree, Mary and Robert Lee developed some sort of understanding on the subject. And whatever arrangement, spoken or unspoken, the Lees adopted, Robert remained a faithful spouse and a sensitive, warm, sensuous man at the same time.[21]

Lee preferred the company of women to men. Often he seemed preoccupied when in the company of men; he retained that certain shy side of himself when he encountered people he did not know well or numbers of people at once. But on occasions he could join the hearty camaradarie of men. Sometimes Lee shared with males the clever wit and quick mind that he usually reserved for women.

One good example of Lee at home in a barracks atmosphere occurred at Fort Hamilton and concerned the unlikely topic of liturgical practice in the Anglican Church. At that time American Episcopalians were debating the Oxford or Tractarian movement, which advocated "High Church" liturgics and a return to many of the forms and features of Roman Catholicism. At the center of this controversy was the English theologian Edward Bouverie Pusey, who spoke and wrote in favor of the Oxford movement. Puseyism became a divisive issue within many American parishes. Lee, who was a member of the vestry at St. John's Church, attempted to avoid debate about the matter. He was decidedly "Low Church" himself and likely opposed Puseyism.

At a gathering of officers one evening at Fort Hamilton the discussion became especially intense. Henry J. Hunt, a lieutenant who like Lee declined to take sides in the dispute, recalled that Lee seized the floor and addressed him in mock solemnity:

I am glad to see that you keep aloof from the dispute that is disturbing our little parish. That is right, and we must not get mixed up in it; we must support each other in that. But I must give you some advice about it, in order that we may understand each other. *Beware of Pussyism! Pussyism* is always bad, and may lead to unchristian feeling; therefore beware of *Pussyism!*

It is true that Puseyites were also "pussy-cats" in nineteenth-century slang. But the vulgar meaning of "pussy" was in vogue too and makes better sense in the context in which Lee spoke. For some time thereafter, Lee repeated, "Beware of Pussyism!" whenever he saw Hunt.[22]

While Lee flexed his social maturity and made various accommodations for what seemed to him to be his wife's limitations as spouse and parent, he also grew rich. At the close of his service at Fort Hamilton, he was quite "comfortable" by nineteenth-century standards, in terms of his personal income.

The United States Army and the Congress had done little to make Lee "comfortable" during this period. In the wake of the Panic of 1837, Congress looked long and hard at military salaries and made cuts. In 1843, Robert Lee wrote his brother Carter, "I never felt poorer in my life & for the first time in my life I have not been able to pay my debts. Last year my pay was cut down $300 & the year before $500." In 1846, he informed his brother, "My pay seems to decrease as my children increase. The first has been reduced to $1350 & the second raised to 7."[23]

Officers in the United States Army earned money in accord with a complicated series of acts and appropriations, some of which dated back to 1802. Each officer earned a stated amount per month, plus subsistence (calculated in a prescribed number of rations per day at 20 cents per ration per day), plus forage for the officer's horses (again, the number of horses varied with rank and service), plus the cost and care of servants, plus an additional ration for every five years served. In 1841, the Secretary of War reported that Captain R. E. Lee received $1,817. In 1842, the Secretary reported that an officer of Lee's rank, branch, and years of service received $1,379. And in 1844 Lee should have received $1,374, an amount reduced to $1,350 in 1846, as Lee informed his brother.[24]

Dollars, of course, have relative value. When Lee began his service in the Engineer Corps, civilian engineers were earning from two to three times more money per year. However, by the 1840s salaries of civilian engineers had sunk to approximately the level of Lee's.[25]

Living so often at Arlington reduced the Lees' expenses considerably. The house Lee rented in Brooklyn cost $300 per year. When Custis began formal schooling, his father paid $100 per semester (which included room and board) and a little more for lessons and books in French. Later, when Rooney went to Harvard, his expenses were $200 per semester, plus spending money, which he always seemed to need.[26] In 1846 the Lees were still able to live on Robert Lee's pay and allowances from the government ($1,350). For the education of the children, Lee depended upon the proceeds from invested money, what he termed "my private income."[27]

Robert Lee's private income began with his mother's bequest of thirty slaves to her three sons. Carter, Smith, and Robert Lee divided this bequest in some way, and Robert hired out some of his slaves and probably sold the others. In 1835 he retained only one of the original number, a woman named Nancy Ruffin whom he rented to his father-in-law to work on his plantation White House in New Kent County, Virginia. Nancy Ruffin had three "illegitimate" children whom Lee presumably hired out as well.[28]

Money from the sale and rent of slaves, together with any savings from his pay and allowances, Lee invested. During the 1830s he bought stock in banks, principally the Bank of Virginia and the Bank of the Valley of Virginia. Following the Panic of 1837 Lee became disillusioned with banks and began to diversify. He bought canal and railroad bonds, and he bought state bonds (Virginia, Ohio, and Kentucky). His friend Henry Kayser in St. Louis was especially helpful with advice about prudent and profitable investments in the expansive West. By 1846 Lee's portfolio had a market value of $38,750 and yielded a bit more than $2,000 per year, or around 5 percent.

In addition Lee owned or claimed land. He owned a third interest in a tract of land in Floyd, Virginia, from his mother's estate, some land in Hardy, Virginia, from his father, and a third interest in a claim against the government for land which may have belonged to his father's estate. Lee's landed wealth was not significant compared with his personal wealth. The only parcel for which there was a buyer, the Floyd property, might yield him $2,500, if Carter Lee consummated the sale. Otherwise, Lee owned land no one seemed to want.[29]

Two circumstances during the period 1841–46 no doubt reminded Lee of his family's past financial follies. Soon after he left St. Louis, the bank with which he had dealt claimed that Lee was $4,000 overdrawn and refused to honor one of his checks. Lee pursued the matter with calm, cold diligence and eventually demonstrated that the bank cashier, not he, had erred.[30]

The second reminder that careless handling of money could cost him came from the Paymaster General's office. It seemed that Lee had drawn his pay twice for the months of May and June in 1845. Lee investigated his records and discovered that he had in fact received pay twice for those months. He immediately refunded $265.40 to the government, asserted absolute innocence of any deceit, and could only blame an attack of "bilious fever" for his errors. Lee wrote that the incident "caused me more mortification than any other act of my life." Lee's superiors, all the way to the commanding general of the Army, believed him innocent, and the Paymaster General asserted, "Capt. Lee is as honorable a gentleman as any in the land."[31]

One other event from this period proved that Lee had become mature and shrewd in the ways of the world. In 1842, Lee's uncle/cousin Bernard Carter (his mother's brother, who married his half sister Lucy Grymes) died and in his will named Lee executor of the estate. Surely Bernard Carter had meant to honor his nephew/cousin and had made him executor out of respect for Lee's prudence and integrity. But Lee realized that the task would require thankless labor for an extended period, and so he declined in favor of his brother Carter. Lee was right. Here was a familial obligation fraught with nothing but trouble, as Carter Lee soon discovered. Robert Lee knew his limitations and knew when and how to say emphatically no.[32]

In 1846, at age thirty-nine, Robert Lee could and probably did take pride in his financial acumen. He had begun his adult life with a professional education, a modest bequest in human property from his mother, and little else. Seventeen years later he had a wife, seven children, professional status, and the means to support his family if he were to die tomorrow. Thus far in his life Lee had exorcised the ghost of Light Horse Harry.

In his correspondence at least, Lee the neo-Federalist Whig was as niggardly with his opinions on political issues as Lee the capitalist was with his assets. Family and friends generally knew Robert Lee's orientation and point of view, so he usually referred them to the newspapers for recent political developments and made no comment himself. Opinions he had, however.

When his friend Henry Kayser encountered opposition in 1845 to his reappointment as city engineer in St. Louis because he was not a "native"

American, Lee wrote: "There ought to be no 'native party' in this country. All ought to be Americans in feelings & acts & more than that none can be."[33]

To his father-in-law, Lee sent a newspaper with an account of the Anti-Slavery Society's annual meeting in New York. He wished Custis to "see to what extent some men are carried by their evil passions—which indeed is calculated to excite some apprehensions for the peace & prosperity of the country." Custis would see, Lee continued, "that they contend for the ruin of the present American Church & the destruction of the present Union. That the pulpit is denounced as the great stronghold of slavery. The founders of the Constitution & the fathers of the Revolution *Swindlers,* in accomplishing that which after fifty years trial is found to be a *curse* and not a blessing."[34]

Lee opposed nativist politics in the 1840s and believed that "evil passions" incited some abolitionist activities. Neither attitude is all that surprising. The novelty of these examples is their rarity in a correspondence preoccupied with personal experiences and the activities of friends and family members. Lee was less than absorbed with politics in the traditional sense, associated with elections, taxes, laws, and the like.

Yet Lee was intrigued and active in the politics which concern the relationships of people and power. Armies, like other organizations and institutions, are political entities, and armies in the absence of wars are often intensely political. In his profession Lee was extremely careful to avoid the appearance either of sycophancy or of overweening ambition. Nevertheless he seemed fascinated with the distribution and fluxuation of power and influence within the Army, and within the limits of strictest propriety he acted to improve his own prospects and those of his friends.

In March 1845 Lee was working for Colonel Totten in Washington, and his friend Jack Mackay had been ill and wanted to remain on assignment in Savannah. Lee went to work for him. "I have endeavored to get from your Col. [Chief of the Topographical Engineers], whether in the failure of the appr[opriations] your services would be required elsewhere. He is too deep for me, I can't fathom him. A deep sea line can find no bottom. But I have pumped Swift freely who gives out so bold a stream as to fill your pail at once. He says he knows of nothing to call you away from Sav[annah]." Later Lee was able to wring similar assurances from Mackay's superior.[35]

Very soon after Lee began his assignment at the Narrows (June 1841), Winfield Scott became General in Chief of the United States Army. Very much a Virginian, Scott was fifty-five years old and a veteran of thirty-three years of distinguished military service which commenced with a captain's commission directly from President Thomas Jefferson. Scott had been an American hero since the War of 1812 and had serious support to become the Whig nominee for President in 1840 and 1844. He stood six feet, five inches and weighed 230 pounds when only nineteen years old, and Scott had been adding pounds ever since. Florid in flesh, dress, and prose, Scott visited West Point in 1839 and impressed a brand new plebe named Ulysses S. Grant as "the finest specimen of manhood my eyes had ever beheld."[36]

Lee encountered Scott as a colleague in June 1844 when both men served on the Board of Visitors to the Military Academy, examined the first class of cadets, and reviewed the operation of the school. Those two weeks made an impression upon Lee. He was not quite so awed as Grant in 1839; but he clearly admired Scott and remained loyal to him during subsequent periods when allegiance appeared impolitic.[37]

By 1846, Lee had pursued his career for seventeen years—twenty-one with his apprenticeship at West Point. As an Engineer officer he was engaged in constructing things; but in the larger context of his service Lee had been a consumer. Like other officers in peacetime, Lee had been maintained at public expense in order to produce security for his country. During Lee's service the Army had conducted campaigns against the Black Hawk and against the Seminoles and periodically rattled sabers in hopes that Great Britain would hear. These were less than major conflicts, however, and Lee was a direct participant in none of them.

In 1846, though, the United States launched a significant war against Mexico. Now the Army would earn its living. Soldiers would do what they had been preparing to do since the Battle of New Orleans in 1815: they would fight.

Already Lee had put his wishes in writing. In June 1845, as the Texas boundary dispute which would provoke the conflict intensified, Lee stated to Totten, "In the event of war with any foreign government I should desire to be brought into active service in the field with as high a rank in the regular army as I could obtain. If that could not be accomplished without leaving the Corps of Engineers, I should then desire a transfer. . . ."[38]

After that Lee waited. He waited while expansionist President James K. Polk seemed to manipulate the boundary dispute into a diplomatic crisis and then into war. Then he waited while an American army led by Zachary Taylor won impressive victories in northern Mexico. Lee watched the Democratic administration wonder what to do about the fact that the nation's newest hero Taylor and General in Chief Scott were both Whigs. For a time Lee seemed to worry that the United States had won the war without him.

Lee believed that his fate depended upon Scott. To Mackay he wrote in late June 1846, "I have been very anxious to join the army in Mexico, and had hoped to have joined Gen. Scott this fall at least." But Scott had accommodated his enemies in the administration with what became known as his "hasty soup" letter to the Secretary of War. Lee called it "the most suicidal act that ever a man was guilty of, and all from allowing himself to become excited by the reports . . . of his evil wishers."[39]

Scott's letter simply stated that he had received a letter from the Secretary "as I sat down to take a hasty plate of soup." When quoted in print, however, the letter made Scott appear ludicrous and in the context of the tension in Washington seemed to ruin his chances of commanding in Mexico or anywhere else.

But the campaign in northern Mexico failed to produce victory, and Scott had believed all along in a drive upon Mexico City. So the Polk administration hoped that two Whig generals would cancel each other, and dispatched Scott. And Scott moved Lee.

Maybe the two weeks at West Point had left an impression; more likely Totten recommended Lee. Whatever the rationale, Lee received orders for Mexico in August 1846 and left as soon as possible.[40]

At this juncture Lee wrote his will, the only will he ever made. Aboard a steamboat from New Orleans to Port Lavaca on the Texas coast, he wrote to Mary Lee at Arlington and reminded her where he had stored their furniture, who had charge of his securities, and what were the provisions of his will. He admonished her about disciplining the children—"Set seriously to work upon the dear little creatures & see what you can make of them." Lee even offered his counsel about the boys' shoes—"You will ruin their feet as well as your purse if you do not attend to this yourself." As Lee wrote this, his new mare Creole and his Irish servant Jim Connally were swimming from the steamboat toward the beach. Next day they would all begin the journey to San Antonio in search of the Army and then the war.[41]

Some months earlier Lee had written to nine-year-old Rooney and left him some thoughts in the event that his father did not return from this conflict. Lee wrote down a story, a parable, which revealed the father more than it inspired the son.

A young lad of about Rooney's age named Harry who lived in the mountains of New Hampshire went into the snowy woods with his father to cut firewood. Harry's task was to haul the wood back to their home on a horse-drawn sled. While Harry was en route, a large limb fell upon his father and pinned him to the frozen ground. When Harry returned, he soon realized that his father was dead. After a moment's thought Harry began to cut the limb with his ax. Having freed his father's body, the boy rolled the corpse onto the sled and drove it home to his mother. Once the mother recovered from her shock and grief, "she thanked God who had given her so good and brave a son."[42]

This was indeed a grisly tale, but it was the only parable Lee told that survives. The obvious moral was a plea to Rooney to be "good and brave" if his father should not return from Mexico. But Lee's grim parable possessed larger meaning as well. Life is uncertain, sometimes beyond human control, says the story. Evil occurs. When bad things happen, people—Harry in this case—have the obligation to respond. To the limits of human capacity, people should take control and make the best of bad situations. People should be agents of redemption, even in circumstances such as Harry's when redemption seemed pretty remote.

In many ways, Lee was this Harry. He was certainly not Light Horse Harry. He encountered, even expected, frustration; but he usually retained his poise and coped. He accepted his life and dealt with its vagaries in the most positive ways that he could. Lee was that nine-year-old in the woods with a frozen father.

9

"I Have Done No Good"

CAPTAIN ROBERT E. LEE went off to war aboard a steamboat in the company of sixty-six mules and one pretty young white woman. He and the white woman occupied "Ladies Private Apartments" (beyond the notice, "Gentlemen are not admitted") where a "sable chambermaid" attended them.

Bizarre symbols and circumstances these were for a would-be warrior. Lee could hardly have conjured less auspicious portents for his journey to combat. He did explain them to his family.

His "fair companion," the young white woman, was traveling with her child in search of her spouse, who was a soldier. She was determined to follow him to the war. The black woman had become her "confidant[e] as well as guardian."

Lee children often hopped into bed with their parents. So Robert wrote to his wife, "I was dreaming of you all last night & thought daughter [Mary] was in the bed with me & I was wondering how she should be so small when lo & behold when I awoke in the mor^g I found it was little Agnes."

Also aboard the steamboat were some "laggard volunteers" in transit to the Army, more than $60,000 entrusted to Lee's care as courier, and Lee's new mare Creole hurriedly purchased in New Orleans. Lee's Irish servant Jim Connally was ill and already sorry he had agreed to come along. This queer amalgam of people, animals, and property were all heading for San Antonio to join the army commanded by Brigadier General John E. Wool.[1]

Like most of the men and supplies gathered at San Antonio, Lee and his various companions traveled by ship from New Orleans to Port Lavaca, Texas, and then overland to San Antonio. From there Wool was supposed to lead an expedition to Chihuahua, a major commercial city in western Mexico about 200 miles due south of El Paso. For the sake of roads, water, and provisions, however, Wool would have to take a circuitous route south-southwest from San Antonio to Parras, considerably south of Chihuahua, and then march northwest for many miles in order to reach his objective.[2]

What Wool really wanted to do was join forces with Zachary Taylor in

northeastern Mexico and fight the principal Mexican army commanded by
General Santa Anna. The Chihuahua campaign was pretty clearly of subordinate importance in the emerging strategic plan for the war. While Taylor
operated against Santa Anna in northern Mexico, another army commanded
by Stephen W. Kearny marched to Santa Fe in what became New Mexico and
then to California.

Still in the background at this point (September 1846) was the commanding general of the United States Army, Winfield Scott, and his insistence upon
a campaign via Vera Cruz against Mexico City. Democratic President James
Polk restrained Scott because he hoped for victory without the effort and
expense of an expedition to Mexico City and because Scott was a prominent
Whig and a known aspirant for the presidency. Unfortunately for Polk, Taylor, too, was a Whig whose political ambition developed in rough parallel with
his reputation as a military hero. For the moment, though, the Polk administration believed that the thrusts of Kearny and Taylor would suffice to secure
victory and territorial conquest required to fulfill the nation's Manifest Destiny.[3]

To Lee, as he struggled to reach San Antonio before Wool and his army set
out south, the strategic machinations in Washington seemed to portend a
minor role as a staff officer in an ancillary campaign. Still he seemed pleased at

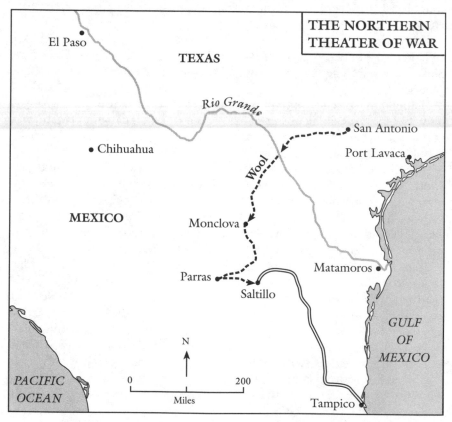

the prospect of adventure and intrigued by new sights and experiences.

A Daguerreotype made before he left for the war shows Lee in the fullness of midlife manhood. Presumably taken when he was thirty-nine, the picture reveals Lee's strength and energy. His hair is still long, covering the top of his ear in waves, but receding somewhat from his high forehead. The sideburns are gone now, and Lee has a neat mustache. The Daguerreotype displays a man of fashion who, as his later feats would demonstrate, was also a man fit for the rigors of battle.[4]

After one night at Port Lavaca, Lee, Jim, Creole, and two mules began the long slog through "Hog Wallow" prairie to San Antonio. They arrived shortly before Wool began his march on September 29, 1846.

Lee had the good fortune to miss much of the friction between Wool, the strict regular disciplinarian, and his army, composed for the most part of volunteers. Tension persisted, however, and whenever the men stopped moving for any length of time, trouble ensued. Indeed, throughout the war and within each American army, volunteers and regulars tended to resent each other only slightly less than they did the enemy. Because he was a staff officer and not in direct command of troops (line officer), Lee remained more or less insulated from these quarrels.[5]

At San Antonio, Lee's comrade Engineer Captain William D. Frazer had constructed pontoons from which to build bridges over Mexican rivers. When Lee arrived, he and Frazer attempted with limited success to acquire tools (picks, shovels, and such) with which to improve roads and build bridges.[6]

Lee and the Engineer Company, as it came to be called, did perform some construction during Wool's advance into Mexico and afterward. But the most important assignments for Lee and his fellow Engineer officers were not construction projects. For the first time in American history, United States armies marched on foreign soil and fought battles in an alien land. Maps were few and often unreliable, and Mexican guides for obvious reasons were even fewer and even less reliable. What Wool and Lee's subsequent commanders required of the Engineers was reconnaissance, accurate information about roads, rivers, terrain, and the enemy. Consequently Engineer officers very quickly made themselves indispensable and found themselves not only recommending routes and evaluating enemy positions but also offering informed advice about strategy and tactics.[7]

Wool's army on the march consisted of 1,400 men and 188 wagons; because he could transport no provisions for them, Wool left behind two regiments of Illinois Volunteers with instructions to follow the main force later. The army covered the 164 miles between San Antonio and the Rio Grande in two weeks. At the river (near Eagle Pass) was a small body of Mexican troops, who withdrew as Frazer and Lee fashioned a "flying bridge" (i.e., a platform drawn across the river on ropes). On October 12, Wool's army crossed into enemy country. Lee wrote home, "There has been a great whetting of knives, grinding of swords, and sharpening of bayonets ever since we reached the river."[8]

After a respite and some reorganization, Wool set out south once more on

October 16 and marched 105 miles to Santa Rosa, paused for a week there, and then pressed on to Monclova. The army arrived before Monclova on October 30, and soon afterward Wool received orders from Zachary Taylor to halt. On September 23, while Wool was preparing to leave San Antonio, Taylor and his army had won a major victory at Monterrey, and in the aftermath of the battle had agreed to an armistice of eight weeks. Wool was about to cross the armistice line, and the agreement was supposed to remain in effect for another four weeks.

So the army encamped outside Monclova and waited. During this halt the two Illinois regiments arrived, boosting Wool's force above 2,000. But many people then and most historians since have considered Taylor's armistice a mistake. Within Wool's army enmity between volunteers and regulars flared as the volunteers chafed at more drill and training. Even Lee, sounding like a volunteer, wrote with some presumption and little patience, "I am one of those silly persons when I have any thing to do I can't rest satisfied till it has been accomplished."[9]

Lee also expressed broader vision. "If then they [the Mexicans] were so crippled by the battle of Monterey [sic], by all means advantage should have been taken of our success, & perhaps the whole Mexican Army would have fallen into our hands," he wrote Mary Lee. "Whereas I now fear," he continued, "time has been given them to recover at least partially from that blow and that when hostilities are resumed, they will be found stronger & we weaker from the respite. At least such will be the case with Genl Wool's Army, for we consume our provisions faster than we can collect them. . . ."[10]

Near the end of November Wool finally received orders to leave Monclova and march to Parras. Also among Wool's instructions was permission to forget the expedition to Chihuahua. On November 23, the army began a grueling trek over deserts and mountains which ended on December 5 at Parras. Now Wool and his men were at last within the war zone after a journey from Port Lavaca, San Antonio, the Rio Grande, Santa Rosa, Monclova, to Parras of more than 700 miles. Taylor's army was at Saltillo and Monterrey to the east. Santa Anna with a Mexican army of 25,000 men was plotting a major offensive at San Luis Potosí, 200 miles to the south. Throughout December 1846 and January 1847 rumors provoked alarms and frantic preparations among the U.S. forces in northern Mexico.[11]

Still Lee had yet to experience combat. He had ridden those 700 miles with Wool's army and spent months in enemy country without hearing a serious shot fired. He had worked hard, though. His scouting duties required Lee sometimes to be in his saddle by 3:00 A.M. and often to ride 50 to 60 miles per day.

During his service with Wool, Lee rode three horses. The small but wiry dun mare Creole he had brought with him to San Antonio from New Orleans. He acquired another mare in Mexico, a sorrel that remained unnamed. "I like mares for riding horses," he wrote his sons. "They are more docile & intelligent than horses. . . ." Lee's other mount was a sturdy bay male he purchased in San Antonio. Lee's servant Jim Connally usually rode the horse and christened him "Jim."[12]

Lee's letters home from Wool's army contained vivid descriptions of the places, pastimes, customs, and people he encountered on the march. At times he seemed as much a tourist as a soldier. Here are some samples.

During an expedition to purchase food, Lee discovered that "Several of the young women were quite pretty. Fine teeth & eyes Small feet & hands & in their simple dress of a chemise & petticoat looked quite interesting." Mexican people in general Lee pronounced "an amiable but weak people, primitive in their habits & tastes."[13]

Lee was less critical regarding Mexican food and announced that "their cooking on the whole is pretty good." He ate some bread "as fine . . . as I have ever tasted."

While Wool was in camp near Monclova, the general occupied the home of a wealthy Mexican landowner and included Lee in his officers' mess. "The dinner," Lee explained, "is El Mexicano"—rice or vermicelli "highly peppered & seasoned"; then boiled beef with cabbage, pumpkins, sweet potatoes, white beans, and corn; then another meat dish with bread and gravy; then still more meat (chicken, kid, or mutton) with pecans and raisins; next a pâté with more pecans and raisins; then black beans; and finally watermelon for dessert.[14]

"Recollect," Lee wrote "that the everlasting pepper enters into all these. . . ." Mexican red peppers were for him "as hot as a coal of fire." In contrast was "the cup of chocolate, which winds up the feast." "You know," Lee wrote, "I never liked chocolate, in fact could never drink it until I came here, but I find it delightful."

The Mexican wolves were impressive. "They surround our camp every night. Are aroused by the lights at Reveille & keep up a concert of howling till scattered by the gray approach of mor^g."[15]

Youngest son Rob (now three) must have mailed his father some fishhooks. Lee asked Mary Lee to "Tell him the Mexicans are dreadfully alarmed at his fishhooks & are running away."

Near Parras he observed, "There are some large estates here, on which there is a union of wealth, poverty, plenty, want, elegance & sloveness [sic] as with us." Lee visited one such estate owned by brothers, one of whom had attended school in Bardstown, Kentucky, and welcomed the invading officers. "The parlour, dining room & drawing room, the only rooms I was in, must have been each 40 ft. long & 20 high. All handsomely furnished, Scarlett & muslin curtains to the windows & doors, sofas, mirrors (small) some paintings etc." On the estate lived 1,200 peons who toiled in extensive vineyards to produce wines and brandies and an income per year of $50,000. "Pretty good," thought Lee, "for a country of this sort."

The master of the estate treated some of the officers, including Lee, to a dinner at which "There was a profusion of wines & liquors, & the preserved peaches (whole) & Charlotte Russe was perfectly delicious."[16]

To Custis and Rooney (William), Lee wrote on Christmas Eve 1846 from

Saltillo. Among other things he told them of a recent alarm, the rumored advance of Santa Anna's army. He was with the "pioneers" (engineers) working on a road through the mountains when a courier rode into his camp at midnight with a summons for Wool to march immediately from Parras to Saltillo to meet an anticipated attack from Santa Anna. The next morning Lee dispatched his pioneers and cavalry escort and set out himself for Parras and Wool. He rode fifty miles and reached Parras at dark, only to learn that Wool and his staff had already started for Saltillo. Lee paused only long enough to feed his horse (the sorrel mare) and then rode into the dark after Wool. He found the general and his party encamped eight or ten miles along the road. Next morning Wool sent Lee (on Creole, this time) after the troops he had sent toward Saltillo to redirect them to a new rendezvous. "The Evg [evening] after this . . . I had ridden *Jim* all day & at night news reached Genl Wool that Santa Anna would reach Aqua Nueva [17 miles south of Saltillo] that night, 9 miles from him, I mounted Jim again, who had had a few hours rest & his supper, & started off to see if Santa Anna was there." Lee took a road different from his cavalry escort and so rode alone in search of the enemy: ". . . I trotted on keeping a sharp lookout . . . & reached Aqua Nueva without seeing anyone." On his way back to camp Lee encountered his escort, sent one rider to Wool with news of his solitary scout, and led the rest beyond Aqua Nueva to make sure Santa Anna was not advancing. "This I did & did not get back to camp till 10 o'clock next day, having ridden some 50 miles that night."

Lee told this story of riding and scouting during several nights and days ostensibly in praise of his mounts: "Now you will know they are *good* horses." But his story also reveals Lee's stamina and energy. Although he had yet to see combat, Lee's experience at war was not all Charlotte Russe and hot chocolate.[17]

On the morning after Lee wrote to his older sons about his adventures while investigating reports of Santa Anna's advance—Christmas morning— another alarm came to Wool's camp. But no army approached, and at one o'clock in the afternoon Wool dismissed his troops. Then the feasting commenced—eggnog, evergreens, oranges, chickens, turkeys, and many toasts.[18]

Still rumors persisted that the Mexican army was on the march about to attack the invaders from the United States. Zachary Taylor supposedly told a captain who said he had seen a force of 20,000 Mexican soldiers and 250 pieces of artillery en route, "Captain, if you say you saw it, of course I must believe you; but I would not have believed it if I had seen it myself." Much later an acquaintance quoted Lee describing a scouting foray as having been convinced that he saw in the moonlight a vast hillside dotted with the tents of Santa Anna's horde. For reasons he could not explain, Lee remained on the scene and discovered in daylight that the "tents" were in fact grazing sheep.[19]

Other rumors swept through Wool's army as well. The most persistent involved Winfield Scott and his plan to land an army near Vera Cruz and march on Mexico City. These rumors proved to be grounded in fact. And in mid-January 1847 Lee received orders to join Scott's headquarters at Brazos.

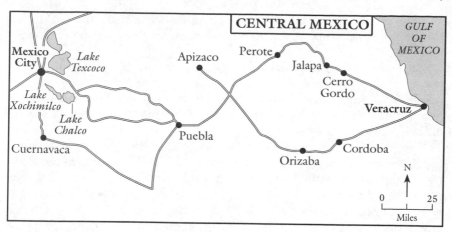

So on his fortieth birthday (January 19) Lee rode Creole toward his first experience in combat. Jim Connally, purged of many of his creature comforts, but "fat, ruddy & corpulent, as when he first came from Ireland," accompanied him. They rode 250 miles, arrived in fine condition, and Lee went to work on Scott's staff.[20]

Colonel Joseph G. Totten, Chief of the Engineer Corps, was with Scott as senior Engineer officer. However, Lee joined Totten, Lieutenant Colonel Ethan Allen Hitchcock, and Captain Henry Lee Scott to form what Scott called his "little cabinet," the inner circle of the general's advisers. Scott was embroiled in preparations and frustrated by delays, and his staff doubtless shared the commander's moods.

On February 15, Scott sailed with his staff to Tampico, and on February 20 they continued down the coast of eastern Mexico to the island of Lobos, rendezvous for the invasion force and fleet. Lee remained aboard the ship *Massachusetts* for over two weeks while men and ships made ready for the landing near Vera Cruz.[21]

While the *Massachusetts* rolled at sea, Lee spent some of his enforced confinement writing letters. He shared a stateroom with his good friend Joe Johnston; but, Lee wrote, "my poor Joe is so sick all the time I can do nothing with him." So Lee wrote to relieve the tedium, and some of his letters are interesting indeed.[22]

To his mother-in-law, the pious Mary Custis, Lee poured forth evangelical agony. Reflecting upon his life thus far, he lamented, "I have done no good. I hope I have escaped any great crime." He missed his children and bewailed his separation from them—"Nothing can compensate me for that." Reconciled to his duty, Lee concluded, "Still here I must remain ready to perform what little service I can & hope for the best." Then he protested, "But I did not sit down to impose upon you my troubles. Those I must keep to myself & will therefore speak of something else."[23]

To his oldest sons, Custis (fourteen) and Rooney (nine), Lee delivered admonitions to grow "in goodness and knowledge, as well as stature." When he returned home, he said, he would be happy or miserable in accord with their performance while he was away. "You must do all in your power to save me pain."[24]

Somber thoughts these were, and less than healthy, too. "I have done no good." "These [my troubles] I must keep to myself." And then to lay responsibility for his happiness or misery upon his young sons—"save me pain"—imposed quite a burden upon the boys. In these letters Lee seems troubled indeed.

But when he let go of pain and admonitions and did "speak of something else," the tone of his letters changed radically. Lee told his mother-in-law of his travels and the sights he had seen. "The approach . . . to Tampico is very pretty, & the town presents its best appearance from the water." He told his sons about Mexican boys playing and swimming, of donkeys and ponies, of a grand parade for General Scott, and about preparations for landing men and horses in the invasion. Clearly Lee was enjoying his new experience and the adventure of making war. "I shall have plenty to do . . . and am anxious for the time to come, and hope all may be successful."[25]

Lee's letters at this juncture revealed important themes in his life. He continued to be concerned about control—not only control of himself, but his capacity to control the lives of other people. He seemed obsessed with righteousness and redemption. He wrote the words he was supposed to write and sought beyond his words to redeem his deeds. By his actions and example, he strove to mold the lives of his children. When Lee told his sons that they possessed the power by their conduct to render him happy or miserable, he told the truth.

Juxtaposed with all this concern for control and his fervor to redeem the human condition, Lee also yearned for freedom. In Mexico, he was free from the complicated responsibilities of his various family roles (husband, parent, son-in-law, uncle, brother, et al.), and he was free to expand his experience and to assert his worth as soldier and person.

Lee's desire for control and freedom at once was paradoxical, and this paradox was and is universal. The tension so associated was hardly unique to Lee. But within Lee's life the tension between control and freedom was especially acute and all but constant, even though most of the time he kept his troubles to himself. In Mexico Lee fretted about his children and their education and development. But in Mexico the overriding fact of war offered Lee resolution for his tensions. Now he found freedom in doing his duty.

Meanwhile, back in northern Mexico Santa Anna's army at last advanced upon Taylor's and Wool's forces, rendered fewer by the demands of Scott's expedition. The Mexicans attacked near Buena Vista; Taylor responded; and the United States forces withstood the onslaught. Intense fighting took place on February 22 and 23, and on February 25 Santa Anna determined to retreat. Taylor's victory at Buena Vista concluded major operations in the north and left Santa Anna (albeit with a beaten army) free to focus his attention upon Scott's campaign against Mexico City.[26]

While their comrades were fighting for their lives at Buena Vista, the officers and men of Scott's invasion force were saluting George Washington's Birthday and toasting their own prospects for victory off Lobos. Finally on March 3, 1847, Scott's small armada started south once more, and on March 9 initial landings began at Collado Beach, about two miles down the coast from Vera Cruz. Within a few hours, Scott's entire army (8,600 men) were ashore, and to the surprise of everyone involved, the landings were absolutely unopposed.

Lee landed on the beach with Scott's entourage on March 10 and soon thereafter joined a council of war to discuss the best way to assault the fortified city and its castle. Time was a factor. Scott knew that he had to take Vera Cruz and begin the march inland before the arrival of yellow fever *(vomito)* season on the coast. Scott also knew that an immediate, direct attack upon Vera Cruz by infantry would be extremely costly in lives for the attackers. Consequently Scott proposed to take Vera Cruz by "regular" approaches—to besiege instead of storm. The "little cabinet" agreed and plans for the investment began.

Already elements of Scott's army occupied a perimeter around Vera Cruz on the land side of the city. Lee and other Engineer officers began a vigorous reconnaissance to select sites for batteries of big guns to shell the city. As they scouted, work gangs were wrestling artillery pieces—"heavy metal," in the jargon of the day—through the surf and over the dunes. A succession of cold fronts, "northers," blew through the region bringing rain and high winds to hamper the work. And Mexican cavalry patrols continued to probe the perimeter. Yet the greatest vexation for the invaders was the smallest—the myriad midges known as sand fleas that attacked the attackers. Lee had encountered such critters at Cockspur Island; but he had acquired no immunity whatsoever.[27]

One evening about a week after beginning the investment, Lee and First Lieutenant P. G. T. Beauregard were returning from a reconnaissance mission beyond friendly lines and came suddenly into a tiny clearing in the chaparral. Another man confronted them and spoke a challenge. Then, with the words barely out of his mouth and as Lee and Beauregard tried to reply, the man pointed a pistol at Lee. At a range of no more than twelve feet, he fired.

Flash, explosion, and smoke filled the clearing. Reacting to instinct, Lee and Beauregard lunged for the man, then held and disarmed him. He was a United States volunteer soldier, a member of an artillery unit that had had the outpost duty in the sector.

Lee examined himself and found that the ball had singed his uniform, but nothing else. The ball had passed between Lee's body and his arm.

The soldier claimed he was lost, and Lee and Beauregard escorted him to his unit. Thereafter the two officers suspected their assailant had been a deserter. However, they never investigated the matter.[28]

If Lee reflected later upon his first genuine experience under fire, he probably chuckled. He was the soldier who had sailed to war, supposedly the ultimate masculine exercise, in the company of mules and sharing with a woman

"Ladies Private Apartments." Now he had had the great good fortune to survive a pistol ball fired at him pointblank. But Lee's maiden experience as a target in a war zone had come at the hands of a member of his own army.

On the afternoon of March 22, after a pro forma surrender demand and a pro forma refusal, Scott's guns opened fire on Vera Cruz. Ships of the United States Navy joined the bombardment soon after the opening rounds. Firing continued the following day and increased in intensity as the army prepared more batteries and guns for action. Guns from Vera Cruz responded; but they proved generally ineffective against the well-designed batteries of the attackers.

Lee, at this point, was hard at work upon another battery, only 700 yards from the city's walls and stocked with the heaviest metal available. Scott had conferred with Commodores David Conner and Matthew Calbraith Perry on March 21, the day before the bombardment began, and secured the services of six naval guns (three 32-pounders and three 8-inch shell guns) and crews to serve the weapons.

Scott gave the orders to Lee to prepare the naval battery for action no later than March 24. So Lee had to order sailors who had just heaved their big guns ashore and through the sand to the site to dig trenches and plant sandbags around the battery. The seamen were not pleased and complained that they had come to fight Mexicans, not to burrow in the ground. Lee insisted and even appealed to the authority of his orders from Scott. The naval battery opened fire about ten o'clock on the morning of March 24.[29]

Gun crews from the fleet took turns serving the pieces; Lee directed the fire. The fire from these guns was devastating, and Mexican gun crews concentrated their fire upon this battery which most menaced their city.

By ironic coincidence one of the naval officers present with one of the gun crews was Smith Lee. So Robert Lee first saw combat in the company of his brother. Yet young Robert seemed to feel more the responsibility for the safety of his older brother. "No matter where I turned," Robert recalled, "my eyes reverted to him, and I stood by his gun whenever I was not wanted elsewhere. Oh! I felt awfully, and am at a loss what I should have done had he been cut down before me. I thank God that he was saved. He preserved his usual cheerfulness, and I could see his white teeth through all the smoke and din of the fire."[30]

By four o'clock in the afternoon (March 24) the naval battery had about spent the ammunition available, so the sailors stood down. Later, the officer who had most resisted the digging and sandbagging told Lee that he was right to insist upon fortifying the position. "I suppose the dirt did save some of my boys from being killed or wounded," he admitted. But he protested that he had "no use for dirt banks on shipboard—that there what we want is clear decks and an open sea. And the fact is, Captain, I don't like this land fighting, anyway. It ain't clean!"[31]

Among the naval officers and men who arrived that evening to continue the bombardment the next day (March 25) was Raphael Semmes, destined later to command the C.S.S. *Alabama*. Firing resumed early on March 25 and once more took a terrible toll upon the coral walls of Vera Cruz and its forts.

And within the city shells from the several batteries outside had wreaked havoc.

To hasten his victory at Vera Cruz, Scott planned a general infantry assault upon the city. However, soon after the bombardment resumed on March 26, the fifth day of the firing and the third day for Lee and the naval battery, the defenders of Vera Cruz signaled that they wished to talk about terms of surrender.

Wrangling ensued over saving of face. But on March 27 United States and Mexican negotiators agreed upon terms. Surrender ceremonies took place on the morning of March 29, 1847.[32]

While the negotiations were in progress, Lee prowled the perimeter of Vera Cruz to inspect the damage done by "his" guns. The naval battery in just over two days had fired 1,800 rounds, very roughly a fourth of the 6,700 projectiles launched by Scott's artillery. In a note to Smith Lee, brother Robert assured him, "Your battery (naval) has smashed that side of the town."

In the same note, Robert asked Smith to try to procure for him a "box or two of claret, one of brandy, and four colored shirts." A postscript requested Smith to try to buy a telescope, as he (Robert) had lost his own. The younger brother repeated his relief that Smith had been "saved through that hot fire, I felt awful at the thought of your being shot down before me."[33]

To the degree that he reflected upon his first experience at war, Lee seemed all but blasé about his own danger. To his immediate and extended family he wrote lots of proper prose about sympathy for noncombatant Mexicans in Vera Cruz. "My heart bled for the inhabitants . . . it was terrible to think of the women and children. . . ." He lamented the loss of comrades—"I grieve for the fine fellows. . . ." To Mary Lee he did remark, "The labour of the whole Corps was very arduous in the trenches . . . I am thankful that I have so far stood it."[34]

Such sentiments contrasted sharply with the response of Ulysses S. Grant to the same war when he first heard firing from hostile guns. Long after the event, in his *Memoirs,* Grant recalled, "I felt sorry that I had enlisted."[35]

Lee sent some pretty pretentious pronouncements to his wife—material well suited for publication, or at least circulation within circles of powerful people.

No one at their comfortable homes, can realize the exertions, pains & hardships of an Army in the field, under a scorching sun & in an enervating atmosphere. Still we must press on. The crack of the whip & prick of the Spur stimulates the animals & man's untiring Ardour drives on the whole. It is a great comfort to me to know that you are removed from the whole & I hope well and happy with our dear children & parents around you, I pray that nothing may disturb that repose & that I may in time return to you. As much as I long for that time & as many calls as I have to carry me back, if my life & strength are spared, I must see this contest to an end & endeavor to perform what little service I can to my country.

In the same letter Lee noted that some of his fellow officers had found themselves unfit for the physical strains of the campaign. He also called Mary

Lee's attention to the list of brevets, temporary promotions which in most circumstances would become permanent, bestowed upon friends and acquaintances in the aftermath of the success at Vera Cruz. Lee's friend Joe Johnston was now a lieutenant colonel—ironic, since Lee and the rest of Johnston's friends had nicknamed Johnston "The Colonel" ever since their days at West Point.

Lee knew that Scott had noticed his competence and hard work. But Lee as yet had no brevet to show for his service. "It is a fine thing to have strong friends in Our Govt.," Lee observed, "& I am glad that some of our friends have felt the benefit of it."[36]

From the beginning of the campaign, Scott had planned to press the invasion inland as soon as possible after securing Vera Cruz as the base of his supply line. However, lack of wagons compelled the general to remain at Vera Cruz for two weeks. While Scott chaffed at the delay, he had to confront some of the issues endemic to an army of occupation—such as the resumption of services in the Roman Catholic churches of Vera Cruz. In the process of encouraging religious services, Scott found himself seated on a bench in a large Roman Catholic church on Sunday, April 4, about to celebrate mass. For Scott the conquering general the situation made some sense; for Scott the candidate for President of the United States the circumstance seemed politically suicidal. The overwhelming majority of Scott's potential constituents were militantly Protestant. Yet there he sat at mass with his staff, which included Captain Lee.

Lee's friend from Fort Hamilton Lieutenant Henry J. Hunt happened into the rear of the church, caught Lee's eye, and in response to Lee's nod took a seat beside him on Scott's bench. No one else in the church had the benefit of a bench; the other worshippers either stood or knelt. From the altar came an acolyte with a candle for Scott, who had no notion of what to do with it. Eventually it became clear to Scott and the rest of the officers that they were supposed to participate in a procession around the church with the priests. And this they did.

As Scott and staff awkwardly shuffled into line, Hunt attracted the attention of Lee who walked beside him. Hunt laid a hand on Lee's elbow, endured "a rebuking look," and touched Lee once more.

"What is it?" asked Lee *sotto voce.*

"Captain Lee?" Hunt asked.

"Well?" whispered Lee.

"I really hope there is no *Pussyism* in all this?"

Hunt, of course, was the young officer at Fort Hamilton to whom Lee had delivered his double entendre about the High Church doctrines of Edward Pusey. Now in the ultimate "High Church" circumstance, Hunt returned Lee's favor and reminded Lee of his ribald pun.

"I glanced at him," Hunt recounted. "His face retained its quiet appearance, but the corners of his eyes and mouth were twitching in the struggle to preserve his gravity."[37]

10

"The Gallant, Indefatigable Captain Lee"

ON APRIL 15, 1847, Robert Lee found himself suddenly very much alone among many Mexican soldiers. John Fitzwalter, who was Lee's guide on this expedition, had scouted the region earlier, but obviously not definitively. The two men were standing near a spring when they heard approaching footsteps and voices speaking Spanish.

Fitzwalter bolted. But Lee only had time to drop behind a large fallen tree near the spring. Mexican soldiers came to the spring for water, and when the initial bunch had drunk their fill, others followed to drink and fill their canteens. Lee wriggled as far under the fallen tree trunk as he could.

The procession of thirsty Mexicans continued throughout the long day, while Lee remained motionless and stoic against insects, stiffness, and itches. Some of the enemy soldiers even sat on Lee's log and carried on conversations with their comrades. Others stepped over the log and Lee on their way to and from the spring.

Only at dusk did the parade of Mexicans abate, and Lee made his escape in the dark back to friendly camps. Next morning, however, he returned to the area and continued his mission.[1]

Lee's mission was to try to find some weakness in the defensive line Santa Anna had drawn across the invasion route of Winfield Scott's United States Army. Scott's men had marched inland about 45 miles from Vera Cruz and then confronted a series of well-prepared artillery positions covering the National Road as it passed through an extensive ravine.[2]

Later, Lee described the ground:

The right of the Mexican line rested on the river [Rio del Plan] at a perpendicular rock, unscalable by man or beast, and their left on impassable ravines; the main road was defended by Field works containing thirty-five cannon; in their rear was the mountain of Cerro Gordo, surrounded by intrenchments in which were cannon and crowned by a tower [El Telégrafo] overlooking all. . . .[3]

Within the maze of "impassable ravines" on the Mexican left (north) Lee endured his long day hiding under the fallen tree.

Lee confirmed the possibility of passing the army through these ravines and into the Mexican flank and rear. Based upon this reconnaissance, Scott formulated his plan to attack the Mexican position.

On April 17, Lee guided a division of troops commanded by David Twiggs around the left flank of the enemy army. And on that afternoon Twiggs decided to attack the hill known as Atalaya, because the Mexican troops stationed there had seen Twigg's column. "Charge 'em to hell!" Twiggs ordered, and his men responded. They drove the Mexicans from Atalaya and halfway up El Telégrafo as well.

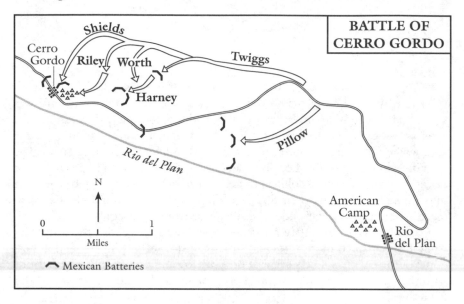

During the night Twiggs ordered guns placed on Atalaya, and Lee supervised the placing. Next morning, April 18, Lee again led Twigg's division toward the rear of Santa Anna's army; Scott had directed Twiggs to secure the road to Jalapa and thus leave the Mexicans no route on which to escape.

Meanwhile, Gideon Pillow, whose chief claim to command of a reinforced brigade was his civilian career as President Polk's law partner, was supposed to attack the right flank of Santa Anna's defense line. Pillow proved to be soft on maps and directions. He was supposed to follow a route which would have shielded his forces from all but one of the Mexican artillery batteries. Instead, Pillow sent his men into the massed fire of three Mexican batteries and saw his assault decisively repulsed. However, the Mexicans soon realized that Scott's army was on their left flank and in their rear, and so they fled or surrendered everywhere.[4]

Lee continued with Twiggs in the pursuit of Santa Anna's demoralized army. To his family, he reported, "All their cannon, arms, ammunition, and most of their men fell into our hands." Had Twiggs continued his flank march on April 17 instead of assaulting Atalaya, he would have trapped even more Mexicans than he eventually did. Nevertheless, the Battle of Cerro Gordo was a clear victory for the United States, and Santa Anna salvaged only about half his soldiers and practically no organization or morale. This was the same Mexican army Zachary Taylor had beaten at Buena Vista less than two months earlier. The Mexican commander even lost his personal carriage, his baggage, and his wooden leg in the chaotic flight from the invaders from the north.[5]

Later Lee and Lieutenant P. G. T. Beauregard found Santa Anna's hacienda, Encero, about nine miles up the road beyond Cerro Gordo, and there discovered a cache of maps and bundles of letters addressed to members of Scott's army previously captured by the Mexicans. Lee and Beauregard kept the maps for future use and had the letters delivered at last to the addressees.[6]

In the wake of the short siege at Vera Cruz, Engineer Lieutenant George B. McClellan recorded in his diary an encounter with his commanding general, Winfield Scott. "I found him writing a dispatch," McClellan wrote. "He seemed to be very much delighted and showed me the last words he had written which were indefatigable Engineers. Then we were needed and remembered—the instant the pressing necessity passed away we were forgotten. The echo of the last hostile gun at Vera Cruz had not died away before it was forgotten by the Commander in Chief that such a thing existed as an Engineer Company." Lee too, seemed to feel abandoned after the battle. Remarking upon the brevets (temporary promotions) some of his friends and comrades had received for their service at Vera Cruz, he wrote, "It is a fine thing to have strong friends in our Govt." So he implied some lament that he lacked such strong friends.[7]

After Cerro Gordo, however, Scott praised McClellan and seven other Engineer officers in his report, and then wrote:

I am impelled to make special mention of the services of Captain R. E. Lee, engineers. This officer, greatly distinguished in the siege of Vera Cruz, was again indefatigable, during these operations, in reconnaissances as daring as laborious, and of the greatest value. Nor was he less conspicuous in planting batteries, and in conducting columns to their stations under the heavy fire of the enemy.

After all, the battle depended upon the route through those impassable ravines which Lee had discovered. Several months later Lee's conduct at Cerro Gordo made him a brevet major from April 18, 1847.[8]

At the time, a week after Cerro Gordo, Lee could only say to his son Custis, "You have no idea what a horrible sight a battlefield is." He then described dead and dying Mexican he had encountered and a young Mexican girl crying for a small boy with a mangled arm, who lay pinned beneath a more seriously wounded Mexican soldier.

Her large black eyes were streaming with tears, her hands crossed over her breast; her hair in one long plait behind reached her waist, her shoulders and arms bare, and

without stockings or shoes. Her plaintive tone of *"Millie gracias, Signor,"* as I had the
dying man lifted off the boy and both carried to the hospital still lingers in my ear.

Immediately following this tender scene, Lee returns to combat and carnage: "After I had broken a way through the chaparral and turned toward
Cerro Gordo I mounted Creole, who stepped over the dead men with such
care as if she feared to hurt them, but when I started with the dragoons in the
pursuit, she was as fierce as possible, and I could hardly hold her."[9]

Lee wrote his personal accounts of Cerro Gordo from Perote, a town on
the National Road over the Sierra Madre range and about 42 miles from the
site of the recent battle. Santa Anna and his remnant army did little to dispute
the advance of Scott's army, and in mid-May Santa Anna abandoned the pre-
tense and withdrew to Mexico City to concentrate his force for a showdown
with the invaders. Scott pressed his advantage and marched his men 60 more
miles beyond Perote to Puebla, a town perhaps 75 miles from Mexico City.
But at Puebla, Scott and his army had to stop. Indeed, the army remained at
Puebla for almost three months.

Part of Scott's problem was his long supply line, which stretched nearly 150
miles back to Vera Cruz. Guerrillas and bandits harassed the transport of
material to Scott and rendered a difficult logistical circumstance much more
so. Eventually Colonel Ethan Allen Hitchcock of Scott's staff hired Manuel
Dominquez, one of the best bandits in Mexico, and 200 of his robber band to
serve as guides, guards, and spies. Hitchcock's ploy proved effective.

The more important reason Scott stopped at Puebla was the anticipated
expiration of the enlistments of most of the volunteers in his army. Some of
the citizen-soldiers reenlisted, but many believed that they had done their duty
and determined to go home. The fact that the army was poised to march on
Mexico City and perhaps to win the war within a few weeks seemed to have no
effect upon men who had done what they agreed to do and who wanted to
return to their homes.

Scott seemed to understand and even started the volunteers who chose not
to reenlist toward Vera Cruz early in order to avoid the worst of the yellow
fever season on the coast. By the end of the first week of June the army at
Puebla numbered just over 7,000 men.

Then Scott wrangled with Washington over replacement and reinforcement. The Secretary of War (William L. Marcy) promised 20,000 more men;
Scott marched from Puebla for Mexico City with 10,738.[10]

While the army paused at Puebla, Lee worked with the maps that he and
Beauregard had discovered at Santa Anna's hacienda. Scott directed Lee and
the chief topographical engineer, Major William Turnbull, to work separately
upon sources of information, to compare notes, and to compose the best map
they could of the country between Puebla and Mexico City.

Lee also spent his evening hours in the company of Scott and his subordinates at levees (receptions) and dinners which the commanding general spon-
sored. Scott could be pompous; he was inordinately occupied with the trap-

pings and ceremony of military service. But he possessed a first-rate mind and wide knowledge. So his "seminars" at dinner were instructive for those officers in attendance.[11]

Finally, on August 7, 1847, Scott's army began the march on Mexico City. Scott decided to abandon his lines of supply and communication and live off the country; he simply did not have sufficient troops to assault Mexico City and garrison the long road to Vera Cruz at the same time. So, with the exception of a small garrison and military hospital left at Puebla, Scott took with him the entire force he had available. This force he divided into four divisions of infantry and artillery and one cavalry brigade. Commanding the divisions were regular Army Brigadier Generals William J. Worth and David E. Twiggs and volunteer Major Generals Gideon J. Pillow and John A. Quitman.

Lee continued in Scott's "little cabinet," now even smaller since the departure of Engineer Chief Joseph Totten following Vera Cruz. And once again Lee had influence beyond his rank or station, because he drew maps and conducted reconnaissance for a campaign in which information about the ground and the enemy was crucial.[12]

Scott's army marched to Ayutla, a town 25 miles east of Mexico City. Lee scouted the most direct route from Ayutla to Mexico City and proclaimed it a possible but costly passage. So Scott resolved to take a slightly less hazardous course via Mexicalzingo. Then Lee and Beauregard reported that a circuitous route around Lakes Chalco and Xochimilco might be better. Scott ordered a detailed reconnaissance and upon receipt of information confirming Lee and Beauregard's report altered his course and set the army in motion on August 15. Two days later, Scott reached the village of San Augustin and once more confronted decisions about where and how to assault Santa Anna's defenses.

The Mexican president/general was no fool, and Mexico City had ample natural defenses. The only routes into the city were raised roadways over the marshy plain that surrounded the high ground on which the city lay. Defensive strongholds covered each road, and a determined Mexican army could make an invader pay an enormous price in blood simply for making an attempt to assault the city. However, Santa Anna's army was much less than determined. Mexican soldiers were inexperienced and ill-led, and the Mexican officer corps tended to be fractious. Although Santa Anna commanded a force perhaps two and a half times larger than Scott's, the Mexican army lacked organization, morale, and discipline. And the Mexican defenders could not be everywhere at once in strength.

Scott realized some of Santa Anna's liabilities; but he could not depend upon his enemy to collapse. Scott chose to maneuver his smaller army, take maximum advantage of surprise, and maintain the initiative throughout the campaign.

On August 18, the day after he reached San Augustin, Scott ordered a reconnaissance up the most direct road to Mexico City via San Antonio and Churubusco. As expected, the Mexican army was across this route in considerable strength.

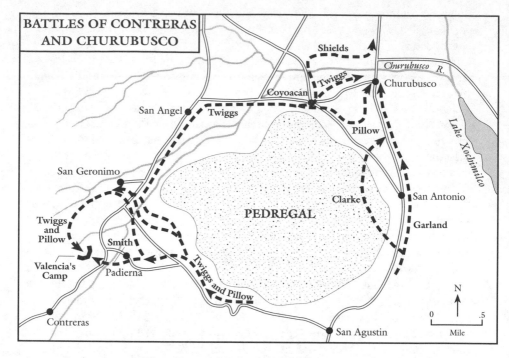

Scott also sent Lee in search of an alternate route to the west. The great obstacle lying between Scott and his goal was a huge lava field, five miles wide and almost as deep, known as the Pedregal. Igneous rocks covered the land form and rendered the terrain almost impassable on foot and apparently impossible for cavalry or artillery. If Lee could find a way through the Pedregal, Scott might be able to avoid a costly confrontation before reaching Mexico City.[13]

Lee, Beauregard, and an escort set out on August 18 along a wagon road into the Pedregal. The wagon road continued for about a mile and then degenerated somewhat into what Lee later called a "military road." Eventually the reconnaissance party pushed to the top of a significant hill (Zacatepec) from which Lee could see a Mexican defensive position on the hills outside the village of Contreras. He could also see the good road that led north through San Angel toward Mexico City. But lots of lava rocks lay between Lee and the Mexicans.

As Lee and the other soldiers picked their way down from Zacatepec, they encountered enemy horsemen and some foot soldiers. The resultant skirmish was brief and concluded when the Mexicans broke away toward Contreras. It was immediately clear to Lee, however, that if Mexicans could walk and ride from Contreras through the Pedregal to him, then he could do the same thing in reverse. He had found a route through the Pedregal and hurried back to Scott with his news.[14]

The commanding general held a council of war that evening (August 18), listened to discussions of routes and strategies, but announced no decision. By morning, though, Scott had determined to make Lee's route a road and use that road via San Angel to bypass Santa Anna's strength at San Antonio. Accordingly, Scott ordered Worth to "demonstrate" in front of San Antonio, but not to attempt any general assault. Quitman's division would guard San Augustin, and Pillow and Twiggs were to support the road construction.

Lee slept some during the night of August 18. Early on August 19, he led about 500 men from Pillow's division over the wagon road he had scouted the day before. Work parties improved the "military road," and by noon they reached the point at which Lee had encountered the Mexican soldiers the previous day. Generals Pillow and Worth with more men and some artillery arrived on the scene.

And then the Mexican guns on the hills of Contreras opened fire. Suddenly this was not a safe place to build a road.

Lee scrambled down the ridge with a regiment of infantry and "selected the best route for the Artillery through the impracticable fields of lava." He found a likely site to place the guns within canister range of the Mexicans, who occupied a ridge just beyond the San Angel road. Between the two forces was a deep ravine and a stream which in Lee's words "rendered a direct attack inadvisable."

Soon the Mexican artillery rendered further exposure of the U.S. guns unwise, and the batteries Lee had placed withdrew to safety. Meanwhile Lee and the other Engineer officers set out to the right with most of the troops on hand to find a way across the ravine and stream in order to flank the Mexicans at Contreras and separate them from the rest of Santa Anna's army. They moved slowly, painfully for about a mile until they found a crossing and then concentrated in the rear of the Mexican position. By this time, however, the day was far spent, and the senior U.S. officer (Persifor Smith) postponed the attack until the next morning.

Neither Scott nor Santa Anna had intended a general engagement for August 19; the battle more or less emerged out of the actions of their subordinates. Santa Anna had ordered his subordinate at Contreras, Major General Gabriel Valencia, to withdraw to a position between San Angel and San Antonio, where with the rest of the Mexican army he could resist Scott's advance from any direction. Valencia refused the order and remained to fight where he, not Santa Anna, would get credit for victory. Scott had intended that Pillow and Twiggs simply open the road through San Angel. When Valencia's artillery began the fight, brigade commanders in Pillow and Twiggs's divisions reacted aggressively, returned the Mexican fire, and found a route into the rear of Valencia's defensive line. Because Pillow was the senior officer on the scene, he accepted the credit for the energetic and spontaneous response of his subordinates.

In the very dark night of August 19, however, the United States troops preparing to assault the Mexican position near Contreras felt alone and vulnerable. Persifor Smith needed to get a message to Scott to inform the command-

ing general of his situation and to ask for a coordinated attack upon Valencia at
dawn from the original front. Smith wanted at least a demonstration from the
lava ridge across the ravine. Lee was the person best prepared to retrace his
steps back across the ravine and across the Pedregal to Scott's headquarters.

> At the request of Genl. Smith, I returned to report the state of affairs to Genl. Scott
> & see if a diversion in favor of the attacking force in rear could not be made by an attack
> in front. On reaching the ravine I found Genl. Shield's brigade . . . and gave him one of
> the men accompanying me to guide him to the village where our troops were biv-
> ouacked. In consequence of the dark night and the impassable nature of the ground I
> did not reach San Augustine [sic] untill between 11 & 12 o'clock, too late in the
> opinion of the Genl. in Chief to withdraw a portion of General Worth's division from
> San Antonio to make the desired diversion.

Scott then dispatched Lee a third time across the Pedregal, again in the
dark, and instructed him to collect any troops he could find and organize a
diversion. Lee left Scott's headquarters about 1:00 A.M. and did find a regiment, a few companies, and some men lost from their commands. The colonel
in command of the regiment managed to move these men to the lava ridge
facing Valencia's guns across the ravine and at first light they commenced
firing and advancing upon the Mexicans.

At the same time, almost as though they had received orders, the three
U.S. brigades in the rear of the Mexicans began their assault. The enemy, in
Lee's words, "soon gave way in all directions, abandoned his artillery, 22
pieces, his packs, ammunition and retreated. . . ." The Battle of Contreras was
over in a very short time at very little cost to Scott's army.

Scott himself arrived in time to witness the rout along the San Angel road.
Then Scott sent Lee to scout the road from San Antonio to Churubusco,
which Lee did, found no Mexicans, and returned to Scott after the assault
upon Churubusco had already begun. Scott then sent Lee to guide two brigades (Shields and Pierce) from the Contreras victory into the rear of the
Mexican army at Churubusco.

So Lee again set out with a mission. As he approached Churubusco he
found the Mexicans in strength at the bridge over the Churubusco River, and
so he deflected the march in such a way as to reach the road to Mexico City at
a point behind the Mexican army. Once more Scott's army had found the flank
and rear of the enemy, all the while exerting pressure in the front. And once
more the Mexicans broke and ran under the pressure. The Battle of Churubusco was another victory for Scott's army, and the Mexican army withdrew to
the gates of Mexico City for a final stand.

Lee joined the pursuit of the vanquished foe. No doubt he slept quite
soundly that night (August 20).[15]

Consider what Lee had done. Early on August 19 he had crossed the
Pedregal, led some of Scott's army into conflict with Valencia's troops, and
then led and directed three brigades into Valencia's rear. Then he had retraced
his steps in the dark and rain back to Scott's headquarters. The same night he

had recrossed the Pedregal, guided the demonstration in Valencis's front, and observed the triumph at Contreras on the morning of August 20. Next he had scouted the road from San Antonio to Churubusco, returned to Scott, and then guided troops to a crucial flank attack on the road beyond Churubusco. Once the enemy was in full flight, Lee had joined the pursuit. He had been awake and active for thirty-six hours (at least), crossed the Pedregal twice in the dark, and led U.S. forces to crucial positions in two separate battles—into Valencia's rear at Contreras and to Santa Anna's flank at Churubusco. After these thirty-six hours, Lee deserved a sound sleep.

In his reports of these battles, Scott wrote of "the gallant, indefatigable Captain Lee" and of Lee "as distinguished for felicitous execution as for science and daring." Later Scott termed Lee's actions during the night of August 19 "the greatest feat of physical and moral courage performed by any individual in my knowledge. . . ." For Contreras and Churubusco Lee eventually received brevet promotion to lieutenant colonel.[16]

In the aftermath of these United States victories the Mexicans requested an armistice, and negotiations directed toward peace began but soon sputtered. Santa Anna used the armistice to reorganize his army and fortify Mexico City. Scott's army occupied Tacubaya; and the *gringos* enjoyed a wary respite.[17]

Lee used some of this lull to write reports of his actions thus far. On August 21, he wrote an account of his activities at Contreras and Churubusco addressed to his immediate superior, the ranking Engineer officer with Scott's army, Major John Lind Smith. On August 22, Lee wrote an informal report to the wife of the Engineer chief in Washington, Joseph G. Totten.

This was a curious thing to do. Perhaps addressing the report to Mrs. Totten was an expedient, an unofficial way to inform Totten without taking the time to compose a formal report. Yet Lee had time; representatives from the Mexican and U.S. armies did not sign the armistice agreement until August 23 and the negotiations over peace did not commence until August 27. A more likely explanation for Lee's report to Mrs. Totten was Lee's desire to tell his and the Engineers' story to the public. Lee expected Mrs. Totten to share his report with one or more newspapers. In fact, it did appear in the Washington *Union,* by way of an assistant in the Engineer office.[18]

The armistice concluded with no immediate prospect for peace on September 7, 1847, and Scott was already pondering and planning his assault upon Mexico City. Reconnaissance on the 7th was vigorous and indicated that the Mexicans were using a complex of stone buildings called Molino de Rey—just outside the fortress, Chapultepec, that guarded the approach from the southwest—as a cannon foundry. They were melting church bells and casting guns, or so rumor had it. Scott became impatient to put a stop to the suspected activity and ordered Worth's division to attack Molino del Rey at dawn on September 8.

The Battle of Molino del Rey that resulted spilled blood to no important purpose. The place was not a cannon foundry, and Scott abandoned the buildings soon after he captured them. In heavy fighting Worth's troops, reinforced as the battle developed, seized, held, and gutted Molino del Rey. But then Scott still confronted the problem of how his army could break into the defenses of Mexico City.

However he proceeded, Scott could anticipate hard fighting. Raised roads flanked by swampy low ground afforded the only access into the city, and the Mexican army guarded each of the four possible roads with artillery and infantry. Moreover, the fight for Molino del Rey demonstrated that the Mexican army could and would fight fiercely for the capital. As reconnaissance continued Santa Anna was strengthening already strong defensive positions.[19]

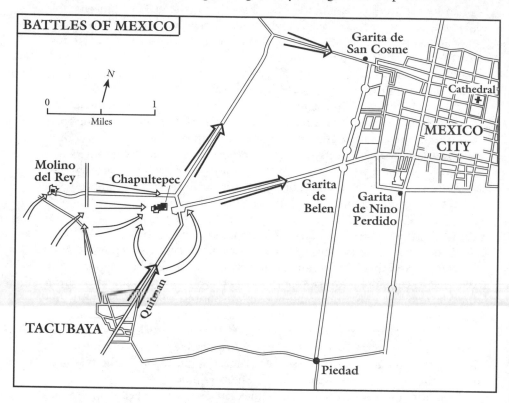

On September 11, Scott held a council of war in the village church at Piedad. Scott favored an attack on the formidable fortress of Chapultepec; if successful, such a stroke would open two roads into the city, and Scott did not believe Chapultepec was as sturdy as it appeared. Pillow opposed the commanding general and favored an assault from the south. The consensus among the Engineer officers (including Lee) was also for an attack from the south. But Beauregard dissented and at Piedad delivered a closely reasoned argument for an attack from the west, i.e., Chapultepec. When Beauregard had completed his presentation, Franklin Pierce, the future President who then commanded a brigade in Pillow's division, announced that Beauregard's statement had caused him to change his mind in favor of an attack on Chapultepec.

Scott, who probably would have done so regardless of anyone else's opinion, then stood and proclaimed, "Gentlemen, we will remain here for further orders—the meeting is dissolved."

As the junior participants filed out of the church at Piedad, Lee's serious labor began in earnest. The campaign required artillery batteries to soften Chapultepec and support the infantry during the actual assault, and Lee had charge of placing these batteries.

Chapultepec began as a rocky mound, perhaps 200 feet above the plain. Brick walls surrounded the stone building on top of the hill, which presented attackers with another solid wall to scale. The fortress and dependent buildings housed a military academy during peacetime; now the place seemed bristling with veteran soldiers.[20]

Lee worked during the afternoon of September 11 upon the first two batteries of guns aimed at Chapultepec. During the night of the 11th he completed the second battery, and on the 12th he brought a third battery into action.

In the afternoon Scott summoned Lee and two other Engineer officers (Beauregard and Lieutenant Zebulon B. Tower) to his headquarters. The commanding general wanted to know the effect of his artillery upon Chapultepec; he wanted to assault the place that evening; he wanted reports from the Engineers several hours ago. Lee and the rest did all that very junior officers could to calm Scott's agitation. And Lee spoke for the trio in an attempt to convince Scott to postpone the attack until the following morning. Scott saw the wisdom in Lee's words. Insufficient daylight remained to organize the assault. The artillery next morning would have an opportunity to wreck any repairs the Mexicans achieved during the night. And a morning attack upon Chapultepec would leave the remainder of the day to exploit any success achieved. Scott then discussed his plans and questioned the Engineers about Mexican strength and strongpoints.[21]

Lee was again at Scott's headquarters that evening to assist the commanding general with briefings and instructions. Then he returned to work at the batteries, repairing some battle damage and preparing the guns for action at daylight on the 13th. At this point Lee had remained awake more than thirty-six hours, and he had no opportunity to sleep during the night of September 12 either.

At dawn the guns began firing once more and continued the bombardment for two hours. When the guns fell silent, the assault on Chapultepec began. Scott wanted Lee with him during the battle. But as the troops moved into position to storm Chapultepec, Lee was with Pillow as a guide. Pillow's division formed for action at Molina del Rey and then advanced across a field, through a grove of cypress trees, to the walls of Chapultepec. As the men moved to the attack, Pillow complained of a wound and called for Worth to reinforce him. So Lee ushered Pillow to a place of safety and relayed Pillow's cry to Worth for help.

The assault upon Chapultepec succeeded brilliantly. The United States forces rushed to the walls and threw up ladders to scale the fortress face. Of course the Mexican defenders poured forth musket balls as the attackers advanced and pushed some of the ladders away from the walls. But the assault troops kept coming and soon streamed over the top. Inside Chapultepec the fighting was grisly—pointblank range, bayonets, screams, and writhing. In less than two hours, before 9:30 A.M., Scott's army controlled Chapultepec, and soon thereafter Scott himself rode to the scene.

Lee was with Scott as he accepted the cheers of his soldiers. No one now knows where Lee was from the time he left Pillow until he arrived at Chapultepec with Scott. Most likely he returned to the commanding general's headquarters, and as he reported later, "was employed by the Genl. in chief in Executing his directions & bringing him news of the events of the day. . . ." From Chapultepec, Scott sent Lee to scout the approach to the San Cosme Gate and to advance the artillery to support the attack upon that point. Lee accomplished these tasks and returned to Scott.

At some time during the day of battle Lee sustained a wound of some sort. It was never a serious wound, but did cost him some blood. By this time he had been awake and working fairly constantly for at least fifty-six hours. So from a combination of exhaustion and loss of blood, Lee found (in his words), "I could no longer keep my saddle." In other words, he fainted.

While Lee recovered, his comrades completed the victory, and Santa Anna with his army abandoned Mexico City during the night of September 13. Next morning at sunrise Lee was back at work doing Scott's bidding, and he rode into the Grand Plaza of Mexico City with the conquering army.

Once more Scott was full of praise for Lee in his report of the victory. And eventually Lee received his third brevet promotion to colonel, for his conduct and courage at Chapultepec.[22]

Lee had been at war for just about exactly one year. He arrived at Port Lavaca, Texas, on September 13, 1846, and next day set out for San Antonio and John E. Wool's army. He had spent eleven months in Mexico; he crossed the Rio Grande on October 12, 1846. Now in the wake of victory, Lee would remain in Mexico for another nine months before he sailed from Vera Cruz toward "home" and his family.

In a sense the victory of Scott's army was too complete. Having humiliated the Mexican army and driven Santa Anna from power, the United States had no one with whom to make peace. The Mexican War also provoked discord within the United States; many people considered "Mr. Polk's War" a slaveholders' plot to expand the slave plantation system; some considered the victory sufficient to claim most of Mexico by right of conquest; and others simply wanted the territory in dispute at the outset of the conflict. So the victors quarreled with each other over the causes of a war now over, over the spoils of victory and the victory of spoils. And the vanquished attempted to salvage honor, all the while distancing themselves from the debacle.[23]

Lee was a keen observer of the various tensions at work, writing to his wife:

"It is true we bullied her [Mexico]. Of that I am ashamed, as She was the weaker party. But we have since . . . drubbed her handsomely & in a manner that women might be ashamed of. They begin to be aware how entirely they are beaten & are willing to acknowledge it. It would be curious now if we should refuse to accept the territory we have forced her to relinquish & fight her three years more to compel her to take it back. It would be marvelously like us."[24]

In tones which anticipated American warriors in future wars, Lee was incredulous that some of his fellow citizens believed his war unjust and thus advocated withdrawal of Scott's army and rejection of the spoils of the victory. "If we have been wrong in our Course," he wrote his brother Carter, "we should have discovered it before." Then he waxed sarcastic. "If this retrograde step would restore us our glorious dead, I should be content. It will rather tend to condemn their devotion to their country & the next step will be to convict them of Suicide."[25]

With the Mexicans, Lee had even less patience. "Such is the egregious folly of this people," he wrote Mary Lee, "that they would talk a year & suffer all the mortification, loss & inconvenience of their present condition . . . [to] Save what they term the national honor. Placing the degradation not in the *deed*, but in the acknowledgement."[26]

To his cousin Anna Fitzhugh (at Ravensworth), Lee offered his solution to the peacemaking impasse. "In my humble opinion," he began, "the administration should have dispatched a treaty proposal as a 'naked instrument' " with a time limit for ratification. If the Mexican government ratified the terms, well and good; if not, "tear up the paper" and "take the country." Under such conditions, Lee believed, "we might reasonably expect, that they would lose no time in ratifying the present treaty." To his old friend Jack Mackay, Lee had written his prescription in the event of conquest: "Open the ports of European immigration. Introduce free opinions of government & religion. Break down the power & iniquity of the church. It is a beautiful country & in the hands of proper people would be a magnificent one." "I might make a rough diplomatist," he admitted, "but a tolerably quick one."[27]

At this point in Lee's life, might made right, and "right" for him meant placing Mexico in "proper," European hands. As for the potential conflict between military objectives and the political process, Lee informed Carter Lee, "It comes hard when you are weaving out your life in this way, to be told it is uncalled for, unnecessary & of no avail." Maybe Lee never quite understood the connection between the "fine opinions of government" he said he valued and the Army as servant of those "free opinions of government." More likely he was simply expressing his frustration with the Polk administration and the effect of the peacemaking process upon the Army and himself.[28]

While the U.S. government was trying to decide what to do with the spoils of victory, the U.S. Army in Mexico engaged in similar intrigues for smaller stakes. At issue in the Army were reputations and rank.

Only three weeks after Chapultepec, Lee observed to Mackay:

We are our own trumpeters, & it is so much more easy to make heroes on paper than in the field. For one of the latter you meet with 20 of the former, but not till the fight is done. The fine fellows are too precious of persons so dear to their countrymen to expose them to the view of the enemy, but when the battle is *won,* they accomplish with the tongue all that they would have done with the sword, had it not been danger-ous so to do.[29]

Soon the "heroes on paper" had their say in American newspapers, and from a flurry of charges and countercharges came a court of inquiry and a court-martial.

The court of inquiry investigated accusations that Scott was involved in a scheme to secure peace through bribery. Even though the court exonerated Scott, the charge gave Polk the excuse he needed to relieve Scott from com-mand.

Scott brought charges in the court-martial against Worth, Pillow, and Colonel James Duncan for various sorts of insubordination. At the core of the proceedings were questions about who should receive credit for doing what during the recent campaigns.[30]

Lee protested to his brother Carter, "I have done all in my power to allay the feelings of the parties from the first, but without success." He counted Worth, Duncan, and Scott as his friends and blamed Pillow for provoking the incident. Indeed, Pillow had made a series of outrageous claims in pseudony-mous letters to American newspapers. So the court spent considerable time hearing evidence about whose idea it was to do what when.[31]

Both sides called Lee to the witness stand. The defense (Pillow, Worth, and Duncan) made Lee admit writing his narrative of Cerro Gordo to Mrs. Totten, though Lee protested innocence of any intent to have his letter pub-lished. The prosecution (Scott) called upon Lee to substantiate Scott's version of the truth about various command decisions. Lee's careful testimony never attacked Pillow directly. But in private conversation Lee seems to have told fellow staffer Ethan Allen Hitchcock plenty about Pillow's "wound" at Cha-pultepec, and Hitchcock wrote his own "private" letter to the *New York Sun* charging, among other things, that Pillow's wound was bogus.[32]

As Lee predicted from the outset, none of the officers involved gained anything as a result of the trial. The proceedings served primarily to amplify ill feelings already present in the Army and to convince Lee and others that the Polk administration meant to reward Scott's services by destroying his reputa-tion.[33]

To his father-in-law, Lee wrote, "The treatment which Genl. Scott has res'd [received] satisfies me what those may expect who have done their duty. It will be better for me to be classed with those who have failed." Of course Lee knew that he had done more than his duty in Mexico, and he wanted rewards appropriate to his accomplishments.

At the time he wrote to Parke Custis, Lee believed he would receive the brevet promotions for Cerro Gordo. "So that if I performed any services at Vera Cruz or at the battles around the capital, they will go for naught," he complained. Lee then gave examples of greater advancement for officers less deserving than himself, all the while protesting. "I presume however that their Services exceeded mine which I know to be Small." His message to Custis was clear despite the humble facade. Lee wanted his due, and he knew the Army well enough to know that he had better not squander this opportunity. Robert Lee was an ambitious man.

Intrigues, pettiness, and politics once more provoked Lee to question his career. "I wish I was out of the Army myself," he told Custis. And to Carter Lee he wrote that he would "make a strong effort" to leave the Army. But once more he remained in uniform—most likely because he could find nothing that he liked any better and because he knew he was a very good soldier.[34]

A story often told about Lee while he awaited peace in Mexico City has him absent from a gathering of officers who wanted him to join them over wine. John B. Magruder (then Captain) sought Lee and found him working on a map he was making.

"This is mere drudgery," Magruder said, "make somebody else do it and come with me."

"No," Lee responded, "no, I am but doing my duty."

No doubt the incident occurred, and maybe the circumstances were just as Magruder described them. Nevertheless, Lee's duty during those nine months he remained in Mexico was not all that arduous. He did make maps; but this was his only assigned task. His time was mostly his own.[35]

Before breakfast Lee usually took a walk or a ride, sometimes with "my lady friends." He did make friends among émigré Europeans who lived in or near the city. So he visited his friends and wrote to his daughter Agnes about an afternoon with a little girl named Charlollita whose mother was French and father English. And to his daughter Annie, he wrote about an "English Gentleman here, with whom I dine very often."

Lee also undertook excursions in the manner of a tourist to various sites in central Mexico. With other officers, for example, he visited Desierto, an abandoned Carmelite monastery in the mountains. Legend had it that a beautiful woman managed to penetrate the walls of the place and put the monks to flight. Lee, however, speculated that only an ugly woman could so disturb their contemplation. Lee took other trips as well, both with company and alone.

Even when he did little more than make maps and drawings, he worked in the palace.[36] And he had his servant Jim Connally to perform errands and chores. Duty was not all that difficult in Mexico.

Lee learned a lot during the twenty-one months he spent in Mexico. These lessons of his initial experience with actual combat and his first war conditioned his life and career thereafter.

Most important among the lessons from experience was increased confidence in his capacity as a soldier. Lee learned and confirmed that he was much more than a capable, conscientious engineer; he was a warrior of uncommon ability.

At Vera Cruz he had conducted reconnaissance, planted artillery batteries, and directed the fire of the naval battery—the guns which were most decisive in forcing swift capitulation upon the fortified city. At Cerro Gordo, he had found a route through "impassable ravines" and guided a column of troops to deliver the decisive flank attack. At Contreras and Churubusco, he had discovered a path through the Pedregal, led a force into the Mexican rear at Contreras, directed fire against the Mexican front, and accompanied U.S. units on a drive into the Mexican flank at Churubusco. Before Mexico City, he had surveyed the ground and the enemy, counseled the commanding general out of a premature attack, planted batteries of guns, and guided troops to the initial assault. Lee had played a crucial role in each of Scott's victories and had had the maximum impact possible for a staff officer.

His work at reconnaissance—during Wool's march from the Rio Grande to Parras and throughout Scott's campaign from Vera Cruz to Mexico City—revealed Lee's extraordinary talent for "reading" terrain. He seemed to understand the ground at a glance and to possess a sense of the relation between one terrain feature and another.

Lee's assignments and performance during critical periods of Scott's campaign bore witness to his stamina and physical fitness. Other officers became sick; some men collapsed from exhaustion; Lee seemed to be what Scott called him—"indefatigable."

Nor was Lee the only person who learned what an outstanding officer he was. Lee's superiors also noticed his talent and performance and praised him accordingly. Scott, especially, was impressed with his young staff officer and later said that Lee was "the very best soldier I ever saw in the field." Scott, wrote an officer who knew him well, "had an almost idolatrous fancy for Lee, whose military genius he estimated far above that of any other officer of the army." Scott suggested that in the event of war, the government should insure Lee's life for $5 million a year. Despite the machinations of the Polk administration, Scott continued in ultimate command of the United States Army until 1861. So Lee hereafter served an organization whose chief regarded him as a "military genius."[37]

If the first important lesson Lee learned in Mexico was confidence in his own ability, the second he learned from Scott. From his commanding general Lee learned that a small army can defeat a larger opponent. To do so, however, the smaller force must make maximum use of its ability to maneuver. Scott taught Lee to take risks, but to calculate them carefully and act upon accurate reconnaissance. Scott taught Lee to act decisively and to ignore timid counsel from subordinates. Ever outnumbered, Scott had won because he had maneuvered and had taken risks. He had gleaned all the information available about the country and the enemy; then he had made decisions and acted upon those decisions, often in the face of conventional wisdom or against a consensus of his subordinate commanders.

From hindsight it is easy to see that Lee learned at least one negative lesson from the Mexican War—a precept he would have been wise to forget. Scott, like Napoleon and other nineteenth-century military thinkers of consequence, was an apostle of offensive action. To engage in war was to attack; a defensive posture was only useful to gain time and opportunity to resume the offensive. Scott's campaign in Mexico certainly seemed to demonstrate the efficacy of the offense. Against Santa Anna's troops, determined attacks succeeded. The first several men up the scaling ladders at Chapultepec may have suffered injury or death; but eventually the attackers got over the walls, and ultimately the attack produced victory.

Offensive success in Mexico, however, depended upon two factors—the state of morale, training, and leadership within the Mexican army, and the musket. Morale, training, and leadership in Santa Anna's army were generally poor; hence Scott's troops, many of whom followed officers trained at West Point and a core group of whom were regulars (not volunteers), prevailed in their assaults. Muskets were the principal weapon of infantrymen on both sides of the Mexican War. This weapon required at least thirty seconds to load and fired a single round ball from a barrel with a smooth bore. Muskets were not very accurate and had a maximum range of about 100 yards. All of this meant that defenders armed with muskets might fire one, maybe two, shots at attackers before those attackers closed with the defenders and began a bayonet melee. In such a circumstance, well-trained, well-led, determined attackers had a distinct advantage.

Lee and many of his contemporaries accepted their experience of offensive success in Mexico as universally valid. The Mexican experience confirmed Napoleonic teaching and rendered reliance upon offense an article of faith in the military mind. What veterans of the Mexican War forgot or failed to emphasize were the factors which allowed attackers to succeed in Mexico—the poor state of Santa Anna's army and the use of muskets as primary infantry weapons.[38]

One final lesson Lee learned from his experience in Mexico involved politics. He already knew about intra army politics; but now he saw the frenzy of men determined to make the most of whatever they had done during the war. Lee's letter to his father-in-law indicates that he was not immune from the scramble for rank. In Gideon Pillow, however, Lee observed someone who in Scott's appraisal was "the only person I have ever known who was wholly indifferent in the choice between truth and falsehood." Pillow, too, was one of the species "political general," an officer whose claim to command rested upon connections to political influence rather than military experience or talent. Lee also watched Winfield Scott humbled on the heels of his victory because he continued at odds with the President.[39]

No doubt Lee resolved to be careful with presidents, to avoid "political generals," and to know better than naively to assume that merit wins rewards. He retained his faith in offensive action. From Scott he learned to maneuver, risk, and act decisively upon available information. And his own performance in Mexico was a lesson. Lee had proven himself an outstanding officer—in his own eyes and in the estimation of significant others.

Lee left Mexico on June 9, 1848, aboard the steamship *Portland* from Vera Cruz with a full load of troops. With him was his horse Grace Darling, his servant Jim Connally, and Jim's dog Jack. Lee never related the fate of Creole and his other horses; he secured Grace Darling in Mexico and clearly liked her. He traveled by water up the Mississippi and Ohio Rivers to Wheeling and then boarded a train, leaving Jim to follow with the horse and dog. On June 29, Lee reached Washington. He had been away for nearly two years (twenty-one months).

Somehow the returning hero missed connection with the carriage sent for him from Arlington. But Lee secured a horse and rode across the Potomac and up the long hill to Arlington. As he approached the house, no one inside recognized horse or rider. Lee's hair had begun to turn gray and "furrows" had opened on his face. First to know that the rider was Lee was Spec the dog. The little terrier raced across the porch and into the yard barking with joy.

Soon Lee was in the entrance hall greeting his family. Then he realized that he had not seen his youngest son (four and a half years old now), Rob.

"Where is my little boy?"

In the background, behind the adults, Rob had been watching his father's homecoming. Now the father strode toward Rob—and picked up Rob's playmate Armistead Lippitt by mistake.[40]

Lee had set out for the war with mules and someone else's wife and child. The first person to shoot at Lee was a member of his own army. When he returned, at first only his dog knew him, and Lee himself confused a neighbor's child with his own son and namesake. Between such embarrassments, however, he was indubitably "the gallant, indefatigable Captain Lee."

11

"*I Am Fond of Independence*"

"HERE I AM ONCE AGAIN," wrote Robert Lee to his brother Smith on the day after his homecoming from Mexico, "perfectly surrounded by Mary and her precious children. . . ." Again Lee was back at Arlington, the semi-permanent houseguest in the home of his in-laws the Custises.

For the time being, Engineer Chief Joseph G. Totten (now a brigadier general) attached Lee to his office in Washington and assigned to him completion of the various maps Lee had begun in Mexico. Lee had returned from the war a genuine war hero, certainly within the officer corps, if not in the public mind. His reward was respite. For several months he puttered about the Engineer office in the War Department and lived at "home."[1]

Arlington House was a full house during the summer of 1848. When all the Lees were in residence, at least nine people slept in four bedrooms on the second floor in the central section of the house. Mary and Robert occupied a large room with adjoining dressing room on the southeast corner. Across the hall on the southwest corner was the bedroom and dressing/play room for the three younger girls: Anne (nine), Agnes (seven), and Mildred (two). The boys—Custis (nearly sixteen), Rooney (eleven), and Rob (not quite five)—slept in the front room on the northeast corner. Oldest daughter Mary (now thirteen) had her own room on the northwest corner; but she often shared space with visitors, the most frequent of whom was cousin Martha Custis Williams (Markie).

Mary and Parke Custis by this time had retreated to the north wing (first floor) of the house. There they resumed residence in the rooms they had used during the years when the wings were the only portions of Arlington House yet built (1804–18). The winter kitchen was in the basement of this wing.

On the first floor of the central section of the house was the family parlor (where Mary and Robert Lee had been married) and the family dining room. Across the central hall was another potential parlor, which the Custises used for storage.

In the south wing was Custis's studio/office, a large auxiliary studio, another storeroom, and the "Camelia House"—an enclosed porch for plants. Behind the house were smaller structures used for the summer kitchen, storage space, stables, barns, and slave quarters.[2]

Tradition holds that the Custises possessed many more slaves than there was work to do. In 1857 no less than ninety slaves lived at Arlington, and in 1850 the census taker listed nineteen free mulattos residing on the place. Yet Custis did no extensive commercial planting at Arlington; he engaged in sufficient general farming to sustain the people, black and white, who lived there. In 1857 at Arlington, there were 28 mules, one jenny (female donkey), three horses, 28 oxen, 66 cattle, 73 sheep, and 101 hogs. Arlington's African Americans kept the house reasonably clean and more or less in order. They tended the garden, grounds, and livestock, cooked and served meals, and performed seasonal tasks such as building fires in the winter and preserving produce in the summer.[3]

Jim Connally probably had charge of the family horses. He groomed and saddled Grace Darling, Lee's last warhorse from Mexico, and he cared for Santa Anna, a white pony Lee had had shipped from Mexico for young Rob.[4]

Custis had other estates in Virginia—White House on the Pamunkey River and Romancock in King William County for commercial agriculture.

ARLINGTON HOUSE 1848 - 1852

Second Floor

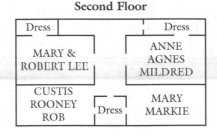

Main Floor

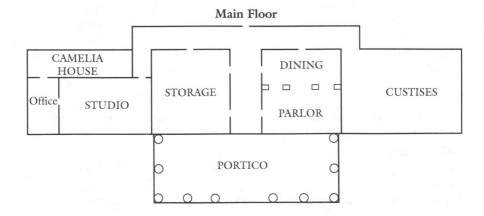

Managers and overseers supervised slaves and acres and supposedly rendered an honest accounting and the profits due to Custis. At age sixty-seven (in 1848), Custis still spent most of his time dabbling with projects he rarely completed. During this period he did have the portico steps repaired; but his plan to repave the portico with hexagonal bricks languished. Mary Custis was sixty in 1848; though she was frequently ill, she retained her piety and her unselfish devotion to her family.[5]

Young Rob's earliest memories of his father and family life date from this time. His namesake, Rob recalled, was "active, strong, and as handsome as he had ever been." Indeed, young Lieutenant Cadmus Wilcox pronounced Lee "the handsomest man in the army" at this point.

And he had developed a sense of presence about him. Because he was quiet, taciturn in the company of men, and because he seemed absorbed in his own agenda and not much inclined to follow fads or fancy, Lee inspired respect. He was shy and concerned about self-control, but these traits only magnified his magnetism. As Rob recorded, "It began to dawn on me that every one else with whom I was thrown held him high in their regard."

Later in life Rob wrote that "I always knew that it was impossible to disobey my father." Lee did work to inculcate in his children his own obsession with self-control. But he mingled standards and sternness with less rigid, less orthodox qualities.

Lee the father probably bestowed and certainly used playful nicknames for his children. Custis was "Boo" or "Mr. Boo"; Mary was "Daughter"; Fitzhugh of course was "Rooney" or "Roon"; Anne was ever "Annie"; Agnes was "Wigs"; Robert became "Rob," "Robertus," or "Brutus"; and Mildred was "Precious Life" or "Life."

Lee encouraged the younger children to jump into bed with him in the morning. Rob remembered that they would then "lie close to him, listening while he talked to us in his bright, entertaining way. This custom we kept up until I was ten years old or older."

With the older children Lee ran family races and entered high-jumping competitions at the standard he set up in the yard. He played with his children and when he kissed them, he kissed them on their mouths. Lee involved himself in his children's activities—maybe to discover vicariously elements of the childhood he had missed while he "carried the keys" and cared for his mother in his own youth. Whatever the source, Lee was certainly a loving parent, filled with good intentions.

Rob also remembered that his father "was very fond of having his hands tickled, and, what was still more curious, it pleased and delighted him to take off his slippers and place his feet in our laps in order to have them tickled." In the evening Lee told stories to his younger children while they tickled his feet. And if they became so absorbed that they neglected their task, Lee stopped to declare, "No tickling, no story!"[6]

As the summer of 1848 waned, General Totten gave Colonel Lee a serious assignment. The afterglow of the Mexican War was over. Lee was assigned to establish the foundation for a fort to protect Baltimore from attack by water. In 1814, Fort McHenry had been sufficiently strong to protect the city from British ships (and so to inspire "The Star Spangled Banner"). But the old fort was now too old and too close to Baltimore to repeat the favor, and Engineer surveys of the Patapsco River recommended construction of another fort off Sollers' Point, further downstream. So in mid-November Lee reported for duty and took some long looks at the site. He saw only mudflats. After two weeks Lee concluded that he could accomplish nothing until the following spring, and so he returned home to spend December and Christmas at Arlington.[7]

Soon after the first of the year (1849), however, Lee had to leave his family once more to pursue his profession. On his return from Mexico, Totten had restored Lee to his former position on the Board of Engineers for Atlantic Coast Defenses. Early in January, Lee and his fellow board members (one of whom was Sylvanus Thayer, former Superintendent of West Point) journeyed to Mobile and boarded ship for a voyage along the Gulf Coast, around Florida, and up the Atlantic coast as far as Cumberland Island off Georgia. Lee did not return home until some time in March.[8]

Once more he came close to Cumberland Island without visiting Dungeness and seeing his father's grave. In one letter written during the trip to Mary, Lee offered a narrative of one segment of the coasting voyage. He sailed on the U.S. schooner *Phoenix*—"I have never been to Sea in a small vessel before. . . ." They had been to Apalachicola and then visited St. Marks—"Found more moschitoes [sic] than people & grounded in the channel. . . ." Leaving St. Marks the *Phoenix* encountered a severe storm—"We had to lay to under a treble reefed foresail." Lee remained below deck, "as long as I could stand it & then sat on deck, watching the big waves tumbling around us."

When Lee returned to Arlington, he then had to go back to Baltimore to commence work on what became Fort Carroll. In the interim the family had tried and failed to secure an appointment to West Point for Custis. Lee determined to renew the effort for the following year; Custis was, after all, not yet seventeen. To enhance his chances, Custis abandoned his classical education and went to study science and mathematics with Benjamin Hallowell in Alexandria, just as his father had done.[9]

In Baltimore, Lee arranged to live at 908 Madison Avenue in a three-story townhouse which was still under construction. An uncle, William Wickham, owned the house, so Lee could not exert too much pressure for his relative to hasten the work. Still, he fretted that he could not settle himself and his family into his duty station. During the spring and summer of 1849 Lee lived alone in Baltimore and commuted to Arlington on weekends when he could.[10]

As usual the summer was humid and hot. In June, Lee commented on summer weddings, "Tell Miss E. she must insist on her Capt G. waiting till fall. I think she is too feeble to encounter so much happiness till cooler weather. And then no body can eat cake & good things with the thermometer at 100° but flies." On a Saturday evening at Sollers' Point he told Mary Lee that his only amusement was "killing muskitoes [sic] & watching kittens playing with their tails." "It is impossible to read," he wrote. "The light brings so many insects in the house that it is intolerable & the ev^n is devoted to contemplation."[11]

The task at Sollers' Point was challenging at first. Lee found solid footing for his fort forty-five feet down into the mud below low tide. So he contracted for construction of a pile driver and a crane, dug a well to secure fresh water for men and machines (steam), and built platforms over the area on which he built cofer dams, and intended to construct sea walls. Subsequently Lee used a diving bell, designed a machine to saw piles to a uniform height under water, and constructed a dredge to grade the surface of the shoal below the surface. After three seasons of work (1849, 1850, and 1851), he had the site ready to support a masonry fort.[12]

During August of 1849, just as he began to make some progress on the site, Lee encountered interruption. He became ill. And in the midst of illness he had to attend meetings of the Board of Engineers for Atlantic Coast Defenses in Newport, Rhode Island. He wanted Mary and some of the children to make the trip with him; but she declined.[13]

Lee's symptoms—sporadic fever principally, with attendant aches—sound like malaria, perhaps contracted in Mexico, maybe at Sollers' Point. He left Arlington in uncertain health and traveled by train, then boat, to Philadelphia where he spent a feverish night and pressed on to New York. At the Irving House, friends tried to dissuade Lee from continuing his journey until he felt better. However, he "preferred having it over & if I was to be sick thought it better to be laid up here [Newport] than in N. York." So he boarded a boat for Newport and as if to endorse his decision to continue the trip, his fever suddenly broke. Lee "slept tolerably" until he arrived at Newport and secured a room at Ocean House.[14]

He managed to attend meetings of the board and had charge of the minutes of that body. He also sampled the society of the 300-plus visitors at Ocean House. But Lee's disease continued to afflict him with fevers, pain, and weakness. He had other duties after the board adjourned on August 22; but his doctor firmly advised Lee to remain and rest. So Lee sought and received a release from other obligations from Washington and tried to recover.[15]

Lee was unused to illness; he had always been nurse to others. He never quite trusted doctors, though he obeyed their instructions and abided by their restrictions. Lee disliked medicine, too, and much preferred to depend upon his body and a healthy regimen to work a cure. In this instance he took the quinine his physician prescribed, but blamed the medicine for being "on my back pretty much all day" on August 27.

When upright and between fevers, Lee did a little work (completing the minutes of the board meeting) and paid some social calls. But he was an impatient patient. "I spend a stupid time here," he wrote Mary Lee. "Bore the young ladies of my acquaintance . . . & am bored in my turn by other people." His doctor warned him against exposure to the sun and the night air. "So when am I to go out?"

Finally Lee secured his physician's permission to leave Newport and go to

West Point. There he continued his quinine and stayed at Cozzens, a new hotel about a mile below the Point. Winfield Scott was also at Cozzens, and he and Lee enjoyed a protracted visit. Then Lee headed south again and after a stop in New York returned to Baltimore.[16]

If malaria was indeed the source of Lee's fevers and discomfort during August 1849, he seems to have recovered completely, because he worked steadily at Sollers' Point and accomplished much during the remainder of the year. In addition, he moved his family into the house on Madison Avenue in Baltimore, enrolled the children in various schools, attended Mount Calvary Episcopal Church regularly, and engaged in an active social life in the city.[17]

Robert Lee's older sister Ann still lived in Baltimore with her husband William Louis Marshall. The Marshalls offered immediate entree to social circles in the city. And Lee wrote to Senator Jefferson Davis to urge his brother-in-law's reappointment as U.S. District Attorney for Baltimore.[18]

Davis, likely in late 1849, had recommended Lee as potential commander of a revolutionary army in Cuba. Cubans generally resented Spanish colonial rule on their island, and some exiles sought aid among other Americans in the United States. A Cuban revolutionary junta approached Davis, and Davis referred the rebels to Lee, who listened to their plans. Then Lee sought counsel from Davis; especially at issue in Lee's mind was his oath as an officer in the United States Army. He did not feel at all comfortable joining another army while obligated to his own country. Davis must have sustained this conviction or at least was unable to convince Lee otherwise, for Lee declined the command.[19]

Early in 1850 Lee renewed the family campaign to secure an appointment to West Point for Custis, who was now seventeen and responding well at Hallowell's school in Alexandria. To support the application, Lee sent to the Adjutant General a report from Hallowell and described his oldest son as "strong, active & healthy; and of irreproachable morals." Lee also wrote to Winfield Scott, asked him for a letter to the President, and understanding that Custis "gives some promise of making a good soldier." Custis's qualifications and Lee's influence proved sufficient to secure an at large appointment for "Mr. Boo." He became a plebe in July 1850.[20]

Although the Lees now lived in Baltimore, they still spent much time at Arlington. And after visiting her parents at Christmas (1850), Mary Lee lagged behind after her husband returned to duty and then wrote that her father wanted her to remain still another week. Robert Lee was tactful. He explained that although he would miss his family, he would be "very glad" for her to prolong her stay because that would "give much happiness to you and to them [the Custises]." However, Lee wrote that he was concerned that Mary (the daughter) would miss a week of school. "We must not for our own pleasure lose sight of the interest of our children." Then he asked his wife to adhere to her original schedule or send Daughter to him.[21]

When he lived alone, Lee became especially susceptible to fantasies. He enjoyed the company of bright young women, and during this period of his life he began in earnest what became a lifelong relationship with Martha Custis

Williams—"Markie." She was Mary Lee's first cousin and at some distance also a cousin of Robert Lee. Their correspondence had begun in 1844, and Lee had gone to great pains to secure and send to Markie her father's sword belt after his death in Mexico at the Battle of Monterrey. Markie was an orphan, eighteen years younger than Robert Lee. During the winter of 1852 she moved her belongings to Arlington and lived with Daughter (Mary) in the northwest bedroom.

In the spring of 1851 Lee wrote to Markie:

You have not written to me for nearly three months. And I believe it is equally as long since I have written to you. On paper Markie, I mean, on paper. But oh, what lengthy epistles have I indited to you in my mind! Had I any means to send them, you would see how constantly I think of you. I have followed you in your pleasures, & your duties, in the house & in the streets, & accompanied you in your walks to Arlington, & in your search after flowers. Did you not feel your cheeks pale when I was so near you? You may feel pale Markie, You may look pale; You may even talk pale; But I am happy to say you never write as if you were pale; & to my mind you always appear bright and rosy.

Friendship with Markie was important to Lee; he was open and honest with her. In her company, real or imagined, he was most himself. He was free.[22]

That April (1851) Lee found some excuse to visit West Point and see his son. He heard good news from the officers and instructors about Custis's performance. But the young man must have been homesick and to his father he must have seemed unsure of his capacity. Lee wrote to his oldest son soon after he returned to Baltimore and devoted the first page to encouraging words. He wrote about *"strength," "fortitude," "industry," "firm resolve," "courageous heart,"* and more. In conclusion, though, Lee simply asked Custis to make his best effort. "I shall then be content & you must not be disappointed."

Then, having disposed of his proper paternal admonitions, Lee filled page two of his letter with a charming account of his homecoming. He had arrived in the city by train at 5:00 A.M. and after storing his trunk, strolled through the quiet streets toward his home. Lee let himself into the house and climbed the stairs to the room where Mary was sleeping.

The door was locked & it took some little time to rouse her. But instead of admitting me, and opening the door, she prevented my entrance saying that Emma Randolph was in there. So we had to make our salutations in the passage & I determined to go up & see the children. I found both Mary's . . . & Rooney's doors locked. After some loud knocks Mary's was opened & allowing sufficient time for the opener to get under cover, I asked if I could enter. There was no answer, so I walked in & found M[ary] sound asleep & some person by her side buried in the bed with their head completely covered. I saw it was too *long* for any of the children, & . . . waking M[ary] she informed me it was cousin Cornelia Randolph. I had then to beat a retreat from there & commenced applying at Rooney's door. After a little time it was opened & stepping in, there laid R[ooney] sound asleep in the middle of the bed, Mildred on one side of him & Rob crawling in on the other. Upon investigation, I discovered that Rooney on coming up to bed, had caught up the two little children from their room & put them into his bed

& fearful lest his mother when she came up might recapture them had locked his door. I did not venture to examine farther into the house. . . . After a reasonable time we all assembled at the breakfast table & laughed over the adventures of the mor^g.

Lee followed his amusing story with some news of comings and goings among people known to Custis.

But by the bottom of page three the father was lapsing again into preachment. "I was much pleased," he proclaimed, "with the good order of your room & the healthy & happy appearance of all of you. I hope it will continue. Cleanliness, temperance & order is [sic] very promotive of health & cheerfulness."

Then Lee wrote of a visit from the father of his brother-in-law William Louis Marshall. The old (seventy-nine) man enjoyed himself and the dinner. "But though I had prepared for him my oldest & best wine, he would not taste a *drop*. Cold water he said was his only drink." As if he feared Custis might miss the message, Lee concluded, "His temperance habits had been of great avail to him. It [temperance] benefits everyone."[23]

There is a tension in this letter to Custis quite similar to the tension within the author. Lee tries to convey his concern over control and offers noble words and a stirring example to guide his son. However, he also relates the story of his encounter with strange and mysterious bedfellows and so reveals himself as playful parent in his accessible family. Like most people then and since Lee lived in search of a balance between control and freedom, between "ought to" and "want to," between obligations and opportunities. His father's example and his mother's teachings, among other factors, made the tension especially acute for Lee. For much of his youth he had been able to rely upon necessity—associated with economic circumstance, schooling, and his mother's ill health—to regulate his life. Then the discipline of West Point and his profession served the same purpose during Lee's young manhood. He obeyed orders and so avoided choices. Now, however, in midlife Lee had reached the stage within the military in which he gave more than followed orders.

Approximately six weeks after Lee wrote his letter to Custis, some of his words assumed an incredible irony. Very late in May an inspection of Custis's room at the Academy revealed a cache of liquor. Possession of alcohol was a serious offense: Custis confronted the possibility of expulsion.

Custis and his roommates emphatically denied any connection with the liquor or knowledge of its presence in the room. Then the situation became complicated for all concerned. Tradition within the corps at West Point permitted a cadet to escape punishment for an offense, if every member of the miscreant's class took a pledge not to commit the same offense for the year. A movement to take such a pledge began among Custis's classmates. The young Lee was generally popular and possessed a splendid academic record at the time. But Custis was especially close to a set of Southern cadets and led a faction that "cut" (shunned) their classmate Oliver Otis Howard. Howard was a priggish young man from Maine. He had arrived at the Academy in September, instead of July, and so had avoided the rigors and hazing of the summer encampment. Howard had a top hat, a cane, a supurb mind, and other features deemed affectations in cadet society. He had associated with a cadet "cut" by the corps, and many suspected that Howard was an active abolitionist. Now that Custis was vulnerable, would Howard and perhaps other less popular cadets be willing to take a pledge to salvage his career at West Point? Moreover, if Custis accepted the pledge from his classmates, would he then have to admit guilt? If so, he would pronounce himself guilty of something he had insisted he had not done. And if he now admitted guilt, would that mean that he had lied earlier? If so, his lie might constitute another offense that demanded expulsion. Custis was in trouble.[24]

Robert Lee was shaken and alarmed over the potential disgrace of his oldest son. He tried to counsel Custis, but seemed to be confused about the facts of the case. Custis explained the situation in greater detail and clarity. Still the elder Lee seemed to doubt his son's credibility. "Your assertion that the liquor was brought into your room without the knowledge or consent of any of your roommates was one of great comfort," Lee wrote. But he added, "It is inexplicable to me how it came there, for in my day, it was not so plenty [plentiful?] as to be thrust upon those who did not desire it, & I feel confident that no one would have thus intruded upon my room without my consent."

Having vented these feelings, Lee turned his attention to the matter of the pledge from Custis's classmates. Custis himself had already stated that he would not accept a pledge from his fellow cadets to escape punishment for an offense he had not committed. Lee sustained his son's course. "I am opposed to the theory of doing wrong that good may come of it," he wrote. "I hold to the belief that you must act right whatever the consequences."

Just in case Custis reconsidered, however, Lee elaborated his feelings about the pledge issue. He said that he would not hesitate to take a pledge in order to save a worthy comrade; to save himself by way of a pledge from his class was a very different matter. "I am fond of independence," he stated. "It is that feeling that prompts me to come up strictly to the requirements of law & regulations. I wish neither to seek or receive indulgence from any one."[25]

By the time Lee wrote out his counsel, the Academy had determined Custis's fate. Custis escaped with 8 demerits. Clearly the officers involved accepted the young man's assertion of innocence and imposed demerits to impress upon him his responsibility for the contents of his room. Custis completed his plebe year ranked second in his class—behind Oliver Otis Howard.[26]

As is often the case, the father's advice to his son reveals more about the father than the son. Significant was Lee's assertion, "I am fond of independence." Therefore he adhered "strictly to the requirements of law & regulations." Here was another expression of the tension between freedom and control; Lee obeyed in order to be independent—controlled himself to liberate himself. This apparent paradox was hardly new to Lee, because he read it many, if not most, of the days of his life. The Collect for Peace from the Morning Prayer Service in the Episcopal Book of Common Prayer speaks to God, "whose service is perfect freedom," and says much the same thing that Robert Lee wrote to his son Custis.[27]

Small wonder that Custis complained in March of melancholy. Robert Lee wrote once again to his son, and once again revealed his own philosophy:

Shake off those gloomy feelings. Drive them away. Fix your mind & pleasures upon what is before you. . . . All is bright if you will think it so. All is happy if you will make it so. Do not *dream.* It is too ideal, too imaginary. Dreaming by day, I mean. Live in the world you inhabit. Look upon things as they are. Take them as you find them. Make the best of them. Turn them to your advantage.

Sad thoughts, Lee observed, "will sometimes come over us. . . . They are the shadows to our picture. They bring out prominently the light & bright spots. They must not cover up *all.* They must not *hide* the picture itself." Use the shadows, Lee advised, "as a medium through which to view life correctly."

Then he offered a broader perspective: "All that is bright must fade & we ourselves have to die." In this context Custis would do well to enjoy the light and bright while he could. And in the context of certain darkness sooner or later, "shadows" in the present should not seem so significant.[28]

Most of the time Lee took his own advice. He made the best of whatever was and refused to take himself or his troubles too seriously.

Nevertheless, Lee told Mary Custis, "God punishes us for our sins here as well as hereafter. He is punishing me for mine through my children. It is there I am most vulnerable, most sensitive." At this juncture Lee was a troubled, frustrated parent. He obviously cared deeply about his children; but as they grew older, he confronted his increasing incapacity to control their lives.[29]

Indeed, in May 1852 the War Department reminded Lee of how little control he had over his own life. Lee received orders to assume the duties of the Superintendent of West Point the following September. Once before he had declined duty at the Academy. Now he protested that the task required "more skill & more experience than I command," and through Totten he asked the Secretary of War to reconsider. When he received no response to his request after a month, Lee resigned himself to his fate. He did inform Totten, however, that he had "never undertaken any duty with such reluctance."[30]

Lee seemed to consider his new assignment a "snake pit" of professional politics from which he could not expect to emerge unpoisoned. Shortly before he assumed his new duties, Lee wrote to veteran Academy Professor Dennis Hart Mahan and confessed "the reluctance I have felt towards my new position from the beginning to which my motives & actions were liable to be subjected. . . ." In addition to the pettiness which Lee associated with the task of superintending West Point, he confronted the presence of his oldest son there as a cadet.[31]

Mexico must have seemed long ago and far away as Lee prepared to undertake an assignment he considered onerous. Still, he did go to West Point and assume command. On September 1, 1852, the man who had expressed increasing anxiety about his role as father became parent to the entire corps of cadets.

12

"The Climate Is as Harsh to Me as My Duties"

A
s usual Robert Lee went alone to his new post, a solitary advance party for Mary Lee and the children. He had visited West Point during those twenty-three years since his graduation in 1829—as a member of the Board of Visitors in 1844 and as an unofficial visitor on other occasions, one of them as recent as April 1851. Now in August of 1852 Lee returned with reluctance to be the Superintendent of the United States Military Academy.

At West Point everything and nothing had changed. None of the principal buildings Lee had known as a cadet still stood. North and South Barracks were gone, and a new cadet barracks stood in their place. The messhall and the Academy (classroom) building were new. A cadet hospital, built since Lee's time, was old enough to be inadequate. A library and observatory facility, the band barracks, the chapel, and an artillery and ordnance laboratory building all dated from the period since 1829, and only two members of the faculty who had taught at West Point when Lee was a cadet were still teaching there in 1852.[1]

Of course the plain, the Hudson River, and the beauty of the place remained. Although he had left the Academy in 1833, Sylvanus Thayer still lived in spirit there in 1852. Thayer's Academic Board, composed of department heads and the Commandant of Cadets, still governed the Academy and tended to be self-perpetuating. Thayer-minded men selected other Thayer-minded men to replace Thayer-minded men. Consequently Thayer's curriculum, recitations, reports, regimen, and discipline continued with little important alterations at the Point.

An Academy mystique sustained the status quo. Cadets at best endured the Academy for four years. Then on that June day when they became graduates, they underwent a mystical transformation: They loved West Point. Graduates had bonded with one another and prevailed. Now they insisted that future generations of young men should have the same opportunity to suffer and

survive that they had experienced. And Academy graduates were often in positions to ensure that little or nothing changed at West Point.[2]

Superintendent Lee had little chance to make much impact upon the place.
The case of the cadet dress cap is a good example of the resistance to innova-
tion at West Point. Cadets and common sense had objected to the cap for
decades; Lee attempted to change the design. "The present Cadet uniform
dress cap is heavy, harsh & uncomfortable to the head," he wrote. "The black
patent leather crown, when exposed to the hot sun in summer is particularly
objectionable, causing headache, dizziness, etc." Lee proposed a slightly different design that was lighter, cooler, and better fitting. He even went so far as
to secure estimates from hatmakers in New York and arrange to have a model
prepared. However, these efforts accomplished nothing; the traditional cap
continued in use during Lee's time.[3]

One major change did occur at West Point during Lee's tenure as Superintendent. In response to continued recommendations from the Board of Visitors, the curriculum prescribed a five-year instead of four-year course. Lee,
however, had little to do with the alteration beyond preparations to implement the five-year curriculum.[4]

Otherwise, Lee did manage to implement a revised disciplinary system
which prescribed dismissal for any cadet who acquired 100 or more demerits
within a six-month period. The old system (Thayer's), which set the limit at
200 for an entire year, remained in effect. But Lee contended that in practice
that system encouraged cadets to make mischief and ignore regulations until
such time as their demerit total neared the 200 mark. Only then did those in
jeopardy make concerted efforts to adhere to disciplinary standards. The six-
month standard, Lee asserted, would compel cadets to observe the regulations
with greater care and consistency.[5]

Lee carried on the tradition among superintendents of requesting funds for
physical improvements at the Academy. He asked for a new riding hall, new
stables, an addition to the hospital, more officers and faculty quarters, and a
gasworks to light the barracks. He presided over a revised edition of the regulations for the Academy that clarified and codified the wisdom of the Academy
Board. And he fought the good fight against political interference with the
systems of academic and disciplinary dismissal. Lee lost this fight while Charles
M. Conrad, who was Secretary of War to March 1853, insisted upon reinstat-
ing young men possessed of influential families. However, Jefferson Davis
succeeded Conrad and rather vigorously upheld decisions of the Academic
Board.[6]

Regulations and tradition made the Superintendent of the Military Academy directly responsible for many of the routine operations at West Point and
all of the extraordinary incidents in the lives of about 50 members of the
academic and military staff and roughly 250 adolescent and post-adolescent
males in the corps of cadets. To illustrate Lee's duties and vexations at West
Point, consider the career of Cadet James McNeill Whistler, the son of George
Washington Whistler, an Academy graduate and career officer who died in

Russia in 1849. Young Jimmy secured an appointment to West Point and enrolled in July 1851. Jimmy's mother Anna was living in Scarsdale, Westchester County, and within a month of assuming his duties at West Point, Lee had to respond to her request for a leave for her son to bid her goodbye on the eve of a trip to Europe. Lee agreed, but for a shorter leave than Anna Whistler had requested. Before he wrote to her, however, Lee consulted Whistler's professors and the schedules of the boats and trains on which the young man would travel. And Whistler's mother was not the only parent who requested some indulgence.[7]

By year's end Whistler had collected 116 demerits, more than the number mandating his dismissal. However, Lee and the Commandant of Cadets had the discretionary authority to examine demerit records and excuse some infractions if the cadet's general conduct and potential justified the mercy. Lee exercised his authority, expunged 39 demerits, and salvaged the young man's career for the moment.[8]

The following spring (1853) Whistler became seriously ill, and Lee wrote again to Anna Whistler informing her that her son was not responding to treatment in the cadet hospital. Medical leave and a summer of convalescence restored the young man, and on August 31, Lee informed Anna Whistler that her son had that day appeared before the Academic Board and passed the examination he had missed the previous June. He stood thirty-second in his class, but first in drawing, at the time.[9]

During Whistler's second class (third) year, Lee had to write a letter to Engineer Chief Joseph Totten urging a favorable response to Whistler's request for permission to receive "some articles of underclothing" from his mother. So responsible was the Superintendent for everything that happened at West Point that a colonel and a general had to correspond about Whistler's underwear.[10]

But that June (1854) Whistler was principal in what was probably the shortest examination in the history of West Point. Second Lieutenant Caleb Huse commenced Whistler's chemistry examination by asking the cadet to discuss silicon. "I am required to discuss the subject of silicon," Whistler responded. "Silicon is a gas." "That will do, Mr. Whistler," interrupted Huse. In thirteen words Whistler failed chemistry and flunked out at West Point. Much later Whistler insisted, "Had silicon been a gas, I would have been a major general."[11]

Superintendent Lee then had to do what he termed "the most unpleasant office I am called on to perform—the discharge of those cadets found deficient at the examination." Whistler and eight other unfortunates climbed into an omnibus wagon bound for the dock and the afternoon boat to New York on June 29, 1854.

Whistler himself did not return to the Point, but his petition to take another examination in chemistry was on Lee's desk within a week. So Lee had to review once more Whistler's record in chemistry and conduct. Having done so, Lee could find reason neither to reexamine Whistler in chemistry nor to excuse enough of his demerits to prevent Whistler's mandatory dismissal. "I can only regret," Lee concluded, "that one so capable of doing well should so have neglected himself & must now suffer the penalty." So instead of becoming a major general, Jimmy Whistler became an artist and immortalized his mother Anna in the portrait entitled *Arrangement in Grey and Black.* [12]

Of course all cadets were not as troublesome as Whistler. Indeed, one of the unfortunate circumstances associated with being Superintendent was the large amount of time and energy expended on the relatively few young men who were often in academic or disciplinary difficulty. Lee seldom had time for cadets who studied diligently and accommodated regulations; he interacted most with those most in trouble. Consequently Lee or anyone in his position might easily fall into a skewed perception of cadets in particular and the human condition in general.

Lee's involvement in Cadet Whistler's case and his active intervention in Whistler's demerit record were typical. He fretted about discipline and seemed to worry about each miscreant. Lee held an office hour each day from 7:00 to 8:00 A.M. for cadets. He listened then to excuses and concerns from the young men, and he summoned to listen to him those cadets whose records indicated a need for reform.

Most likely Lee's most difficult disciplinary situations involved his nephew Fitzhugh Lee, Smith's son. Young Fitz—along with others—on December 16, 1853, was careless enough to be captured returning to West Point at 5:00 A.M. Fitz Lee's companions were in civilian clothes and in possession of liquor. Even though Fitz was in uniform and had no liquor in his possession when apprehended, he was in grave danger of dismissal. His classmates came to his rescue, however, and unanimously took a pledge not to commit the same offense (absent without leave). Superintendent Lee wrote Secretary of War Davis, "I believe experience has shown the happiest results from these specific pledges and I therefore recommend it to your favorable consideration." In this case Davis refused to accept the pledge and ordered a court-martial, which imposed severe punishment short of dismissal upon Fitz Lee.

Nephew Fitz had to forego his furlough the following summer and remain at West Point. He had 197 demerits on his record in July 1854 when he was again caught attempting to sneak back into camp at 2:30 A.M. Yet again Fitz's classmates took the pledge not to attempt unauthorized leave (for the next academic year). Again Superintendent Lee wrote Secretary of War Davis and recommended mercy. This time Davis accepted Lee's recommendation, and Fitz Lee went free. He graduated ranked forty-fifth in a class of forty-nine in 1856. By then his uncle was half a continent away from West Point. [13]

Lee adopted the West Point regimen to the point of imposing Academy standards upon his ten-year-old son Rob in the Superintendent's quarters. Rob had his own room and his father taught him how to maintain it as though it were in the barracks. "He at first even went through the form of inspecting it," Rob recalled, " . . . I think I enjoyed this until the novelty wore off."

One day as Lee and his youngest son were taking their customary afternoon ride, Rob remembered, "We came suddenly upon three cadets far beyond the limits. They immediately leaped over a low wall on the side of the road and disappeared from our view. We rode on for a minute in silence; then my father said: Did you know those young men? But no; if you did, don't say so. I wish boys would do what is right; it would be so much easier for all parties!" Lee adhered to the traditional standards and rules at West Point; but his heart did not seem to support the code.[14]

Some of Lee's ambivalence about military discipline surfaced in a letter he wrote to Markie just over a year after he began his duties at West Point. Markie had asked his advice about the best school for her younger brother Orton. Lee mentioned a number of institutions—one in Sing Sing, St. James's College in Maryland, Virginia Military Institute, William & Mary, and what became Episcopal High School in Alexandria, Virginia. Then he introduced the relative merits of a school in the country versus a school in a city and implied that the former offered fewer temptations. "Young men must not expect to escape contact with evil," Lee counseled, "but must learn not to be contaminated by it. That virtue is worth but little that requires constant watching & removal from temptation." As Lee wrote this, he was quite well aware that "constant watching" and "removal from temptation" were hallmarks of the West Point system.[15]

Although he was not known for his insight, Jefferson Davis displayed rare understanding when he later wrote of Lee that he "was surprised to see so many gray hairs on his head, he confessed that the cadets did exceeding worry him, and then it was perceptible that his sympathy with young people was rather an impediment than a qualification for the superintendency." Lee would likely have agreed with Davis's observation. He once wrote about discipline at the Academy: "Cadets can neither be treated as school boys or soldiers." At West Point Lee confronted an institutional response to his personal quest for the balance between control and freedom.[16]

Like all American military installations, West Point belonged to the citizens of the United States. Especially did graduates of the Academy feel their ownership. Prominent public servants and Army officers of high rank expected special welcome at the Point. Army commander Winfield Scott certainly adopted West Point as his own, even though he never attended the Academy.

As Superintendent Lee felt an obligation to entertain cadets, and opened his quarters to Custis, his friends, and other invitees every Saturday afternoon. Agnes Lee recorded in her journal, "We also arrange for cadet suppers every Sat. evening, they to be sure need not be very exquisite but must be just right for Papa's scrutinizing eye." And Lee gave "he dinners," as he called them, for officers and faculty.[17]

In addition to the entertaining he wanted to do, Lee was liable for all sorts of official social functions as Superintendent. He explained one such obligation in the course of a letter to his cousin Anna Fitzhugh. "I must now go home to receive Prof^r Mitchell . . . just returned from Europe & who [is] calling on me this mor^g in the midst of my papers. I had to ask him to dine with us, though I knew it would not be convenient. . . . But, the Prof^rs ideas are so elevated that I hope his thoughts will rise above our frugal table."[18]

Another intrusion claimed Lee's attention in the midst of a letter to Markie. He returned to the letter and explained:

I have been interrupted by the arrival of Genl Scott, who with his son in law & daughter, Mr. & Mrs. Hoyt & some friends called upon the Supt. He has had therefore to conduct them into the library, order a salute in honour of the Comm^g Genl shew them around the Academies, & conduct them in presence of the Battery, which has just belched forth its thunder. The Genl has now gone to my quarters under Major Porter's escort, to repose till dinner, when I shall again have the pleasure of his company, & the gentlemen of his suite, with such of our natives as I can collect to do them honour. As my servants have rec^d but short notice for their preparation for dinner, I fear the Genl will again have an opportunity of taking, if not hasty, at least a thin plate of soup, & but for an Arlington ham & some of my Shanghai chickens, which I had purposed for my solitary dinner, I should be in doubt whether their hunger could be appeased, as ten additional guests will have to be provided for. But having given all the required directions, I will wait with patience & *hope* for their execution.[19]

At least Lee's liability for instant dinner parties took no toll upon his wry sense of humor.

Lee had been at West Point eighteen months when he remarked in a letter to cousin Anna Fitzhugh that the plain was still "hard frozen" in April and despite the date, "we are apparently in the midst of winter." Then he added, "The climate is as harsh to me as my duties & neither brings any pleasure."[20]

Yet Lee did derive some benefit from his tenure at West Point, whether or not he understood or acknowledged it at the time. The Scott connection continued, for example. However thin the soup Lee served Scott, the Superintendent remained in Scott's favor and became indeed his protégé.

Lee also had the benefit of working with the Academic Board at West Point. The board and its powerful role in the life of the Academy rendered Lee unable to work any major changes. But the Academic Board also made the difficult decisions, so Lee did not have to. During Lee's term and for most of the period before the Civil War, three men dominated the Academic Board: mathematics professor Albert E. Church; physical scientist William H. C. Bartlett; and military scientist Dennis Hart Mahan. Church and Bartlett were assistant professors when Lee was a cadet; Mahan had returned to West Point for good the year after Lee's graduation. Lee apparently never challenged this trinity and may have learned some professional lessons from Mahan.[21]

Lee tended to read French military histories, treatises, and manuals, and to study the campaigns of Napoleon as interpreted by Baron Henri Jomini and then reinterpreted by Napoleon himself. The Superintendent made good use of the Academy library, and his contact with the faculty and various visitors broadened his professional vision. At some point Lee must have confronted Mahan and his military wisdom. Among other ideas, Mahan insisted that field fortifications (trenches) were vital to "modern" warfare. Later in life Lee demonstrated affinity with such an emphasis—an understanding that may have begun at the Point.[22]

While at West Point, Lee also increased his personal wealth substantially. He purchased more bonds from the states of Virginia and Missouri, the cities of Pittsburgh and St. Louis, the New York & Erie and the Hudson River Railroads. These bonds paid 6 and 7 percent, and with his other investments in bank stock, canal bonds and stock, railroad bonds, and state bonds, raised the value of Lee's invested capital to $64,500 by the spring of 1855. (Nine years earlier, in 1846, Lee's invested capital totaled $38,750.) On a base military salary of $2,628 per year, Colonel Lee was becoming a rich man.[23]

However harsh Lee's duties at West Point seemed to him, as Superintendent he had the advantage of maintaining contact with Scott, of interacting with some strong minds and at least one bright mind among the faculty, of having a second portrait of himself painted by Robert W. Weir, and of increasing his personal wealth. He enjoyed regular visits from Custis while he was a cadet and saw his son finish first in his class in 1854. Like his father, Custis joined the Engineer Corps, and like his father went first to work on the southeastern coast, roughly 100 miles south of Savannah on Amelia Island, in extreme northern Florida.[24]

Some time during the fall of 1852 Mary Lee journeyed up from Arlington to join her husband in the Superintendent's quarters. She brought her two youngest children, Rob and Mildred, with her. Mary and Rooney came too, but then went off to schools—Rooney in New York City, Mary to Pelham Priory in Westchester County. Annie and Agnes remained at Arlington with the Custises and their governess/teacher Susan Poor. So at West Point that fall and winter were Mary Lee, Robert Lee, Rob, Mildred, and Cadet Custis.[25]

The following spring (1853) tragedy struck the dispersed family: Mary Custis died suddenly in April. In poor health of late, she complained of a headache one day, saw a doctor the next, but appeared in no danger. The following day, April 23, the doctor returned and pronounced her dying. Mary Lee received a telegram with the sad news and left West Point immediately for Arlington. Meanwhile, Mary Custis could only worry about her daughter's reaction to her own impending death—" 'how terribly she will be shocked when she hears this.' " Mary Lee arrived in time to attend her mother's funeral on April 27.[26]

Robert Lee was deeply grieved. On the day of his mother-in-law's burial he wrote to his wife, "The more I think of our irreparable loss the greater is my grief. But it is for you, your poor father, for myself, the children, relatives, friends, & servants I grieve. Not for her. She has gone from all trouble, Care & Sorrow to a happy immortality." Lee could not leave his duties at West Point, but he tried to comfort and counsel his wife in writing, if not in person. He reported receiving a letter from daughter Mary "full of attachment for her Gr^n mother & penitence for the pain & sorrow she had occasioned her." Rooney also wrote—"He is a dear affectionate boy. Full of good impulses & kind wishes. We must not expect him to be exempt from the thoughtlessness & love of pleasure peculiar to youth." Custis, too, tried to comfort his father—"His feelings are deep & do not show on the surface."[27]

At Arlington, Parke Custis was still distraught, only able to leave his house for a drive in his carriage in early June. Mary Lee cared for her father, and Robert Lee took care of Rob and Mildred. He went to New York City and purchased mourning clothes for the children and also made the transition from winter carpeting to summer straw matting on the floors in the Superintendent's quarters. He urged his wife to organize everyone at Arlington and bring them to West Point. However, his father-in-law protested that he was not yet well enough for the trip. So Robert Lee went instead to Arlington with Rob and Mildred in mid-July. Custis had to remain at the Academy that summer; Mary and Rooney joined their family a few days after their father and youngest siblings arrived.[28]

On July 17, the first Sunday after the Lees (minus Custis) were reunited at Arlington, the family attended Christ Church, Alexandria. The Right Reverend John Johns, Episcopal Bishop of Virginia, was present and preached a sermon. Then Robert Lee and two of his daughters, Mary and Anne, presented themselves for confirmation. In a brief service Bishop Johns laid his hands upon their heads and prayed over them.

After learning his catechism at his mother's knee before he could read; after attending the Episcopal Church quite regularly and serving on the vestry of St. John's Church, Brooklyn; after speaking and writing for many years the rhetoric of evangelical Protestants and Low Church Anglicans, at age forty-six Lee finally, formally joined the church. Why did he wait so long?[29]

Lee was the product of strong religious impulses within his family and community. He revered the church, at least the Protestant Church, and appropriated its language and the essentials of its doctrine. But Lee was a very private person, and his religious response was private as well. He avoided sectarian exclusivity and believed expansively. Lee did proper things and said correct words; but his piety was practical, grounded in this world, however much he intoned or wrote his litany about dead souls rising to joy in heaven.

Lee certainly believed in sin. Had the church not taught the doctrine of original sin, Lee would have invented it. The human condition was flawed, he believed, and the fatal flaw was absorption with self. Conversely Lee believed that "the great duty of life" is "the promotion of the happiness & welfare of our fellow men." Good Christians, Lee believed, attempted to make selflessness a habit and eventually an instinctive response to any situation. But even the best Christians failed in this effort because of the evil inherent in human beings. So God resolved this dilemma with His grace and forgiveness.

Although Lee couched his beliefs in evangelical rhetoric, he believed beyond evangelicalism. Lee's response to God was selflessness, self-control, and service to others. God's response to Lee was freedom.[30]

Lee's religious life underwent no significant change following his confirmation. He presented himself to Bishop Johns to acknowledge his relation to the church. He probably also wanted to support his daughters' conviction, and he wanted to honor his mother-in-law's piety.

Back at West Point he still appeared dressed and ready to walk to chapel with his family. Mary Lee was often late. Rob remembered, "When he could wait no longer for her, he would say that he was off and would march along to church by himself, or with any of the children who were ready." Inside the chapel Lee sat near the front and center—and dozed through the sermon. The preacher and chaplain at the Academy was William T. Sprole, a Presbyterian, who, according to Agnes, was "a little hard on the cadets & too pointed in his remarks." Perhaps for these reasons Lee quite often took his family to Holy Innocents, which according to Agnes was "a little episcopal chapel—very pretty but a little too much like a catholic one, about a mile & a half from West Point property." Drawing Professor Robert Weir designed the building and sold paintings to finance its construction. When Lee the Superintendent went the extra mile to attend Holy Innocents, he made a clear statement about sermons that were "a little hard on cadets."[31]

When the Lees had returned to West Point in August 1853, they took Parke Custis with them. He enjoyed himself, went to Niagara Falls with his son-in-law, and returned to Arlington in the fall. The following summer, 1854, the Lees returned to Arlington for a relatively short visit there.

During the next academic year (1854–55) Congress stirred in response to the responsibility of the Army for protection of white settlers on the western frontier. In March, Congress authorized four new regiments (two infantry and two cavalry), and very soon after that Secretary of War Davis announced that Colonel Lee would be second in command of one of the cavalry regiments.[32]

After more than a quarter century in the Engineer Corps, Lee was going to join a combat arm of the United States Army. He was going to command troops instead of advise commanders. This was a major shift in his career.

Lee wrote and said lots of words to rationalize the transition to himself and others. But certainly since his experience in Mexico, Lee had been preparing himself for this change of course. One index of the direction he was taking was his record at the West Point library. Lee believed in purposeful reading; moreover, he had trouble with his eyes during his period at the Point so he probably read more purposefully than ever. He checked out books about and by Napoleon, not engineering tomes. Lee aspired to command and had been thinking of battles instead of battlements for some time.[33]

To Markie, his confidante, Lee lamented his separation from his family. "The change from my present confined & sedentary life, to one more free & active, will certainly be more agreeable to my feelings & serviceable to my health," he admitted, and added, "You know Markie how painful it will be to part from you."[34]

On March 31, 1855, Lee ceased to be Superintendent at West Point; but he and his family lingered into April, packing or selling belongings and saying goodbyes. On April 9, the Monday after Easter, they all left together in a downpour and started south for Arlington.[35]

In spite of his misgivings, Lee had had a successful tour of duty at West Point. In June 1854 the Board of Visitors reported Lee's "eminent qualifications," and asserted that his feats of heroism in Mexico "have lost none of their lustre in the exalted position he so worthily fills."[36]

The Board of Visitors in 1853 included in its report a paean for the cadets:

"No men living are required to be more industrious. It is the crowning excellence of the institution that arrangements are made by which all their time is suitably employed. They, while here, have no time to contract vicious habits." Lee, however, was somewhat more skeptical. He once commented perceptively to a friend that "Cadets deceive themselves sometimes by thinking they study, when in reality they do not, & are satisfied by reading over or devoting a reasonable time with their lessons. You know the difference between that & *understanding*. . . ."[37]

13

"The Question Which I Have Staved Off for 20 Years"

VERY EARLY IN HIS CAREER Lieutenant Robert Lee vented frustration upon his good friend and one-time mentor Andrew Talcott. "I am waiting, looking and hoping for some good opportunity to bid an affectionate farewell to my dear Uncle Sam," Lee wrote. "And I seem to think that said opportunity is to drop in my lap like a ripe pear, for d——l a stir have I made in the matter." For twenty years no ripe pear dropped into Lee's lap; nor did he make sufficient stir to seize an opportunity for a career outside of the military. Then something did drop into Lee's lap.[1]

Lee made an important decision about his career when he embraced his transfer from the Engineer Corps to the Cavalry in the spring of 1855. He probably thought he would see action on the western frontier against Comanche warriors who had for some time been retaliating against the incursions of American settlers on land traditionally Native American hunting grounds. To Markie Williams he wrote about his expectations of a life "more free & active" than his "confined & sedentary" existence at West Point. What Lee actually did for the next two and a half years hardly matched those expectations.[2]

Lee was supposed to be second in command of the new Second Cavalry regiment, for which he now had the permanent rank of lieutenant colonel (his brevet or temporary rank continued colonel). In command of the Second Cavalry was Colonel Albert Sidney Johnston, who was four years older than Lee, a West Point graduate (1826), and veteran of the Black Hawk and Mexican wars. Johnston had also fought in the Texas revolution and served the Lone Star Republic as secretary of war. However, now the Army was unable to find Johnston, and so Lee had to go in his place, first to Louisville, then to Jefferson Barracks near St. Louis, to coordinate recruiting and begin organizing the regiment.

Mary Lee remained at Arlington with her father and the younger children (Annie, Agnes, Rob, and Mildred). Mary the daughter (now twenty) had recovered from a foot problem that had plagued her for some time, and was caring for her father's sister Ann Marshall in Baltimore. Custis continued on duty at Amelia Island in Florida. And Rooney had gone off to Harvard following a failed attempt to get him into West Point.[3]

Johnston eventually materialized, and Lee expected a chance to return to Arlington in the process of settling his accounts, left open since 1848. Instead, he lingered at Jefferson Barracks during the late summer and then received orders to serve on courts-martial at Forts Leavenworth and Riley in Kansas. By the time he returned to Jefferson Barracks on November 21, 1855, his regiment had departed for duty in Texas, and he still had to go to Washington. Consequently Lee traveled from St. Louis to Texas via Washington.[4]

Having transacted his official business in the War Department, Lee then secured permission to continue in Virginia until after the first of the year. He may have relaxed at Arlington during some of December 1855; but much of his time and energy he had to devote to family business. He and Mary Lee had begun some long overdue renovation at Arlington House. G. W. P. Custis finally relinquished some of his control over the place, which had become more and more shabby with each recent year. Lee arranged to install a furnace to heat the house and took advantage of the necessity to knock holes in walls to repaint rooms downstairs. The Lees also furnished the large parlor (a storage room heretofore) with furniture they had purchased and used in Baltimore and West Point.

Lee's father-in-law needed help as well with his business affairs at White House and Romancock. Custis's manager/agent on these two 4,000-acre estates, Francis Nelson, had presented Custis a huge balance due statement for the ten years he had had charge of the farms. Custis had never exercised much supervision; indeed, he had likely not visited his properties in years. As it happened, Nelson was not much more efficient than his employer, and he lacked vouchers and receipts to support his claim.[5]

Lee set out for White House by train on December 5, arrived December 7, and found Nelson absent and the place in poor condition. He then went over to Romancock and once more discovered Nelson absent. Still having never confronted Nelson, on December 13 Lee went to Richmond and checked on Nelson's accounts with various millers there. Then Lee boarded the train once again, returned to Arlington for a couple of days, then journeyed to Baltimore to examine Nelson's record of wheat sales there. He returned to Arlington on December 19 and began trying to unravel the paper record of Nelson's management of White House and Romancock. By New Year's Day, 1856, Lee had done what he could with the incomplete records he had, and he had discovered discrepancies amounting to $6,078.95.[6]

Of course Lee realized he was paying the price for many years of neglect on the part of his father-in-law. But he seemed to direct his resentment at Nelson and told Custis not to let the situation "annoy you or interfere with your happiness." To Mary Lee he wrote later and advised, "As regards your household arrangements & what concerns your father's comfort & welfare, as well as your own, you must yourself act & not rely on him or wait for me. . . . At his age & present state of life, persons prefer their matters being accomplished by others, if *well* & satisfactorily performed."[7]

Lee also realized that he could not complete the cleansing of Custis's Augean stables before he would have to resume his own professional duties. So he consulted his distant relative William F. Wickham, who lived near Hanover Court House which was also near Richmond, and on Wickham's recommendation appointed William Overton Winston his agent to render as true an accounting as possible and settle with Nelson. Lee did try once more to secure Nelson's records; but once more Nelson was remiss, and so Lee charged Winston with the task and asked Nelson in writing to cooperate.[8]

Meanwhile the Army found work for Lee to do. He went to Carlisle Barracks, Pennsylvania, to sit on a court-martial, returned to Arlington for a week, then went to West Point for another court-martial. By the time Lee returned to Arlington, he had spent a month in travel and courts-martial. Finally, on February 12, 1856, Lee set out for Texas to join his regiment. He did spend another week en route in Virginia working on his father-in-law's affairs. Then he traveled by train to New Orleans, by boat to Indianola, by stagecoach to San Antonio, and by horseback to Fort Mason (100 miles NNW of San Antonio). Lee reported for duty to Johnston at Fort Mason on March 25, 1856— just over a year after he received his orders to join the Second Cavalry.

Johnston put Lee on the trail again. Lee's more-or-less permanent assignment was to command two squadrons of the Second Cavalry stationed at Camp Cooper, another 150 miles north of Fort Mason. So Lee set out once more on March 31, arrived at Camp Cooper on April 9, and assumed command there on April 13.[9]

Camp Cooper was indeed a camp. Located on the Clear Fork of the Brazos River, it was essentially four rows of tents which sheltered the four companies of troopers. A single line of tents perpendicular to the others formed officers' quarters, and just behind these was Lee's tent as commanding officer.

Within the camp, the ground was relatively level; pecan, elm, and ash trees grew along the riverbanks. Beyond, the country was dry and stark. Rocky cliffs defined the river valley, and away from the river itself only mesquite, chaparral, hackberry, and prickly pear rose above the level of grasses. Lee described the region as he saw it in May, before the summer drought: "The country is fertile & rolling, lightly timbered, & the deer & antelope luxuriate in the abundant grass. We are far beyond civilization."

Lee lived simply on the plains, as he explained to his daughter Agnes. "On the right of the entrance of the tent, stands an iron camp bed. On the left a camp table and chair. At the far end a trunk. On the side near the entrance a water bucket, basin & broom. Clothes hang around within easy reach of all points, & a sword & pistol very convenient. A saddle & bridle stand at the foot of the bed on a wooden horse. What more could it or ought it to contain!" Behind Lee's tent was a kitchen, behind that an improvised henhouse, and behind that he staked his mare Mary. Initially, Lee paid a woman named Jane $15 per month to do his cooking and washing. Later in his sojourn on the

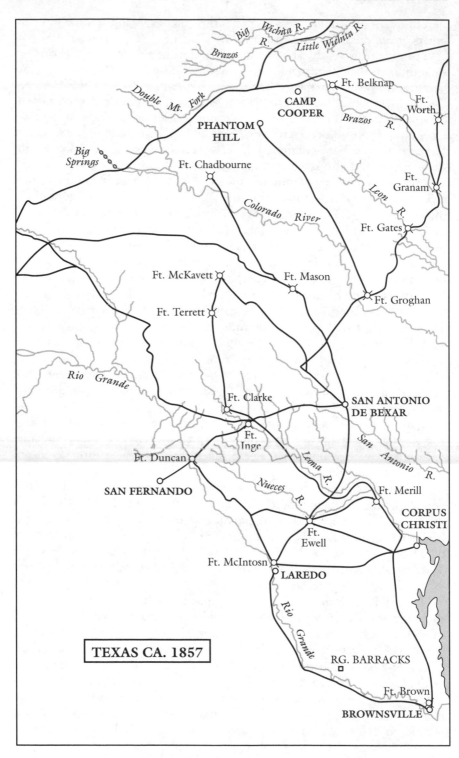

Big Wichita R.
Brazos R.
Little Wichita R.
Double Mt. Fork
Ft. Belknap
CAMP COOPER
Ft. Worth
Brazos R.
PHANTOM HILL
Big Springs
Ft. Chadbourne
Leon R.
Ft. Granam
Colorado River
Ft. Gates
Ft. McKavett
Ft. Mason
Ft. Groghan
Ft. Terrett
Rio Grande
Ft. Clarke
SAN ANTONIO DE BEXAR
Ft. Inge
San Antonio R.
Ft. Duncan
Leona R.
SAN FERNANDO
Nueces R.
Ft. Merill
CORPUS CHRISTI
Ft. Ewell
Ft. McIntosn
LAREDO
Rio Grande
TEXAS CA. 1857
RG. BARRACKS
Ft. Brown
BROWNSVILLE

plains, he hired someone named Theodore Kremer to cook for him at $20 per month.[10]

One reason that Camp Cooper and Lee were on the Texas plains was just downstream—a semi-permanent settlement of 577 Comanche. These people supposedly lived on their reservation, and agents appointed in Washington tried to induce nomads to take up agriculture. The Second Cavalry was present to support the Indian agents and to protect white settlers and reservation Comanche against other Comanche (perhaps 1,000) who roamed and raided beyond the reservation boundaries.

Very soon after Lee arrived to assume command, he had a visit from Catumseh, chief of the neighboring village. Lee wrote to his wife, "We have had a *talk,* very tedious on his part & very sententious on mine. I hailed him as a friend, so long as his conduct & that of his band entitled him to it, but would meet him as an enemy, the first moment he deserved it." On April 12, Lee returned Catumseh's call. Then the chief told Lee he had six wives, and Lee said of the Comanche, "Their paint & ornaments make them more hideous than nature made them & the whole race is extremely uninteresting."[11]

Lee's judgment of his Comanche charges did not improve with time. He wrote of his government's attempt to "humanize" them—as though they were less than human as they were. He wrote his old friend Eliza Mackay Stiles, "We are on the best of terms with our neighbors, the Comanchees, & I am happy to believe that there is no love lost between us. I see more of them than I desire. . . ."

Asked to call upon Ha-Tem-a-see, a chief who was quite ill, during May, Lee rode into the village. "The explosion among the curs, children & women was tremendous." A medicine man appeared and attempted to inform Lee that he must remove some of his clothing before seeing the patient. In time Lee realized that his cravat was the offending item and so he took it off.

> The lodge was carpeted with buffalo robes. The sick man was stretched on his couch with his wives & servitors [attendants] around him. His shield, bow and quiver were suspended on the outside, near which stood his favorite horse, ready to be slain, to bear the spirit of his master to the far hunting ground. I thought him laboring under an attack of pleurisy—administered a loaf of bread and some sugar, of which I knew him to be very fond . . . & told him I would send a man to complete his cure. So in the eve, the *Dr.* rode down with his steward and drugs, & cupped him pretty freely, which I hope will restore him. Perhaps the lancet has only reserved for the bullet the task of dispatching him.

Beneath the mock heroic in this letter to Eliza Stiles lies Lee's general contempt for the Comanche. In Lee's mind these people occupied a rung of the evolutionary ladder somewhere below Mexicans. He would carry out his government's policy toward them but neither learn nor care more about them than his duty required.[12]

In June 1856, Lee launched a punitive expedition from Camp Cooper against a marauding band of Comanche reportedly led by a chief named

Senaco. He divided his force to cover more territory and swept up the Brazos, Colorado, and Wichita Rivers northwest of Camp Cooper. One of Lee's detachments found five Indians, killed two warriors, and captured a woman. Lee and the rest of his force saw no Indians and no indications that Indians had been in the region for years. Although he did not know so at the time, this expedition would be Lee's lone foray against hostile Comanche. He wandered for hundreds of miles in the West Texas wilderness from June 13 to July 23—forty days of fruitless searching. The biblical symbolism would be wonderful if Lee had returned from the wilds with some new revelation or renewed spiritual strength. But he returned only to discover that Camp Cooper looked much like the barren plains he had traversed, writing to Mary Lee, "The grass is parched & our hopes for a few cabbage plants & roasting ears [of corn] have passed away. . . . The worst is the Clear Fork no longer deserves its title & is converted into fetid, Stagnant pools." The wilderness followed Lee home.[13]

Moreover, the news from Virginia was uniformly bad. Winston had had no success settling Nelson's accounts at White House and Romancock. Lee wrote Winston immediately and instructed him to settle in accord with "the data before you according to the rules & custom in such cases."

Mary Lee was ill, but vague about her symptoms; she informed her husband that she was planning to go to one of the mineral springs/spas in western Virginia on the advice of her physician. Lee despaired. "At this distance I can do nothing for you," he wrote. "You must make your arrangements & carry out your own plans. I am at a loss however to know where you will get funds for your journey, as it seemed from your letter, that you have deprived yourself of those you had in possession, before you knew how you could replace them."

Also in Mary Lee's letter was the news that Mildred Lee Childe, Robert Lee's younger sister, had died in Paris. "Though parted from her for years, with little expectation of but a transient reunion in this life," Lee reflected, "this Sudden, harsh & terrible Separation has not been the less distressing. . . ."

In addition, Mary reported that she had dutifully deposited some interest payments from her husband's invested money. But she failed to say precisely for how much the deposit was or into which bank she deposited the money. "You must be very particular dear Mary," Robert Lee wrote, "when you deal in money matters. You know I cannot draw upon a bank unless I know *where* the money is, & its *exact* amount." Somewhat later that fall Lee had a check returned to him because of his wife's carelessness. Then he tried again to teach her that he or she simply could not "give checks on Banks & not have [sufficient funds] to meet them. People may think I am endeavoring to *Swindle.*"[14]

There was also the chronic problem of Rooney and Harvard. The collegiate career of Lee's second son inspired classic stereotyping from his classmate Henry Adams:

Tall, largely built, handsome, genial, with liberal Virginian openness toward all he liked, he had also the Virginian habit of command and took leadership as his natural habit. No one cared to contest it. None of the New Englanders wanted command. For a year, at least, Lee was the most popular and prominent young man in his class, but then seemed slowly to drop into the background. The habit of command was not enough, and the Virginian had little else. He was simple beyond analysis; so simple that even the simple New England student could not realize him. No one knew enough to know how ignorant he was; how childlike; how helpless before the relative complexity of a school. As an animal, the Southerner seemed to have every advantage, but even as an animal he steadily lost ground.

Adams responded to Rooney's Virginia provincialism with a full measure of Massachusetts provincialism:

Strictly, the Southerner had no mind; he had temperament. He was not a scholar; he had no intellectual training; he could not analyze an idea, and he could not even conceive of admitting two; but in life one could get along very well without ideas, if one had only the social instinct. Dozens of eminent statesmen were men of Lee's type, and maintained themselves well enough in the legislature, but college was a sharper test.

Adams knew three Virginians at Harvard and thus extrapolated from this sample his wisdom about Southerners.[15]

However, Lees and at least one Custis agreed with much of what Adams wrote. Rooney's maternal grandmother Mary Custis did not seem to let her considerable affection for Rooney interfere with her capacity to know and tell the truth. Near the end of her life, she wrote to Custis Lee, "Rooney I think will never do for any of the learned professions." She believed Rooney needed to be "under . . . [his father's] eye till old enough to be on his own hook as the saying is."[16]

Robert Lee delivered a series of judgments about Rooney's life at Cambridge. Of his academic standing and standards, Lee proclaimed, "It is the *Substance,* not the *Show* I desire for him. If he cannot, or will not attain the former, I wish him to abandon the chase of the latter." In the same letter Lee stated, "It is time he began to think of something else besides running about amusing himself, & I wish him to do so at once." Later Lee announced, "He thinks entirely of his pleasures, & not of what is proper to be done. I fear he pursues the same course at College. . . ."

Yet Lee the father often softened his criticism and admitted that his son was "ready to acknowledge his fault & take the blame, & is frank & affectionate." And when Rooney wrote of his despair at performing so poorly and being so far removed from his family, his father responded, "If you could hear the beating of my heart for you, in the long wakeful hours of night; & feel the anxious throbbing of my brain for your future, during the busy hours of the day, you would find little cause to say that you had lost a 'devoted father.' . . ." To Rooney's mother, Lee wrote, "He gives me many anxious days & sleepless nights & adds more than years to the grey hairs in my head. Always affectionate & apparently disposed to do right, he is yet thoughtless, impulsive & is guided more by his feelings than his reason."

This was the same son who at age eight sliced off the ends of two fingers. At that time Lee wrote down phrases like "fruits of disobedience," "evil ways," and "ruined for life," but all the while he was writing doom, he was acting out love. He sat with the boy throughout long nights to tend the dressings on his injured fingers. Lee's deeds said more than his words.

Now Lee had harsh things to say about Rooney—"thinks entirely of his pleasures," "running about amusing himself," and more. But once more Lee's actions possessed significance beyond his words. For when he had written the words, Lee wrote checks to support his son at Harvard, to give Rooney freedom to decide for himself what to do with his life.[17]

Less than three weeks after Lee returned from his expedition against the Comanche band he never saw, a courier brought him orders to sit on a court-martial at Ringgold Barracks, on the Rio Grande near Rio Grande City, 730 miles from Camp Cooper, "almost the farthest point in the Dept. they could send me." "Truly," he wrote to Eliza Stiles, "there is no rest for the wicked."

The trial began at Ringgold Barracks, moved to Fort Brown (near Brownsville), and continued interminably for four and a half months. The substance of the case was inconsequential. Lee and the other members of the court consumed an enormous amount of time listening to lawyers wrangling and waiting for witnesses to appear. Finally on February 18, 1857, the court adjourned *sine die,* and Lee began his trek back to Camp Cooper.[18]

He got as far as San Antonio after a journey Lee calculated at 387 miles. There, on March 6, Lee received orders to sit on another court-martial, this time at Indianola on the Texas coast between Corpus Christi and Galveston. Lee rode in a stagecoach from San Antonio to Indianola, spent ten days there, and again boarded a stagecoach for San Antonio. Soon after he arrived at Camp Cooper, orders to sit on yet another court-martial followed him. This time Lee was president of the court and also "host"; the court met at Camp Cooper.[19]

From September 2, 1856, until May 5, 1857 (eight months), Lee underwent his own species of trial by court-martial. And during the two years since he left West Point, Lee had traveled an incredible amount. His itinerary for the past two years looked like this:

> West Point; Arlington; Louisville; St. Louis (Jefferson Barracks); Fort Leavenworth; Fort Riley; Fort Leavenworth; St. Louis (Jefferson Barracks); Arlington; White House; Romancock; White House; Richmond; Arlington; Baltimore; Arlington; Carlisle Barracks; Arlington; West Point; Arlington; White House; Hanover Court House; Richmond; San Antonio (via New Orleans, Galveston, and Indianola); Fort Mason; Camp Cooper; Wilderness (up the Brazos, Colorado, and Wichita in search of Comanche raiders); Ringgold Barracks; Fort Brown; San Antonio; Indianola; and Camp Cooper.

Mary Lee continued her decline in general health, and her rheumatism was fast rendering her an invalid. She went to mineral springs each summer; but any relief she experienced proved temporary. Robert Lee encouraged her to go and counseled her to "indulge yourself in as much mental enjoyment as circumstances will permit" and so "turn as far as possible your affliction to your benefit."

This latter phrase became a theme in Lee's life. To various people, at various times Lee said: " . . . there is nothing stable on earth," "Live in the world you inhabit," "When a thing *is done* we ought always make the best of it," "We make a great deal of our own happiness and misery in this world," and "turn . . . your affliction to your benefit." In time Lee would have increasing opportunities to take his own advice.[20]

Rooney Lee resolved his problems with higher education at Harvard during the summer of 1857. With ample assistance from his father's friendship with Winfield Scott, Rooney secured a direct commission as second lieutenant in the infantry and bade farewell to Cambridge. His father thanked Scott profusely, spoke of Rooney's "ardent desire for this high privilege," and repeated Scott's manly assertion that " 'boys are only fit to be shot.' "

To Mary Lee, Lee expressed the hope that Rooney would "no longer exclaim against his fate; but set himself to work diligently to prepare himself for his duties. . . ."[21] Lee did point out that Rooney's direct commission placed him ahead of those young men who had entered West Point the year Rooney tried and failed to gain admission. But he still fretted that two of his sons had chosen his profession. At the time, Custis was on duty in San Francisco, and from what Lee could learn, Rooney's regiment was destined for California as well. "We can scarce hope to see much of them in this world. Probably they and I will never meet again."[22]

Even as his oldest children began to leave home and make their own way in the world, Lee thought long and deeply about parenthood. Some of these thoughts he expressed to his wife, like these inspired by his experience at Fort Brown:

My little neighbors on either side of me are as regularly uproarius [sic], and their mothers, who seem to have entire charge of them, are as incompetent, or indifferent as ever, to their proper management. They are consequently miserable themselves, and annoying to others. I have seen so much bad home-training that I have become an advocate for infant schools where children can be gathered together under well trained instructors, and taught to practice politeness, gentleness, courtesy, and regard for the rights of others . . . the necessity and advantage of self-denial and self-control, can be forcibly exemplified and their exercise confirmed into habit. This exercise, this habit, is the true means of establishing a virtuous character, so far as it can be accomplished by human means.[23]

How did Lee propose to inculcate these happy habits in children? The answer appears in an essay he wrote in the rear of a diary he was then keeping. There Lee advocated teaching by example. He insisted that physical punishment and verbal abuse were counterproductive. Children, Lee believed, "should be governed by *love* not *fear*. . . . " "When love influences the parent," he wrote, "the child will be activated by the same spirit. . . . Dissimilar as are characters, intellects, and situations, the great duty of life is the same, the promotion of the happiness and welfare of our fellow men." This statement, of course, transcends child rearing.[24]

About the time Lee became accustomed to Rooney's new career, the young man (now twenty) made another major change in his life. He became engaged to marry Charlotte Wickham. It was Mary Lee who informed Lee (who had had no letter from Rooney in months), adding that the bride's grandfather had given his blessing, and that although "the affair had been going on for a long time," the couple planned to wait two or three years for the wedding.[25]

Lee was less than pleased. "Charlotte is a sweet amiable child," he replied, "but I fear is ill calculated in health or from education to follow the drum over our western prairies. I hope you have told her of the hardships of a soldiers life & the privations to which she will be exposed in a marching Regt." Lee likely worried that Charlotte (nicknamed "Chass") Wickham suffered from the tuberculosis which had killed both of her parents. He also worried about the maturity of the couple. "They are both mere children," he wrote Mary Lee, "each requires some staid person to take care of them."

Then Robert Lee told Mary Lee about the sort of woman he had in mind for Rooney:

There is a kind of widow here that I was going to recommend to Rooney. She seems to be a strong minded American woman with the benefit of Texas habits. I was invited to her house to a musical party, but declined. About a week afterwards, I thought it incumbent on me to return the compliment by a call. I found the house & made myself as agreeable as I could for about 5 minutes, when as I rose to depart, she took me out in her garden to see her corn & potatoes by *Starlight*. But she had waked up the wrong passenger. I told her I had no knowledge of horticulture, & took no interest in agriculture in Texas. I have not seen her since, but I think she has had some other musical parties. She has some sons & daughters. She would take care of a man finely. Those are the kind of women tell *Chass* a man wants in the army.

Eventually, almost two months after he learned of Charlotte and Rooney's intentions, Lee wrote to Chass and said all the proper words. He welcomed her into the family and promised to "guard and watch over you with the care of a father." In time Lee did indeed develop great affection for Charlotte and embraced her as a daughter. For this moment, though, Charlotte Wickham was one more worry in a series of concerns about a son who seemed estranged from the family and adrift in the larger world.[26]

When not focused upon the trials of his family, Lee thought about the tribulations of his country. He still read newspapers avidly and kept current in national politics. Certainly the year 1857 offered sufficient fuel for Lee's thoughts. Just north of him "Bleeding Kansas" continued to be a national wound, and sectional agitation seemed to permeate the American mind.

Lee the Whig nationalist no longer had a political party of national scope; but like others of his temper he clung to Whig principles and despaired of sectional divisions. To his brother-in-law Edward Childe, Lee proclaimed, "I know no other Country, no other Government, than the *United States* & their *Constitution.*" But of course Lee's use of the pronoun "their" implied his acceptance of at least some degree of state sovereignty and his rejection of the Union as a monolith.[27]

Villains in the sectional drama were, in Lee's eyes, "certain people of the North" who were committed to "interfere with & change the domestic institutions of the South." In other words the abolitionist attack on slavery was the fundamental cause of American malaise. "Their object is both unlawful & entirely foreign," and emancipation "can only be accomplished by *them* through the agency of a civil & servile war."

Lee's views on slavery continued to be enlightened within very severe limits, as he revealed in an important letter to Mary Lee written in late 1856:

In this enlightened age, there are few I believe, but what will acknowledge, that slavery as an institution, is a moral & political evil in any Country. It is useless to expatiate on its disadvantages. I think it however a greater evil to the white than to the black race, & while my feelings are strongly enlisted in behalf of the latter, my sympathies are more strong for the former. The blacks are immeasurably better off here than in Africa, morally, socially & physically. The painful discipline they are undergoing, is necessary for their instruction as a race, & I hope will prepare & lead them to better things. How long their subjugation may be necessary is known & ordered by a wise Merciful Providence. While we see the Course of the final abolition of human Slavery is onward, & we give it all the aid of our prayers & all justifiable means in our power, we must leave the progress as well as the result in his hands who sees the end; who Chooses to work by slow influences; & with whom two thousand years are but as a Single day.[28]

Lee himself continued to own slaves. As recently as August 1852 he had appointed an agent in Washington for the supervision of "my Servant man Philip Meriday." Crucial to his views was his perception of racial hierarchy. Africans and African Americans Lee considered below white people on his evolutionary scale—perhaps somewhere above Comanches, but beneath Mexicans.

In holding these beliefs Lee was much in step with most Americans, and his abhorrence of slavery in the abstract probably placed Lee among more enlightened Americans. But he did not accept any responsibility to act upon his belief that slavery was "a moral & political evil." To the contrary, he observed, "Is it not strange that the descendants of those pilgrim fathers who crossed the Atlantic to preserve their own freedom of opinion, have always proved themselves intolerant of the Spiritual liberty of others?"[29]

On October 21, 1857, major news from Arlington interrupted Lee's musings and his professional duties as well. He received a telegram announcing the death of his father-in-law. By this time Custis had been dead for eleven days; he contracted pneumonia, lingered for four days, and died as he had lived—with pomp and passivity.[30]

Lee realized that he would have to go to Arlington. He secured two months' leave, sold Mary the mare, and left San Antonio on October 24, arriving at Arlington at 1:00 P.M. on November 11. Lee also realized that he would soon have to decide whether to return to his military duties or resign his commission and take charge of the family estates in Virginia. To Albert Sidney Johnston he wrote of his necessity "to repair to Washington immediately." Then he added, "I can see that I have at last to decide the question, which I have staved off for 20 years. Whether I am to continue in the Army all my life, or to leave it. . . . My preferences which have clung to me from boyhood impell me to adopt the former course, but yet I feel that a mans family has its claims too."[31]

At this juncture Lee likely did not know the specific terms of his father-in-law's will. He did know that Mary Lee was an only child, and now both of her parents were dead. Arlington, White House, Romancock, and more lands totaling more over 5,000 acres plus at least 150 slaves would pass from Custis to his heir or heirs.

From his experience living at Arlington and his dealings with Nelson, who had mismanaged Custis's lands for so long, Lee was well aware that the estate was anything but a ripe pear. But whatever it was, it was most certainly in Lee's lap now.

14

"How Hard It Is to Get Contentment"

L ATER IN LIFE Robert Lee developed a litany which he repeated to many
people about "a small farm" earning his "daily bread" from the earth,
and leading a "tranquil" life. His son Rob remembered, "He often said
that he longed for the time when he could have a farm of his own,
where he could end his days in quiet and peace." When George Washington
Parke Custis died in 1857, Lee had a splendid opportunity to have all the land
he could want and to till the soil to his heart's content. "Quiet and peace" were
not as easily available.[1]

Custis had written his own will, presumably without consulting legal counsel, and he performed this task about as well as he did most things—not well at
all. He left his daughter Mary Lee a life estate in Arlington; at her death the
place would belong to Custis Lee, together with all the George Washington
silver, furnishings, and relics. Custis left White House to Rooney and Romancock to Rob. The Lee daughters (Mary, Anne, Agnes, and Mildred) were to
get $10,000 each from the sale of Smith Island and other properties, and
income from the operation of the farms remaining in the estate (Arlington,
White House, and Romancock). Once Custis's executor accomplished the
sales, collections, and distributions, the executor was to emancipate all the
Custis slaves. Whatever else happened, the emancipation had to occur within
five years of the date of Custis's death.

To his son-in-law, Custis left one lot in Square 21, Washington, D.C.
Custis also named Lee first among four executors, probably expecting him to
perform the chore. In fact Lee did fall heir to the task and worked at it for the
rest of his life.[2]

Most obvious among the difficulties associated with executing these bequests was the financial state of the estate. Custis died heavily in debt, and his
creditors inundated Lee with requests for payment; in March 1858, Lee estimated the debt at $10,000 and hoped that was all of it. The man who oper-
ated the mill at Arlington, for example, claimed wages for the last six years; but
when Lee attempted to rent the mill to obtain some cash, he found that it
needed repairs equal to two year's rent ($800). All of Custis's property, espe-

cially Arlington, was in sad condition and required money expended now in order to make money later. Smith Island and the other properties Custis wished sold would not begin to bring enough to pay the $40,000 in bequests to Lee's daughters. So someone was going to have to become a farmer, at least for a while, to generate the cash. Custis Lee continued on duty with the Army in California; Rooney had orders for the Utah expedition against the Mormons (an occupation ordered by President James Buchanan, who declared the Mormons in rebellion against the United States); and Rob who was now fourteen remained in school in Fauquier County, Virginia. So Colonel Lee became a farmer.[3]

Early in February 1858 he visited White House for the first time in two years. In his diary Lee noted, "buildings dilapidated, no funds, no corn," and then, "went to Romancoke—found things there were more dilapidated than at White House—nothing looking well." For the moment the only positive move Lee could make was to change the name "Romancock" to "Romancoke" to make the place sound better to genteel ears.[4]

It is difficult to know what legacy Custis intended for his son-in-law. He may have been intent upon preventing Lee from laying hands on any significant portion of his estate. Considerations of wealth, wills, and Lees may have awakened fears that Robert Lee might follow his father's example, squander the estate, and leave Mary Lee and the children destitute. Most likely Custis assumed that Lee wanted to continue his military career and use his wife's home as his base. Regardless of what Custis assumed or intended, the effect of his will was to throw Lee a token bequest and to burden him with unfulfillable obligations for the rest of his life. In response to his father's profligacy, Lee had saved rigorously, invested wisely, and accumulated substantial net worth. Lee's reward for this prudence was more debt than he had ever imagined at the behest of his father-in-law.

Son Custis in California, however, attempted to change the distribution of property in his father's favor. Custis executed a deed which transferred his title to Arlington to his father and mailed the document to Arlington in February 1858. Lee demurred. He thanked Custis profusely, but insisted that "it would not be right" to rearrange the way in which Custis had elected to bestow his property.[5]

Still, Custis's will might have made Lee a member of the landed gentry in Virginia and a rich man, too. Had he so chosen, Lee could have taken control of all the land in the estate—certainly until Rooney decided what he wanted to do with White House and Rob was old enough to take charge of Romancoke. Then Lee could still have managed Arlington for Mary Lee during her life and perhaps might have acquired more land and wealth in the process. That would surely have been Light Horse Harry Lee's plan. But that was the very reason Robert Lee could not pursue such a course.

Lee chose not to become a planter and instead to remain in the Army. "I am no farmer myself & do not expect to be always here," he wrote to someone who was helping him find an overseer.

"Dear Cousin Anna what am I to do," he asked Anna Fitzhugh soon after he had surveyed the situation. "Custis I fear could not support his Grd fathers name & place as he desired. Everything is in ruins & will have to be rebuilt. I feel more familiar with the military operations of a campaign than the details of a farm."

Compounding Lee's problems with the estate was his wife's failing health. During the year and nine months Robert Lee had been in Texas, Mary Lee had become quite crippled with arthritis. Lee confided to his aunt, "I fear Mary will never be well enough to accompany me in my wandering life. . . ."

For the moment, though, Lee's wandering would be limited. He secured an extension of leave to December 1858. He speculated about freeing the Custis slaves—when and how should he make the emancipation? Then he began playing the role of slaveholder and planter.[6]

One way or another the Arlington slaves learned that Custis had freed them in his will. They were surprised to learn from Lee that their freedom depended upon his capacity to fulfill other bequests in the will. They became much less willing workers, even as Lee was trying to make Arlington productive and profitable.

One way to respond to unservile slaves was to sell or rent them. In January 1858, the traditional time for hiring, Lee managed to "hire out" (rent) six men and five women. Rent for their labor promised more cash for the estate, which Lee badly needed. But three of the men, Lee reported, "returned the first day on account of the work being too hard. Among them is Reuben, a great rogue & rascal whom I must get rid of some way."

Mary Lee was more candid in her analysis of the circumstances at Arlington. She wrote to an acquaintance, "Scarcely had my father been laid in his tomb when two men were constantly lurking about here tampering with the servants & telling them they had a right to their freedom *immediately* & that if they would unite & *demand* it they would obtain it. The merciful hand of a kind providence & their own inertness I suppose prevented an outbreak." She then wrote of "a host of idle & thankless dependents," and asserted, "We should be most deeply indebted to their *kind friends* the Abolitionists if they would come forward & purchase their time & let them enjoy the comforts of freedom *at once.*"[7]

In May 1858 Robert Lee wrote to Rooney and admitted, "I have had some trouble with some of the people. Reuben, Parks, Edward . . . rebelled against my authority—refused to obey my orders, & said they were as free as I was etc. etc. I succeeded in capturing them however, tied them & lodged them in jail. They resisted till overpowered & called upon the other people to rescue them."

Soon after this incident Lee informed William O. Winston, who had helped him settle Francis Nelson's accounts for Custis at White House and Romancock, that he was sending three male slaves to Richmond under guard. Winston was to rent them if possible to someone in the city. If Winston could find no one to take the men, he was to hire them out on some farm or send them to work at White House. Quite likely the three men were Reuben, Parks, and Edward.

Lee the novice planter continued to have troubles with his slaves. The following summer (1859) at least two Arlington slaves attempted to flee to freedom in Pennsylvania. Captured in Maryland, the runaways returned under guard to Arlington, and from there Lee sent them elsewhere.[8]

Fugitive slaves, Arlington, and the Custis connection with George Washington attracted attention. On June 24, 1859, Horace Greeley's *New York Tribune* printed two anonymous letters written from Washington about Arlington slaves and slaveholder Lee.

One correspondent identified as "A." suggested that the five-year time limit was an invention of Custis's heirs and alleged that slaves at Arlington had been deprived of their customary opportunities to earn money for themselves, had had to exist on a half-peck of unsifted meal per week, and had "been kept harder at work than ever." When two men and a *woman* ran away, "A." claimed that Lee ordered the captured fugitive males given thirty-nine lashes and himself administered thirty-nine lashes to the woman's bare back. The second letter, written by "A Citizen," charged that Custis was the father of fifteen of his slaves and then repeated the story of Lee's punishment of the recaptured runaways.[9]

Lee read the letters, said of his father-in-law Custis, "He has left me an unpleasant legacy," and said to his son Custis, " . . . I shall not reply." But someone did respond to the letters in the *Tribune,* termed them a "malicious attack," and suspected "A." and "A Citizen" to have been two of those "meddling scoundrels who immediately after Mr. Custis's death went over from Washington City and tried to induce the negroes upon the Arlington estate to run away." The writer railed at the "concealed assassins of character" who had written the anonymous letters, and signed the rejoinder "JUSTICE."[10]

However much Lee disliked slavery in the abstract and found his experience as a slaveholder distasteful, he accepted the peculiar institution as a source of labor and a means of racial subordination. While Rooney was trying to decide what to do about his military career, his engagement to Charlotte Wickham, and his inheritance at White House, Lee informed his son that his future in-laws had promised to "supply you with hands" when the slaves on his farm became free. When Rooney did begin farming at White House and became an active slaveholder, Lee had advice for him about "his people." He wrote, "attend to them & give them every aid & comfort in your power & they will be the happier." After lamenting a fire at a neighbor's place, Lee counseled, "I trust you will so gain the affection of your people, that they will not wish to do you any harm."[11]

Lee professed himself eager to set free the Custis slaves; however, he realized that to accomplish all the bequests and conditions of the will, he would need an authoritative determination of the priorities he should assign to each. Therefore he asked the Circuit Court for interpretation and guidance and asked the Army to extend his leave. Winfield Scott extended Lee's leave until May 1859 and then again until October 1859.[12]

Early in 1859 Rooney finally decided to resign his commission, marry Charlotte Wickham, and move to White House. The wedding took place on the evening of March 23 at Shirley, where Rooney's paternal grandparents had married in 1793. Mary Lee was physically unable to make the trip from Arlington. Robert Lee, however, was delighted to escort two of his daughters and two other young women to Richmond, where Rooney, brother Carter Lee, various Wickhams, and a Carter joined the party for the short trip to Shirley.

Relatives, friends, and neighbors filled the house, and the wedding was prelude to an extended, happy houseparty. One local guest called Robert Lee "decidedly the most striking person in the room." At fifty-two he still sparkled in social settings and outshone men and women half his age. Lee remained three days among the merrymakers and then resumed his role of caretaker on three estates.[13]

Quick to learn the pessimism of farmers regarding the weather and crops, Lee termed his wheat harvest at White House in 1859 a "great failure—much straw but little grain." He told Rooney, "A farmer's work is never done," began to give him advice about plowing, and in fact offered all his sons counsel about agriculture for the rest of his life.

By fall 1859 Lee could see a logical conclusion to his labors in Virginia. He had paid all the debts of the estate except those owed to him, and he had the three farms in reasonably good operating condition. Rooney moved himself and Chass to White House, from which he could supervise Romancoke as well. Lee used his influence to get Custis assigned to the Engineer Corps office at the War Department so Custis could live at Arlington, care for his mother and the farm, and commute to Washington as necessary. At this point all the Lees worked for the Custis estate and channeled any profits from farming into the legacy fund for the Lee daughters. Once that fund reached $40,000, Lee could make the distributions the will mandated and emancipate the Custis slaves. In the event five years passed without collecting sufficient funds for his daughters' bequests, Lee would have to emancipate the slaves; but October 10, 1862, seemed a time far off to all concerned.[14]

On the morning of October 17, 1859, Lee was working away at Arlington and preparing to return to Texas when a rider approached the house. First Lieutenant James Ewell Brown (J.E.B.) Stuart came with a message from the War Department: Colonel Lee was to report at once.

Stuart had happened to be in the War Office attempting to sell an invention (a device to assist cavalrymen to mount and dismount their horses while wearing a saber) when he heard rumors of trouble at Harpers Ferry. A mob estimated at up to 3,000 people had seized the United States arsenal and armory located there, and many in the mob were black. If rumors proved true, a slave revolt was in progress. Stuart followed the stories to the office of Secretary of War John B. Floyd and included himself in discussions of what to do about the disturbance. When Floyd determined to send for Lee, Stuart volunteered to carry the summons.

Friend and classmate of Custis Lee at West Point, Stuart was no stranger to Lee homes. He had attended those Saturday suppers at the Superintendent's quarters, and he had ingratiated himself with the entire family. He was a bundle of energy whose love for show and carefree manner sometimes obscured his capacity as an intensely professional soldier. Stuart was twenty-six years old; already he was a mature cavalry officer. Now he told Lee what he knew about Harpers Ferry and speculated about courses of action. Lee left Arlington with Stuart at once; he did not even take the time to change from his civilian clothes.

They went to the War Office and from there to see President James Buchanan. From these visits a plan emerged. The government would dispatch troops to Harpers Ferry; Lee would lead them; and the expedition would leave as soon as possible.

The troops available were one company of marines from the Washington Navy Yard and four companies of Maryland Militia. Lee was to meet the marines at Relay House, about eight miles from Baltimore, and advance to Harpers Ferry by railroad. Stuart again volunteered, this time to serve as Lee's aide. Lee accepted, and Stuart managed to secure a uniform coat and sword. Lee remained in the civilian clothes in which he had left Arlington.

The two officers arrived at Relay House too late for their rendezvous with the marines, who had already departed. So Lee sent instructions by telegraph for the troops to wait for him a mile outside of the town, and he and Stuart boarded a locomotive to follow the advance to Harpers Ferry. They rode the Baltimore & Ohio line back through Baltimore and then west, eventually up the north bank of the Potomac River to the confluence of the Potomac and Shenandoah Rivers, a journey of about 84 miles. Harpers Ferry occupies a wedge of land south of the Potomac, west of the Shenandoah.[15]

About 10:00 P.M. on October 17, Lee joined his followers and began to learn something reliable about the situation. The previous night approximately eighteen men—some black, most white—had taken hostages and seized the arsenal and armory. On the morning of the 17th, local citizens responded to alarms and began a pitched battle with the intruders. As the day wore on, some of the raiders fled, and some died in the increasingly uneven battle with townspeople and mustered militia units. By the time Lee arrived, only a few of the insurgents remained alive in Harpers Ferry, barricaded into a firehouse located on the armory grounds, surrounded by militia troops and citizens. No one knew how many raiders or hostages were inside the engine house. Indeed, no one seemed to care very much, now that the insurgents were at bay. The assault on Harpers Ferry had become a circus. Local folk were firing random rounds at the makeshift fort and into the bodies of the raiders killed earlier. Rumor had it that the leader of the attack upon the town was an old man named Smith.

Lee listened to these imprecise stories and then took charge of the situation. He ordered Lieutenant Israel Green, who commanded the marines, to march his men into Harpers Ferry and to surround the firehouse, a small building perhaps thirty by thirty-five feet with two sets of heavy double doors. Then Lee instructed the militia companies and private citizens to leave the immediate area. He stationed Virginia and Maryland Militia troops around the armory grounds so that those inside the engine house could see that they had no chance to escape.

Having secured the area, Lee then confronted the problem of how to subdue the remaining insurgents with the least risk to their captives. He wanted to act as soon as possible, but decided to wait until daylight to decrease the chances of harming the hostages. By 2:00 A.M. on the 18th Lee had formulated a plan. He wrote a note addressed to "the persons in the armory buildings," assuring them that they could not escape and demanding immediate surrender. If "the persons" resisted and he had to assault the engine house, Lee warned that he could not "answer for their safety." He gave the note to Stuart and asked him to deliver it to the people in the engine house under a flag of truce when Lee gave the word. Lee told Stuart to discuss no terms except surrender and in the event of impasse to signal the storming party, which would be ready to rush the building.[16]

Lee did not believe the insurgents would comply with his demand. So he prepared to enforce his ultimatum. He called together the commanders of the Virginia and Maryland Militia forces and Green of the marines and asked them for a storming party. The militia officers declined the honor, explaining that their men were citizen-soldiers; they deferred to the professionals for this task. Lee then requested Green to undertake the mission of "taking those men out." Green said he would be honored to do so and selected two teams of twelve men each from his command.

Green and Stuart established a signal between them which Stuart would give in the likely event the insurgents refused to surrender. Then Green instructed his two storming parties in accord with Lee's instructions. He armed the men with sledgehammers, forbade them to load their weapons, but ordered bayonets fixed. Lee wanted no shooting for fear of harming the hostages.

At seven o'clock in the morning the drama began. Lee, still in civilian clothes, stood on a small rise only forty feet in front of the firehouse. Green and the marines stood nearby, and Stuart was ready with Lee's note and his white flag. Crowded into a very confined area behind Lee and in front of the engine house were militia troops and civilians estimated at 2,000 people.

Stuart waved his white flag and strode to one of the doors of the engine house. He watched the door open slightly and then stared into the muzzle of a cocked cavalry carbine. Characteristically undaunted, Stuart read out Lee's note and looked past the carbine barrel into the face that peered from the gloom of the engine house: wrinkles, a haunted expression, and those piercing coals in his eye sockets. "Mr. Smith" was John Brown. Stuart had encountered the old abolitionist in Kansas, and he recognized the memorable face immediately.

As Lee had predicted, Brown immediately attempted to use the captives to secure their freedom. And some of hostages added their voices to Brown's appeals for softer terms. Then a loud voice from the engine house called out,

"Never mind us, fire!" Lee recognized the speaker as Lewis W. Washington, a cousin of George Washington. "The old revolutionary blood does tell," Lee stated, more to himself than to anyone else. After more wrangling and proposed deals, Stuart became convinced that Brown and his followers were not going to surrender. So he stepped back quickly and waved his hat at Green. And Green launched his attack.

Marines rushed to the doors of the engine house and pounded them with their sledgehammers. Trapped raiders fired shots through the doors at the sounds of the pounding. But neither the sledgehammer blows nor the shots had much effect. Green's attack had stalled very soon after it began.

In desperation, Green shouted to his reserve group of twelve marines to pick up a wooden ladder lying nearby and use it as a battering ram. The men hurried to comply and launched themselves and the ladder at one of the doors. The first blow had no effect, and the troopers retreated for another try. This time the ladder splintered boards and punched a small hole in one of the doors on the right side near the ground.

Inside the engine house Brown fired his carbine at the opening. As soon as his men extracted the ladder, Green slipped through the hole. Other marines followed as rapidly as they were able; in the process two of the men suffered gunshot wounds, one of them mortal. Green was adjusting his eyes to the smoky gloom inside the engine house when the hostage Washington pointed out Brown, who was attempting to reload his weapon. The lieutenant had only his dress sword with him; he swung the blade at Brown's head and inflicted a gash in his neck. Then Green tried to run Brown through; but he struck something hard, likely Brown's belt buckle, and the sword bent nearly double without doing any damage. Finally Green pummeled Brown's head with the hilt of his sword until Brown collapsed into unconsciousness.

By this time Green's men had killed two of the insurgents with bayonets and captured two others. Those at the scene stated that the action lasted only three minutes from the time that Stuart waved his hat. Brown had held thirteen hostages inside the engine house. They were very dirty and weak from hunger. But not one of them was hurt in the assault.[17]

John Brown's raid on Harpers Ferry was barely over before the posturing began. Virginia Governor Henry A. Wise hastened to Harpers Ferry and sent a telegram before him ordering Lee to "grant no terms." Wise questioned Brown himself and insisted that he be tried in a Virginia court for treason against the state, murder, and inciting a slave insurrection.[18]

Brown, when he recovered consciousness, donned a cloak of martyrdom and finally protested, *"Let them hang me. . . .* I am worth inconceivably more to *hang* than for any other purpose."[19]

Eventually, on December 2, 1859, Brown did hang for his crimes. Edmund Ruffin, the aging secessionist crusader, spent fourteen hours on a train and rendered himself by his own admission "ludicrous" by weedling his way into the Virginia Military Institute Cadet Corps to gain a good view of Brown's execution. In his own way, Ruffin was every bit as much a zealot as was Brown.[20]

But Brown's soul would continue to march in the American consciousness. He had compelled his countrymen to confront slavery as an immediate, moral issue. Some people denounced Brown's means but applauded his goal; others became convinced that all those who opposed slavery shared Brown's thirst for blood in order to accomplish abolition. Brown and the incident at Harpers Ferry demonstrated the pent-up power of ideology in both North and South.

Lee wrote in his report of events at Harpers Ferry that the raid "was the attempt of a fanatic or madman. . . ." Because Lee was neither fanatic nor mad, he little understood those qualities in other people. In this instance he underestimated the emotional repercussions of an irrational act, and the rapid escalation of sectional tensions came as a surprise to him. Yet the focus upon Brown and the role of his raid in rousing sectional passions too often obscures Lee's part in the crisis. In the midst of confusion and frenzy, Lee was able to impose control. He took charge of a very serious situation in which desperate men held hostages in a small space from which escape was impossible. He acted carefully and decisively at once, capturing John Brown and rescuing his hostages unharmed. Lee's actions attest the strength of his will and his capacity for leadership.[21]

On November 29, 1859, Lee returned to Harpers Ferry with Federal troops to foil any of the rumored attempts to rescue Brown before his execution. No such attempt materialized, so Lee and the troops remained idle in Harpers Ferry while the hanging took place near Charlestown. In January 1860, Lee testified before a congressional committee investigating the raid but only had to answer a few questions about his list of Brown's followers.

He anticipated orders to return to Texas, indeed had expected them since October of 1859. Finally, on February 9, 1860, the Army ordered Lee to San Antonio to command the military Department of Texas. So once more he left his family to pursue his duty.[22]

Lee had worked hard at making the three family plantations productive during the two years he had been a planter. But he did not seem to be as effective as a slaveholder as he was a farmer. Maybe the Custis slaves were as lazy and undisciplined as Mary Lee insisted they were. Whatever the cause, Lee had trouble making them work. Slaves did not respond to regulations and orders like soldiers, and Lee could not try them by court-martial. At base slavery was a simple, stark relationship between people, grounded in power and dependence. Within this relationship the ultimate appeal was neither to law nor custom nor even justice; the ultimate appeal was to force—physical violence enacted as punishment. Since he disapproved of slavery in general, Lee likely lacked the stomach to resort to torture.

Lee also disliked confrontation in human relationships. He could rise to crisis and embrace combat, but in his day-to-day life Lee tended to avoid conflict and sometimes went to great lengths to do so. Because some of the Custis slaves felt betrayed by their dead master's heirs and executor, they were less than servile. Lee never really confronted the circumstance, maybe because he understood the resentment of people told they would be free who were still chattels. He dealt with assertive slaves by not dealing with them; he got rid of them, rented them elsewhere. He also hired overseers to interact directly with "the people," as he called them, committed to his charge.

Two years as a major slaveholder soured Lee on the system, and like other Southerners, he tended to blame the victims. Ten years later, when African Americans were free, Lee counseled his son Rob, "You will never prosper with the blacks, and it is abhorrent to a reflecting mind to be supporting and cherishing those who are plotting and working for your injury. . . ." Times had changed significantly when Lee wrote this bitter judgment. But "reflecting" minds before emancipation perceived inherent conflict between slaveholders and slaves, as well as later between former slaveholders and freedmen.[23]

In San Antonio, Lee could advise at long range and leave the immediate tasks of planting and slaveholding to sons and overseers. He must have preferred this arrangement because he chose it, rather than resign from the Army and remain in Virginia.

In San Antonio, Lee did not have to confront his wife and children except in letters. He may have preferred this arrangement, too. In August 1860, Lee wrote to his daughter Annie, now twenty-one:

God knows how often I think of you and long to see you. If you wish to see me you will have to come out here, for I do not know when I will be able to go in there. It is better too I hope for all that I am here. You know I was very much in the way of everybody and my tastes and pursuits did not coincide with the rest of the household. Now I hope everybody is happier.

These were devastating pronouncements. Especially were they devastating for Lee the father and would-be scion of an increasing tribe. Chass and Rooney produced Lee's first grandchild in March 1860 and named their son after Lee. The child did not survive youth, however.[24]

In Texas, Lee tended the administration and deployment of too few troops against too many Comanches, Kiowas, and Mexican bandits. He stabilized the situation regarding Comanches and Kiowas as best he could and then led an expedition against the bandit Juan Cortinas. With a company of cavalry Lee rode to the Rio Grande in search of Cortinas and his band. Cortinas disappeared into northern Mexico, and Lee had to satisfy himself with patrolling the border and writing threatening letters to Mexican officials. He spent two months (March 15 to May 17, 1860), considerable energy, and reaped little more than frustration. He summarized his campaign for Rooney upon his return to San Antonio: "I could not catch Cortinas, which I very much regret, but drove him to the mts. & dispersed his party. I also gave the Mexican authorities to understand that if they permitted him to molest our frontier again, I should cross the river in force & they must take the consequences." At San Antonio, Lee found two months of correspondence and Army paper to consume his time. He wrote for two complete days, then reported, "It will take me some days yet to despatch them."[25]

During this sojourn in Texas, Lee did not enjoy his usual robust health. He had a cold in April and wrote to his wife of his ailment, "I still feel its rheumatic effects & that in my right arm seems stationary. It is not very bad, yet enough to add to my complaining mood & make me less satisfied with myself. How hard it is to get contentment. . . ." To confirm his mood, Lee wrote of the residents of Brownsville, "They have made their calls & I have returned them. So we are mutually satisfied. . . . You know too I am a great advocate of people staying at home & minding their own affairs, & am indisposed to trouble strangers." Lee was still gregarious; but he was also still shy with people he did not know well, and he did not suffer fools gladly at all.

Lee complained of the fleas and mosquitoes, concerned especially that "I am so extremely awkward in catching them, that they mock my efforts."

"Rheumatism" was still making him uncomfortable two months later. Pain troubled him particularly in his right arm, which "makes it more objectionable for a soldier." But such pain may also have had cardiovascular origins. In July he was sick again; fever confined him to his room. By then it was so hot that Lee was amazed "a man has energy to be sick."

Because Lee considered his assignment in San Antonio temporary, he did not hire a cook and establish a household. He ate in a boardinghouse and had to "suffer all the annoyances that a person of my unfortunate temperament must undergo in such an establishment in such a Country & such a population." He complained, "I am far from comfortable in my present situation."[26]

Lee shared an uncharacteristic amount of gloom with his family while in Texas this time. But characteristic whimsy enlivened his letters even as he complained. To Agnes, he reported 100° heat for three weeks in San Antonio and 108° for two hours on June 6.

Still the young women find it favourable for matrimony. They select the cool hours for the occasion & one some short time since took the quiet season of 1 a.m., repaired to the church, woke up the priest & enjoyed I hope a long day of happiness. A young widow a few days since, wishing to follow in the footsteps of her prudent predecessor, but being unable to sit up quite so late, appointed 10: P.M. for the happy period which the good priest thought more reasonable, & then went home in the moonlight with her new husband. We live in a fast age & all seasons must be improved.[27]

All the while Lee was sweltering in San Antonio, back "in the states" (as Lee referred to the rest of the country) the campaign for President accelerated. This was not politics as usual. Parties and candidates committed to sectional interests seemed ascendent, and in the fall, of course, Abraham Lincoln carried every Northern state and won the presidency. Southerners threatened secession; indeed, South Carolinians had called a convention which well might unratify the United States Constitution and declare the state an independent republic.

Lee was a long way away from the action, and his newspapers reached him two weeks after their publication. Moreover, in December 1860 he received orders to relinquish command of the Department of Texas and return to his regiment. This meant he would likely be even further removed from news about the fate of the country.

"Things look very alarming from this point of view," he wrote Rooney in early December. "As an American citizen," he continued, "I prize the Union very highly & know of no personal sacrifice that I would not make to preserve it, save that of honour." He wrote precisely the same words on January 16, 1861, to Annette Carter, one of his special young female friends, the daughter of his first cousin Charles Henry Carter. And he repeated his no-sacrifice-save-honor line to Markie Williams on January 22, 1861.

Lee changed his wording in these letters as well. To Annette Carter, he said, "If the Union is dissolved, I shall return to Virginia & share the fortune of my people." To Markie Williams, Lee amended "share the fortune" to read "share the misery of my native state," and added, "save in her defense there will be one soldier less in the world than now."[28]

By this time Lee had moved to Fort Mason and assumed active command of the Second Cavalry. However, military administration had broken down and the troopers had missed paydays. Lee summed up the situation succinctly, "No pay No money & waiting upon the turn of events." To Mary Lee, he wrote blaming the secession crisis on democracy:

As far as I can judge from the papers we are between a State of anarchy & Civil war. . . . It has been evident for years that the country was doomed to run the full length of democracy. To what a fearful pass it has brought us. I fear mankind for years will not be sufficiently christianized to bear the absence of restraint & force.

Lee also wrote the same day, "The South, in my opinion, has been aggrieved by the acts of the North. . . . I feel the aggression, and am willing to take every proper step for redress." Then, after repeating his "sacrifice everything but honour" phrase one more time, he pronounced: "Secession is nothing but revolution." Later in this letter he added, "Still, a Union that can only be maintained by swords and bayonets, and in which strife and civil war are to take the place of brotherly love and kindness, has no charm for me."[29]

Very soon after Lee wrote out these views of the secession situation, a convention of elected Texans on February 1, 1861, dissolved the link with the United States and for the second time in twenty-five years proclaimed Texas an independent republic. And on February 4, a convention of delegates from six of seven seceded states (South Carolina, Mississippi, Alabama, Georgia, Louisiana, and Florida) met in Montgomery, Alabama, to form a Southern republic. Within five days the delegates had written a provisional constitution, elected a provisional president and vice president, and resolved themselves into a provisional Congress. The Confederate States of America was decidedly de facto.

As the crisis became critical, Lee received orders to leave his post and report in person to Winfield Scott in Washington. He packed his belongings, said his goodbyes, and left Fort Mason on February 13. His first stop was San Antonio on February 16. There he learned that his superior David Twiggs had given the military property for which he was responsible to Texas Militia and had left town. Texas Rangers controlled San Antonio when Lee arrived at two o'clock on the afternoon of February 16. "Has it come so soon to this," Lee said when he learned the circumstances.

After he registered at the Road House Hotel, Lee changed into civilian clothes and went to his former headquarters, perhaps to find out his status as an officer of the United States attempting to travel in the Republic of Texas. He remained in San Antonio for several days and encountered no difficulty in leaving to resume his journey to Washington. While in San Antonio Lee told one friend, "I shall resign and go to planting corn," and said to another, "If Virginia stands by the old Union, so will I. But if she secedes (though I do not believe in secession as a constitutional right, nor that there is a sufficient cause for revolution), then I will follow my native State with my sword, and, if need be, with my life." Clearly Lee seems to have had few doubts about his ultimate allegiance at this juncture.[30]

On March 1, Lee arrived at Arlington in time for dinner. Within a week or so, he reported to Scott, and the two Virginians closeted themselves in Scott's office for three hours. No one knows precisely what they discussed. Scott surely informed Lee that he would very soon have the permanent rank of colonel and command of the First Cavalry regiment. But he did not have to summon Lee from Texas to tell him he was to be promoted. So they probably spoke of secession and prospects for war, and Lee probably expressed ambivalence about the situation but also conviction in his intention to follow the course Virginia chose.[31]

Meanwhile on March 4 Abraham Lincoln became President of the United States; a convention continued to meet in Richmond and debate the fate of Virginia; and Confederate President Jefferson Davis continued to construct his government and act as though his new nation were an accomplished fact. Lee read about these events in newspapers, but otherwise took no part in the unfolding drama. He did accept his promotion to colonel in the United States Army, and he seems to have ignored the offer of a commission as brigadier general in the Confederate army made by Southern Secretary of War Leroy Pope Walker.[32]

In mid-April the sectional impasse broke in a hurry. Lincoln had always insisted upon retaining government property in the South, because he insisted that secession was illegal and thus had not happened. On April 8, Lincoln decided to dispatch supplies to Fort Sumter, the installation in Charleston Harbor still tenuously occupied by United States troops. And on April 12, in accord with orders from Davis in Montgomery, P. G. T. Beauregard opened fire on the fort to compel its surrender. The Sumter garrison surrendered on April 14, and next day Lincoln called for 75,000 volunteers to quell rebellion. Davis called for 100,000 volunteers to defend his nation from impending invasion.

On April 17, Lee received two invitations. Scott wished to see him on the 18th, and so did Francis P. Blair, Sr. Blair was the scion of an influential political family, a close friend of the President, and father of Lincoln's Postmaster General. Whatever Blair said, Lincoln was prepared to do. And what

Blair did was offer Lee command of the army formed in response to Lincoln's call to arms. Here was an opportunity for greatness, glory for the taking—and Lee declined. Blair persisted; Lee stood firm; and the meeting was over. Lee then called upon Scott and discussed the same topic. Still Lee the Virginian insisted that he could not wage a war against his own people. Obviously Scott the Virginian could at least plan such a campaign, even if he were no longer up to the rigors of command in the field. Yet Scott probably understood Lee's feelings, though he did not share them, and the meeting concluded amicably.

On the day Lee received his communications from Blair and Scott (April 17), the Virginia convention became a secession convention. Hitherto moderate delegates pounced upon Lincoln's resort to "coercion" in the wake of Fort Sumter's fall and stampeded out of the Union. When Lee made his calls on the 18th, he did not know what had happened in Richmond. He read the news on the morning of April 19, most probably in Alexandria, and the report was confirmed that evening in at least one other newspaper.[33]

It must have been agonizing for Lee that night at Arlington thinking of what he must do. He was leaving the army he had served for nearly thirty-two years; moreover, Lee was leaving the United States, the legacy of his father and that pantheon of heroes in his father's generation. He believed he had no other option.

Shortly after midnight Lee made his move. He wrote a letter to his mentor Scott, thanking him sincerely and informing him of the decision to resign his commission at once, adding, "I shall carry to the grave the most grateful recollections of your kind consideration, and your name and fame will always be dear to me." Lee wrote another letter, one sentence, to Secretary of War Simon Cameron: "I have the honor to tender the resignation of my commission as Colonel of the 1st Regt. of Cavalry."

Then he went downstairs to join Mary Lee. "Well, Mary," he said, "the question is settled. Here is my letter of resignation and a letter I have written General Scott."

Some time that same day Lee wrote to his sister Ann Marshall in Baltimore and to his brother Smith in Washington to inform them of his course. Lee knew that his sister adhered to the Union, and thus he explained, "With all my devotion to the Union, and the feeling of loyalty and duty of an American citizen, I have not been able to make up my mind to raise my hand against my relatives, my children, my home." Smith needed to know the reason he had resigned at this time, the importance of resigning while not under orders. To quit in the face of a mission, Lee and others considered less than honorable.[34]

Also on April 20 Lee received a message from Judge John Robertson of Richmond, who wished to meet with him. Robertson was close to Virginia Governor John Letcher; Lee offered to meet him at 1:00 P.M. the following day in Alexandria.

April 21 was a Sunday. Lee and one of his daughters attended Christ Church in Alexandria, and then he waited for Robertson. The meeting miscarried; but that evening Robertson sent a letter to Lee at Arlington by messenger. Robertson spoke for Governor Letcher; the governor wanted Lee to come to Richmond the next day (April 22). Lee agreed to go and then spent the last night he ever would spend at Arlington.

On Monday morning, April 22, Lee boarded a train in Alexandria and rode to Richmond with Judge Robertson. When they reached the capital city, Lee went first to the Spotswood Hotel, secured a room, and soon thereafter went to Capitol Square to see the governor.

Letcher was very direct. He asked Lee to accept command of "the military and naval forces of Virginia" and the rank of major general. Lee accepted. In a short period of time Robert Lee resigned from the United States Army and very soon afterward joined another army committed to conflict against the United States.

Then and since many people have analyzed Lee's decisions. To a large extent his motives were exactly what he said they were. He believed the North had abused the South. He said that he still hoped for harmony and that he did not believe secession to be constitutional; but his version of harmony depended upon conciliation by the North, and the constitutionality of secession mattered little after Virginia made secession a fact.[35]

At base Lee was more Southern than he was American, at least in terms of the way the majority of Americans defined "American" in 1861. He believed in social hierarchy, however much he tempered his belief with generosity and *noblesse oblige.* He was a politically conservative neo-Federalist Whig who did not believe the world was ready for democracy. He believed slavery was evil; but he owned slaves and resented criticism of the South's peculiar institution. He may not have believed in state sovereignty; but he did believe that Southern rights were in peril. Lee would likely have asserted that he and other Southerners remained the "real" Americans; the North had departed from traditional American values and the faith of the Founding Fathers. Certainly Lee shared these and more characteristic feelings and beliefs with other Southerners.

During his journey toward disunion, Lee insisted that he was prepared to sacrifice anything to preserve the Union—except honor. Honor forbade Lee from deserting his family, friends, and community. Loyalty sprang from blood and bonds; in such a context the Union was a mere abstraction. " . . . I have not been able to make up my mind to raise my hand against my relatives, my children, my home." Lee believed what he wrote to his sister, and he acted upon his conviction.[36]

At several important junctures in his life Lee had taken action to avoid confrontation and conflict. In a curious way this was another such instance. When Mary Lee and her mother left Fort Monroe to go visiting in 1833, Lee proclaimed himself "happy as a clam in high water." In 1837, Lee fled his in-laws, bureaucratic pettiness, and small children to go to work in St. Louis. When Custis slaves were recalcitrant, Lee got rid of them—hired them out elsewhere. He returned to Texas in 1860 and observed that he had been "very much in the way of everybody" at Arlington and that his "tastes and pursuits did not coincide with the rest of the household." He hoped, now that he had departed, that "everybody is happier." In these and other circumstances Lee had escaped unpleasantness when he could.

Had Lee chosen to remain in the United States Army or had he resigned and only raised corn while other men fought and died, he would have elected infamy. He would have had to spend the rest of his life explaining his actions to deaf ears. And not the least of a legion of accusers would have been his own wife, who became a fiercely partisan Confederate. Robert Lee would have been most in danger in his own bed. In a real sense, Lee went to war in order to avoid conflict.

He said he only wanted some land to farm in peace and quiet. But he rejected ample acres in the Custis estate and remained a soldier. Now for the sake of personal peace and domestic quiet, Lee would leave home to do battle.

15

"Can Anybody Say They Know His Brother?"

"INVITATION," said the five men who came to call; but the occasion was very much a command performance. The five were a committee of delegates from the convention which had voted Virginia out of the United States on April 17 and continued to sit and act like conservative radicals. They came to Robert E. Lee's new office in the Virginia Mechanics Institute at Nineth and Franklin Streets to invite and escort the man they had made a major general and given command of Virginia armed forces to the Virginia capitol to appear before the convention.

Lee genuinely disliked crowds and public occasions; he avoided both whenever he could. On the evening he arrived in Richmond and accepted this command, a large crowd of local citizens gathered before the Spotswood House to cheer him. In place of Lee, the crowd got Richmond Mayor Joseph Mayo, who explained that Lee appreciated the display of support but had too much work to do to make an appearance. Lee had even more work to do now; yet he realized that an appearance before the convention was part of his work, and so he aquiesced with as much grace as he could muster.[1]

Speaking for the committee was Marmaduke Johnson, whom Richmond voters had elected to the convention as a staunch unionist. The stridently secessionist Richmond *Examiner* had characterized Johnson as "the sleek fat pony from Richmond, who neighed submission; one master for him was as good as another; what he went in for was good feeding; and he believed he could get that from Old Abe as well as anybody else." Johnson responded to this slander by trying to shoot *Examiner* editor John M. Daniel on a Richmond street. Daniel returned the fire, but neither antagonist hit the other. Only the intervention of the Mayor's Court and imposition of a $3,000 bond prevented further violence.[2]

Around noon Lee accepted the inevitable and followed his escort to the capitol to endure his public appearance. When they arrived, the first thing they did was stand and wait.

Lee stood in the rotunda near the statue of George Washington by Jean Antoine Houdon in the Classical Revival public temple designed by Thomas Jefferson where Governor Light Horse Harry Lee had confronted his rebellious legislature.[3]

After Lee became a legend, some of those who saw him during the spring and summer of 1861 remembered a noble specimen of manly grace and martial form. And in Lee's case hindsight was nearly accurate. He was fifty-four years old; but he looked younger. Moreover, Lee could look like someone important without affectation. Walter H. Taylor, who served on Lee's staff, recalled meeting Lee early in May 1861. "Admirably proportioned, of graceful and dignified carriage," wrote Taylor, "with strikingly handsome features, bright and penetrating eyes, his iron-gray hair closely cut, his face cleanly shaved except for a mustache, he appeared every inch a soldier and a man born to command." Almost everyone who saw Lee for the first time remarked upon his dignity; few people knew that his reserved manner was a facade surrounding a shy man who had trained himself to be proper instinctively when he encountered others.[4]

Lee certainly looked like a soldier, and that was important at this stage. He acted like a soldier, too; after all, he began learning how soldiers act at West Point almost thirty-six years ago. Lee's first task was to mobilize an army and navy for Virginia. But what would he then do with these forces? Would he live up to his reputation in the field? Most people believed that Lee was a great commander, because Winfield Scott and others who should know said he was. But the substance on which to base any belief in Lee was quite slim.

Lee had devoted most of his career to building forts and other engineering projects. His record during the Mexican War was impressive, but Lee had been a staff officer then. He had never led troops in battle. In fact the only times Lee had ever commanded in anything remotely resembling combat were his two expeditions in Texas: one against Comanche marauders in the summer of 1856 and the other in search of Juan Cortinas and his band of Mexican bandits in the spring of 1860. On neither expedition did Lee even see anyone hostile, except for one Comanche woman captured by one of his detached cavalry squadrons. The largest force Lee had ever commanded in the field was four cavalry squadrons.

The only time Robert Lee actually commanded in person during combat occurred against John Brown at Harpers Ferry. Then he directed the assault upon the fire engine house—as many marines and militia as he wanted against Brown and four of his followers in a "battle" which lasted all of three minutes.

Nor was Lee quite as physically fit as he appeared. During his most recent tour of duty in Texas, he had suffered more colds, one of the worst of which afflicted him in June. He had begun to suffer too from "rheumatism" (which may have in fact been cardiovascular problems) to the point that his right arm "feels stationary." And he had complained about his health, something he had rarely ever done before.

Nevertheless, in Richmond in the spring of 1861, Lee impressed people with "his erect and muscular frame, firm step, and the animated expression of his eye." They believed that Lee was a skillful soldier because everyone said he was; and Lee gave them no cause to believe otherwise.[5]

So Lee stood at the rear of the hall of the Virginia House of Delegates and acknowledged the friendly eyes of convention delegates and governor. And while he stood, convention president John Janney read to him a prepared address.

Janney, a Whig from Loudon County sixty-one years old, had spoken and voted against secession. He was up to this occasion, however, and commenced by telling Lee and everyone present what they already knew—that amid searching of souls and gnashing of teeth delegates to this convention had stumbled into secession—that now Virginia confronted the armed might of the United States—and that Virginians were determined "that no spot of her [Virginia's] soil shall be polluted by the foot of an invader." Janney spoke of Westmoreland County, invoked the memory of George Washington and Lee's "own gallant father," and pronounced some contorted prose about "first in war," "first in Peace," "first in the hearts of your countrymen." He closed with more references to Washington, swords, and scabbards, and commanded Lee to "fall with it [his sword] in your hand rather than the object for which it was placed there should fail."

Then it was Lee's turn; he was reserved and brief.

Mr. President and Gentlemen of the Convention: Profoundly impressed with the solemnity of the occasion, for which I must say I was not prepared, I accept the position assigned me by your partiality. I would have much preferred had your choice fallen on an abler man. Trusting in Almighty God, an approving conscience, and the aid of my fellow-citizens, I devote myself to the service of my native State, in whose behalf alone will I ever again draw my sword.

It was pretty much a pro forma speech; but it was just about the only speech Lee ever made. After more applause Janney abandoned the chair so that convention delegates might meet and greet Lee. Then everyone sat down and listened to a speech from Vice President Alexander Stephens. Eventually Lee was able to return to his new office and live up to all the rhetoric.[6]

Very soon he suffered another interruption; the Vice President wished to see him. So Lee hiked back toward Capitol Square to the Ballard House at Fourteenth and Franklin Streets to call upon Stephens. The Vice President was five years younger than Lee, but he seemed much older because of his chronic ill health and diminutive stature. Within a year he would become disillusioned with the administration and spend much of his time back home in Georgia. At this point, however, Stephens was concerned about his government's relations with Virginia in general and with Lee in particular. He hoped that the convention would agree to act as though Virginia were a Confederate state, even though Virginian voters still had the final decision on the matter in a referendum to be held within a few weeks. Most especially did Stephens want to secure Lee's loyalty to the larger cause of the Confederacy. Lee more than satisfied Stephens that he would not obstruct the formation of a national army and military posture. Nor would he quibble or quarrel about matters of rank and status in the new Southern army. He would mobilize Virginia and cooperate in any ways that he could with the administration. Stephens was pleased; Lee only wanted to get on with his task.[7]

During the next few weeks Lee mobilized 40,000 troops, 115 field artillery pieces, 15 coastal defense batteries, and one ship. When he had begun, the Virginia Militia units totaled 18,400, and this army existed only on paper. Many of these citizen-soldiers were unarmed; most of them were absolutely untrained; and almost all of these men until very recently had considered the militia an essentially social organization.[8]

On May 3, 1861, Governor Letcher issued a call to arms; by then Lee was more or less prepared to accept volunteers for his army. He had officers ready at designated points about the state to receive volunteer companies (about 100 men). He had plans for arming and equipping the men and some hopes regarding their training. He employed, for example, cadets from the Virginia Military Institute (VMI) to drill and instruct volunteers who reported to Camp Lee near Richmond. Elsewhere Lee relied upon experienced officers to conduct training so as to transform citizens into soldiers.

Meanwhile Lee remained cognizant of the threat of invasion by the United States. So he attempted to assemble troops at several sites he deemed crucial to the defense of the state: Harpers Ferry, Manassas, Culpeper Court House, Gloucester Point, Norfolk, Alexandria, and Yorktown. Lee also knew that invasion via water was likely. So he planted guns along Virginia's rivers, and in this endeavor he had the able assistance of his old friend and once commanding officer Andrew Talcott.[9]

Experience was the common denominator of the officers Lee placed in command; he wanted professional soldiers who could transform enthusiastic civilians into some approximation of soldiers. Accordingly Benjamin Huger, a Charlestonian with thirty-six years of service in the United States Army, now commanded at Norfolk; Thomas J. Jackson, a West Point graduate most recently on the faculty at VMI, was in charge at Harpers Ferry; John Bankhead Magruder, a veteran of the Seminole and Mexican Wars, commanded on the peninsula between the James and York Rivers; and so on down the roll of Lee's principal subordinates.

When Joseph E. Johnston reported for duty, Lee assigned him to Harpers Ferry over Jackson, and for the moment Johnston seemed satisfied. He had outranked Lee and every other Confederate officer in the United States Army, and he did not suffer slights, real or imagined, with much grace at all. But Johnston and Lee had been West Point classmates and friends, and for the time being at least that friendship overrode the politics of command.[10]

Lee established his headquarters in the Virginia Mechanics Institute at Ninth and Franklin, only two blocks from the Spotswood Hotel where he continued to reside. Eventually the Confederate War and Navy Departments would occupy the entire building. For now Lee and his staff only used the top floor.

To assist him in this frenzy of mobilization, Lee had his former Commandant of Cadets at West Point, Robert S. Garnett, who acted as chief of staff. John A. Washington, nephew of George Washington and known to Lee in northern Virginia, joined Lee's staff in early May. Pennsylvania-born but South Carolina–connected, George Allen Deas resigned from the United States Army, drifted south, and also joined Lee's staff. "The New York clubs were so unpleasant now for Southern men," Deas explained to an audience of socialites in Charleston. Walter Herreu Taylor, a young (not quite twenty-three) militia officer with VMI training and connections with friends of Governor Letcher, became the fourth and final member of Lee's first staff. Others assisted in specific tasks or for short periods; Garnett, Washington, Deas, and Taylor served throughout the mobilization, and Taylor would remain with Lee throughout the war.[11]

During his administration of Virginia's mobilization Lee remained mostly in Richmond. He did manage brief visits to Norfolk, Manassas, and the lower peninsula between the James and York Rivers. His family members were significantly more mobile. Both older sons and his brother Smith joined Lee's armed force: Custis as an engineer; Rooney as a cavalry officer; and Smith as a captain in the Virginia navy. His daughter Mary moved about but settled at Kinloch for a time. Agnes came to Richmond, visited Rooney's in-laws and Chass at Hickory Hill (just a few miles north, near Hanover Court House and also near Rooney's camp), and visited White House. Annie usually stayed with Chass at White House or Hickory Hill. Rob continued at the University of Virginia in Charlottesville. Mildred remained with her mother, and Mary Lee had to move about a lot.[12]

Arlington became very soon unsafe for rebels, so by mid-May Mary Lee and Mildred retired to Ravensworth and then with daughter Mary to Kinloch. All the while Robert Lee advised moving sooner and farther than Mary Lee and her daughters did move. Mary Lee then became anxious about Arlington and "her people" she had left there. She discovered that Federal troops had occupied the place, that she would have to obtain a pass to visit her home, and that most likely she would be denied that pass. In a rage Mary Lee wrote a scathing letter to the officer in charge: "It never occurred to me . . . that *I* could be forced to sue for permission to enter my *own home*. . . ." She railed about the "outrage" of "military occupation" and Federal troops "committing such enormities there upon every *defenseless* person they meet," and described herself as "homeless," unable to gain access to funds deposited in Alexandria banks and thus deprived of "means for my support." She asked for dispensations for a few of the elderly slaves at Arlington and permission for some of her slaves to bring themselves and some of her belongings to her, and she concluded with a prayer "that God may ever spare you & yours the agony and inconvenience I am now enduring."

Union General Irvin McDowell responded with tact and conciliation the same day. Mary Lee could indeed return to her home if she so chose; her wishes regarding her slaves he had already fulfilled; and would she please accept his sympathy. McDowell, however, might have spared his energy and ink.

Mary Custis Lee had learned about civil war. The home at issue on the home front was her home; Yankees had defiled sacred soil; and so her wrath was mighty and destined only to grow.[13]

Robert Lee was powerless to mollify his wife. "Our private distresses," he wrote, "we must bear with resignation like Christians & not aggravate them by repining. . . ." But even as he wrote, he surely suspected that Mary Lee would repine. In contrast to Robert Lee's stoic resolve to accept whatever was and make the best he could of it, Mary Lee bore her ample afflictions with less than good grace and raised repining to the level of art.[14]

In this instance Robert Lee had little time to reflect upon Arlington occupied and his wife uprooted. His circumstance in the spring of 1861 he pretty well summarized in a telegram to Jefferson Davis on May 7, clearly in response to a summons from the President to come to Montgomery to discuss defending Virginia and defining his role in the Confederate military:

> GENERAL JOHNSTON SICK. I CANNOT BE SPARED. SENATOR [R. M. T.]
> HUNTER, ON THE WAY TO MONTGOMERY, IS FULLY INFORMED OF PLANS
> AND WATER DEFENCES AT NORFOLK. SUFFICIENT LAND DEFENCES IN
> PROGRESS. TROOPS SUFFICIENT, UNINSTRUCTED: OFFICERS NEW. MY
> COMMISSION IN VIRGINIA SATISFACTORY TO ME.

Lee not only had little time to ponder his personal problems or make public appearances; he had no time to promote himself with the President. So he remained in Richmond and continued the labors of mobilization.[15]

Walter Taylor much later recalled this period in Lee's service: "His correspondence, necessarily heavy, was constantly a source of worry and annoyance to him. He did not enjoy writing; indeed he wrote with labor, and nothing seemed to tax his amiability so much as the necessity for writing a lengthy official communication; but he was not satisfied unless at the close of his office hours every matter requiring prompt attention had been disposed of."[16]

Official correspondence was not Lee's only vexation in Richmond. He had also to deal with an ample amount of pettiness regarding appointments and plans. On May 14, for example, the man who claimed credit for firing the first shot in this war came to Lee's office on an urgent errand. Edmund Ruffin, planter-agronomist turned radical, came up to Richmond from his plantation Beechwood on the James River to protest the person and performance of Harrison H. Cocke, an aged naval officer who was constructing a river fort (Fort Powhatan) on the James below Richmond ("incompetent, worthless for command," "the most abject of submissionists & sycophants to northern power"). Ruffin failed to secure an audience with Governor Letcher, and then with the Governor's Advisory Council, so he came to see Lee. "After some conversation," Ruffin recorded in his diary, Lee asked him to submit his complaint in writing, which Ruffin did immediately. Lee promised to investigate; Ruffin did note later that Cocke had lost his command.[17]

Two days after his interview with the man who commanded all Southern troops in Virginia, Ruffin dispatched a telegram to Jefferson Davis: "FOR SAL-

vation of our cause come immediately and assume military command."
Nor was Ruffin the only person who asked the President to act out his constitutional role as commander in chief. "No one admires Gel. Lee more than I
do," wrote Albert Taylor Bledsoe, an old friend of Davis then on the faculty of
the University of Virginia, "but I fear he is too despondent. His remarks are
calculated to dispirit our people. . . . "Noble and glorious as he is," Bledsoe
continued, "I fear he does not know how good and how righteous our cause is
and consequently lacks one quality the times demand." Thus, Bledsoe told
Davis, "All eyes and all hearts, turn to you."[18]

When Lee made rare remarks about the prospects of the Confederacy in
the impending war, he told people what they did not want to hear. His aide
Walter Taylor claimed that Lee "alone, of all those then known to me . . .
expressed his most serious apprehensions of a prolonged and bloody war. . . ."
Lee, Taylor recalled, "looked upon the vaporific declamations of those on each
side who proposed to wipe their adversaries from the face of the earth in ninety
days as bombastic and foolish."[19]

But Lee seemed much less than a charismatic leader at this time. D. G.
Duncan, who appears to have been in Richmond to send reliable information
to the President and Secretary of War Leroy Pope Walker (in effect to spy),
had very few encouraging words to say about Lee. "Have conversed with
General Robert E. Lee," Duncan informed Walker very soon after Lee assumed command. "He wishes to repress enthusiasm of our people." Several
days later Duncan reported that "Chaos and confusion reign here . . . I learn
General Lee is troubled about rank. . . ." And two days after that, Duncan
wrote to Walker about "treachery." "Great dissatisfaction prevails here. . . . I
doubt if there are 5,000 Virginians armed and equipped."[20]

President Davis did of course come to Richmond. He came with his entire
government and made Richmond his capital. Davis came to the probable seat
of war to demonstrate his government's commitment to Virginia. The Confederate Congress voted to move the capital from Montgomery on May 20;
Davis signed the resolution on May 21 and arrived in Richmond with the
vanguard of his administration early on the morning of May 29.[21]

Lee was at Manassas Junction inspecting troops when Davis reached Richmond. On his way by rail back to the city Lee's train paused at Orange Court
House, and a crowd formed to see and hear him. At first Lee did not respond
to calls for him. Finally he stepped out of the car and according to the Richmond *Whig,* "said he had much more important matters on his mind than
speech-making; advised all who were in service to be drilling, and those who,
for good reasons, were not, to attend to their private affairs and avoid the
excitement and rumors of crowds. . . ." However valid were these views, Lee
once more closed himself and offered his constituents no more than somber
platitudes. He knew what the crowd at Orange did not—that war is somber
business—and he would not pretend otherwise.[22]

When Lee returned to Richmond during the evening of May 29, he found
the city agog over the arrival of Varina and Jefferson Davis. Lee realized that

his command in Virginia (of all Confederate forces within the state) was temporary. In accord with Davis's insistence, all state troops were to become members of the national army, and the Confederate government would appoint and assign principal officers within that army. Indeed, in little more than a week (June 8, 1861) Governor Letcher issued a proclamation transferring Virginia's army and navy to the Confederate States. Then Lee became a general with neither an army nor an assignment. "I do not know what my position will be," he wrote Mary Lee on the day after he relinquished his command; and he claimed that he preferred becoming a civilian.[23]

For the time being he remained in Richmond at the Spotswood House with his new neighbors the Davises, and he did whatever needed doing. Never did Lee receive orders for what he did during the next several weeks. He simply made himself more and more useful to President Davis. The two men were almost the same age. Lee was slightly older, but Davis had been a year ahead at West Point. Both had served with distinction in the Mexican War, albeit in different theaters. Davis had recommended Lee to leaders of a Cuban revolutionary junta as a possible military leader, then probably advised Lee against the adventure. Davis had been Secretary of War while Lee had been Superintendent of West Point (1852–55), and so they had corresponded frequently and worked closely together.[24]

Now Davis began to listen to Lee's advice about defending Virginia. At first it was only natural for Davis to consult the architect of Confederate defensive positions in the state. So Lee's information and opinion had been useful in assigning P. G. T. Beauregard to Manassas in May. But once Lee had no specific duties, Davis seemed to use him as a sort of household staff officer. Accordingly, when Beauregard hatched a grandiose scheme involving thousands of nonexistent troops, logistical sophistication far beyond Confederate capacity, and the complete cooperation of enemy armies, Lee was present to introduce some notion of reality and to dissuade serious consideration of Beauregard's fantasy. Davis attended whatever seemed to be the most significant theater himself; the President considered his military experience and instincts the most important contributions he could offer his new nation.[25]

When the first major battle of this young war occurred at Manassas/Bull Run on July 21, Lee remained in Richmond and waited for news from the front. That news, of course, was wonderful indeed for the Confederacy. Near the end of a long day of fighting, a fresh brigade of Southern troops appeared on the Federal flank and provoked a withdrawal of Union units which soon became a chaotic rout. "Night has closed upon a hard fought field—Our forces have won a glorious victory," began Davis's telegram, which was the way Lee and others in Richmond learned the news.[26]

Many Southerners believed that the fighting on July 21 had won the war and established the independence of the Confederacy. Lee knew better. He continued to speak of the war as a long, destructive struggle. He realized better than most people the liabilities which the Confederacy brought to the conflict. And he was aware of the full measure of failure that afflicted Southern military fortunes in places other than Manassas/Bull Run.[27]

One such theater where Confederate efforts had foundered was western (later West) Virginia. There in mid-July Federal General George B. McClellan had led a successful assault upon the Southern defensive line, and sent Confederate forces reeling before him. In the fighting Lee's friend and recent chief of staff Robert S. Garnett had lost his life at a place called Corrick's (sometimes spelled Carrick's) Ford in the Cheat River Valley on July 13. The situation was stable in late July primarily because the Federals had not taken advantage of their victories and pressed the campaign.

In effect the Confederates had several "armies" in western Virginia, separated by rugged terrain and the incredible egos of some of the men who commanded there. Lee's next task, assigned to him verbally by President Davis, was to go to the scene and impose some military sense upon the situation. Did Lee possess the authority of command? Did Lee go only to consult and coordinate? No one seemed to know—least of all Lee himself.[28]

Once more Lee's situation was enigmatic, much as it had been ever since he arrived in Richmond to accept command of the armed forces of Virginia. He had conducted the mobilization in Virginia with efficiency and energy; fully one fourth of the Southern troops involved in the victory of Manassas/Bull Run were Virginia troops organized, armed, equipped, and instructed by order of Robert Lee. But even as he directed the mobilization, Lee knew that he was working himself out of a place in this war. And after relinquishing his fledgling force to the Confederacy, Lee's limbo compounded while he worked as an unassigned general for the President. Now Lee had a defined mission; but his role and authority continued in question.[29]

Walter Taylor remembered of this period with Lee in Richmond: "After a day's work at his office he would enjoy above all things a ride on horseback. Accompanied by one or two of his military household, he would visit some point of interest around Richmond, making the ride one of duty as well as pleasure."[30]

On one such occasion Lee encountered Mary Chesnut, wife of South Carolina Congressman and presidential aide James Chesnut. Mary Chesnut was riding in a carriage with Martha Stanard, a prominent and clever Richmond widow.

A man riding a beautiful horse joined us. He wore a hat with somehow a military look to it. He sat his horse gracefully, and he was so distinguished at all points that I very much regretted not catching the name as Mrs. Stanard gave it to us. He, however, heard ours and bowed as gracefully as he rode, and the few remarks he made to each of us showed he knew all about us.

Martha Stanard, "in ecstasies of pleasurable excitement," chatted with the horseman as though he were a "big fish." In the course of her banter, she suggested that he was ambitious.

He remonstrated—said his tastes were of the simplest. He only wanted a Virginia farm—no end of cream and fresh butter—and fried chicken. Not one fried chicken or two—but unlimited fried chicken.

To all this light chat did we seriously incline because the man and horse and everything about him was so fine looking. Perfection—no fault to be found if you hunted for one. As he left us, I said, "Who is it?" eagerly.

"You do not know! Why, it is Robert E. Lee, son of Light Horse Harry Lee, the first man in Virginia"—raising her voice as she enumerated his glories.

"All the same," Mary Chesnut concluded thoughtfully, "I like Smith Lee better, and I like his looks, too. I know Smith Lee well. Can anybody say they know his brother? I doubt it. He looks so cold and quiet and grand."[31]

At the same time Lee was trying to know and understand his role as a Confederate, many Confederates were trying to know and understand Lee. They were no more successful than he.

16

"Never Fought a Battle...
Pious Horror of Guerrillas...
Extreme Tenderness of Blood"

SNOW FELL UPON the Confederate Army of the Northwest during the night of August 14–15 at Valley Mountain, (now West) Virginia. One Southern survivor of the campaign claimed, with justifiable hyperbole, that "it rained 32 days in August" and that he had seen "dead mules lying in the road with nothing but their ears showing." A more reliable account from the future Episcopal Bishop of West Virginia recalled rain during thirty-seven of forty-three days he camped at Valley Mountain.[1]

Robert Lee wrote letters to his family from Valley Mountain in "all my winter clothes," plus his overcoat, and said among other things, "Now it is pouring, & the wind, that has veered around to every point of the compass, has settled down to the northeast"—"It rains here all the time, literally"—"Rain, rain, rain, there has been nothing but rain"—"The cold too has been greater than I could have conceived."[2]

With rain and cold came sickness—measles mostly, with subsequent complications, plus typhoid fever. "Some regiments [1,000 men]," wrote Lee, "have not over 250 for duty, some 300,500, or about half. . . ." Later he observed, "Now those on the sick list would form an army." Walter Taylor remained on Lee's staff throughout the war and saw more than his share of hardship. "But never," he later reflected, "did I experience the same heart-sinking emotions as when contemplating the wan faces and the emaciated forms of those hungry, sickly, shivering men of the army at Valley Mountain!"[3]

Lee had left Richmond on July 28, 1861, a week after the great Confederate victory at Manassas/Bull Run, to oversee operations in northwestern Virginia where recent victories belonged to the Federals. With Lee on the train from Richmond to Staunton on July 28 were only two other officers, Colonel John A. Washington and Lieutenant Walter Taylor, and two slaves—Meredith, a cook from White House, and Perry, who had worked in the dining room at Arlington. The three officers slept in a single tent, and on at least one cold night Lee and Taylor slept together to take advantage of their body heat and combined blankets. They ate from tin plates and bowls and drank from tin cups. In the field Lee's regimen was Spartan in the extreme.[4]

Waiting for Lee in the mountains was William Wing Loring, whom Lee had dispatched to command the Army of the Northwest following the Confederate defeat at Rich Mountain and the death of the former commander (and before that Lee's chief of staff) Robert Garnett at Corricks Ford. Loring had been fighting wars since the age of fourteen when he enlisted to kill Seminoles in the Everglades. He had lost an arm in the Mexican War, and at the time he resigned from the United States Army to come south, Colonel Loring outranked Lee.[5]

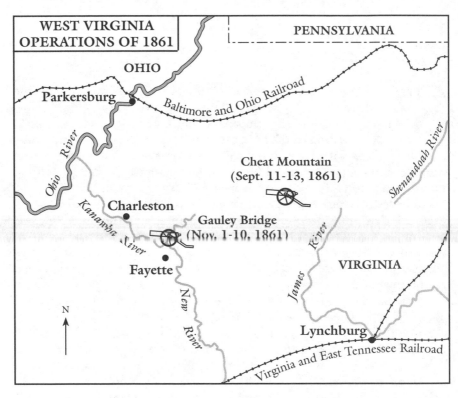

The strategic significance of Northwest Virginia lay principally in its roads, passes, and gaps, which offered access to more important places. The region was sparsely populated by very independent people whose ultimate loyalties often lay with themselves and who seemed to resent armies from either side. Both Federal and Confederate forces had to contend with local "bushwhackers," and Lee informed his wife, "Our citizens beyond this [point] are all on their side." Federal presence in the region threatened control of the Staunton-

Parkersburg Turnpike, the James River Turnpike, and the Virginia Central Railroad and thus entree to the Shenandoah Valley and the Virginia Piedmont. Conversely, if the Confederacy controlled Northwest Virginia, Southern armies might menace the Baltimore & Ohio Railroad, the Ohio River, and potentially western Pennsylvania and Ohio.[6]

Lee's Mexican War comrade George B. McClellan had made sufficient reputation in western Virginia to secure command of the principal Union army in the East. While Lee was packing to travel west, McClellan was paying his first call upon Abraham Lincoln in Washington.

McClellan "immediately" began forming his staff, which eventually numbered sixty-five officers. Succeeding McClellan in western Virginia was his former subordinate William S. Rosecrans, who, like McClellan, had used his training at West Point to launch a civilian career in engineering. Now Rosecrans was a brigadier general in command of far-flung forces in what was currently a backwater of the war; yet this same circumstance had launched McClellan's rapid rise to prominence.[7]

Rosecrans's army held, in Lee's words, "a long front, extending from the Potomac to the Kanawha." Strongpoints along this line were on Cheat Mountain and at Gauley Bridge (at the confluence of the New and Gauley Rivers). "The only way of breaking up this long line of the enemy," Lee stated, "is to assume the offensive, which I regret to say we are not prepared to do." The rains had rendered roads impassable and so compelled the Confederates to disperse their forces in order to distribute provisions, and allow horses to graze. Offense required concentration. But even had the Southerners concentrated, the men were too sickly to do more than defend themselves. So Lee counseled caution, even as he endorsed in principle the necessity to attack.[8]

Loring and that portion of his army at or near Valley Mountain focused attention upon the Federal fort atop Cheat Mountain. Indiana and Ohio regiments had been laboring on the mountain for several weeks, established a formidable set of works, and felled trees to clear fields of fire. Lee estimated that the Federals in the vicinity numbered 12,000 to 15,000 men—an estimate that was generous by about 3,000 or 4,000. He counted about 10,000 "effective" troops in Loring's force of almost 14,000.[9]

To the southwest, perhaps 70 miles as the crow flies, was the Federal stronghold at Gauley Bridge and 4,500 troops, with several thousand more nearby. Confronting the enemy here were about 7,500 Confederates commanded by Generals John B. Floyd and Henry A. Wise, both of whom were former governors of Virginia. Floyd had also been Secretary of War in James Buchanan's administration; Wise had often been a member of Congress. Both men were avid secessionists. Floyd recruited a brigade of soldiers; Wise raised and equipped a "Legion" (a body of infantry, artillery, and cavalry). But zeal for the Confederacy did not necessarily make them great military chieftains—or even adequate commanders. And compounding their mutual inexperience was the scorn they shared for each other.[10]

It is difficult now, and was impossible then, to define Lee's role in northwestern Virginia. On August 31, the Confederate Congress confirmed a list of five full generals in the Confederate army, including Lee. Among this five, Samuel Cooper, who served throughout the war as Adjutant and Inspector General (the President's principal staff officer), held the highest rank as determined by date of commissions, followed by Albert Sidney Johnston, Robert E. Lee, Joseph E. Johnston, and P. G. T. Beauregard. So Lee outranked everyone in the army except Cooper and Albert Sidney Johnston. In the Northwest he signed orders and correspondence as "General Commanding" and clearly possessed the authority to do and command others to do whatever he wanted.

However, his verbal understanding with the President, as Lee acted out that understanding during the campaign, seemed to indicate that his role was more that of coordinator or consultant. He took no immediate command of any troops, neither Loring's army, Floyd's brigade, nor Wise's "Legion." He urged and suggested; he did not order. Not even in the midst of the protracted quarrel between Floyd and Wise did Lee assert his rank or any authority. Moreover, a letter to Lee from Cooper in Richmond sustains the interpretation of Lee's role as other than commander. Cooper spoke for President Davis: "He has not ceased to feel an anxious desire for your return to this city to resume your former duties. . . . Whenever in your judgement circumstances will justify it, you will consider yourself authorized to return." These were not words for an officer with a specific command.

Acting the part of consultant/coordinator also allowed Lee to avoid conflict and confrontation. This was important to him; he shrank from "scenes" in which he was compelled to assert rank or authority. He sought harmony. He preferred to suggest and depend upon others to recognize the wisdom of his suggestions and to act upon his advice out of enthusiasm instead of obligation. This was his pattern as husband and parent in his personal life; he simply adopted it as a leadership style in his professional life.[11]

From the beginning of his sojourn in the Northwest, Lee exhorted Loring to concentrate his troops and attack the Federals on Cheat Mountain. Loring, however, failed to respond, and at least one contemporary believed that Loring resented Lee's presence and rank, and thus his counsel. Lee resolved this unpleasantness on August 6 by leaving Loring's headquarters at Huntersville, moving forward to Valley Mountain, and establishing his own headquarters there. Leaving Loring, however, did not advance the cause of an attack; Lee had sacrificed his best military instinct for the sake of personal peace and quiet. Meanwhile the rain, cold, and state of the roads impeded operations, and Loring did little to expedite any attack upon the Federals.[12]

Loring had a good plan which called for his forces to maneuver down the Tygart's Valley River, then around the Cheat Mountain stronghold, attack and defeat the Union troops at Huttonsville, and thus isolate the enemy on Cheat. Eventually the Federals on the mountain would surrender or starve, and the Confederates could claim a major victory without having to assault the strength of their enemy. Lee endorsed the idea, but again stressed the need for speed and surprise in the course of achieving the obvious.

From Valley Mountain, though, Lee, assisted by his son Rooney's cavalry, scouted routes by which Loring's men might directly approach the Federal works on Cheat Mountain. Perhaps he recalled the Pedregal in Mexico or the assault upon Chapultepec and sought to surprise the enemy by moving troops over "impossible" ground and attacking in strength where least expected.

Then, as if thinking had made it so, Lee received a report of a route through the mountains terminating at an unguarded point overlooking the Federal works on Cheat. The pathfinder in this instance was a civilian surveyor who twice traversed the route undetected. On the second trip Colonel Albert

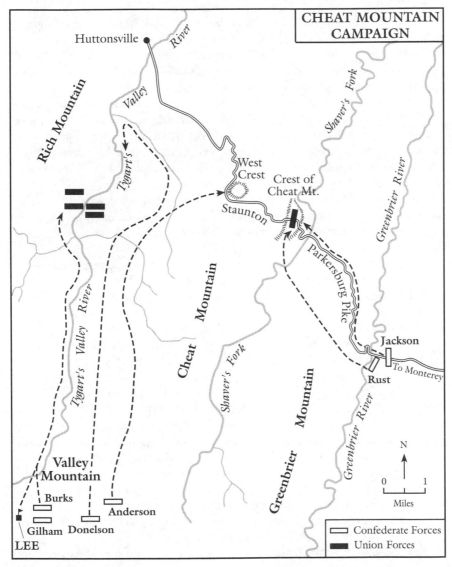

Rust, who commanded the Third Arkansas Infantry Regiment, accompanied the surveyor and concluded that he could lead his troops over the difficult ground and launch an assault on the Cheat Mountain stronghold.[13]

Lee was intrigued; Loring was elated. So from a series of notes between Loring and Lee emerged an attack order. The plan incorporated Rust's surprise attack upon an unsuspecting Cheat Mountain garrison and the march down the valley of Tygart's Valley River to seize Huttonsville. Success depended in large measure upon Rust's approach march; his surprise attack had to be a surprise. Accordingly, the firing associated with Rust's attack was the signal for every other commander associated with the offensive to commit his men to battle.

During the first week of September the rain abated; roads dried; and spirits elevated. On September 8, the Confederate plan of attack became an order issued by Loring. Next day Lee added his order encouraging the men—"great principles"—"eyes of the country . . . upon you"—"your homes"—"right of self government"—"the progress of this army must be forward."[14]

On September 11, the Confederates began to move into position for an attack at dawn on September 12. Lee and Taylor rode in the wake of the troops assigned to sweep down the eastern side of Tygart's Valley River. They slept in the woods on the night of September 11–12 and nearly blundered into a Federal cavalry patrol next morning as Lee hurried toward high ground where he could survey the valley.

Rain resumed falling and the temperature plunged. By dawn on the 12th, men and equipment were soaked and cold. But, wonder of wonders, every Confederate column was in place to launch the attack, and the Federals were still unaware of their peril.[15]

Albert Rust had had a long, frantic night. The rain compounded the difficulty of his march, though it did muffle the noise of 1,500 to 1,600 scrambling men. Rust was a large man physically and a big man politically back in Arkansas. He lacked military experience and training, however, and his responsibility in this fairly intricate plan of attack proved too much for him.

Early on the morning of September 12, Rust's troops captured some Federal pickets, and teamsters. As it happened, this success set the stage for failure. The prisoners, when interrogated, claimed that the Federal garrison on Cheat Mountain numbered 4,000 to 5,000 men, and Rust believed the exaggeration. Rust also believed that he saw impregnable field fortifications, heard artillery in motion, and smelled disaster. Rust himself went close enough to the enemy position to become convinced that the garrison was alarmed and alert for action. Then he called a meeting of his principal subordinates and listened while they "declared it would be madness to make an attack." So Rust called off his assault and withdrew his command. And because Rust never attacked, the other Southern columns never attacked. The assault on Cheat Mountain was a well-conceived, competently prepared fiasco. Loring's army retreated from the brink of victory, and the Federals remained in place.[16]

Lee acknowledged the defeat. "I can not tell you," he wrote Mary Lee, "my regret and mortification at the untoward events that caused the failure of the plan." To Governor Letcher, he admitted, "It is a grievous disappointment to me, I assure you." Lee still blamed "untoward events"—chiefly the weather—and resolved, "We must try again."[17]

In public, before the soldiers, Lee offered euphemism raised to infinite power. On September 14 he issued a special order calling the aborted attack a "forced reconnaissance" and boasting of success in exposing the "natural approaches" and the "nature of the artificial defenses." He had experienced "much gratification at the cheerfulness and alacrity displayed by the troops in this arduous operation." The commanding general closed his message with a flourish, praising the "promptitude" exhibited by the men and asserting that "promptitude" in the preliminaries of battle "gives assurance of victory when a fit opportunity offers."[18]

Surely Lee gave thought to his authorization from the President through Cooper to leave Loring's hapless army and in so doing shake the mud from his feet. Not only had the attack on Cheat Mountain failed; in the course of events on September 12, Lee's principal staff officer John A. Washington became one of the few soldiers on either side killed in action on a day distinguished by inaction. Washington was riding with Rooney Lee performing reconnaissance when some Union troops fired upon the pair from ambush. Washington and Rooney Lee's horse went down, and Lee escaped becoming a casualty by leaping aboard Washington's horse and dashing away. Thus far the campaigns in these mountains had killed half (two of four) of Lee's original staff (Garnett and Washington).[19]

While Lee was enduring his frustration before Cheat Mountain, Rosecrans had been active on the Gauley. The Federal commander had reinforced his troops stationed in the Kanawha Valley and on September 10 attacked Floyd's Confederates at Carnifax Ferry. Floyd called upon Wise for help; but Wise did not help. Nevertheless Floyd's brigade held firm throughout the day. Because he believed he had confronted many more men than in fact he had, Floyd retreated that night to the southern bank of the Gauley and later withdrew further east. Each time Floyd ordered Wise to join him, Wise either ignored the order or offered some excuse for remaining where he was. This circumstance, together with Rosecrans's reinforced force in the Kanawha Valley, demanded Lee's personal intervention.

With Taylor and some cavalry, Lee rode out to the scene, about 70 miles to the southwest. Lee and his escort, of course, were not crows, so they rode many more than 70 miles through the mountains and reached Floyd's headquarters at a place called Meadow Bluff on September 21. There Lee learned that Wise was still insubordinate, still insistent that his position was the better for receiving Rosecrans's attack.[20]

So Lee began to survey the ground and learn as much as he could about the strength and intentions of the enemy. He rode forward on September 24 to Wise's headquarters on Sewell Mountain and found there some elements of Rosecrans's Federals nearby and serious disorder within Wise's Legion. As the

"General Commanding" looked over the Legion, a young lieutenant asked him who the ordnance (weapons and ammunition) officer was and where such essential supplies were kept. Lee vented cold, controlled rage. "I think it very strange, lieutenant, that an officer of this command, which has been here a week, should come to me, who has just arrived, and ask who his ordnance officer is and where to find his ammunition. This is in keeping with everything else I find here—no order, no organization, nobody knows where anything is, no one understands his duty!" The weather continued consistent, as Lee wrote to Mary Lee on September 26. "It is raining heavily. The men are all exposed on the mountain, with the enemy opposite to us. We are without tents, and for two nights I have lain buttoned up in my overcoat."[21]

What Lee discovered at Sewell Mountain compounded his problems. Wise's Legion was in terrible shape. Wise himself had no notion of how to act the part of an officer, much less how to command a combined arms force the size of a small brigade. His response to Floyd's orders were letters to Lee including such remarks as, "I solemnly protest that my force is not safe under his [Floyd's] command." But by some primitive instinct or by luck, Wise had indeed selected and occupied a better position from which to confront Rosecrans.

So now Lee had to assure Floyd that he was correct about Wise's abject insubordination and then inform Floyd that Wise was right and he wrong in the choice of ground on which to resist an imminent attack. Whatever Lee did or said, he seemed assured of making an enemy of Wise or Floyd or both. Again Lee was in the midst of personal conflict and he did not like it. He already possessed specific authority from the President to transfer Wise and his Legion anywhere he wanted, and he already had information from Cooper about troop units designated to replace Wise's men. Lee never exercised this authority, however, perhaps because he expected Rosecrans to attack before the replacement units could arrive (from Lynchburg), more likely because he continued to shrink from personal conflict and confrontation.[22]

Lee tried to resolve his dilemma by convincing Floyd of the merits of Sewell Mountain and hoping Floyd would recognize the obvious wisdom of uniting his brigade with Wise's Legion on the better ground. In his own way Floyd was no better a subordinate than Wise; Floyd's response to his troubles with Wise was to write to Davis and ignore such matters as channels of military communication and chains of command. Yet Floyd's unmilitary behavior finally helped Lee out of his awkward circumstance. On September 25, Floyd received a curt note addressed to Wise from Secretary of War Judah P. Benjamin instructing Wise to transfer "everything under your command" to Floyd and to report to the Adjutant General (Cooper) in Richmond "with the least delay." Clearly Davis recognized the problem and dealt with it by removing Wise.

But Wise still treated the very clear instructions of the Secretary of War as though they were negotiable. Lee at length convinced Wise to obey. Wise insisted that he complied with Benjamin's order only because Lee advised him to do so, not because he followed orders.[23]

With Wise out of the way, Lee convinced Floyd to untie the two commands and augmented the defensive position on Sewell Mountain with Loring's troops as they arrived. Convinced that Rosecrans still outnumbered him significantly, Lee organized a defensive position and hoped the enemy would oblige him by attacking. During the first few days of October, Rosecrans seemed about to cooperate. Then on the night of October 5–6, the Federals withdrew. So the campaign in the Kanawha Valley came to inconclusion and Confederate arms accomplished no more than at Cheat Mountain.

Lee remained for about three weeks near the scene of the stalemate that left most of western Virginia in Federal control. Then near the end of October he made his way back to Richmond and the President. Davis later claimed that he never blamed Lee for his failure in the mountains and that Lee, when pressed, explained his troubles and implored the President to keep these explanations to himself.[24]

However, silence was the one thing Lee could not control. Henry A. Wise owned a major portion of the Richmond *Enquirer* newspaper, among other assets, and his son Obediah Jennings Wise was an editor. *Examiner* editor John M. Daniel was an aide to Floyd during the campaign. After the campaign proved a major failure, Lee reminded Mary Lee, "I am sorry . . . that the movements of the armies cannot keep pace with the expectations of the editors of papers. I know they can regulate matters satisfactorily to themselves on paper. I wish they could do so in the field. . . . I hope something will be done to please them."

Rumors circulated that Lee and his wife had separated. The *Enquirer* printed a rumor that Rosencrantz (Shakespeare's minor villian in *Hamlet* and the way newspapers often spelled Rosecrans) had surrendered to Lee, and it continued to claim victory at Cheat Mountain almost a month after the non-battle. The *Whig* mentioned Lee as a strong candidate to succeed Secretary of War Leroy Pope Walker. But when Confederate scribes eventually sorted fantasy from fact, many concluded that Lee's reputation was largely inflated and that he had failed the test of combat in western Virginia.[25]

Edward A. Pollard, an editor with the Richmond *Examiner,* undertook to produce instant history in his series of histories of each year of the war. In *The First Year of the War,* Pollard concluded about western Virginia: "The most remarkable circumstance of this campaign was, that it was conducted by a general who had never fought a battle, who had a pious horror of guerrillas, and whose extreme tenderness of blood induced him to depend exclusively upon the resources of strategy, to essay the achievement of victories without the cost of life."[26]

But worse than idle rumors and negative criticism in the daily press and sarcasm in a journo-history of the war was the collective judgment within the army. One Tennessean wrote, in the aftermath of the campaign, "Well, at the end of seven days' marching and starvation, we go back to Valley Mountain, the whole affair having proved a failure—in the opinion of our brigade, chiefly from the old fogyism and want of pluck among the Virginians. Never were men more sick of Virginia and Virginians than we are." One Virginian with an inflated understanding of Floyd's capacity wrote his fiancé, "It was scandalous that Genl. Lee did not attack the Yankees at Big Sewell. Had Genl. Floyd been in command of the whole force, he would have killed or taken every one of them." Seemingly overnight Lee, Virginia's anointed warrior, had become "Granny Lee," too timid and genteel for the dirty work of war.

Lee's three months in the mountains had not been wholly unproductive. Lee had left Richmond in July a brigadier general in the Confederate army; he returned a full general, the third highest ranking officer. Lee also found a horse in western Virginia. At Sewell Mountain he noticed a four-year-old gray stallion then named Jeff Davis and spoke to the owner about buying the animal. Later that autumn, in South Carolina, Lee did buy the horse, now called Greenbrier, for $200. Lee renamed him Traveller, rode him for the rest of the war, and raised him to the pantheon of warhorses. Lee also grew a beard in western Virginia which he retained for the rest of his life. Appropriately, the beard appeared gray; at the same time it matched Lee's Confederate uniform and reflected his worries during the campaign.[27]

Lee made lessons of his experiences over the mountains. He demonstrated an appreciation of the stamina, courage, and common sense of volunteer soldiers in the Southern army. He did admire their "promptitude," and he tried to communicate his empathy in the two special orders he addressed to the entire command. Anecdotes eventually made their way east of the mountains in which for example Lee secured a plug of chewing tobacco for a young soldier brash enough to ask him for it, and cajoled an officer into overlooking the offense of a sentry asleep. Lee's concern for the men of the army inspired his quiet wrath when he found officers unwilling or unable to care for their needs or to lead them effectively.[28]

Lee discovered the deflation when an army poised to attack did not attack. By definition moments of truth are rare. He reinforced his resolve to accept the chance for victory and not to shrink from opportunities to act.

Lee also learned about people in this campaign, and some things he did not like. His subordinates were, for one reason or another, incompetent commanders. Lee lacked the temperament to confront Loring's jealousy, Floyd's inexperience, or Wise's insubordination. But none of the three, nor Rust either, was in Virginia by the time the next campaigning season opened. Lee could not permit himself to get visibly angry with these men when they failed. But he could indeed get rid of them, and he did.

Beneath that benign veneer of good manners and thoughtfulness was Lee's professional zeal; he did not excuse stupidity, slovenliness, or sloth. "Granny Lee" might not confront fools to their faces in public or in writing; but General Lee did not suffer fools for long in his army.

17

"Low-Country Gentlemen Curse Lee"

SINCE THAT GLORIOUS July afternoon at Manassas/Bull Run the war had not gone well for the Confederates, and prospects were not improving. Lee himself bore some of the blame for flaccid prospects in western Virginia, and when he returned to Richmond to serve President Jefferson Davis, Lee learned firsthand how weak seemed Southern arms in relation to the Northern foe.[1]

With his sole surviving staff member Lieutenant Walter Taylor and two slaves, Meredith and Perry, Robert Lee reached Richmond on Halloween 1861. Mary Lee was living at Shirley, the family home of Robert Lee's mother not too far down the James River from Richmond. Lee had not seen his wife since he left Arlington last April 22 on the journey that took him to war.[2]

But even as the Lees planned a reunion, the war again intervened. For some time the Federal navy had been fitting out a coasting expedition at New York. Late in October these vessels joined a variety of troop transports in Hampton Roads (the mouths of the James, Nansemond, and Elizabeth Rivers), and on October 29, the fleet of 75 vessels and 12,000 troops sailed out of Hampton Roads into the Atlantic. On November 1, Confederate Secretary of War Judah P. Benjamin became convinced that the invasion expedition was bound for Port Royal, South Carolina. If successful, a Union capture of Port Royal and the barrier island of Hilton Head offered a refueling and refitting station for the South Atlantic blockading squadron, a base for the capture of Savannah and/or Charleston, and at least the opportunity to sever the railroad linking Savannah and Charleston . . .

Benjamin responded to this series of threats by creating a military department of the coasts of South Carolina, Georgia, and Eastern Florida, and installing Lee as departmental commander. Lee left Richmond in a hurry on November 6 and arrived on November 7 just in time to learn that Port Royal had fallen that afternoon.[3]

He established his headquarters at a place called Coosawhatchie, situated on the river with that name which flows eventually into Port Royal Sound, and also located on the Savannah & Charleston Railroad. To Benjamin, Lee re-

ported: "The enemy having complete possession of the water and inland navigation, commands all the islands on this coast, and threatens both Savannah
and Charleston, and can come in his boats within 4 miles of this place [Coosa-
whatchie]." In a letter to his daughter Mildred a few days later, Lee managed
to be even more lugubrious. "Another forlorn hope expedition. Worse than
western Virginia."[4]

The new commander was appropriately appalled by his new command.
And the feeling was very much mutual.

When Jefferson Davis decided to send Lee to South Carolina, failures in
western Virginia still tainted him. As Davis later stated, "The clamour which
then arose followed him when he went to South Carolina," and as a consequence Davis believed it necessary "to write a letter to the Governor of that
State, telling him what manner of man He [Lee] was." Davis also wrote to
Georgia Governor Joseph Brown with the same message. That the President
should have to write letters of recommendation for Lee when assigning him a
new command speaks volumes about Lee's reputation, or lack of it, at this
juncture.[5]

At Coosawhatchie Lee could not rely alone upon Davis's confidence; the
President's recommendation carried little weight in the midst of continued
reversals. And the military circumstance all but dictated failure. Lee discovered
the sad facts of his situation during an inspection trip of the coast from
Charleston to Fernandina undertaken within two weeks of his arrival. To
daughters Annie and Agnes he reported, "I have been down the coast as far as
Amelia Island to examine the defenses. They are poor indeed & I have laid off
work enough to employ our people a month. I hope our enemy will be polite
enough to wait for us. It is difficult to get our people to realize their position."
He continued to travel and to issue instructions, but experienced increased
frustration in the process.[6]

Nature seemed in conspiracy against Confederate capacity to defend this
coastal region. Barrier islands lay miles from the mainland separated from the
major landmass by salt marshes, sounds, and meandering tidal streams, and
separated from each other by wide channels. The Federal navy enjoyed dominance in these waterways as in the near-shore waters and ocean beyond. To
defend this coast, the Confederates would have to mount batteries of guns
everywhere, and the new nation (or any nation for that matter) did not have
enough guns with enough range to cover every channel, sound, and creek.[7]

So Lee had to choose carefully the points he could defend and erect defensive positions. However, the longer he remained on the deep southern coast,
the fewer became those places for which sufficient troops and guns were available.

Throughout his four months in command Lee fretted about the will and
commitment of the officers and men with whom he worked.

"The people [here] do not seem to realize that there is war. . . ," he wrote
to Annie, and three weeks later, to his son Custis, "I am dreadfully disap-

pointed at the spirit here. They have all of a sudden realized the asperities of war, in what they must encounter, & do not seem to be prepared for it." Lee speculated to Mary Lee that this phase of the war might well be God's game with the Southern people. "It is necessary we should be humble & taught to be less boastful, less selfish, & more devoted to right & justice. . . ." And to Annie on March 2, 1862, he said, "Our people have not been earnest enough, have thought too much of themselves & their ease, & instead of turning out to a man, have been content to nurse themselves & their dimes, & leave the protection of themselves & families to others."[8]

In the course of his command on the coast Lee felt compelled to say and write bad news to people who did not wish to confront the consequences of war. He had to inform South Carolina Governor Francis W. Pickens that a brigade of militia which on Pickens's paper numbered 3,420 in reality had only 1,531 men present for duty. "The strength of the enemy, as far as I am able to judge, exceeds the whole force that we have in the state. It can be thrown with great celerity against any point, and far outnumbers any force we can bring against it in the field."[9]

To Georgia Governor Brown, Lee explained the necessity of abandoning St. Simon and Jekyll Islands and the mainland port of Brunswick. "I find it impossible to obtain guns to secure it as I desire, and now everything is required to fortify this city [Savannah]."[10]

Unfortunately, the barrier islands Lee had to abandon in Georgia produced sea island cotton, and some very wealthy and powerful families had had to evacuate themselves and their slaves in the face of the Federal invasion. The coastal region of South Carolina produced not only sea island cotton but also enormous quantities of rice, and more wealthy and powerful families there had had to flee inland. Lee the departmental commander not only had no plans to recover these valuable lands; he insisted that the Confederacy forsake this region for the duration of the war. He proposed to destroy Brunswick to prevent the enemy from using its harbor and buildings. He determined to withdraw up the various rivers to points at which Confederate guns would match Federal gunboats—"taking interior positions, where we can meet on more equal terms. All our resources should be applied to those positions."[11]

Lee's plan was expedient and wise at once. But many of those people immediately involved were unimpressed. Mary Chesnut observed, "Low-country gentlemen curse Lee and Drayton [Thomas Fenwick, commander at Port Royal] alike." Edmund Ruffin, after conversations with some South Carolinians, concluded, "Gen. Lee . . . though reputed to be an accomplished & great officer . . . is, I fear, too much of a red-tapist to be an effective commander in the field." Lee's principal subordinate at Charleston, Roswell P. Ripley, described as "a big fat whiskey drinking loving man," came to despise Lee (one of very few people who ever did). Governor Pickens described Lee to the President as "quiet and retiring" and observed, "His reserve is construed disadvantageously." Pickens also informed Davis, "I do not know if it prevails elsewhere in the Army, but I take the liberty to inform you that I fear the feeling of General Ripley towards General Lee may do injury to the public service. His habit is to say extreme things even before junior officers, and this is well calculated to do great injury to General Lee's command." Lee persisted in the face of criticism, however, and by the time he left the region he had begun to establish a chain of practical defensive positions.[12]

But in the meantime troubles continued to come in battalions. On December 11, Lee and some members of his staff were eating dinner at the Mills House in Charleston when a series of fires in the city roared into what became the Great Conflagration of 1861. The men adjourned to the roof of the hotel and watched as the flames spread through the city and came nearer and nearer the Mills House. Finally they decided to flee, and about midnight Lee carried someone's baby down some back stairs, through the cellar, and out into the street. There they commandered a carriage and sped away to the battery, where Lee secured rooms for them for the rest of the night in a private home. The fire spared the Mills House but little else in a broad swath from the Ashley to the Cooper Rivers. Eventually Lee donated $300 to the relief fund established in the city.[13]

On December 20, first anniversary of South Carolina's secession from the Union, the Federal navy sank the "Great Stone Fleet"—derelict ships loaded with rock—in the main channel of Charleston Harbor. Lee reported the event to the Secretary of War and called it "unworthy of any nation," "the abortive expression of the malice & revenge of a people which they wish to perpetuate by rendering more memorable a day hateful in their calendar." Somehow, such outrage seems more than a little bogus from a person himself in the process of obstructing rivers and destroying any resource which his enemies might use.[14]

In January 1862 the Confederacy's very tenuous claim to Kentucky collapsed only a month after Congress admitted that state to the Southern republic. The Battle of Mills Springs compelled Albert Sidney Johnston to draw his "Kentucky Line" in southern Tennessee.

On February 7, in an action reminiscent of Port Royal, the Federals landed 10,000 troops on Roanoke Island in North Carolina. Next day Southern defenders commanded by Henry A. Wise fought a token battle and ignominiously surrendered.

Later the same month two more of Lee's old nemeses, Gideon Pillow and John B. Floyd, combined with Simon B. Buckner to lose Forts Henry and Donelson on the Tennessee to the Federal invasion force of Ulysses S. Grant. If possible the Confederate failures at Henry and Donelson were more ignominious than at Roanoke Island, and both debacles inspired investigations by the Confederate Congress.[15]

And ever since the previous summer George B. McClellan had been assembling and training near Washington the largest army ever in North America. McClellan was cautious to the point of inertia; but sooner or later McClellan's horde would march, and each day it did not made the next day more ominous.

Lee of course absorbed all of this bad news while he worked hard at his plan to arrest the invasion of the coastal region in the Deep South. Yet his personal fortunes seemed synchronized with Confederate fortunes of war. He realized by now that he would never again live at Arlington. To his wife he wrote, "As to our old home, if not destroyed, it will be difficult ever to be recognized. Even if the enemy had wished to preserve it, it would almost have been impossible. With the number of troops encamped around it, the change of officers, etc. the want of fuel, shelter, etc., & the dire necessities of war, it is vain to think of its being in a habitable condition. I fear too books, furniture, & the relics of Mount Vernon will be gone. It is better to make up our minds to a general loss."[16]

Mary Lee received this letter at White House, one of her father's properties now controlled by her second son Rooney. White House and Romancoke, the other working plantation in G. W. Parke Curtis's estate, were still encumbered by the terms of the will that required substantial legacies for the Lees' daughters and freedom for all the Custis slaves within five years. From Coosawhatchie Lee continued to try to settle the Custis estate, which only promised to leave him homeless.

He confessed to his oldest son, Custis, "I expect to be a pauper if I get through the war." His investments in city, state, and railroad bonds in the North seemed likely losses, almost certainly subject to confiscation, and Lee's holdings in Southern bonds would depreciate in value even in the best of circumstances.[17]

Lee did speculate about using what funds he might salvage from his Virginia Bank stock to purchase what remained of Stratford. He told Annie and Agnes that buying his birthplace had "always been a great desire of my life." To Mary Lee he wrote, "In the absence of a home, I wish I could purchase Stratford. That is the only other place that I could go to, now accessible to us, that would inspire me with feelings of pleasure & local love. You & the girls could remain there in quiet. It is a poor place, but we could make enough cornbread & bacon for our support, & the girls could weave us clothes. I wonder if it is for sale & at how much."[18]

Speculation and Stratford were logical associations in Lee's mind with his visit in January 1862 to his father's grave at Dungeness on Cumberland Island. He remained only "a few moments," picked a flower, and then left the grave of the man he never knew and whose life he had spent much of his own trying to live down. This was Lee's first pilgrimage to his father's grave; he never returned until the year in which he himself was dying.[19]

Over thirty years ago Lee had served in this region as a young lieutenant, fresh from West Point. He revisited some of the scenes of his youth and found some of his old friends as well. Catherine Mackay, mother of his classmate Jack Mackay, still lived in Savannah. And her daughter Eliza Mackay Stiles, whom Lee had courted casually, was in the city on an extended visit. She insisted upon mending some of Robert's shirts, and her company likely enlivened his life in Savannah as it had so many years earlier.[20]

Lee visited Fort Pulaski downstream from Savannah near the mouth of the

Savannah River. He had worked hard all those years ago to build Cockspur Island on which the fort rested—25 million bricks called "as strong as the Rocky Mountains" when finished in 1847. Lee left this command just over one month before Pulaski fell. He had directed construction at Fort Jackson, much closer to the city, in the event the Pulaski garrison succumbed to a siege; but he anticipated no genuine danger any time soon. Pulaski fell because no one expected rifled artillery (Parrot and James rifles) to be as effective as it was. In thirty hours the Federals blew away the supposed security that all that labor and all those bricks had promised. Fort Pulaski was one more object lesson that Lee's world and life were much in flux.[21]

As if to underscore the instability in Lee's Confederate career, on March 2, 1862, the President dispatched a telegram to his journeyman general: "If circumstances will in your judgement, warrant your leaving, I wish to see you here with the least delay." Both Davis and Lee understood that this was not an invitation but an order. Lee received the summons on a Sunday; he responded the same day and told the President that he would leave on Tuesday morning (March 4).[22]

Lee had made enough of an impression in Charleston to inspire rumors of his fate in Richmond. The consensus, following the lead of "Hermes," the Richmond correspondent of the Charleston *Mercury*, believed that Lee would become Davis's Secretary of War.[23]

The *Mercury* reported that Lee set out for the Confederate capital on Wednesday, March 5, which made symbolic sense; that day was Ash Wednesday in 1862, the beginning of the penitential Christian season of Lent. Lee did not become Secretary of War as the President shuffled his cabinet in the hope of prosecuting the war more efficiently and assuaging his political critics. Instead, Lee once more was "charged with the conduct of military operations in the armies of the Confederacy"—whatever that meant. He still had no command and possessed only the power of suggestion. Maybe Davis anticipated a role as chief of staff for a President acting out his constitutional prerogative as commander in chief. If so, he failed to communicate his idea to Lee and apparently appointed Lee to an intentionally nebulous post in order to frustrate the will of Congress, which was to legislate a commander in chief other than Davis.[24]

A general order of the Secretary of War on March 13 prescribed and announced Lee's new position. On March 14, Lee wrote Mary Lee, "I do not see either advantage or pleasure in my duties," and to his brother Carter, "I fear I shall be able to do little in the position assigned me & cannot hope to satisfy the feverish & excited expectation of our good people."[25]

By the time he wrote this pessimistic assessment Lee had no doubt discerned the political implications of his appointment and despaired of the machinations of Davis and Congress. He also knew more than he wanted to know of the desperate plight of his country. In his inaugural address as President under the permanent Constitution on February 22, Davis had proclaimed that moment "the darkest hour of our struggle." But when Lee arrived in

Richmond about two weeks later, the hour must have seemed darker still. Southern armies continued to lose battles, and McClellan's huge army would soon begin to move. As the military campaigning season loomed and Federal forces multiplied, the terms of enlistment of many, if not most, of the volunteer soldiers in the Confederate army were about to expire. These men intended to go home. The Confederacy within another month or two would become a nation at war without an army.[26]

Lee summarized the crisis confronting himself and his country quite well to Mary Lee: "In the present condition of affairs no one can foresee what may happen, nor in my judgment is it advisable for any one to make any arrangements with a view to permanency or pleasure." In the midst of gathering gloom, he could only resolve to "do my best." But Lee's best had accomplished precious little thus far during this war. He would have only had to be human to question his decision, made less than a year earlier, to cast his lot with this make-believe nation and to serve among this collection of fools masquerading as an army.[27]

No rational person, knowing what Lee knew, would have given the Confederate States of America any but the longest odds of surviving the summer. Lee was a rational person. But at this point his actions were not so much rational as they were existential. He persisted in trying to help an all but discredited government—and more besides. He offered his last son to a cause which seemed already lost.

Rob Lee did not have to join the army. He had wanted to enlist the previous April; but his father had refused his consent. Now amid renewed recruiting clamor, the Secretary of War specifically exempted students and faculty from the University of Virginia where Rob was enrolled. But Rob insisted, and his father relented.

On the Ides of March, 1862, Lee the full general took Lee the aspiring private to secure his uniform and equipment. Then Rob went alone to enlist in the Rockbridge Artillery. Much later Robert E. Lee, Jr., remembered that, "though he was very careful in providing me with the least amount [of baggage] he thought necessary, I soon found by experience that he had given me a great deal too much." Rob set out for his unit and for war on March 22, "in good spirits with two of his comrades." His father wrote his mother, "I think he ought to have had another pair of pants.[28]

18

"Lee Is Audacity Personified"

THE SAME DAY Robert Lee informed his wife that their youngest son had joined the war at age nineteen, he summarized the Southern perspective of a war going badly. "Our enemies are pressing us everywhere & our army is in the fermentation of reorganization," he wrote. He added, "I pray the great God may aid us & am endeavouring by every means in my power to bring out the troops & hasten them to their destination." But then this man so much in touch with a military circumstance growing daily more desperate changed the subject to shirts, and wrote twelve sentences about mending his shirts and enlarging collars and cuffs.

One factor in Lee's easy transit from national crisis to matters mundane was his incredible capacity to cope—to make the best of practically any situation and to resist the temptation to brood or bewail his fate. With the Confederacy nearly *in extremis* and his career, family, life, and world in grave danger, Lee could satisfy himself that he had done all he could do, invoke blessings from God, and try to secure some shirts that fit.[1]

Of course Lee wrote other letters during this spring of 1862. He wrote to the commanders of the various bodies of troops stationed about Virginia, and in consultation with the President attempted to concentrate Confederates in order to confront the Federal invasion. Union General George B. McClellan seemed to be transporting his entire army, more than 100,000 men, by water to Fort Monroe at the tip of the Peninsula (between the York and James Rivers). From there McClellan could threaten Norfolk, a significant Southern port cum naval yard, and/or Richmond. So Lee and the Confederates could only react when McClellan committed his host in one direction or another.[2]

When he was not responding to "enemies . . . pressing us everywhere," Lee became involved in the "fermentation of reorganization" within the Southern army. For some time now Confederate officials, elected and appointed, had worried about those expiring twelve-month enlistments and the prospect of facing the campaigning season of 1862 with a dissolving army. Congress had legislated all manner of inducements (furloughs, elections of officers, et al.) to try to retain the army intact. The War Department had imposed new requests for troops upon state governors. But none of these measures seemed enough; in the face of increasing national peril the army was shrinking.

Lee, with encouragement from Davis, began thinking seriously about a policy mandating national military service for white Confederate males between ages eighteen and forty-five. He delegated writing a draft law to Charles Marshall, a lawyer in civilian life who joined Lee's staff soon after he returned to Richmond from Coosawhatchie. It was Lee who produced the first draft of the Conscription Act, the first ever in North America, that the Congress adopted on April 16.

Most important for the immediate crisis was the provision of the act which bound those already in the army to remain. In the political negotiations that attended passage of conscription by Congress, many sensitive issues surfaced, and the execution of the law provoked all manner of conflict within the nation. In his memoir of the war, Marshall railed at the exemption policies and officer elections Congress enacted. No doubt Lee, too, took a dim view of common soldiers electing their commanders. But for the draft, though, there would likely have been many fewer common soldiers and thus no Confederacy beyond the spring of 1862.[3]

Conscription was the radical act of a desperate government on the verge of collapse. The only good news in Richmond had come from an unlikely source, the Southern navy. Bereft of ships and short on the materials and facilities from which to construct ships, the Confederate navy had launched a sea monster—the ironclad C.S.S. *Virginia,* built over the hull of the U.S.S. *Merrimack.* On March 8, 1862, the *Virginia* attacked Union ships off Newport News and destroyed two formidable vessels. Next day, however, the U.S.S. *Monitor,* a Federal ironclad, challenged the *Virginia* and fought her to a stand-off draw. As long as the *Monitor* remained in Hampton Roads, the *Virginia* could not destroy Federal ships at will (in fact she destroyed no more ships at all). But as long as the *Virginia* remained afloat, the Union navy did not dare to try to steam past the Confederate ironclad and into the mouth of the James River. This circumstance caused a pause in McClellan's invasion plan, which assumed Federal control of waterways.[4]

Nevertheless, the heroics of the men who made and sailed the *Virginia* seemed only to have delayed the inevitable. During the first week of April, McClellan joined his army at Fort Monroe, and the United States War Department closed its recruiting offices, firm in the belief that the government already had quite enough soldiers to quash the rebellion.[5]

Meanwhile, John Bankhead Magruder who commanded about 10,000 Confederate soldiers on the Peninsula realized that the enemy outnumbered his force by more than ten to one and outgunned him by an even larger margin. "I have made my arrangements to fight with my small force," Magruder wrote Lee, "but without the slightest hope of success." Another installment of Magruder gloom proclaimed, "Reinforcements come very slowly, and will probably be too late." On April 5, Magruder left his headquarters at

Yorktown and retreated to a house on the James River "to seek some days of quiet absolutely necessary to restore my health."[6]

On April 12, after consulting the President, Lee issued orders incorporating Magruder's command and the approximately equal number of men at Norfolk commanded by Benjamin Huger into the larger army of Joseph E. Johnston. "The Colonel," Lee's friend and classmate who was now a general, commanded the principal Confederate field army in Virginia. Until March 8–9 Johnston's army occupied the position established the previous summer on Bull Run near Manassas. Then Johnston withdrew to Culpeper Court House. The move was essentially sound; from Culpeper, Johnston could confront Federals advancing upon Richmond from Washington or from Fort Monroe with greater facility than he could from Manassas. But although the President had endorsed the move in principle, Johnston acted without informing Davis until five days after the fact, and the Confederates had destroyed immense quantities of supplies which Johnston declared impossible to transport. Now Johnston would have to move again to meet McClellan somewhere before Richmond.

And constantly in the back of the Confederate military mind was another Federal army commanded by Irvin McDowell, still in the vicinity of Washington. Here were 45,000 more Federals poised to fall upon Richmond from the north, if Johnston overcommitted his army against McClellan to the east of the capital.[7]

The immediate question became where to confront McClellan. After Johnston had had a chance to inspect Magruder's defensive line at Yorktown, he told President Davis that the position was untenable. Davis then convened a council of war on April 14 to discuss courses of action. In the President's office at about 11:00 A.M. were Davis, Johnston, Lee, Secretary of War George W. Randolph, and Johnston's senior subordinates, Generals Gustavus W. Smith and James Longstreet. Johnston repeated what he had told Davis about Magruder's Yorktown line. Then the debate began. Smith advocated holding Richmond against McClellan with as small a garrison as possible while the bulk of the Confederate army marched on Washington, Baltimore, maybe Philadelphia, and perhaps New York. Longstreet, too, seemed to share Smith's vision of invading the North. Johnston advocated a more moderate course: concentrate all available troops and fight the Federals in front of Richmond. Lee and Randolph insisted that the Peninsula was as good a place as any to face McClellan, and Randolph especially expressed concern about abandoning Norfolk without firing a shot. Davis acted as moderator and at 6:00 P.M. suggested a break and change of venue.

In accord with the President's wish, the council reconvened at seven o'-clock at the Executive Mansion. There the wrangling continued until 1:00 A.M., at which point Davis announced the conclusion. Johnston's army would march from Culpeper through Richmond and into Magruder's works at Yorktown. The Confederates would begin this campaign attempting to hold the lower Peninsula and Norfolk at once. Since he was the person charged with all this holding, Johnston was wary. But he left the fourteen-hour council of war resigned to go through the motions the President prescribed.[8]

March and April of 1862 were grim months for Confederate arms throughout the nascent nation. While the Davis administration and Lee the President's aide of necessity focused most of their attention and concern upon Federal threats growing ever closer to the capital, disasters multiplied elsewhere—indeed everywhere. In addition to defeats at Port Royal, Mill Springs, Roanoke Island, and Forts Henry and Donelson, Confederates lost at New Berne, North Carolina, Pea Ridge (Elkhorn Tavern), Arkansas, Shiloh (Pittsburg Landing), Island Number Ten (in the Mississippi River), Fort Pulaski, and New Orleans. Was the war already lost?[9]

In Virginia, the final stronghold of the Southern Confederacy, prospects seemed no better. A sample of Lee's counsel to his correspondents in command reveals the depth of the crisis.

To Magruder on March 29, Lee wrote, " . . . a call for reinforcements comes from every department. It is impossible to place at every point which is threatened a force which shall prove equal to every emergency."[10]

A telegram on April 10 to John C. Pemberton, who had succeeded Lee in command of the Department of South Carolina, Georgia, and Eastern Florida, announced a pressing need for troops in the West. "Send, if possible. . . . If Mississippi Valley is lost Atlantic states will be ruined."[11]

On April 18 Lee wrote to Henry Heth and Humphrey Marshall, who commanded troops in western and southwestern Virginia, respectively. He spoke of contingencies requiring them "to fall back toward Lynchburg" and "to fall back upon Abingdon," and advised Marshall "to ascertain the best route into North Carolina."[12]

From Pemberton in South Carolina on April 20 Lee requested more troops to meet the enemy in Virginia, and confessed, "I have no arms to send from here but pikes [spears!]."[13]

To Thomas J. Jackson in the Shenandoah Valley on April 21, Lee confided, "[Confederate] Genl. [Charles W.] Field has abandoned Fredericksburg, burned the bridges over the Rappahannock and retired fourteen miles south of the town."[14]

Precisely one month after he wrote to tell his wife, "Our enemies are pressing us everywhere," Lee wrote her again, "The enemy is pressing us on all sides." This time he added, "I hope a kind Providence will protect us & drive them back." Lee seemed to retain little faith that the Southern army was capable of much protecting or driving. He discussed Mary's need to flee from White House to a place of greater safety, mentioned several alternatives, and again "recommended a more distant move to Carolina or even Georgia."[15]

Yet even amid such sad tidings Lee could still laugh. In his letter to Mary he completed his advice about flight and then suggested that Rooney's wife Charlotte (Chass) sell the corn and wheat stored at White House. "She will have to manage for her husband now." Then he invited Chass and Life ("Precious Life," i.e., Mildred) to come and stay with him in Richmond. "There is to be a wedding to night," he added, and named the bride and groom. "Did you ever hear of such a thing! In such times to think of such trivial amusements!" Of course it is possible that Lee wrote these last two sentences in righteous indignation. But in the context of Lee and this letter, it is more probable that he wrote tongue-in-cheek to ridicule such pretension and maybe to mock his wife as well.[16]

Johnston's army did make the march from Culpeper to Yorktown. There Johnston commanded about 55,000 men and knew that McClellan outnumbered him two to one. Lee could hardly have been surprised to hear dissatisfaction from Johnston about the position his army occupied. From Richmond, Lee was in no position to make suggestions; but he did ask Johnston for his views and promised "to lay them before the President."

Thus began a pattern of Lee acting as an intermediary between Johnston and Davis. By this time Davis had become convinced that Johnston was insubordinate, and Johnston was just as convinced that Davis was a meddlesome, overbearing politician. So Lee was a buffer between two sensitive egos— softening in translation the criticism that President and general leveled at each other. In so doing Lee's common sense and his inherent recoil from conflict served the Confederate purpose.[17]

McClellan was cautious; moreover, he underestimated his advantage at Yorktown. But he would not delay his assault on Johnston's lines forever. As the Federals prepared for a massive attack, Johnston determined to withdraw back up the Peninsula on May 3–4 and fight some other day when his chances of success seemed more sanguine. The Confederates fought a rear-guard battle at Williamsburg on May 5, but continued to retreat until very near Richmond.

Johnston's withdrawal left Benjamin Huger and his 10,000 troops at Norfolk isolated and vulnerable; Lee coordinated Huger's withdrawal and the evacuation of Norfolk. Indeed, Lee seemed more aware than anyone else in Richmond of the "domino effect" of Johnston's retreat. The withdrawal from Yorktown exposed Norfolk; the evacuation of Norfolk in turn left the *Virginia* a ship without a port and doomed her to destruction by her own crew on May 11 (although Lee had tried to launch the ironclad against Union ships in the York River, so to render the *Virginia*'s final cruise victorious). Without the *Virginia* on guard, the James River lay open to Federal gunboats, and the James was navigable all the way to Richmond.

So Lee assigned his son Custis the task of somehow preventing the Federals from steaming up the James and assailing the capital from the river. At Drewry's Bluff, a scant seven miles from the city, the Confederates sank obstructions in the channel and mounted guns on the eighty-foot-high bank. Huger's refugees from Norfolk and the crew of the *Virginia* made ready to meet the *Monitor,* another ironclad, and three wooden ships as they steamed up the James in mid-May.[18]

"The loss of the *Virginia* has produced such profound sensation that all personal considerations are smothered," Lee wrote his wife on May 13. Lee resuscitated his own personal considerations sufficiently to withdraw all his money from the bank and entrust it and his bonds to James H. Caskie, a family friend with whose family daughter Mary was living. These facts he told his wife; Custis knew the details. "I have considered the matter maturely," Lee wrote; the letter was in effect a codicil to his will, written in the event he perished with the Confederacy.[19]

By the time Lee wrote this letter, Mary Lee had left White House, destined to become the principal river port and supply depot for the Federal army. She had fled before the invading army. Some months earlier her husband had written her from Coosawhatchie, "This place is too exposed to attack for the residence of a person as hard to move as you are. You would be captured while you were waiting 'a moment.'" Now Mary Lee waited "a moment" at the home of a neighbor a few miles from White House, and the Federals engulfed her in their advance toward Richmond. So now all the Lee property (Arlington, White House, Romancoke) and Mary Lee, too, were behind enemy lines.[20]

Jefferson Davis had already insisted, on May 9, that Varina Davis leave Richmond for Raleigh, North Carolina. Secretary of War Randolph had already ordered the government's archives loaded into railroad cars to expedite an evacuation. Congress adjourned and the members scattered. Virginia Governor John Letcher called a mass meeting of Richmond's citizens on May 15 to organize volunteers for local defense. The governor taunted the enemy— "Shell and be damned!" Richmond's Mayor Joseph Mayo swore he would never surrender the city. Beyond the taunting and swearing most Richmonders could hear the guns booming down at Drewry's Bluff. One moment of crisis was at hand.[21]

At some time during the alarm President Davis convened his cabinet and requested Lee's presence at the meeting. Davis was adamant that McClellan should never lay siege to Richmond. He planned to evacuate his capital in order to save the army, the capital, and the government at once. Davis seemed committed to fight forever for Southern independence and convinced that sooner or later his enemies would tire, lose the will to continue the war, and accept the inevitability of the Confederacy.

So the question for Lee was simple: in the event Richmond fell, to what place should Johnston's army retreat to make another stand? Lee answered the question; he recommended occupying a line along the Staunton River, 100 miles away to the southwest. But then Lee blurted out his own conviction: "Richmond must not be given up; it shall not be given up!" Postmaster General John H. Reagan saw tears in Lee's eyes, and later asserted that he never saw Lee display greater emotion.[22]

The crisis of May 15 passed without action from Lee, Davis, or anyone else in Richmond. The obstructions of Drewry's Bluff did bar the *Monitor*'s passage up the James, and Southern gunners managed to disable the *Galena,* the second Union ironclad. The three Federal wooden ships did not dare enter the fray. For the moment, at least, Richmond was safe, and the enemy vessels withdrew downstream. Of course none of this naval drama much affected

McClellan's army, and so the larger crisis continued.[23]

Having expressed his conviction so vehemently in the cabinet meeting, Lee was able to do very little during the next two weeks to save the Confederate capital. He continued to defuse the volatile relationship between Johnston and Davis. On May 18, for example, Lee wrote to Johnston that the President urges that "private houses be not taken for the use of the army without the consent of the owners and to their discomfort, as it has been stated to him . . . has been done, *no doubt without your knowledge."* In the same letter Lee added, "As you are now so convenient to the city the President wishes you to confer with him upon your future plans, and for that purpose desires you to see him at his office." Clearly Johnston had reported little or nothing of his intentions to Davis; nor did he respond to Davis's invitation to come to his office. On May 21, Lee again wrote to Johnston with "suggestions." He said, "The President desires to know the number of troops around Richmond, how they are posted, and the organization of the divisions and brigades; also the programme of operations you propose." Lee realized it might not be "prudent to commit it to paper," and so once again, "I would respectfully suggest that you communicate your views . . . personally to the President. . . ." In time Johnston did share some of his plans with Davis, most satisfactorily via Lee. Yet Davis never seemed to know anything consequential until after it had happened.[24]

There was irony indeed in the fact that during this period in which Lee tried so unsuccessfully to communicate with Johnston, he was able to exchange advice and confidences quite freely with one of the most secretive commanders in American military history: Thomas Jonathan Jackson. "Stonewall" Jackson commanded in the Shenandoah Valley. With Lee's suggestions and ample encouragement, Jackson waged a brilliant campaign against Federal forces many times stronger than his Valley Army. More than most Confederates Lee realized that Jackson's success in the Valley might convince the enemy high command to withhold McDowell's army from the campaign for Richmond. If the Federals believed that Jackson posed a threat to Washington, then McDowell just might remain in northern Virginia. "Whatever movements you make against [Union General Nathaniel P.] Banks do it speedily, and if successful, drive him back towards the Potomac, and create the impression as far as practicable that you design threatening that line," Lee instructed Jackson on May 16. Jackson responded, attacking Banks at Front Royal on May 23, at Newtown on May 24, and then at Winchester on May 25. Banks's army, once 20,000 men, streamed to the Potomac, and Abraham Lincoln recalled McDowell from his march to join McClellan.[25]

Even without McDowell's 45,000, McClellan still commanded an army of more than 100,000 men by now within the suburbs of Richmond. Johnston commanded between two thirds and three fourths of McClellan's numbers, and he knew that he must find an opportunity to attack while he still had some space within which to maneuver. The result of Johnston's resolve was the Battle of Seven Pines/Fair Oaks on May 31.

Henry ("Light-Horse Harry") Lee, III, portrait by Gilbert Stuart. Father of Robert E. Lee, Henry Lee was a hero in the Revolutionary War, Governor of Virginia, Member of Congress, and rascal (1756–1818).
The Library of Virginia

Portrait of Robert E. Lee at age 31, painted in Baltimore by William E. West in the spring of 1838.
Virginia Historical Society

Robert E. Lee in 1850 or 1851 at age 43 or 44, after the Mexican War before his cavalry command in Texas, shortly before he became Superintendent of the United States Military Academy at West Point. *Valentine Museum*

Stratford Hall, birthplace of Robert E. Lee. Built during the 1740s by Thomas Lee, the house remained in the Lee family until 1822. Robert E. Lee only lived at Stratford from 1807 until the summer of 1810, but he continued to think of the place as "home." *Museum of the Confederacy*

Mildred Childe Lee (1846–1904), known within the family as "Precious Life," was the youngest child in the Lee family, and likely the most vivacious.
Virginia Historical Society

Robert E. Lee, Jr. (1843–1914) was "Rob" within the family. He volunteered to serve in the Confederate Army as a private and later joined the staff of his brother Rooney.
Virginia Historical Society

"Romancoke" in King William County, Virginia, belonged to George Washington Parke Custis and, at his death in 1857, passed to his grandson Robert E. Lee, Jr., when he reached the age of twenty-one. *Washington and Lee University*

Mildred Childe Lee as an adult managed the family household after her father's death and resented photographs and stories of him from the brief period in his life when he was old and ill. *Museum of the Confederacy*

Mary Custis Lee, the daughter (1835–1918), was seemingly the most independent of the children. However, in later life she enjoyed the distinction of being "the last surviving daughter of Robert E. Lee." *Virginia Historical Society*

Agnes Lee (1841–1873), although afflicted with neuralgia herself, took care of her mother during the war and accompanied her father on his "farewell tour" in 1870. *Museum of the Confederacy*

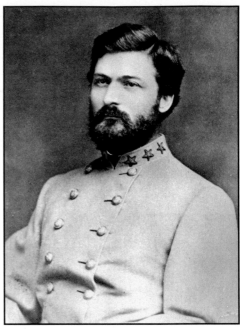

Above, left: William Henry Fitzhugh ("Rooney") Lee (1837–1891) was a capable cavalry commander for J. E. B. Stuart during the war and a United States Congressman thereafter.
Valentine Museum.

Above, right: George Washington Custis Lee (1832–1913), whose nickname was "Boo" or "Mr. Boo" within the family, was the oldest child of the Lees. He spent his time during the war on the staff of Confederate President Jefferson Davis.
Museum of the Confederacy

Stephen Dill Lee, James Ewell Brown Stuart, and George Washington Custis Lee, a photograph most likely taken soon after their graduation from West Point in 1854.
Virginia Historical Society

Arlington, Washington City P.O.
20 Apl 1861

Lt Genl Winfield Scott
Commd U.S. Army

Genl

Since my interview with you on the
18 Inst: I have felt that I ought not longer
to hold my Commission in the Army, I therefore
tender my resignation which I request you will recommend
for acceptance. It would have been presented
at once but for the struggle it has Cost me to
Separate myself from a Service to which I have devoted
all the best years of my life, & all the ability
I possessed. During that time, more than a quarter of a century
I have experienced nothing but Kindness & Consideration
from my Superiors & the most Cordial friendship
from my Comrades. To no one Genl have I been
as much indebted as to yourself for kindness &
Consideration, & it has always been my ardent
desire to merit your approbation. I shall carry
with me to the grave the most grateful recollection
of your kind Consideration, & your name & fame
will always be dear to me. Save in the defence of my native State
my most earnest wishes for the Continuance of
your happiness & prosperity. believe me
most truly yours
R E Lee

Draft copy of Robert E. Lee's letter of resignation from the United States Army.
Museum of the Confederacy

THE SOUTHERN ILLUSTRATED NEWS.

Vol. I. RICHMOND, SATURDAY, JANUARY 17, 1863. No. 19.

ROBERT EDMUND LEE,

COMMANDER-IN-CHIEF OF THE CONFEDERATE FORCES.

[W. B. CAMPBELL, Engraver.]

[FROM A PHOTOGRAPH BY REES, TAKEN TEN YEARS AGO.

On the opposite page:
Southern Illustrated News,
January 17, 1863, features a
version of the photograph
of Robert E. Lee taken
after the Mexican War
before his tour of duty at
West Point. *Museum of the
Confederacy*

In full dress uniform with
his sash and sword, Robert
E. Lee posed for J. Vanner-
son in early 1864.
Valentine Museum

Hd Qtrs Army of No. Va
19th April 1865

Gen Orders No 9

After four years of Arduous Service
Marked by unsurpassed courage and fortitude the
Army of No. Va. has been compelled to yield to
overwhelming numbers & resources.

I need not tell the brave Survivors of so many
hard fought battles who have remained Steadfast
to the last, that I have consented to the result
from no distrust of them

But feeling that valour and devotion could accomplish
nothing that would compensate for the loss that must
have attended the continuance of the contest, I determined
to avoid the useless sacrifice of those whose past services
have endeared them to their countrymen,

By the terms of the agreement officers and men can return
to their homes and remain until exchanged, you will
take with you the satisfaction that proceeds from the
conciousness of duty faithfully performed and I earnestly
pray that a mercifull god will extend to you his
blessing and protection with an unceasing admiration of
your constancy and devotion to your country and a
grateful rememberance of your kind and generous consideration
for myself I bid you an affectionate farewell

R E Lee
Genl

General Orders #9, April 9, 1865, Robert E. Lee's farewell address to his army, drafted
by his aide Charles Marshall. *Museum of the Confederacy*

Robert E. Lee on Traveller, September 1866. Lee purchased the horse during the fall of 1861 for $200, rode him throughout the war, and remained devoted to the animal afterward.
Washington and Lee University

Robert E. Lee, Jr. (1843–1914), William Henry Fitzhugh ("Rooney") Lee (1837–1891), and George Washington Custis Lee (1832–1913), Lee sons in mature life, none of whom ever quite escaped the shadow of their famous father.
Virginia Historical Society / Washington and Lee University

Mary Custis Lee (1807–1873). Never very robust, Lee's wife suffered from arthritis, which rendered her an invalid from 1863. *Washington and Lee University*

On the opposite page: Mathew Brady photograph of Robert E. Lee taken in Richmond on April 16, 1865, only a few days after Lee's return from Appomattox. *National Archives / Museum of the Confederacy*

The Lee residence in Richmond from January 1864, until the summer of 1865, was previously "The Mess" when rented by son Custis and some of his bachelor friends. *Stratford Hall*

The President's House at Washington College. Built from standardized plans, the house did, however, boast conveniences such as central heat and incorporated features like the porch on three sides of the main floor to accommodate the Lees. The interior of the President's House, below, reflects the Victorian decor in style when the Lees lived there. *Washington and Lee University photos*

The parlor. Compare with the absence of ornamentation in Lee's study. Below:
Lee's study at Washington College as he left it before he died. The simple decor
contrasts with the Victorian ornamentation in the President's House.
Virginia Historical Society / Washington and Lee University photos

Perhaps the final photograph of Robert E. Lee, taken in 1870 when
he was, or was almost, sixty-three years old. *Virginia Historical Society*

Lee was a spectator, much as he had been all spring. Neither he nor the President knew anything about Johnston's plans beyond his general intention to attack some time soon. Lee did ride out to the east of Richmond on May 31 and found to his surprise a major battle in progress. By chance President Davis also rode out to find Johnston and discovered Lee and combat instead.

Johnston spent much of that day attempting to unscramble considerable confusion caused in part by his own haste and secrecy in planning the attack. Seven Pines/Fair Oaks was an abortive attempt to attack two corps (of five) of McClellan's army that were south of the Chickahominy River and partially isolated from the rest of the Federal army by torrential rains which had washed out bridges over the river. The fighting produced 6,000 Southern casualties (5,000 Federal) and did not much alter the positions of the armies. But as daylight faded, Joe Johnston fell, struck by a ball in the shoulder and seriously wounded in the ribs by a shell fragment. Davis and Lee both looked down at the fallen general as he lay in pain on a litter; both wished him well.[26]

Later that evening Lee and Davis rode back to Richmond with their staff officers. En route the President informed Lee that he would inherit command of Johnston's army.

Unless Davis wished to assume the command himself (a prospect that he probably considered quite seriously), the President really had no one else to whom he could entrust the army. Gustavus W. Smith was next senior to Johnston, had succeeded him in command, and would continue in charge overnight. But Smith's health was wretched and on June 1 Smith confirmed the President's judgment by suffering a total collapse on the field. The army required decisive leadership immediately, and Lee was the only available general with knowledge of the situation. Davis had worked with Lee; he believed that he and Lee looked at the war alike. To a degree, they did. To the degree they did not, and Lee had better sense than to let Davis discern the fundamental difference.[27]

Robert Lee assumed command of the army he rechristened the Army of Northern Virginia on June 1, 1862. That same day Johnston's battle at Seven Pines/Fair Oaks wound down with no interference from the new commander. Lee withdrew his army from contact with the enemy and had the troops resume the positions near Richmond they had occupied on May 30. Then he set the men to work digging defensive positions and improving the positions already in place east of Richmond.[28]

Most of the soldiers believed "Granny Lee" was acting out his nickname once again. Now they dubbed Lee the "King of Spades" and grumbled about warriors being assigned the work of slaves. Lee heard the complaints and wrote his mind in a stream-of-consciousness letter to the President. "Our people are opposed to work," he lamented. But just such hard labor had brought the Federal army where it now was, and the example of the Roman legions still lived in their roads and fortifications extant in Europe. "There is nothing so military as labour," Lee concluded, "& nothing so important to an army as to save the lives of its soldiers."[29]

Lee's nicknames revealed how little most people really knew about him. One of the best descriptions of Lee at his accession to command came from Lee himself in a letter to his daughter-in-law Chass:

My coat is of gray, of the regulation style and pattern, and my pants of dark blue as is also prescribed, partly hid by my long boots. I have the same handsome hat which surmounts my gray head (the latter is not prescribed in the regulations) and shields my ugly face, which is masked by a white beard as stiff and wiry as the teeth of a [cotton] card. In fact, an uglier person you have never seen, and so unattractive is it to our enemies that they shoot at it whenever visible to them, but though age with its snow has whitened my head, and its frosts have stiffened my limbs, my heart you well know, is not frozen to you, and summer returns when I see you.[30]

One of Lee's subordinates offered observations much less romantic in a letter to his father:

Genl. Lee . . . is the grandson [wrong] of Col. Harry Lee of Revolutionary fame. He is a large, stout man, somewhat inclined to corpulency, & probably 55 years of age. He makes no show or parade and rides about from one point to another as quietly as a farmer would ride over his farm.[31]

From brief service on Lee's staff, Joseph Christmas Ives—who was then serving on the President's staff—did grasp the most essential fact about the new commander. Ives was discussing the strategic situation with Edward Porter Alexander, former aide to Johnston and later in command of artillery in the Army of Northern Virginia. Alexander lamented the fact that the enemy held the initiative, and he asked Ives if Lee had the capacity to win in such circumstances.

Alexander, if there is one man in either army, Federal or Confederate, who is, head & shoulders, far above every other one in either army in audacity that man is Gen. Lee, and you will very soon have lived to see it. Lee is audacity personified. His name is audacity. . . .

Ives appeared prescient within a few weeks, and Alexander never quite understood how Ives could know Lee so well.[32]

Lee had learned to dare from his mentor Winfield Scott. In Mexico, Scott had always the inferior force in unfamiliar country with the obligation to pursue the offensive. Lee appreciated Scott's bold strategy and probably developed a confidence in attacking that made him miscalculate against an enemy well led and armed with rifles instead of much shorter-range muskets.[33]

Lee had also observed this war for more than a year. Ever since Manassas/ Bull Run, he had mentally absorbed and emotionally digested an all but unbroken string of defeats. Too well he knew the peril in which his army and his country now lay. He also knew that Confederate armies would never enjoy anything near parity with their enemies in numbers of men and quantity of resources; Lee knew that the Confederacy was desperate.

Lee's fate was much associated with the Confederacy. He had three sons committed to the same cause. His wife was somewhere behind enemy lines, like all the property in land that was supposed to support himself and his children in some degree of style. A letter from Mary Lee informed him that their young grandson (child of Chass and Rooney) had died. His invested wealth offered only tenuous promise of surviving the collapse of the Confederacy or confiscation by his enemies. Certainly Lee was free to risk and to dare; and one source of Lee's freedom was the very little he had left to lose.[34]

Like Jefferson Davis, Lee had a sophisticated sense of Southern strategy. Like Davis, Lee had come to embrace the concept of an offensive defensive. Abandoning the notion of defending every inch of Southern soil, both men were willing to endure invasion. Both believed that resourceful Confederate commanders might choose their time, place, and circumstance, and strike an exposed enemy army. Lee's appreciation of the Confederacy's military disparity (present and increasing) with the United States and his understanding of the will to conquest among his Northern enemies produced a sense of urgency in his strategic thinking. If the Confederacy were to have a chance of winning this war, Southern arms must fight and win a climactic campaign. And the longer such a campaign were delayed, the more difficult a "battle of annihilation" would become. Consequently, within hours of assuming command, Lee began plotting the utter destruction of McClellan's army. While most Southerners simply sought to drive the enemy from the suburbs of Richmond, Lee's goal was much more ambitious: he planned to obliterate his enemy.[35]

As soon as possible Lee left his offices in the War Department (the former Mechanics Institute) and moved in with his army. His headquarters had been the home of Mary C. Dabbs, a widow who had moved to Richmond for safety's sake, and left her farm, High Meadows. The house was a side hall plan, two-story brick structure on Nine Mile Road about a mile and a half due east of Richmond. "Dabb's House" (instead of Dabb's) was an unpretentious place, and Lee's personal staff was correspondingly small. He retained Robert H. Chilton and A. P. Mason from Johnston's staff and brought A. L. Long, Charles Marshall, Charles S. Venable, T. M. R. Talcott, and Walter H. Taylor with him from Richmond. These men were now his "family."[36]

Two days after assuming command (on June 3) Lee assembled the generals within his army at "The Chimneys," further out on Nine Mile Road. This was not a happy gathering; it certainly reinforced Lee's sense of crisis. Some subordinates suggested drawing their lines closer to Richmond because some of the position was already within range of Federal artillery. Lee said little during the discussion, but afterward remarked, "If we leave this line because they can shell us, we shall have to leave the next for the same reason, and I don't see how we can stop this side of Richmond."[37]

By June 5, Lee had made up his mind. That day he began his custom of informing the President solicitously, regularly about the situation and his intentions. In contrast to Johnston, Lee was quite careful to keep Davis appraised of his plans and to tell Davis some of what he (Davis) wanted to hear, along with much of what he (Lee) wanted Davis to hear.

Lee's letter to Davis was very much a ramble, most unlike a closely reasoned position paper; but within this military mélange Lee revealed the expanse of his vision and the audacity of his intent.

> After much reflection I think if it was possible to reinforce Jackson [in the Valley] strongly, it would change the character of the war. This can only be done by the troops in Georgia, South Carolina & North Carolina. Jackson could in that event cross Maryland into Pennsylvania. It would call all the enemy from our Southern coast & liberate those states. . . . McClellan will make this a battle of posts. He will take position from position, under cover of his heavy guns, & we cannot get at him without storming his works, which with our new troops is extremely hazardous. You witnessed the experiment Saturday [Seven Pines/Fair Oaks]. It will require 100,000 men to resist the regular siege of Richmond, which perhaps would only prolong not save it. I am preparing a line that I can hold with part of our forces in front, while with the rest I will endeavour to make a diversion to bring McClellan out. . . . I . . . have written up [to Josiah Gorgas, Chief of Ordnance] to see if I can get made an iron battery on [railroad] trucks with a heavy gun, to sweep the country in our front. The enemy cannot move his heavy guns except on the railroad. You have seen nothing like the roads on the Chickahominy bottom. . . . Our position requires you should know everything & you must excuse my troubling you.[38]

Lee did manage modestly to reinforce Jackson; but the grand offensive into Maryland and Pennsylvania with his Valley Army augmented by troops from the Carolinas and Georgia had to wait. Lee's prediction that McClellan would let his big guns do the heavy work in his campaign was incredibly accurate. Ten days after Lee wrote Davis about McClellan's "battle of posts," McClellan wrote his wife, "I will push them in upon Richmond & behind their works—then I will bring up my heavy guns—shell the city & carry it by assault."[39]

Buried in his collected reflections on the situation was Lee's bold plan: Hold the Federals outside of Richmond with the defensive works the troops were now preparing. The better the earthworks, the fewer men it would require to keep McClellan at bay. With two thirds of his army Lee proposed to attack the Federal right flank and drive the enemy from his works. And into the rear of McClellan's right flank Lee planned to unleash Jackson's Valley Army following a rapid, secret march from the Shenandoah.

Here was ample audacity. If the Federals realized how thin were Lee's lines in front of Richmond, they could storm into the city, capture Lee's government, cut Lee's lines of supply and communication, and then watch Lee starve for a while on the Chickahominy bottom before receiving the surrender of his floundering army. If Federal commanders in the Shenandoah Valley should follow Jackson over the mountains, they could then assault Jackson's rear while Jackson was supposed to be attacking McClellan. If Washington allowed McDowell's army to march south, then 45,000 Union troops would flank Lee's flank attack. Lee gambled that none of these possibilities would occur. He gambled that his offensive would seize the initiative from his enemies. The desperation of a war all but lost justified Lee's gamble.

Lee proposed his intention as a specific plan to the President on June 10. "I think this is our surest move," he wrote, and urged Davis, "Please consider this immediately and decide." Davis acquiesced—very likely because he knew he had no real choice.[40]

A prudent person in June 1862 would have given the Confederacy scant chance to survive the Peninsula Campaign. Lee and Davis seemed to be playing a game—pretending they still had a nation and an army. Was Lee simply going through the motions that pride prescribed before he accepted the inevitable?

19

"The Federal Army
Should Have Been Destroyed"

B Y JUNE OF 1862 Mary Lee had seen more of the enemy than her husband. While Robert Lee was in an office in Richmond thinking about Federals, his wife was out in the countryside living among Yankees.

During her migration from Arlington to the homes of her relatives in northern Virginia, to White House in Tidewater, Mary Lee had remained a step ahead of her enemies. But they were closing fast. When she left White House, Mary Lee posted a note on the front door of the house:

> Northern soldiers who profess to reverence Washington,
> forebear to desecrate the home of his first married life, the
> property of his wife, now owned by her descendants.

Federal troops stationed at White House, which became a principal port and supply depot, honored her request for the next month or so. The Federals overtook the author of the note at the home of a friend nearby and treated her with a courtesy she did not return.[1]

So with her daughters Annie and Mildred, Mary Lee moved again, this time to Marlbourne in Hanover County, one of the plantations of Edmund Ruffin, the aged radical who claimed to have fired the first shot in the war. Ruffin was elsewhere at the time, and Mary Lee remained for several weeks with his daughter who lived on the place. Again the enemy encompassed her as they advanced toward Richmond. Again the Federals left Mary Lee undisturbed within their lines, although some of them were concerned that she was spying on them.

Finally, Mary Lee decided to move once more through enemy lines to Richmond. This time on June 10 she traveled to George B. McClellan's headquarters, thence with a Federal escort to the Meadow Bridges over the Chickahominy River, and from there with a Confederate escort to Richmond. At this point in her life she could barely hobble from her arthritis; she was a year away from a wheelchair. But she certainly displayed indomitable spirit throughout her odyssey.[2]

Near the conclusion of her wandering, Mary Lee lost her only grandchild, Rooney and Chass's infant son. Mary informed Robert Lee on June 6, and he answered her letter on June 10, some time before he learned of her safe arrival in Richmond.

These facts and dates are consequential, because on June 22 Robert Lee wrote to his daughter-in-law, told her of Rooney's recent exploits, answered questions about his own appearance, and concluded with a request that she "Kiss your sweet boy for me. . . ." Lee had forgotten that his grandson, Charlotte's "sweet boy," was dead! Clearly his mind was focused upon other matters.[3]

Robert Lee had not seen Mary Lee since before the war—since April 22, 1861, when he left Arlington for Richmond and command of the armed forces of Virginia. Now, after more than thirteen months, several duty assignments, and considerable family trauma, Lee was too busy to greet the refugees. "I am strongly tempted to go in to see you," he wrote on the day Mary Lee arrived. "My constant duties here alone prevent, & preparations for the anticipated movement of troops will detain me. I will go up to see you as soon as I can." It is difficult to determine when Robert and Mary Lee did reunite. He wrote to her on June 25, "It is . . . impossible for me to see you," and on July 9, "I shall come in when I can but I have much to do & do not know when that will be." Surely he was able to pay her a visit some time soon after her arrival.[4]

But, as in the case of his grandson, Lee was too intent upon the impending campaign to expend much attention upon his wife. Duty called and took priority. At long last this war had brought resolution to the tension between freedom and control that Lee seemed to feel so acutely. Because Lee was finally in command of an army in the field, he had some charge of the events that conditioned his life. He was free to risk, to fail, to win. His understanding of what he ought to do was very nearly one with his idea of what he wanted to do. And what he wanted to do was to strike a decisive blow before it was too late.

Lee planned to stave off the mass of McClellan's army with Benjamin Huger and John B. Magruder's divisions, about 25,000 troops in well-prepared field fortifications. Then, with the rest of the army—perhaps 47,000 men—he would attack the Federal right flank north of the Chickahominy River and unleash Stonewall Jackson and his Valley Army upon the rear of the enemy. Finally he would force the Federals out of their works and destroy them in the chaos of the rout. This was Lee's plan. To make plan into reality he had a great deal of work to do.

The same day that Mary Lee and her daughters passed through the lines and into Richmond, J. E. B. Stuart was at Dabb's House to speak with Lee about the Federal right flank. A cadet when Lee was Superintendent at West Point, and Lee's aide at Harpers Ferry in 1859, Stuart now commanded all the cavalry in the Army of Northern Virginia. With his brigade of horsemen he controlled whatever space lay between armies to discern dispositions and strength of the enemy and to deny the enemy any such knowledge about friendly forces. Stuart had already spent a night behind enemy lines and spoken to one of his spies. He had also dispatched John S. Mosby, a private soldier whom Stuart believed had potential, to scout Totopotomoy Creek to see if the enemy flank extended that far. Now Stuart and Lee discussed a significant cavalry expedition to confirm Stuart's belief and Lee's hope that the Federal right flank was vulnerable.

Lee sent an order the next day (June 11), and at 2:00 A.M. on the morning after that Stuart roused his staff and proclaimed, "Gentlemen in ten minutes every man must be in his saddle!" Stuart had already readied 1,200 troops, and on June 12 they rode north out of Richmond to Ashland, rested for part of the night, and then started east down the Southern bank of the Pamunkey River to Old Church. At this juncture Stuart knew that the Federals did not occupy this region in strength; their flank was "in the air." But at Old Church Stuart decided to continue his reconnaissance all the way around the Federal army. And he did—100 miles in just over three days with but one casualty. Stuart's "Ride Around McClellan" demonstrated that the Confederates were still dangerous, and Stuart's panache disguised his mission and thus deceived McClellan. Stuart was an instant hero in a country desperate for anything but more bad news.[5]

Jeb Stuart was not alone in the Southern pantheon. "Stonewall" Jackson pressed his advantage in the Shenandoah Valley, won smashing victories at Cross Keys (June 8) and Port Republic (June 9), and wrote to Lee, "Circumstances greatly favor my moving to Richmond in accordance with your plan." Lee passed the letter along to the President with the comment, "I think the sooner Jackson can move this way, the better," and the counsel, "We must be secret & quick."[6]

Lee crossed his Rubicon on June 16 when he ordered Jackson to the Pamunkey. On Monday morning, June 23, Lee summoned his principal subordinates to come to Dabb's House that afternoon. About three o'clock two men rode into the yard. One of them walked into the house, encountered someone from Lee's staff, and learned that the commanding general was at work in his office just behind the parlor/adjutant general's office. The man walked back into the yard, propped himself against the fence, and covered half of his face with the bill of his cap. The Valley Army was en route. Jackson had arrived.[7]

He had begun his journey at one o'clock that morning, ridden fourteen hours and 52 miles on a series of horses. He had been careful not to commence his ride on Sunday. When he went inside to meet with Lee, he accepted only a glass of milk with which to refresh himself.[8]

Joining Lee and Jackson at Dabb's House that afternoon were Daniel Harvey Hill (West Point, Mexican War, educator recently made a major general, abrasive), Ambrose Powell Hill (West Point, Mexican War, distinguished at Williamsburg, now a major general), and James Longstreet (West Point, Mexican War, major general, blundered badly at Seven Pines/Fair Oaks). These were the men upon whom Lee depended to crush McClellan's army; Jackson, the Hills (they were not related), and Longstreet would command the troops assaulting the Federal right flank. Coordinating their marches and attacks was absolutely crucial.[9]

Participants in this council of war had emerged from a reorganization/ purge of Johnston's army. In three weeks Lee had made changes that rendered the Army of Northern Virginia more his own. Gustavus W. Smith had commanded his own division plus the entire left wing of Johnston's army; now he was resting, never again to command in the field with this army. Longstreet had commanded Johnston's right wing; he retained command of his division (added three regiments) and so shared in Lee's reorganization of the army into a collection of divisions instead of two wings and a reserve. A. P. Hill inherited two of Smith's brigades. D. H. Hill still commanded five brigades in his division; but his number of infantry regiments increased from twenty-one to twenty-three, and he now had an artillery battalion that he had not had at Seven Pines/Fair Oaks. Jackson was new to the organization although he now had two brigades once commanded by Smith. Lee had done some significant shifting, and for this moment at least, these four men were winners; Smith was the principal (and permanent) loser. The reorganization had also expanded the size of the army. Lee, who had never commanded in combat, began this campaign with 92,400 men.[10]

When Lee closed the door of the second-story room and convened the council of war, he explained his thinking about the impending campaign. He said that he wanted the four commands represented in the room to sweep down the north bank of the Chickahominy driving and destroying the Federal army as they advanced. Then Lee left the room to allow his subordinates to determine among themselves who would take which road and what would be the timetable of the attack. When Lee returned, he agreed with the routes and times selected, and dismissed the council at dark on the 23rd. Jackson left to ride again to his army.[11]

On June 24, Lee wrote out his attack order—General Orders No. 75. The order called for Jackson to begin his march toward battle at 3:00 A.M. on June 26. When Jackson arrived in the rear of the enemy and his arrival generated the sounds of firing, the Hills and Longstreet would launch attacks upon Mechanicsville. Confederate troops were supposed to sweep down the northern bank of the Chickahominy picking off the Federals as they left their works and sought safety. The campaign depended upon Jackson's arrival; firing from Jackson's sector was the signal for everyone else.[12]

The campaign just east of Richmond on the Chickahominy became known universally as the Seven Days, so-called because the two major armies remained in contact, engaged in combat, for seven consecutive days.

Day One
Wednesday, June 25, 1862
OAK GROVE *or* KING'S SCHOOLHOUSE

McClellan attacked! It was a probing advance against Huger's works across the half-mile or so which separated the two armies due east of Richmond. Such an attack was precisely what Lee feared most; if the enemy realized how thin

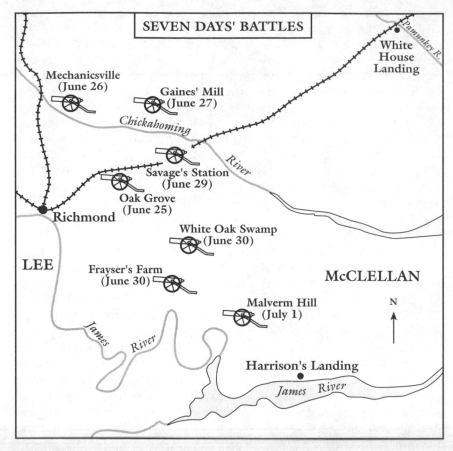

were Huger's lines in front of the capital, they would surely mount a serious assault and sweep into the city. Moreover, if McClellan knew enough to attack here (down the Williamsburg Road), did he also know about Lee's "surprise" attack forming on the Federal right flank?

Lee rode out the Williamsburg Road to watch the action around noon. He did not like some of what he saw and informed Davis, "The affair on the whole was not well managed." On the other hand, "The general behavior of the troops was good," and the Federals did not reach near enough to Huger's trenches to discover his strength or lack of strength in this sector. In a series of sharp fights among several brigades the Federal front moved a little closer to Richmond, perhaps a few hundred yards.

Lee could only hope that McClellan did not know the Confederate troop dispositions; as it was, McClellan became convinced that day that he faced 200,000 rebels, and he heard rumors, too, of Jackson en route. Lee, of course, knew none of this and wrote Davis, "I fear from the operations of the enemy . . . that our plan of operations has been discovered to them." He implored Huger the next morning to "Hold your trenches to [until] night at the point of the bayonet if necessary."[13]

The day had been muggy, with intermittent, misting rain. As the battle ceased, so did the rain, and as the sun set, people in Richmond witnessed a rainbow off to the east over the earthworks of Lee's army. Many believed it was a portent, and indeed it was, if hoping could make it so. Lee may or may not have seen the rainbow; he was never much of a mystic and doubtless desired evidence of approaching good fortune firmer than bands of refracted light. Whatever the omens, Lee wrote to the President that evening, "I have determined to make no change in the plan."[14]

Day Two
Thursday, June 26
MECHANICSVILLE

Jackson had only reached Ashland, a village 15 miles due north of Richmond, on June 25. In a note to Lee he blamed high water and mud and promised to resume his march the following day at 2:30 A.M. Jackson had left himself a long, hot journey into battle. To be where he was supposed to be to do what he was supposed to do, Jackson would have to march 15 miles, deploy his troops for battle, engage the enemy (on or near Beaver Dam Creek), and then somehow inspire men who had done all these tasks to pursue a presumably beaten foe down the north bank of the Chickahominy. And this presupposed that Jackson knew the road systems near Richmond or had adequate maps, neither of which was true. Lee could still hope that Jackson would arrive with his army in time to contribute to the battle on June 26; but such hope depended more on fantasy than fact. Very likely, though, Lee himself lacked sufficient knowledge of the roads and accurate enough maps to realize the dimensions of Jackson's challenge. So Lee continued to believe that his concerted attack upon the Federal right flank would occur on the 26th. Accordingly, Lee's staff packed their papers and informed President Davis that Lee's headquarters would be on the Mechanicsville Turnpike.[15]

Lee rode to the bluff overlooking the valley of the Chickahominy; from this vantage point he could see some of Mechanicsville just over the river and some of the troops who were ready to launch his attack. He could see or sense that everyone on the south bank of the Chickahominy was ready.

They simply waited for Jackson to arrive; Lee's order read: "As soon as the movements of these columns are discovered, Genl. A. P. Hill will cross the Chickahominy near Meadow Bridge and move . . . upon Mechanicsville, and the passage across the [Mechanicsville Turnpike] bridge opened, Genl. Longstreet with his division and that of Genl. D. H. Hill will cross the Chickahominy. . . ." They waited all morning, through midday, and into the afternoon, and still no one "discovered" anything from Jackson's columns. The Southern soldiers "lay on their arms," or more likely lay on the grass in the shade with their weapons nearby.

While the men tried to relax, the Confederate high command tried to be busy. President Davis, Secretary of War Randolph, and their staff members rode out from Richmond to watch the action. Now there was no action. Lee should have been some combination of nervous, worried, and frustrated. If so, he did not show his concern to those around him. The afternoon wore on with only rumors to stir the monotony.

Finally, after 3:00 P.M., probably closer to 4:00 P.M., Lee heard rifle fire from the northwest, the direction of Meadow Bridges. Next he saw Federal soldiers retreating to Mechanicsville, and the firing increased, and then a line of skirmishers in gray appeared. Lee at last knew what was happening. "Those are Hill's men," he stated, and then said to Longstreet, "General, you may now cross over." The day of battle was far spent; but at least the battle had finally begun.[16]

A. P. Hill's troops did open the way for Longstreet and D. H. Hill to cross the Chickahominy and move on to Mechanicsville via the turnpike. And A. P. Hill's troops did sweep through the little crossroads village and continue to the east toward Beaverdam Creek. But then it became clear that something was dreadfully wrong. The Confederates encountered a very strong, in fact impenetrable, Federal position along Beaverdam Creek. That should have been all right, because Jackson should have been in position to attack the Federal line from the flank and rear. But Jackson was nowhere in evidence.

A. P. Hill had not "discovered" Jackson's approach; he launched his attack presumably on the assumption that Jackson would soon arrive. In fact, Jackson spent a long and confusing day on the march and never came closer than three miles to the enemy battle line on Beaverdam Creek. Jackson reached a road junction known as Hundley's Corner about 5:00 P.M., heard the sounds of battle south of him, elected to stop, spend the night where he was, and try to sort out the situation the following day. So all those who were at Mechanicsville waiting for Jackson's arrival on the Federal flank were waiting in vain.[17]

Soon after Jackson began making camp at Hundley's Corner, Lee, who knew nothing of Jackson's whereabouts or intentions, rode down the hill to the Mechanicsville Turnpike across the Chickahominy and into the village. He picked his way toward Beaverdam Creek and stood in a field to view the futile attempts of five brigades to storm the Federal line. The attackers confronted more or less open space raked by artillery fire, then a tangle of felled trees (abatis) on the western bank of the creek, then the creek itself, and ample Yankees in prepared positions on the eastern slope/bluffs of the creek valley.

Artillery shells were exploding around the small rise where Lee stood, and then he noticed President Davis with his entourage of civilians standing nearby. He rode over to the party, and addressed Davis, "Who is all this army and what is it doing here?"

The commander in chief responded, "It is not my army, General."

To which Lee countered, "It is certainly not my army, Mr. President, and this is no place for it."

"Well, General," said Davis, "If I withdraw, perhaps they will follow me," and he led the civilians out of Lee's sight at last.

No Confederates belonged anywhere near this Federal position. But having committed himself to combat under these circumstances, Lee believed that he must make the effort, if only to retain the initiative, and there was still time for Jackson to appear and transform the situation on Beaverdam Creek. Jackson, of course, did not appear, and the series of spirited attacks all sputtered in the creek bottom until darkness came with mercy to stop the carnage. In order to carry out Lee's offensive, 1,475 Southerners had become casualties (killed, wounded, missing, or captured), almost four times the Federal loss.

Lee remained at Mechanicsville until 11:00 P.M. on the night of June 26 and then rode back up the turnpike and up the hill to his headquarters. Many things had miscarried that day. But Lee believed he had no choice except to renew his attacking the following day.[18]

Day Three
Friday, June 27
GAINES'S MILL

Lee had not expected battle near Mechanicsville. He had assumed Jackson's arrival would preclude the enemy from making a stand at Beaverdam Creek; in fact if Jackson had done what Lee anticipated and maintained his place on the far left of the Southern sweep down the Chickahominy, the Valley Army would have been in position to flank any Federal line on any creek en route. Obviously the first task for Lee the next morning was to establish contact with Jackson. In anticipation of doing that, Lee ordered his subordinates to continue attacking on June 27 and sent Walter Taylor to find Jackson.

When the Confederates probed the battle line of the evening before, they found the Federals in the final stages of withdrawing from Beaverdam Creek. Lee was in Mechanicsville by then, and he decided that the enemy would next make a stand at Powhite (pronounced POW-hite) Creek. Thus Lee began working to locate and align his divisions for the approach and attack.[19]

Meanwhile Jackson's first action in the Seven Days occurred. Some of his artillery fired on soldiers approaching from the direction of Beaverdam Creek and managed to hit two men from A. P. Hill's division. Everyone involved was sorry for the incident (especially the two wounded "friends"); but the action seemed poetically correct in hindsight.

Jackson was at Walnut Grove Church when Lee rode out to meet him in the late morning. The two generals conferred for a time, and Lee directed Jackson to advance upon the assumed Union position via Old Cold Harbor. Jackson found a local guide who put his columns on the most direct route—which was not the road Jackson was supposed to take. So Jackson backtracked a mile and a half and was once again late.

While Jackson marched and countermarched through the countryside, A. P. Hill found the enemy. Federal corps commander Fitz John Porter, whose troops (initially about 30,000) occupied this portion of McClellan's front, had established a defensive line almost as strong as the one on Beaverdam Creek. Porter's men were in strength, not behind Powhite Creek, but at Boatswain's Swamp about a half-mile further east, near Gaines's Mill. This stream did not appear on any of the maps of the region, and so the Southerners had difficulty all day attempting to reconcile maps with reality. Given the choice they preferred blank space, and no stream, on the map; but there it was, another swampy creek with felled trees, enemy infantry earthworks on the far bank, and enemy artillery behind them.

Lee established his field headquarters at Selwyn, the home of William Hogan, and from there he tried to monitor the movements of his troops. But Lee was altogether ignorant of A. P. Hill's attacks and the nature of Porter's lines behind Boatswain's Swamp. He did ride forward in the early afternoon and began to understand the situation. Meanwhile A. P. Hill's Confederates were bearing the brunt of the punishment in revealing the Federal position, which as it followed Boatswain's Swamp faced more north than east and so frustrated Lee's design to flank Porter.

Finally Jackson emerged, and Lee rode to brief him on the situation. It was time for a concerted assault, all of Lee's available troops against Porter's position. Jackson sent the message to his subordinates: "Tell them this affair must hang in suspense no longer; sweep the field with the bayonet!" Maybe Jackson knew; maybe he did not know that soldiers in this war seldom came close enough to their enemies to use their bayonets. Still he spoke of combat very close and personal, and his exhortations struck a responsive chord.[20]

Lee ordered the general advance some time around 6:00 P.M. The attack was much less than a coordinate surge; but it became general and in the gathering twilight the Confederates broke through. John Bell Hood's brigade usually gets credit for first smashing through the enemy works; but the breach was probably pretty general. The Federals fled in disorder increased by an ill-conceived cavalry charge ordered by Union General Philip St. George Cooke, who was J. E. B. Stuart's father-in-law and destined for duties at desks after this day. Soon after 7:00 P.M. Lee knew that he had at last won a victory. The day was too far spent to follow up his success that evening; but he would press the issue tomorrow.

President Davis had again been near the scene watching some of the action during the afternoon. Lee, however, had to savor his letter informing Davis, "Profoundly grateful to Almighty God for the signal victory granted to us, it is my pleasing task to announce to you the success achieved by this army today."

Lee had managed to focus his superior numbers in this sector and overwhelm Porter's corps. But of course this was precisely what Lee intended, to strike with strength against the enemy's fractions. On June 27, the Federals suffered 6,837 casualties; the Confederates lost 7,993. Lee could hardly afford many more victories like Gaines's Mill.[21]

Day Four
Saturday, June 28

Saturday, June 28, was almost an exception to the constant, rolling combat that characterized the campaign. The battle concluded at dark the night before had shattered organization in both armies, and soldiers remained awake sorting themselves most of the night. The Federals reeling in near rout fell back across the Chickahominy. Lee's attacking divisions consolidated north of the river. The principal action on June 28 was an ill-fated rebel attack at Garnett's Farm near Old Tavern by Secretary of State–turned–General Robert Toombs.

Lee himself awoke at Selwyn on the morning of June 28 eager to learn his enemy's intentions. He dispatched Stuart and a substantial force of cavalry to the Richmond & York River Railroad. If McClellan still intended to supply his army via the Pamunkey River and the railroad, Stuart had a wonderful opportunity to raid and wreck. If McClellan had abandoned his supply line, Stuart would discover the fact and so reveal the Federal intent to change his base to the James or retreat down the Peninsula.

Stuart reached the railroad with little difficulty and next morning (June 29) with Rooney Lee pressed on to White House, "now in ashes and desolation." So it was clear that McClellan had severed this umbilical cord. The Federals were withdrawing; now was the moment to destroy McClellan's army. But first Lee had to discover McClellan's route; he needed to know in which direction to launch his divisions in the drive for the kill. During the afternoon reports of enemy activity—and the absence of it—convinced Lee that McClellan was heading for the James River, changing his base of supply without entirely abandoning the Peninsula.[22]

Lee best summarized his understanding of the situation and intentions on June 28 in a letter to President Davis written the morning of the 29th:

After the enemy had been driven from the left [north] bank of the Chickahominy on the 27th instant, he seemed to have determined to abandon his position on the right [south] bank & commenced promptly & quietly his arrangements for its evacuation. His intention was discovered but his proposed route could not be ascertained. . . . Having however discovered that no movements were made on his part to maintain or recover his communications with York River . . . his only course [it] seemed to me was to make for James River & thus open communications with his gunboats and fleet. Though not yet certain of his route, the whole army has been put in motion. . . .

At his new headquarters in the Gaines House, Lee went to bed early (11:00 P.M.) in anticipation of the busy, bloody work of the pursuit.[23]

Day Five
Sunday, June 29
SAVAGE STATION

Lee took a risk in mounting a vigorous pursuit toward the James. If McClellan were planning to withdraw down the Peninsula or were luring Lee into a trap, Lee would pay dearly for his assumptions. But Lee well calculated his risk, and his assumptions proved correct. McClellan, in the belief that he and not Lee was outnumbered and in peril, was acting to "save" his army and save his dignity by changing his base from the Pamunkey to the James.

In direct pursuit of the Federal rear Lee dispatched his freshest troops, the divisions of Magruder and Huger that had been holding the lines most directly between the Federal army and Richmond. Jackson and D. H. Hill, Lee sent to the left (north) of Magruder and Huger. A. P. Hill and Longstreet were supposed to march south, then southeast, to intercept the Federal march the following day (June 30). If all went according to Lee's plan his entire army would converge upon the Federals as they marched, and Lee would have his battle of annihilation near a stream known as White Oak Swamp.

In Lee's mind at least this day, June 29, was Magruder's day. Lee envisioned rapid pursuit with rested soldiers and a rear-guard action that would arrest McClellan's withdrawal and set up the general engagement. Magruder (with Huger, D. H. Hill, and Jackson as necessary) would fight while A. P. Hill and Longstreet marched.[24]

Magruder, though, was unwell—severe stomach problems—and unsure of his assignment. He marched slowly, encountered the enemy, and called for reinforcements. Lee wrote Magruder what for Lee was a harsh rebuke,

I regret much that you have made so little progress today in the pursuit of the enemy. In order to reap the fruit of our victory the pursuit should be most vigorous. I must urge you, then, again to press on his rear rapidly and steadily. We must lose no more time or he will escape us entirely.

In his defense Magruder did confront a numerically superior foe to his front. Huger was slow to move in support of Magruder's right flank. And Jackson spent all day on June 29 rebuilding Grapevine Bridge over the Chickahominy, so Magruder had no one to support his left.

At last Magruder attacked; the result was the Battle of Savage Station (on the Richmond & York River Railroad). It was a sharp fight in which the Confederates inflicted 914 casualties while suffering 444. But Magruder's tardiness and caution upset Lee's timetable for running his enemy to ground.[25]

Then and since people have speculated about the cause of Jackson's behavior on June 29. Why did he sit down and suck lemons and allow the reconstruction of Grapevine Bridge to proceed at so leisurely a pace? "Fog of War," stress fatigue, fanatical observance of the Sabbath, simple confusion, and more have been offered to explain Jackson's inaction. Whatever the reason, Jackson should have joined Magruder and Huger on the blunder list for frustrating Lee's plan to destroy McClellan's army.[26]

Day Six
Monday, June 30
WHITE OAK SWAMP / GLENDALE

Lee still had a chance to overrun his enemies, but his margin for error was small. The Army of Northern Virginia would have to act in concert, and Lee seemed to resolve to do his own staff work this time. In contrast to previous battles when he ordered troop movements and dispositions from his headquarters and then adjourned to the field to watch the action, Lee was himself much on the move on June 30.

He rode out to Savage Station at 3:30 A.M., met Jackson, and then spoke with Magruder. During the mid- and late morning Lee was several miles to the south of Savage Station on the Darbytown Road conferring with A. P. Hill, then Longstreet. Lee remained with Longstreet during the early afternoon, met with President Davis who had ridden out to find the action, and both men reluctantly obeyed A. P. Hill's order to retire to a position of greater safety. Then Lee rode a couple of miles to the south to view Federal columns retreating to safety and to urge Theophilus Holmes to hurry troops and guns to strike the enemy before they reached the James River and the support of their gunboats. Soon after that Lee was back with Longstreet and A. P. Hill committing two of his divisions to battle against a larger number of Federals.

If nothing else Lee learned this day that he could not manage complex operations all by himself. Despite his riding, conferring, meeting, and urging, the Federals escaped his trap. The major combat, attacks and counterattacks near the crossroads community of Glendale on ground locally identified as Frayser's Farm, involved only two Confederate divisions. Huger, Magruder, and Holmes seemed always to be late or lost or both. And Jackson was hopeless. He did nothing—most probably because his exhausted body ordered his mind, in no uncertain terms, to stop and rest. Rest Jackson did—all day, while McClellan's army marched away.

Day Six of the Seven Days cost the Confederates 3,673 casualties, the Union 3,797. Because the Southern army did most of the attacking, however, the Confederates had about twice as many men killed and many more wounded.

Lee had had the chance to overtake and overwhelm an enemy in full retreat. Next day someone expressed the fact that McClellan would escape. Lee responded with rare vitriol, "Yes, he will get away because I cannot have my orders carried out!"[27]

Day Seven
Tuesday, July 1
MALVERN HILL

The Federal army was in prepared positions on Malvern Hill. Not all that much hill by inland standards, Malvern Hill did rise from the Tidewater plain, and creeks with steep banks and marshy bottoms flowed on either side with the effect of accentuating the rise and of defining Malvern Hill as a field of battle. D. H. Hill knew something of the terrain from a chaplain in his division and remarked to Lee on the morning of July 1, "If General McClellan is there in strength, we had better let him alone."

Lee was tired and feeling unwell during the morning; he asked Longstreet to stay at his side in the event he needed help with the demands of the day. With Longstreet, Lee rode to view the enemy and this imposing hill. They saw a formidable position indeed, and they saw dozens of Union guns covering the ground with infantry in strength. Lee agreed that an assault on this position would be suicide.[28]

But Lee's vision extended beyond Malvern Hill to Harrison's Landing, where McClellan had other prepared positions and gunboats to support him. At Malvern Hill the Federals would have to make one last stand; if they held here, then they could retire to the James and safety at Harrison's Landing. This was Lee's last chance to destroy McClellan's army.

So Lee looked for some way to make Malvern Hill into Chapultepec, and around midday Longstreet seemed to have discovered that way. He found positions on the right and left of the Confederate line which appeared appropriate for massing Southern artillery. If Southern guns could pound the enemy line into impotence, then a coordinated infantry assault might break through. Lee's army might then chase the Federals to the James River and render Harrison's Landing a massive killing ground instead of the sanctuary McClellan intended.

Nearest the small rise on the Confederate right where Longstreet proposed to plant Southern artillery was the brigade of Lewis A. Armistead, a veteran officer with a distinguished record in Mexico and a recent promotion for his service at Seven Pines. Armistead would be in a position to assess the effect of the Southern guns; thus Armistead would begin the infantry assault and so signal the rest of the army to attack. Lee's order, prepared by Robert Chilton, read: "Batteries have been established to rake the enemy's lines. If it is broken, as is probable, Armistead, who can witness the effect of the fire, has been ordered to charge with a yell. Do the same."

This directive began making the rounds about 1:30 P.M. Soon afterward Confederate artillery began firing. But instead of massed batteries, a pathetically few guns opened on the Federal lines. And the Union response was devastating; very few of the few Confederate guns survived to continue firing, and it became clear that the general attack would not take place.[29]

Lee persisted, though. He rode off with Longstreet to the left of his lines to try to find a way to flank the Federals on Malvern Hill. In fact Lee did find some ground which seemed to offer a way to flank the enemy and alter the situation considerably.

By now it was approaching 4:00 P.M., and as Lee rode to organize his flanking movement, couriers found him and brought fresh news. The Federals seemed to be retreating, one message said, and another reported that Armistead's brigade had advanced and driven back the Federals to its immediate front. Without corroborating either report, Lee abandoned his flanking plan and ordered a general attack.[30]

What resulted was a gallant disaster. Federal guns and troops were not retreating; they remained in place to mow down the series of frontal assaults mounted in accord with Lee's order. One grand sweep involving all the Confederates at the same time might have overwhelmed the Federal line. But that was not what occurred. The Southern infantry attacked in piecemeal, offering the enemy the opportunity to focus fire upon a relatively few attackers at a time. Artillery fire was decisive: this was one of the few battles in the entire war in which artillery was such a crucial factor. D. H. Hill, who had warned early in the day about attacking Malvern Hill, delivered the verdict when the day was over. "It was not war," Hill stated. "It was murder."[31]

Lee himself rendered his own judgment in the aftermath of Malvern Hill. He encountered Magruder after dark as Magruder was about to try to sleep. "General Magruder, why did you attack?" Magruder responded, "In obedience to your orders, twice repeated." Lee spoke no more and rode away into the darkness.[32]

Malvern Hill was a mismanaged macabre farce. Never again would Lee make so many errors of judgment, sins of omission and commission, in a single day. Then and since people have asked why. Why did Lee order an attack in that place against such obvious strength? On incredibly flimsy indications that his enemy might be withdrawing, Lee committed his army to suicide. But he did not in fact commit his entire army, because in his haste to take advantage of what in hindsight seems like a fantasy, Lee did not take the time or care to involve more than a fraction of his forces. Why?

Of course he was and had every right to be exhausted on this the seventh day of the Seven Days. His request that Longstreet stay close to him that morning was an index of how infirm Lee felt even early in the day. But more important than exhaustion or illness was Lee's obsession with victory complete. He was convinced that he must destroy his enemy if the Confederacy were to have a chance to win this war and thus Southern independence. Lee had come this far, led his army to this point, and this was their last chance to win not just a battle or a campaign but the war. This was the moment of truth, and Lee would not shrink.

In Richmond and elsewhere Confederate Southerners rejoiced in the victorious campaign and raised up Lee as war hero. Lee published a general order filled with praise and gratitude for the men of his army:

> On Thursday, June 26th, the powerful and thoroughly equipped army of the enemy was entrenched in works vast in extent and most formidable in character within sight of our capital.
>
> Today the remains of that confident and threatening host lie upon the banks of James River, thirty miles from Richmond, seeking to recover, under the protection of his gunboats, from the effects of a series of disastrous defeats.

In his report of the campaign to his wife, Robert Lee confided, "Our success has not been as great or complete as I could have desired. . . ." And in the official report to his government, Lee stated, "Under ordinary circumstances the Federal Army should have been destroyed."[33]

Some time during the morning after Gaines's Mill, young Rob Lee was taking advantage of the respite in marching and fighting to snatch a nap beneath a gun caisson. A member of the Rockbridge Artillery, Rob had endured the Valley Campaign with Jackson, the rapid ride/march to the vicinity of Richmond, and battle the previous day. Suddenly he felt a series of prods from an artillery sponge-staff and became rudely awake. Rob scrambled out from under the caisson in a daze and looked around. He saw men in clean uniforms mounted on sleek horses and then he saw his father, the commanding general.[34]

A couple of weeks earlier Lee the general had been too busy to greet Mary Lee the refugee after an absence of more than thirteen months. A few days ago Lee the grandfather had forgotten that his grandson was dead. Now Lee the father sought out his son the soldier in the wake of a great battle. The stress of preparation and strain of anticipation were over; the battle was at hand, and the elder Robert Lee was again complete.

20

"We Cannot Afford to Be Idle"

HINDSIGHT REVEALS that the Seven Days Campaign before Richmond marked the beginning of *annus mirabilis,* the year of wonder, in Southern military fortunes. Exactly one year after Malvern Hill, elements of Lee's army went looking for shoes in a quiet Pennsylvania town named Gettysburg. Between Malvern Hill and Gettysburg the Army of Northern Virginia and its commander achieved amazing martial feats and came on occasion to the very brink of winning this war.

Hindsight, however, is a very mixed blessing in historical narrative; sometimes knowing what happened next can skew the story and obscure historical insight. Whatever else he was, Robert Lee was not prescient. In the wake of the Seven Days, Lee could neither know his destiny nor even imagine *annus mirabilis.* His actions indicate that he seriously doubted that the war would last another year.

During those long months before he came to field command, Lee had witnessed an almost unbroken series of Southern failures. He was impressed, perhaps inordinately so, with the numbers and material resources the enemy could bring into the field against him; he realized that this disparity in strength would only grow with time. Thus he acted upon the conviction that victory in this conflict would have to be decisive and soon or not at all. So even before he returned to his headquarters at Mrs. Dabbs's farmhouse in July 1862, Lee began to reorganize his army and make plans to maintain the momentum of his recent victories. He did not undertake extensive, long-term reforms—regarding the production of maps, reorganization of the artillery, or expansion of his staff, for examples—probably because he did not believe that the war would last long enough for such reforms to reach fruition.[1]

In the reorganization of his army after the Seven Days (which continued the reorganization begun after Seven Pines), Lee's priority was personnel. This emphasis upon installing the right people in subordinate commands sprang directly from Lee's style of leadership, which was becoming manifest as he acted out command.

Somewhat later in life Robert Lee confided to a Prussian visitor the essential feature of his leadership. "I plan and work with all my might to bring the troops to the right place at the right time," he said; "with that I have done my duty. As soon as I order the troops forward into battle, I lay the fate of my army in the hands of God."[2]

Lee believed that his active participation in the conduct of a battle "would do more harm than good. It would be a bad thing if I could not rely on my brigade and division commanders." Here was the military expression of traditional Southern honor, state rights, and individualism; the commanding general planned and launched the army into battle, but then left the conduct of combat to those who commanded component units of the army. In one sense Lee abdicated his authority once he committed his army to battle.

Yet Lee's style of leadership was consistent not only with the peculiar Southern preference for personal as opposed to institutional relationships, but also with the limitations in communication, with the size of armies, and with the scope of battlefields in this war. Lee and his adversaries usually depended upon mounted couriers and written messages to communicate in combat; armies in this war were already ten times larger than Winfield Scott's expeditionary force in Mexico; and generals now measured battlefields in miles instead of yards. In such circumstances Lee's concept made realistic sense. Moreover, Lee's exercise of leadership was consistent with Lee's life. He had learned how to be a commanding general following Scott into Mexico, and Scott's technique then was much like Lee's now. Lee also favored subordinates who had professional military experience—officers who presumably knew what to do in combat. And Lee's leadership was quite in keeping with his personality; he recoiled from confrontation and conflict and much preferred to lead from consensus, at some distance from the hurly burly.

In the aftermath of the Seven Days Campaign, though, Lee revealed once more that his discomfort with confrontation and conflict did not in the least inhibit his capacity to analyze the actions of his subordinates and act upon the results of this analysis. "It would be a bad thing if I could not rely on my brigade and division commanders"; now was the time to purge the army of unreliable subordinates.[3]

Benjamin Huger had led a division during the Seven Days. Less than two weeks after Malvern Hill, Huger became something called "inspector of artillery and ordnance in the Army of the Confederacy."

John Bankhead Magruder had conducted a skillful bluff along his "Yorktown Line" during the early phase of the Peninsular Campaign and commanded in the Seven Days. Magruder had said he wanted assignment in the trans-Mississippi, which was a good thing, because two days after Malvern Hill, Magruder began the transit which enabled him to spend the remainder of the war in Houston, Texas.

Theophilus H. Holmes had commanded the Department of North Carolina and thus led a division in the Seven Days Campaign. He, too, went into "exile" as commander of the Trans-Mississippi Department.[4]

The Hills, Ambrose Powell and Daniel Harvey, in essence remained in place within the reorganized Army of Northern Virginia. James Longstreet and Stonewall Jackson advanced to what amounted to corps command as leaders of the two "wings" of the new army.

In these two latter men Lee seemed to recognize the Janus face of his own military personality. Longstreet seemed to Lee to be steady and dependable, the consummate professional. Jackson, on the other hand, had been by turns brilliant (in the Valley) and useless (Mechanicsville and White Oak Swamp). But Jackson was a killer, possessed of the same sorts of aggressive instincts which obsessed Lee.[5]

At the same time that Lee labored to recast his army, some of his lieutenants were also at work in the uncertain arena of martial politics. Former Secretary of State Robert Toombs challenged D. H. Hill to a duel when Toombs failed to receive a promotion to major general for his service during the Seven Days. Longstreet and A. P. Hill feuded in print, in Richmond newspapers, over the relative merits of their valor in the recent combat. Hill requested a transfer from Longstreet's command; Longstreet acceded; but Lee, as was becoming his pattern, tried to ignore the quarrel in hope that the acrimony would go away.[6]

When Lee renamed his army the Army of Northern Virginia, he began to make it his own. Reorganization now continued this process, and Lee also acted methodically to expand his autonomy in the eastern theater of the war and his influence in strategic policy elsewhere.[7]

To Jefferson Davis, Lee wrote informative missives and shared reports of Federal activities. He also made suggestions about strategy in other theaters of the war. "If the impression made by [General John H.] Morgan in Kentucky could be confirmed by a strong infantry force, it would have the happiest effect." Then Lee listed major commands and commanders who might indeed "confirm" Morgan's cavalry raids in Kentucky, and so planted the notion of an offensive in Kentucky in the President's mind.[8]

Of course in the wake of his rapid accession to power and influence Lee left some disgruntled comrades. Gustavus W. Smith had lost his composure, nerve, and capacity to act on the battlefield of Seven Pines. But Smith retained his capacity to carp while he languished on sick leave, and he attempted to enlist another wounded warrior, Joseph E. Johnston, in the ranks of an anti-Lee cabal. Smith wrote to Johnston in mid-July and poured forth complaints. He had spoken with Lee on June 21, and Lee had evaded any mention of Jackson's army coming to join the fight against McClellan. Lee had said nothing about reinforcement from North Carolina either, and Smith reminded Johnston that when they were in charge, Lee would not even discuss reinforcement for their army from anywhere. Then Smith launched a tirade about Lee's insistence upon a surgeon's certificate from Smith as a condition for extending Smith's leave. He had received a note from Lee, "first a layer of sugar three lines, then two lines telling me to forward a certificate, and three more lines of sugar." When he had spoken with Lee in person, Lee had been "semi-pious, semi-official, and altogether disagreeable." Smith concluded, "If provoked much further I will tear the mask off of some who think themselves wonder-fully successful in covering up their tracks."[9]

Johnston had too much sense to take Smith very seriously; but he did cherish the notion that Lee was simply substituting for him until he was sufficiently recovered to resume command of "his" army. Johnston was already jealous of his old chum's success; he resented Lee's apparent favor with Jeffer-son Davis; and Johnston's concern for his own importance would only in-crease as his physical condition improved.[10]

Lee continued to be Johnston's friend, maybe more so than was prudent. But Lee also well realized the tension that existed between Johnston and the President, and he was not above turning that enmity to advantage. When Lee eventually left his headquarters at the Dabbs's farm, he was careful as usual to inform Davis of his plans and the troop dispositions he had made to ensure the security of the capital. Lee concluded his letter:

I will keep you informed of everything of importance that transpires. When you do not hear from me, you may feel sure that I do not think it necessary to trouble you. I shall feel obliged to you for any directions you may think proper to give. I learn that Genl. Johnston will soon return to Richmond. He is riding on horseback every day & is gaining his strength rapidly.

Why did Lee suddenly change his subject in the midst of making arrangements to mount a major campaign? Maybe his reference to Johnston's recovery was an idle afterthought. More likely he was reminding the President that his relationship with his principal army commander had not always been this satisfactory. Lee needed Davis's support and here was a veiled plea for con-tinued cooperation between commander and commander in chief—in terms Davis well understood.[11]

All the while Lee worked to recast his army and gain strategic control of the war in Virginia, his enemies, too, were maneuvering for position and power. George B. McClellan remained at Harrison's Landing with his huge army. Secure within a fortified perimeter, supplied by water, and supported by naval guns, McClellan was safe. McClellan and his army only 23 miles from Richmond still posed a threat to the Confederate capital. But although McClellan spoke and wrote about renewing his campaign, he never acted upon his expressed intentions.[12]

Meanwhile another would-be saviour of the Union appeared in northern Virginia. John Pope (West Point class of 1842, veteran of the "old" Army, and recently victorious at New Madrid and Island No. 10 on the northern Missis-sippi River) came east to command something called the Army of Virginia, composed of Federal troop units previously stationed in the Shenandoah Val-ley or held before Washington. Pope soon served notice that he intended to alter and intensify the course of the war. On July 14, he issued orders to his army. He hoped to challenge the officers and men of his new command; in fact he insulted them. "Let us understand each other," Pope began. "I have come to you from the West, where we have always seen the backs of our enemies;

from an army whose business it has been to seek the adversary and to beat him when he was found; whose policy has been attack and not defense." Then Pope's new order offered an unveiled attack upon George B. McClellan. "I desire you to dismiss from your minds certain phrases. . . ," Pope wrote. "I hear constantly of 'taking strong positions and holding them,' of 'lines of retreat,' and of 'bases of supply.' Let us discard such ideas. The strongest position a soldier should desire to occupy is one from which he can most easily advance against the enemy. . . . Let us look before us, and not behind."

More important than the bluster of Pope's initial address to his army was a series of general orders he issued soon afterward. In effect these orders said that this Federal army would take its supplies from the countryside, would hold local residents responsible for any guerrilla activity or sabotage directed against the army, would impose loyalty oaths upon all male civilians and treat violators with "the extreme rigor of military law." Thus far during this war the Union command in Virginia—McClellan—had attempted to restrict the conflict to rebel armies and to exclude civilians and their property (including slaves) from the effects of combat. Pope meant to change this policy, and he did so with the approval of United States Secretary of War Edwin M. Stanton and President Abraham Lincoln.[13]

Within the Confederacy, Southerners reacted with outrage and Southern editors were free with words and phrases like "diabolical," "enemy of humanity," and "atrocity." At Dabb's Farm Lee was concerned by this new intensity in the war. He wrote to his daughter Mildred that her brother, Rob, was "off with Jackson & I hope will catch Pope & his cousin Louis Marshall [Lee's nephew, who had joined the Union army]. I could forgive the latter for fighting against us if he had not have joined such a miscreant as Pope."[14]

Already Lee had dispatched troops to confront Pope's new force threatening northern Virginia; on July 13, the day before Pope issued his initial address to his army, Lee sent Jackson with his own and Richard S. Ewell's division (about 12,000 men) to Gordonsville. To Jackson, Lee wrote in late July, "I want Pope to be suppressed. The course indicated in his orders if the newspapers report them correctly cannot be permitted and will lead to retaliation on our part. You had better notify him [Pope] the first opportunity." Lee also wrote a letter of protest to Henry Halleck, who was now Federal general in chief, using words like "robbers and murderers" to describe Pope and his soldiers. If the Federals began killing civilians, Lee threatened, then the Confederacy would select an equal number of captured Federal officers and have them "immediately hung." He had no choice but to accept "the war on the terms chosen by our enemies until the voice of an outraged humanity shall compel a respect for the recognized usages of war."[15]

How much of Lee's indignation at this juncture was rhetorical and how much of it was real is difficult to determine. He certainly preferred to fight an enemy burdened with supply lines and problems in logistics; he relied upon spies and intelligence gleaned from people loyal to the Confederacy who lived near or behind Union lines; and later in the war, at least, Lee rejoiced in the successes of guerrilla warriors like John S. Mosby. "The recognized usages of war" gave advantage to Lee and his cause, and so he supported them.

At the same time Lee declared himself capable of accepting "usages" more vicious. What Lee likely feared most was a deterioration (from Lee's perspective) of this war into a general guerrilla conflict. As his campaigns during the summer of 1862 amply demonstrated, Lee not only accepted, he embraced the bloodshed and destruction of his profession. But for Lee warmaking was very much a profession, too important to entrust to untrained amateurs. His professional nightmare was amateurs in charge, running amok, out of control, in unrestrained guerrilla warfare. So Lee tried to keep the war under control until he could win it.[16]

Having sent Jackson to "suppress" Pope, Lee then had to reinforce Jackson in order to give him the means for his mission. Meanwhile McClellan sallied forth once more from Harrison's Landing. On August 5, the Federals reoccupied Malvern Hill; Lee advanced from Richmond to contest a renewal of McClellan's threat to the capital; and then on August 7 the Federals withdrew again to Harrison's Landing. Now Lee was confident that McClellan would never attack Richmond from the east, and he soon learned that McClellan's troops were abandoning the Peninsula to reinforce Pope. McClellan was fast becoming a general without an army, and Pope's force would soon outnumber the huge army McClellan had brought to the Peninsula.[17]

To harry McClellan, interrupt his communications and supply lines on the James River, and otherwise frustrate the orderly withdrawal of his troops, Lee had assigned D. H. Hill, who commanded about 12,000 troops designated as the Department of North Carolina in Virginia. Lee tried to goad Hill into action—"this does not satisfy the object I had in view"; "we must set to work vigorously to prepare to arrest their progress"; "please cause all the wood in the woodpiles accessible to their boats to be burned"; "I regret to hear of the feeble conduct of your Cavalry. . . . I hope you will see to its organization and instruction"; "I hope you will lose no opportunity of damaging the enemy in every way." But Hill seemed less than resourceful in his efforts.[18]

On August 9, Jackson attacked Pope at Cedar Mountain (about 17 miles north of Gordonsville) and claimed victory. The battle, however, was essentially indecisive, save for the 1,418 Confederates and 2,403 Federal who became casualties.

Although he congratulated Jackson "most heartily" on the "victory," Lee began immediately moving Longstreet's wing of the army north and prepared to take the field himself. Some index of the concern Lee felt for Richmond's safety lay in his decision to leave Gustavus Smith in command of the Confederates guarding the capital.

Lee and his "military family" had lived at Mary Dabbs's house on the Nine Mile Road since Lee's accession to command on June 1. They had gone to the field during the Seven Days, but returned to stay from July 9 until the departure by train for Gordonsville, and then camped near Orange Court House at 4:00 A.M. on August 15.[19]

By the time Lee and the staff had settled into camp, Lee knew the worst: McClellan had evacuated Harrison's Landing with uncharacteristic speed, and his columns were en route into northern Virginia. By August 17 Lee realized that his best, perhaps only, chance to "suppress" Pope would have to happen very soon, before McClellan's troops arrived en masse to reinforce him or McClellan threatened Richmond from some port (Fredericksburg?) on the Rappahannock. He wrote to the President on the 17th to share what he knew of the situation. "It appears certain that General McClellan's force has escaped us," Lee announced. "I feel greatly mortified. . . . He ought not to have got off so easily." Lee blamed D. H. Hill, declaring him "not entirely equal to his present position." "Left to himself," Lee observed, "he seems embarrassed and backward to act." Lee recommended replacing Hill in command, but then confessed, "I blame nobody but myself" for McClellan's easy exit. "We must lose no time in preparing to meet him wherever he may appear," Lee asserted.[20]

Rumor established Pope's strength already at 92,000 men. Lee did not believe this estimate, "though I believe he is very big." Actually at this time (August 17), Lee and Pope commanded armies of roughly equal size, 55,000 troops. But McClellan's 90,000 men in transit could swell Pope's army to three times the size of Lee's within a matter of days. As Lee confided to Mary Lee, "We shall have a busy time."[21]

Having learned about as much as he could of Pope's strength and troop dispositions, Lee committed the Army of Northern Virginia to a campaign grounded in maneuver, designed to compel the enemy to fight on his terms and terrain and to maintain the momentum seized during the Seven Days. So the rivers, streams, mountains, and ridge lines of northern Virginia became components in what resembled a giant game of chess with enormous stakes.

Lee's initial gambit against Pope, however, was a thorough failure. Lee planned a swift crossing of the Rapidan River, then a march around Pope's left (east) flank to Culpeper Court House, at which point the Army of Northern Virginia would have been on Pope's supply and communication line to Washington (the Orange & Alexandria Railroad), and Pope would have had to fight on Lee's terms. A comedy of errors nearly cost J. E. B. Stuart ignominious capture and did provide Pope with a copy of Lee's order for the maneuver. Delays also hampered the operation, and Pope withdrew to the north bank of the Rappahannock before Lee completed crossing the Rapidan.

Stuart redeemed his embarrassment over his near capture on August 22 when he conducted an all-night raid upon Catlett's Station on the Orange & Alexandria behind Pope. Stuart's troopers, in Lee's words, "accomplished some minor advantages," among which was the capture of some of Pope's correspondence confirming the Federal plan to unite the armies of Pope and McClellan under Pope. Lee needed a new plan, and he needed it in a hurry.[22]

August 24 was a Sunday, and on this day Lee rode to the little village of Jeffersonton in search of Jackson. Early on that sunny afternoon the two men spoke alone. Lee proposed sending Jackson with his entire wing of the army upon a bold expedition deep into the enemy rear. Jackson responded with enthusiasm. One of his staff officers recalled him inscribing a crude map in the dirt with his boot. Someone overheard Jackson proclaim that he would march at once.[23]

Lee's plan was daring to the brink of recklessness. Jackson's wing, 23,000 men, moved at dawn on August 25 up then across the Rappahannock west of the Bull Run Mountains to Orleans and Salem Court House that night. On August 26, Jackson turned east down the Manassas Gap Railroad, through Thoroughfare Gap, and reached Bristoe Station (on the Orange & Alexandria Railroad) that evening. At Bristoe Station the Confederates amused themselves—and Jackson—causing train wrecks on Pope's principal supply line, while Stuart and his cavalry pressed on to Manassas Junction, where the Federals had their major supply depot. Next day (August 27) Jackson's troops swept into Manassas and probably thought they had discovered Confederate heaven—acres of ammunition, food, and creature comforts collected there for Pope's army—an ironic reward for following that strange Calvinist who commanded them. The Southerners gorged themselves, carried away all they could, and burned the residue in a huge holocaust to whatever gods presided over their great fortune.

On August 28, the fourth day of his expedition into Pope's rear, Jackson sought security. He marched his troops across the ground made sacred thirteen months earlier at the First Battle of Manassas/Bull Run and arrayed them in an unfinished railroad cut at the base of a terrain feature known as Stony Ridge near Sudley Springs. There, in effect, he waited for Pope to find him.[24]

Meanwhile Lee rode with Longstreet's wing of the army in Jackson's wake. They began the march a day later than Jackson, reached Orleans on August 26, Salem Court House on August 27 (while Jackson's men were pillaging Manassas), and on August 28 they were advancing through Thoroughfare Gap against Federal opposition that compelled Lee to stop and maneuver in difficult terrain against enemy guns. Here was Pope's opportunity to make Lee pay dearly for dividing his lesser force in the face of a stronger enemy. If Federal troops and guns could hold Thoroughfare Gap long enough to delay a reunion of Longstreet and Jackson, the two wings of Lee's divided army, then Pope, whose numbers were only growing, might overwhelm by turns Jackson and then Longstreet almost at his leisure. But Pope did not understand his chance, did not support a determined defense at Thoroughfare Gap, and by dawn of August 29, Lee and Longstreet were east of the Bull Run Mountains with only two brigades of Union cavalry between them and Jackson.[25]

Lee, of course, understood quite well the implications of his dilemma at Thoroughfare Gap. Yet he displayed little or no anxiety that members of his staff recalled. In fact, while Longstreet's men sought some alternate route through the gap, Lee accepted an invitation to dinner at a nearby home. A. L. Long of Lee's staff later explained this blasé behavior as an example of the "absence of any overmastering anxiety" and also remembered that Lee ate heartily and conversed genially during the meal. It is also possible that Lee was acting out a rather healthy form of fatalism. This was not the Pedregal lava field in Mexico; he was not responsible for finding the flank of those Federal gunners; he had dispatched other men to do that. And while his subordinates sought some way out of the impasse at the pass, Lee could only wait. If he were unable to help at Thoroughfare Gap, he might as well help himself to a proper dinner, and so he did.[26]

On August 29, Longstreet continued his march toward Jackson, while Jackson's wing bore the brunt of Pope's assaults on Stony Ridge. For reasons that still defy rational explanation, Pope seemed to forget Longstreet's proximity and focus almost entirely upon Jackson. By noon Longstreet's men were on the Warrenton Turnpike within a very few miles of Jackson's position, and still the Federals all but ignored them.

As Longstreet's troops closed upon the Federals, Lee rode far forward to see what he could see. But soon he returned to his staff and announced, "A Yankee sharpshooter came near killing me just now." Then he showed his aides his cheek and a scratch where a bullet had grazed his face.

This scare—possibly Lee's closest call with death on a battlefield—did not dampen his ardor to take full advantage of the situation and attack Pope's apparently exposed left (south) flank. But Longstreet demurred—three times during the course of the day. Each time Lee could discern some logic in waiting, and so he acceded to postponing an assault. In the interim Jackson's men took a significant pounding during a long, bloody afternoon.

By contrast August 30 opened with inaction in the lines, and Lee feared that he had lost his opportunity to strike. He summoned Longstreet, Jackson, and Stuart to him and established contingency plans in the event Pope did not renew the fighting. Whatever Pope did or did not do, Lee was ready.[27]

As it happened Pope did precisely what Lee most wanted him to do; about 1:30 P.M. he committed virtually his entire army to another assault upon Jackson's position at Stony Ridge. It was almost as though Pope planted his soldiers like wheat in long rows before Jackson's position. And then Lee ordered Longstreet forward with the scythe in the form of five infantry divisions and ample artillery. Jackson's weary defenders reversed roles with the Federals and swept forward to join the massive attack. And the harvest was rich indeed. When darkness and exhaustion concluded the day, Pope's army was still in flight beyond Bull Run.[28]

Lee followed closely behind his army's advance during the long afternoon, and at the end of it he rode with his staff to a hilltop and surveyed the scene for long moments as daylight faded. He sat Traveller very near some artillery pieces that had only recently ceased firing, and one of the young gunners, "face and hands . . . blackened with powder—sweat . . . garments . . . ragged and stained with the red soil of the region," approached the officers and spoke to a member of Lee's staff.

"General, here is some one who wants to speak to you." Lee turned and looked down. "Well, my man, what can I do for you?"

"Why, General, don't you know me?"

Here was Rob once more in the aftermath of victory. The father laughed at his son's appearance and rejoiced that he was uninjured. But the family reunion was brief; Lee had to decide what to do the next day.[29]

Lee made camp on the field, listened to reports of the situation, and sent a telegram to the President:

THIS ARMY ACHIEVED TODAY ON THE PLAINS OF MANASSAS A SIGNAL VICTORY OVER COMBINED FORCES OF GENLS MCCLELLAN AND POPE

The message continued, and Lee, if anything, understated in terming Second Manassas a "signal victory." In a letter to Davis written the same day (August 30), Lee claimed that he had wanted "to avoid a general engagement." But the engagement on August 30, 1862, was general indeed (costing 9,500 Confederate and 14,500 Federal casualties throughout the campaign), and the victory was one of Lee's greatest. Confronted with an enemy force slightly larger than

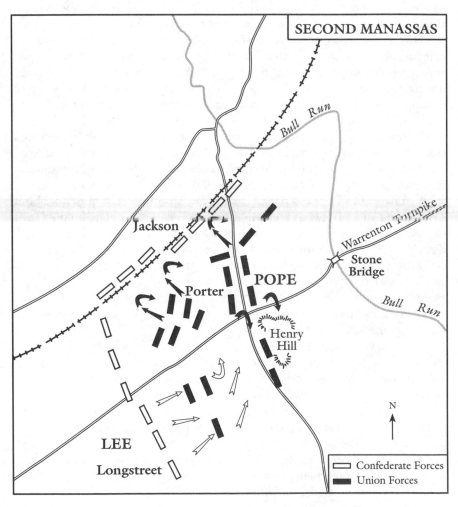

his own, Lee had divided his army, made maximum use of disciplined marching and mountains to screen his movements, and seized the initiative with a series of bold maneuvers. Lee so baffled and threatened Pope that the Union general did not know where his own forces were, much less Lee's army. Then Lee launched his general engagement; the attack swept the field; and Pope's army reeled back into the defenses of Washington.[30]

Next morning Lee was still seeking ways to exploit his victory; but several circumstances seemed to conspire against accomplishing the annihilation he sought. Once relieved of his fantasies about what was happening, Pope led a competent withdrawal, and as his troops fell back, they fell in with reinforcements arriving from McClellan's army. Lee's soldiers, Jackson's men especially, were almost without rations and for the moment pretty well fought out. On September 1, for example, Jackson's wing spent most of the day marching only three miles, encountered a Federal force smaller in numbers at Chantilly, attacked the inferior enemy, and suffered a general repulse. Nor did the weather cooperate with Lee's zeal to press his advantage. Rain pelted the armies during the night (August 30–31) and continued the following day. Not only did sodden roads impede the pursuit; they made it more difficult for supplies to overtake the hungry Confederates. Much later Lee explained his inability to take better advantage of the situation quite simply, "My men had nothing to eat . . . they had had nothing to eat for three days."[31]

The rain on August 31 drove Lee into his rubber suit—overalls and poncho—while he rode forward and conferred with Longstreet and Jackson. At some time during the day Lee was standing among his staff with Traveller's reins over his arm. Then came an alarm: "Yankee cavalry!" One witness remembered being startled by a crowd of prisoners in the course of being herded to the rear appearing suddenly over a nearby embankment. Whatever the cause, Traveller reared; Lee lunged for the reins, tripped over his overalls, and fell forward. Instinctively he broke his fall with his hands and in the process broke a bone in one of them and sprained them both. Quickly fitted with splints and a sling, the commanding general was doubtless embarrassed. He also suffered for weeks from an inability to ride, write, and even dress himself unassisted. For a time the general would have to follow his army in an ambulance.[32]

Lee's enemies were, as he observed, "weakened and demoralized." But the Federal forces were essentially "safe" across the Potomac within prepared defenses before their capital. McClellan reemerged from beneath his professional cloud to reorganize the army that was again his and to incorporate within it fresh recruits. Pope was soon on his way to the Department of the Platte in Minnesota to direct operations against Sioux warriors.

Lee eschewed any appetite for attacking or investing Washington; such a course would amount to fighting on the enemy's terms and turf with an army inferior in size and resources. He directed his ambulance to the village of Dranesville on September 3, and at his field headquarters on the Leesburg-Alexandria Turnpike announced his decision to lead the Army of Northern Virginia into Maryland. To Jefferson Davis, Lee offered all candor:

The army is not properly equipped for an invasion of an enemy's territory. It lacks much of the material of war, is feeble in transportation, the animals being much reduced, and the men are poorly provided with clothes, and in thousands of instances are destitute of shoes. Still we cannot afford to be idle, and though weaker than our opponents in men and military equipments, must endeavor to harass, if we cannot destroy them. I am aware that the movement is attended with much risk, yet I do not consider success impossible, and shall endeavor to guard it from loss.[33]

Lee envisioned the Army of Northern Virginia conducting a campaign of liberation in Maryland and had reason to hope that some Marylanders would flock to his banner. He invited former Maryland Governor Enoch L. Lowe to join his expedition, issued a proclamation calling Maryland a "conquered province" and stating his army's mission as "throwing off this foreign yoke," and gave stern orders against "excesses" and "depredations." Lee insisted that his army pay for supplies in Maryland and hoped that his scrupulous policy would enable Confederate supply services to feed and refit the army in enemy country without alienating Marylanders. But Lee was realistic enough to state, "I do not anticipate any general rising of the people in our behalf." He did suggest to the President that his invasion—"the present posture of affairs"—offered the opportunity "to propose with propriety . . . the recognition of our independence." At the very least, Lee reasoned, such a proposal, if refused in Washington, might influence the congressional elections in November to the detriment of the Lincoln administration and its commitment to continue the war.[34]

In his quaint, modest way, Lee was staking his claim to become the Father of a new country—the nineteenth-century George Washington. To redeem Light Horse Harry Lee's misdeeds and restore the family fame, Robert Lee would become his father's hero.

Ample irony attended the fact that Jefferson Davis was attempting to win this war and Southern independence in much the same way Washington had won the Revolution. Davis was convinced the Confederacy could win by not losing and outlasting his enemies' commitment to conquest. In Davis's mind the most important battle in this war, as had been the case in the Revolution, was the last battle, and so he was willing to wait for a Yorktown.

Lee never openly disputed Davis's vision of victory; he would not have remained in command had he done so. Rather, he attempted to bend the President, to secure from Davis the authority and resources to win the war a different way. Lee believed that time was as formidable an enemy as the United States Army, that he must win quickly if he were to win at all. His army was smaller and his resources fewer; and the disparity would only increase with the passage of time and thus render the chances of victory more and more remote.

Having admitted to Davis that his army was ill-prepared for an invasion, Lee conducted his campaign in Maryland anyway. When he wrote to the President, Lee stated that his goal was "to harass" his enemy and later added the verb "annoy" to describe his purpose. Lee certainly hoped that his presence north of the Potomac would draw Federal troops from Virginia, and as it happened, when the Federals failed to evacuate Harpers Ferry, Lee sent Jackson and half the army to drive them out. But Lee's measured words about modest goals sound like obfuscation when compared with his actions. He began the Maryland campaign with maneuver while the Federal army licked its wounds within the defenses of Washington. Soon or later, though, Lee knew that McClellan or someone else would lead the Union army out of Washington to confront him. When that happened, words like "harass" and "annoy" became quickly moot; deeds demonstrate that Lee intended to fight. He led his army north in the hope of fighting and winning a major battle in the enemy's country.

Although his swollen hands precluded him from doing so much as signing his name, Lee wrote dictated daily letters to Davis, all with the apparent purpose of informing the commander in chief and securing his blessing for acts already undertaken by the time the President received Lee's letters. Lee proposed crossing into Maryland in his letter of September 3. On September 4, Lee declared himself "more fully persuaded of the benefits that will result from an expedition into Maryland. . . ." Accordingly, "I shall proceed to make the movement at once, unless you should signify your disapprobation." That same day, presumably after Lee posted his letter to Davis, elements of his army crossed the Potomac into Maryland. And Lee announced that he proposed "to enter Pennsylvania," too, "unless you should deem it inadvisable upon political or other grounds." On September 5, Lee informed Davis that "this army is about entering Maryland," although many of his troops were already there, and on September 6, he sent a telegram announcing that "Two divisions of the army have crossed the Potomac. I hope all will cross today." On the 7th, Lee wrote to Davis that "all the divisions of the army have crossed the Potomac. . . ." Next day Lee issued his proclamation "To the People of Maryland" offering them liberation by way of his army; Davis sent Lee his version of such a proclamation on September 7, a week before he was even able to read Lee's document.[35]

Then on September 9 when Lee had established his headquarters at Frederick, he received a message from Davis stating his intention to join Lee and the army in Maryland. Lee responded diplomatically—"I should feel the greatest satisfaction in having an interview with you and consulting upon all subjects of interest"—but negatively—"I cannot but feel great uneasiness for your safety should you undertake to reach me." He informed Davis that he was severing his lines of communication east of the Blue Ridge Mountains; thus the President would not be able to travel a secure route. Lee even dispatched his aide Walter Taylor to amplify the cautions of his letter and dissuade Davis from undertaking the journey. As vehemently as possible Lee let Davis know that he did not want him with the army during this campaign. Lee was trying to win the war; Davis could only get in his way.[36]

By the time he wrote to Davis on September 9, Lee had already decided upon his next move and prepared Special Orders No. 191 to direct the action. On September 10 the Army of Northern Virginia would march from Frederick west to Middletown, and then divide to march in four different directions.

Longstreet with two divisions (John Bell Hood's and D. R. Jones's) was supposed to press on to Boonsboro west of South Mountain. There he was supposed to halt; but in fact Longstreet turned north and moved to Hagerstown in response to a rumored advance of some Pennsylvania Militia from Chambersburg.

Jackson with three divisions (A. P. Hill's, Alexander Lawton's, and J. R. Jones's) was to recross the Potomac, march on Martinsburg, and then move down the Baltimore & Ohio Railroad to take part in a recapture of Harpers Ferry. The Federals held the town with about 12,000 troops commanded by Dixon S. Miles.

Lafayette McLaws would command two divisions (his own and R. H. Anderson's) and march south from Middletown to seize Maryland Heights, across the Potomac from Harpers Ferry. His divisions would then "capture the enemy at Harpers Ferry and vicinity."

John G. Walker and an undersized division (about 3,000 men) was supposed to recross the Potomac east of Harpers Ferry and seize Loudoun Heights, across the Shenandoah River from Harpers Ferry. Then, Walker would cooperate with Jackson and McLaws in taking Harpers Ferry.

D. H. Hill with his division was to act as rear guard for the army. When Longstreet moved north to Hagerstown, however, only Hill and Stuart's cavalry remained at Boonsboro where all these disbursed Confederate columns were to rendezvous. Lee's schedule for the operation was ambitious. He wanted Harpers Ferry in Confederate hands by Friday, September 12. Then presumably Lee expected to concentrate to give battle to McClellan should he challenge.[37]

Lee's plan contained in Special Orders No. 191 went awry, figuratively and literally, almost from the beginning. The worst thing that happened was that Special Orders No. 191 fell into Union hands. On September 13 two Federal soldiers at Frederick found a copy of Lee's order wrapped around three cigars. The order was an extra copy, intended for D. H. Hill by virtue of his heretofore independent command. Precisely how the "lost order" became lost is not as important as the fact that George B. McClellan read it on September 13. Lee knew about the loss of the document on the morning of September 14 though the agency of a friendly ear near McClellan's headquarters. The information was theoretically out of date; but Lee's subordinates were behind his schedule and even more scattered than his order indicated. McClellan possessed the opportunity to fragment the Army of Northern Virginia into quite small pieces and win the war in a matter of days.[38]

Even before McClellan read Lee's plan, however, Lee's army was in major disarray. Troubles began in the ranks and seemed to radiate throughout the chain of command. The word Lee had used at the outset of the Maryland campaign to describe his artillery and draft horses and mules, "reduced," still applied to the animals and described his soldiers as well. One who saw them pass recorded:

They were the dirtiest men I ever saw, a most ragged, lean, and hungry set of wolves. Yet there was a dash about them that the Northern men lacked. They rode like circus riders. Many of them were from the far South and spoke a dialect I could scarcely understand. They were profane beyond belief and talked incessantly.[39]

Most of these men did not ride "like circus riders"; they walked, and as Lee admitted, they walked without shoes. They walked in hot, dry weather, as it happened, and they seemed seldom able to find enough to eat. This was "the green corn campaign" in the army's collective memory; crippling hunger vied with diarrhea as the major malady among the men. A resident of Shepherdstown who observed troops on the march throughout the war period recalled these men at this time:

When I say that they were hungry, I convey no impression of the gaunt starvation that looked from their cavernous eyes. . . . I saw the troops march past us every summer for four years, and I know something of the appearance of a marching army, both Union and Southern. There are always stragglers, of course, but never before or after did I see anything comparable to the demoralized state of the Confederates at this time. Never were want and exhaustion more visibly put before my eyes, and that they could march or fight at all seemed incredible.

Many of Lee's men did find it impossible to march or fight, so they quit the campaign—straggled or deserted. On September 13, Lee reported to Davis, "Our ranks are very much diminished, I fear from a third to a half of the original numbers. . . ." Available evidence indicates that "half" was the more accurate estimate of defections in the army. So alarmed did Lee become that he recommended to the President the appointment, in effect, of a mobile court-martial to travel with the army and ensure "more promptness and certainty of punishment."[40]

Lee's generals, too, seemed to share the army's military malaise. In the first place Lee did not have nearly enough generals; attrition had left brigades and some divisions woefully ill-led. And the generals Lee did have seemed determined to arrest each other. Longstreet placed Hood under arrest and ordered him to Culpeper. Then Jackson renewed a quarrel with A. P. Hill, placed him under arrest, and relieved him of command. Lee intervened to keep Hood with the army and on September 14 restored him to command. Hill, too, remained with his troops, but awaited Jackson's pleasure regarding charges and a court-martial.[41]

Of course it mattered very little who arrested whom if McClellan's army moved with dispatch to destroy the Army of Northern Virginia. In fact McClellan moved slowly to take advantage of his fantastic good fortune. Nevertheless, on September 14 two Federal corps overwhelmed D. H. Hill's division at South Mountain and poured through Turner's Gap. The same day another Union corps mauled the few troops McLaws could post at Crampton's Gap. Now Lee's army was in genuine peril. He directed an immediate concentration-cum-withdrawal, west through Sharpsburg, then across the Potomac.

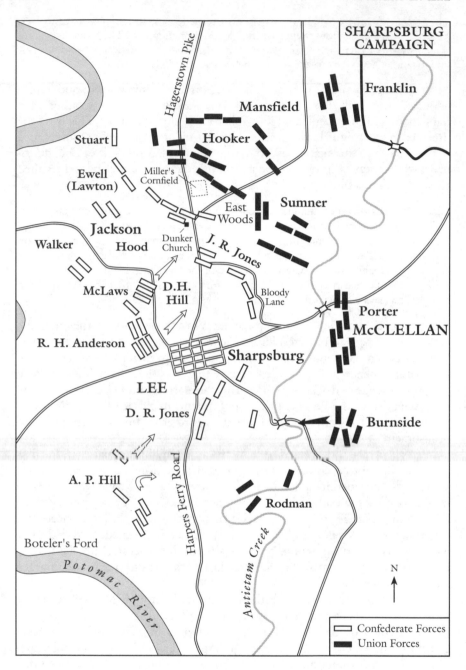

Lee was at Hagerstown with Longstreet and came with him down the valley of Antietam Creek to Keedysville on September 15 and then three miles west to Sharpstown. He planned initially to use Boteler's Ford at Shepherdstown to cross the Potomac. But at 9:00 A.M. on September 15, Jackson received the surrender of Harpers Ferry and very soon thereafter began his march to rejoin Lee. McClellan's advance was characteristically cautious. So Lee called a halt at Sharpstown and decided to have his battle there on a line of hills behind (west of) Antietam Creek, between the creek and the town.[42]

"We will make our stand on those hills," he said to some of the troops as they approached the position. Hindsight, if nothing else, compels the question, Why? Why did Lee decide to stand and fight an enemy he knew would have many more men and more guns than the Army of Northern Virginia with the Potomac River at his back and only one ford in the event he needed a route of escape? Any answer must depend upon conjecture. Maybe Lee believed that he would have to fight McClellan somewhere and soon and so chose here and now. Maybe he was afraid that his army would only grow weaker from a lack of rations and an increase in straggling if he attempted to maneuver more, and so elected to fight before his strength eroded still further. Maybe Lee believed that his defensive position would be sufficiently strong to achieve a Malvern Hill in reverse: let the Federals bleed themselves to death attacking him this time. Lee, more than anyone, knew the cost of offensive operations in this war; perhaps the stand at Sharpsburg was his attempt to pursue an offensive goal—the destruction of the enemy—by means of defensive tactics. Whatever Lee thought about his situation, one conclusion is pretty obvious. He believed he could win.[43]

McClellan's actions since reading the copy of Lee's Special Orders No. 191 offered grounds for hope. McClellan had delayed his march when speed was essential, and once in motion the Army of the Potomac moved with very deliberate speed. Having seized the gaps in South Mountain, McClellan did not press his advantage, and even as Lee posted his troops behind Antietam Creek and anxiously awaited the arrival of half his army from Harpers Ferry, McClellan seemed bent upon withholding an attack until his enemy were ready to receive him.[44]

Longstreet with three divisions of infantry (Hood, D. H. Hill, and D. R. Jones) and Stuart's cavalry took up positions in Lee's defensive line on September 15. On the afternoon of September 16, Lee wrote to Davis, "Part of Genl Jackson's corps has reached us, and the rest are approaching, except Genl A. P. Hill's division left at Harper's Ferry to guard the place and take care of public property." Although McClellan's vanguard had opened Turner's and Crampton's Gaps on September 14, the Army of the Potomac consumed the next two days getting ready to exploit the advantage. As Lee wrote Davis on the 16th, "The enemy have made no attack up to this afternoon, but are in force in our front."[45]

The battle began at dawn on September 17 when Federal General Joseph Hooker sent his corps slamming into Lee's lines near the northern extremity of the position between the creek (Antietam) and the town (Sharpsburg). At least three horrendous battles took place outside of Sharpsburg during that fateful day.

In the morning, attack, counterattack, and desperate concentration occurred north of the town and left to legend sites such as the East Wood, the corn field, the West Wood, and Dunker Church. Lee was present and committed all the troops and guns he could assemble to stem the Federal tide. In so doing he all but stripped the rest of his line; but he wrested a tactical stalemate from the first battle.

During the middle of the day the fighting shifted to the center of Lee's position and raged across a sunken road which became "Bloody Lane." Once more Lee used every man and gun he could find to prevent disaster. Most likely disaster for the Army of Northern Virginia would have occurred despite Lee's efforts had not McClellan recoiled from the carnage and withheld a final assault.

The third battle took place in the afternoon across the banks of Antietam Creek south of Sharpsburg. Once more the fighting was vicious, and the creek ran red with blood near Burnside's Bridge. At the moment when Lee had sent every available Confederate into action and still could not stop the Federal advance, A. P. Hill arrived from Harpers Ferry and led a counterattack that saved the day and the Army of Northern Virginia.[46]

September 17, 1862, proved to be the bloodiest single day of the entire war. Of the 39,000 troops Lee commanded at Sharpsburg/Antietam, 10,318 one fourth, were casualties (1,546 killed, 7,754 wounded, 1,018 missing). Federal losses were even greater, 12,410 total casualties (2,108 killed, 9,549 wounded, 753 missing); but McClellan's army numbered 71,500.[47]

Lee had been fortunate indeed. His troops and subordinate commanders had risen to the occasion and performed heroically. McClellan had sent his assaulting forces into battle by turns, and so permitted Lee to shift his defenders and counterattackers along interior lines to meet each new threat. McClellan had also shrunk from moments of truth, when one last surge might well have shattered Lee's lines. Lee should not have offered battle on September 17 at Sharpsburg; he very nearly lost his army and the war.

On the day following the heinous bloodletting before Sharpsburg, Lee kept his army in place. Once more McClellan possessed and allowed to pass a golden opportunity to annihilate the Army of Northern Virginia. A concerted attack against Lee's right flank would most likely have succeeded in cutting off the Confederates from Boteler's Ford and any chance of orderly withdrawal. But both armies remained inert on September 18, and during the night Lee directed a successful retreat through Boteler's Ford back into Virginia.[48]

Desperation at Sharpsburg/Antietam compelled Lee to abandon his distant stance as strategic director on the battlefield. On September 17, he had had to absorb himself in tactical decisions—when and where to send reinforcements, where to place artillery, and the like. The results of Lee's tactical decisions demonstrated his capacity to direct the action, even with bandaged hands and his arm in a sling. He had been engaged at critical times and places, and his army survived.[49]

However, three stories have emerged from accounts of Lee's day at Sharpsburg/Antietam that transcend testimony to his tactical mastery.

During one lull in the fighting Lee and Longstreet were standing on a rise surveying Federal lines when D. H. Hill rode up to join the discussion. Longstreet cautioned Hill to dismount as Union artillery was active. Hill declined, and shortly afterward an enemy shell interrupted the conversation and took the front legs from under Hill's horse. The animal was in shock, quivering on its fore knees, its back slanted forward toward the ground. Hill tried to dismount; but the severe angle of the horse's back rendered Hill's attempts "ludicrous." Hill's dilemma inspired "a roar of laughter from the persons present" and the "merriment" continued until, acting upon Longstreet's advice, Hill hoisted a leg over the pommel of his saddle and succeeded in dismounting. Witnesses to Hill's "adventure" did not record the fate of the horse.[50]

At another time during the day Lee was en route from one sector of his line to another when he and his staff surprised a straggler who had stolen a pig. Here was a soldier who had abandoned his comrades in the midst of a momentous battle and compounded his crime by stealing a pig. When Lee encountered the man, he had already killed the pig and was carrying the carcass away with him. Such a brazen display "threw the general into a hot passion." Lee ordered members of his staff to arrest the soldier and take him to Jackson with instructions to shoot him for desertion and theft. As it happened, Jackson decided to let the enemy carry out the execution: he dispatched the condemned soldier into the front ranks of one of his hotly engaged units.[51]

Some time likely during the long afternoon, Lee stood on a small hill with members of his staff when the commander of a mauled artillery battery approached him to ask for instructions. The battery had lost three of its four guns as well as men and horses. But Lee told the battery commander to recast his men and horses to serve the remaining gun and return to the fight. One of the gunners still fit for fighting was young Rob Lee, who took advantage of this chance to greet his father. "General, are you going to send us in again?" Rob asked.

"Yes, my son," Lee replied, "you all must do what you can to help drive these people back." Rob Lee remembered that his father pronounced this sentence "with a smile."[52]

21

"It Is Well That War Is So Terrible"

Two WEEKS IN September of 1862 may indeed have marked the "high tide" of Confederate hopes for victory and independence. All the while the Army of Northern Virginia invaded Maryland, Braxton Bragg and elements of the Army of Tennessee marched through Kentucky. The contrast with the previous spring when the Confederacy seemed on the brink of collapse was striking in the extreme.

But Bragg's campaign in Kentucky sputtered, and after an inconclusive battle at Perryville on October 8, the Army of Tennessee retired to Tennessee. And after Sharpsburg the Army of Northern Virginia also returned home to northern Virginia to lick its wounds and restore shattered ranks. Throughout the Confederacy September 18 was, by proclamation of the President, a day of "public thanksgiving to God" for the successes of Southern arms. But in the wake of failed invasion, the Southern war became suddenly more desperate.

In Washington on September 22, Abraham Lincoln issued the preliminary Emancipation Proclamation announcing his intention to free all slaves in rebel territory on January 1, 1863. In so doing Lincoln boldly redefined the Union he sought to save as a union sans slavery. From this point the United States could never again revert to status quo ante bellum.

In London, Lord Palmerston's government withdrew from the brink of proposing with France to mediate the American war. Rather than risk embroiling themselves in the conflict the British decided to let North and South "exhaust themselves a little more." Never again would a European power come as close to intervention.[1]

At Richmond the *Examiner* understood what had happened. In response to Lincoln's proclamation, the editor announced: "What we have hitherto seen is but the prelude of the war which will now begin—the war of extermination."[2]

At Robert Lee's headquarters Walter H. Taylor wrote his sister about the battle before Sharpsburg, "We do not boast a victory—it was not sufficiently decisive for that." And later Taylor added, "I believe my chief was most anxious to recross into Maryland but was persuaded by his principal advisors that the condition of the army did not warrant such a move." Later, in his report of the campaign, Lee stated: "The condition of our troops demanded repose. . . ."[3]

At this moment Lee used his own repose to contemplate peace. He still could not write; his injured hands precluded letters to his family. So Lee took advantage of a visit from Custis to dictate some personal letters to Annie and Agnes, who were at a place called Jones Springs near Warrenton, North Carolina. "I heartily join you in sincere gratitude to Almighty God for granting such success as he has seen fit to our arms," Lee dictated, "and pray and trust that his blessings and favors may be continued until an honorable peace is accomplished, and *the whole Country instead of being joined in strife with each other shall unite in praise & serving him* [emphasis added]." Maybe Lee was indulging in some mystical religious fantasy. Maybe his reference to "the whole Country" was a Freudian slip. But he certainly seemed to envision peace predicated upon reunion—the very sort of settlement that events of the last few weeks had rendered impossible. Perhaps Lee knew that, too, and merely repeated a litany that he believed would comfort his girls.[4]

Whatever resolution to this war Lee now envisioned required him to win victories, and to do that he had to rehabilitate the Army of Northern Virginia. This he did with extraordinary speed during the early autumn of 1862, thanks in no small part to the respite from combat George B. McClellan offered him. Lee found ways to feed his men and find shoes and other supplies for them. Fulfilling such fundamental needs improved morale and made discipline easier. Never again would the Army of Northern Virginia suffer from straggling on the scale of the Maryland Campaign.[5]

Between October 26 and November 2, McClellan did finally cross the Potomac and march into Virginia. To counter the incursion, Lee again divided his army; Stonewall Jackson and his corps (about 40,000) remained in the Shenandoah Valley, while Lee accompanied Longstreet and his corps (about 45,000) to Culpeper Court House. Lee explained his intentions to Secretary of War George Randolph: "I think it preferable to baffle his designs by maneuvering rather than to resist his advance by main force," and to Custis: "I am operating to baffle the advance of the enemy & retain him among the mountains until I can get him separated [so] that I can strike at him to advantage."[6]

From the beginning of his Confederate service Lee acted as though he were serving in a foreign war. He assumed that he would rarely if ever be able to see his family, and he consistently placed his duty to the army ahead of familial or personal concerns. Once he adopted this code, he was free to focus upon the army and relieved from any awkward decisions about family obligations. He delegated as many financial affairs as possible to Custis, corresponded regularly with Mary Lee and his daughters, and otherwise acted as though he were in Mexico instead of Virginia.

During the early autumn of 1862 Lee had reason to feel secure about his family. Custis continued to serve on the President's staff in Richmond. Rooney received a promotion to brigadier general and took on Rob as a member of his staff with the rank of first lieutenant. Mildred, who was now sixteen, was in school at St. Mary's Academy in Raleigh, North Carolina. She was homesick and unhappy at St. Mary's, but Lee believed she was where she belonged. Daughter Mary was on a protracted visit with friends Richard Stuart and his wife at Cedar Grove on the Northern Neck. When the Federal army moved east, Mary was behind enemy lines. But J. E. B. Stuart's cavalry patrols maintained sporadic, word-of-mouth contact with the commanding general's oldest daughter; Lee forbade written communication for fear of reprisals in the event of interception by the enemy. Agnes usually remained with her mother, and the two women resided "temporarily" at Hickory Hill with Chass and her family. Mary Lee was ever more crippled from arthritis, and Agnes suffered from neuralgia; but both mother and daughter seemed to take good care of themselves.

Lee wrote (via Custis) to his wife on September 30 with strong counsel about her residence: "I do not like your establishing yourselves in Richmond. It is a bad place for six unprotected women, and I think your visit had better be made as short as possible." He considered the capital "not healthy" and was concerned about "a whirl of agitation and excitement" in the city. "Unless from necessity, I will not be near Richmond, and therefore you will see nothing of me." Mary Lee read her husband's advice and soon after moved to Richmond. She "visited" the James Caskies, whose daughter Norvell was a good friend of Agnes, until June 1863; and in October 1863 she rented a house on Leigh Street in Richmond for the family.[7]

But tragedy struck in October 1862 at Jones Springs in North Carolina where Annie contracted typhoid fever. Agnes was with her, and when Annie's condition became critical, Mary Lee and a relative came to nurse her. They could make her as comfortable as possible and no more. Annie Carter Lee died on the morning of October 20, 1862, at age twenty-three.[8]

Lee learned of the death of his daughter at his headquarters near Culpeper Court House. Lee read his mail as usual, mail containing a letter announcing Annie's death, and then called for Walter Taylor to give instructions about some matters of army administration. Taylor went about his chores, but returned to Lee's tent soon after to find the general "overcome with grief, an open letter in his hands." Only after business as usual would the stoic Lee allow himself emotional release. A month later Lee confessed, "In the quiet hours of the night, when there is nothing to lighten the full weight of my grief, I feel as if I should be overwhelmed."[9]

Family news was bad again later in the fall; Chass gave birth to a sickly daughter who died unchristened in December. And Chass herself seemed to be ill much of the time. Lee wrote to his daughter-in-law regularly and attempted to cheer her. Indeed, he wrote his first letter with his injured hand to "My beautiful Chass" on October 19.[10]

Lee did receive a letter through enemy lines from Martha Custis Williams (Markie). Almost two months old when Lee read it on October 1, the letter related a visit to Arlington House and the general desolation she found at their home, now occupied by Federal troops. Lee replied at once with the aid of an amanuensis (apparently Custis). "There is much I would say, but it is so uncertain whether you would ever read it, that I forbear," Lee dictated; "We shall have to resign ourselves to non-intercourse until peace is once more restored to this distracted land."[11]

The net effect of family affairs and deaths upon Lee is difficult to calculate. Although he continued to lose loved ones and the fruits of his labor, Lee bore his losses with apparent good grace and made the best of his situation. But the toll upon even his stoic psyche must have mounted, and challenges to his emotional equilibrium multiplied.

Whatever storms roiled inside Lee during this period he kept very much inside himself, and his military family noticed only his mirth at the time. On one evening in his camp Lee flipped open a tent flap and interrupted the discussion of a mathematical problem between T. M. R. Talcott, Lee's staff engineer, and artillery chief Edward Porter Alexander. Also in the tent was Lee's aide Charles Marshall, and just as Lee looked inside, Marshall was pouring a very stiff drink "neat" into a glass from a demijohn he had slung over his shoulder. Alexander recalled that Marshall appeared "utterly reckless & dissipated" in this pose, and after Lee left, Marshall was concerned about what the general thought of what he had seen. Next morning Marshall mentioned having a headache. Lee observed, "Too much application to mathematical problems at night, with unknown quantities of X & Y represented by a demijohn & tumbler, was very apt to have for a result a head ache next morning."

Alexander also remembered his response to being in Lee's company at Culpeper and after: "I valued Gen. Lee's approval & good opinion far more than general reputation or even high rank in our volunteer army." Alexander's awe was hardly unusual; the Army of Northern Virginia was developing a corporate version of the same feeling for its commander.[12]

Soldiers responded to Lee's efforts to rebuild the army. On October 10, Lee's army numbered 64,273; on October 20, the effective strength was 68,033. By November 10, the number of men was 70,909, and on December 10, Lee could count 78,511. Lee once more paid attention to personnel. To Cadmus Wilcox, who requested a transfer from the Army of Northern Virginia, Lee wrote, "I require your services here. You must come & see me & tell me what is the matter. I know you are too good a soldier not to serve where it is necessary for the benefit of the Confederacy." To the Secretary of War, most probably in answer to a query, Lee sent a telegram: "I have no position in this army for Genl. Loring." Lee well remembered Loring from that disastrous campaign in western Virginia in 1861.[13]

On October 10 through 13 J. E. B. Stuart led a raid on Chambersburg, Pennsylvania, which netted numerous horses and elevated morale in the army and nation. Stuart's bold adventure fed McClellan's caution as he advanced over the Blue Ridge Mountains to Warrenton. Lee still retained Jackson's corps in the Shenandoah Valley to threaten McClellan's flank.[14]

McClellan, however, proved most vulnerable in Washington, where Lincoln refused to understand his failure to take advantage of the victory at Sharpsburg/Antietam. Then when McClellan marched so slowly in pursuit of Lee, Lincoln gave up and on November 7 removed McClellan from command. In his place to command of the Army of the Potomac Lincoln installed Ambrose E. Burnside. Thirty-eight years old, graduate of West Point, veteran of six years' service in the "old" Army, Burnside had failed in a weapons-manufacturing business in Rhode Island and worked for McClellan when he was chief engineer with the Illinois Central Railroad. During this war Burnside had led the expedition which captured Roanoke Island, North Carolina, and commanded a corps in McClellan's army. Like McClellan, Burnside was "deliberate"; his major blunder thus far as a combat commander occurred at Antietam when he insisted upon using "Burnside Bridge" to cross the creek, although his troops later discovered they could wade the stream in several places nearby. Burnside's obsession with his bridge cost crucial time and numerous lives and would prove to be a portent of restricted vision to come.[15]

Lee learned of the change of commanders within twenty-four hours and greeted McClellan's demise with regret—"we always understood each other so well." Then he remarked, "I fear they may continue to make these changes till they find some one whom I don't understand." Next, as if to prove that Burnside was someone he understood quite well, Lee correctly predicted that the Federals would drive on Fredericksburg as a stepping stone for another assault upon Richmond. The first "grand division" of Burnside's army began the march toward Fredericksburg from Warrenton on November 15; Lee sent a regiment of cavalry and some artillery to Fredericksburg later on the same day. Burnside's forces began arriving at Falmouth across the Rappahannock from Fredericksburg on the night of November 17, and on November 19 the Federal army was still on the march toward concentration. On the morning of November 19, Lee wrote to Stonewall Jackson that J. E. B. Stuart was convinced that "Burnside's whole army had marched for Fredericksburg." The next day Lee sent a telegram to the President:

I THINK BURNSIDE IS CONCENTRATING HIS WHOLE ARMY OPPOSITE
FREDERICKSBURG[16]

Still Lee delayed ordering Jackson to him and instead only suggested that he move east of the Blue Ridge Mountains. Actually Lee had some pretty good ideas for Burnside; one of the best involved a rapid move by water to the southern bank of the James River. This was the same plan Lee had feared McClellan might adopt during the Peninsula Campaign; such a move attended by the capture of Petersburg would severely limit Richmond's access to the rest of Confederacy and would have the effect of threatening to besiege the Southern capital.[17]

Burnside, however, lacked Lee's imagination and intended simply to cross the Rappahannock, possess Fredericksburg, and march directly for Richmond. He intended to move rapidly, but he had encountered difficulty with his Engineer Department in securing pontoons with which to construct bridges over the Rappahannock. So Burnside and his army had to wait; and while the Federals waited, Lee set to work preparing a masterful defensive position.

Lee arrived in the small city (4,000 inhabitants) at the falls of the Rappahannock on November 20 and immediately confronted a threatened artillery shelling from Stafford Heights just over the river. All he could do was to help the residents evacuate Fredericksburg; he could not prevent the bombardment, and he did not choose to try to defend the city. In 1862, Fredericksburg was a cluster of buildings on the south bank of the Rappahannock. Federal guns already in place on Stafford Heights dominated the town and effectively precluded any serious attempt to hold the place. Lee realized that if he made a stand here, that stand would have to be in the hills at some distance from the river. It probably galled Lee that his enemies were swarming over Chatham, the Fitzhugh estate where Robert Lee may have proposed marriage to Mary Custis. Currently residing at Chatham was Ambrose Burnside.

For his own headquarters Lee selected a grove of trees about halfway between Fredericksburg and Hamilton's Crossing on the Richmond, Fredericksburg & Potomac Railroad. He continued to be puzzled about Burnside's intentions, daring to hope that the Federals would cross the Rappahannock and mount a frontal assault against well-prepared Confederate defensive positions, but alert to his adversary's options. As long as Burnside delayed doing anything, Lee used the respite to improve his defensive line. That line was more than seven miles long and followed the forward slopes of the series of ridges and hills which lay parallel to the river, roughly a half-mile from the town, between one and two miles from the river.[18]

Lee took special care with the placement of his 306 artillery pieces. On one occasion in his travels over the field he found a battery poorly positioned and learned from the battery commander that his own adjutant, Robert Chilton, had placed the guns. Lee's neck turned red, his head jerked, and he commented, "Colonel Chilton takes a lot upon himself." Another time, Lee overruled Edward Porter Alexander and insisted that he place some guns behind the top of a ridge on Marye's Heights in order to increase their range. As it happened, the guns Lee located "never fired a shot at their distant view, but thousands of rounds into infantry swarming over the canister & short range ground. . . ." And later Alexander felt bold enough about his vindication to remind the battery commander in a voice loud enough for Lee to overhear.[19]

Lee did not have his troops prepare extensive earthworks along his defensive position, and this was very curious. The "King of Spades" seems to have been baiting Burnside into attack. The ground itself, without much improvement, was incredibly strong, so Lee did (or did not do) what he could to lure Burnside into an assault. Burnside relied upon balloons for reconnaissance and did not know much about the surface of the ground. So he launched his offensive precisely where Lee wanted him to.

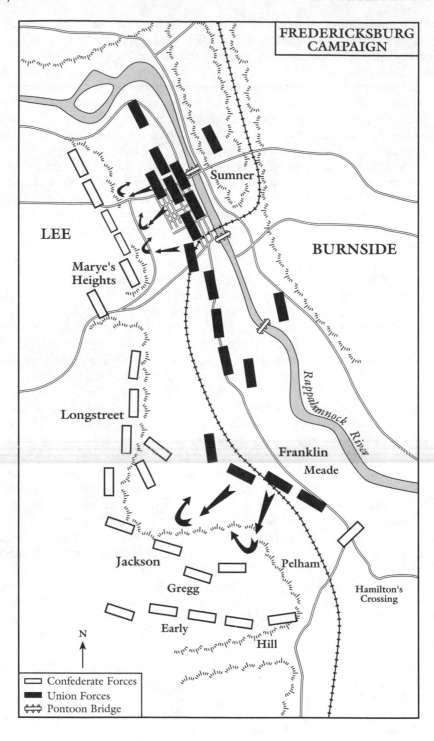

FREDERICKSBURG
CAMPAIGN

Sumner

LEE

BURNSIDE

Marye's
Heights

Rappahannock River

Longstreet

Franklin

Meade

Jackson

Pelham

Gregg

Hamilton's
Crossing

Early

Hill

N

☐ Confederate Forces
■ Union Forces
⛏ Pontoon Bridge

Federal troops commenced building their pontoon bridges during the night of December 10–11. In the daylight of December 11, however, Confederate rifleman William Barksdale's Mississippi Brigade made bridge building almost impossible by shooting the Federals as they tried to work in the river. Finally Burnside ferried enough soldiers across the Rappahannock to chase the Mississippians from Fredericksburg; but the effort cost the Federals an extra day. On December 12, Burnside at last finished crossing the river and occupied the town. Lee used the time to concentrate his army along the defensive line he had selected. He also crept forward to watch with Jackson and Heros von Borcke, a giant Prussian who served on J. E. B. Stuart's staff. They advanced to within a few hundred yards of their enemies, who were "working like beavers in digging rifle-pits and erecting works for their artillery." Confirmed in his belief that Burnside intended his primary attack to come from Fredericksburg, Lee slipped away from his precarious outpost and returned to a vantage point behind his lines known as Lee's Hill, from which he could survey most of the field.

That night (December 12–13) Lee permitted no campfires, and the men suffered from bitter cold. Next morning fog concealed everything to the front; but the enemy was making ready, and everyone knew it. Jackson once more promised to "give them the bayonet." Then the fog began to lift, and foes could see each other.[20]

The plain between Fredericksburg and the line of hills where Lee had planted his army was full of Federals. The Union troops had to advance under fire and cross a significant drainage ditch. Then the attacking ranks had to cross more open ground to confront a sunken road which formed a perfect four-foot trench for Southern infantry. Behind the sunken road Marye's Heights rose precipitously, studded with artillery and more infantry. The assault disintegrated into murder.[21]

Lee watched the enemy founder, and then saw his own men leap from their cover to chase their fleeing foes. "It is well that war is so terrible," he said; "we should grow too fond of it!"[22]

Again and again the Federals formed and charged. Each time they died and recoiled. "General," Lee said to Longstreet who was by his side, "they are massing very heavily and will break your line I am afraid." "General," Longstreet responded, "if you put every man now on the other side of the Potomac on that field to approach me over the same line, and give me plenty of ammunition, I will kill them all before they reach my line." He did.

The danger lay on the right of Lee's line, and Jackson's men had to endure hard fighting, thrust and counterthrust, in order to hold their ground. But Burnside seemed to focus his attention exclusively upon Marye's Heights, determined to break Lee's lines there. Alexander assured Longstreet, "A chicken could not live in that field when we open upon it," and he proved correct. Burnside ignored his troops on the Confederacy's right, and they remained available, but inert for most of the day.[23]

Lee concentrated on Marye's Heights and watched the slaughter. Here was

Malvern Hill in reverse—what Lee may have intended at Sharpsburg. Lee watched John Pelham of Stuart's horse artillery drag two guns into the open and blast a Federal division to a standstill and then duel four Federal batteries with one Napoleon gun until Pelham himself was serving his piece. "It is glorious to see such courage in one so young!" exclaimed the commanding general. Then he watched Longstreet's veterans slaughter the assaulting Yankees until darkness stopped the battle. Lee liked what he saw.

Jackson wanted to launch a night attack. But even Jackson paused when enemy guns opened upon the field where so many had fallen. Then he canceled his plan.[24]

Lee was convinced that Burnside would renew his attacks the next day, and so he ordered his troops to dig. Finally he was ready to throw up field fortifications. A captured Federal courier had with him instructions from Burnside to his subordinates to assault Marye's Heights again in the morning. Longstreet at least believed his rebels would completely destroy the Army of the Potomac if the Federals complied. But Burnside's subordinate commanders dissuaded him, and during the night of December 14–15, Lee's enemies retreated back across the Rappahannock. The Federals lost 12,653 men, almost 11,000 killed or wounded; Lee's army suffered 5,377 casualties, about 4,700 of whom were killed or wounded.[25]

In a letter written on December 16 to his wife, Lee reflected best upon his victory at Fredericksburg. "Their hosts covered the plain & hills beyond the river, & their numbers to me are unknown," he wrote. "Still I felt confidence we could stand the shock and was anxious for the blow that has to fall on some point, & was prepared to meet it here. . . . This morning they were all safe on the north side of the Rappahannock. They went as they came, in the night. They suffered heavily as far as the battle went, but it did not go far enough to satisfy me. . . . The contest will have to be renewed. . . ."[26]

Burnside wanted to renew the contest immediately and plotted a winter campaign on the Rappahannock. He hoped to move his army upriver (west), cross the stream, and then descend upon Lee's flank and rear at Fredericksburg. The Army of the Potomac did not commence Burnside's maneuver until January 20, 1863; but the continued Federal concentration and the preparations attendant to a winter campaign compelled Lee to vigilance while he attempted to discern Burnside's intentions.[27]

Lee revealed his strategic thinking at this period in a letter to Gustavus W. Smith, who commanded forces protecting Richmond. Lee seemed to feel he needed to explain the war to Smith, who was asking for reinforcements from Lee's army. "It is as impossible for him [the enemy]," Lee wrote, "to have a large operating army at every assailable point in our territory as it is for us to keep one to defend it. We must move our troops from point to point as required, & by close observation and accurate information the true point of attack can generally be ascertained." Later in his letter, Lee added, "Partial encroachments of the enemy we must expect, but they can always be recovered, and any defeat of their large army will reinstate everything."[28]

On Christmas Day Lee revealed his general mood when he wrote to Mary

Lee. Lee's Christmas epistle, 1862, was a classic: a plea for peace linked with zest for war combined with his extraordinary capacity to make the best of whatever circumstances in which he found himself.

But what a cruel thing is war. To separate & destroy families & friends & mar the purest joys & happiness God has granted us in this world. To fill our hearts with hatred instead of love for our neighbors & to devastate the fair face of this beautiful world. I pray that on this day when "peace & good will" are preached to all mankind, that better thoughts will fill the hearts of our enemies & turn them to peace. The confusion that now exists in their counsels will thus result in good. Our army was never in such good health & condition since I have been attached to it & I believe they share with me my disappointment that the enemy did not renew the combat of the 13th [Fredericksburg]. I was holding back all that day, & husbanding our strength & ammunition for the great struggle for which I thought he was preparing. Had I divined that was to have been his only effort, he would have had more of it. But I am content. We might have gained more but we would have lost more & perhaps our relative condition would not have been improved.[29]

As Christmas passed and the new year approached, Abraham Lincoln made good on his promise to issue an Emancipation Proclamation on January 1, 1863. Before and after Lincoln's stroke, Lee professed his abhorrence of slavery—but ever in the abstract and always conditioned by his conviction that African Americans occupied some evolutionary level below that of white people. In this instance Lee did not respond, either to Lincoln's preliminary Emancipation Proclamation of September 22, 1862, or to the effective Emancipation Proclamation issued on New Year's Day, 1863. Irony attends the fact that Lee himself became an emancipator and issued his own liberating proclamation three days before Lincoln.

The objects of Lee's proclamation were the slaves once owned by George Washington Parke Custis. In accord with his father-in-law's will, on December 29, 1863, Lee the executor of the estate did "manumit, emancipate and forever set free from slavery" the slaves at Arlington, White House, and Romancoke, as well as those slaves Lee had hired out in other places. Lee's deed of emancipation listed each person by name, at least 170 people, and he meticulously searched his memory and records to make sure he missed no one.[30]

To be sure, Lee was a limited emancipator. The Custis will established a five-year time period within which his executor had to act, and Lee technically exceeded that period if reckoned from the date of his father-in-law's death in October 1857. Like Lincoln, who emancipated only slaves in rebel regions, Lee freed many slaves over whom he had no control. Most of the Arlington slaves, for example, were already free by virtue of Union occupation. "Those that have been carried away," Lee wrote to Mary Lee, "I hope are free & happy. I cannot get their papers to them & they do not require them." Lee also insisted that those slaves who remained "on the farms" should "work as usual." He did propose "to devote the net proceeds of their labour for the year to their future establishment." And Lee conceded, "Any who wish to leave can do so."[31]

Throughout this emancipation exercise Lee seemed characteristically torn between his fairly rigid racial assumptions combined with his concern for good order and control on the one hand, and his abiding ethical principle that "the great duty of life" is "the promotion of the happiness & welfare of our fellow men." In the end, however, he most often elected ethics over order and did what he could to render his emancipation absolute and irrevocable. In the aftermath of emancipation, Lee hired Perry his personal servant and George his cook each for $8.20 per month and hoped "they will be able to lay up [save] something for themselves."[32]

The war had changed during two campaigning seasons in 1861 and 1862. In his journo-history *The First Year of the War,* published near the end of 1862, Edward A. Pollard asserted, "The war has given to the States composing the Confederacy a new bond of union," and "the demand for our independence admits of no alteration or compromise." Defeat, Pollard insisted, would yield "confiscation, brutality, military domination, insult, universal poverty, the beggary of millions, the triumph of the vilest individuals in these communities, the abasement of the honest and industrious, the outlawry of the slaves, the destruction of agriculture and commerce, the emigration of all thriving citizens, farewell to the hopes of future wealth, and the scorn of the world." Pollard proclaimed a bitterness that continued to grow and fester and a desperation that gripped both South and North as sacrifice mounted and victory seemed still remote.[33]

Certainly Robert Lee's life had undergone significant change, too, during those past two years. Two years ago Lee had commanded a regiment of United States cavalry on the plains of Texas. Since that time he had become a full general in command of a huge army. He had also lost one of his children, two grandchildren, and most of the money and property he had labored thirty years to accumulate and develop. To Mary Lee, he observed, "I have no time to think of my private affairs. I expect to die a pauper, & I see no way of preventing it."

Despite the volatile fortunes of an enormous war and cataclysmic changes in his personal life, Lee himself remained very much a constant. He continued on duty in his winter camp with, as he told his wife, his "military family at sunrise & at dusk in the evenings, with their tin plates & cups freezing to their fingers out of doors enjoying their sup & tough biscuit. . . ." And he pronounced his own benediction on Christmas Day when he stated quite simply, "I am content."[34]

22

"From Such a Scene...Men...
Rose to the Dignity of Gods"

ROBERT LEE WAS A SHY MAN and genuinely modest as well. "You can give
Fitzhugh's [Rooney's] autograph to those persons desiring mine," he
wrote his wife early in 1863. "It is worth more." But fame overtook
Lee despite his best efforts to avoid it. In January 1863, for example,
the venerable magazine *Southern Literary Messenger* published a sketch of Lee
by the "Prince of Correspondents," Peter W. Alexander, variations of which
had appeared in the Columbus *Daily Times,* the Knoxville *Daily Register,* and
the Mobile *Daily Advertiser and Register.* Covered first among "Confederate
Chieftains," in Alexander's eyes Lee was "in the prime and vigor of physical
and intellectual manhood" at age fifty-five.

He is six feet in height, weighs about one hundred and ninety pounds; is erect, well-
formed, and of imposing appearance; has clear bright, benignant black eyes, dark gray
hair, and a heavy gray beard. He is exceedingly plain in his dress, and one looks at his
costume in vain for those insignia of rank for which many officers show such a weakness. He wears an unassuming black felt hat, with a narrow strip of gold lace around it,
and a plain Brigadier's coat, with three stars on the collar, but without the usual
braiding on the sleeves. He travels and sleeps in an ambulance, when the army is in
motion, and occupies a tent when it is stationary, and not the largest and best house in
the neighborhood, as is the custom of some officers. In a few words, he cares but little
for appearances, though one of the handsomest men in the Confederacy, and is content to take the same fare his soldiers get.

Alexander continued to describe Lee in terms even he must have appreciated:
"Gen. Lee, though not possessing the first order of intellect, is endowed with
rare judgement and equanimity, sagacity, great self-control, and extraordinary
powers of combination. Like Washington, he is a wise man and a good
man. . . ."[1]

Of course Lee likely never saw Alexander's piece about him. He did realize
that he had become very much a public person, but still received with a naive

wonder gifts sent him from admirers ("I have recd. from a kind lady in Alaba. a beautiful pair of socks, which to show I must wear some day without my boots. Another has sent me a hat"). Certainly he had matters beyond new-found fame to occupy him during the early months of 1863.[2]

Winter was hard that year. Lee mentioned significant storms of January 22 and 27 in letters to the President and Secretary of War. On February 6, he told his daughter Agnes, "We are now in a liquid state at present. Up to our knees in mud. . . ." On February 20, he wrote about "a heavy storm of three days, snow, sleet & rain," and added, "though Perry had entrenched me, the water night before last broke through my tent." Three days after, Lee complained, "The weather now is very hard upon we poor bushmen. This morning the whole country is covered with a mantle of snow full a foot deep." The railroad that day, he wrote, "brought me a young french officer, full of vivacity & no english, ardent for service with me. I think the appearance of things will cool him, if they do not, the night will, for he brought no blankets." On February 28, Lee told Custis, "We have mud up to our eyes," and a month after that he noted, "The weather has been wretched. More unpleasant than any other part of the winter. The earth has been almost fluid. . . ."[3]

Lee worried about his wife's crippling arthritis during the cold season, and about Agnes and her neuralgia. He wrote rather often to Agnes that winter, perhaps out of concern for her emotional as well as physical well-being. Agnes had long admired Markie Williams's brother William Orton Williams, and Orton had spent a portion of the Christmas season at Hickory Hill with the Wickhams (Chass's family), Agnes, and her mother. Tradition has it that both Mary and Robert Lee thought Orton Williams unstable and not a suitable suitor for Agnes. Rumor had it that he drank heavily, and he had shot a subordinate soldier the previous spring when the man questioned an order. William Orton Williams had changed his name, to Lawrence Williams Orton. Agnes and the young man went for lengthy horseback rides at Hickory Hill; but "after a long session in the parlor . . . he [Williams/Orton] came out, bade the family goodbye and rode away alone." Lee never mentioned the man in his solicitous letters to Agnes. Apparently he did not have to write down his counsel.[4]

Lee was less successful in imposing his influence upon the government in Richmond. He expressed his frustration with the Commissary Department and reduced rations for his men, but received only indirect countercomplaints from Commissary General Lucius B. Northrop.[5]

Lee also tried to impress Richmond with his need for more troops. "The success with which our efforts have been crowned, under the blessing of God, should not betray our people into the dangerous delusion that the armies now in the field are sufficient to bring this war to a successful and speedy termina-tion," Lee wrote to Secretary of War James A. Seddon. To Custis, who Lee knew would represent his thinking to the President, as well as the War Office, Lee wrote, "Nothing now can arrest during the present [United States] admin-istration the most desolating war that was ever practiced, except a revolution among their people. Nothing can produce a revolution except systematic success on our part. What has our Congress done to meet the exigency? I may say extremity, in which we are placed!" Then Lee asked, "Cannot Genl [Louis T.] Wigfall do something for us with Congress?"[6]

Strain and frustration took a toll upon Lee in winter quarters at Fredericksburg. His worries affected him and that worried him, too. He wrote to Agnes on February 6, "The only place I am to be found is in camp, & I am so cross now that I am not worth seeing anywhere."

Walter Taylor found the general in foul humor one day when he had to bring some tedious correspondence to Lee's attention. Taylor knew that Lee "had a great dislike to reviewing army communications . . . ," and on this occasion, "he was not in a very pleasant mood; something irritated him, and he manifested his ill-humor by a little nervous twist or jerk of the neck and head, peculiar to himself, accompanied by some harshness of manner." Taylor presented the necessary papers as expeditiously as he could. But "in disposing of some case of a vexatious character, matters reached a climax; he became really worried. . . ." Taylor, caught up in Lee's mood, "petulantly threw the paper down at my side and gave evident signs of anger. Then, in a perfectly calm and measured tone of voice, he said, 'Colonel Taylor, when I lose my temper don't you let it make you angry.' "[7]

Lee complained to Custis that "Cong.[ress] seem to be labouring to pass laws to get easy places for some favorite or constituent or get others out of active Service. I shall feel very much obliged to them if they will pass a law relieving me from all duty & legislating some one in my place better able to do it." Lee added a postscript to this letter: "I fear you will think I am in a bad humour & I fear I am."[8]

This concern about Mary Lee's health continued. Lee repeated his lament that he could do nothing to ease her suffering in practically every letter to her. "I fear you are very imprudent," he wrote, "& that unless you are careful, you will reduce yourself to confinement altogether."[9]

Lee also rated his own health "indifferent" in early March. "I fear," he wrote his wife, "I may be unable in the approaching campaign to go through the work before me." A few days later he complained, "Old age & sorrow is wearing me away, & constant anxiety & labour, day & night, leaves me but little repose." Although he wrote his wife quite regularly, she scolded him for not writing more often. "You forget how much writing, talking & thinking I have to do," he reminded her, "when you complain of the interval between my letters."[10]

Then, in late March, Lee became seriously ill. He visited Richmond to consult with the President in the middle of the month, between the 12th and 18th. He returned to his camp and learned of a sharp cavalry fight on March 17 at Kelly's Ford on the Rappahannock, in which Rooney had had a horse shot from under him, and the gallant John Pelham, whose exploits Lee had so admired during the Battle of Fredericksburg, had been killed. He informed Mary Lee on March 27, "I have felt so unwell since my return as not to be able to go anywhere. I have been suffering from a heavy cold which I hope is passing away." A week later (April 3) Lee termed his malady "a violent cold" and blamed it upon his sojourn in Richmond—"either . . . going in or coming out of a warm house, perhaps both. . . ." Then the physicians summoned to treat Lee's ailment became concerned about "some malady which must be dreadful if it resembles its name. . . ," and ordered the general to leave his headquarters and take to a bed in a house.[11]

The Yerby family who lived nearby made a room available and Lee brought Perry his hired servant to attend him. The doctors "have been tapping me all over like an old steam boiler," he complained to Mary Lee, and "my handsome aides ride over with the papers after breakfast which I labour through by 3 P.M. . . ." After several days of care, pills, and "a complete saturation of my system with quinine," Lee was "still confined to my room."[12]

His symptoms included a cough, fever, elevated pulse rate, and "a good deal of pain in my chest, back, & arms." The pain "came on in paroxysms, was quite sharp," and Lee compared his condition to an amalgam of Mary Lee's arthritis and Agnes's neuralgia. On April 11, after nearly two weeks in his room at the Yerbys' home, Lee had a pulse rate "still about 90," and he was so weak that he described his "pins" as "remarkably unsteady." He returned to his headquarters on April 16, but on April 19 wrote Mary Lee, "I am feeble & worthless & can do but little." And on April 24 Lee confessed to feeling "oppressed by what I have to undergo for the first time in my life."[13]

Throughout his illness, Lee was by force of will a patient patient. One of his physicians, in a letter to his children, lauded the general as "so noble a specimen of men," describing him as "a tall robust, fine-looking man . . . always polite and agreeable, and thinking less of himself than he ought to. . . ." Lee was a shy person who followed doctors' orders because he wanted to get well, but whose experience with his wife's maladies left him skeptical about physicians and medicines. Resident at the Yerby home were two generations of Yerbys, plus refugees from Fredericksburg; Lee could never decide whether two or three families shared his convalescent quarters. He wrote his honest feelings, very much tongue-in-cheek, to Agnes: "You know how pleased I am at the presence of strangers. What a cheerful mood their company produces. Imagine then the expression of my face & the merry times I have."

Lee believed that "fresh air & exercise" would cure most ailments, and his condition did improve rapidly once he was again able to follow his own regimen. But he never completely recovered from the illness of March and April 1863. In October he himself insisted, "I have felt very differently since my attack of last spring, from which I have never recovered." And during the last year of his life Lee still referred to his "first attack in front of Fredericksburg."[14]

What most probably began that spring in 1863 was angina pectoris, diagnosed as rheumatism and/or inflammation of the pericardium (the membrane enclosing the heart). Lee likely suffered from atherosclerosis, gradual constriction of the blood flow in his arteries. Whatever the precise diagnosis, the illness in March 1863 signaled the onset of cardiovascular problems that would become more serious and eventually provoke a stroke, the complications of which proved fatal.[15]

What absorbed Lee most upon his return to headquarters on April 16 was the impending campaigning season. Soon after Ambrose Burnside's "Mud March" ground to a halt in late January, Lee learned that Burnside had gone to Washington "to consult the military oracles at the Federal seat of Government. Sunday I heard of his being closeted with President Lincoln, Secretary [of War Edwin M.] Stanton & Genl. [Henry W.] Halleck. I suppose we shall have a new move, around next week." The new move was a new commander; into Burnside's place came Joseph Hooker, who had graduated from West Point in 1837 and served with distinction in the Mexican War. Lee probably best remembered Hooker for his testimony on behalf of Gideon J. Pillow against Winfield Scott in the unseemly court-martial after that war. In this war Hooker had been an aggressive division and corps commander and had earned the nickname "Fighting Joe" for his performance at Williamsburg and elsewhere. Hooker had campaigned for this post and undermined Burnside behind his back; but he embarked upon his command of the Army of the Potomac with considerable energy and enthusiasm.[16]

Thus far, during the snow, sleet, and rain of February and March, Hooker had generated sound and fury and little else. Lee offered his commentary to Agnes in early February: "Genl Hooker is obliged to do something. I do not know what it will be. He is playing the Chinese game. Trying what frightening will do. He runs out his guns starts his wagons and troops up & down the river & creates an excitement generally. Our men look on in wonder, give a cheer, & all again subsides 'in statu quo ante bellum.' " The fight at Kelly's Ford on March 17 seemed to portend hot work for the cavalry; yet throughout the winter J. E. B. Stuart's horsemen had maintained their dominance of both fords and fields between the two armies. As April waned, however, and the earth and roads began to dry, Lee knew that Hooker would cease playing games, Chinese or otherwise, and commit more than his cavalry to battle.[17]

On April 19, Lee shared with his wife his thinking about the war in 1863. "I do not think our enemies are so confident of success as they used to be," Lee wrote. "If we can baffle them in their various designs this year & our people are true to our cause & not so devoted to themselves & their own aggrandisement, I think our success will be certain. . . . If successful this year, next fall there will be a great change in public opinion at the North. The republicans will be destroyed. . . ." Of course for this vision to become reality, Lee realized that he would have to win victories against long numerical odds.[18]

For the moment, he would have to confront Hooker's army without James Longstreet and two veteran divisions (John Bell Hood's and A. P. Hill's). These troops and others were in extreme southeastern Virginia, east of the Blackwater River near Suffolk. Lee had sent Longstreet in mid-February to counter Federal reinforcement (Burnside's corps) in the region and to collect supplies for the army. Longstreet's performance in independent command explained why Lee tended to remain with him instead of Jackson during army

operations. Longstreet seemed incapable of initiative or action when left to his
own devices. He asked Lee what he should do; Lee told him, "You must act
according to your good judgement," or words to that effect; and then Longstreet did little.[19]

The absence of Longstreet's detached force left Lee with 60,892 men in the
Army of Northern Virginia on the Rappahannock. Across the Rappahannock,
Hooker commanded 133,868 in the Army of the Potomac. Fortunately for
Lee, neither general knew with precision at the time the strength of his oppo-
nent.[20]

Hooker launched his offensive on April 29 with a series of river crossings.
Federal cavalry swept on a wide arc around Lee's left (west) and then rode well
into the Confederate rear with the mission of disrupting Lee's communications and supply lines. Federal infantry (two corps commanded by John Sedgwick) crossed the Rappahannock below Fredericksburg and threatened Lee's
dispersed units very near the commanding general's headquarters. Five Federal
army corps marched up the river, crossed the Rappahannock (and the Rapidan), and then moved upon Lee's left flank in overwhelming strength.[21]

Initially Lee had no notion of how to respond to all this activity and said as
much to the President and to Adjutant and Inspector General Samuel Cooper
in a series of telegrams:

> HE IS CERTAINLY CROSSING IN LARGE FORCE HERE, AND IT
> LOOKS AS IF HE WAS IN EARNEST
>
> I HAVE NOTHING TO OPPOSE ALL THAT FORCE UP THERE . . .
>
> THEIR INTENTION I PRESUME IS TO TURN OUR LEFT &
> PROBABLY GET INTO OUR REAR
>
> . . . IT LOOKS LIKE A GENERAL ADVANCE, BUT WHERE THE
> MAIN EFFORT WILL BE MADE I CANNOT SAY

By early evening of April 29, however, Lee had begun to act. He ordered
Jackson to concentrate behind the line the army had occupied in December
against Burnside and assigned one division (McLaws's) to hold that line along
Marye's Heights against Sedgwick's Federals who had crossed the Rappahannock. Lee ordered the division commanded by Richard H. Anderson to move
upriver to the Confederate left as far as the little crossroads community of
Chancellorsville.[22]

Anderson did reach Chancellorsville; but when he did, he encountered the
vanguard of Hooker's flanking force and withdrew to form his defensive line
nearer Fredericksburg at a place known as Tabernacle Church. By noon on
April 30 Lee had developed his plan and telegraphed the War Department in
Richmond.

> . . . I DETERMINED TO HOLD OUR LINES IN REAR OF
> FREDERICKSBURG WITH PART OF THE FORCE AND ENDEAVOR
> WITH THE REST TO DRIVE THE ENEMY BACK TO THE
> RAPIDAN[23]

Jubal Early with his division, plus one of McLaws's brigades (about 10,000 men), drew the assignment of holding the lines at Fredericksburg. With the rest of his army Lee marched west toward Chancellorsville and Hooker's advancing columns.

Lee's principal advantage at this point in the developing campaign was Stuart's cavalry. Since Hooker had sent the best of his cavalry on the protracted raid into the Confederate rear, he had too few horsemen with him to

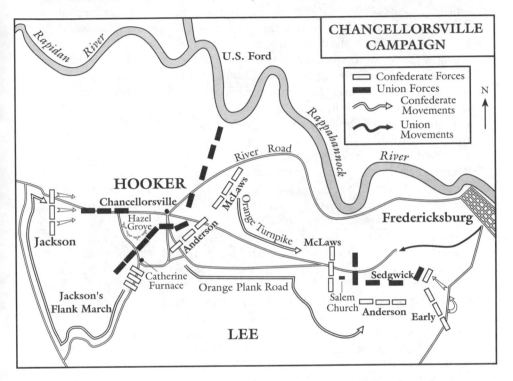

perform the necessary reconnaissance for his offensive. Stuart "owned" the space between the two armies. That space in which the armies maneuvered also favored Lee, because this region west of Fredericksburg was heavily wooded, appropriately called "the Wilderness." Such tangled terrain reduced Hooker's numerical superiority: the Federals could deploy only so many troops in the few clearings and two major roads in the area.[24]

The armies clashed in earnest on May 1 along the Turnpike and Orange Plank Road just east of Chancellorsville. Hooker ordered a general attack for two o'clock in the afternoon. Then, instead, for no understandable reason, he ordered his army to recoil and take up a defensive position around Chancellorsville. Maybe Hooker simply possessed too many advantages—balloons; telegraph wires; numbers of men, rations, guns, horses, supplies, forage—and became confused attempting to manage his largess. More likely Hooker simply lost his nerve. Whatever the cause, the Federal army abdicated the initiative during the afternoon of May 1. Hooker wrote, "The major-general commanding trusts that a suspension in the attack today will embolden the enemy to attack him." He also said, "If his communications are cut, he must attack me. I have a strong position."[25]

Robert Lee was indeed thinking about attacking Hooker's army at Chancellorsville. While Jackson's troops pressed the retiring Federals back toward their positions around the Chancellor House, which was about all there was to Chancellorsville, Lee rode off to his right. He discovered enemy troops and difficult ground all the way to the river, so he rode back to the intersection of the Plank Road and the road that led to Catherine (Iron) Furnace, where he encountered Jackson. Both generals dismounted, left the road, and sat on a log in a grove of pine trees. Jackson reported that the Federal position at Chancellorsville was strong and becoming more so as Federals felled trees in front of their earthworks. Lee recounted his own reconnaissance on the right and asked the obvious question: "How can we get at those people?" Jackson was convinced that the Federals were going to abandon their flank offensive and recross the river the following day. Lee disagreed.

While Lee and Jackson huddled on their log, Stuart arrived with one answer to Lee's quandary. Fitz Lee had ridden to the far left (Hooker's right) and found the Federal flank very much "in the air," unsecured by any natural obstacle or even by troops in any state of readiness. The question then became how to get some formidable body of troops in position to strike that exposed flank. Lee's map of the area was primitive at best. Nevertheless Lee and Jackson studied the map as they absorbed Stuart's news, agreed that someone should attack Hooker's right, and concurred that Jackson should be that someone.

"General Stuart will cover your movement with his cavalry," Lee promised.

"My troops will move at four o'clock," Jackson declared.

Jackson's declaration in this case belonged in the class with his "sweep the field with the bayonet!" bombast. At this point the question still remained about a route to the Federal flank, and until Stuart and the staff officers assigned to answer that question reported, talk about moving troops was premature. Both Lee and Jackson used the next few hours to sleep. When Lee awoke, he found Jackson huddled before a campfire sipping coffee that A. L. Long of Lee's staff had found for him in another bivouac nearby. Lee joined Jackson and Long, and soon Jed Hotchkiss, topographical engineer from Jackson's staff, and the Reverend B. T. Lacy, a chaplin familiar with this area, rode into the makeshift command post. Hotchkiss had a map and a route, plus the promise of a guide for the difficult portion of the march.

Lee studied Hotchkiss's sheet and turned to Jackson. "General Jackson," he asked rhetorically, "what do you propose to do?"

"Go around here."

"What do you propose to make this movement with?"

"With my whole corps."

"What will you leave me?"

"The divisions of Anderson and McLaws."

"Well, go on."[26]

Lee well knew what he was saying. In this instance Jackson was his alter ego; in a real sense Lee conducted a dialogue with himself. He knew the Federals outnumbered him significantly. He had already divided his smaller army in the face of a larger enemy. Now he was compounding his risk. Jubal Early and 10,000 men remained in front of Fredericksburg; he, Lee, would have about 17,000 facing Chancellorsville; and Jackson would march into the Wilderness with 26,000 in the hope of finding Hooker's exposed right flank. All day on May 2, while Jackson's corps was en route, Hooker had 73,000 troops concentrated at Chancellorsville and 23,000 more men poised before less than half their number at Fredericksburg. This was audacity to the point of madness. By all odds at day's end, the Army of Northern Virginia would cease to exist.

While Jackson gave the orders that put his corps in motion, Lee rode away to make sure he filled the gaps in his lines Jackson's men would leave when they marched. Lee returned to the intersection of the Plank and Catherine Furnace Roads in time to watch Jackson's corps depart. Jackson himself rode with his staff near the front of his column. Lee and Jackson met alone, sat their horses, and spoke briefly. Then Jackson was gone, and the desperate gamble began.

May 2, 1863, was a very long day. Jackson's flank march covered 14 miles and consumed most of twelve hours. Meanwhile Lee directed what might best be described as an aggressive defensive battle before Chancellorsville. He made Hooker believe, likely because Hooker wanted to believe, that he intended two mutually exclusive courses of action. By turns Hooker became convinced that Lee would attack him at Chancellorsville and then that Lee would retreat.[27]

What Lee in fact intended he wrote down in a dispatch to President Davis some time around midday on May 2. It was a masterpiece of understated restraint, as though his enormous gamble were battle as usual. "I find the enemy in a strong position at Chancellorsville and in large force," Lee began. "We succeeded yesterday in driving the enemy from in front of our position at Tabernacle Church, on all the roads back to Chancellorsville, where he concentrated in a position remarkably favorable for him," Lee reported, and then added almost parenthetically, "I am now swinging around to my left to come up in his rear." Then, Lee changed the subject and relayed some information he had recently received about cavalry operations in western (West) Virginia.[28]

Finally, at last, as the day was waning, Lee heard what he had waited all day to hear—Jackson's guns, sounds of battle in the Union rear. Jackson's corps crushed the exposed Federal flank while Lee directed attacks against Chancellorsville in order to keep his enemies from supporting each other. Lee listened throughout the evening and knew that his gamble had been successful so far.[29]

Later, while he was trying to sleep, he heard bad news. R. E. Wilbourn, the signal officer on Jackson's staff, awakened the commanding general to tell him that Jackson had been severely wounded. Command of his corps had passed to Stuart, because A. P. Hill was also wounded and Robert Rodes had demurred. Lee pulled on his boots and summoned his staff; his day on May 3 had begun, and it was not yet 3:00 A.M.

Wilbourn mentioned Jackson's intention to seize Hooker's escape route and so trap the Federals in a killing zone. "These people must be pressed today," Lee exclaimed. He thought of Stuart commanding infantry for the first time in his life, of the absolute necessity to reunite his army, and of the opportunity to maintain his initiative and punish his enemy. He composed a message to Stuart—"glorious victory achieved thus far . . . prosecuted with the utmost vigor . . . enemy given no time to rally . . . they must be pressed . . . dispossess them of Chancellorsville . . . let nothing delay the completion of the plan. . . ."

Lee found a picnic basket a woman had sent to him and removed some food for Wilbourn's breakfast. When the young officer offered details about Jackson's wounds, Lee stopped him, "Ah, don't talk about it; thank God it is no worse!" Then Lee asked for details of the troop dispositions on the other side of the enemy.

Jed Hotchkiss arrived, and Lee learned more from him about friendly and enemy forces. Hotchkiss tried to tell Lee more about Jackson, but Lee interrupted, "I know all about it and do not wish to hear any more—it is too painful a subject." Then Lee directed another note to Stuart to reinforce his first message. "Keep the troops well together and press on . . . work by the right wing, turning the positions of the enemy so as to drive him from Chancellorsville, which will again unite us . . . proceed vigorously."[30]

At first light on May 3, Stuart launched his attack from the west; Lee responded with assaults from the east and south. Hooker had withdrawn into a tight perimeter around Chancellorsville; clearly he had no clue to his golden opportunity to strike the divided Confederates.

The previous night, amid the confusion of Jackson's wounds, changing commanders, and uncertain battle lines, Stuart had dispatched Edward Porter Alexander to find positions for his artillery. From 9:00 P.M. (May 2) until 3:00 A.M. (May 3) Alexander scouted the woods; but only on the day of battle did he discover Hazel Grove, a cleared ridge from which the Confederates could fire into the Federals clustered about Chancellorsville. Stuart ordered thirty guns to Hazel Grove, and Alexander recalled, "the position turned out to be one of great value. It gave us fire over a larger part of the Chancellorsville plain, & we could even see the Chancellorsville house from it, about 2,000 yards away."[31]

Some time soon after nine o'clock that morning Joseph Hooker was standing on the porch of the Chancellor House when an artillery ball struck and split the column nearest him. Hit by a large timber from the column, Hooker tumbled off the porch to the ground. He was dazed, and later when he insisted that his aides help him mount his horse, was still confused. Pain in his head soon compelled Hooker to dismount and lie down. Brandy, he recalled afterwards, revived him; however, some witnesses insisted that the last thing Hooker needed that morning was more alcohol. He never relinquished command of the Army of the Potomac; yet his only orders were to fall back, and Hooker's daze endured.[32]

Shortly before Hooker's mishap on the porch of the Chancellor House, his chief of staff Daniel Butterfield, "though not directed or specially authorized to do so," took it upon himself to communicate by telegraph with President Lincoln. In a brief masterpiece of understatement and double negative, Butterfield informed his president, "I think it not improper that I should advise you that a battle is in progress." Butterfield amplified his news in subsequent telegrams, but at 8:00 P.M. still could "give no general idea of how affairs stand." He did promise the commander in chief that he would "try after awhile to advise you if an interval occurs"—i.e., if he could spare the time.

For his part Hooker dispatched a message to Lincoln at 1:30 P.M. and reported "a desperate fight yesterday and today, which has resulted in no success to us." Lincoln revealed his exasperation in a telegram to Butterfield at 4:35 P.M.—"Where is General Hooker? Where is Sedgwick? Where is [cavalry commander George] Stoneman?"[33] Lee sent only one telegram to his president on May 3:

Yesterday Genl Jackson with three (3) of his divisions penetrated to the rear of the enemy & drove him from all his positions from the wilderness to within one (1) mile of Chancellorsville. He was engaged at the same time in front by two (2) of Longstreet's divisions. This morning the battle was renewed. He was dislodged from all his positions around Chancellorsville & driven back towards the Rappahannock, over which he is now retreating.[34]

Lee was premature in his report of Hooker's retreat across the Rappahannock. Actually Hooker formed another perimeter defense and repeated orders for Sedgwick to advance upon Marye's Heights and Lee's rear. Sedgwick did manage to drive Early's troops from their position before Fredericksburg and compel Lee to send reinforcements (McLaws's division) to Early. The next day (May 4) Lee attacked Sedgwick, drove him into a perimeter defense, but did not destroy his corps as Lee intended. On May 5, Lee returned his attention to Hooker and prepared to attack in force. But on May 6 Hooker led his army back over the Rappahannock to safety and concluded the campaign.[35]

Staff member Charles Marshall was present on the morning of May 3 when Lee rode Traveller from Hazel Grove to Chancellorsville in the wake of his victorious men.

The scene is one that can never be effaced from the minds of those who witnessed it. The troops were pressing forward with all the ardour and enthusiasm of combat. The white smoke of musketry fringed the front of the line of battle, while the artillery on the hills in the rear of the infantry shook the earth with its thunder, and filled the air with the wild shrieks of the shells that plunged into the masses of the retreating foe. To add greater horror and sublimity to the scene, Chancellor House and the woods surrounding it were wrapped in flames. In the midst of this awful scene, General Lee . . . rode to the front of his advancing battalions.

This was Lee's moment. He had taken an army only half the size of his adversary, divided his force in the face of the enemy, divided it again, and then concentrated his columns to accomplish victory now nearly complete. Lee's army still drove its foes, and Lee had joined his men in victory. Marshall continued:

One long, unbroken cheer, in which the feeble cry of those who lay helpless on the earth blended with the strong voices of those who still fought, rose high above the roar of battle, and hailed the presence of the victorious chief. He sat in the full realization of all that soldiers dream of—triumph; and as I looked upon him in the complete fruition of the success . . . I thought that it must have been from such a scene that men in ancient days rose to the dignity of gods.

Lee had this moment with the cheers of his men before the Chancellor House ablaze in the full flush of his triumph. He had achieved greatness, and he knew it.[36]

Soon would come reports of Sedgwick's advance in his rear. Later would come the frustration of his failure to annihilate Sedgwick's corps, and Hooker, too, would make good his escape over the Rappahannock.

Then once more Lee would have to recast his army, renew his labors, and confront his foes in the face of longer odds against him. Experience had taught him that such was the way of this imperfect world. Fame was fleeting; reality was flawed; life involved making the best of finite circumstances. Virtue consisted of bringing grace into adversity and giving selflessly among the multitude of takers. This was Lee's larger greatness—greatness that transcended Chancellorsville.

In his moment of glory, in the midst of firing and cheers, a courier brought Lee a message. It was a note from Jackson expressing his congratulations and informing Lee of his injuries. Reality intruded: Jackson's wounds were serious. Maybe Lee sensed that within another week Jackson would be doing whatever Calvinists do in the Elysian Fields while he remained with the Army of Northern Virginia to define more battlefields. Beyond this one triumphal moment in the chaotic wilderness of war, Jackson, not Lee, "rose to the dignity of gods."

23

"Too Bad! Too Bad! OH! TOO BAD!"

Thiey had sat Traveller and Little Sorrel on the morning of May 2, 1863, near the crossroads and spoken briefly to each other—doubtless very practical, professional words. Then Stonewall Jackson pointed down the Catherine Furnace Road and kicked his horse into a trot, while Robert Lee watched him leave. Lee never saw Jackson again.

After he awoke on May 3 to the news of Jackson's wounds, Lee had refused to listen to details, protesting, ". . . it is too painful a subject." He dictated a note to Jackson from Chancellorsville expressing the wish that he had been "disabled in your stead." And he continued solicitous about Jackson's well-being and insisted that Jackson's staff move their chieftain to a place of greater safety than the field hospital at Wilderness Old Tavern. When Lee learned that Dr. Hunter McGuire had had to amputate Jackson's left arm, he observed, "He has lost his left arm; but I have lost my right arm."[1]

Upon hearing of Jackson's death on May 10, Lee did everything that was fitting and proper—sent the remains to the capital, directed an escort of honor to meet the train, and published a general order "with deep grief" replete with praise for Jackson's "indomitable courage and unshaken confidence in God. . . ." Privately Lee wrote his son Custis, "It is a terrible loss. I do not know how to replace him"; and he once said of Jackson, "Such an executive officer the sun never shone on. I have but to show him my design, and I know that if it can be done it will be done. No need for me to send or watch him. Straight as the needle to the pole he advances to the execution of my purpose."[2]

But Lee never saw or spoke to Jackson after the moment at the crossroads on the morning of May 2. He never visited his faithful lieutenant during the week that Jackson lived following his fall before the mistaken volley of his own troops. For the first few days, of course, Lee was very busy with the Army of the Potomac; however, after Joe Hooker retreated across the Rappahannock on May 6, Lee was free to think beyond imminent combat. But although he made his headquarters briefly at Guiney's Station very near where Jackson conducted his campaign for his life, Lee did not go to see Jackson. Instead, he returned to his former headquarters near Fredericksburg, to begin reorganizing his army and planning his next campaign.

Lee revealed himself when he told Jed Hotchkiss, "Ah, Don't talk about it," as Hotchkiss wanted to explain more about Jackson's wounds. Lee knew that Jackson was lost to him for an indefinite period; that was enough. He could not allow himself to dwell upon pain; he would think about Jackson whole or not at all. And so he mourned Jackson's loss and reorganized the Army of Northern Virginia for an invasion of Pennsylvania.[3]

On May 14, two days after Jackson's body left Richmond for burial at Lexington, Lee arrived in the capital to meet with Jefferson Davis and his cabinet. Despite the recent victory at Chancellorsville, the military prospect looked quite bleak. Vicksburg, Mississippi, was the principal concern. John C. Pemberton and 30,000 Confederates held Vicksburg, the last viable Southern stronghold on the Mississippi River; but Federal General Ulysses S. Grant threatened with at least twice as many troops. Joseph E. Johnston, installed by Davis as theater commander in the West, seemed unsure of his role and authority beyond the 25,000 troops he commanded in person. Even as Lee and Davis conferred, Grant captured Jackson, Mississippi, and prevented Johnston from reinforcing Pemberton. By the end of May, Grant would lay siege to Vicksburg, and Johnston would continue unsure of his role and authority.[4]

To meet the emerging crisis at Vicksburg, some highly placed Confederates, most notably Texas Senator Louis T. Wigfall, P. G. T. Beauregard, and James Longstreet, favored a "western concentration." The plan was vague but generally involved Lee assuming a defensive posture in Virginia, Longstreet with his corps marching into middle Tennessee to reinforce Braxton Bragg's army, and Johnston joining Longstreet and Bragg to overwhelm the Federal army there commanded by William S. Rosecrans. Then the concentrated Confederates would relieve the pressure on Vicksburg by assailing Grant's lines of communication and supply.

Lee favored a different plan. He hoped that Johnston would realize his opportunity to shift troops, orchestrate his own western concentration, and attack Grant at Vicksburg. Meanwhile, Lee wanted all the men he could muster for an offensive in Pennsylvania. He wanted to feed his army and animals with provisions secured north of the Potomac rather than have to depend upon the fought-over fields of Virginia and the inefficient services of the Confederate commissary. He wanted to carry the war into the enemy's country and thus defend the Confederacy from Pennsylvania instead of in Virginia. And regardless of what Lee said or wrote to Davis, what Lee did make clear was his desire to fight a climactic battle on Northern soil. He still sought a showdown, a battle of annihilation that would end the war in a single afternoon. If Lee could invade the North and win decisively there, Vicksburg would matter very little.[5]

On the eve of his march north, June 10, Lee wrote an ironically revealing letter to the President. The subject of this letter was peace: Lee implored Davis to explore any and all opportunities to "give all the encouragement we can, consistently with truth, to the rising peace party of the North." He was concerned with the intransigence with which some Confederate editors and politicians had greeted the prospect of peace with reunion. "Should the belief that peace will bring back the Union become general," Lee observed, "the war would no longer be supported, and that after all is what we are interested in bringing about. When peace is proposed to us it will be time enough to discuss its terms, and it is not the part of prudence to spurn the proposition in advance, merely because those who wish to make it believe, or affect to believe, that it will result in bringing us back to the Union." He was well aware that Davis remained adamant for independence. But once the war ceased, many things were possible.

Lee's rationale for advising the President to remain open to proposals of peace was very similar to his reason for invading Pennsylvania:

Conceding to our enemies the superiority claimed by them in numbers, resources, and all the means and appliances for carrying on the war, we have no right to look for exemptions from the military consequences of a vigorous use of these advantages, excepting [divine intervention]. . . . While making the most we can of the means of resistance we possess . . . it is nevertheless the [better?] part of wisdom to carefully measure and husband our strength, and not to expect from it more than in the ordinary course of affairs it is capable of accomplishing. We should not therefore conceal from ourselves that our resources in men are constantly diminishing, and the disproportion in this respect between us and our enemies, if they continue united in their efforts to subjugate us, is steadily augmenting.

So Lee encouraged a negotiated peace before the growing disparity in strength enabled the United States to secure peace by conquest. The same circumstance drove Lee to Pennsylvania in search of a signal victory before the increasing Union preponderance rendered any victory impossible.[6]

Lee would have denied it vehemently, but he seemed to fancy himself as some combination of George Washington and Prince Metternich. Had he had his way, he would have been revolutionary general and architect of the Union restored. Because Lee was also both modest and shrewd, he never revealed more than indirect hints of such paradoxical fantasies to Davis or anyone else.

By the time Lee returned from Richmond to his headquarters at Hamilton's Crossing near Fredericksburg, he had resolved the problem of how to reorganize his army without Jackson. "I have for the past year felt the corps of this army were too large for one commander," Lee wrote Davis. "Each corps contains when in fighting condition about 30,000 men. These are more than one man can properly handle & keep under his eye in battle. . . . They are always beyond the range of his vision & frequently beyond his reach. The loss of Jackson from the command of one half the army seems to me a good opportunity to remedy this evil." Lee then proposed recasting the Army of Northern Virginia into three corps of three divisions each.

Longstreet already had commanded a corps composed of half the army, so he should be able to lead one of the new, smaller corps. Lee usually pitched his own tent very near Longstreet's in order to advise his "Old War Horse" and when necessary to prod him into action. Longstreet had been ineffective in independent command during his recent campaign before Suffolk. But Lee appreciated Longstreet's simple strength—the Old War Horse was steady under fire—and his professional experience.[7]

To command the remnant core of Jackson's corps Lee nominated Richard Stoddert Ewell. "Old Bald Head" was a forty-six-year-old professional officer, a West Point graduate (1840) and Mexican War veteran who had lost a leg with Jackson at the Battle of Groveton in August 1862. Lee lauded Ewell as "an honest, brave soldier, who has always done his duty well."[8]

The third member of Lee's new trinity was Ambrose Powell Hill. Lee called the thirty-seven-year-old major general "the best soldier of his grade with me." Hill's finest moment in this war had come late in the afternoon of September 17, 1862, when his division had saved the Army of Northern Virginia before Sharpsburg. But as a result of a much lesser moment when he was a cadet at West Point, Hill still suffered complications of gonorrhea, and his health would decline over time.[9]

Lee wrote to Davis, "I do not know where to get better men than those I have named." Nevertheless, some grumbled at Lee's reorganization and accused Lee of favoring Virginians over officers from other states. The promotion of A. P. Hill, for example, Lee made over the heads and claims of two major generals more senior than Hill—North Carolinian D. H. Hill and Georgian Lafayette McLaws. Longstreet, too, disagreed with his commander in more than grand strategy; something, most likely the reorganization, prompted Longstreet to conspire with McLaws to leave the Army of Northern Virginia. Indeed, Longstreet was writing to McLaws about such prospects on the same day (June 3) that Lee began the march which ended in Pennsylvania.[10]

Having completed his reorganization and seen his nominations rapidly accepted by the President and confirmed in Congress, Lee began moving his army. He took some care to ensure that a sufficient force protected Richmond in case Hooker elected to attack the capital instead of following the Southern army northward. Lee also recalled Longstreet from Southeastern Virginia and then on June 3 sent two of his three corps (Ewell and Longstreet) westward to Culpeper Court House. Lee himself left his headquarters at Hamilton's Crossing on June 6, camped beside the road that night, and arrived at Culpeper Court House on the morning of June 7.[11]

Later that day Lee answered an old invitation from J. E. B. Stuart to come and review his cavalry division. Stuart had already held one grand review on June 5; it had been quite a show—spectators arriving on special trains, horsemen charging artillery batteries in mock combat, women swooning, and then dancing under the stars. But of course for the commanding general Stuart would repeat the performance on June 8. He appeared on the field near Fleetwood Hill with his horse and himself draped in flowers. John Bell Hood, invited to come "and bring your people"—meaning his officers—arrived with his entire infantry division. Despite some complaints from the troopers at having to parade again for Stuart's pleasure, the review went pretty well. Lee wrote to Mary Lee about the spectacle, "It was a splendid sight. The men & horses looked well. . . . Stuart was in all his glory. Your sons & nephews well & flourishing."[12]

After the review Stuart's horsemen made ready to march. Lee planned to cross the Blue Ridge Mountains and move north down the Shenandoah Valley; Stuart's cavalry would guard the gaps and passes in the Blue Ridge so as to screen this march from the Federals. But on June 9, very early on the morning after Stuart's grand review, Federal cavalry disrupted Stuart's departure.

Union General Alfred Pleasonton mounted 10,000 cavalrymen and an attack upon the equal number of Confederate troopers under Stuart's command. Two brigades of Federal infantry supported the mission, which was a reconnaissance in significant force designed to "disperse and destroy" Stuart's horsemen. The Federals crossed the Rappahannock at Beverly and Kelly's Fords and caught Stuart very much by surprise. Brandy Station, the largest cavalry battle ever in North America, became a contest for control of Fleetwood Hill, and Stuart prevailed, but just barely.[13]

Lee learned of the battle in progress via hasty notes from Stuart and assured his cavalry commander that ample infantry was nearby if necessary. However, Lee did not want his enemies to discover that he had moved two thirds of his army from Fredericksburg to Culpeper, and so he hoped that Stuart could contain Pleasonton's incursion without exposing Southern strength. This much Stuart did; but Brandy Station served notice that Federal cavalry had achieved parity with Stuart's troopers. And Brandy Station opened Stuart to criticism from the press, the public, and even from within the Army of Northern Virginia.[14]

Lee had ridden to the scene and watched some of the action from the cupola of a house near the battlefield. Late in the afternoon he rode forward for a closer look, and encountered his son Rooney being carried to the rear with a bullet wound in his leg.

Lee satisfied himself that the wound, though serious, was not mortal. He later arranged for Rooney to travel to Hickory Hill, Chass's family home, to recuperate. Rob, because he was his brother's aide, also went to Hickory Hill to attend Rooney.

The Battle of Brandy Station was a tactical draw. Stuart was able to hold his ground on Fleetwood Hill and to prevent Pleasonton from discovering the disposition of Lee's infantry; but Stuart felt the censure directed toward him and seemed determined to rectify his poor image to himself and others. For the moment, though, Stuart had to lick his wounds and screen the march of Lee's army.[15]

Lee spent the next few days at Culpeper attempting to allay fears in Richmond that he was leaving the capital defenseless. He refused to allow Brandy Station or anything else to interfere with his plans to invade the North, and on

June 10, the day after Brandy Station, Lee started Ewell's corps for the Valley. He ordered Longstreet to march northward on June 16 and A. P. Hill to follow Longstreet "as closely as you can." Then, on June 17, Lee himself left Culpeper and joined the march.

Hooker, meanwhile, had withdrawn from the Rappahannock and concentrated the Army of the Potomac between Lee's army and Washington. Consequently the Army of Northern Virginia was free to roam western Maryland and southern Pennsylvania almost at will. The Confederates remained dispersed in order to live off the country. Lee forbade "unnecessary or wanton injury to private property" and insisted upon paying for all the food, supplies, and forage his men required—in Confederate money.[16]

Lee crossed the Potomac on June 25, after most of his troops. That same day he abandoned his communications with Richmond and took advantage of one final opportunity to urge President Davis to assemble an army at Culpeper and install P. G. T. Beauregard in command. Lee wanted to bring Beauregard up from Charleston with some of his troops and concentrate "idle" units from Virginia and the Carolinas in northern Virginia. At the very least, he reasoned, a Confederate army at Culpeper would cause Washington to pause before dispatching the entire Army of the Potomac to Pennsylvania. In the best circumstance Lee might be able to fight a major battle against an army equal in numbers to his own, win that battle decisively, and then coordinate with Beauregard a march on Washington and/or Baltimore. Lee's plan had the effect of raising the military stakes significantly and inviting a climactic campaign here and now. Three times Lee all but begged Davis to adopt his proposal; but the President rejected the plan as too difficult logistically.[17]

Still Lee hoped for a showdown battle that would win the war. Isaac R. Trimble, who had commanded a brigade in Ewell's division and suffered a wound at Second Manassas, overtook the army as he attempted to return to duty, and traveled for a few days with Lee. Trimble's journal kept during this period records some of Lee's statements made on the march to Pennsylvania. While still in Virginia, Lee told Trimble:

We have again out-maneuvered the enemy, who even now don't know where we are or what are our designs. Our whole army will be in Pennsylvania the day after tomorrow leaving the enemy far behind, and obliged to follow us by forced marches. I hope with these advantages to accomplish some signal result, and to end the war if Providence favours us.

Later, on June 27, Lee even pointed out the region around Gettysburg as the probable site of the impending battle. Trimble believed, "I repeat his words nearly verbatim":

Our army is in good spirits, not over fatigued, and can be concentrated on any point in twenty-four hours or less. I have not yet heard that the enemy have crossed the Potomac, and am waiting to hear from General Stuart. . . . They will come up, probably through Frederick; broken down with hunger and hard marching, strung out on a long line and much demoralized, when they come into Pennsylvania. I shall throw an overwhelming force on their advance, crush it, follow up the success, drive one corps back and another, and by successive repulses and surprises before they can concentrate; create a panic and virtually destroy the army.[18]

Lee waited a long time "to hear from General Stuart," whose instructions were to screen the army's march, watch Hooker, and rejoin the army in Pennsylvania. On June 23, however, Lee left to Stuart's discretion the route he would take when he rode north. Stuart decided to "ride around" Hooker, to cross the Potomac between the enemy and their capital and rendezvous with his own army with fresh laurels from his coup. But Stuart was late from the outset; he did not cross the Potomac until June 28. And no sooner did Stuart cross the Potomac than he encountered a long wagon train ripe for capture. So Stuart rode at the pace necessary to escort 150 wagons. He also lost any idea of the whereabouts of two very large armies, even as he rode between them. Because Lee never did hear anything important from Stuart's cavalry, he never knew the Federal strength or location with any confidence.[19]

Lee did learn that Hooker had crossed the Potomac not long after he did so, and so the concentration began. Ewell's troops were scattered—at Carlisle, York, and some units all the way to the Susquehanna River; Longstreet and A. P. Hill were at or near Chambersburg, west of South Mountain. On June 28 the Confederates began coming together.[20]

Very early that same morning George Gordon Meade awoke to find himself in command of the Federal army. Meade had graduated from West Point in 1835 and devoted most of his life to military service. He advanced to command of the Army of the Potomac from corps command principally because Abraham Lincoln and his military chief of staff Henry Halleck were unsure of Hooker's capacity to lead the army in this period of crisis. The incident which provoked the change of command at this moment was Hooker's demand for reinforcements and his insistence that Lee outnumbered him. In reality the Army of the Potomac numbered 93,500 men; the Army of Northern Virginia marched into Pennsylvania with about 75,000 troops. Lee believed that his enemies outnumbered him two to one; but he knew that his president would not reinforce him, and he had already made his plea that Davis assemble an army to draw troops away from the Army of the Potomac.[21]

Lee learned of Meade's accession to command and his enemy's approximate whereabouts from Henry T. Harrison, who was a "scout" (a.k.a. spy) in Longstreet's employ. Although Lee had already recalled Ewell, this new news added urgency to the concentration. On June 29, Lee remarked, "Tomorrow, gentlemen, we will not move to Harrisburg, as we expected, but will go over to Gettysburg and see what General Meade is after." Lee also observed, "General Meade will commit no blunder in my front, and if I make one he will make haste to take advantage of it."[22]

As his soldiers assembled on June 29 and 30, Lee still fretted about Stuart and wondered about the strength of Meade's army. But with or without Stuart, Lee was determined to have his battle and directed his concentration accordingly. He had not gone to all this trouble and come this far only to recoil just when a climactic battle seemed possible.

So Lee rode with Longstreet down the road from Chambersburg through Cashtown to Gettysburg on the morning of July 1. In contrast to recent rains, bright sunshine adorned this day. When Lee heard rumbling ahead, he knew that the noise was not thunder, but more than likely artillery. He left Longstreet and pressed on toward the sound.[23]

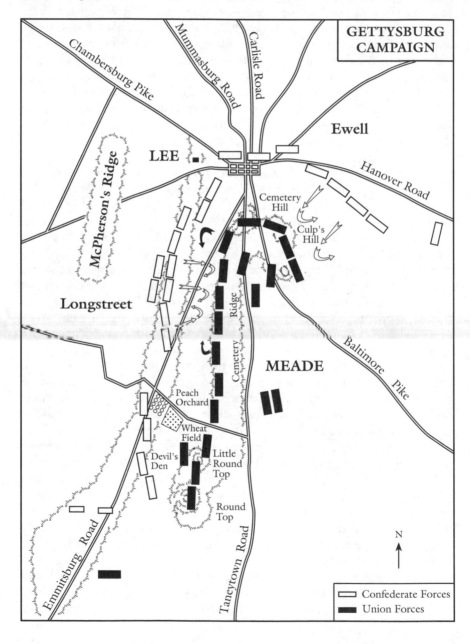

The day before, James J. Pettigrew had led his Confederate brigade down this same road in search of a supply of shoes reported to be in Gettysburg. Pettigrew, however, encountered Federal cavalry west of the town and so withdrew to Cashtown. Today (July 1) the Southerners marched in greater strength and found not only Federal cavalry, but infantry as will. A "meeting engagement" (collision) ensued, and by the time Lee arrived on the scene soon after 2:00 P.M., the fight was six hours old, and involved four Confederate divisions and two Federal corps.[24]

This was not what Lee wanted to see—fractions of his army engaged before most of his troops had reached the field. Accordingly, Lee restrained his subordinates and explained, "I am not prepared to bring on a general engagement today—Longstreet is not up." But even as Lee was studying terrain and troops before him, the situation changed dramatically. While two divisions of Hill's corps engaged the Federals on the ridges west of Gettysburg, Ewell's corps began arriving from the north to join the fray. The result of this stroke of Southern good fortune in time and place was a battle line with half the Confederates at a right angle from the other half and the Federals caught between the two. Lee then ordered attacks and watched his troops drive the enemy from Gettysburg in confusion.[25]

Generations of military historians have described the important features of the ground around Gettysburg in terms of a giant fishhook. Lee and his staff stood upon Seminary Ridge (named for the Lutheran Theological Seminary just south of the road) and looked almost due east at Gettysburg about a half-mile away. Slightly south of the town was Cemetery Hill and beyond that Culp's Hill and another unnamed hill further to the south. The unnamed hill was the barb of the fishhook; Culp's Hill and Cemetery Hill formed the great curve of the hook. Due south of Cemetery Hill was Cemetery Ridge, which formed the shank of the fishhook. At the position of the eyelet of the fishhook were two rounded hills (likely carved by glaciers) known later as Little Round Top and Big Round Top. In front of these hills was a boulder field of glacial tailings known as Devil's Den. The entire fishhook is four miles long from barb around the curve to the eyelet at the end of the shank. Seminary Ridge where Lee stood was roughly parallel to the long axis of the fishhook one mile to the west.[26]

Lee saw the Federals as they withdrew from Gettysburg scramble up Cemetery Hill, and he readily appreciated the value of that high ground. Consequently he dispatched his staff member Walter H. Taylor to inform Ewell "that it was necessary to press 'those people' in order to secure possession of the heights and that, if possible, he wished him to do this."[27]

That afternoon Longstreet joined Lee and his staff on Seminary Ridge and spent some time studying the terrain before them. During a lull in the activity, Longstreet said to Lee, "If we could have chosen a point to meet our plans of operation, I do not think we could have found a better one than that upon which they are now concentrating. All we have to do is throw our army around by their left [south], and we shall interpose between the Federal army and Washington. We can get a strong position and wait, and if they fail to attack us we shall have everything in condition to move back tomorrow night in the direction of Washington, selecting beforehand a good position into which we can place our troops to receive battle next day . . . the Federals will be sure to attack us. When they attack, we shall beat them, as we proposed to do before we left Fredericksburg, and the probabilities are that the fruits of our success will be great." These were the words Longstreet later remembered saying (or one of his versions of those words). He also insisted that he and Lee had agreed to fight a defensive battle (*à la* Fredericksburg) in Pennsylvania.

Whatever Longstreet said, Lee responded with words to the effect, "No, the enemy is there, and I am going to attack him there." That should have concluded the debate.[28]

Meanwhile Ewell seemed in a quandary down at Gettysburg. He had Lee's instructions via Taylor to seize the high ground "if possible," but amid the uncertainty and confusion he decided that it was not possible. Ewell determined to await the arrival of his final division before he attacked again. Trimble, the general without a command, was with Ewell and protested the inaction. "Give me a division," Trimble said, "and I will engage to take that hill." Ewell refused. "Give me a brigade," Trimble begged, "and I will do it!" Again Ewell said no. "Give me a good regiment," Trimble implored, "and I will engage to take that hill." Once again Ewell declined, so Trimble stormed away in disgust.[29]

Late in the afternoon Lee rode into Gettysburg to confer with Ewell. By this time capture of Cemetery Hill was no longer at issue; Ewell had exercised his discretion in response to discretionary orders, and now the Federals were on the heights in strength. Lee wanted to discuss plans for the next day. Ewell had no enthusiasm for attacking Cemetery Hill; consequently Lee decided to make the principal attack on the right with Longstreet's corps and use Ewell to "demonstrate" on the left.

That evening Lee established his headquarters in a small house behind Seminary Ridge near the Chambersburg Pike. He pondered his position, altered Ewell's orders, and later changed them again. He instructed Ewell, who had ridden out to him, to attack Culp's Hill.

Longstreet also visited Lee that evening and again suggested that Lee pivot the entire army and march south to some defensive position between Meade and Washington, there to refight Fredericksburg. Again Lee rejected this counsel and ordered Longstreet to attack the Federal left. Longstreet was not pleased, and later pronounced Lee in a "desperate mood."

By the time Lee was able to lie down for a few hours of sleep, he believed he had settled his plans for the next day (July 2). Since some of A. P. Hill's divisions had borne the heaviest fighting on July 1, Hill's corps would only "threaten" the Federal center. The primary action would occur on the flanks— Longstreet on the right, Ewell on the left. Since some of Longstreet's divisions were still arriving, Longstreet would launch the attack; his guns would signal Ewell to advance. Lee had no idea how many Federals were in front of him, but it did not require genius to realize that enemy strength would increase with time. Thus it was imperative to commence the Confederate attack as soon as possible on July 2, before Meade had his entire army at hand and in place.[30]

Lee was awake very early on July 2; at 4:00 A.M. he sent his engineer staff officer Samuel R. Johnston to conduct a reconnaissance of the enemy's left flank on Cemetery Ridge and the Round Tops. As soon as it was daylight, Lee began looking for Longstreet's advance, and he waited for quite a long time. Longstreet did arrive, significantly later than dawn, and his troops were deployed for marching, not fighting. One more time he stated his case for conducting a defensive battle, and once again Lee overruled him. But Longstreet still chose to argue an issue already decided. Lee left the fruitless discussion and walked off by himself, away from the conflict.

When he returned to the cluster of officers gathered at his observation point on Seminary Ridge, Lee spoke again about the projected attack and shared the results of Johnston's reconnaissance mission. Johnston had found no Federals in the area between Seminary and Cemetery Ridges and none on Little Round Top either. Lee believed that he had instructed Longstreet to deliver his attack as soon as possible.

Having done so, Lee rode into Gettysburg to find Ewell and survey his front. From the cupola of the almshouse Lee could see that Cemetery Hill was a poor target for offensive action. So in subsequent discussions with Ewell, Lee asked him to assault Culp's Hill when Longstreet's guns opened fire. Then Lee returned to Seminary Ridge. Throughout the mid-morning he continued to listen for Longstreet's guns, expecting the attack on Cemetery Ridge and the Round Tops to occur at any moment—"What can detain Longstreet? He ought to be in position by now."[31]

After some searching Lee found Longstreet and his troops about 11:00 A.M. and asked the obvious question. Longstreet made some excuse and then received from Lee a direct order to attack. And Longstreet did attack—five hours later. In the interim Longstreet literally dragged his feet in a circuitous approach march. By the time his corps came into position, reports of the location of the enemy were ancient, and so Longstreet had to alter the plan of the attack and move troop units accordingly.

Longstreet acted out petulance on July 2. The previous afternoon, when Lee had announced his intention to attack if Meade was still there, Longstreet countered, "If he is there tomorrow it will be because he wants you to attack." He seemed determined to do everything in his power within the letter of military law to render his dire prophecy self-fulfilling. No one can know what would have happened had Longstreet attacked earlier in the day. But as it happened, the officers and men of Longstreet's corps paid a high price for attacking when they did.[32]

The men in Longstreet's corps pressed their assaults with furious intensity. John Bell Hood's division crushed the left flank of Daniel Sickles's Union corps in the Peach Orchard, fought through Devil's Den and up the front of Little Round Top. Federal troops arrived on Little Round Top only minutes before Hood's men and managed to drive them off in frenzied fighting. Lafayette McLaws's division eventually pushed the Federals out of the Peach Orchard and up the slope of Cemetery Ridge. R. H. Anderson's division from A. P. Hill's corps also participated in the attack and some of these troops managed to break through the Federal line on Cemetery Ridge. They were too few, however, to maintain the breach.

Indeed, the entire Confederate attack on July 2 featured uncoordinated assaults, and the Southerners were unable to exploit the tactical successes they won. This was especially true on the Confederate left where Ewell's troops attempted to storm Culp's and Cemetery Hills. Men from Jubal A. Early's division, for example, reached the crest of Cemetery Hill, but had to fall back for lack of timely support.[33]

Lee spent the afternoon and early evening sitting alone on a stump at his lookout point on Seminary Ridge. He spoke with A. P. Hill and A. L. Long of his staff; but most of the time he simply watched the action through his field glasses. During the entire time he only sent one message and received one report—a signal from Longstreet at 7:00 P.M.—"We are doing well."[34]

A visitor did arrive that afternoon; J. E. B. Stuart rode to see Lee and report that his cavalry had reached the field. "Well, General Stuart, you are here at last," Lee supposedly said in a tone tantamount to rebuke. Stuart had learned of the battle at Gettysburg while he was at Carlisle and had ridden since midnight to rejoin the army. Of course he knew less than anyone present about the strength and location of the enemy and so was essentially useless to Lee. Stuart's actions in the Gettysburg campaign only served to inspire one of Lee's classic euphemisms in his report—"The movements of the army preceding the battle of Gettysburg had been much embarrassed by the absence of cavalry."[35]

From his observation point on Seminary Ridge Lee could not see much of the fighting in the Peach Orchard, Devil's Den, or on Little Round Top. He did watch one of his brigades storm through the Federal line atop Cemetery Ridge, and he knew that his subordinates had erred in not coordinating their attacks. He saw nothing that discouraged him from renewing his assault on Meade's army the following day and issued orders to Longstreet and Ewell to attack again the next morning.

On July 3, Lee did not wait for Longstreet to form for the attack; the commanding general rode over to confer with Longstreet very early that morning. "General," Longstreet greeted Lee, "I have had my scouts out all night, and I find that you still have an excellent opportunity to move around to the right of Meade's army and maneuver him into attacking us." Surely Lee was tired of hearing this constant refrain from Longstreet. Given the advantage of hindsight Longstreet's plan sounds like a good idea at first hearing. But, as Lee later pointed out, very real logistical problems made Longstreet's proposal impossible. An army living off the surrounding country cannot simply sit and wait in one place for the enemy to attack. Even if Lee were able to extricate his army and move the component units without exposing them to attack on the march, his men and animals would have starved while Meade's army watched. Longstreet argued an alternate plan that seemed certain to yield disaster; Lee insisted upon his own plan that he believed had every chance of success.

Overruled, Longstreet then informed Lee that his corps could not attack again; if Hood's and McLaws's divisions were moved to make the attack, the enemy would advance in those sectors of the Confederate line they vacated. Lee accommodated his recalcitrant subordinate in this discussion. Longstreet's third division, commanded by George E. Pickett, had only recently reached the field. Pickett's fresh troops would lead the attack. But in place of Hood's and McLaws's divisions, Lee substituted Henry Heth's division and two brigades of Dorsey Pender's division, both from A. P. Hill's corps. Longstreet would direct the assault, not at Meade's left flank, but at the center of the Federal line on Cemetery Ridge.[36]

Longstreet later said that he told Lee, "That will give me fifteen thousand men. I have been a soldier, I may say, from the ranks up to the position I now hold. I have been in pretty much all kinds of skirmishes, from those of two or three soldiers up to those of an army corps, and I think I can safely say there never was a body of fifteen thousand men who could make that attack successfully." Lee then became "a little impatient" and insisted that Longstreet follow his orders. Longstreet did so, but admitted, "my heart was heavy. . . ."[37]

Lee spent most of the morning with Longstreet and A. P. Hill riding along the line settling details. He designated a small grove of chestnut oak trees near the crest of Cemetery Ridge as the goal of the troops attacking. If Pickett and the men who followed him could break through the Federal line near those trees, Meade's army would be ripe for rout.

Around noon the generals had done about all they were able to do to prepare the assault. Unfortunately Ewell had already moved again against Cemetery and Culp's Hills and so disrupted the coordination in the attacks. Yet, although the Confederates failed again to take the high ground, by their threatening presence they prevented Meade from shifting troops to meet Longstreet's attack.[38]

At 1:00 P.M. the Confederate artillery began firing. Edward Porter Alexander, Longstreet's artillery chief, had 159 guns, and he fired for almost an hour at the ridge. Federal guns responded, and Alexander recalled, "Lots of guns developed which I had not before been able to see, & instead of saving ammunition, they were surely trying themselves how much they could consume." Alexander swept his front with his field glasses and concluded that "it was madness" to charge that ridge. Then Alexander knew that he was running short of ammunition and at 1:25 P.M. dashed off a note to Pickett. "If you are coming at all," he wrote, "You must come at once, or I cannot give you proper support. . . ." Ten minutes later Alexander sent a second note: "For God's sake come quick. . . . Come quick or I can't support you." In the interim between these notes, Alexander noticed enemy gun crews moving their guns to the rear, and the volume of fire from Cemetery Ridge slackened considerably. He hoped that his own fire had damaged those guns; but he feared that they or some exactly like them would return when the infantry started forward. But if Pickett were to come now and move quickly, he might be on the ridge before the enemy guns could return and open fire. "If they don't put fresh batteries there in five minutes," he said, "this will be our fight."[39]

Pickett did come out of the woods behind Alexander's guns, and the rest of the attacking force followed. For long moments the Confederates transformed the blood and filth of war into spectacle. Clear of the woods and into the open they came. "Up, men, and to your posts! Don't forget today that you are from old Virginia!" It looked like a ceremony. "Now, Colonel for the honor of the good Old North State, forward." Regimental colors flapped in a soft westerly wind. "Attention, Second Battalion, the battalion of direction! Forward, guide center! March!"

Then the guns began firing again. Men began to fall. "Close up!" From Seminary Ridge to Cemetery Ridge the Confederates had to advance about a mile to reach the small groove of chestnut oaks. From this perspective Cemetery Ridge is a very gentle slope; the elevation is about forty feet above the depression between the ridges. A slight dip in the terrain permitted the Southerners to re-form their lines within 200 yards of the low stone wall that protected the Federals. "My God! They're dressing ranks."

Still they pressed forward in the face of withering fire from the blue infantry. They reached the low stone wall. "Come on boys, give them the cold steel!" Some of the Confederates, very few of them, broke through the Federal line. But their enemies fell back and kept firing at them. Indeed, Federals were shooting the attackers from three directions. Less and less Confederates confronted more and more Federals as each minute passed. Southern survivors either turned and retreated or stopped fighting and surrendered. Lee's momentous attack had failed.[40]

Lee watched Pickett's charge from Seminary Ridge. He saw lots of smoke and confusion, but could generally follow the action. Long before the attack stalled and died, Lee rode forward alone and joined Alexander and his gunners. Lee saw the backwash of the battle as wounded, scared men from broken regiments streamed toward him. Later, when he knew that the day, and perhaps the war, was lost, Lee tried to rally the survivors against the counterattack he expected from Meade.

"All this will come right in the end; we'll talk it over afterwards; but, in the meantime, all good men must rally. . . .

"General Pickett, place your division in the rear of this hill, and be ready to repel the advance of the enemy. . . .

"Your men have done all that men could do; the fault is entirely my own. . . .

"Never mind, General, all this has been my fault—it is *I* that have lost this fight and you must help me out of it the best way you can."

These words and more Lee spoke in the aftermath of the disaster on Cemetery Ridge. The entire attack consumed only an hour or so. Now, suddenly, Lee had to plan a retreat. He knew he must withdraw; he only hoped that

Meade would allow him to do so. During the evening of July 3 he spent time with A. P. Hill at Hill's headquarters, then after midnight he rode to his own headquarters to give instructions to cavalry officer John D. Imboden, to whom he assigned the duty of escorting his supply wagons and ambulances back to Virginia.[41]

Imboden was waiting when Lee arrived about 1:00 A.M. "He was almost too tired to dismount," Imboden remembered, and "The effort betrayed so much physical exhaustion that I hurriedly rose and stepped forward to assist him, but before I reached his side he had succeeded in alighting, and threw his arm across the saddle to rest, and fixing his eyes upon the ground leaned in silence and almost motionless upon his equally weary horse,—the two forming a striking . . . group. The moon shone full upon his massive features and revealed an expression of sadness that I had never before seen upon his face."

Lee remained in this posture for long moments and said nothing. Then Imboden broke the awkward silence. "General," he offered, "this has been a hard day on you."

Raising his head and turning to Imboden, Lee responded, "Yes, it has been a sad, sad day to us." Then he lapsed again into silence.

Finally, Imboden stated, "After perhaps a minute or two, he suddenly straightened up to his full height, and turning to me with more animation and excitement of manner than I had ever seen in him before . . . he said in a voice tremulous with emotion:

'I never saw troops behave more magnificently than Pickett's division of Virginians did to-day in that grand charge upon the enemy. And if they had been supported as they were to have been,—but, for some reason not yet fully explained to me, were not—we would have held the position and the day would have been ours.' "

Lee fell silent for a time and then said "in a loud voice," "Too bad! Too bad! OH! TOO BAD!"[42]

Lee had spent much of his life coming to terms with adversity and making the best of any circumstance in which he found himself. Gettysburg was certainly his sternest challenge so far. He confronted all the emotions that attend defeat and failure not only within himself, but also in others for whom he felt responsible. He faced this devastation when he had been physically unwell. It is significant that he chose to sleep in a house during this expedition, another index of his tenuous state of health. As he did with Imboden, Lee absorbed the devastation of Gettysburg, pulled himself together, and continued to cope in the retreat back across the Potomac and after.[43]

But what of Lee's assertion about Pickett's men that, "if they had been supported as they were to have been," the Confederates would have won the battle? Had Lee intended or ordered supporting columns to follow Pickett's charge? And if he did, why did none join the attack?

During the unseemly acrimony among then ex-Confederates after the war was long over and Lee was dead, one claque of officers insisted that Longstreet was to blame for what happened at Gettysburg because, among other reasons, he did not dispatch a second wave of attackers to support and exploit Pickett's breakthrough. Longstreet insisted that his divisions (Hood's and McLaws's) had to remain in place to protect the Confederate right flank. Such a contention, however, implies that Longstreet had the option to include some or all of these troops in the attack plan. If he had, Lee might have lost his army and the war that afternoon. Lee might well have won Gettysburg and the war, had Longstreet augmented Pickett's charge with strong supporting units. And that, of course, was what Lee had come to Pennsylvania to do—fight a climactic battle that would decide the war, one way or the other.

Edward Porter Alexander, who otherwise criticized Lee for attacking where he did on July 3, later expressed his opinion that heavier attacking forces would have gained victory that day. "What we did, under all our disadvantages, with only 9 brigades in the storming column," Alexander wrote, "surely justifies sanguine anticipations of what might have been done by 22, at a more favorable locality & with more artillery." Beyond a certain point, such speculation crosses the border of enlightenment into daydreaming. What occurred on the afternoon of July 3, 1863, cannot happen in history in some contrafactual fantasy.[44]

But the events of that overanalyzed afternoon were not inevitable simply because they happened. Lee was absolutely accurate when he accepted blame for Confederate defeat at Gettysburg. It was all his fault. Blunders on the part of Lee's subordinates, however, do mitigate Lee's guilt. Stuart rode off into nowhere with his captured wagons and left Lee blind in the presence of his enemies. Ewell turned timid on July 1 and chose to remain in Gettysburg rather than seize the commanding ground on Cemetery Hill. Longstreet acted out his prolonged pout on July 2 and attacked Meade's left flank only after giving the Federals enough time to accumulate and implant ample defenders. And someone, most likely Longstreet, did not organize and order forward any supporting force to augment Pickett's charge.

Lee sought a showdown battle in Pennsylvania. He confronted the moment of truth at Gettysburg and never flinched. William Faulkner spoke to the circumstance in *Intruder in the Dust:*

It's all now you see. Yesterday wont be over until tomorrow and tomorrow began ten thousands years ago. For every Southern boy fourteen years old, not once but whenever he wants it, there is the instant when it's still not yet two o'clock on the July afternoon in 1863, the brigades are in position behind the rail fence, the guns are laid and ready in the woods and the furled flags are already loosened to break out and Pickett himself with his long oiled ringlets and his hat in one hand probably and his sword in the other looking up the hill waiting for Longstreet to give the word and it's all in the balance, it hasn't happened yet, it hasn't even begun yet, it not only hasn't begun yet but there is still time for it not to begin against that position and those circumstances which made more men than Garnett and Kemper and Armstead [sic] and Wilcox look grave yet it's going to begin, we all know that, we have come too far with too much at stake and that moment doesn't need even a fourteen-year-old boy to think THIS TIME. MAYBE THIS TIME with all this much to lose and all this much to gain:

Pennsylvania, Maryland, the world, the golden dome of Washington itself to crown with desperate and unbelievable victory the gamble, the case made two years ago; or to anyone who ever sailed even a skiff under a quilt sail, the moment in 1492 when somebody thought THIS IT IS; the absolute edge of no return, to turn back now and make home or sail irrevocably on and either find land or plunge over the world's roaring rim.[45]

Defeat at Gettysburg was Lee's fault—in part because he decided to risk boldly and lost, but principally because of who Lee was. He was a soldier who preferred to suggest rather than order, a general who attempted to lead from consensus and shrank from confrontation. He insisted upon making possible for others the freedom of thought and action he sought for himself.

Lee enabled Stuart to decide to ride completely around McClellan in June of 1862. Lee honored Longstreet's opinion that he should delay his attack on Pope's flank at Second Manassas, and the attack was probably more successful for the postponement. Lee sent Ewell down the Shenandoah Valley with only the request to "Keep me advised of your progress," and Ewell responded by recapturing Winchester and taking 2,300 prisoners. Stuart, Longstreet, and Ewell were the same subordinates who failed Lee in Pennsylvania. They failed for the same reason they had succeeded: Lee left them free to act upon their own initiative.[46]

Lee chose not to maintain Stuart upon a short tether. He did not unequivocally order Ewell to capture Cemetery Hill. Lee did not relieve Longstreet from command or follow him around to make sure he did what Lee wanted done. Lee was the commanding general; he was responsible for the failure at Gettysburg, and he knew it.

Perhaps at some late hour of the night Lee remembered his conversation with Jackson at a very early hour of the morning of May 2, 1863.

"What do you propose to do?"

"Go around here."

"What do you propose to make this movement with?"

"With my whole corps."

"What will you leave me?"

"The divisions of Anderson and McLaws."

"Well, go on."

That was a long time ago.

24

"I Was Influenced by the Bribe"

THE "GLORIOUS FOURTH" of July, 1863, in the vicinity of Gettysburg was principally glorious for resident flies and other creatures that feasted upon the cornucopia of carrion spread over the land. Robert E. Lee roused himself and his subordinates to organize a defensive position on Seminary Ridge. While the Army of Northern Virginia prepared to march south, Lee gave himself and his soldiers the satisfaction of daring George G. Meade and the Army of the Potomac to renew battle.

Soon after noon the heavens opened, and rain fell in torrents throughout the afternoon and evening. If this downpour were absolution for the three days of carnage just past, the Southerners cursed the sacrament. One of them recalled:

The rain fell in blinding sheets; the meadows were soon overflowed, and fences gave way before the raging streams. During the storm, wagons, ambulances, and artillery carriages by hundreds—nay, by thousands—were assembling in the fields along the road from Gettysburg to Cashtown, in one confused and apparently inextricable mass. As the afternoon wore on there was no abatement in the storm. Canvas was no protection against its fury, and the wounded men lying upon the naked boards of the wagon-bodies were drenched. Horses and mules were blinded and maddened by the wind and water and became almost unmanageable. The deafening roar of the mingled sounds of heaven and earth all around us made it almost impossible to communicate orders, and equally difficult to execute them.

With concern did Lee note the tardy disorder with which John D. Imboden and his cavalry started the long train of empty wagons and wounded men west toward Cashtown and Chambersburg.[1]

Thousands of Lee's soldiers did not leave Gettysburg with Lee. Captured or missing were 5,150, and numbers of wounded men remained to seek treatment from the surgeons of the enemy. Official reports listed Confederate casualties at 2,592 killed, 12,709 wounded, and 5,150 captured or missing—a total of 20,451. An accurate count would be higher, perhaps 28,000. Also among those soldiers who did not return South with Lee were about 5,000 who left their comrades and fell in with Imboden's wagons and wounded. Some of these men eventually returned to their units; others became prisoners; and still others simply quit the war and returned home. Lee lost a full third of his army—one of every three men who crossed the Potomac with him was no longer with the army by dark on July 4. And those who did remain faced the prospect of marching and fighting for their lives should Meade mount a determined pursuit.

As it happened, Meade followed Lee's retreat cautiously during the week after Gettysburg. Tense times there were, however, as Lee's army contended with heavy rains, Federal cavalry, and extremely high water in the Potomac River.[2]

Wounded Confederates suffered. Imboden vividly remembered the agony experienced in his train of wagons: "Many of the wounded in the wagons had been without food for thirty-six hours. Their torn and bloody clothing, matted and hardened, was rasping the tender, inflamed, and still oozing wounds. Very few of the wagons had even a layer of straw in them, and all were without springs. The road was rough and rocky. . . . The jolting was enough to have killed strong men. . . ." Imboden also remembered the sounds of his journey—"cries and shrieks."

"Oh God! Why can't I die?"

"My God! Will no one have mercy and kill me?"

"Stop! Oh! for God's sake, stop just for one minute. Take me out and leave me to die. . . ."

"I am dying! I am dying! My poor wife, my dear children, what will become of you?"[3]

Soldiers still whole slogged along through the muck and confusion of the retreat. But Meade, in the words of a Confederate staff officer, "pursued us as a mule goes on the chase of a grizzly bear—as if catching up with us was the last thing he wanted to do." Finally on July 13 and the early hours of July 14, Lee's army managed to get across the Potomac through a rising ford near Williamsport and over a makeshift bridge near Falling Waters. More rain "in showers, sometimes in blinding sheets," complicated the passage, and Longstreet recalled, "The best standing points were ankle-deep in mud, and the roads halfway to the knee. . . ."[4]

By this time Lee had already had very bad news from home. On June 26, the same day Lee rode from Hagerstown, Maryland, into Pennsylvania, raiding Federal cavalry charged Hickory Hill, the Wickham family home just north of Richmond, and captured Rooney Lee. He was convalescing with his wife and brother (Rob) with his in-laws from a bullet in his thigh sustained at Brandy Station on June 9. When Lee the father learned of the calamity, Rooney was already at Fort Monroe.[5]

Lee found time to write his wife and family; but he could counsel only stoic resignation in the face of Rooney's plight. Then Lee had to direct a rapid march up the Shenandoah Valley and through gaps in the Blue Ridge Mountains (Chester and Thornton's) to reach Culpeper in order to block Meade's march toward Richmond. By the end of July, though, in Lee's words to President Davis, "The enemy now seems to be content to remain quiescent, prepared to oppose any offensive movement on our part." And for his part, Lee was hardly prepared for "any offensive movement." He had to convert soldiers into farmers and millers in order to feed his army—"obliged to send men and horse, thresh the wheat, carry it to the mills, and have it ground."[6]

Meanwhile, the Confederate people were coming to terms with the recent course of the war. About the same time that the torrential rains were beginning at Gettysburg, Union General Ulysses S. Grant rode with his troops into Vicksburg whose defenders had just surrendered. Pundits then and since have debated the strategic significance of the fall of Vicksburg. But however significant Vicksburg had been as a bastion on the Mississippi River, the fall of the city cost the Confederacy 30,000 soldiers and their attendant weapons. Vicksburg also provoked renewed feuds within the Southern high command, especially between Jefferson Davis and Joseph E. Johnston.[7]

Contemporary conclusions about Gettysburg were less clearly defined. As late as July 17 the Richmond *Examiner* was still insisting that Southern arms had prevailed at Gettysburg. On July 16 the Charleston *Mercury* proclaimed, "Lee is master of the situation."

By July 30, though, the *Mercury* said of the Pennsylvania campaign, "It is impossible for an invasion to have been more foolish and disastrous. It was opportune neither in time nor circumstance." The *Mercury* also printed the rumor that Lee had demanded trials by court-martial for some brigadier generals whose conduct had been "delinquent," that President Davis had refused to authorize the trials, and that Lee and Davis were much at odds over the matter. None of this in fact happened.[8]

Adverse criticism of Lee at Gettysburg appeared in ink, as well as print. Texas Senator Louis T. Wigfall, generally perceived by Lee and others as a great political ally of the Confederate military, wrote Alabama Senator Clement C. Clay about Lee's "blunder at Gettysburg" and "his utter want of generalship." That Davis sustained Lee in the wake of failure according to Wigfall was only one more demonstration of the President's incompetence.[9]

Lee himself seemed none too sure about what he had achieved or failed to achieve in his second major invasion of the North. While he was still in Maryland waiting for the Potomac to fall and so permit his withdrawal, Lee wrote to Mary Lee, "You will have learned before this reaches you that our success at Gettysburg was not as great as reported. In fact, that we failed to drive the enemy from his position & that our army withdrew to the Potomac." Five days later, back in Virginia, Lee revised his expectations and pronounced his campaign a success. He had returned to Virginia, he told Mary, "having accomplished what I purposed on leaving the Rappahannock, viz., relieving the Valley of the presence of the enemy & drawing his army north of the Potomac. . . ." "The enemy," he explained, "after concentrating his forces in our front began to fortify himself in his position, bring up his local troops, militia, etc., & all those around Washington & Alexandria. This gave him enormous odds. It also circumscribed our limits for procuring subsistence for men & animals, which with the uncertain stage of the [Potomac] river rendered it too hazardous for us to remain on the north side." Much later in his life, Lee returned to these same themes to explain Gettysburg in a conversation on April 15, 1868, with William Allan (a Colonel of ordnance during the war and a fierce defender of Lee thereafter), who made notes of Lee's words. Again Lee stressed the advantage of seizing the initiative, luring the Federals out of Virginia, and then the difficulties of securing food and fodder in the face of the enemy. By this time Longstreet was claiming that he and Lee had reached an understanding not to fight an offensive battle in Pennsylvania as one of the conditions attending the invasion. Lee not only denied the existence of such an arrangement; he told Allan that he was sure Longstreet had never made such a statement.[10]

Lee heard and read some of the carp directed toward him; indeed, President Davis sent him a clipping from the Charleston *Mercury* containing an uninformed critique of Gettysburg. Lee responded to Davis, "The object of the writer & publisher is evidently to cast discredit upon the operations of the government & those connected with it & thus gratify feelings more to be pitied than envied. To take notice of such attacks would I think do more harm than good, & would be just what is desired."

In this same letter to Davis, Lee offered the clearest insight into his thinking about Gettysburg:

No blame can be attached to the army for its failure to accomplish what was projected by me, nor should it be censured for the unreasonable expectations of the public. I am alone to blame, in perhaps expecting too much of its prowess & valour. It however in my opinion achieved under the guidance of the Most High a general success, though it did not win a victory. I thought at the time that the latter [victory] was practicable. I still think if all things could have worked together it would have been accomplished. But with the knowledge I then had, & in the circumstances I was then placed, I do not know what better course I could have pursued. With my present knowledge, & could I have foreseen that the attack on the last day would have failed to drive the enemy from his position, I should certainly have tried some other course. What the ultimate result would have been is not so clear to me.

Not only did he believe he was going to win at Gettysburg; under similar conditions, Lee would do the same thing again.[11]

Some of the other ways in which Lee attempted to come to terms with his defeat at Gettysburg were less reasoned and magnanimous than his reply to the President. On August 8, Lee offered his resignation to Davis. "The general remedy for the want of success in a military commander," Lee observed, "is his removal." Then he continued:

I have been prompted by these reflections more than once since my return from Pennsylvania to propose to Your Excellency the propriety of selecting another commander for this army. I have seen and heard of expression of discontent in the public journals [newspapers] at the result of the expedition. I do not know how far this feeling extends in the army. My brother officers have been too kind to report it, and so far the troops have been too generous to exhibit it. It is fair, however, to suppose that it does exist, and success is so necessary to us that nothing should be risked to secure it. I therefore, in all sincerity, request Your Excellency to take measures to supply my place.

Lee then mentioned his health, "the growing failure of my bodily strength," his "attack" of the previous spring, and his perception that he was "more and more incapable of exertion." He also praised the President's support and "nothing but kindness from those above me," during his tenure with the army.

Some of Lee's words and phrases smack of pro forma gesture—proffered resignation following a defeat designed to elicit from Davis an expression of confidence for the future. But at some level, Lee's resignation was genuine. He did question his capacity to meet the physical challenges of active command in the field. Had Davis accepted Lee's resignation and replaced him in command, Lee would certainly have felt relieved from multiple burdens. And maybe, too, Lee realized that Gettysburg had been a moment of truth, his last serious chance to win this war.[12]

The President soon rendered all such speculation ahistorical; he implored Lee to "take all possible care of yourself," and stated: "To ask me to substitute you by some one in my judgement more fit to command, or who would possess more of the confidence of the army, or of the reflecting men of the country, is to demand an impossibility." So whatever the Confederacy did with the Army of Northern Virginia in the aftermath of Gettysburg, Lee would have to do.[13]

The President, seeking to assume moral high ground, proclaimed August 21 as a day of "fasting, humiliation, and prayer" for the nation. In so doing, Davis encouraged the belief that this war was a spiritual trial for the Southern people. Defeat in battle was a call to cleansing and greater piety; God would aide only with a righteous people. Lee, too, repeated this evangelical liturgy of Southern civil religion. "Soldiers!" he wrote in conjunction with the President's proclamation, "we have sinned against Almighty God. We have forgotten His signal mercies, and have cultivated a revengeful, haughty, and boastful spirit. We have not remembered that the defenders of a just cause should be pure, in His eyes; that our times are in His hands, and we have relied too much on our own arms for the achievement of our independence."[14]

Lee also confronted that certain manifestation of frustration and disaffection within the army—desertion—in the wake of his campaign in Pennsylvania. The President attempted to restore men to the ranks by declaring an amnesty and pardoning all those who returned to duty within twenty days. Davis had forgotten how soldiers think, however, and many men used his amnesty as an opportunity to visit their homes. Lee's solution was a system of furloughs designed to reward faithful service and improve morale. But Lee also believed that trials and executions were the only genuine remedy for desertion. Later in the year he berated Secretary of War James A. Seddon on the subject:

I beg leave to express my serious apprehension of the consequences of a relapse into that lenient policy which our past experience has shown to be so ruinous to the army, and in the end so much more cruel to the men. . . . I fear that pardons, unless for the best of reasons, will not only make all the blood that has been shed for the maintenance of discipline useless, but will result in the painful necessity of shedding a great deal more. I hope I feel as acutely as any one the pain and sorrow that such events occasion, and I am sure that no one would more willingly dispense with them if they could be avoided, but I am convinced that the only way to prevent them is to visit the offense, when committed, with the sternest punishment, and leave the offender without hope of escape, by making the penalty inevitable.

Lee did resort to firing squads that fall. Despite amnesty, furloughs, and executions, however, the Army of Northern Virginia recovered strength very slowly and only exceeded 60,000 men by the very end of August. And soon after that Lee faced the prospect of detaching about a third of his army for operations elsewhere.[15]

The President wanted to discuss with Lee "military questions of a general character," and so summoned him to Richmond on August 24. What Davis really wanted was to send Lee over the Appalachian Mountains to command the western theater of the war. Disaster for Southern arms in the West had not stopped with the fall of Vicksburg. In middle Tennessee William Rosecrans and his Federal army maneuvered Braxton Bragg and the Army of Tennessee out of Tullahoma, out of Chattanooga, and finally out of Tennessee. Lee remained in the capital throughout the last week of August, "in the hot & badly ventilated rooms in the various departments." He returned to the army during the first few days of September, only to have to go again to Richmond to confer with the President.

Lee did not want to go west; he pointed out to Davis that he knew nothing about the Army of Tennessee or its strategic circumstance. Health had to be a factor as well: Lee was even then suffering from "a heavy cold" which he associated with his errand in Richmond. Lee also remembered that he had been sending incompetent and/or contentious officers west throughout two campaigning seasons; he had no desire to encounter these men again. So he assured the President that he would "submit" to Davis's decision, but made clear his desire to remain in Virginia.

Not only did Lee want to continue with the Army of Northern Virginia; he proposed to engage the army in offensive operations. "I can see nothing better to be done," Lee wrote to Longstreet, whom he left in command, "than to endeavor to bring General Meade out and use our efforts to crush his army while in its present condition." Gettysburg had certainly not tempered Lee's conviction that he would have to destroy one or more enemy armies in order to win this war.[16]

But the crisis in the West seemed to require significant response from Richmond. And Lee's contribution to the response was Longstreet's corps. Two brigades from Longstreet went to Charleston to bolster Beauregard in the face of renewed Federal pressure there. The rest of Longstreet's troops (with substitutions for George E. Pickett's shattered division) began leaving Lee during the first week of September. By September 10, the strength of Lee's army was down to 46,000 men and so appeared to preclude offensive operations. In such situation Lee could only counsel an attack upon Rosecrans as soon as possible.[17]

In fact Bragg did attack Rosecrans at Chickamauga Creek in Northwest Georgia on September 19 and 20. Indeed, Bragg won a stunning victory at Chickamauga, but then failed to take advantage of his success. Lee reacted to the news from Chickamauga almost as though he were prescient: "I was rejoiced yesterday to learn . . . of the complete victory gained by Genl Bragg. I hope he will be able to follow it up, to concentrate his troops & operate on the enemy's rear. . . . Longstreet can successfully move to E[ast] Tennessee, open that country . . . & thence rejoin me. No time ought now to be lost or wasted. Everything should be done that can be done at once, so that the troops may be speedily returned to this department." Lee, of course, was his own advocate in this counsel to Davis; he wanted his army at full strength to seek some decisive victory in Virginia. As it happened, though, Bragg simply sat upon what seemed to be commanding ground outside Chattanooga with the Army of Tennessee and dispatched Longstreet into East Tennessee, where he conducted a long, fruitless campaign against Knoxville. Longstreet would not return with his corps to Lee until April of 1864.

In September 1863, Lee only knew that Longstreet's corps would be in Tennessee for some time longer, and consequently he adopted an essentially defensive posture behind the Rapidan River. But then in response to Bragg's victory at Chickamauga, the Federals shifted two corps from Meade to Rosecrans at Chattanooga. Lee learned of the transfer and began immediately to seek an opportunity for offensive action. Meade still outnumbered him (about 77,000 to 47,000); but the disparity was much less than it had been. Lee wanted to strike a blow.[18]

In this case Lee was unwell while he pondered his autumn offensive. The "heavy cold" caught during his sojourn to Richmond in late August and Lee suffered from pain—diagnosed as rheumatism, lumbago, or sciatica, but most likely provoked by angina pectoris—during September and October.

His plan was reminiscent of the campaign against Pope in August 1862. On October 9, Lee sent Ewell's and A. P. Hill's corps west, across the Rapidan and then around Cedar Mountain beyond Meade's right flank. Lee hoped to interpose his army between Meade and Washington and compel his enemy to give battle in the open. He himself, as he later related, "had to be hauled in a wagon" for the first two days of the march. Thereafter he felt well enough to ride.[19]

Meade responded to Lee's flank march by withdrawing toward Washington. So the campaign became a race to determine whether Lee could overtake and assail all or part of Meade's army. Lee's troops were at Madison Court House on October 10, reached Culpeper on October 11, crossed the Rappahannock River on October 12, and halted at Warrenton on October 13. Then on October 14 Lee rode with Ewell, whose corps advanced via farm roads toward the Orange & Alexandria Railroad and Meade's line of retreat. A. P. Hill and his corps marched a more direct route toward Bristoe Station about a mile distant. As they marched, Hill's troops captured 150 stragglers from the Federal Third Corps, so Hill knew he was close on the heels of the enemy retreat.[20]

When Hill reached Bristoe Station, he saw his quarry in the process of crossing a small creek known as Broad Run. He seized the opportunity to attack and hurried his leading division (Henry Heth's) into an assault. But as Hill's men advanced upon the enemy at Broad Run, an entire Federal army corps arrayed in a railroad cut on the Confederate right flank opened a murderous fire. Suddenly the chase became an ambush. Gouverneur K. Warren commanded the Federal Second Army Corps; all Warren had to do was order his subordinates to face left and commence firing into the rebel flank. The railroad cut along which the Yankees were marching became a field fortification.

Hill's soldiers wheeled about, faced Warren's men, and charged the railroad cut. But the Confederates were targets at Bristoe Station—two brigades against an enemy corps.

By the time Lee reached the scene, the uneven fight was over, and he had sustained 1,361 casualties. Once Ewell's corps and the rest of Hill's troops arrived, the Confederates were ready for anything the Federals could do. Meade, however, continued his retreat to Centreville and established a firm defensive line. Lee then decided to fall back to the Rappahannock and destroy the Orange & Alexandria Railroad tracks as he withdrew. En route Stuart had the satisfaction of luring Federal cavalry into his trap and driving his rivals in what became known as the "Buckland Races." Otherwise, the Bristoe Station Campaign was for Lee an exercise in frustration.[21]

In his immediate report to the President from Bristoe Station, Lee termed Hill's attack "a severe skirmish" having no "decisive or satisfactory result." Later, when he endorsed Hill's report of the action, Lee spoke of "disaster." Certainly Hill should have been more careful and should have reconnoitered sufficiently to have discovered all those Yankees lined up in the railroad cut. But Hill only did what Jackson would probably have done—sacrificed caution for speed and aggressive action. At Bristoe Station, though, audacity failed Hill and Lee.

Lee's verdict on Bristoe Station was as charitable as he could render it. He and Hill rode over the field on the morning after the battle. At the conclusion of Hill's narrative, Lee simply stated, "Well, well, General, bury these poor men and let us say no more about it."[22]

Lee began his withdrawal to the Rappahannock on October 18; Meade followed, and in a rare night attack on November 7 captured Lee's fortified bridgehead where the Orange & Alexandria Railroad crossed the Rappahannock. As a consequence, Lee withdrew from the Rappahannock to the Rapidan and began to settle into winter quarters.[23]

Then Meade determined to try one more time to strike a decisive blow before winter set in for sure and rendered movement on any scale for any extended period impossible. Meade maneuvered east down the north bank of the Rapidan and on November 26 began crossing the river in strength beyond

Lee's right flank. Meade hoped to drive a wedge of his soldiers between Hill's and Ewell's Confederates and then to destroy each isolated corps in turn.

Lee was alert to the Federal threat, however, and he anticipated Meade's maneuver. By the time the Army of the Potomac had crossed the Rapidan and wheeled west to find Lee's flank, Lee had moved his men and fortified a north-south line along the west bank of Mine Run, a creek that flowed north into the Rapidan. The armies discovered each other on November 28: Lee ordered his troops to expand and extend their defensive positions; Meade probed the Southern lines seeking weakness. On November 29, Meade made ready to attack Lee's lines on both flanks; Lee continued to improve his earthworks. On December 1, Meade and his subordinates aborted the anticipated Federal assault. Lee's defenses were too formidable to assail.[24]

Lee had been hoping that Meade would attack, and when he did not, Lee determined to seize the initiative himself. "They must be attacked," he said, "they must be attacked." Lee then decided to maintain his fortified line along Mine Run, in effect to use his trenches to fix the Federals in place in his front. He ordered two divisions from Hill's corps (Anderson and Wilcox) to leave the defensive line, march to Meade's left flank, and launch an attack down the Federal line of battle on the other side of Mine Run. The Confederates surged forward soon after daylight on December 2—and found little more than trees in front of them. The previous afternoon Meade had ordered a withdrawal back over the Rapidan; by the morning of December 2, the Army of the Potomac was north of the river, thinking about winter quarters.

The Mine Run Campaign revealed Lee's renewed appreciation of field fortifications; he used trenches to occupy a numerically superior enemy and to release his flanking force to deliver the attack. However clever were his stratagems, Lee was much frustrated with the empty results of Mine Run. "I am too old to command this army," Lee announced; "we should never have permitted those people to get away."[25]

While Lee had been in the field contending with Meade's advance, bad news spread across the South from Chattanooga. There Bragg had been content to concentrate the Army of Tennessee on Missionary Ridge and essentially ignore the transformation of the Federal forces in the city below. Grant came to Chattanooga, relieved Rosecrans, and restored Union supply lines. On November 25, the day before Lee rode out to meet Meade, Grant unleashed a series of thrusts against Bragg in his Missionary position—with predictable results. The Army of Tennessee suffered ignominious defeat and stumbled routed into Dalton, Georgia, to lick its wounds.

Lee responded to the sad tidings with counsel for Davis. He advised the President to "concentrate as large a force as possible under the best commander to insure the discomfiture of Grant's army." For "best commander" to take charge of the concentration and enact the discomfiture, Lee nominated P. G. T. Beauregard, who then commanded the defenses of Charleston.

As Lee likely feared, Davis wanted him to take command at Dalton, at least until he could restore good order and esprit de corps to the Army of Tennessee. But Lee did not want to go. He replied to the President's query with several reasons why he would be an unwise choice to command the Confederacy's western army. That army needed a permanent, not *ad interim,* commander. Lee knew that the high command under Bragg had been a veritable snake pit of personal hatreds and petty jealousies and feared that he himself "would not receive cordial cooperation." Lee also observed that Ewell was "too feeble" to assume command of the Army of Northern Virginia; so if Lee left, Davis would then have to find someone to replace him from outside the incumbent officer corps.[26]

On December 9 the President answered Lee's letter with a summons to Richmond, and Lee resigned himself to an assignment at Dalton. He wrote a note to Stuart as he prepared to leave: "I am called to Richmond this morning by the President. I presume the rest will follow." He informed Stuart that "I expect to be back"; but he believed his return would be only a visit to gather his staff and his belongings for the journey to Georgia.

Somehow Lee managed to convince Davis to retain him in command in Virginia. The task took several days; but on December 16, Joseph E. Johnston became the commanding general of the Army of Tennessee. Davis rejected Lee's preference for Beauregard, but probably selected Johnston at Lee's behest. When Mary Chesnut, who was very much the confidante of important Confederate officials, heard of Johnston's appointment, she noted in her diary, "General Lee had this done."[27]

Between conversations with the President, Lee visited his new home for the first time. Mary Lee had rented a house on Leigh Street between Second and Third Streets (later numbered 210 East Leigh Street) in late October. There she was living with Agnes and Mary among borrowed furnishings. Robert Lee was less than satisfied with the arrangement; he wrote to Mildred, who was still at St. Mary's School in Raleigh, "How she [Mary Lee] will get along in Richmond by herself I do not know." Chief among Lee's complaints about the house on Leigh Street was that the place had no room for Rooney's wife Charlotte. Chass was not well and hadn't been so for some months.[28]

Lee had not seen his wife for a long time—about seven months. When Lee had visited Richmond in late August and early September, Mary had been in the mountains in search of relief for her arthritis pains and for Chass's generally poor health. She had begun her travels in style, in a private railroad car fitted for her comfort. Her mode of travel was an index of her increasing invalidism, however, and by now she was reduced from crutches to a wheelchair.[29]

Mary Lee's physical infirmity took an increasing toll upon her disposition and judgment. From time to time Robert Lee seemed to feel obliged to offer her thoughtfulness lessons. "You forget how much writing, talking & thinking I have to do," he wrote in March 1863, "when you complain of the interval between my letters. You lose sight also of the letters you receive." A few months later he wrote, "I see though you are relapsing into your old error, supposing that I have a superabundance of time & have only my own pleasures to attend to. You do not recollect that after an absence of some days, that matters accumulate formidably, & that my attention is entirely engrossed in public business. I am unable therefore . . . to write to you. . . ." Lee also chided his wife about her habit of sending her letters to him by individuals whom she knew were traveling in his direction. He gave her an example of one such letter bearer who arrived by train at Orange, had to walk two miles to Lee's head-quarters, then walk back to Orange, and forgo his supper in the process. "Your fancy for writing by private opportunities," Lee wrote, "I fear gives your mes-sengers much trouble & does not expedite the delivery of your missives." He then explained that if Mary would simply send her letters to the Adjutant and Inspector General's office, he would receive them the next day.[30]

In Richmond, Lee had to witness his wife's physical decline. He also real-ized that his beloved Chass would not likely get well. Lee later reflected, "I have been oppressed with sorrowful forebodings, parting with Charlotte. She seemed to me stricken with a prostration I could not understand." Indeed, Charlotte Wickham Lee died soon after Lee returned to the army. Rooney Lee was not able to comfort his dying wife; he remained a prisoner of war, by this time at Fort Lafayette in New York.[31]

Lee did have the chance to see his other children in Richmond during his December visit. Mildred was home from her school, and she remained with her mother during 1864. Agnes continued to live with her mother and con-tinued to suffer from neuralgia. Daughter Mary was also in Richmond, and Custis still served on President Davis's military staff, although he periodically said he wanted more active duty in the field. Rob, who had been an aide to Rooney, awaited his brother's exchange and served with his cousin Fitzhugh Lee.[32]

During the interlude in Richmond Lee could count the cost to himself and his immediate family of this terrible war and the fateful year about to end. His wife was crippled beyond taking care of herself; a son languished in prison; his only daughter-in-law was about to die.

His own health had deteriorated and angina made physical exertion pain-ful. Lee did not know about angina pectoris, but he felt its pain nonetheless. And he had gained weight to the point that he no longer inspired women to call him the best-looking man in the army. When he requested new uniform jackets, Lee advised, "Get any pattern to fit a big old man & cut them large. Measure Custis & give an extra size or two."[33]

Very soon the United States would seize Arlington for delinquent taxes, a formality that only codified the fact of Federal confiscation. Here was one more reminder of the sacrifice this war had exacted from the Lees. Lee's own estimate of his net worth in late 1863 ironically arose from his inability to pay his taxes. He had inquired in vain for assessors, gatherers, and collectors "as a matter of right and conscience," and also because "I see by the papers that unless a man pays by the 9th of September he is charged double." He wrote to Custis, upon whom he usually relied to transact his business in Richmond, "I have nothing now not in the hands of the enemy, except $5,000 in Confederate States' bonds, which are not taxable I believe, and $5,000 or $8,000 in N.C. bonds, I forget which. . . ." Other than these and some bonds from the old United States, "I own three horses, a watch, my apparel and camp equipage. You know the condition of the estates of your grandfather [G. W. P. Custis]. They are either in the hands of the enemy or beyond my reach. The negroes have been liberated, everything swept off them [the estates], houses, fences, etc., all gone. The land alone remains a waste."[34]

The war was going badly. On December 31, 1863, the Richmond *Examiner* proclaimed: "Today closes the gloomiest year of our struggle." The campaigns of the fall just past—Bristoe Station and Mine Run—seemed to confirm what Lee could not admit even to himself: Gettysburg had been his last chance at victory.[35] The future seemed fraught with illness and loss for Lee, his family, and his country.

Certainly Lee had ample cause for frustration and despair, personal and professional. Yet he continued capable of exhibiting grace under all but overwhelming pressure. During 1863 at least Lee retained his poise and sense of perspective. He maintained his sense of humor and resisted the temptation to take himself too seriously. Here are some examples.

Even while he reorganized his army following the Chancellorsville Campaign, he thought to invite a woman who lived near his camp to attend a review of some of his infantry divisions. "I understand it will be near where the cavalry was reviewed & have thought you might like to see it if convenient," Lee wrote Elizabeth Taylor. He added, "I know the soldiers would like to see you & those sweet little Gwathmeys, their mother & any friends."[36]

Only five days after submitting his resignation to Jefferson Davis, Lee wrote again to Elizabeth Taylor, who was ill. "I am deeply grieved at your condition & wish I could do anything to relieve it." Then he did do what he could: "I send to you your nephew [on furlough]. He can be spared but for a little time: but I hope he can make arrangements satisfactory to you. Unless we can keep back the enemy, all will be lost."[37]

In the midst of the Bristoe Station Campaign, a number of young women called upon Lee while he was at Culpeper. One of their number accused the others of visiting the headquarters of Federal General John Sedgwick when he had held Culpeper. Lee looked grim, but said to the company:

I know General Sedgwick very well. It is just like him to be so kindly and considerate, and to have his band there to entertain them.—So, young ladies, if the music is good, go and hear it as often as you can, and enjoy yourselves. You will find that General Sedgwick will have none but agreeable gentlemen about him.[38]

In December while Lee was preparing to leave his headquarters, perhaps for the final time, to go to see the President in Richmond, he received a note from Lucy Minnegerode and Lou Haxall, who called themselves "your two little friends":

We the undersigned write this little note to you our beloved Gen. to ask a little favor of you which if it is in your power to grant we trust you will. We want Private Cary

Robinson of Com. G. 6th V. Mahone's Brig. to spend his Christmas with us, and if you will grant him a furlough for this purpose we will pay you back in thanks and love and kisses.[39]

The commanding general then wrote to Private Robinson and informed him that his brigade would have seven to ten days of leave, which included Christmas Day. And from Richmond he wrote to his "two little friends":

I rec'd the morning I left camp your joint request for permission to Mr. Cary Robinson to visit you on Xmas, and gave authority for his doing so, provided circumstances permitted. Deeply sympathizing with him in his recent affliction it gave me great pleasure to extend to him the opportunity of seeing you, but I fear I was influenced by the *bribe* held out to me, and will punish myself by not going to claim the thanks and love and kisses promised me. You know the self denial this will cost me. I fear too I shall be obliged to submit your letter to Congress, that our Legislators may know the temptations to which poor soldiers are exposed, and in their wisdom devise some means of counteracting its influence. They may know that bribery and corruption is stalking boldly over the land, but may not be aware that the fairest and sweetest are engaged in its practice.[40]

Lee had his limits, however. When he made the trip to Richmond on December 9 and subsequently retained his command of the Army of Northern Virginia, he might have remained in the capital and spent Christmas with his family. Davis made the decision to send Johnston to Dalton on or about December 15, and Lee certainly deserved another ten days with his family. He had not spent a Christmas with them since 1859, and all was quiet on the Rapidan. But on December 21 Lee left his family and returned to his army. Why?

Lee's aide Walter Taylor believed that Lee insisted upon doing his duty before fulfilling his personal wishes to set the example for his men. Devotion to duty and desire to set an example were factors in Lee's decision to leave his family before Christmas. But there were probably other factors as well. In Richmond, Lee attracted many well-wishers and visitors to whom he had little to say. He was uncomfortable with strangers and shy in public. And his family members may have depressed him with their maladies and demands on him and each other. Maybe he returned to the war in order to find peace and quiet. In a sense, when Lee left his family and returned to his headquarters, he resolved his various personal problems by ignoring them—or at least confronting them at long range—and refocusing his attention on his army.[41]

There were problems he could not help. So he returned to the mud.

25

"We Must Never Let Them Pass Us Again"

OON AFTER Robert Lee left Richmond to spend Christmas 1863 with his army, Mary Lee moved with her daughters into "The Mess." The nickname given this handsome Greek Revival house on East Franklin Street (707) may have described the place when Custis Lee and several other bachelor officers lived there. But Mary Lee transformed the house rented from John Stewart into what Mary Chesnut termed "an industrial school." "Everybody so busy," the lively diarist recorded after pressing a call upon Mary Lee, "Her daughters were all there, plying their needles, and several other ladies. . . . When we came out: did you see how the Lees spend their time! What a rebuke to the taffy parties!"[1]

Robert Lee still disapproved of his wife residing in the Confederate capital. "I consider Richmond not a suitable place for you," he wrote, "nor ought any one to be there unless business or occupation for the Country compelled them. In addition to other considerations you run the hazard of assault & siege, which you are not in a condition to undergo." He was concerned that The Mess on Franklin Street would only offer "more care" to his wife, but conceded "advantages"—presumably more space—to other members of the household.[2]

During his infrequent sojourns in the capital during the winter months of 1864, Lee stayed with his family in the "new" house. But even the larger residence sometimes overflowed with Lees and their friends and relatives. In mid-February, Mary Chesnut recorded: "General Lee told us what a good son Custis was. Last night [February 15, 1864] their house was so crowded Custis gave up his own bed to General Lee and slept upon the floor. Otherwise General Lee would have had to sleep in Mrs. Lee's room." Robert Lee seemed to have contrived this opportunity to inform Mary Chesnut and her circle of friends that he no longer slept with his wife. And telling such news to these people was tantamount to publishing the fact in a newspaper. But Mary Chesnut also observed that "Cousin Robert holds all admiring females at arm's length." However much this war had altered Lee's life, the tension between freedom (in this case to titillate) and control (to hold at arm's length) in Lee's persona persisted.[3]

At his headquarters near Orange, Lee devoted an inordinate amount of time and energy attempting to feed, clothe, and equip his army. In late January, for example, after fruitless correspondence with Commissary General Northrop and Quartermaster General Lawton, Lee informed Secretary of War Seddon, "Short rations are having a bad effect upon the men, both morally and physically. Desertions to the enemy are becoming more frequent, and the men cannot continue healthy and vigorous if confined to this spare diet for any length of time. Unless there is a change, I fear that the army cannot be kept together." Two days later Lee wrote his wife, "I have had to disperse the cavalry as much as possible to obtain forage for their horses. . . . Provisions for the men too are very scarce, & what with light diet & light clothing I fear they suffer. But still they are cheerful & uncomplaining. I received a report from one division the other day . . . that over 400 men were barefoot & over 1000 without blankets."[4]

Thus it was appropriate that Mary Lee directed efforts at her "industrial school" to produce knitted socks and gloves for the troops. The rented house on Franklin Street already had a history in relation to socks. Norman Stewart, the Scottish immigrant who built the house in 1844, reportedly had his servant unravel his old socks in order to darn his newer socks. Mary Lee emulated Stewart's thriftiness and drove her daughters and friends to help warm the feet of her husband's infantry. By May 2, 1864, she had generated 392 pairs for the Stonewall Brigade alone.

Of even greater significance was the obsessive interest Robert Lee displayed in Mary Lee's production: within a sample of fourteen extant letters that he wrote his wife between January 10 and May 2, 1864, only one letter did not contain some reference to socks. Moreover, Lee pointed out that "There were 67 pairs . . . instead of 64 as you supposed"; "the number of pairs scarcely ever agrees with your statement"; "there were only 23 pairs & not 25 as you stated. I opened the bag & counted them myself twice. . . ." The spectacle of the commanding general of the Army of Northern Virginia counting pairs of socks is at least ludicrous. Surely Lee had more important chores to perform. But perhaps he was acting as he had in the spring of 1862, when the Confederacy seemed doomed and Lee preoccupied himself with giving instructions to his wife about how to sew his shirts. Confronted with massive problems, most of which he could not solve, Lee tended to refocus his attention on simpler matters over which he did have some influence.

Lee's obsession was also most probably an index of the degree of stress he endured in his prolonged and increasingly difficult command. Well he realized that his enemies were growing stronger while he grew weaker. He had tried and thus far failed to win the war before this dynamic overwhelmed him and his army. Now he confronted a struggle daily more challenging, while his strength and resources diminished.[5]

Some good news came to Lee at Orange during the early months of 1864. His son Rooney finally returned south from Federal prison at Fort Lafayette, New York, after eight months of captivity. Released from his status as a hostage during late 1863, Rooney Lee managed to qualify for exchange in February 1864 and rejoined J. E. B. Stuart's cavalry command on March 29.[6]

Lee also retained his sense of humor during this bleak period when he wrote his wife, "The young men have no fondness for the society of the old Genl. He is too sombre & heavy for them." Mildred Lee, who was now eighteen and living at The Mess with her mother and sister, attempted during the winter to make a family pet of a captured squirrel. She named the little rodent Custis Morgan in honor of her brother Custis and of John Hunt Morgan, the daring Confederate raider who "will not stay in his cage." Indeed, Mildred's pet generated considerable mischief in the household. Lee assumed a mock intolerance regarding Custis Morgan and suggested "Squirrel soup thickened with peanuts. Custis Morgan in such an exit from the stage would cover himself with glory." He prescribed squirrel soup on other occasions for family members as well as wounded soldiers, and once instructed Mildred, "If you would immerse his head under the water for five minutes in one of his daily baths, it would relieve him & you of infinite trouble."[7]

Custis Morgan's namesake Custis Lee was himself restless during the winter, anxious to uncage himself from service on President Davis's staff for a more active post. Yet Custis's desire for more conspicuous service alternated with fits of self-doubt. He tried and failed to secure an assignment as Chief Engineer in his father's army; he declined commands in the Shenandoah Valley and at Richmond; then he tried to secure an appointment as chief of staff to his father. The father attempted to help his son. He encouraged Custis to accept command at Richmond and supported his application to become Chief Engineer. "You refuse command because you have no experience in the field," Lee wrote. "I appreciate the motives," he added, "But until you come in the field you never will gain experience." Lee did not support Custis's attempt to become his chief of staff, however. He protested that such an assignment would appear to be, in fact would be, nepotism; and he objected to the appearance. Quite likely Lee objected to the fact as well; he seemed to share doubts about Custis's capacity to perform in the crises and confusion that attended operations. Lee also liked having Custis with the President where Custis could speak for his father and keep him abreast of Davis's moods and thoughts. So Custis continued to serve the President and continued to chafe periodically in his assignment.[8]

Within his own family, the commanding general enjoyed the luxury of declining the services of an officer he sensed was unqualified for weighty responsibilities and the joy of welcoming back to duty another officer of proven talent. In the officer corps of the Army of Northern Virginia such circumstances were uncommon indeed in early 1864. During two campaigning seasons in which Lee had commanded the army, the attrition of combat had taken a heavy toll.

One year earlier Lee had commanded twenty-eight brigades on the eve of Chancellorsville. Among those who commanded those brigades, only eleven continued in place a year later. Three had risen to command divisions; five were dead; four had transferred; three were wounded; one, John R. Jones, had apparently feigned a wound; and one (William Smith) had been elected Governor of Virginia.

Of the six division commanders who were Lee's subordinates at Chancellorsville, three remained in place (Richard H. Anderson, Robert E. Rodes, and Jubal A. Early). Two (Lafayette McLaws and Raleigh Colston) had transferred, and one (A. P. Hill) had risen to corps command.

At Chancellorsville, of course, Lee lost "Stonewall" Jackson, his most capable corps commander. Longstreet had been in southeastern Virginia a year earlier with two divisions. Now he was again with Lee after his second unsuccessful attempt at independent command (at Knoxville). The reorganization of the army after Chancellorsville had produced two new corps commanders, A. P. Hill and Richard S. Ewell, both of whom were still with Lee in 1864. But both men provoked more concern than confidence. Hill had been little more than present at Gettysburg and then had blundered at Bristoe Station. Ewell's health was much less than robust—the stump of his amputated leg continued to trouble him, and he acted like a lovesick adolescent at times over his new young wife. Lee made a point of telling Ewell in writing of his concern for Ewell's capacity to undergo the physical rigors of the campaigns upcoming. Lee left any decision to remove himself from command squarely up to Ewell. "I do not know how much ought to be attributed to long absence from the field, general debility, or the result of your injury," Lee wrote Ewell on January 18, 1864, "but I was in constant fear during the last campaign that you would sink under your duties or destroy yourself . . . you now know from experience what you have to undergo and can best judge of your ability to endure it; I fear we cannot anticipate less labor than formerly." Between these lines Lee seemed to be suggesting that Ewell leave the war gracefully.[9]

Lee's lieutenants, then, were a questionable crew in 1864. Of three corps commanders only Longstreet gave Lee evidence of competence. But many knowledgeable people then and since have doubted Lee's judgment regarding his "Old War Horse," and Longstreet lasted less than three days during the spring campaign before falling wounded before the fire of his own troops.

Only half of the division commanders who served with the army a year ago remained with their commands. And neither John Bell Hood nor George E. Pickett who had been with Longstreet last spring were with Lee this spring.

Half the number of brigade commanders from the spring of 1863 still commanded in the Army of Northern Virginia during the spring of 1864. This ratio remains roughly accurate if those brigade commanders with Longstreet the previous spring be included. By many standards Lee's was a veteran army; but in terms of general officers, a clear majority of his principal subordinates were new to their level of command in 1864.

J. E. B. Stuart's cavalry was the apparent exception to all this attrition and inexperience. Wade Hampton, Fitzhugh Lee, and Rooney Lee had each served with Stuart for two years. Hampton and Rooney Lee had survived wounds and captivity respectively to return in time for the campaigns of 1864. But Stuart's horses were worn down and many fewer than before. And Stuart himself would suffer a mortal wound before the impending campaign was a week old.[10]

On April 18, Lee estimated that the enemy army across the Rapidan numbered 75,000 men. Fortunately for him, Lee did not know that he faced 119,-000 Federals; he knew that his own army included only 64,000 soldiers. Lee would conduct the campaigns of 1864 pretty consistently outnumbered two to one. Of course one reason for these adverse odds was Lee himself. In his zeal to fight a showdown battle and his zest for taking risks, Lee had spilled an enormous amount of Southern blood. One modern estimate places Lee's losses in battle from the Seven Days through Mine Run at 81,000 men—nearly one fifth of the total number Lee commanded in all of his battles thus far. There was cruel irony in the fact that Lee's disparate attempts to win the war before his enemies mobilized their superior numbers and resources and only accelerated the process he most feared—the effects of prolonged attrition upon the weaker Confederacy.[11]

Lee did not choose to dwell upon blood or irony as he prepared for the resumption of active campaigning in the spring of 1864. He did think and plan as creatively as he could in the hope that expanded vision might compensate for dwindling troops and supplies. He offered some of his ideas to Davis on February 3. "If we could take the initiative & fall upon them unexpectedly," Lee proposed, "we might derange their plans & embarrass them the whole summer." Then Lee suggested two bold options:

If Longstreet could be strengthened or given greater mobility than he now possesses he might penetrate into Kentucky where he could support himself, cut Grant's communications so as to compel him at least to detach from Johnston's front, & enable him [Johnston] to take the offensive & regain the ground we have lost. I need not dwell upon the advantages of success in that quarter. . . . Longstreet can be given greater mobility by supplying him with horses & mules to mount his infantry. He can only be strengthened by detaching from Beauregard's, Johnston's, or this army.

Lee's second strategic option was not quite so grandiose.

If I could draw Longstreet secretly & rapidly to me I might succeed in forcing Genl Meade back to Washington & exciting sufficient apprehension, at least for their own position to weaken any movement against ours. . . . WE are not in a condition, or never have been, in my opinion to invade the enemy's country with a prospect of permanent benefit. But we can alarm & embarrass him to some extent & thus prevent him undertaking anything of magnitude against us.[12]

The prospect of Longstreet, the "Old War Horse," mounting his infantry on horses and mules and then leading a mongol horde of rebels sweeping across the blue grass like a nineteenth-century Kahn should have amused President

Davis. It probably did not, because Davis rarely found amusement in anything. As Lee likely believed he would, the President elected Lee's second option. Lee himself wrote to Longstreet to point out the problems inherent in a mounted invasion scheme—"your proposition is attended with many difficulties . . . I now do not see how they can be overcome." In early April, Longstreet began the movement to rejoin Lee and fight the Federals in Virginia.

One good reason for Lee's (and Davis's) decision to make a major stand in Virginia instead of the West was the arrival of Ulysses S. Grant on the eastern front. Made general in chief of all Federal armies in March, Grant decided to pitch his tent near Meade and exercise his new command while directing operations against Lee.[13]

Rumor of Grant's transfer to command the Army of the Potomac had reached Lee back in December 1863. As late as March 25, 1864, Lee questioned the assumption that Grant would direct the principal Union campaign against the Army of Northern Virginia instead of Joseph E. Johnston and the Army of Tennessee. He counseled Davis, "We should hold ourselves in constant readiness to concentrate as rapidly as possible whenever it may be necessary, but do nothing without reasonably certain information except prepare." What Lee did not realize was the capacity of the United States to launch a concerted campaign and assail both major Confederate field armies with Federal armies in excess of 100,000 troops.[14]

Already, however, an ominous portent of the sort of war in store for Southerners during 1864 had occurred. On February 29, Lee was in Richmond conferring with Davis when reports of a significant body of Union cavalry on the march reached the capital. He soon boarded a train to return to Orange and to direct operations against the enemy horsemen from his headquarters. Lee almost learned far more than he wanted to know about the Federal raid: a detachment of Federal cavalry came very near to intercepting the train on which Lee was traveling. At Orange, Lee discovered that as many as 3,600 Federals were loose behind his lines, pursued by only 300 Confederate cavalrymen. Next day (March 1) about 3,000 Yankees commanded by Hugh Judson Kilpatrick rode down the Brook Turnpike to the intermediate line of defense before Richmond. A desultory action ensued; then Kilpatrick broke off the engagement and began a retreat down the Peninsula.

Later that same afternoon a smaller force of Federals challenged Richmond's defenses from the west, met repulse, and dashed away in the growing darkness. The next night, March 2, some home guard volunteers and Confederate cavalrymen on leave ambushed about one hundred Federal troops in King and Queen County, killed the enemy commander, and captured many of the raiders.

The dead officer was Ulric Dahlgren, and on his body were documents indicating that the raiders' intention had been to kill Jefferson Davis and his cabinet, to release Federal prisoners of war, and to burn Richmond. Newspapers in Richmond and elsewhere printed the alleged text and howled for the execution of the captured raiders as murders and arsonists. Lee, too, was righteously indignant and spoke of the Kilpatrick-Dahlgren Raid as a "barba-·rous & inhuman plot." But he advised against executions or retaliation on the obvious grounds that none of the raiders had translated their intentions into deeds. Lee also feared a chain reaction of reprisals that would soon get out of control.

When Lee joined people on both sides of the war who recoiled from assassinating civilians and burning cities as "unchristian & atrocious acts," he betrayed his essential innocence as one of the generation of Americans that introduced "total war" all the while protesting horror over the acts that defined the concept. Whether Lee liked it or not, the war was turning obviously ugly. And the looting, burning, and random killing on both sides would only accelerate during 1864.[15]

"Enemy has struck his tents. Infantry, Artillery, and Cavalry are moving toward Germana and Ely's Fords," said Lee's telegram to Richmond on May 4.

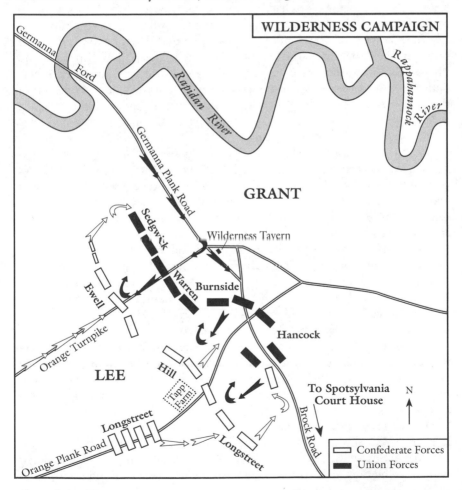

WILDERNESS CAMPAIGN

The campaigning season of 1864 had commenced in earnest.[16]

Lee had already decided not to contest his enemy's crossing of the Rapidan. He wanted to catch the Federal columns in that tangle of trees and undergrowth known as the Wilderness; numbers counted for very little on the few roads and small amount of open land in this region. The Wilderness was a briar patch, and Lee was Brer Rabbit. Grant/Meade would have to march through the Wilderness in order to travel south from the fords used to cross the Rapidan. Accordingly, Lee ordered Ewell and Hill to plunge into the Wilderness and strike the Federals as they marched. Longstreet, however, was at Gordonsville, 42 miles away, so stationed in the event Grant elected to try to turn Lee's other (left) flank. Lee ordered Longstreet to him and hoped he would arrive in time to deliver a concerted blow with Ewell and Hill.[17]

Meanwhile first Ewell then Hill encountered the enemy on May 5. Ewell was moving east on the Orange Turnpike when battle broke out in the morning. Lee rode with Hill along the Orange Plank Road, but he soon realized that his two advancing corps had lost contact with each other. About a mile of wilderness and Wilderness Run (creek) separated Ewell's right from Hill's left. Lee rode forward with Hill and Stuart to try to find Ewell or the Federals or both. At a field that was part of a farm belonging to the Widow Tapp, Lee and his companions dismounted to survey the ground in this rare open space. Suddenly a line of blue-coated soldiers emerged from the woods to the left of the Confederates. Had these men seized the moment, they could have easily captured or killed Lee, Hill, and Stuart. But while the three Southerners were still within range the Federals withdrew.[18]

Lee then attempted to shift one of Hill's divisions (Cadmus M. Wilcox's) further left to establish contact with Ewell's units. But as the Confederates pressed past the Tapp farm, the Federals attacked, and very soon Lee and Hill had all they could do to maintain some semblance of a battle line across the Orange Plank Road. Hill was brilliant throughout the day, shifting troops and responding to an enemy who outnumbered him 40,000 to 15,000.

By nightfall, however, Hill was exhausted and unwell. His men were not much better after prolonged marching and furious fighting all day. But someone should have reorganized the Southern troops and imposed order upon Hill's ragged front. Hill was ill, Lee was busy planning the next day's action, and Longstreet's corps would arrive soon. So Hill let the men rest wherever they happened to be and said Lee had so ordered.

Lee established his headquarters on the Tapp farm, a few hundred yards in the rear of Hill's chaotic battle line. There he learned that Ewell had enjoyed greater success than Hill; his front was stable. That gap still existed between Ewell and Hill; but Longstreet's anticipated arrival around midnight promised an opportunity to attack in strength and drive the enemy into the Rapidan. Lee's emerging battle line extended very roughly upon a north-south axis. Longstreet was approaching as Hill had come down the Orange Plank Road and with him was Richard H. Anderson's division of Hill's corps. Lee determined to send these fresh troops around the Federal left flank and then launch an attack similar to Jackson's a year ago at Chancellorsville. But such plans assumed Longstreet's early arrival. And Longstreet was late.

At 5:00 A.M. the next morning, May 6, the Federals attacked and quickly overran Hill's troops closest to them. That disarray in Hill's lines from the evening before suddenly became costly indeed. On Hill's left Cadmus Wilcox watched his division melt away before the determined attack of the enemy.[19]

Lee recognized all the indications of impending rout, and dispatched Walter Taylor to order the officers in charge of the supply wagons to hitch up the teams and prepare for a rapid retreat. He stood in the Orange Plank Road and tried to turn his beaten men around and get them back into battle.

"My God, General McGowan," Lee shouted to Samuel McGowan, "is this splended brigade of yours running like a flock of geese?"[20]

Then in the swirling confusion of movement, the sounds of guns, and the smoke of battle, Lee saw soldiers striding against the tide of Hill's men heading to the rear. The vanguard of Longstreet's column was here—at the absolute last moment before Hill's line evaporated.

"Who are you, my boys?" Lee asked

"Texas boys," was the response.

"Hurrah for Texas," Lee called. "Hurrah for Texas."

Lee guided the troops into line, and rode at their heels as they swept forward to the attack. Then the men realized that Lee was about to charge with them and those near the general turned to him,

"Go back!" they shouted. "Lee to the rear!"

For long moments Lee was oblivious to these cries; he seemed possessed. Then, at last, Charles Venable of his staff caught Traveller's bridle and led Lee out of the line of battle.[21]

Longstreet continued what Lee had started and drove his corps plus Anderson's division down the Orange Plank Road until his momentum slowed in the face of stiffening Federal resistance. Hill recovered his shattered units and led them toward Ewell, thus becoming the center of the Confederate line. By 11:00 A.M. the line of battle was stable, approximately where it had been the night before.

But Longstreet was not finished attacking. He ordered one of his staff officers, G. Moxley Sorrel, to assemble four brigades on the far right of his line. Then while Longstreet renewed his assault down the Orange Plank Road, Sorrel would launch an attack upon the enemy (left) flank and accomplish Lee's original plan for this battle. The attack began auspiciously enough: Federals fell back and felt their left flank begin to collapse as the brigades Sorrel had assembled surged forward. Then Longstreet fell before a volley of fire by his own men. A mine ball ripped through his neck, front to back, and he commenced to cough blood with every breath he took.[22]

Almost one year earlier, very near this place, in the midst of a similarly bold flank attack, Jackson had sustained a mortal wound in like manner. Now Longstreet was down and his attack stalled. Lee tried to oversee the recovery of momentum lost, but to no avail. The moment had passed; hindsight suggests it was Lee's last.

Late in the afternoon Lee rode to Ewell's headquarters on the left and

authorized an attack on the Federal right flank led by John B. Gordon. But it
was too late in the day. Gordon achieved some success before darkness compelled the Confederates to withdraw.

Next morning, May 7, both armies remained in place along the five-mile
line of battle now soaked with blood and seared with flames of burning undergrowth. At the Widow Tapp's house Lee hoped that Grant would attack him
again; Grant, however, had other plans. Lee spent most of May 7 riding from
one end of his line to the other and back again trying to discern Grant's
plans.[23]

In his published reminiscences, written long after these events, John B.
Gordon has Lee tell him on the morning of May 7, "Grant is not going to
retreat. He will move his army to Spotsylvania." By attempting to enhance
Lee's mystique and making him seem clairvoyant, Gordon actually trivialized
the deductive process Lee pursued for much of the day on May 7. The conversation Gordon claims occurred that morning most probably never happened.
Lee was no psychic; he was a brilliant strategist.

Grant believed Lee's present lines too strong to assault, so the Army of the
Potomac would likely maneuver. The question was where. At Ewell's headquarters Lee learned that the enemy had withdrawn his right (northern) flank;
thus it seemed that Grant intended to abandon his link with German Ford.
This Union commander would not retreat after defeat as the others before him
had done. Then Lee received a report of Federal cavalry near Todd's Tavern, a
point down the German Plank/Brock Road which extended southeast to New
Spotsylvania Court House, a critical road juncture on the route south. Finally
at Hill's headquarters Lee heard of an observation of Grant's guns moving off
to the Federal left—the direction of New Spotsylvania Court House. So a
combination of keen insight and hard work led Lee to predict Grant's next
move. Accordingly, he ordered Richard H. Anderson, whom he had installed
in Longstreet's stead in command of the First Corps, to withdraw at dark (on
May 7) and march for New Spotsylvania Court House. Hill and Ewell would
follow.

Next morning, May 8, the Confederates confirmed that fact that the Federal army was in motion and soon corroborated Lee's deduction about Grant's
destination. The campaign became a race to the right, and Lee joined the
march to Spotsylvania.[24]

En route Lee heard from A. P. Hill that he had become too sick to continue in command of his corps. Hill had a high fever and suffered intense
pain every time he tried to walk. Riding a horse was out of the question. He
insisted upon remaining with the army, however, and made a bed for himself
in an ambulance to follow his men to Spotsylvania. Lee elevated Jubal Early to
command Hill's corps. Now he had lost two of three corps commanders, and
the one who remained (Ewell) was the officer Lee had believed not able to
stand the vigors of an active campaign.

Fitz Lee's Confederate cavalry conducted a masterful delaying action
before the Federal infantry advancing upon Spotsylvania on the morning of

May 8. And when the Federals reached the vicinity of the little village, they found Anderson's (Longstreet's) corps waiting for them. Lee had won the race to Spotsylvania; now he had to hold the place. But as Anderson had arrived just in time to bar the way to the road junction, Ewell reached the scene just in time to support Anderson in repulsing the Union attack.[25]

Lee was awake at 3:00 A.M. on May 9, his usual hour to rise during this

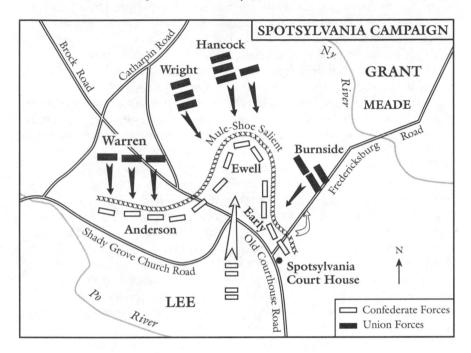

campaign, and his priority was establishing a defensive line around Spotsylvania. Felled trees opened avenues of fire for artillery and infantry and also impeded the advance of enemy troops in an attack. Behind the belt of tree trunks and branches (abattis), the Confederates dug trenches and gun positions. This line of field fortifications around Spotsylvania eventually stretched seven and a half miles, although Lee's army never occupied more than about five or six miles of trenches at any one time. All of this presaged the trench warfare Lee would later conduct at Petersburg. The principal anomaly in Lee's well-designed defense system was a huge salient (protrusion) at the northern extremity. Terrain and vegetation dictated what the Confederates termed the "Mule Shoe" during the initial phase of the battle; Lee had plans to straighten the line but needed time to cut down more trees and erect earthworks across the base of the salient. Meanwhile he stationed Ewell's entire corps around the extension of his line.[26]

On May 9, Grant probed the left of Lee's lines and attempted to turn the Confederate flank. Also on May 9, Philip Sheridan's Union cavalry, 10,000 horsemen, commenced a protracted raid behind the Southern lines apparently directed at Richmond. Sheridan cared more about Stuart's Confederate cavalry than about Richmond, however. His mission was to lure Stuart into open country and "thrash hell out of him." Stuart followed Sheridan; he could not allow his enemy to roam unmolested through central Virginia. But Stuart took less than half of Sheridan's strength in the pursuit.[27]

On May 10, while Stuart and Sheridan dashed southward toward Richmond, Grant attacked with massive numbers during the late afternoon. The first assault struck Anderson's line and suffered a bloody repulse. But just after 6:00 P.M. another concerted attack breached the left (western) perimeter of the Mule Shoe and captured men and guns within the Southern works.

While he heard reports of the Union penetration, Lee made ready to dash to the threatened sector and rally the defenders. Venable and Walter Taylor prevailed upon the commanding general to remain in his place. "Then you must see to it that the ground is recovered," Lee responded. So Taylor mounted and galloped into the Mule Shoe, where he grabbed a flag and himself led a counterattack. When darkness fell, the Confederates finally expelled the last of the Federal intruders and reclaimed their works.[28]

Grant did not attack on May 11, and his quiescence, combined with activity in the Federal rear, convinced Lee that his adversary was about to maneuver again. Lee tried to prepare his troops to block Grant's way if he headed south toward Richmond or to attack Grant's columns if they marched eastward toward Fredericksburg. Lee even ordered his artillery out of the Mule Shoe so that displacing the guns would not impede the march he anticipated next day.

In this case Lee outsmarted himself. He made assumptions, then adopted conclusions based upon his assumptions, and then attempted to anticipate his enemy's course of action. His assumptions were wrong. Grant had no intention of moving; he intended to attack some more.

Very early on May 12 overwhelming numbers of Federal soldiers rushed the Mule Shoe. The guns Lee had ordered withdrawn were silent in the Confederate defense; in fact, the attackers captured some of the guns as Confederate artillerists attempted to bring them back into the salient. The attack was immediately successful, and the attackers threatened to overrun Ewell's corps and in so doing drive a wedge between Anderson and Early.

Lee heard the firing soon after he finished breakfast, and hastened toward the Mule Shoe. As he rode he encountered men running toward him in flight from disaster.

"Shame on you men, shame on you," Lee shouted.

Soon Lee learned the worst: the enemy was deep into the Mule Shoe. He sought out his generals, urged them to rally their men, and directed troop units to sectors of the field where the Federal threats were greatest. Once more Lee prepared to lead a countercharge himself and again Lee's soldiers refused to move until he withdrew. "Lee to the rear!" came the calls. "Go back!" Moxley Sorrel reported that on one occasion during the day Traveller reared, and while horse and rider were in the air a cannon ball whizzed beneath the horse's girth. Had Traveller not been on his hind legs, the ball would surely have hit and likely killed the general.

But late in the day Lee once again rode forward with a brigade of infantry about to enter the battle. "For God's sake, go back!" they cried. "Go back, General."

By this time the "Mule Shoe" had become the "Bloody Angle" amid some of the most awesome fighting in the entire war. Here was Pickett's Charge at Gettysburg lasting all day. From dawn when the Federals first charged out of the morning mist until after dark men clawed at each other across the parapet that defined the Bloody Angle. The firing was so intense and continued so long that an oak tree twenty-two inches in diameter toppled to the forest floor, felled by the myriad mine balls that struck the trunk.

Lee decided to construct another fortified line of earth and logs across the base of Bloody Angle/Mule Shoe. But troops in contact with the enemy had to sustain the combat along the old line until the new set of works was ready. Finally, after midnight, the men fell back and groped into the new trenches.[29]

During that terrible day, May 12, Lee learned more bad news—J. E. B. Stuart was dying. He had outrun Sheridan in the race to Richmond and awaited the heavy Federal column at Yellow Tavern on May 11. In the fight that ensued that afternoon, Stuart suffered a mortal wound; he died in Richmond the following evening. Lee grieved. "A more zealous, ardent, brave & devoted soldier than Stuart, the Confederacy cannot have," he wrote Mary Lee on May 16. Not until May 20 did Lee have the opportunity to announce Stuart's death to the Army of Northern Virginia.[30]

Four days of rain followed the slaughter on May 12; in fact it rained on May 12 too, but few of the soldiers involved in the battle seemed to notice. On May 13, Grant planned a bold maneuver on Lee's right flank; two Union corps began a march after dark from the Union left all the way around to positions on and beyond Lee's right (southeast of Spotsylvania). Rain retarded the Federal march, however, and Lee countered by shifting Anderson's corps from the left of his line to the right flank and extending his earthworks all the way to the Po River, over two miles south of Spotsylvania. Some of Early's troops "handsomely repulsed" the attacks on May 14. Undaunted, Grant then moved two corps from his extended left flank back to his right and ordered attacks in the sector of the Mule Shoe again. Lee responded, and Ewell's troops "easily repulsed" the attacks on May 18.

Lee renewed his concern that Grant might move undetected beyond the Confederate right and interpose the Army of the Potomac between Lee's army and Richmond. Accordingly, on May 19 Lee ordered Ewell forward in what amounted to a reconnaissance in force. Ewell convinced Lee to probe for the Federal right flank instead. But Ewell left his artillery behind and stumbled into a serious fight. Compelled to retreat in haste, Ewell was able to verify that the Federals were still in place.

But the next day Grant began moving again—again to the south and east.

So Lee moved as well—this time south of the North Anna River—and he established another firm defensive position on May 22.[31]

Hill pronounced himself fit to command on May 21; but he remained unwell, and Ewell, too, was unsteady. Then on May 24 Lee succumbed to a virulent attack of diarrhea that confined him to camp. He lay on his cot and said to no one in particular, "We must strike them a blow—we must never let them pass us again—we must strike them a blow."

Lee's defensive position on the North Anna was ingenious; as Grant approached, his army divided into thirds separated by the river. Had Lee not been very ill with his intestinal malady, he would have had the chance to strike that blow.[32]

Grant, however, soon realized his vulnerability and set his army in motion once more. Again he moved south and east, and again Lee countered his adversary's maneuver. Feeling not much better, Lee rode south and established another line—this time along Totopotomoy Creek, only nine miles from Richmond.

For the first time during this campaign, Lee established his headquarters at a house and slept indoors. While Grant was discovering that Lee's works were too strong to assail directly, Lee conducted a campaign for reinforcements. Already he had drawn John C. Breckinridge from the Valley and George E. Pickett's division from the James River. Lee had in mind combining forces with P. G. T. Beauregard, who by now had thwarted a Federal campaign south of the James. But Beauregard initially refused to cooperate. Lee was in no mood to debate with Beauregard or anyone else. To Beauregard, Lee telegraphed, "The result of your delay will be disaster," and then he used the same word—"disaster"—in a telegram to the President. Robert F. Hoke's division from Beauregard's command started for Lee's army that same evening.

Lee still wanted to strike a blow to destroy Grant's army before Grant achieved siege. To Hill he wrote, "The time has arrived in my opinion, when something more is necessary than adhering to lines and defensive positions. We shall be obliged to go out and prevent the enemy from selecting such positions as he chooses. If he is allowed to continue that course we shall at last be obliged to take refuge behind the works of Richmond and stand a siege which would be but a work of time. You must be 'prepared to fight him in the field. . . .'" Meanwhile, Lee extended his lines to the southeast; they extended from Totopotomoy Creek to the Chickahominy River at Grapevine Bridge.[33]

Maybe Grant became frustrated; he had maneuvered skillfully, and still Lee barred his way. At any rate Grant decided to assault the center of Lee's long defensive line in hopes of breaking through and opening the road to Richmond at the same time he split Lee's army in half.

The result of Grant's feeling and thinking was the Battle of Cold Harbor on June 3. Grant believed he could break the seven-mile-long defensive curtain Lee had drawn before Richmond. He erred. The attack was a bloody debacle, and by mid-morning it was clear that the Army of Northern Virginia had prevailed. In the aftermath the Federal survivors simply dug holes where they were, and the short-range trench war began again as it had at Spotsylvania.[34]

By this time the campaign, really a rolling battle in which the antagonists never did break contact, was a month old. Lee had maintained a stalemate; he had tried to achieve much more than stasis. Lee still believed that he had to destroy his enemy, and from that perspective his campaign was thus far a failure. Grant had lost at least 50,000 men, nearly 1,700 casualties per day. Lee's casualties were less but consequential, perhaps as many as 32,000 or one half his army on May 4.[35]

Most eloquent among the many words written about the casualties in the Army of Northern Virginia during the campaign of 1864 so far was a letter one of those casualties wrote from Spotsylvania to his father in Mississippi:

> This is my last letter to you. I went into battle this morning as courier for General Heth. I have been struck by a piece of shell and my right shoulder is horribly mangled

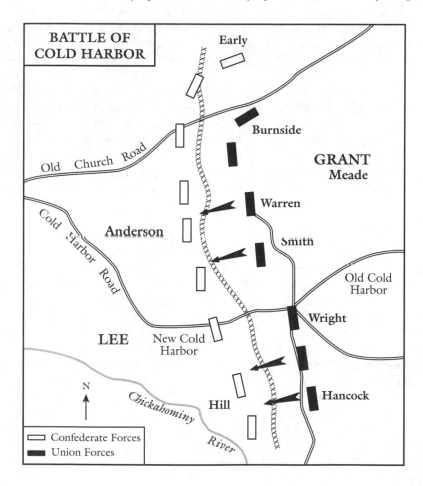

and I know death is inevitable. I am very weak but I write to you because I know you would be delighted to read a word from your dying son. I know death is near, that I will die far from home and friends of my early youth but I have friends here too who are kind to me. My friend Fairfax will write you at my request and give you the particulars of my death. My grave will be marked 58 that you may visit it if you desire to do so, but is optionary with you whether you let my remains rest here or in Miss. I would like to rest in the grave yard with my dear mother and brothers but It's a matter of minor importance. Let us all try to reunite in heaven. I pray my God to forgive my sins and I feel that his promises are true that he will forgive me and save me. Give my love to all my friends my strength fails me. My horse and my equipment will be left for you. Again a long farewell and you. May we meet in heaven.

> Your dying son,
> J. R. Montgomery[36]

As for Robert Lee to this point in 1864, far more eloquent than anything he wrote or said were his actions. On four separate occasions during the fighting in the Wilderness and around Spotsylvania Lee was about to launch himself into the fury of combat. Each time those nearby—staff officers, subordinate commanders, and common soldiers—restrained him. "Lee to the rear"; "Go back, General Lee." Men grasped Traveller's bridle and physically turned Lee around.

What was happening in these instances? Did Lee reveal a "death wish" when he prepared to charge with the Texans in the Wilderness, when he heard of the Federal penetration of his lines on May 10, when twice on May 12 he was about to lead counterattacks into the Mule Shoe at Spotsylvania? Was Lee so frustrated with the course of the war that he elected to die at the head of an infantry charge? All things of course are possible; but it is improbable that Lee consciously or otherwise chose to end his life in some grandiose romantic gesture.[37] War was Lee's profession. "Those people" were his enemies; he wanted to win.

The "Lee-to-the-rear" incidents were also indications of a more practical circumstance of Lee's command. No longer could he trust his subordinates to react in battle as he desired. Lee believed that he had to take charge and take action himself. He explained this problem to A. P. Hill at Spotsylvania, when Hill became furious at Ambrose Ransom Wright for bungling a mission with the brigade he commanded. "These men are not an army," Lee explained to Hill, "they are citizens defending their country. General Wright is not a soldier; he's a lawyer. The soldiers know their duties better than the general officers do and they have fought magnificently. Sometimes I would like to mask troops and then deploy them, but if I were to give the proper order, the general officers would not understand it; so I have to make the best of what I have and lose much time in making dispositions. You understand all this, but if you humiliated General Wright, the people of Georgia would not understand. Besides, whom would you put in his place? You'll have to do what I do: When a man makes a mistake, I call him to my tent, talk to him, and use the authority of my position to make him do the right thing the next time."[38]

While Yankee soldiers stormed into the Mule Shoe, Lee had no time to call someone to his tent and talk to him; so he attempted to perform difficult tasks himself rather than delegate them to others. But Robert Lee could not win the war all by himself. For Lee, the gratification of a "death wish" would have constituted cowardice. Had he suffered a mortal wound in the Wilderness or at Spotsylvania, he would probably not have made any grandiloquent pronouncements on his deathbed. More likely he would have said much the same things J. R. Montgomery wrote to his father from Spotsylvania. But Lee had no father; he would have said them as a prayer.

26

"I Go to Petersburg"

OLD HARBOR HAS NO HARBOR—the little village is many miles from water navigable by vessels larger than canoes. The name probably derives from the old English term for a tavern at which travelers might secure lodging without food.

Once before the Army of Northern Virginia and the Army of the Potomac had clashed at Cold Harbor: First Cold Harbor is an alternate name for Gaines's Mill, June 27, 1862. About Second Cold Harbor on June 3, 1864, Robert E. Lee made the matter-of-fact report to Jefferson Davis: "So far every attack of the enemy has been repulsed. His assaults began early this morning, and continued until about 9 o'clock." Charles S. Venable of Lee's staff later wrote that "The victory of the 3d of June, at Cold Harbor, was perhaps the easiest ever granted to Confederate arms by the folly of Federal commanders." June 3 was the Confederate President's birthday; he did not expect a gift as expensive as this battle from Ulysses S. Grant. Confederate casualties were less than 1,500; the United States lost 7,000 men at Second Cold Harbor.[1]

In the aftermath of most battles, it had become customary for the defeated commander to send a message through the battle line accompanied by a "flag of truce" (i.e., white flag) requesting a suspension of shooting to allow the contending armies the opportunity to bury the dead and carry away the wounded. After Second Cold Harbor no flag of truce appeared on June 3 or June 4; so the corpses began to rot under the summer sun, and the cries of wounded men for relief swelled to wails.

Then, after noon on June 5, Grant sent a message to Lee proposing that unarmed litter bearers from both armies advance to collect their respective wounded. "It is reported to me," Grant stated, "that there are wounded men probably of both armies, now lying exposed and suffering between the lines." Grant's suggestion was considerably less than the usual truce to bury the dead; Lee decided to make an issue of this departure from protocol. "I fear that such an arrangement will lead to misunderstanding and difficulty," Lee responded. "I propose therefore, instead, that when either party desires to remove their dead or wounded a flag of truce be sent as is customary." Lee well knew that his dead and wounded lay within his lines; the rotting bodies and wounded men whose cries for help had become whimpers by this time between the lines were all Yankees.

Undaunted, Grant, having lost the battle, still tried to win the truce. "I will send immediately, as you [!] propose," Grant informed Lee, "to collect the dead and wounded between the lines of the two armies, and will also instruct that you be allowed to do the same."

"I do not make myself understood. . . ," Lee replied. He had not requested a truce. If Grant wanted one, he must ask, "by a flag of truce in the usual way."

So late on June 6 Grant did the "usual" thing and asked Lee to suspend hostilities. Lee concurred. When the burial details and litter bearers advanced on the morning of June 7, four days after the battle, they found only two wounded men alive; the rest had somehow made it to Union lines or died. Pride commanded a high price; this time Lee compelled Grant to pay.[2]

All the while this verbal combat continued at Cold Harbor, the war resumed elsewhere. In the Shenandoah Valley on June 5, Union General David Hunter with 15,000 troops defeated and killed Confederate cavalryman William E. Jones and then occupied Staunton. Then, on June 7, Grant unleashed Philip Sheridan and numerous cavalry to wreck the Virginia Central Railroad. And still P. G. T. Beauregard reported dangers in his sector south of the James River.[3]

To this flurry of Federal activity Lee responded as well as he was able. He wanted to concentrate troops in his army and try to destroy Grant. "It is apparent," he wrote to the President, "that if Grant cannot be successfully resisted here we cannot hold the Valley. If he is defeated it can be recovered." But Lee admitted that he had no immediate plan to defeat Grant, so he decided to detach elements of his army to confront Hunter and Sheridan.

On June 7 he dispatched John C. Breckinridge with 2,100 troops to Lynchburg, and on June 13 he sent Jubal A. Early with his corps (8,000 men) to the Valley. Lee envisioned Early marching down the Valley to pose a threat to Washington and thus compel Grant to respond. After Sheridan, Lee sent Wade Hampton and Fitz Lee with 4,700 troopers. Beauregard, Lee tried to ignore; he believed that Beauregard's fears were phantoms. "Telegrams of Genl Beauregard received," Lee wrote Braxton Bragg, now Davis's military adviser. "I am aware of no troops having left Genl. Grant's army." But on June 14 Lee detached Robert Hoke's division for Drewry's Bluff on the James and thence to Petersburg.[4]

The disbursement of these troops bore some early fruit. On June 11-12, Hampton defeated Sheridan at the Battle of Trevilian's Station. Early drove Hunter across the Alleghany Mountains out of the Valley, and then Early commenced a march down the Valley that threatened Washington. But Lee's various detachments reduced his own strength to perhaps 28,000 men and so limited his options when confronting Grant. And Grant was not idle.[5]

Lee for a long time had anticipated a Federal army crossing the James River and operating against Richmond from the south. Before he assumed command in the field, he predicted that George B. McClellan would "move his army to the James River." During the winter of 1862–63 while Ambrose E. Burnside commanded the Army of the Potomac, Lee wrote the President, "I think by spring if not before they will move upon James River." On June 11, 1864, Lee wrote Davis that he thought Grant was "strengthening his defenses to withdraw a portion of his force, and with the other move to the James River." Then on June 14, Lee informed Davis, "I think the enemy must be preparing to move south of James River."[6]

Finally Lee's prediction came true. During the night of June 12, Grant began his movement to the James while Union cavalry established an impenetrable screen of mounted units to conceal the march. By June 16, Grant had his entire army south of the James and advancing upon Petersburg. Both Grant and Lee realized that possession of Petersburg was vital to the retention of Richmond. Through Petersburg ran all but one railroad connecting Richmond with the rest of the Confederacy. If Grant could capture Petersburg, he would very nearly have the Confederate capital in a state of siege. Only time and tenacity would stand between Grant and victory.

Even though Lee was well aware of Grant's capacity to strike at Petersburg, he had to be certain of his enemy's intention before crossing the James River himself. Grant also had the capacity to feint toward Petersburg, and if Lee accepted the deception, Grant could lead the Army of the Potomac into Richmond all but unopposed. Lee had to be very careful.[7]

P. G. T. Beauregard not only commanded the defenses of Petersburg; he also held a defensive line at Bermuda Neck across the major bow in the James River north of Petersburg known as "Bermuda Hundred." At Bermuda Hundred within the bow was Benjamin F. Butler's Army of the James. Beauregard had effectively isolated Butler; but in so doing Beauregard had extended the defensive line he had to maintain. And Beauregard had not numbers anywhere near those necessary to confront the Federal horde approaching Petersburg.

Lee knew that Grant had once again moved south and east; but he did not know how far Grant had moved. So on June 13 Lee shifted his army to a new defensive position from White Oak Swamp to Malvern Hill, while he continued to seek accurate intelligence about Grant's intentions.[8]

There followed a frenzy of telegraphic messages among Lee, Beauregard, and Richmond (Secretary of War James Seddon and presidential adviser Braxton Bragg). It is tempting to imagine these members of the Confederate high command in high states of excitement bending over telegraph operators and reading dispatches in some nineteenth-century anticipation of E-mail. Alas, the reality was not quite so dramatic. On June 9, Lee sent a telegram to Bragg at 4:45 P.M. informing him that Lee had just received Bragg's telegram of 1:00 P.M. On June 15, Beauregard announced by telegraph at 11:15 P.M. that he had abandoned his Bermuda Hundred line; Lee did not receive the message until 2:00 A.M. At one point Lee wrote to Bragg that "Couriers seem to reach me from Richmond more promptly than telegrams." Lee said of his note, "I intended the foregoing for the telegraph, but send it by courier to save time."[9]

Nevertheless, a sample of the notes and telegrams that passed among prominent Confederates between June 12 and June 18 forms an intriguing narrative. On June 12, Lee wrote briefly to Mary Lee about family and friends and informed her that while he commanded an army in the field, "I do not require night shirts." Lee also wrote to Confederate Adjutant and Inspector General Samuel Cooper to recommend relieving Richard S. Ewell from his corps command for the sake of his health and reassigning Ewell to command the defenses of Richmond. Then on June 13 the tone of Lee's correspondence became more urgent. He announced to Secretary of War Seddon the cavalry victory at Trevilian's Station and the disappearance of Grant's army from Lee's front. Beauregard wrote to Bragg about "seven transports with troops passed up James River," and, "four more steamers have passed up river with troops," and, "it is rumored Grant intends advancing from south side."[10]

JUNE 14, 7:15 A.M. Beauregard to Bragg—". . . my position here critical. With my present force I cannot answer for consequences."

JUNE 14, 10:00 A.M. Beauregard to Lee—"Petersburg cannot be reinforced from my small force in lines of Bermuda Hundred Neck without abandoning entirely that position."

JUNE 15, 7:00 A.M. Beauregard to Bragg—" . . . my position more critical than ever. . . . Can anything be done in the matter?"

JUNE 15, 9:30 A.M. Beauregard to Bragg—" . . . enemy have attacked my outposts in force . . . it is an 'on to Petersburg. . . .' "

JUNE 15, 11:45 A.M. Beauregard to Bragg—"We must now elect between lines of Bermuda Neck and Petersburg. We cannot hold both. Please answer at once."[11]

JUNE 15, 12:20 P.M. Lee to Bragg—"Unless . . . I am better satisfied, I shall remain where I am today, as the enemy's plans do not seem to be settled."[12]

JUNE 15, 9:11 P.M. Beauregard to Bragg—"Re-enforcements not having arrived in time, enemy penetrated lines. . . ."

JUNE 16, 9:40 A.M. Lee to Beauregard—"Please inform me of condition of affairs."

JUNE 16, 10:30 A.M. Lee to Beauregard—"Your dispatch of 9:45 received. It is the first that has come to hand. I do not know the position of Grant's army, and cannot strip north bank of James River. Have you not force sufficient?"[13]

JUNE 16, 7:30 P.M. Lee to Davis—"I have not learned from Genl Beauregard what force is opposed to him in Petersburg, or received any definite account of operations there, nor have I been able to learn whether any portion of Grant's army is opposed to him."[14]

JUNE 16, 9:45 P.M. Beauregard to Bragg—"Enemy made two attacks on our lines this afternoon. They were repulsed with loss."

JUNE 17, 6:00 A.M. Lee to Beauregard—"I am delighted at your repulse of the enemy. Endeavor to recover your lines. Can you ascertain anything of Grant's movements?"

JUNE 17, NOON. Lee to Beauregard—"Until I can get more definite information of Grant's movements I do not think it prudent to draw more troops to this [south] side of the river."

JUNE 17, 3:30 P.M. Lee to Rooney Lee—"Push after enemy and endeavor to ascertain what has become of Grant's army."

JUNE 18, 12:30 A.M. Beauregard to Bragg and Lee—"Enemy in large force . . . attacked heavily our lines at 6:30 P.M. Affair lasted until 11:30 P.M. Enemy was finally repulsed at all points."

JUNE 18, 12:40 A.M. Beauregard to Bragg and Lee—"All quiet at present. I expect renewal of attack in morning. My troops are becoming much exhausted. Without immediate and strong re-enforcements results may be unfavorable. Prisoners report Grant on the field with his whole army."

JUNE 18, Lee to Early at Lynchburg—"Grant is in front Petersburg. Will be opposed there. Strike as quick as you can and if circumstances authorize, carry out the original plan [march down Valley], or move upon Petersburg without delay."[15]

JUNE 18, Lee to Davis—". . . it is pretty certain that Grant's whole force has crossed to the south side of the James River. . . . I have ordered all the troops over towards Petersburg, leaving the outer defenses of Richmond in charge of Genl G. W. C[ustis] Lee. . . . P.S. I go to Petersburg."[16]

Beauregard had ample reason to express anxiety. On June 16, he had 14,000 men with which to confront 48,000 Federals. On June 18, Beauregard commanded 20,000 in the morning, 38,000 that afternoon against attacks, morning and afternoon, by 95,000 Federal troops. Beauregard exercised all the skill and good luck he possessed and held the city until Lee's troops and Lee arrived.[17]

Located about 23 miles south of Richmond, Petersburg occupied the south bank of the Appomattox River perhaps 10 miles from the confluence of the Appomattox with the James. About 18,000 people, half of them white and half of them black, lived in Petersburg in 1860. When Lee arrived in the city, he made his headquarters in the yard of Mrs. Shippen, an "invalid lady," who with her husband owned a farm called Violet Bank on the north bank of the Appomattox River near the Richmond-Petersburg Turnpike.[18]

Confederate earthworks extended north-south just east of Petersburg. But Lee's entire defensive line now ran 26 miles from White Oak Swamp southeast of Richmond to Chaffin's Bluff on the north bank of the James, then across Bermuda Hundred Neck to the Appomattox, and south of that river before Petersburg to the Jerusalem Plank Road. Because Grant had more troops and resources, as soon as he established his own line of field fortifications opposite Lee's he began to extend his line and reach toward Lee's roads and railroads south of Petersburg.[19]

On June 22, Grant sent two Federal corps around Lee's right flank, across the Jerusalem Plank Road and perilously close to the Welden Railroad that linked Petersburg with Wilmington, North Carolina, and Charleston,

South Carolina. To counter this threat, Lee committed A. P. Hill's corps to a counterattack, and Hill's men responded with fury. The Confederates drove themselves between the two flanking Federal corps and then drove the enemy back in considerable confusion at significant cost. The battle near the Jerusalem Plank Road added 3,000 more Union casualties to the 10,000 already inflicted at Petersburg.[20]

After June 22, the war became a duel of trench systems for the rest of the summer. In both armies soldiers improved their field fortifications until they became all but impregnable. The situation at Petersburg was technically not a siege; Lee retained rail and road contact with Richmond and the rest of the Confederacy. But he did not have space or opportunity in which to maneuver. He had to keep his men in the trenches in order to protect his army, his government, and his country.[21]

Jubal Early quoted Lee as saying shortly before Early set out for the Valley and his eventual raid on Washington, "We must destroy this army of Grant's before he gets to James River. If he gets there, it will become a siege, and then it will be a mere question of time."[22]

Why, then, did Lee submit to the quasi-siege at Petersburg? Some of the answer is that he had no choice in the matter. Lee had to hold Petersburg in order to hold Richmond, and President Davis was loathe to abandon his

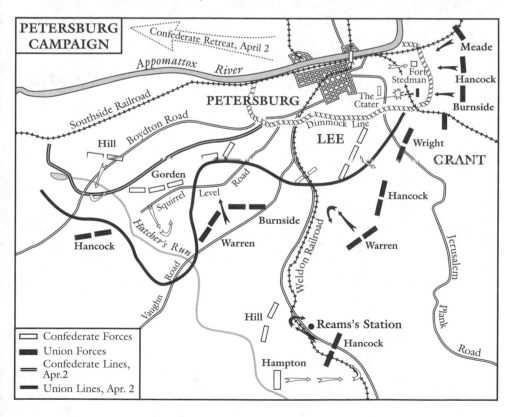

capital. But more important than the desire to retain Richmond was a tragic irony: the Army of Northern Virginia depended upon its trenches to compensate for its inferiority in men and material vis-à-vis the Army of the Potomac. Lee had roughly half the number of troops Grant commanded. Support services within the Confederate army had never been very efficient (excepting ordnance), and a static army is easier to feed and equip than an army in motion. The trenches in front of Petersburg that gradually grew longer—north toward Richmond and southwest around Petersburg—were in one sense a trap. Trenches precluded maneuver and compelled Lee to fight a war of attrition. But those same trenches kept Lee's army alive and intact against overwhelming odds.

The metaphor is Thomas Jefferson's, and Jefferson used it to describe holding slaves, but it applies as well to Lee and trenches at Petersburg: Lee was holding a wolf by the ears. However discomforting it may be to grasp those ears while looking at the wolf's vicious teeth and listening to the wolf's snarls, one action is much more discomforting—letting go. So Lee's army remained in its trenches and the war in Virginia settled into a succession of Second Cold Harbors.

27

"Ah! But He Is a Queer Old Genius"

O N JULY 22, 1864, Robert E. Lee's faithful aide Walter Herren Taylor wrote to his sweetheart Betty Saunders;

Those scamps in the trenches . . . pass their time circulating these preposterous stories & find some credulous enough to lend a listening ear, I should not omit to mention that Burnside has some thousands of negroes under ground—not dead & buried—mining our works. Some of our fellows actually overheard them digging some fifteen feet deep & about as many yards in front of our lines of entrenchments. At least so they say. No doubt these important facts will be announced to the public ere long as was the death of Grant.

Ulysses S. Grant remained quite healthy during 1864; but "Those scamps in the trenches" every once in a while stumbled upon rumors possessing more than a modicum of truth.[1]

On July 30 at 4:40 A.M. the Federals detonated 8,000 pounds of gunpowder planted beneath Confederate works east of Petersburg. A regiment composed mostly of coal miners from Pennsylvania had dug a tunnel 511 feet long under the Southern trench system and ventilated the shaft by an ingenious system of fires and baffles. The explosion created a huge hole, perhaps 200 feet by 70 feet in area and 25 feet deep, known as the Crater, and the blast opened a gaping gap 500 feet wide in the Confederate trench line.[2]

Lee hurried to the scene once he realized what had happened and drew reinforcements from the right of his line. He watched the action from the Gee House on the Jerusalem Plank Road only 500 yards from the Crater. The conduct of the battle by the enemy was as wretched as their pyrotechnics had been brilliant. Instead of exploiting the opening in the Confederate line of battle, the Federal troops simply crowded into the Crater. As the Confederate troops nearby recovered and reinforcements arrived, the Southerners were able to seal the breach and blast away at the massed targets still within the Crater. By mid-morning the Battle of the Crater was over, and Grant had sustained 4,400 casualties; Lee lost about 1,500 men.[3]

Among the doomed Union units that charged into the Crater on July 30 was a division of African American troops, the first black soldiers that most of Lee's men had ever encountered in battle. The racial factor seemed to stir the Southerners to frenzy. One South Carolinian wrote to his sister, "He charged with his Nigro Troops that come yelling like Devils crying, 'No quarter.' They got to the works. Our troops charged them, got back to the works, killed five hundred negroes and took two prisoners and set them to work. We took [prisoner] 1,000 white troops." Edward Porter Alexander observed, "Some of the Negro prisoners, who were originally allowed to surrender by some soldiers, were afterward shot by others & there was without doubt, a great deal of unnecessary killing of them." Phoebe Pember, a matron at Chimborazo Hospital in Richmond, dated increased bitterness among her patients to the active participation of African American troops at the Crater.[4]

Lee made no comment that has survived regarding this murder of prisoners by his troops. Later, during the fall of 1864, he restated his government's policy that runaway slaves when captured as prisoners would perform forced labor until reclaimed by their owners. Black soldiers "taken by us, who are not identified as the property of citizens or residents of any of the Confederate States are regarded as prisoners of war, being held to be proper subjects of exchange. . . ." It is now impossible to know how much Lee knew about the killings at the Crater. If Alexander, a staff officer, Milton Barrett, the South Carolinian common soldier, and Phoebe Pember, a hospital matron, be any index, the murders were pretty common knowledge. If Lee knew that his men had shot prisoners of war, he chose to do nothing about the outrage. By this point in the war, Ulric Dahlgren's unfulfilled fantasies of the previous spring to kill Jefferson Davis and his cabinet and to burn Richmond, termed "a barbarous and inhuman plot" by Lee at the time, must have seemed pretty tame on the savagery scale.[5]

The Battle of the Crater was only one attempt by the combatants to break the siege at Petersburg and restore mobility to this war. Lee's dispatch of Jubal Early and his small army toward Washington was another. Yet Lee seemed strangely resigned to his trenches, even in the early stages of the siege. To Mary Lee, he wrote, "Grant seems so pleased with his present position that I fear he will never move again." To President Davis, Lee said, "I have no idea that Grant will evacuate his position unless forced. It is one from which he can attack us at three points, as he may select, & our success will depend upon our early information & celerity of movement, as we have not troops sufficient to guard all points." And Lee asked his son Custis, "Where are we to get sufficient troops to oppose Grant? . . . His talent & strategy consists in accumulating overwhelming numbers."[6]

Most likely Lee realized that the Army of Northern Virginia could not long survive outside of field fortifications that compensated for its inferior numbers. His major concern at the outset of this new phase of the war was his capacity to feed his troops. On June 26, he explained to the President: "I think I can maintain our lines here against Genl Grant. He does not seem disposed to attack, and has thrown himself strictly on the defensive. I am less uneasy about holding our position than about our ability to procure supplies for the army. I fear the latter difficulty will oblige me to attack Genl Grant in his entrenchments, which I should not hesitate to do but for the loss it will inevitably entail. A want of success would in my opinion be almost fatal, and this causes me to hesitate in the hope that some relief may be procured without running such a great hazard."[7]

The war was going badly for the Confederacy on many fronts during the summer of 1864. The worst news came from Georgia, where Joseph E. Johnston was waging a defensive campaign against the armies of William T. Sherman. Johnston had withdrawn behind the Chattahoochee River into the defensive works at Atlanta, and the President was impatient. In fact, Davis had all but convinced himself to change commanders—to relieve Johnston and replace him with John Bell Hood. "It is a bad time to release the commander of an army situated as that of Tennessee," Lee telegraphed Davis. "We may lose Atlanta and the army too. Hood is a bold fighter. I am doubtful as to other qualities necessary." That evening (July 12) Lee expanded upon his telegram in a letter. "We must risk much. . . . he wrote; "Concentrate all the cavalry in Mississippi & Tennessee on Sherman's communications" . . . "fall back on Augusta" . . . "Hazard . . . communication to retain the country." As for Hood, Lee called him "a good fighter, very industrious on the battle field, careless off. . . ." Then Lee pointed out that William J. Hardee "has more experience in managing an army." Five days later President Davis relieved Johnston and installed Hood in his place, precisely the reverse of the course of action Lee counseled.[8]

In Virginia the war had become static; both combatants depended upon trench systems that became ever more elaborate with time. But even though the field fortifications did not move except to extend and expand, the troops were often on the march from one point on the line to another. And because the armies remained in place in close proximity, combat occurred daily along the line of battle. Typical of the activity in the trenches is this report from Bushrod Johnson's division on November 3, 1864:

I have nothing new to report this morning. General R. E. Lee inspected the line occupied by this division on yesterday. Three men deserted from [Henry A.] Wise's brigade last night. A deserter from the [U.S.] Second Corps came into our lines this morning.

The following casualties are respectfully submitted: Wise's brigade, wounded, 1; [Archibald] Gracie's brigade, killed, 1.

Of course the soldier from Gracie's brigade who died that day, along with his family and friends, would have had reason to challenge the assertion that "nothing new" had happened. But that, too, was a symptom of what the war had become.[9]

Here follows a chronicle of Lee's campaign in front of Richmond and

Petersburg. Crucial events in the extended semi-siege there were. But the essential story involves events in staccato sequence—the whole was very much the sum of parts.[10]

JULY 1, 1864: Lee wrote to Mary Lee, who had finally heeded her husband's plea to leave Richmond. She had moved with Mildred and Agnes for a "visit" at Bremo in Fluvanna County west of Richmond, the estate of John Hartwell Cocke, who was an influential planter and social reformer. A skirmish just north of the James continued the battle known as First Deep Bottom.[11]

AUGUST 1: Another skirmish at Deep Bottom concluded the action there. Walter Taylor went to view the Crater during a truce called to bury the dead and pronounced the sight "gruesome indeed." Taylor remembered, "portions of the bodies . . . were . . . protruding from immense blocks of earth. . . . The bottom of the pit or crater was covered with dead, white and black intermingled. . . ."[12]

AUGUST 5: Lee went to Richmond to consult with the President and decided to reinforce Early with a division each of cavalry (Fitz Lee) and infantry (Kershaw).[13]

AUGUST 7: Lee returned to Violet Bank by train after only obtaining a "glimpse" of Custis and daughter Mary in Richmond.

AUGUST 9: Confederate saboteurs returned the favor of the Crater. Two men managed to plant explosives on a Union transport ship at City Point (where the Appomattox River joins the James) and the resultant blast killed 43 men, injured 126, and pelted Grant with debris. Lee, meanwhile, had to write to President Davis about the lack of soap in his army and threats to the "health, comfort & respectability" of the men.[14]

AUGUST 11: Lee rode up to the Howlett Line that stretched across Bermuda Neck and watched Federals at work on a projected canal across Dutch Gap. He ordered artillery fire directed upon the laborers.[15]

AUGUST 13: Lee returned to the Howlett Line.

AUGUST 14: Federals attacked north of the James and for a time seized the Southern works at Fussell's Mill. Lee had to move troops and recall Hampton's cavalry to secure the sector.

AUGUST 15: Lee rode up to Chaffin's Bluff and established his headquarters there. Fighting continued sporadically at places like Gravel Hill and Bailey's Creek, and along the Charles City and New Market Roads. On this day Rob Lee suffered what became a minor wound while serving with his brother Rooney's cavalry division near White Oak Swamp.

AUGUST 16: Federal pressure on Lee's left provoked Lee to telegraph Davis to call out the reserves in Richmond to occupy the outer defense line. Sharp fighting recovered the Confederate line, however, and Lee was able to inform Secretary of War Seddon, "We now occupy our original position."[16]

AUGUST 18: On the same day that Lee planned to establish his headquarters at Chaffin's Bluff north of the James, Grant unleashed a concerted attack upon the Weldon Railroad south of Petersburg. Lee had long believed that the Federals would capture this rail line; now they had struck. Lee sent reinforcements south of the James, and battle joined at Globe Tavern, Yellow House, and Blick's Station.

AUGUST 21: Lee made a concerted attempt to recover the Weldon Railroad. He lost. By this time Lee knew that Union Admiral David G. Farragut had control of Mobile Bay.

AUGUST 25: Lee won the Battle of Reams Station but relinquished the battlefield and the railroad at dark. Now he had to transport supplies 20 miles by wagon from the Weldon Railroad Station at Stony Creek that lay south of Federal control of the tracks.[17]

SEPTEMBER 2: This day William T. Sherman's army marched into Atlanta. Hood retreated and hoped to fight another day. Lee addressed a long letter to Davis about the desperate need to increase the size of the Army of Northern Virginia: "Our ranks are constantly diminishing by battle and disease, and few recruits are received. The consequences are inevitable. . . ." The Federals pressed a reconnaissance down the Weldon Railroad.[18]

SEPTEMBER 3: There was an "affair near Sycamore Church" in which the First District of Columbia Cavalry regiment lost one man killed, three men wounded, three men and six mules captured.[19]

SEPTEMBER 10: A division of Federal infantry seized a line of rifle pits at the Chimneys on the Jerusalem Plank Road near Petersburg.

SEPTEMBER 18: An "affair at Coggin's Point," about five miles down the James from City Point became better known as "the great beefsteak raid." Hampton's cavalry captured 2,500 head of cattle.

Lee informed Mary Lee, "We shall want for the army all the socks we can get, so you need not fear having too many. Put the girls to knitting."

SEPTEMBER 23: After advancing to the outskirts of Washington in July, Early's small army had had to retreat before Philip Sheridan's Federals. A series of defeats in the Valley compelled Lee to send Kershaw's division to Early.[20]

SEPTEMBER 29: Grant directed in person an attack north of the James that carried Fort Harrison. Lee rode to Chaffin's Bluff, ordered the Richmond reserves to action, and tried to recapture Fort Harrison. Indeed, he begged his attacking troops three times to retake the earthwork; each rush was unsuccessful. Meanwhile at the other end of the line Federals advanced to the southwest and fought at Popular Springs Church and Peebles Farm to consolidate their extension of the seige lines beyond Petersburg.

SEPTEMBER 30: Once more Lee tried to recapture Fort Harrison and once more failed in the attempt. The Confederates constructed another earthen strongpoint, Fort Gilmer, to counter enemy retention of Fort Harrison.[21]

OCTOBER 7: Lee again directed operations north of the James on the Charles City and New Market Roads. As he reported, the enemy "was found strongly entrenched, and was not dislodged."[22]

OCTOBER 13: Lee reported an enemy advance east of Richmond "repulsed in every attempt." A Federal brigade commander involved in this battle claimed that his men "repulsed the enemy's every onset, even taking the offensive and capturing one prisoner, whom they brought in."[23]

OCTOBER 19: James Longstreet returned to duty from his convalescence from wounds at the Wilderness; Lee assigned him command of troops north of the James.[24]

OCTOBER 20: Lee learned of Sheridan's victory over Jubal Early at Cedar Creek. Early softened the news as best he could; but his loss of twenty-three guns was some indication to Lee that Early's defeat was severe.[25]

OCTOBER 25: Lee wrote to Mary Lee at Bremo and again advised her not to return to Richmond "in the present uncertainty of events."[26]

OCTOBER 27: Again Grant attacked both Confederate flanks. Longstreet met and dispersed an attempt to turn his left flank near the Williamsburg Road. From Popular Springs Church south of Petersburg, the better part of three army corps swept northwest in an attempt to seize the Southside Railroad. Hampton's cavalry and Hill's infantry met this thrust on the Boydton Plank Road near Burgess's Mill on Hatcher's Run. The Confederates exploited flaws in Union coordination and forced the Federals to withdraw.[27]

NOVEMBER 1: Lee moved his headquarters from Chaffin's Bluff to the Beasley House on High Street in Petersburg, as both armies took up winter quarters of sorts within their respective trench systems.[28]

NOVEMBER 2: Lee wrote to the President and again bewailed his understrength. Grant, he estimated, would soon have 150,000 men. "Unless we can obtain a reasonable approximation to his force I fear a great calamity will befall us. On last Thursday at Burgess' Mills we had three brigades to oppose six divisions. On our left [north of the James] two divisions to oppose two corps. The inequality is too great."[29]

NOVEMBER 12: Lee wrote Mary Lee that she might as well "make up your mind that Mr. Lincoln is reelected President" and "we must therefore make up our minds for another four years of war." Lincoln had indeed won reelection on November 8, and so faded the last substantive hope that war weariness in the United States might secure independence for the Confederate States.[30]

NOVEMBER 21: Lee wrote to Hampton to ask about the "practicability of striking Grant a blow, either this side [south] or the north side of James River. . . ."[31]

NOVEMBER 25: Lee wrote to his wife about socks; this year he intended to have an officer in Richmond (to which Mary Lee had now returned) collect the socks, ship them to another officer at Petersburg, who would deliver them to a third officer to distribute. Lee also noted that he had had to move his headquarters again. The Beasleys rented their house to someone else, so Walter Taylor secured Edge Hill, "a very good abode about 1 1/2 miles from Petersburg, south of the Appomattox, belonging to a Mr. Turnbull, who had sent his family off for fear of Genl Grant & his missiles."[32]

DECEMBER 9: Hampton's cavalry with Hill's infantry nearly thwarted a Federal foray down the Weldon Railroad. Other Federals advanced to Hatcher's Run and retired.

DECEMBER 16: Hood, having wasted his army in frontal assaults at Franklin, Tennessee, on November 30, confronted George H. Thomas and Federal defenders of Nashville. The resultant battle eliminated the Army of Tennessee as an effective force.

DECEMBER 20: Confederate troops evacuated Savannah, Georgia, and Sherman's army concluded "the March to the Sea" from Atlanta.[33]

DECEMBER 25: Lee attended church services in Petersburg on Christmas Day, encountered his former staff engineer T. M. R. Talcott, and brought him "home" to headquarters for a dinner of turkey and potatoes. "My young family [the staff] had gone to more pleasant feasts."[34]

JANUARY 8, 1865: Lee was counting socks again. He wrote to his wife on this day that he had counted twice the pairs in her most recent shipment and found forty-five instead of the fifty pairs she claimed. Almost as afterthought about the day he noted, "The enemy made several attempts to drive us in but failed."[35]

JANUARY 11: Lee responded to a letter from legislator Andrew Hunter requesting Lee's opinion upon the use of African American troops in the Confederate army. "I think therefore," Lee stated, "we must decide whether slavery shall be extinguished by our enemies, and the slaves used against us, or use them ourselves at the risk of the effects which may be produced upon our social institutions. My own opinion is that we should employ them without delay." Moreover, Lee wrote that he favored "giving immediate freedom to all who enlist," and mentioned also bounties (money or land) to attract black men to Southern service. Lee's opinion was important in the efforts of the Davis administration to arm and free slaves.[36]

JANUARY 12: Lee was reduced to making a direct plea to the "Farmers East of the Blue Ridge" for food for his army. He promised to "pay promptly for all supplies delivered under this appeal."[37]

JANUARY 15: Fort Fisher, which guarded the crucial blockade-running port of Wilmington, North Carolina, fell to Federal hands.

JANUARY 19: On Lee's fifty-eighth birthday he called to Longstreet's attention the results of inspections within his corps during December. The inspectors discovered much to improve, and Lee wrote of soldiers "reported to be unsoldierly & unmilitary, lax in discipline and loose in military instruction"; of officers "not informed of the condition and wants of the men"; and of public property and animals "not well attended to."[38]

JANUARY 27: Lee wrote to Seddon about "the alarming frequency of desertions from this army." He pointed out that Hill's corps had lost fifty-six men in three days and blamed poor morale upon the "want of food."[39]

JANUARY 30: Lee expressed his fear to Davis that "with our present force here, Grant will be enabled to envelope Richmond, or turn both of our flanks, & I see no way of increasing our strength."[40]

JANUARY 31: In accord with a recent act of Congress, the President appointed and the Senate confirmed Lee as general in chief of the Confederate armies. Lee continued to direct the operations of the Army of Northern Virginia.

FEBRUARY 3: Aboard the *River Queen* on Hampton Roads, Confederates

Alexander H. Stephens, John A. Campbell, and R. M. T. Hunter met with Abraham Lincoln and his Secretary of State, William H. Seward. They discussed prospects for a negotiated peace, but foundered on the question of an independent Confederate States of America. The Hampton Roads Peace Conference adjourned without achieving peace.

FEBRUARY 5: Grant sent two army corps with cavalry toward Lee's right flank, by now well south west of Petersburg. Lee responded, and the Battle of Hatcher's Run commenced.

FEBRUARY 6: Fighting continued at Hatcher's Run (also known as Dabney's Mill, Armstrong's Mill, Rowanty Creek, and Vaughn Road). Confederate General John Pegram was killed leading his division; he was barely thirty-three years old and had been married for eighteen days.

FEBRUARY 7: Federal troops entrenched in extended positions near Hatcher's Run, and the alarm on Lee's flank subsided for the moment. Engaged in the battle were 35,000 Union troops and 14,000 Confederates.[41]

FEBRUARY 11: Lee wrote his sympathy to Hetty Cary Pegram, recently the widow of John Pegram. As was usual in such circumstances, Lee wrote of the "peace & rest" the dead person had achieved, and observed, "We are left to grieve at his departure, cherish his memory & prepare to follow."[42]

FEBRUARY 17: Both Columbia and Charleston, South Carolina, fell to the Union troops commanded by Sherman, who seemed headed for a union with Grant.

FEBRUARY 22: Acting as commander in chief, Lee assigned Joseph E. Johnston to command the remnant Army of Tennessee retreating before Sherman.

FEBRUARY 24: Lee wrote to John C. Breckinridge, named Secretary of War to replace Seddon on February 6, about "the alarming number of desertions" from his army. Walter Taylor estimated an average of a hundred men per day were deserting. Lee understated, "These desertions have a very bad effect upon the troops that remain and give rise to painful apprehension."[43]

FEBRUARY 25: Lee sent a telegram to Richmond refusing to suspend the execution of a convicted deserter. "Have reexamined case, & he is not entitled to mercy," Lee asserted, and added, "Hundreds of men are deserting nightly and I cannot keep the army together unless examples are made of such cases."[44]

MARCH 2: Lee wrote to Grant about "the possibility of arriving at a satisfactory adjustment of the present unhappy difficulties by means of a military convention," and offered to meet with Grant to discuss the matter. To Davis, Lee confessed that he was "not sanguine" about the prospect for peace by these means. He was right.[45]

MARCH 4(?): Lee was in Richmond to confer with the President and enjoyed a rare reunion with his family at The Mess on Franklin Street. After dinner he paced the room looking very grave. "Well, Mr. Custis," he said to his oldest son, "I have been up to see the Congress and they do not seem to be able to do anything except to eat peanuts and chew tobacco, while my army is starving. I told them the condition the men were in, and that something must be done at once, but I can't get them to do anything, or they are unable to do anything."[46]

MARCH 13: The Confederate Congress finally passed the law authorizing the recruitment of black men for Confederate armies. The act did not provide for emancipation; indeed, it attempted to preserve the relationship of master to slave.

MARCH 14: In response to a query from Breckinridge, Lee wrote his thoughts about implementing the act authorizing African American troops. He suggested using white officers and black non-commissioned officers in black units, and he insisted that the new recruits be on the "footing of soldiers, with their freedom secured."[47]

MARCH 18: Desertions since February 15 reduced Lee's army by almost 3,000 men, almost 8 percent of the total strength.[48]

MARCH 25: Lee attempted a last attack—at Federal Fort Stedman due east of Petersburg. Here he hoped to break through Federal trenches and roll up at least a portion of the enemy's lines. Initially, the assault led by John B. Gordon in the early morning was a significant success; the rebels captured Fort Stedman and perhaps three fourths of a mile of the Yankee trench system. But the Southerners could not expand their gains, and in the face of impending counterattacks from Union reinforcements, Gordon withdrew. The battle was over by 8:00 A.M., and Lee had lost another 4,000 soldiers in the process of inflicting 1,500 casualties upon Grant.

MARCH 29: The spring offensive Lee knew that Grant would launch occurred early. Two Federal infantry corps plus Sheridan's cavalry began the march to get behind Lee's right flank, well beyond Hatcher's Run.

MARCH 30: Grant's massive flanking movement continued to develop. Sheridan was at Dinwiddie Court House; the infantry beyond the Boydton Plank Road.

MARCH 31: Pickett's reinforced division, transported by rail west of Petersburg, joined Fitz Lee's cavalry division at Five Forks. Lee constituted a mobile command of about 10,600 men with which to confront Grant's flank march. And Lee was on the field when the Confederates repulsed the Federals between Dinwiddie Court House and Five Forks.

APRIL 1: Pickett and Fitz Lee withdrew to Five Forks and established a defensive position at the important road junction. During the afternoon, while Pickett and Fitz Lee were absent at a shad bake, the Federals attacked in overwhelming force. Within two hours, Lee's mobile force beyond his right flank was no more.[49]

APRIL 2: Federals advanced to the attack in every sector of the battle line and achieved breakthroughs at several points. Lee sent a telegram to Breckinridge: "I see no prospect of doing more than holding our position here till night. I am not certain that I can do that. If I can I shall withdraw tonight north of the Appomattox, and if possible . . . withdraw the whole line tonight from James River." Then he set to work ordering evacuation. The siege was over; it had concluded the way Lee had feared. Now began the flight.[50]

By the time the Army of Northern Virginia began to dig its trenches around Petersburg, Robert E. Lee had become a legend. Detractors there

were; but Lee's record of victories during the two previous years had inspired
vaulting confidence within the army and throughout the country. And as the
siege of Petersburg and Richmond protracted while military disasters multiplied elsewhere, Lee became even more revered as some sort of miracle maker.
He had wrested triumph from impending doom in the past; surely he would
do so again. Only afterward did Lee become a suffering saint, the South's
Christ figure; in the trenches Lee was still a Southern Joshua.[51]

In contrast to the confidence he inspired in the army and elsewhere, Lee
must have felt enormous frustration while he endured the siege at Richmond
and Petersburg. He was, after all, a career officer; he cared about his professional performance; he defined himself as a soldier; and he knew that his
chances for success were becoming slim. Lee manifested his mounting frustration in his relations with people and in his attitude about the war. Here follow
some examples.

Perhaps most revealing are the letters during this period of Lee's adjutant
Walter Taylor to his future wife Betty Saunders. In July, Taylor expressed
indignation that someone had asked about him whether " 'Walter had altered
any because of his high position.' " "In the first place," Taylor wrote, "a Lieutenant Colonelcy is not such an exalted position even though the individual is
at the right hand of the 'greatest man of the day' and privileged to receive his
[rectangle cut out of page—noun deleted]." Taylor's sarcasm was unsubtle.[52]

On August 1, Taylor wrote:

The General and I lost temper with each other yesterday and of course, I afterwards was
disgusted at my allowing myself to be placed in such a position where I appear to such
disadvantage. I couldn't help [it] however, he is so unreasonable and provoking at
times; I might serve under him for ten years to come and couldn't *love* him at the end of
that period. I don't intend though to take up my paper and your time with any account
of my grievances concerning the "Greatest and best (?) man living!" . . . Ah! but he is a
queer old genius. I suppose it is so with all great men.[53]

When Lee moved his headquarters from Violet Bank to the Beasley House
in Petersburg, Taylor had charge of the relocation. He recalled, "I, of course,
selected a place where I thought he would be comfortable, although I firmly
believe he concluded that I was thinking more of myself than of him. I took
possession of a vacant house, and had his room prepared with a cheerful fire,
and everything made as cozy as possible. It was entirely too pleasant for him
for *he is never so uncomfortable as when comfortable*" (emphasis added).

Then when Lee moved again to Edge Hill, the Turnbull House west of
Petersburg, Taylor wrote, "I am finely fixed in the parlor with piano, sofas,
rocking-chairs and pictures—capital surroundings for a winter campaign." Initially, Taylor expected to claim "one of the miserable little back rooms"; but
Turnbull convinced him to take over the parlor. Lee looked around the house
and found Taylor settled in the parlor. " 'Ah, you are finely fixed,' Lee remarked. 'Couldn't you find any other room?' 'No,' I replied, 'but *this will do;* I
can make myself tolerably comfortable here.' He was struck dumb with amaze-
ment at my impudence and soon vanished."[54]

Edward Porter Alexander told another story about Lee and his staff during the siege. Lee intended to ride north of the James to superintend some action, and Alexander remembered 2:00 A.M. as the time of departure. Alexander was ready to travel at 1:30 A.M. when Charles Venable of Lee's staff appeared.

"Come on! The Old Man is out here waiting for you & mad enough to bite nails."

"Yes," Venable said, "two o'clock was the hour he told us all last night, but now he swears he said one. And he scolded everybody & started off all alone, & with scarcely any breakfast because nothing was ready. I overtook him & the rest of the staff are coming along as fast as they can get their horses."

Alexander approached Lee. "Good morning, General Alexander," Lee said. "I had hoped to find you waiting in the road for me on my arrival."

"Yes Sir! I was all ready & might have been here just as well, but you told me last night that you'd start at two o'clock. . . ."

"One o'clock was the hour, Sir, at which I said I would start!"

"I misunderstood you then, General, I thought you said two."

"One o'clock, Sir, was the hour!" Then Lee changed the subject, "Well Sir, have you gotten a guide who can direct us on the best cross-roads to reach the Darbytown Road?"

"No, General, as the subject was not mentioned I supposed no guide would be needed & I would only have to follow you."

"Well, Sir, when I was a young man & had a march to make in the morning, I never went to bed until I had procured some citizen of the neighborhood who could conduct me."

Alexander tried to explain that the route was not at all complicated. Then Lee said, "Well, we will have to make the best of it. Col. Venable, will you ride ahead then & guide us."

But Venable was engrossed in conversation and did not hear Lee. So Lee turned to one of his couriers, "Evans, I will have to ask you to act upon my staff today, for my officers are all disappointing me."[55]

On another occasion during the siege Lee asked an officer about some work he had ordered; the officer said the task was completed. So Lee suggested that they ride to the site and see the finished work. But when they arrived, they discovered very little accomplished. The officer explained that he had given instructions, and his subordinates had told him they had done the job.

"We must give our personal attention to the lines," was Lee's judgment. Then the commanding general apparently changed the subject and made some flattering remarks about the horse the embarrassed officer was riding. The officer told him the horse belonged to his wife.

"A magnificent horse indeed," Lee said, "but I should not think him safe for Mrs.——to ride. He is entirely too spirited for a lady and I would urge you by all means to take some of the mettle out of him before you suffer your wife to ride him again. And, by the way, general, I would suggest to you that *the rough paths along these trenches would be admirable ground over which to tame him."* (italics in the original)[56]

Georgia Senator Benjamin H. Hill remembered a conversation with Lee during the siege in which Lee claimed to have discovered a "fatal mistake" Southerners had made in founding the Confederacy. When Hill inquired about the mistake, Lee replied:

Why, sir, in the beginning we appointed all our worst generals to command the armies, and all our best generals to edit the newspapers. As you know, I have planned some campaigns and quite a number of battles. I have given the work all the care and thought I could, and sometimes, when my plans were completed, as far as I could see they seemed to be perfect. But when I have fought them through I have discovered defects, and occasionally wondered I did not see some of the defects in advance. When it was all over, I found by reading a newspaper that these best editor-generals saw all the defects plainly from the start. Unfortunately, they did not communicate their knowledge to me until it was too late.[57]

On the same evening in March when Lee delivered his tirade about congressmen eating peanuts, chewing tobacco, and ignoring the needs of his army, Lee also told his son: "Mr. Custis, when this war began, I was opposed to it, bitterly opposed to it, and I told these people that, unless every man should do his whole duty, they would repent it; and now (he paused slightly as if to give emphasis to his words) they will repent."[58]

Many of the memories people had of Lee during the long siege at Petersburg and Richmond were somber. Alexander, for example, recalled his mission to hurl exploding shells into the ill-fated "canal" across Dutch Gap. Lee told him that the Yankees were reported to have taken Southern prisoners of war into the ditch to discourage Alexander's artillery fire. Lee did not wish to "flinch," lest the enemy next resort to using women and children as shields. So he insisted that Alexander double the volume of shells and supervise the aiming of his weapons to ensure that his gunners did not flinch. Lee wanted it "hotter in the Dutch Gap than it had ever been before."[59]

These were the symptoms of Lee at bay before Richmond and Petersburg. Incidents such as these inspired an image of Robert E. Lee as rigid, inflexible, and aloof. In outline at least much of this image is no doubt accurate. Lee was shy; he accepted confrontation only when so provoked that he overreacted; he likely made the transit from belief that he would have to win the war all by himself to concern that he was the only person in the Confederacy genuinely committed to fighting at all. He inspired Grant to say of him, "He was a large, austere man, and I judge difficult of approach to his subordinates."[60]

Quite possibly Lee's health, especially his cardiovascular system, was a factor in his sometimes sour disposition during this period. Taylor spoke of Lee's health being "somewhat impaired" during the final year of the war and also pointed out that only at Petersburg did Lee consent to live in a house instead of a tent. Another member of Lee's staff, Armistead Long, believed that Lee "had aged somewhat in appearance since the beginning of the war, but had rather gained than lost in physical vigor from the severe life he had led." On Lee's face, Long saw "the ruddy hue of health," and "he seemed able to bear any amount of fatigue, being capable of remaining in his saddle all day and at his desk half the night." Surely the strain of his responsibilities and his declining fortunes in this war took their toll upon Lee, physically as well as emotionally. His eyesight was not as good as it had been; Mrs. Churchill J. Gibson, wife of the Rector of Grace Church, Petersburg, gave Lee a new copy of the Book of Common Prayer with larger print. He had gained weight, and what Long saw as "the ruddy hue of health" in Lee's face others described as "florid." But to ascribe Lee's disposition during this period to a physiological condition would be pure speculation in the absence of more evidence.[61]

What certainly afflicted Lee at Petersburg was the frustration of a professional soldier trapped in a circumstance that every day seemed less sanguine. He had not abandoned hope; he had known desperate situations before and made victories happen (e.g., Seven Days). But in this case Lee knew that agony of knowing ways to punish his enemy, perhaps even to extricate his army from the debilitation of the siege; yet he lacked the troops, resources, and resourceful subordinates to do what he knew.

If nothing else, Lee probably wanted to end this war with a bang instead of a whimper. He acted out his desire on March 25 in his attack upon Fort Stedman. Had Lee had a "death wish," this was certainly his opportunity to gratify it. However, he simply stood by and watched the attack succeed, then sputter and fail.

What likely kept Lee as stable as he was during the extended trauma of siege in 1864 was the experience of his entire life. He·had known frustration before—in his childhood, in many of his assignments before 1861, in his career generally, in his marriage, in his children, in his efforts to manage the Custis properties, in his execution of Custis's will, and more. Small wonder Lee expressed his sympathy to bereaved friends and relatives as he did: the dead go to glory; the living must endure more of this "vale of tears." Lee knew more than he wanted to know about enduring in a world imperfect.

In the past Lee's great strength had been his resilience, his capacity to confront his fortune, fate, or whatever and to make the best of circumstances, no matter how bad. Some of his genius as a soldier had been his creative talent at turning adversity to his advantage—before Richmond in 1862, at Second Manassas, at Chancellorsville, and elsewhere.

At Petersburg, more people than Lee were frustrated and disconsolate. So they remembered Lee in context and told stories about him that reflected their mood as well as his. The stories during this period emphasize sacrifice, duty, and other stoic virtues. One exception is Long's tale of Lee remaining under artillery fire in order to pick up a baby sparrow and replace the bird in its nest. Here was Lee selflessly trying against odds to bring redemption to the battlefield. But Long, who told the story, and J. William Jones, who repeated it, emphasized Lee's "love for the lower animals," his concern for the helpless, and "a heart so tender."[62]

Amid the general gloom and impending doom of Petersburg Lee did display, along with many manifestations of his frustration, his redemptive instincts. One example sprang from a visitation to Lee by a group of young women from Richmond. They wanted his judgment about parties and dances in such dire times. What did Lee think about the propriety of parties? "Why, of course . . . ," Lee said. "My boys need to be heartened up when they get their furloughs. Go on, look your prettiest, and be just as nice to them as ever you can be!"[63] The best example of Lee attempting to redeem disaster occurred at one of the worst of times with one of the least likely people. On April 2, Lee's headquarters was absorbed in the frenzy of preparations for evacuation and retreat. Indeed, the headquarters evacuated about midday before the threat of a Federal column and moved to the inner defenses of Petersburg. Late that afternoon, only a few hours before the army was supposed to march, Walter Taylor asked to be excused for the evening. He and Betty Saunders wanted to be married that night in Richmond. According to Taylor, Lee "expressed some surprise at my entertaining such a propose at that time. . . ." After all, Lee had the smallest of staffs; as adjutant, Taylor was responsible for orders and reports; and a fairly significant, very intricate, operation was supposed to begin very soon. But the "queer old genius," "so unreasonable and provoking at times," whom Taylor knew he could never love, in Taylor's words, "promptly gave his consent."[64]

28

"I Would Rather Die a Thousand Deaths"

A. P. HILL was dead. On the morning of April 2 he had ridden from a meeting with Lee into Federal troops who had recently pierced Hill's lines. Hill and his courier were attempting to intimidate two Yankees into surrender when the Federals called their bluff at a range of less than twenty yards. Hill had lived a long time in pain. Mercy attended his death: the rifle ball tore through his heart and out of his back. Hill spun around in his saddle and crashed face first to the ground already dead.

Robert Lee burst into tears when he heard the news. "He is now at rest," Lee pronounced, "and we who are left are the ones to suffer." During the week that followed Hill's death on April 2, Lee was more right than he knew. Considerable suffering lay ahead for the Army of Northern Virginia.[1]

Walter Herren Taylor and Elizabeth Selden Saunders were married. Having secured Lee's leave to leave the headquarters as the headquarters was about to leave, too, Taylor commandeered the locomotive of an "ambulance train" and overhauled another train bound for Richmond. Taylor's courier followed with the horses. When Taylor arrived in Richmond, the government, the army, and anyone else able to do so either had fled or were fleeing the Confederate capital. Walter and Betty had made careful plans, however, and during the early minutes of April 3, 1865, the Reverend Dr. Charles Minnigerode, Rector of St. Paul's Church, blessed the marriage in the presence of some family and friends at the home of Lewis D. Crenshaw on West Main Street.

By the time Taylor set out to fulfill his promise to rejoin Lee, it was four o'clock in the morning. Most of the official Confederates (government and military) had left; a mob of residents were looting warehouses containing military rations of food, and lapping and scooping from gutters the whiskey that flowed from barrels dutifully broken to prevent people from drinking it. Fires raged out of control in much of the city, as Taylor and his courier rode over Mayo's Bridge to the south bank of the James.[2]

Meanwhile, the Army of Northern Virginia marched at 8:00 P.M. Lee mounted Traveller and rode across to the north bank of the Appomattox River, posted himself at a fork in the road, and helped direct traffic while his troops filed past in the dark. At most Lee commanded 30,000 men; the army retained 200 guns and moved with 1,000 wagons. But of course Lee commanded these soldiers, weapons, and supplies only if they were able to disengage from the general battle that had continued for most of April 2, march through the dark over unfamiliar roads, and rendezvous at Amelia Court House on April 4. Lee planned to have rations ready at Amelia and move on from there to Burkeville, junction of the Danville and Southside railroads. Then Lee hoped to march (or perhaps ride) down the railroad to Danville and a union with Joseph E. Johnston and the residue Army of Tennessee.

Lee made or revealed no specific plans for his movements beyond Burkeville; the junction with Johnston was essentially inference. Clearly Lee's principal task now was to escape from Grant's army; until he accomplished that, any plan was pure conjecture.

Lee did have reason to hope that the Federals would not pursue him aggressively. Certainly George B. McClellan and George G. Meade had been cautious following their successes at Sharpsburg (Antietam) and Gettysburg. But Grant was neither McClellan nor Meade. Still the Federals faced a formidable challenge to occupy Petersburg and Richmond, to leave their established lines of supply and communication, and to maneuver masses of men who had been sealed in trenches for nearly ten months.[3]

On the morning of April 3 as Lee rode west with Longstreet, the Confederates were once more in open country out of the labyrinthine trench systems and for the moment at least beyond Grant's grasp. By dark the vanguard of Lee's retreat had marched 21 miles, and Lee had had word from all of the various commands that had escaped from Petersburg and had heard no discouraging words from units that had been north of Petersburg and the James.[4]

On April 4, however, the retreat began to unravel. When Lee rode into Amelia Court House, he found no food for his men. He had ordered rations to Amelia from Richmond. In effect Lee had moved his base of supplies from Richmond to Danville, and he planned to feed the army from rations sent by rail as he marched. If he were able to follow this plan, Lee's supply line would grow shorter each day the army marched, and Grant's supply line would lengthen if he tried to follow. But Lee's sound planning meant nothing if the army went hungry, and on April 4 the army was already hungry.

It is now impossible to know what happened to Lee's directive to deliver food to Amelia Court House, if in fact a written order ever existed. If the retreat from Petersburg had ever been more than a desperate gamble, this failure to have rations ready for the troops at Amelia Court House would rank with the loss of Special Orders No. 191 during the Maryland Campaign of 1862 or the several blunders at Gettysburg among the hypothetical impondera-

bles of the Confederate War. On April 4, those absent rations were crucial to
Lee and his soldiers. Because Lee found no rations at Amelia Court House, he
had to stop his march and dispatch foraging parties with wagons into the
countryside. All this consumed time, and Lee could not afford time. He spent
twenty-four hours in foraging forays, collected very little food, and later concluded, "This delay was fatal, and could not be retrieved."[5]

While details of men searched the surrounding country in relatively fruitless foraging, more troops arrived, and finally Lee learned that Richard S.
Ewell was nearby with his troops from the defenses of Richmond. However
much Lee needed to bring his army back together, in this case the troops were
concentrating where Lee could not feed them, and the crisis increased as each
new body of soldiers reached the rendezvous.

On April 5, Lee ordered the march resumed and hoped that the trainload
of rations ordered up from Danville would meet the column. By this time
many of the soldiers were weak from hunger, and the horses that carried the
cavalry and pulled wagons, gun carriages, and caissons were struggling with
their burdens. Straggling and freelance foraging increased as Lee's thin ranks
constantly shrank.

Then Lee's worst fears materialized; about one o'clock that afternoon, as
Lee and Longstreet approached Jetersville, they discovered Philip Sheridan's
cavalry ahead of them. Rooney Lee shared the bad news: two corps of Federal
infantry were throwing up field fortifications across their projected path.

Edward Porter Alexander remembered, "I never saw Gen. Lee seem so
anxious to bring on a battle in my life as he seemed this afternoon." Battle was
clearly one of Lee's options—perhaps a showdown fight before even more
Yankees overtook his army—the Army of Northern Virginia would overrun its
enemies or die trying in the most literal way possible. But the more Rooney
reported his observations, the clearer it became that attack would be futile. So
Lee decided to change his route of march; his immediate objective became the
village of Farmville, to which he ordered supplies sent from Lynchburg. As it
happened, I. M. St. John, the new commissary general, reported later on the
5th that he had 80,000 rations at Farmville. Speed was essential, more so now
than ever. Lee had to break free from Federal infantry that had outmarched
and overtaken him. He had to keep his troop units together to fight off cavalry
attacks. And he had to get to Farmville before the enemy in order to feed the
men. Lee ordered an all-night march for April 5–6.[6]

To the degree that regiments, brigades, divisions, and corps still existed in
the Army of Northern Virginia, Longstreet's corps led the way, followed by
Richard H. Anderson (who now commanded his old division and what was
left of the divisions of George E. Pickett, Bushrod Johnson, and Henry
Heth), Ewell (with his contingent of Richmond defensive forces and reserves),
and John B. Gordon (now in command of what had once been Ewell's corps).
Many of these troops units were very nearly imaginary; Ewell's reserve force all
but evaporated en route as 6,000 men became less than 3,000. And when this
confused column attempted to move, a gap opened between Pickett's division

and the units ahead of him, effectively dividing the army.[7]

Disaster came at Sayler's Creek, a tributary of the Appomattox River, just east of Farmville. Lee witnessed it. He rode back to a ridge above the creek, and there he saw the remnants of almost half of his army in desperate flight from the enemy.

"My God! has the army been dissolved?" Lee asked rhetorically.

Anderson and Ewell had had to deploy infantry in battle formations to combat the assaults of Union cavalry, and the gap between the two halves of

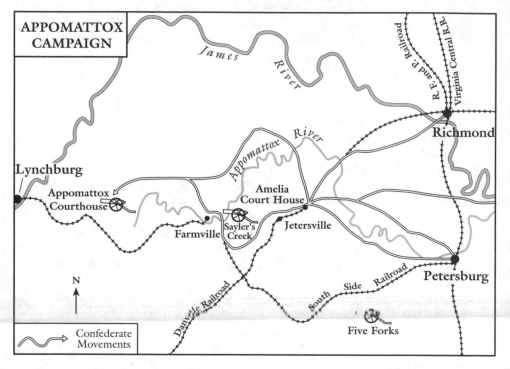

the army widened. At Sayler's Creek a Federal infantry corps overtook the stragglers and surrounded them. Within a very short while roughly half of Anderson's corps and all of Ewell's men were lost to Lee's army; some were killed or wounded; most were captured. What Lee saw from the ridge was the backwash from an uneven battle, broken men in flight from an enemy that seemed omnipresent.

With Lee was William Mahone and a division of soldiers; Lee directed Mahone to face his troops toward the valley of Sayler's Creek and stem Federal pursuit. Lee then seized a battle flag and began to try to rally those scared, sad men stumbling past him. Mahone returned to him, took the battle flag, and took over the task of restoring order and organization to the fugitives. Lee raised his field glasses and began to think about what to do now.

Then a Confederate general officer "of exalted grade" emerged from the rout. One of Lee's staff officers called the commanding general's attention to his dispirited subordinate. Lee never averted his eyes. He was in search of some solution to the problem in which this disgraced officer had participated.

"General," Lee said to the man, "take those stragglers to the rear out of the way of Mahone's troops. I wish to fight here."[8]

While Lee with Mahone was attempting to stem the tide and cover the rear of the army, Gordon was engaged in another frantic fight on Sayler's Creek just downstream from Lee's position. Already Gordon had lost many of the wagons he had been trying to guard; now he fought to save what remained of his command. Lee ordered Mahone to hold his ground on the ridge line above Sayler's Creek until the survivors had made their way across the Appomattox River and into Farmville. Then Mahone was to follow, and the engineers left in Lee's army were supposed to burn the two bridges spanning the river.

This day, April 6, had been worse than sad. Lee lost perhaps 8,000 men; Ewell and Lee's son Custis were among the Confederates captured; the Army of Northern Virginia now numbered no more than 12,000 infantry and 3,000 cavalry. Grant had 80,000 soldiers at or near the scene. And to crown the day of debacle, the Confederates waited too late to burn one of the bridges over the Appomattox River. Instead of finding rations and respite in Farmville, the men had to continue the march, grab whatever food they could, and as Lee later admitted, "All could not be supplied." Needless to say, Lee reacted to this "blunder with . . . warmth and impatience."[9]

On April 7, Lee's troops slogged ahead with decreasing speed. The roads were muddy from rains; both men and animals were weaker; the force was so small that men had to march with the artillery and wagons to protect them; and periodically during the afternoon Lee had to stop and deploy infantry to keep the Federals at bay. Dark on April 7 found Lee with Longstreet only about three miles beyond Farmville near a place called Cumberland Church.[10]

During the evening a courier found Lee and handed him a message received through enemy lines. It was from U. S. Grant.

General: The results of the last week must convince you of the hopelessness of further resistance on the part of the Army of Northern Virginia in this struggle. I feel that it is so, and regard it as my duty to shift from myself the responsibility of any further effusion of blood, by asking of you the surrender of that portion of the C. S. Army known as the Army of Northern Virginia.

Lee read the note and handed it to Longstreet, who read it and returned it to Lee with the two-word judgment—"Not yet."[11]

Lee was not so sure. At the very least he wanted to know his options, so he wrote out a response and dispatched it to Grant without revealing its content to anyone present.

I have read your note of this date. Though not entertaining the opinion you express of the hopelessness of further resistance on the part of the Army of N. Va.,—I reciprocate your desire to avoid useless effusion of blood, & therefore before considering your proposition, ask the terms you will offer on condition of its surrender.[12]

The wagons, such as they were, kept rolling through the dark and reached New Store before midnight. The infantry resumed the march during the night and cavalry assumed a rear guard. Now the goal was Appomattox Station on the Southside Railroad. There Lee hoped to feed his troops once more and then attempt to break through the Federals and strike for Danville.[13]

By this point in the retreat, however, the soldiers sensed an end to this corporate agony. Alexander began to hear calls from his artillery batteries: "Don't surrender no ammunition!" His gunners were determined to fire all the shot and shells they had before the end.

On April 8, pressure from the Federals relaxed to the point that the Southerners marched "uninterrupted." This was "the first quiet day of the march, since leaving Amelia." There was an ominous cause for the quiet, though: pursuing columns were marching along roads parallel to Lee's route in an effort to reach Appomattox before Lee did.[14]

During the morning of the 8th Lee took advantage of the tranquility to lie down on the ground to rest. Artillery staff officer William Nelson Pendleton found Lee and imposed upon his peace to speak for a group of officers that had gathered the previous evening and decided the time had come to surrender. Although educated at West Point, Pendleton was more than anything else a tedious, loquacious cleric (Episcopal) disguised as chief of artillery. Lee heard his message and emphatically disagreed. The precise tone and tenor of Lee's response varies with the several accounts of the incident. Lee did fail to tell Pendleton that he had already commenced negotiations of sorts with Grant and in them used the word "surrender." As Alexander observed, "I believe that Gen. Lee took no one into his confidence as to his intentions, or as to this correspondence with Gen. Grant; preferring as his hand became the harder to play, to play it more & more alone."[15]

On the afternoon of April 8, Lee took time to dispense justice upon three of his senior subordinates. He relieved from command and removed from his army Richard H. Anderson, George E. Pickett, and Bushrod Johnson. The more information Lee learned about Pickett's actions at Five Forks on April 1 (i.e., leaving his command to attend Thomas Rosser's shad bake), the more culpable this broken man seemed to have been in the virtual destruction of his division. After Sayler's Creek on April 6, Johnson told Lee that the enemy had decimated his division. But soon after Johnson's report, Lee encountered Henry A. Wise and his brigade of Johnson's division very much intact. Obviously Johnson had fled his command in the course of the battle. Anderson may have been that general officer "of exalted grade" whom Lee had so summarily dismissed in the wake of Sayler's Creek. At any rate, this trio felt Lee's wrath, and Lee's righteousness endured to the end of his tenure in command.[16]

Some time after dark on April 8, Lee received his second communication from Grant:

GENERAL,—Your note of last evening in reply to mine of the same date, asking the conditions on which I will accept surrender of the Army of Northern Virginia, is just received. In reply I would say that, peace being my great desire, there is but one condition I would insist upon,—namely, that the men and officers surrendered shall be disqualified for taking up arms again against the government of the United States until properly exchanged. I will meet you, or will designate officers to meet any officers you might name for the same purpose, at any point agreeable to you, for the purpose of arranging definitely the terms upon which the surrender of the Army of Northern Virginia will be received.

Lee pondered his reply and then wrote a very curious note to Grant:

I recd at a late hour your note of today. In mine of yesterday I did not intend to propose the surrender of the Army of N. Va.—but to ask the terms of your proposition. To be frank, I do not think the emergency has arisen to call for the surrender of this Army, but as the restoration of peace should be the sole object of all, I desired to know whether your proposals would lead to that and I cannot therefore meet you with view to surrender the Army of N. Va.—but as far as your proposal may affect the C.S. forces under my command & tend to the restoration of peace, I shall be pleased to meet you at 10 A.M. tomorrow on the old stage road to Richmond between the picket lines of the two armies.

Lee seemed to suggest that they raise the stakes, in effect, and discuss "the C.S. forces under my command" (i.e., all Confederate armies) and "the restoration of peace." Did Lee propose that he and Grant negotiate the end of the war then and there? Grant could find out if he appeared at ten o'clock the next morning on the old stage road.[17]

Not long after he sent his note through the lines to Grant, Lee convened a council of war among his surviving subordinate commanders, Longstreet, Gordon, and Fitz Lee. These men led the two infantry corps and all the cavalry left with the Army of Northern Virginia—perhaps 10,000 men altogether.

Lee stood by a fire; Longstreet sat on a log; Gordon and Fitz Lee lounged on a blanket. Lee summarized their circumstance, read the notes from and to Grant, and asked the obvious question—what to do next. The answer, in retrospect, seemed obvious—attack. Trust trial by combat one last time.

But, and this was important, if Federal infantry were in force behind the Federal cavalry known to be blocking the route of march, then surrender was the only answer. Enemy infantry in strength in front of Lee's army, together with the infantry in the rear of the column, would mean that the Confederates were essentially surrounded by an overwhelming Federal force. The only alternative to surrender would then be suicide.

Longstreet was to protect the rear, while Fitz Lee's horsemen and Gordon's infantry attacked the Federals in front. The troops were supposed to move at 1:00 A.M.; but Fitz Lee, with Lee's blessing, delayed the advance until 5:00 A.M., almost first light.[18]

After a short nap, Lee dressed himself in the best uniform he possessed, complete with a red silk sash and sword, neither of which he usually wore. He rode to the front, which was not far away, and stationed himself on a hill behind Gordon's troops. He heard the firing, but saw little of the ensuing fight. Finally, about 8:00 A.M., Lee sent his staff officer Charles Venable to find out what was happening.

Venable discovered that Gordon's assault had succeeded at first. But as the Confederates advanced, Lee reported later, "A heavy force of the enemy was discovered opposite Gordon's right, which, moving in the direction of Appomattox Court House, drove back the left of the cavalry and threatened to cut off Gordon from Longstreet. His [enemy] cavalry at the same time threatening to envelop his [Gordon's] left flank, Gordon withdrew. . . ." When Venable returned to Lee, Gordon's message was, "Tell General Lee I have fought my corps to a frazzle, and I fear I can do nothing unless I am heavily supported by General Longstreet's corps."

Lee listened to this and proclaimed, "Then there is nothing left me but to go and see General Grant, and I would rather die a thousand deaths."[19]

For members of the Army of Northern Virginia, the war was over. Most of them had sensed that end for some time. A week earlier, while the army was attempting to maintain a position in Petersburg long enough to evacuate the city under cover of darkness during the night of April 2, a staff officer noticed Lee "handsomely dressed," and another soldier believed Lee's uniform was new. Maybe Lee had dressed himself for surrender even then. But knowing the end was near and coming to emotional terms with defeat were very different matters. Someone heard Lee exclaim, "How easily I could be rid of this, and be at rest! I have only to ride along the line and all will be over!" Soon he regained control and professed, "But it is our duty to live."[20]

At some point during this interim between defeat and surrender, Edward Porter Alexander appeared. Lee sat down upon a log and said to him, "Well here we are at Appomattox, & there seems to be a considerable force in front of us. Now, what shall we have to do today?"

Alexander just happened to have a very firm answer to Lee's question; he had been thinking about such a contingency for some time. He was, as he remembered, "wound up to a pitch of feeling I could scarcely control." He had made up his mind "that if ever a white flag was raised I would take to the bushes."

Lee heard Alexander's plan and passion to "scatter like rabbits & partridges in the woods & they could not scatter so to catch us." Then Lee demonstrated that he, too, had thought about a guerrilla alternative to surrender. He had had to consider a guerrilla phase of this war, because he knew that Jefferson Davis was committed to just such a recourse. Lee rejected the partisan alternative, however; he had from the beginning believed that the South's best chance lay in decisive victories in conventional battle. Lee feared anarchy far more than Yankees, and his concern for the social order saturated his response to Alexander.

Suppose I should take your suggestion & order the army to disperse & make their way to their homes. The men would have no rations & they would be under no discipline. They are already demoralized by four years of war. They would have to plunder & rob to procure subsistence. The country would be full of lawless bands in every part, & a state of society would ensue from which it would take the country years to recover.

Then the enemy's cavalry would pursue in the hopes of catching the principal officers, & wherever they went there would be fresh rapine & destruction.

And as for myself, while you young men might afford to go to bushwhacking, the only proper & dignified course for me would be to surrender myself & take the consequences of my actions.

When Lee completed his statement, Alexander recalled, "Then I thought I had never known before what a big heart & brain our general had."[21]

Soon it became time to keep the appointment with Grant that Lee had proposed the previous evening. Four horsemen rode down the old stage road. George W. Tucker, the courier who had ridden with A. P. Hill the day Hill was killed, led the way with a white flag, followed by Lee and Walter Taylor and Charles Marshall from Lee's staff. They met not Grant, but a Federal staff officer with a note from Grant, dated April 9.

GENERAL: Your note of yesterday is received. As I have no authority to treat on the subject of peace the meeting proposed for 10 A.M. today could lead to no good. I will state, however, General, that I am equally anxious for peace with yourself, and the whole North entertain the same feeling. The terms upon which peace can be had are well understood. By the South laying down their arms they will hasten that most desirable event, save thousands of human lives, and hundreds of millions of property not yet destroyed. Sincerely hoping that all our difficulties may be settled without the loss of another life. . . .[22]

Lee dictated his reply to Marshall; but as he did, a rider approached from Lee's rear at top speed. John Haskell, sent by Longstreet with orders to ride so fast as to kill his horse if necessary, brought a message to Lee that Fitz Lee thought he had discovered a route by which the army might escape. "What is it? What is it?" Lee asked, and then, "Oh, you have killed your beautiful mare! What did you do it for?" Haskell told Lee in private the nature of his errand; but Lee determined to continue his negotiations to surrender. As if to reinforce his resolve, guns commenced firing from the Federal side. Lee's note read:

I received your note of this morning on the picket line whither I had come to meet you and ascertain definitely what terms were embraced in your proposal of yesterday with reference to the surrender of this army. I now request an interview in accordance with the offer contained in your letter of yesterday for that purpose.

Lee offered to wait for an answer and asked that the Federals suspend hostilities until Grant read his note. The Federal officer could only promise to deliver the note and return with a reply. Grant was difficult to find that morning; he seemed inclined to repay Lee's actions over a truce after Second Cold Harbor with interest.

As Lee doubtless wondered what to do next, a second message arrived from Longstreet. Fitz Lee's escape route was not as clear as he had believed at first.

On Longstreet's front, Union Cavalry General George A. Custer decided to preempt his commanding general and try to bully Longstreet into surrendering to him. "Well, Sheridan & I are independent here today," Custer told Longstreet, "& unless you surrender immediately we are going to pitch in." Longstreet was unimpressed. "Pitch in as much as you like," he responded.

While Lee waited in the road, Federal infantry advanced to the attack in accord with orders no one had or could countermand without Grant's permission. Lee dispatched another note: "I ask a suspension of hostilities pending the adjustment of the terms of surrender of this army, in the interview requested in my former communication today." The situation became tense. Someone shouted for Lee to get out of the way of the Federal infantry; a major bloodbath seemed about to commence.[23]

Lee did withdraw within his lines, and at the last moment before the shooting began in earnest, George G. Meade, who still commanded the Army of the Potomac, sent a note proclaiming a truce based upon the imminent surrender. Meade also suggested that Lee write another note to Grant through another point in the enemy line in the hope that he might receive it more rapidly. Accordingly, Lee dictated a third note to Grant:

General, I sent a communication to you today from the picket line whither I had gone in hopes of meeting you in pursuance of the request contained in my letter of yesterday. Maj. Gen. Meade informs me that it would probably expedite matters to send a duplicate through some other part of your lines. I therefore request an interview at such time and place as you may designate to discuss the terms of the surrender of this army in accord with your offer to have such an interview contained in your letter of yesterday.[24]

Whether he intended to or not, Grant was requiring Lee to grovel just to receive the opportunity to surrender his army. But Lee was well aware that war, the resort to physical force, is by definition a suspension of rules, laws, and civilized behavior. Victors can impose their will upon the vanquished. If his decision to "take the consequences of my actions" compelled Lee to humble himself, so be it. And, in accord with Lee's conviction that "the great duty of life" was "the promotion of the happiness & welfare" of others, Lee likely believed that his personal pride was a small sacrifice, if he could salvage the honor of his army.

Meade's truce and the search for Grant left Lee nothing to do until Grant responded to one or more of his notes. He rode back within his lines, stood alone in an apple orchard, and eventually said, "I would like to sit down. Is there any place where I can sit near here?" Alexander heard these words and hurried to fashion a seat from fence rails under an apple tree. There Lee sat for nearly three hours.[25]

Then Orville E. Babcock of Grant's staff appeared with a message from Grant:

Your note of this date is but this moment (11:50 A.M.) received. In consequence of my having passed from the Richmond and Lynchburg road to the Farmville and Lynchburg road I am at this writing about four miles west of Walker's church, and will push forward to the front for the purpose of meeting you. Notice sent on this road where you wish the interview to take place will meet me.

Lee collected Marshall and his courier Tucker and rode with Babcock to Appomattox Court House.

Lee assigned Marshall the duty of finding a place to meet with Grant. Marshall settled upon the home of Wilmer McLean. This man had had a home near Manassas; one of the first artillery rounds fired in this war had crashed into McLean's kitchen. After the Second Battle at Manassas, McLean had decided to remove himself and his family away from the war zone. McLean had moved to Appomattox Court House to escape combat; but now the war had found him again.

Lee rode into McLean's yard, dismounted, and entered the house. He settled in the parlor to the left of the front door and awaited Grant. After a half-hour, Grant appeared. He was dressed in "rough garb," fresh from the field, spattered with mud. Lee was "in full uniform which was entirely new and was wearing a sword of considerable value." Both generals had clothed themselves carefully as they wanted others to see them—Grant no less than Lee.[26]

For a time the two men spoke of mutual experiences in the Mexican War. Then Lee shifted the conversation to the transaction at hand, and Grant wrote down terms of the surrender.

In accordance with the substance of my letter to you of the 8th instant I propose to receive the surrender of the Army of N. Va. on the following terms, to-wit:

Rolls of all the officers and men to be made in duplicate, one copy to be given to an officer designated by me, the other to be retained by such officer or officers as you may designate. The officers to give their individual paroles not to take up arms against the government of the United States until properly [Lee confirmed that Grant had intended writing "exchanged" after "properly"] and each company or regimental commander sign a like parole for the men of their command.

The arms, artillery, and public property to be parked and stacked and turned over to the officer appointed by me to receive them.

This will not embrace the side arms of the officers, nor their private horses or baggage. This done each officer and man will be allowed to return to their homes not to be disturbed by United States authority so long as they observe their paroles and the laws in force where they may reside.

Lee liked what he read. He did point out that Confederate cavalrymen and artillerists owned the horses they rode or drove. After some pause Grant agreed to allow the men who claimed a horse or mule to take the animal with them. Lee was pleased.

Lee asked Marshall to write out his response:

GENERAL: I have received your letter of this date containing the terms of surrender of the Army of Northern Virginia as proposed by you. As they are substantially the same as those expressed in your letter of the 8th instant, they are accepted. I will proceed to designate the proper officers to carry the stipulation into effect.

Lee and Grant, once they had signed these documents, shook hands. Lee bowed to all present and strode onto the porch. "Orderly! Orderly!" Lee called, and Tucker brought Traveller. Lee helped replace the bridle and mounted. Grant appeared on the porch of the McLean House. Seeing Lee about to depart, the Federal took off his hat; others did the same. Lee tipped his own hat, turned Traveller, and rode away.[27]

Lee returned to his troops one last time. They greeted him with an amalgam of love and awe. He had arranged with Grant to have rations of food delivered to these men, many of whom had not received rations since they had left Petersburg a week ago. Lee tried to speak to his soldiers; but his words were lame—I have done my best for you . . . go home and be good citizens. It made no difference; the soldiers provided the eloquence. They wanted to hug him; they settled for a touch and some expression of their affection. Then one of the men said, "Farewell, General Lee. I wish for your sake and mine that every damned Yankee on earth was sunk ten miles in hell!" The day required some benediction.[28]

Lee went into the orchard by himself and paced. Soldiers and strangers came and went; Lee spoke very little. He seemed in "one of his savage moods," and his staff officers knew better than to disturb him. He was coming to terms with defeat, surrender, the end—almost forty years of career and life gone.[29]

Lee needed to grieve. He had seen and known so much death and loss. In four years he had lost almost all that he owned and many whom he loved. A daughter was dead, along with a daughter-in-law and two grandchildren. His wife had become an invalid, and he knew his own health had declined dramatically. Arlington was gone. And Lee had mourned so many of his men—Robert S. Garnett and John A. Washington from his first staff; Stonewall Jackson at Chancellorsville; Dorsey Pender, Richard B. Garnett, Lewis A. Armistead, William Barksdale, and James Johnston Pettigrew at Gettysburg; Jeb Stuart, Dodson Ramseur, John Pegram, A. P. Hill, and many more—more than 650,000 soldiers on both sides.

He was a soldier; he should have been accustomed to death. But this war had produced not only death in the immediate family. It concluded with the death of Lee's extended family—the Army of Northern Virginia. Surrender was death raised to an enormous power. Lee would need to grieve a long time. But at last the suffering was over, and he was at rest.

29

"After Four Years of Arduous Service"

ROBERT LEE WAS A PRESENCE. What he did and was far surpassed anything he ever wrote or said. Eloquence was not foremost among Lee's many attributes. He made very few speeches during his life, and nearly forty years of military service reduced his formal prose to passive voice and professional cliché. So Lee entrusted the composition of his farewell address to the Army of Northern Virginia, General Orders No. 9, to Charles Marshall of his staff.

The words were Marshall's; but the sentiments belonged to Lee, and the message was simple and direct.

After four years of arduous service, marked by unsurpassed courage and fortitude, the Army of Northern Virginia has been compelled to yield to overwhelming numbers and resources.

I need not tell the brave survivors of so many hard fought battles, who have remained steadfast to the last, that I have consented to the result from no distrust of them.

But feeling that valor and devotion could accomplish nothing that would compensate for the loss that must have attended the continuance of the contest, I determined to avoid the useless sacrifice of those whose past services have endeared them to their countrymen.

By the terms of the agreement officers and men can return to their homes and remain until exchanged. You will take with you the satisfaction that proceeds from the consciousness of duty faithfully performed, and I earnestly pray that a Merciful God will extend to you His blessing and protection.

With our increasing admiration of your constancy and devotion to your country, and a grateful remembrance of your kind and generous considerations for myself, I bid you all an affectionate farewell.[1]

Such was Lee's closure with his army.

Little else remained to do. Lee and the members of his staff secured their paroles as prisoners of war, and Lee designated officers to execute the surrender of his army. Visitors came and went about the headquarters, and subordinates submitted their reports of the army's final campaign.[2]

One of the last tasks Lee completed before leaving Appomattox was his report to Jefferson Davis. Lee waited three days to write to Davis and promised a detailed report later. The letter Lee wrote on April 12, however, was pretty complete, and in it Lee took pains to justify his decision to surrender the army:

. . . The enemy was more than five times our numbers. If we could have forced our way one day longer it would have been at a great sacrifice of life; at its end, I did not see how a surrender could have been avoided. We had no subsistence for man or horse, and it could not be gathered in the country . . . the men deprived of food and sleep for many days, were worn out and exhausted.[3]

When Lee did write again to Davis on April 20, he offered less details, but a broader view of the war and the Confederacy. "A partisan war may be continued," he wrote, "and hostilities protracted, causing individual suffering and the devastation of the country, but I see no prospect by that means of achieving a separate independence. . . . To save useless effusion of blood, I would recommend measures be taken for suspension of hostilities and the restoration of peace." Lee accepted the verdict of arms; he knew the war and the cause were lost. Davis never seemed to come to terms with such realities.[4]

Lee remained at Appomattox as long as his soldiers did; he was in the vicinity when the survivors stacked their arms in what became a moving ceremony celebrated in Joshua L. Chamberlain's *Passing of the Armies;* but Lee did not witness the event.

Then it became time to do something else, so some time on April 12 Lee commenced the journey back to his family in Richmond. Walter Taylor, Charles Marshall, and Charles S. Venable rode with Lee, and they retained the headquarters wagon and the ambulance in which Lee had sometimes ridden when ill or afflicted with "rheumatism." Giles Cooke, another member of the staff, was sick and so rode in the ambulance until he left Lee and headed home. The "trustworthy Burt" drove the ambulance, and "Bryan" Lynch still served as mess steward and prepared food for the company. Venable soon parted to return to his family in nearby Prince Edward County. But other Confederate veterans joined and left Lee's party over the 100-plus miles between Appomattox Court House and Richmond.

On the third night of the journey, Lee reached his brother Carter Lee's farm in Powhatan County, but slept (for the final time) in his tent, because Carter's house was crowded. During the morning of April 15, Rooney Lee overtook his father and the procession increased to twenty horses.

Lee entered Richmond from the south in the midst of a strong April shower and passed at once into the portion of the city most thoroughly burned in the evacuation fire on April 2. Some citizens saw the horsemen, and word spread that Lee had come home from the war. Lee tipped his hat to those who greeted him but rode the most direct route to 707 East Franklin Street and the house in which his wife and family had lived for just over fifteen months. When he arrived, he dismounted Traveller, gave the reins to someone else, bowed to the bystanders, went inside, and shut the door.[5]

In the beginning he slept a lot, and left his house very little. His wife and two of his daughters were there; Custis had arrived in Richmond before his father; and Rooney, too, remained in the city with the family. Rob was missing. He had learned of the surrender and gone to Greensboro, North Carolina, where Davis and the government had paused in their flight. Rob then decided to follow the family example, surrender, and secure his parole. So he reached Richmond about two weeks after his father arrived.[6]

In Richmond many people wanted to see Lee. Matthew Brady took his picture; Thomas M. Cook of the *New York Herald* interviewed him; and an Irish veteran of Lee's command of the Second U.S. Cavalry tried to kiss him. Very soon Lee's family established a roster of doorkeepers to screen visitors and protect Lee from his fame. When he wanted exercise, Lee had to take walks at night to avoid presumptuous people. This shy man for whom social contact with people he did not know well required significant effort had not been in Richmond long at all when he resolved to leave the occupied Confederate capital as soon as he was able.

Lee's landlord John Stewart informed him that he owed no rent for as long as he wanted to remain, and if Lee insisted upon paying rent, Stewart insisted upon taking payment in Confederate currency, as such were the terms of the original contract with Custis Lee.

Lee had never owned his home during thirty-three years of married life. He had depended upon Mary Lee's life interest in Arlington to provide a more or less permanent place for his family. But now Arlington was gone—rendered uninhabitable by the many graves of Federal solders that covered the land. Lee harkened back to a familiar refrain: he only wanted "some little quiet home in the woods, where I can procure shelter and my daily bread, if permitted by the victor. I wish to get Mrs. Lee out of the city as soon as practical."[7]

Lee could expect to salvage some money from his investments prior to the war. And some of the Custis properties still belonged to his sons Rooney and Rob, or so Lee believed, so perhaps this was his chance to do what he had many times said he wanted to do—buy some land, build a small home, and become a humble farmer.[8]

But complications threatened Lee's bucolic fantasy. As Lee should have known, civil wars often end in acrimony and executions. At Appomattox, Lee could believe he had surrendered himself and his army on favorable terms and thus concluded his quarrel with the United States. Grant shared with Lee the hope that North and South would resume "business as usual," and a United States would revert to status quo ante bellum. But for four years Lee had been a rebel, and during three of those four years he had established himself as the most troublesome rebel the United States ever confronted. As long as the war continued, Lee was a paroled prisoner of war. When the war ended, though, Lee could no longer be a prisoner of war; no one can be a prisoner of a war that does not exist. What would become of Lee when his parole no longer protected him?

Early on the morning of the day Lee rode into Richmond (April 15),

Abraham Lincoln died of a gunshot wound in his brain inflicted by John Wilkes Booth in the cause of Southern vengeance. Lincoln was suddenly a martyr, and understandable hysteria swept through the North. If in the flush of impending victory anyone had forgotten that treason was a serious matter, Booth certainly recalled attention to the issue. At the very least some hangings seemed in order. And the most logical candidates for execution were the most prominent traitors. After Jefferson Davis, surely Robert E. Lee was a very likely candidate.

On May 10, Federal cavalrymen captured Davis in flight near Irwinville, Georgia. Davis then was deposited in a cell at Fort Monroe, Virginia, while the United States decided what to do with him.[9]

What did this portend for Lee? On June 7, a Federal jury in Norfolk, Virginia, indicted Lee for treason. But Lee clung to the belief that his parole protected him and in effect absolved him from such proceedings. On June 13, Lee stated his case to Grant: "I had supposed that the officers and men of the Army of Northern Virginia were, by the terms of the surrender, protected by the United States Government from molestation so long as they conformed to its conditions." Lee included in his letter to Grant his application to President Andrew Johnson for amnesty and pardon that Johnson had required of prominent Confederates: "Being excluded from the provisions of the amnesty and pardon contained in the proclamation of the 29th ult., I hereby apply for the benefits and full restoration of all rights and privileges extended to those included in its terms."[10]

Lee counseled other Confederate Southerners to do all they could to regain their full civil rights. He believed that they could more quickly recover from the war and the stigma of disloyalty if they displayed wholehearted cooperation with the victors. He realized that recalcitrance would only make a bad situation much worse.

Throughout this trying period when Lee had to confront the consequences of his adherence and contribution to the Southern rebellion, he insisted that he had committed no inconsistency. His explanation, perhaps best expressed in a letter to P. G. T. Beauregard, is extraordinary.

True patriotism sometimes requires of men to act exactly contrary, at one period, to that which it does at another, and the motive which impels them—the desire to do right—is precisely the same. The circumstances which govern their actions change; and their conduct must conform to the new order of things. History is full of illustrations of this. Washington himself is an example. At one time he fought against the French under Braddock, in the service of the King of Great Britain; at another, he fought with the French at Yorktown, under the orders of the Continental Congress of America, against him. He has not been branded by the world with reproach for this; but his course has been applauded.[11]

Such a statement, especially coming from Lee, smacks of rationalization. After all this was the same man who believed the way to deal with desertion was "to visit the offense, when committed, with the sternest punishment, and leave the offender without hope of escape, by making the penalty inevitable." Yet Lee offered other examples of his ethical flexibility. In April 1864, for example, he wrote to Mary Lee about a widow who was debating remarriage. "I think the world generally accords to a woman more respect & esteem," Lee wrote, "who marries but once. There are of course exceptions to this as other rules & there are often valid reasons accepted by all, for departing from it. Every one must judge for themselves in such matters."[12]

Few people then and since have ever associated Robert Lee with existential ethics. Lee did adhere to absolute standards—e.g., "the desire to do right." But within the bounds of rather broad moral and ethical guidelines, Lee followed an ethical code perhaps best described as "situationalist." At least this was how he justified his altered loyalties between 1861 and 1865.

It was ironic that Ulysses Grant resolved the dilemma of what to do about Lee and other Confederate military leaders on the basis of a very rigid standard—the sanctity of Grant's word. Grant agreed with Lee that the terms of surrender precluded trials for treason. Grant believed that such lenient provisions had forestalled a guerrilla war, and he intended to honor his promise. Indeed, Grant threatened to resign if Andrew Johnson abrogated what Grant believed was his pledged word at Appomattox. The President relented, and Grant was able to write Lee on June 20 that he need not worry about standing trial for treason.[13]

While Lee still lived in official limbo regarding the consequences of his Confederate career, he began seriously the search for another home. Around June 1, he mounted Traveller and rode alone east from Richmond, over the Chickahominy, through Mechanicsville, and across the Pamunkey into King William County. He went to a plantation called Pampatike that belonged to Thomas H. Carter, who was a cousin and had recently served as a colonel of artillery in the Army of Northern Virginia. Lee arrived unexpected (and thus uninvited); but in the tradition of Virginia hospitality the Carters welcomed him lavishly and prevailed upon him to extend his visit into several days. Neighbors too invited Lee to dinners, and since Rooney and Rob had lately moved to White House in the vicinity, they joined their father on at least one occasion.

Lee wanted a respite from Richmond; he genuinely enjoyed the informal ease of the countryside; and he liked the elegance his more prosperous relatives could afford. He also wanted advice about where he might settle with his family. Carter suggested Gloucester County if Lee liked salt water or Clarke County in the Piedmont if Lee preferred grass. Lee pronounced in favor of grass and continued to explore the possibility of becoming a farmer.

He also felt free to give advice while he visited at Pampatike. He chided his hosts about the quantity and variety of foods they served—"Thomas, there was enough dinner to-day for twenty people. All this will now have to be changed; you cannot afford it; we shall have to practice economy."

Lee had opinions about using free black labor on Carter's plantation; he advised his cousin to hire white workers. "I have always observed," Lee pontificated, "that wherever you find the negro, everything is going down around him, and wherever you find the white man, you see everything around him improving." The war and the African American troops that had helped defeat him did not seem to change Lee's hierarchical assumptions about race.[14]

But soon after he returned to Richmond, Lee once more confounded those who considered him uncomplicated. The occasion was communion at St. Paul's Church on a Sunday in June. The Reverend Dr. Charles Minnegerode was still rector of the parish; St. Paul's was (and is) just across the street from Capitol Square, and during the war a list of communicants read like a *Who's Who* of the Confederacy. At this particular service, as soon as Minnegerode delivered the invitation to the people to come forward to receive the consecrated bread and wine, a tall, well-dressed, very black man stood and strode to the rail. There followed a pregnant pause. According to one witness, "Its effect upon the communicants was startling, and for several moments they retained their seats in solemn silence and did not move, being deeply chagrined at this attempt to inaugurate the 'new regime' to offend and humiliate them. . . . Dr. Minnegerode was evidently embarrassed."

Then another person rose from the pew and walked down the aisle to the chancel rail. He knelt near the black man and so redeemed the circumstance. This grace-bringer, of course, was Lee. Soon after he knelt, the rest of the congregation followed his example and shuffled in turn to the rail. Once again Lee's actions were far more eloquent than anything he spoke or wrote.[15]

Peace with the United States made possible a resumption of Lee's correspondence and relationships with clever young women. One of the first personal letters he wrote after Appomattox was to "Markie" Williams on May 2, 1865. In one of her letters to him, Markie offered to go with him to Europe; but Lee demurred—"there is much to detain me here, & at present at least it is my duty to remain." He continued:

There is nothing my dear Markie that I want, except to see you, & nothing that you can do for me, except to think of & love me. It would require you to become a Fairy & turn what you touched to Gold to take me to Europe, but I would not desire you to change your nature for my benefit. I prefer you remaining as you are—

In this same letter Lee reported his plan to move to the country—"to Cumberland Co. about six miles from Cartersville on the [James River and Kanawha Canal." Elizabeth Randolph Cocke had offered the Lees a vacant house on her property, about midway between Richmond and Charlottesville. Elizabeth Cocke was related to the Cocke family at Bremo, where Mary Lee and her daughters had spent the summer and some of the fall of 1864. This place possessed the virtue of being accessible by water and so was more accessible to Mary in her invalid condition. And even though Lee told Markie, "I have . . . selected a house. . . . ," as though he had bought it, Elizabeth Cocke's house was rent-free.[16]

On June 28 the family boarded a packet boat on the canal and teams of horses pulled them upstream to a landing near Oakland, where Elizabeth

Cocke lived. The Lees visited at Oakland for a week and made the vacant house, known as "Derwent" (after Derwent water in the English Lake District), ready for habitation. Furnishings came from Oakland; Mary and Robert Lee had never owned much furniture and retained none of that they had purchased or inherited. At last Lee had his little house in the country.

Derwent was a wooden frame house, two rooms over two rooms, front and side porches, dining room in the basement, detached kitchen in the backyard, and another outbuilding suitable for an office. The best feature of the house was the ornamented (doors and millwork) closet in the room to the left of the central hallway which became the Lees' room.[17]

Lee described Derwent to son Rob as "a comfortable but small house in a grove of oaks." To Rooney, Lee wrote, "Our house is small & excessively hot, more so to me than a tent would be. Our neighbors are very kind & do everything in the world to promote our comfort."[18]

Mary Lee described her situation less positively:

You would suppose from the title of this retreat that we are in sight of cool lakes and romantic scenery but it is a little retired place with a straight up house and the only beauty it possesses is a fine growth of oaks which surrounds it. Thro' the kindness of a friend who has given us the use of it, it has been rendered habitable, but all the outbuildings are dilapidated and the garden is a mass of weeds. As we shall probably not remain here longer than a season we shall not attempt to cultivate it. . . . Our future will be guided by circumstances. I dare not look into it, all seems so dark now, that we are almost tempted to think God has forsaken us.[19]

The Lees would not last long in the country.

Lee did enjoy much about this quiet summer at Derwent. He took rides on Traveller and visited friends and relatives. He even began to think about writing a history of his campaigns—not to vindicate himself, he insisted, but to reveal the long odds his soldiers faced in battle and thus to laud the courage and gallantry of the men he had led. He wrote to Walter Taylor to try to secure accurate records, and he opened negotiations with a publisher regarding the publication of his history together with a new edition of his father's memoirs.[20]

Still, Lee needed more to do—some purpose greater than refighting battles lost and some source of income for himself and his family. Mary Lee would likely never feel much better, and she required considerable care now. Custis confronted embarking upon a new career at age thirty-three; he was hoping for an appointment to the faculty at VMI, but spent most of the summer overcoming a case of dysentery. Daughter Mary (now thirty) was alive somewhere; she rarely rejoined the family, but spent most of her time on protracted visits with relatives and friends. Agnes (twenty-four) became quite ill during the summer at Derwent; she had been her mother's primary companion during the war and remained at home wherever home might be. Mildred (nineteen) also seemed destined to continue at home. During the summer of 1865 she absorbed herself in her flock of chickens, read novels, and probably became quite bored. Her father called her his "only reliance & support" at Derwent.

Rooney (twenty-eight) and Rob (twenty-one) spent the summer at White House trying to make something from a crop of corn. Both young veterans had decided to become farmers and try to support themselves on the land they inherited from their grandfather. So in uncertain times Lee the patriarch confronted equally unsettled family plans. He realized that one of the important ways in which he could help his children was monetarily.[21]

In August 1865, which Robert Lee termed "a quiet time . . . delightful to me . . . I fear not so exhilarating to the girls," amid what Mary Lee said was "a quiet so profound that I could even number the acorns falling from the splendid oaks that overshadowed the cottage," as Lee pondered what to do with the rest of his life, to use his metaphor from an early stage in his military career, a ripe pear fell into Lee's lap. Judge John W. Brockenbrough, who a few days earlier had won election as Rector of Washington College in Lexington, Virginia, appeared at Derwent one August day and informed Lee that the board of trustees of Washington College had unanimously elected him president of the college.

Brockenbrough, like Lee, was fifty-eight years old, and unlike Lee had been a Democrat "from infancy." Brockenbrough had served as a Federal judge member of the Confederate Congress, and Confederate States judge. But in Lexington, Brockenbrough was best known for his law school, which he had conducted by himself since 1849 and which eventually became the Washington College Law School.[22]

Brockenbrough made a strong case for the college and for Lee's acceptance of his election, and reinforced his speech with a letter written aboard the packet boat during his return trip to Lexington. The words appealed to Lee: "to make yourself useful to the state, to dedicate your fine scientific attainments to the service of its youth, to guide that youth in the paths of virtue. Knowledge & religion, not more by precept than your own great example— these my dear General are objects worthy of your ambition and we desire to present you the means of their accomplishment." The board of trustees also prevailed upon William Nelson Pendleton, Lee's former artillery chief and Rector of Grace Church, to add his encouragement, and Pendleton, too, appealed to Lee's concern for "the right training of our young men."

The trustees promised a salary of $1,500 per year, plus a residence and garden, and one fifth ($15) of the tuition each student paid ($75). In exchange for this compensation, the president assumed responsibility for administering the college and traditionally taught a course in philosophy.[23]

Pendleton insisted that of the institutions of higher learning in Virginia, "Washington College . . . is perhaps at present most promising." In retrospect son Rob offered a more candid appraisal of Washington College in the summer of 1865:

Its buildings, library, and apparatus had suffered from the sack and plunder of hostile soldiers. Its invested funds, owing to the general impoverishment throughout the land, were for the time being rendered unproductive and their ultimate value was most uncertain. Four professors still remained on duty, and there were about forty students, mainly from the country around Lexington. . . . It was very poor, indifferently equipped with buildings, and with no means in sight to improve its condition.

When Lee sought advice from the Reverend Joseph P. B. Wilmer, later Episcopal Bishop of Louisiana, who was then living in nearby Albemarle County, Wilmer suggested that Lee might aspire to lead "more conspicuous" institutions than Washington College, which then possessed only "local interest." In fact the University of the South at Sewanee, Tennessee, and the University of Virginia each approached Lee about accepting a leadership role with them. Lee impressed upon Wilmer his commitment to enlightenment and his unconcern with the status or prestige of an educational institution.[24]

In the past Lee had expended energy and influence in attempts to avoid association with educational institutions. He had eschewed an assignment as an instructor at the United States Military Academy, done his best to prevent his appointment as Superintendent of the Academy, and transferred from Engineers to Cavalry to hasten the end of his tenure as Superintendent at West Point. But each of those situations involved West Point and the rigidity of barracks life and technical subjects. At Washington College in this period of crisis in Southern higher education, Lee recognized the opportunity to mold the institution himself and work a transformation that he believed to be important.

So after two weeks of pondering Lee wrote his reply to the trustees. At the beginning of his letter Lee listed two reasons why he should not accept his election as president. "I do not feel able to undergo the labour of conducting classes in regular courses of instruction," he protested. And he added that since he was "an object of censure to a portion of the Country, I have thought it probable that my occupation of the position of President, might draw upon the College a feeling of hostility; & I should therefore cause injury to an Institution which it would be my highest desire to advance." So, because he was unable to teach courses and because he did not want "to be the cause of animadversion," Lee believed he should decline the presidency.

Then, in effect, he accepted the position. "Should you however take a different view," Lee wrote, "& think that my services in the position tendered me by the Board will be advantages to the College & Country, I will yield to your judgement & accept it." Of course the board did indeed think that Lee's services would be most advantageous and told him so in resolutions adopted on August 31.[25]

Accordingly, Lee prepared to commence another career and embark upon adventures in education. Mary Lee confided to a friend, "I do not think he is very fond of teaching, but is willing to do anything that will give him an honorable support." The trustees of Washington College doubtless cared more than anything else about Lee's name and fame, and hoped that Lee's association with the college would attract the students and financial support necessary to rescure the institution from oblivion. Lee himself had plans more ambitious than "honorable support" or affecting a benign persona as hero-in-residence. He soon asserted his determination to become an active educator at Washington College.[26]

On September 15, Lee set out alone for Lexington mounted on Traveller and made the journey in "four days' easy rides." He had never seen the town or Washington College before. Lee arrived about 1:00 P.M. on September 18 dressed in a gray suit from which his military insignia and buttons had been removed and wearing his brown hat. Lexington was a small mountain town of about 2,000 inhabitants and an agricultural marketplace dominated by three institutions—Washington College, Virginia Military Institute, and the Presbyterian church. One of the first residents Lee encountered was Professor James J. White, who taught Greek at the college and who insisted that Lee be the guest of White's father-in-law Samuel McD. Reid.[27]

Lee met with the trustees of the college on September 20 and found them solicitous and supportive. The president's residence was currently leased to a physician; after he vacated the place, repairs were in order, so Lee decided to take a room a the Lexington Hotel and wait to move his wife and daughters until he had the house ready for occupancy. Meanwhile, he spent a week at Rockbridge Baths, a mountain spa only 11 miles from Lexington. There Lee nursed his "rheumatic affliction" and took scenic rides with some of his female friends. He returned to Lexington on September 30 and prepared to open Washington College on October 2.[28]

The trustees had grand plans for Lee's installation as president—a brass band, speeches, "young girls robed in white," songs, and more. But Lee took charge and saw to a simpler ceremony—prayer, brief welcomes and an oath, presentation of the keys, and then Lee walked to his office and went to work.[29]

"A fine set of youths," approximately fifty of them, were on hand on October 2 when the college reopened in 1865. In time, 146 students matriculated during the academic year; Washington College denied no one admission that first year and dismissed no one from the academic program.[30]

President Lee did many of those things the trustees hoped he would do. He attracted students, many of whom had served in his army. He solicited contributions to the college, most notably in this year $10,000 from Cyrus McCormick, inventor and manufacturer of the reaper. Lee went to Richmond and asked the Virginia General Assembly to honor some bonds upon which the college depended for operating funds. And he answered his mail, all by himself during this period, thus generating goodwill toward the college.[31]

Lee in fact did considerably more than the trustees expected him to do as president. He injected ideas about expanding and altering the curriculum at Washington College. In December 1865, Lee sent a petition to the Virginia General Assembly to apply for money from the Morrill Act (signed into law the day after Lee's Seven Days Campaign concluded) designed to aid higher education in agriculture and mechanical arts. Specifically, Lee proposed to use the land grant funds to establish and support five new professorships: Practical Chemistry (chemical engineering); Experimental Philosophy (physics) and

Practical Mechanics (mechanical engineering); Applied Mathematics (civil engineering); Modern Languages (French, German, Italian, and Spanish); and History and Literature. In this instance Lee was unsuccessful in securing land grant funds; indeed, he never coaxed Morrill Act money from the General Assembly. But Lee was able to expand the curriculum in the way he envisioned when he applied for these funds, and in so doing he began the transformation of Washington College from a nineteenth-century classical academy to a twentieth-century university.[32]

From the beginning Lee became more involved with the students at Washington College than anyone had expected. Early evidence of Lee's commitment to his students is his letter to his cousin Anna Fitzhugh about his brother Smith's son, Robert. The young man was Lee's nephew; but abundant testimony exists to indicate that Lee took similar interest in students not kin to him.

Robert had interrupted his education, and he arrived late (December) in the academic year to begin his studies at Washington College. "He has commenced his work cheerfully & hopefully," Lee reported, and then added perceptively, "Like most boys, he has heretofore studied apparently, more with a view to his daily recitations than to acquire knowledge, but now that he sees the distinction, I am sure he will alter his course, & after he recalls what is forgotten of his reading, I think he will go on well." Lee counseled Robert into courses in mathematics, Latin, and French. He also "made arrangements for him to commence Greek, as I think it important he should commence as broad a base for the structure of his education as possible." Acknowledging the challenge of such a course load, Lee wrote, "I do not know that he will be able to carry them all on, but he says he is willing to study & try & by Feb. I shall be able to judge what course is best for him."

When Lee wrote his letter, his nephew was living in the President's House with Lee's family. However, Lee noted that Custis, who had now secured the faculty appointment at VMI, had had to live elsewhere for lack of space in the residence. "So Robert can arrange a room in College & I think be less interrupted in his studies than if with us." Lee did assure his cousin Anna, "Rob will take his meals with us, & you may tell Smith, I shall pay the same attention to him, if he will permit it, as if he was my own Son." Again, this student Robert was Lee's nephew; but as president, Lee worked long and hard to learn the names and try to know all the students at his college as if they were family. He perceived himself very much *in loco parentis* in Lexington.[33]

Lee did have concerns about his own sons in the aftermath of war. In many ways the father at fifty-eight adapted to defeat and changed circumstances much better than did his sons at thirty-three, twenty-eight, and twenty-two. Custis seemed to be established teaching engineering at VMI; but the fact that he continued to take his meals with his parents and never seriously pursued a wife and family of his own or, it would seem, his independence as a person, troubled Lee.[34]

Rooney Lee was the first of the Lee males to plunge into a peacetime pursuit. He went to live on his farm, White House, and with Rob's help managed to plant corn during the spring of 1865. This experience seems to have convinced Rooney that he did not want to continue active farming, because during the fall of 1865 he leased all of his arable land (2,000 acres) at White House to a Scottish entrepreneur. Rooney had a lawyer draw up the lease; but one of the stipulations of the agreement was Lee's approval. Unless Rooney's father gave his consent to the terms within three weeks, the lease became null and avoid. Lee the father did have serious questions about the wisdom of the arrangement—"it has occurred to me if Mr Black [the leasee] can pay himself & you, from the proceeds of the land which of course he expects to do, you might do as well, & thus receive the whole profit, & at the end of ten years, your estate would be in better condition than I fear you will receive it; especially as you have to endorse his loan of $10,000, & become responsible for it." But Lee also promised not to stand in his son's way. Rooney's primary concern was labor; he wished someone else to take the risk of hiring farm workers and hoping they would prove dependable. Lee concluded this correspondence with an affirmation: "If you are satisfied with the arrangement, I am, & sincerely hope it may result for the best." But why did Rooney Lee, the twenty-eight-year-old major general, feel the necessity of securing his father's approval before he leased his own property?[35]

The youngest son, Rob, also had a farm he inherited from his grandfather Custis, Romancoke on the Pamunkey River in King William County. However, Rob worked with Rooney at White House during the planting season of 1865. He contracted poison ivy then and later fell victim to some sort of fever. He went to Lexington to recuperate during the fall and returned to Romancoke only on December 20. Robert Lee, Senior, could probably be a formidable father, yet he took pains not to be overbearing. Nevertheless, Lee's students seemed to derive greater benefit from Lee's influence than did Lee's sons.[36]

One of the tasks Lee undertook and took seriously as president was the repair of buildings and grounds at the college. He worked hard enough at this responsibility to ask in his first annual report to the trustees for a proctor to take over this duty in the future. Among his first renovation projects was his own home. When the physician who was renting the president's residence finally vacated the place, Lee became a general contractor. He had to locate workers and materials to repair the roof, fences, and plaster. Then Lee became an interior designer; he had to furnish the house with carpets, curtains, and furniture. He also served as landscape architect and designed the walkways, garden, and planting. He seemed to enjoy these projects and led tours through the house when his wife and family arrived in Lexington on December 2.[37]

At last Lee had a home for himself and his family. But of course the house belonged, not to Lee, but to Washington College. Consequently, in a letter to his brother Smith written barely a month after Lee and his family moved into the president's residence, Lee wrote out a new verse to an old song: "I shall endeavor to get a little farm somewhere & make such preparation as to afford a home to my family in case of necessity, or of my death, that in either event I may not feel that they will be houseless. I should be perfectly content to be with them where I could make my daily bread, 'the world forgetting, by the world forgot.'" Some irony attends the use of this quotation; Lee's mother once used the same phrase about her life at Stratford Hall before Robert Lee was born, and she did not use it to describe perfect contentment.[38]

Lee seemed to make the transition from Appomattox to Lexington with remarkable ease, and by the close of 1865 he had already established himself as a presence in Lexington and savior of Washington College. But in his life oftentimes what Lee said or wrote and especially what other people said or wrote about him—the apparent and obvious—were not most important. During this period from Appomattox to Lexington, Lee said little about his health. His son Rob's words described Lee when showing off the President's House as appearing "bright and even gay."[39]

But Lee still suffered from angina pectoris, and he was developing arteriosclerosis with uncommon rapidity. He became increasingly aware that something was wrong; he probably knew or sensed that his physicians erred in the diagnosis of rheumatism. Lee's arteries were clogging, filling with a substance now known as plaque. But neither Lee nor his physicians knew about plaque—or what produced it.

30

"I Am Considered Now
Such a Monster"

ON OCTOBER 2, 1865, Robert E. Lee took two oaths. Soon after 9:00
A.M. he signed the document required to make him president of
Washington College (originally chartered as Liberty Hall):

I do swear that I will to the best of my skill and judgement, faithfully and
truly discharge the duties required of me by an act entitled, "An act, for incorporating,
the rector and trustees of Liberty Hall Academy," without favor, affection or partiality.
So help me God.[1]

Some other time that day, before a notary public, Lee also signed:

I Robert E. Lee of Lexington, Virginia do solemnly swear in the presence of Almighty
God, that I will henceforth faithfully support, protect and defend the Constitution of
the United States, and the Union of the States thereunder, and that I will in like
manner, abide by and faithfully support all laws and proclamations which have been
made during the existing rebellion with reference to the emancipation of slaves, so help
me God.

The second oath was Lee's Amnesty Oath, a necessary element for the
restoration of all the rights and privileges of United States citizenship. But
neither President Andrew Johnson, nor anyone else in the government, acted
upon Lee's request: his letter to the President of June 13, 1865, and this oath
which Johnson made a requirement subsequent to Lee's initial letter. Lee
simply assumed that someone or ones in the United States government had
decided to answer his request, "No." As Lee observed to his son Rooney back
in July 1865, "I think . . . we may expect procrastination in measures of relief,
denunciatory threats, etc."

In fact, the procrastination Lee predicted continued for 110 years. Lee
became a full United States citizen by act of Congress passed July 22, 1975,
and signed into law by President Gerald Ford on August 5, 1975. The oath Lee
had signed on October 2, 1865, reached Washington and the desk of Secretary

of State William H. Seward. But Seward gave the document to a friend as a souvenir, and Lee's Amnesty Oath disappeared until 1970, when archivists rediscovered the paper in some records of the Department of State in the National Archives. The errant oath, together with Lee's letter to Johnson, completed Lee's application for pardon and restoration of his citizenship, and so inspired the posthumous gesture on the part of Congress.[2]

Lee's lost Amnesty Oath set a symbolic tone for his feelings about the peace of Reconstruction. More than most Southerners, Lee knew the war was lost. Like most Southerners, Lee knew that losing the war meant rejoining the Union. But what Lee and most Southerners never really understood was what the Union had become during those four years of warfare. This was not the Union as it had been in 1860 when the secession process had begun and soon produced the Confederate States of America. The war for Union had transformed the Union. Now the Union was recommitted to humanitarian reform in the form of emancipation and equality for 4 million African Americans. Now the Union was recommitted to industrial capitalism and the role of government as servant of the business class. Ante bellum was a long time ago.

At the surface and in public Lee was extremely circumspect in his statements about the postwar settlement. At some level he was conscious that he had led a rebellion and lost and was very fortunate to be alive. Yet he believed that he had served in a civil war on the side devoted to traditional values and eternal verities, and he never really doubted his cause was right and good. But he was enough of a soldier to accept the verdict of arms. He also revered the old Union that his father and his father's friends founded; he wanted to restore that Union as he had known and loved it. So he counseled resignation and cooperation; indeed, he made himself a monument to making the best of a lost cause.

Early in 1866, Lee received a summons to go to Washington and appear before the Joint Committee on Reconstruction of the Congress. He arrived at the capital on February 16, checked into the Metropolitan Hotel, and discovered to his intense chagrin that Markie Williams was not at Tudor Place, her family home, but in Philadelphia.

Lee did encounter old friends and many curious folk in search of celebrity. One fellow claiming to be a Confederate veteran overwhelmed the efforts of Lee's friends to spare him from pests and boors and demanded to know why Lee had lost the Battle of Gettysburg. "My dear sir," Lee replied, "that would be a long story, and would require more time than you see I can possibly command at present; so we will have to defer the matter to another occasion."

Lee wrote Markie that he felt reticent about calling upon some of his friends in Washington. "I am considered now such a monster," he said, "that I hesitate to darken with my shadow the doors of those I love lest I should bring upon them misfortune."[3]

On February 17, the day after he arrived, Lee appeared in a gray suit before the Joint Committee. Jacob M. Howard, Republican senator from Michigan, began with a series of questions relating to the loyalty or disloyalty Virginians felt toward the United States. Lee was little help; he was "living very retired," he said, and had had "but little communication with politicians." Howard then asked about public debts, Union and Confederate, and Lee was even less able to say or predict what his fellow Virginians thought about these topics. Lee did speak of the Reconstruction process as "restoration," and he expressed enthusiasm for the policy of President Johnson.

Howard moved to questions about the new freedmen. Again Lee was reticent, but said, "I do not think that he [an African American] is as capable of acquiring knowledge as the white man is." And Lee repeated some other stereotypical saws: "They are an amiable, social race. They like their ease and comfort, and, I think, look more to the present-time than to the future."

Next, Howard asked about a hypothetical situation in which the United States were to go to war with a foreign power, England or France, for example. Would Virginians seize the chance to secede again and ally with the enemy? Lee refused to guess what anyone would do in such a circumstance. Howard asked what Lee would do, and Lee responded, "I have no disposition now to do it, and I never have had."

Henry T. Blow, representative from Missouri, took up the interrogation and asked Lee about Johnson's policies and the capacity of Northern people to "go to work among the people." Lee's answers supported the President and suggested that Northern immigrants confine "themselves to their own business and . . . not interfere to provoke controversies with their neighbors. . . ." Then both Howard and Blow asked again about attitudes of Virginians toward the North. "They think," Lee stated, "that the north can afford to be generous."

Blow returned to the circumstance of new freedmen and the proposed constitutional amendment guaranteeing them the right to vote. Lee asserted that "at this time, they cannot vote intelligently," and that black suffrage would "exclude proper representation; that is, proper intelligent people would not be elected."

Lee concluded his testimony by following some leading questions from Blow:

Do you think that Virginia would be better off if the colored population were to go to Alabama, Louisiana, and the other Southern States?

I think it would be better for Virginia if she could get rid of them. That is no new opinion with me. I have always thought so, and have always been in favor of emancipation—gradual emancipation. . . .

Do you think that the State of Virginia is absolutely injured and its future impaired by the presence of the black population there?

I think it is.

And do you not think it is peculiarly adapted to the quality of labor which would flow into it, from its great natural resources in case it was made attractive by the absence of the colored race?

I do.

The process lasted two hours; then Lee was free to go.[4]

Circumspection, indeed refusal to write or speak publicly any sentiments except in favor of cooperation and healing the sectional breach, continued to be Lee's policy. He let his feelings surface from time to time, but never in such a way as to offer his enemies the opportunity to attack him. Mary Lee, however, more than compensated for her husband's silence. While Lee was still in Washington, the day after he appeared before the Joint Committee, Mary Lee wrote her friend Emily Mason, "You will probably see by the [news]papers ere this reaches you that the Genl has been summoned to Washington to appear before the Reconstruction Committee. They should more properly be called the Destruction. . . ." In April, Mary Lee wrote her feelings about Arlington:

I have passed a quiet & tolerably comfortable winter but my heart will never know rest or peace while my dear home is so used & I am almost *maddened* daily by the accounts I read in the paper of the number of interments continually placed there. . . . My home was too beautiful stretched out before their eyes to escape their avarice & covetousness. . . . If *justice* & *law* are not utterly extinct in the U.S. I *will have* it back.

Then, in May, Mary Lee vented her wrath about race:

We are all here dreadfully plundered by the lazy idle negroes who are lounging about the streets doing nothing but looking what they may plunder during the night. We have been raided on twice already but fortunately they did not get a great deal either time. . . . When we get rid of the freedmen's Bureau & can take the law in our hands we may perhaps do better. If they would only take all their pets north it would be a happy riddance.

Some of what Mary Lee wrote to her friend doubtless reflected the emotions of her husband. But Robert Lee rarely let such feelings find expression.[5]

Mary Lee assured her friend, "the Genl is much occupied with his College. . . ." He was indeed. Lee ate breakfast at 7:00 A.M., attended chapel services at 8:00 A.M., and then spent about six hours in his office. He went home for dinner, took a very brief nap, paid calls, and rode Traveller during the afternoon. He had a secretary, Edward C. Gordon, to help with his correspondence from the 1866–67 academic year; nevertheless the volume of letters was enormous. Lee received letters addressed to "Professor Lea" and to "Most noble General, The Hero of the South, Honored Sir." From Richmond came a request from a baseball club to use Lee's name. Lee countered with a suggestion to name the team after Arlington; the members expressed the wish "to see that proud Domain again in the hands of its Rightful owners," and elected Lee an honorary member of the Arlington Base Ball Club.[6]

From the community of Greenway near Rockbridge Baths, Lee received "a New Year's offering" in January 1866. Twenty-five people donated nine hams, two pork shoulders, a turkey, a crock of apple butter, twenty-seven bushels of corn, a crock of quince butter, thirty pounds of buckwheat flour, and more for the Lee larder. They intended to present these gifts on New Year's Day, encountered logistical problems, but rejoiced in the delay since the Lees suffered a burglary in the interim (probably one of the plunderings about which Mary

Lee complained) and so needed the offering even more.[7]

Old comrades in arms also required Lee's attention. For example, Jubal Early sent his commanding general a manuscript of a military narrative to read and presumably endorse. Lee approved the piece in very guarded terms and advised Early to "omit all epithets or remarks calculated to excite bitterness or animosity between different sections of the Country." The closest Lee came to entering the several quarrels among his subordinates about who did or said what and when was a letter to the widow of Stonewall Jackson in which Lee attempted to correct errors in the manuscript of a biography of Jackson by R. L. Dabney.[8]

Thanks to the success of the trustees and professional fund-raisers, Washington College could afford to expand the faculty and extend the curriculum for the growing numbers of students that came to Lexington each fall to attend "General Lee's College." But Lee then had to make the inquiries and find good faculty members. In October 1866, for example, Lee wrote a professor at the University of Virginia to inquire about the facilities necessary to support a course in gymnastics and about "a proper teacher" to initiate the program. To the Reverend Churchill J. Gibson, he wrote to share his hopes for the chair of Mental and Moral Philosophy—"the occupant should not only be a man of true faith, learning and science but should be so thoroughly imbued with the Heavenly principles of the blessed gospel of Christ as to make his holy religion attractive to the young"—to thank Gibson for his nominations, and to make a modest contribution to the building fund of Gibson's church.[9]

Washington College, of course, also embarked upon a building program to expand physical facilities on the campus. Lee was much involved in both the design and construction of a new college boardinghouse, a new president's home, and especially the college chapel. The architect of the chapel, Thomas H. Williamson, who served on the faculty of VMI, wrote his daughter in October 1866, "I have been thrown a good deal with Genl. Lee lately—the building Committee of College got me to design the New Chapel . . . and I have made all the working drawings and written out the specifications, all of which I had to confer with the Genl and explain to him. He often stops at my lot and insists on coming over to help me." Lee also served on the vestry of Grace Church (Episcopal) in Lexington, and the parish pretty constantly had to assume some building or repair project. So Lee, the trained engineer, was often involved in projects beyond his "normal" duties as president of a small college.[10]

To some extent Lee used his numerous obligations and his relative isolation in Lexington to avoid involvement in postwar politics. But the rancor of Reconstruction sought Lee out, made of him more than ever a Southern symbol, and provoked him to private rhetoric only slightly less vitriolic than his wife's.

In January 1867 a groundswell began to develop to make Lee Governor of Virginia, and Richmond *Whig* editor Judge Robert Ould asked Lee to run:

"You are necessary to the state." But Lee feared that his candidacy "would be used by the dominant party to excite hostility toward the State. . . ." He declined.[11]

During the spring of 1867, Congress confronted the Reconstruction and confirmed that President Johnson's policies and actions had been too soft on the South. Accordingly, Congress passed two Reconstruction Acts and overrode the President's veto. These laws compelled former Confederate States to hold conventions to revise their constitutions in ways guaranteeing suffrage to all adult males, and to elect legislatures that would ratify the Fourteenth Amendment (guaranteeing civil rights to new freedmen and barring ex-Confederates from holding office). Only when the Southern states had done these things might Congress readmit them to the Union; until then they were not states, but portions of districts administered by the United States Army.

For nearly two years the states of the former Confederacy had had the opportunity to reconstruct themselves in accord with the policies of Presidents Lincoln and Johnson. As the Joint Committee on Reconstruction discovered, most white Southerners seemed to believe that Reconstruction meant resurrection, a return to status quo 1860. Prominent Confederate generals and political officials won election as governors, representatives, and senators. "Black Codes" abused the civil rights and status of freed persons in the guise of "vagrancy laws." Violence and intimidation enforced the will of the white majority over the aspirations of the black minority to become free in fact as well as in law.

Lee, like the vast majority of white Southerners, did not understand. But he did realize that white Southerners would have to obey the law, and so he counseled those who asked him to make the best of the situation, elect the best convention possible, and endorse the resultant constitution. To Robert Ould, for example, Lee wrote:

I think that all persons entitled to vote should attend the polls & endeavor to elect the best available men to represent them in the Convention, to whose decision everyone should submit. The preservation of harmony & kind feelings is of the utmost importance & all good citizens should exert themselves to secure it & to prevent the division of the people into parties.

He gave the same advice to R. I. Moses in Columbus, Georgia, to Dabney H. Maury in New Orleans, and to others. Lee did insist that his counsel be private and resented any repetition of his views in print. "It is extremely unpleasant to me," he wrote Ould, "for reasons which I think will occur to you, that my name should be unnecessarily brought before the public, and I do not see that any good can result from it. I hope therefore you will not publish my letter, but that you will try & allay the strife that I fear my arise in the State."[12]

Mary Lee felt less compunction to mince words. "What a farce all the proceedings of the Washington Congress are. We have almost ceased to read them. . . . I should think soon all *decent white* people would be forced to retire from that city & give place to the dominant race."[13]

Lexington, Virginia, did not exactly seethe with racial tension during this period. However, on March 22, 1867, five students of Washington College went out in search of a meeting of freedmen. One of the young men, J. A. McNeill, was attempting to peek through a window of the Freedmen's School House when a black man challenged him. Harsh words followed; McNeill drew a pistol and threatened the black man. Then McNeill and his companions left the scene.

The incident provoked a trial in the mayor's court which somehow McNeill eluded. Then the four students implicated in the disturbance had to appear before the college faculty. At this point McNeill also appeared and admitted that he had carried the pistol and acted alone in the altercation with the freedman. The faculty decided to dismiss McNeill from Washington College and to reprimand the other four students. There the matter concluded.[14]

Subsequently, however, Lee acted to forestall any repetition of the incident. Hearing that some students intended "to disturb a Public meeting of the coloured people of Lexington" in November 1869, Lee posted a notice warning all students of the college to "keep away from all such assemblies." Lee observed, "From past experience they [the students] may feel certain, that should any disturbance occur, efforts will be made to put the blame on Washington College."[15]

During the summer of 1867, the Lees made the rounds of now West Virginia spas. Convinced only that travel and a change of scene would help Mary Lee, Robert Lee was enthusiastic about these adventures because he genuinely enjoyed the social whirl at such mountain retreats. He indulged his fondness for young women, delighted in the gossip about belles and beaux, and enjoyed elegant living in the presumed pursuit of healthful waters and baths. At the "Old Sweet," however, Lee became quite ill. He described his debility to Markie as, "It seems to me if all the sickness I ever had in all my life was put together, it would not equal the attack I experienced." He recovered and returned to Lexington, but wrote to Rooney on September 20, "I am still so feeble that I cannot attend to the pressing business connected with the college."[16]

Good news cheered Lee in this sickness: Rooney was engaged to be married again. The bride was Mary Tabb Bolling, known as "Tabb" in the family. The sad news was that Tabb was from Petersburg, and the wedding would take place in the city Lee had left very hurriedly on April 2, 1865. Apparently Lee had serious doubts about returning to Petersburg; he delayed his arrangements, invited bride and groom to Lexington in lieu of his attending, but finally agreed to make the journey and accepted the invitation of William Mahone to be his guest.

As it happened, a summons from a Federal court took Lee to Richmond only a few days before Rooney and Tabb's wedding. The United States had released Jefferson Davis from imprisonment at Fort Monroe in May 1867, and now a grand jury in Richmond would decide whether to indict Davis, and if so, upon what charge. One strategy of the prosecution was to demonstrate that Davis had ordered his generals to make war on the United States and thus Davis was ultimately responsible for the American Civil War and the death and destruction that resulted. If this were so, then the government could try Davis for treason without having to try the millions of former Confederates who in some way supported the rebel cause.

Lee reached Richmond November 25 and some time that evening broke away from friends and well-wishers to visit with Jefferson Davis. Lee found the former President "astonishingly well, and . . . quite cheerful." On November 27, Lee appeared in court, perceived the thrust of the prosecution's case, and countered, "I am responsible for what I did, and I cannot now recall any important movement I made which I would not have made had I acted entirely on my own responsibility." Lee never had to testify again; the prosecution eventually dropped the case.[17]

In Petersburg on November 28 Lee had a wonderful time at the wedding. He wrote his wife (unable to attend) before breakfast the next morning, "Our son was married last night & shone in his happiness. The Bride looked lovely, & was in every way captivating." Evidently, after the wedding, there must have been quite some party. "I believe the plan was for the Bride & Groom to start on their travels this morg., but I doubt whether it will be carried out, as I thought I saw indications of change & purpose before I left, which I had no doubt would be strengthened by the reflections of this morg.," Lee explained. He himself decided to remain in Petersburg another day, before returning to Richmond for more visits and then home to Lexington on December 7. Lee had a very good time and told Rooney, "My old feelings returned to me, as I passed well-remembered spots and recalled the ravages of the hostile shells. But when I saw the cheerfulness with which the people were working to restore their condition, and witnessed the comforts with which they were surrounded, a load of sorrow which had been pressing upon me for years was lifted from my heart."[18]

The year 1868 was especially difficult at Washington College. Lee established a symbolic tone when he wrote Markie on New Year's Day, "My interest in time & its concerns is daily fading away & I try to keep my eyes & thoughts trained on those eternal shores to which I am fast hastening." A series of what should have been non-events seemed to call embarrassing attention to the college at the worst of all possible times.[19]

The process began with a young man named Erastus C. Johnston. He came to Lexington initially in 1865 about the same time as Lee as a member of the American Missionary Association. A former Union soldier committed to educating the new freedmen, Johnston helped start some freedmen's schools and made friends within the African American community in Lexington. Then he opened a store in a rented building and lived on the premises. On February 4, 1868, Johnston took advantage of the cold weather and went ice skating on the North River. He soon sensed that he was unwelcome among the other skaters and skated downriver. About a mile downstream Johnston encountered a group of boys and young men, some of whom were students at Washington College. As he skated past them, they called him names and threatened him; then he reached a dam, rested briefly, and began to skate back upstream, past the crowd that had taunted him.

Again the men and boys on the ice harassed Johnston as he skated among them. A twelve-year-old lad skated very near and called Johnston "a son of a bitch." This was the last straw. In a rage Johnston grabbed his tormentor, pulled a pistol, and promised to shoot the lad if he ever called him that name again.

Then the other men and boys on the scene began to abuse Johnston quite seriously. They tripped him as he attempted to skate away and threw sticks, ice, and snowballs at him. All the while they called him a "damned Yankee," threatened to tar and feather him, and gave him ten days to leave Lexington or they would kill him.

Eventually Johnston was able to scramble out of the riverbed and escape the crowd. He returned to his store and dressed his cuts, scrapes, and bruises. But that night, about 11:00 P.M., some men came to Johnston's store, beat upon the door and shutters, and yelled, "Come out here you damned Yankee son of a bitch! We want to kill you!"[20]

The next day Johnston complained to Lexington Mayor J. M. Ruff, who asked for specific charges against named individuals. Johnston believed that all of his tormentors were students at Washington College and that Ruff was part of a conspiracy to protect the college. So Johnston took his complaint to the officers of the United States Army involved in the administration of Military District number one. In time two general officers investigated Johnston's complaint and in the process spoke to Lee about the incident. Lee conducted his own investigation, discovered that three students at the college had been involved, and either dismissed or allowed them to withdraw from the school. There the matter should have concluded.[21]

Johnston, however, was far from satisfied. He did leave Lexington, moved to Covington, Virginia, and then began to write letters to newspapers in the North. The *New York Independent* printed Johnston's description of life in Lexington, and Johnston's piece began other accounts and opinions about "General Lee's College." A schoolteacher named Julia Anne Shearman complained about being insulted in Lexington—"Never did I walk the streets of Lexington without rudeness in one form or another." Shearman complained especially about "the boys of the aristocratic school of the place," and wrote, "From one set of students, whose boarding-house I was compelled constantly to pass, I habitually received the polite salutation of 'damned Yankee bitch of a nigger teacher,' with the occasional addition of an admonition to take up my abode in the infernal regions."

Various pundits took up the incident and by extension Lee's leadership at Washington College. One editorial in the *New York Independent* railed:

We do not think that a man who broke his solemn oath of allegiance to the United States, who imbued his hands in the blood of tens of thousands of his country's noblest men, for the purpose of perpetuating human slavery, and who was largely responsible for the cruelties and horrors of Libby, Salisbury and Andersonville, is fitted to be a teacher of young men.

Individuals like William Lloyd Garrison, Charles Sumner, Wendell Phillips, John Bright, and Neal Dow, and newspapers including the Yale *Courant,* the *New York Tribune,* the Boston *Transcript,* the Philadelphia *Press,* and the Louisville *Journal* at one time or another criticized Lee and Washington College.[22]

Most unfortunately for the college, the furor over Johnston and attendant public comment coincided with a major fund-raising effort on behalf of Washington College in New York City. Lee attempted to defend the institution. "I think it useless," he wrote to answer one inquiry, "to deny the assertion of the Chicago *Tribune* that Washington College is 'run principally for the propagation of hatred to the Union' for I think no one can honestly believe it." Lee informed another correspondent, "No student has ever been dismissed from Washington College on account of his political opinions." In each case Lee referred critics and friends alike to a letter published in the *New York Tribune* on April 20, 1868, in which an Army officer offered a balanced narrative of the Johnston incident.[23]

Repercussions of the incident had only begun to fade when another potentially explosive event involving students at Washington College occurred. Francis H. Brockenbrough, young son of the judge and rector of the college, on May 8, 1868, became embroiled in a fight with a young black man named Caesar Griffin. The fight concluded when Griffin shot Brockenbrough, wounding him seriously. Brockenbrough was too young to be a student at Washington College; but two of his brothers were students, and his father was of course closely associated with the school. So the students sought out and captured Griffin. They marched the black man to the courthouse with a rope around his neck and seemed intent upon acting out vigilante justice then and there. Several officers of the town and members of the faculty of the college tried in vain to calm the crowd. One witness remembered, "Just then General Lee appeared. Immediately the tumult was hushed, and the General, standing in the midst of the excited throng simply said: 'Young gentlemen, let the law take its course.'" Lee's command restored order and probably saved Griffin's life.

Meanwhile young Brockenbrough seemed on the verge of death, and rumor spread that the young man's death would become a signal for the students to storm the jail, remove Griffin from custody, and kill him. Again Lee acted to forestall violence, and again he was successful. Brockenbrough recovered; Griffin, after some questionable legal maneuvers, served two years in the penitentiary.[24]

Military rule in the South and recriminations rising from the recent war continued to vex Lee. Simon Cameron, first Secretary of War in the Abraham Lincoln administration, said on the floor of the Senate that Lee lied to a friend of Cameron's about his intentions in the secession crisis, accepted command of the United States Army, and then deserted to the Confederacy. Lee felt obliged to write his friend, Maryland Senator Reverdy Johnson, and explain what he in fact had done. The trial of Jefferson Davis continued to come and go from the court docket in Richmond; Lee made an abortive trip to court in June 1868. Davis's possible trial and the indictment against Lee for treason remained factors in Lee's life until the general amnesty of Christmas Day 1868, and the formal abandonment of the indictment for treason on February 15, 1869. Lee had to spend time and energy, but he was able to recover Smith Island for the Custis estate. Rooney and Robert bought the island from the estate for $9,000 and soon sold it at a significant profit ($16,000). In January 1869, one of Lee's students became involved in an altercation with a black man in Lexington, shot and wounded the African American, and then disappeared. Lee and the faculty voted to dismiss the student from Washington College.[25]

During the summer of 1868 Lee again took himself and his family to the mountain springs and spas. At White Sulphur Springs, Lee received letters and entreaties to organize a "Southern" statement from William T. Rosecrans, who wanted something he and his managers might use to aid the Democrats in the elections of 1868. Lee did invite some of his friends and associates to "the White" and made it possible for Rosecrans to speak to them. The result was something called "the White Sulphur paper," and the signatories included Lee, P. G. T. Beauregard, Alexander H. Stephens, and other luminaries.

The paper confirmed that "African slavery" and "the right of a state to secede from the Union" were casualties of the recent war. The authors then asserted: "At the close of the war, the Southern people laid down their arms and sought to resume their former relations to the Government of the United States," and yet "their rights under the Constitution are withheld from them. . . ." Then the statement confronted the core of the problem of Reconstruction—race, "The idea that the Southern people are hostile to the negroes, and would oppress them, if it were in their power to do so." There followed assertions that Southern white people both knew and needed Southern black people and vice versa. "But for influences exerted to stir up the passions of the negroes," the statement continued, "the relations of the two races would soon adjust themselves on a basis of mutual kindness and advantage."

The White Sulphur paper affirmed: "It is true that the people of the South in common with a large majority of the people of the North and West, are, for obvious reasons, inflexibly opposed to any system of laws which would place the political power of the country in the hands of the negro race." Those "obvious reasons" included the conviction that "at present, the negroes have neither the intelligence nor the other qualifications which are necessary to make them safe depositories of political power."

Having consigned African Americans to some subcitizen class, the paper said little else. "The great want of the South is peace," the authors observed. But of course they meant "peace" to restore white conservatives to power in the South, and Lee believed all this. He had been speaking and writing these racial assumptions for years, and Lee the Federalist/Whig had always assumed that the only legitimate government was government by the rich, the well-born, and the able.[26]

The statement composed at White Sulphur Springs in August 1868 may have afforded its authors the satisfaction of expressing their feelings in words and in public. It did not much help the Democratic Party in the national elections that fall. Ulysses S. Grant and Schuyler Colfax carried the election for President and Vice President, and the Republicans retained their control of Congress. So Lee continued to despair for the Union as it had once been and as he believed it should be again. To his twenty-seven-year-old cousin Annette Carter, Lee wrote in March 1868, "I grieve for posterity, for American principles & American liberty. Our boasted self Govt. is fast becoming the jeer & laughing stock of the world."[27]

But these words were not the words people remembered when they recalled Lee after the war. They remembered his Amnesty Oath, his statement about the attitude of Southern people to the Joint Committee on Reconstruction—"They think that the north can afford to be generous"—his advice to "omit all epithets or remarks calculated to excite bitterness or animosity between different sections of the Country," his counsel to fulfill the requirements of the Reconstruction Acts, his determination to remain aloof from politics, to avoid any public presence, and the pronouncement from White Sulphur Springs, "The great want of the South is peace." People who knew him thought of Lee as a suffering saint, the person large enough to rise above human sectional response.

When Lee responded to an invitation to the White House to visit President Grant on May 1, 1869, the conversation was perfunctory, the occasion brief. The sort of story people liked to tell about Lee post bellum involved not a dreary president, but guests from the North in a glittering ballroom at White Sulphur Springs.[28]

During the summer of 1868 some young people from the North appeared at "the White" and found a frosty reception from the Southerners who dominated life and society among the guests. Lee inquired about the aliens, suggested that his young friends welcome them, but encountered reluctance and refusal from the Southerners to whom he spoke. So Lee said to the young women and men who surrounded him, "I have tried in vain to find any lady who has made acquaintance with the party and is able to present me. I shall now introduce myself, and shall be glad to present any of you who will accompany me."

A young woman named Christina Bond responded, "I will go, General Lee, under your orders."

"Not under my orders," Lee protested, "but it will gratify me deeply to have your assistance." Bond recalled:

And so we crossed the great room, but under the brilliant crystal chandelier he paused, and spoke words which went to the soul of his young hearers. He told of the grief with which he found a spirit of unreasoning resentment and bitterness in the young people of the South, of the sinfulness of hatred and social revenge, of the duty of kindness, helpfulness, and consideration of others.

Then the young woman asked, "But, General Lee, did you never feel resentment towards the North?" Christina Bond's story continued:

Standing in the radiance of the myriad lighted crystals his face took on a far-away, almost inspired look, as his hand involuntarily sought his breast. He spoke in low, earnest tones: "I believe I may say, looking into my own heart, and speaking as in the presence of my God, that I have never known one moment of bitterness or resentment."[29]

Lee had become a Christ figure for Southerners. "Blessed are ye when men shall revile you and persecute you and shall say all manner of evil against you. . . ." "Love your enemies, bless them that curse you, do good to them that hate you. . . ."

Lee was a realist. The war was over: he had lost. He did not understand the dimensions of race or the zeal of Northern politicians; but he realized that victors can impose their will upon the vanquished. So he worked within a legal framework that shifted, and he settled in the knowledge that the opportunity for resistance was long gone.

Perhaps the most characteristic act in Lee's response to peace was not crossing a ballroom to try to make his former enemies welcome. It may instead have been his reply to an invitation from the Gettysburg Battlefield Memorial Association to join other officers who fought at Gettysburg to mark on the ground with "enduring memorials of granite the position and movement of the Armies in the field." Lee pled prior commitments and said he would not be able to contribute anything of consequence to the project anyway.

Then he added: "I think it wiser moreover not to keep open the sores of war, but to follow the example of those nations who endeavored to obliterate the marks of civil strife and to commit to oblivion the feelings it engendered."[30]

31

"We Have But One Rule Here"

ENRY S. PLATT was a long way from home and in very deep trouble. He had come to Washington College from St. Louis in 1867 and fallen into some very bad habits. Platt lived and boarded with the family of the Reverend William Nelson Pendleton. But Platt was a Roman Catholic and so attended no church in town, since Roman Catholics were quite few and had no church in the vicinity. Platt might have escaped censure in an academic community out of respect for his religious convictions, but for two circumstances. First, Pendleton had seen a letter from Platt's father instructing his son to attend church, in effect giving the young man dispensation. And second, Platt spent most of his time on Sundays playing cards, something he was of course free to do, but which had the effect of antagonizing the evangelical Pendleton and scandalizing the good Presbyterians who were much in the majority in Lexington.

At the Pendleton table, Platt's manners were "often indecorous"; his language in the house was "shockingly profane" and around the servants "disgustingly obscene." He had also broken glass and defaced walls in the Pendleton home and borrowed money from Pendleton that he had not repaid. Finally, Pendleton informed Platt that he would have to find some other place to live and eat. But Platt was very contrite and promised to mend his ways, if only Pendleton would allow him to remain. So Pendleton took pity on the young man and agreed to give him another chance.

Although he was evidently quite bright, Platt encountered difficulties in his classes as well as at the Pendletons' home. Platt's name appeared on the list of students at Washington College President Robert E. Lee wanted to see in his office in November. Lee had carefully read the reports of the faculty about their students during the month of October 1867. He noticed that Platt was performing poorly and that he had missed an alarming number of classes. Lee had a brief visit with the young man, impressed upon him the necessity of regular attendance, and secured from Platt a promise to attend more faithfully. Lee also wrote to Platt's father expressing concern for the student.

Platt's record improved in November, and Lee again wrote to the young man's father to give him the good news. But Platt was still missing too many classes—eighteen during November—"I have again impressed upon him this necessity, & again he promises amendment. . . ."

In January 1868, the Reverend Pendleton lost all patience with Platt and wrote to Lee that the youth was "too depraved and lost to principle to leave any hope of benefit to him, while to others there is danger of mischief, from his staying longer with me."

Lee then persuaded Adolphus White to take Platt into his home and "watch over him." The faculty of the college reviewed Platt's conduct at the conclusion of the semester, noted that his performance on his examinations demonstrated that "he could acquit himself well if he chose," and resolved to issue a stern warning. On February 11, the secretary of the college sent a formal notice to Platt's father, requesting him to aid in producing in Platt "an immediate and radical change in his attendance and industry or application to studies."

Meanwhile, on February 4, Henry Platt went ice skating on the North River with some other college students. He was one of the gang of students and local boys that harassed Erastus C. Johnston. Indeed, a sheet of notes about students suspected of taking part in the attack on Johnston, apparently in Lee's handwriting, indicates that Platt "acknowledges to have struck Mr. Johnston on the ice." And beside Platt's name on the sheet is a bold X.

So Lee on February 13 wrote again to Platt's father in St. Louis with the sad news that "it is necessary for you to withdraw your son from Washington College." Lee rehearsed some of the background in Platt's abortive career in Lexington, then stated: "He has since however been presented to the Comm'r of this Sub-district, Genl Wilcox, for having been engaged on the 4th Inst: with others in an attack upon a resident of the town, & finding that such was the case, I have concluded that it is necessary for him to leave College." Because Lee was afraid that "it might not be prudent for him to travel alone [from Lexington to St. Louis] & that besides you might wish to place him at some other school," the president decided to "keep him at his studies until I hear from you. . . ."

In St. Louis, J. M. Platt was confused. He received the letter from the secretary of the college on February 17 and immediately wrote to young Henry, enclosing the letter from the faculty, and "commanding him to at once and without delay" to make an appointment to see Lee and with him to arrange to appear before the faculty and "make apology for past conduct with a positive promise to immediately amend his deportment." Then three days later, on February 20, Platt received Lee's letter informing him that his son would have to withdraw from Washington College. The elder Platt missed the significance of what Lee had done for his son in the Johnston incident with General Wilcox; he felt betrayed that the college had asked his son to reform and then only three days later decided that he would have to leave. So Platt wrote Lee a plaintive letter requesting "a further opportunity [for Henry] to prove himself as improved in his conduct as we would wish. . . ." Young Platt's mother had received a letter from a friend in Lexington stating that her son "was not altogether to blame for what occurred" at the Pendletons. Platt proposed that the month of March "will show the Faculty, yourself & Genl Wilxon [Wilcox] that he has changed. . . ." And until Platt had a response to this proposal from Lee, he would "make no further preparations for his return home."

Lee received J. M. Platt's letter on February 27 and was caught in a quandary. He had acted in such a way as to be able to present General Wilcox with a fait accompli: yes, some students were involved in the Johnston affair; we have identified them and dismissed them; you need not bring civil charges against them, as they have already been punished. Now he had on his hands an angry parent and Henry Platt.

Lee resolved his quandary by writing once more to the senior Platt and explaining more clearly what had happened—"It was therefore a question whether he should be dealt with by the Military or College authorities & for reasons that will be obvious to you the Faculty took the matter into consideration." Lee also found someone in Lexington about to take a trip to St. Louis and willing to escort young Platt. So the president lent Platt $50 to pay for his trip and sent him on his way. W. G. Clark, the escort, delivered his charge and assured Lee that the elder Platt was "still the warm friend of yours." J. M. Platt repaid the $50 and thanked Lee profusely. Lee acknowledged the payment, expressing the hope that "while enjoying the society of his parents & the pleasures of home, your son will feel the importance of improving his time & apply himself diligently to his studies." Lee also assured the Platts that he thought the faculty would readmit Henry the following September if he wished to return to Washington College.[1]

Most students and parents of students while Lee was president of Washington College did not communicate with the president as much as the Platts. But President Lee was very much an *in loco* parent to his "boys," and he took seriously the reports of faculty members about student performance for each month. Lee invited troubled or troublesome students to come to his office to talk with him about their classes or conduct. He worked hard at learning the name of each student and speaking to them as he and they went about their errands on campus and in town.[2]

Lee wrote to students' parents to enlist their aid in reforming bad habits. And he received letters from parents requesting all manner of attention to the perceived needs of their sons. One mother, for example, asked Lee to reverse the decision of the faculty and allow her son to attend Washington College for another year. She had heard that her son was paying much attention to Miss Sallie Payne, most likely to the detriment of his studies, and wanted Lee to investigate the woman. "Who is the young lady, Genl? I should like to know something of her family. . . . I cannot conceive of any greater misfortune to my Son, than that of marriage when so young, without any means independent of me, and at present no business qualifications." When Lee had done these things, the woman wanted him to tell her whether her son should continue working in a drugstore or go to college for another year.[3]

On at least one occasion Lee received a request from a general in the United States Army to compel a student to pay a debt owed to a freedman for washing clothes. This far Lee's role as *in loco* parent did not extend. He responded, "I presume that he [the student] is amenable to the ordinary legal processes for the collection of debts. I am not aware of any authority vested in me, as President of the College, to enforce the collection of a debt of this character, but would be glad to have it pointed out to me. It is not the wish of the Faculty that any student should evade a just debt."[4]

In addition to learning the names of as many students as he could and summoning slackers and miscreants to his office, Lee tried to have a few students to tea in his home each day. In later life the "Lee alumni" of Washington College treasured any and all contact they had with Lee during the period when they attended the school. But try as he might to frame structured occasions with students, Lee was still the shy, controlled person he had ever been. Consequently students and others perceived him as aloof, more an eminence or presence than a person. One former student said, "He seemed to avoid contact with men. . . ." A member of the faculty asked if he were "intimate" with Lee. "No, sir, no man was great enough to be *intimate* with General Lee." Many of the students could insist that Lee was a great man; very few were able to offer specific instances of Lee's greatness.[5]

Yet examples of Lee at work with students and faculty members reveal him to have been a remarkable educator. Lee's administration of Washington College was in many ways the antithesis of his superintendence of West Point. Indeed, Lee once said, "The great mistake of my life was taking a military education." On occasions when Lee and General Francis Smith, Superintendent of VMI, marched together in some joint exercise, Lee consistently marched out of step. A faculty member recalled, "He simply walked along in a natural manner, but although this manner appeared so natural, it seemed to me that he consciously avoided keeping step, so uniformly did he fail to plant his foot simultaneously with General Smith or at the beat of the drum."[6]

Lee began his career as college president by revoking the regulation requiring compulsory attendance at chapel. Yet he himself attended chapel every day. He wanted the students to attend because they wished to attend, as he did, not because they had to.[7]

A member of the faculty once quoted some rule from the college by-laws; another faculty member pronounced the rule a dead letter. Lee promptly announced, "Then let it be repealed. A dead letter inspires disrespect for the whole body of laws."

When a professor offered precedent in a matter before the faculty and said, "We must not respect persons," Lee injected, "In dealing with young men I always respect persons, and care little for precedent." Nevertheless, Lee insisted upon clear, firm evidence of offense before he resorted to discipline. At a faculty meeting many voices spoke to the reputation of one student for frequenting bars and becoming habitually drunk. The consensus seemed to favor expelling the young man. Lee then asked if any one person had actually seen the student intoxicated or had actually seen him in a bar. No one had, and Lee then said, "We must be very careful how we are influenced by hearsay. During the war at a time when my physical and mental strain was intense, I was reported to the executive as being habitually intoxicated and unfit for the discharge of my duties." Whether this in fact happened is not important; Lee had made his point and kept the student in school. In the course of a conversation with a rather zealous professor, Lee offered some advice. "Well, sir, always observe the stage driver's rule," he said. "What is that General?" the professor inquired, and Lee said, "Always take care of the *poor* horses." Another Lee maxim was, "As a general principle you should not *force* young men to do their duty, but let them do it voluntarily and thereby develop their characters."[8]

A new student once asked President Lee for a copy of the rules of Washington College. Lee replied, "Young gentleman, we have no printed rules. We have but one rule here, and it is that every student must be a gentleman."[9]

What did Lee mean when he used the word "gentleman"? Found among his papers after his death was the following statement:

. . . the manner is which an individual enjoys certain advantages over others is the test of a *true gentleman*.

The power which the strong have over the weak, the magistrate over the citizen, the employer over the employed, the educated over the unlettered, the experienced over the confiding, even the clever over the silly—the forbearing or inoffensive use of all this power or authority, or a total absence from it when the case admits it, will show the gentleman in plain light. The gentleman does not needlessly or unnecessarily remind an offender of a wrong he may have committed against him. He can not only forgive, he can forget; and he strives for that nobleness of self and mildness of character which impart sufficient strength to let the past be the past.

A true gentleman of honor feels humbled himself when he cannot help humbling others.

A very interesting statement, this; certainly it reveals Lee's convictions about ethics and relationships. But it may reveal more beside. Substitute *"God"* for *"true gentleman"* and Lee has offered an intriguing theological insight. The series of metaphors remains valid, and Lee says what he believes about the nature of God. God, for Lee, is the ultimate manifestation of the "forbearing or inoffensive use of all this power or authority." God, in Lee's understanding, "can not only forgive, he can forget," and if God does not wish to humble people, it follows that God is on the side of exalting them. In this light Lee's statement about the true gentleman is not only code, but credo.[10]

Lee's one-rule standard produced the honor system, which soon became the practical definition of a "gentleman" at Washington College. A gentleman does not lie, cheat, or steal; nor does a gentleman tolerate lying, cheating, or dishonesty in those persons claiming to be gentlemen. The honor system assumes that students enter a form of social contract among themselves and resolve that they will uphold the system. It is an elitist system that depends upon a relatively small, homogeneous student population. But of course in

Lee's time Washington College had a relatively small, homogeneous, generally elite body of students.[11]

In November 1867, an anxious parent wrote to Lee about his son's conduct as a student at the college. The parent stated, "I hope he will be treated by the Faculty, as a *Boy* and not as a man."[12]

During Lee's tenure at Washington College students seem to have been both boys and men. Lee called his students "my boys" and in many ways treated them as children. Certainly his appointments with students in difficult circumstances, academic or otherwise, and his correspondence with parents acted out a conviction that students were boys in need of supervision and constant guidance. And Lee also had a set of admonitions on various topics that served as something very similar to a list of rules. Although he opposed sects and narrow denominationalism and abolished compulsory chapel, Lee made plain his favor toward Christians. "If I could only know that all the young men in college were good Christians I should have nothing more to desire," he proclaimed. Lee also was adamant about effort and a proponent of the work ethic. Of a student in search of the nineteenth-century equivalent of "the gentleman's 'C,' " Lee once said, "He is a very quiet, orderly young man, but seems very careful not to injure the health of his father's son. Now, I do not want our young men really to injure their health, but I wish them to come as near to it as possible." About alcohol, too, Lee could be rigid. He wrote to the "Friends of Temperance" at Washington College, "My experience through life has convinced me that, while moderation and temperance in all things are commendable and beneficial, abstinence from spirituous liquor is the best safeguard of morals and health." Such statements on Lee's part seem grounded in the assumption that his students were very much boys.[13]

But the thrust of Lee's regime at Washington College was to treat the students as much as possible as responsible adults. The case of Henry S. Platt provides a good example: Lee spent much time and energy attempting to let Platt discover for himself that attending classes regularly was a good idea and that behaving in some accord with the expectations of the family that owned and operated his boardinghouse might make his life less complicated.

Further evidence of Lee's commitment to ideas about education perhaps best characterized as "progressive" or enlightened comes from Lee's work within a committee of the Educational Society of Virginia. In 1867, the Society intended to prepare an address or statement of principles for the public, embracing several topics at all levels of education, from primary through postsecondary schools.

Lee served with General Smith of VMI and Professor S. Maupin of the University of Virginia on the subcommittee charged with treating "discipline," and he wrote out a draft of his thoughts for the benefit of the other members. His emphasis was upon parents and teachers as examples for the students, and the inculcation of virtues such as obedience, reverence, and truthfulness as habits. Telling the truth, for example, Lee believed was natural to children and only required reinforcement to become an all but automatic response.[14]

Lee also served on the subcommittee dealing with "instruction" and more general matters with R. L. Dabney and Professor J. B. Minor of the University of Virginia. Lee prepared his draft in January 1867 and began by defining education as broadly as possible. "Education embraces the physical, moral and intellectual instruction of a child from infancy to manhood," Lee wrote, and continued, "Any system is imperfect which does not combine them all. . . ." In accord with his belief in some form of evolution, Lee lauded an educational system that "abases the coarse animal emotions of human nature & exalts the higher faculties and feelings." To secure obedience, Lee posed, "Neither violence nor harshness should ever be used, and the parent must bear constantly in mind, that to govern his child, he must show him that he can control himself." By "patient kindness and gentle admonition," Lee believed, parents can accomplish far more than by resorting to threats and punishment.

Lee also believed that children should leave home and parents once they attained the age at which they could support themselves. Otherwise, if children continued to live with their parents, Lee wrote, "This encourages them in injurious idleness & destroys that spirit of self dependence which is necessary for their advancement in life, and causes them to appear so unreasonable as to depend upon them [parents], after having arrived at the age of being able to think and act for themselves." Lee wrote similar thoughts at other times, and they constituted rare instances of criticism directed toward his own children, however indirectly.

"The choice of profession," Lee wrote in this same draft, "is not of so much consequence as the manner in which it is pursued." If a person possesses "the habits of self control and self denial," then "diligence and integrity" will yield prosperity, and fame and success will attend a business in which "the generality of mankind are interested." These sentiments about education really reveal a great deal of what Lee believed about life. They are mild variants of the "essays" he wrote on blank pages of the diary he kept during the late 1850s and 1860s, and so indicate that Lee must have thought a lot about child rearing, moral training, and education. And he had been developing these ideas for at least the past decade.[15]

Blessed with Lee's name and active leadership, Washington College grew and prospered. Never did the trustees collect as many or as large amounts of donations to the college as they wished; yet given the volatility of the times, the record of contributions secured for the college was enviable. On the eve of the Civil War, Washington College had eighty-three students and five faculty members, one of whom was the president. During Lee's tenure as president, the number of students quadrupled and the faculty increased more than threefold. As one veteran faculty member asserted, "He found it a college, and left it a university. . . ."[16]

Washington College could eventually become a university in the twentieth-century sense because of the significant alterations made in the curriculum during the Lee administration. Before the war, the college had been one of many "classical" schools in the South and the nation. Lee honored this heritage and insisted that his alterations would not erase the commitment to Latin, Greek, and classical literature, the canon of the nineteenth century. Lee knew, however, that many veterans of his army were stomping across barren fields screaming Latin mottoes at mules. He wanted to blend the practical nature of an engineering course at West Point with the enlightened aesthetic of Ovid.[17]

Lee began by introducing elective courses in the place of the lockstep rigidity of the old classical curriculum. Soon he applied for Morrill Act land grant money to establish five new professorships, most of them in science and technology. When he failed to secure funding through the Virginia General Assembly, Lee went to the board of trustees and got what he wanted.

What Lee eventually secured was a number of "schools"—the approximate equivalents in most cases of departments in modern universities. These schools included Latin, Greek, modern languages (French, German, Spanish, and Italian), English, history and literature, moral philosophy, mathematics, natural philosophy, natural history, chemistry, and law and equity. Lee projected schools of commerce and agriculture as well, and recruited students with scholarship aid for a school of journalism. He began a public service program by contracting with Jed Hotchkiss (formerly Stonewall Jackson's topographer) to produce maps of nearby counties. The school of law and equity was John W. Brockenbrough's law school incorporated into Washington College. Lee also began a summer school to supplement and eventually replace the "preparatory class," a remedial course for students unprepared to work at the college level. Finally, Lee had aspirations for a school of astronomy with a telescope, and thoughts about starting a medical school.

Naturally, Lee's innovations attracted negative comment as change usually does. Some of the most negative came from Francis Smith "next door" at VMI, who considered Lee's alterations mere fads and "twaddle." How much Lee inspired these developments and how many of them originated with members of the faculty remain unanswered questions. However, Lee certainly endorsed each projected change and pled each new cause before the board of trustees. And Lee was responsible for hiring the faculty members and encouraging them to think and plan boldly about the future of the college.[18]

All the while Lee carried out his duties as president, including the tradition of attending oral examinations, he was himself attempting to be some sort of scholar. He spent significant time trying to assemble sufficient material to write his history of the campaigns in Virginia during the late war. He despaired of the project, though, when much of the material he needed for his history proved unavailable.[19]

Lee did produce a new edition of his father's *Memoirs of the War in the Southern Department of the United States,* part of his ongoing effort to know his father. If Lee came to terms with Light Horse Harry Lee when he composed the biographical sketch that introduces the new edition, he kept it to himself; the sixty-eight pages of biographical sketch are pretty pedestrian and quite uncritical. Lee repeated all the old myths that obscured his father's shortcomings. "In the year 1811 he removed with his family to Alexandria for the purpose of educating his children," Lee wrote, saying nothing of his father's time in jail for debt or of the fact that his father's oldest son (Henry) had reached the age at which he owned Stratford Hall, or that Light Horse's wife refused to live at Stratford any longer. Lee the son wrote down filiopietism in the stilted, formal prose he thought correct and proper for such a tome. He appended his father's letters from the West Indies to his older brother (Carter) and assigned the proceeds of the book to Carter. Lee completed his editorial chores in June 1869 and saw the published results later that same year.[20]

Lee's years at Washington College marked what in reality was his third career. He had spent seventeen years after he graduated from West Point working as an engineer, and as his efforts at St. Louis displayed, Lee was a very good engineer. From his journey to Mexico and his participation in the Mexican War, Lee was very much a soldier for the next seventeen years of his life. Then in 1865 he became an educator. Yet Lee still identified himself as a soldier.

One of Lee's students who later became an instructor at Washington College came first to the school in 1860 and returned in 1866 after four years in the Army of Northern Virginia. Milton W. Humphreys resumed his academic career with zeal—so much zeal that he injured his health. President Lee noticed that Humphreys was working too hard and told him so. Humphreys acknowledged that he was indeed studying more than was good for his body and explained, "I am so impatient to make up for the time I lost in the army." Then Lee turned immediately red and interrupted the student-veteran, "Mr. Humphreys! However long you live and whatever you accomplish, you will find that the time you spent in the Confederate army was the most profitably spent portion of your life. Never again speak of having lost time in the army."[21] Robert Lee passionately believed this. Milton Humphreys may or may not have believed it. But Humphreys never again spoke of losing time in Lee's army.

32

"I Will Give That Sum"

T HE NEW PRESIDENT'S HOUSE at Washington College was very much Robert Lee's house, although he did not own it; the design originated in a "pattern book," and Lee lived there little more than sixteen months. The Lees moved next door from the old President's House in June of 1869. The new two-story home was architecturally undistinguished, a box with additions and extensions; yet it bore the impress of Robert Lee's influence. The porch that wrapped around the three sides of the first floor was inviting and enabled Mary Lee to roll in her wheelchair from her first-floor bedroom onto the porch and outdoors. Although they never gathered there during Lee's lifetime, Lee's immediate family all fit in the new house. An attached stable placed Lee and Traveller under the same roof with room in the second stall for Lucy Long, Lee's mare, a gift from J. E. B. Stuart, lost to Lee in the chaos of his retreat and surrender and then restored to him in December 1866. Among the outbuildings was a "cow house," a greenhouse, and even a "cat house" for Mildred's feline friends.

The engineering within the house was state-of-the-art. A furnace and air ducts warmed the place in winter, and pumps raised water from two huge cisterns to a tank in the attic and then via pipes and gravity throughout the house. Lee's favorite space was within a deep window of the dining room. He sat and napped there after dinner and from his chair he enjoyed views of the college and surrounding mountains. The new house cost $15,000, no small sum for the small college to spend; but the home and increases in Lee's salary (100 percent from his first year to the second) were the trustees' ways of expressing their appreciation of Lee's efforts and influence in their behalf. Lee's income from salary and percentage of student tuition for the academic year 1866–67 was $4,756.[1]

After just over a month at the new home in Lexington, Mary and Robert Lee went in July 1869 to Rockbridge Baths, where Mary Lee spent the summer. But soon after their arrival, Lee learned bad news: his brother Smith Lee had died unexpectedly; he would have to go to northern Virginia. When Lee reached Alexandria on July 24, he learned that Smith's funeral had occurred the day before. Nevertheless he remained in the area, visited with nephew Fitz Lee and aunt Anna Maria Fitzhugh at Ravensworth. There Lee recalled Ann Carter Lee and said, "Forty years ago I stood in this room by my mother's death-bed! It seems now but yesterday!"[2]

From Ravensworth Lee decided to travel to White House to visit his son Rooney, his daughter-in-law Tabb, and his infant grandson Robert Edward Lee, III, born in February 1869. On Sunday, July 30, the family, plus Rob from Romancoke, attended St. Peter's Church nearby where Martha and George Washington had married. Tabb and Rooney took advantage of the opportunity to have their young child baptized so that Grandfather Lee might participate as godfather in the service. Then Lee escorted mother and son to Rockbridge Baths and went from there with Agnes and Mildred to White Sulphur Springs. He remained at "the White" until the end of August, when he returned to Lexington to prepare for another academic year.[3]

Frank Buchser arrived in Lexington in late September 1869, wearing flowing clothes, a bright neckerchief, a goatee, and a long, waxed mustache. Buchser was forty-one, a Swiss native and a painter. He had been in the United States since 1866, having been commissioned by Swiss liberals to "paint the Union victory in the American Civil War." Buchser first left his homeland after a piano builder in Berne caught Buchser in bed with his daughter. He studied art in Paris and Rome, traveled widely, and returned to Switzerland. A tavern brawl in which Buchser injured a man and confronted prison for it impelled the artist to seek the commission to go to the United States. Thus far in America, Buchser had traveled and painted extensively in the West but had come no closer to executing his commission than doing a portrait of William T. Sherman. He hoped to paint both Lee and Ulysses S. Grant to fulfill his obligation, hence the trip to Lexington.

For reasons difficult to understand Lee seemed to like Buchser, agreed to sit for a portrait, and invited the artist to stay in the President's House while he worked. Buchser wanted Lee to wear his uniform; but Lee refused—"I am a soldier no longer." Instead, Lee posed in the black suit he had purchased for Rooney's wedding; he did agree to display his sword and uniform on a table, however. Buchser worked for three weeks as Lee's schedule permitted, and as the artist worked, he asked questions about the war he had not seen but was supposed to paint. Lee eventually spoke with feeling to Buchser's queries. By the time Buchser completed his portrait—only the third ever done of Lee from life—he had become a committed Confederate and a consummate admirer of Robert E. Lee.

The portrait, celebrated with a party at the President's House on October 18, 1869, is like neither of the others. The face is ruddy to the point of flush, and he appears engaged and alert, as opposed to posed. Lee seemed to have approved of Buchser's effort; the portrait made him look younger and much more alive.

Buchser shipped the painting to his patrons in Switzerland along with glowing words about the subject. In fact, Buchser tried to convince his patrons that his Lee portrait fulfilled his commission. The patrons were not amused by a portrait of a Confederate general in civilian clothes purporting to represent the Union victory. (In time people would appreciate Buchser's work. And in 1989 the portrait was returned to the United States to hang in the Swiss Embassy in Washington, D.C.)[4]

Soon after Frank Buchser left Lexington with his painting, Lee caught another one of his "heavy colds." Any exertion produced pain and now relatively mild exertion produced severe pain. Markie came to visit, and helped to nurse her ailing cousin. On November 27, Lee wrote to thank her:

I am better than when you left & able to attend generally to my duties, though still in the hands of the Drs. You must not think that you were unable to do anything for me while here. You did a great deal & were of the greatest service. You gave me pleasant thoughts & pleasant reflections, & did a thousand things besides. I took one of your prescriptions last night.[5]

Lee believed he was better after the first of the year, and he surely sounded like himself in a letter to Mildred written on January 8, 1870. At issue was a letter "Precious Life" had written the family that was apparently illegible or otherwise obscure.

I received your letter of the 4th. We held a family council over it. It was passed from eager hand to hand and attracted wondering eyes and mysterious looks. It produced few words but a deal of thinking, and the conclusion arrived at, I believe unanimously, was that there was a great fund of amusement and information in it if it could be extracted. I have therefore determined to put it carefully away till your return, seize a leisure day, and get you to interpret it. Your mother's commentary in a suppressed soliloquy, was that you had succeeded in writing a wretched hand. Agnes thought that it would keep this cold weather—her thoughts running on jellies and oysters in the storeroom; but I, indignant at such aspersions upon your accomplishments, retained your epistle and read in an elevated tone an interesting narrative of travels in sundry countries, describing gorgeous scenery, hairbreadth escapes, and a series of remarkable events by flood and field, not a word of which they declared was in your letter. Your return, I hope, will prove the correctness of my version of your annals. . . .[6]

Throughout the postwar period and his illness, Lee maintained contact with his young female friends. Markie visited in Lexington, and Lee also saw her at Rockbridge Baths during the summer of 1869. He counseled her against any resolve "never to marry," and advised, "I hope . . . that you will come to no determination on the subject but leave it an open question to be settled by circumstances. I am sure that no one would make a better wife than you Markie. . . ." As it happened, Markie married at age forty, after Lee's death.[7]

Another of Lee's cousins and correspondents was Annette Carter, who also married at age forty after Lee's death. Lee wrote to her about coming to Lexington for commencement in June 1870. He said, "After the Commencement, I hope certainly to see you, for if you all are not coming to the mountains I will try very hard to get to see you—Let me know then where you will be & what you are going to do during the summer." Lee did spend perhaps as much as a week at Goodwood, Annette Carter's home, in July 1870.[8]

To still another cousin, Caroline ("Carrie") Stuart, he wrote in July 1868:

I have been looking for you and Annette all the spring, and I believe it is the "hope deferred" that made me sick. You ought not to disappoint me, Carrie, for I cannot stand broken promises like the young men. It is a serious matter with me. I enjoyed my visit with Robert very much and wished that you were there all the time. Everything would have gone well then. The leaky house, and flooded spring would not have been felt and his household would have been perfectly satisfactory. You have had such experience of the ill success of my "courtships," that I hardly think you can expect any good results from them. How far has my suit with you prospered, or what encouragement do you suppose it has given me to undertake anything of the kind with another? None; nor have I attempted it.[9]

Charlotte ("Lottie") Haxall was a potential daughter-in-law; in fact she agreed to marry Rob in July 1870. But the father in a sense "courted" Lottie Haxall, too. In November 1868, for example, he thanked her for sending him a picture of herself.

I am delighted my beautiful Lottie at the reception of your picture. It is very much like you & consequently very sweet, silent, not sad, & the eyes averted in pity. It has given me very pleasant thoughts & I thank you sincerely for the pleasure of its company. I cannot however give it the place of my own, which is constantly before me, heightened by my remembrance & highlined by my recollections.

Lee would enjoy the company and correspondence of lively young women to the very end of his life.[10]

During the winter of 1869–70, Lee's disease troubled him seriously. He had always driven himself to do, to go, and to accomplish. He still did. But now all this driving and striving took a toll upon Lee's well-being. In February, he told his daughter Mildred, "I am getting better I hope & feel stronger than I did, but I cannot walk much farther than to the College, though when I get on my horse, I can ride with comfort." To Robert Carter at Shirley, Lee wrote, "I go no where unless called by business: have been sick all winter, an aggravation of an attack I had before Fredericksburg [spring 1863] which I have felt ever since." In March, Lee confessed to a group of men in Alexandria who were trying to make him the president of a new railroad company, "My health has been so feeble this winter that I am only waiting to see the effect of the opening [of] Spring before relinquishing my present position."[11]

The same day Lee wrote to the men in Alexandria he had a candid conversation with William Preston Johnston, son of Albert Sidney Johnston (the general killed at Shiloh) and professor of history and literature at the college. Lee told Johnston about his intention to resign if his health did not improve. When he first came to Washington College, Lee observed, he had no problem walking four miles (to Johnston's house and back); now, although he could walk downhill, "any ascent made it necessary for him to stop and rest, even between the chapel and his house."

Johnston tried to cheer Lee, pointed out that he need not work so hard, and suggested a trip south for a change of scene and rest. Lee's physicians had recommended much the same. The same day Johnston had this conversation with Lee, the young professor spoke with his colleagues William Allan and James J. White about Lee's health. The three men agreed that Lee needed rest and diversion, and they decided to call an informal meeting of the faculty that very afternoon. At 3:00 P.M. the faculty gathered and adopted a resolution calling upon the president to take leave, travel south, and relax for two months. By 5:00 P.M. Johnston, Allan, and White were meeting with Lee to present him with the resolution of the faculty and to try to persuade him to act on their suggestion. But then Johnston began trying to convince Lee to make use of his leave to write his history of the Confederate war, as though such a monumental task were relaxing. Lee demurred on all questions, but said he would consider the resolution of the faculty. He also confided to the three men that "he felt that he might at any moment die."

Most probably the people who had the most influence upon Lee's reluctant decision to take leave from his duties and travel south to find a gentler climate were his two physicians, R. L. Madison and H. T. Barton. Lee explained in a letter to Mildred, "The doctors and others think I had better go to the South in hope of relieving the effects of the cold winter under which I have been labouring all the winter. I think I should do better here, and am very reluctant to leave home in my present condition; but they seem so interested in my recovery and so persuasive in their uneasiness that I should appear obstinate, if not perverse, if I resisted longer. I therefore consented to go, and will take Agnes to Savannah, as she seems anxious to visit that city, or, perhaps, she will take me. I wish also to visit my dear [daughter] Annie's grave before I die."

So father and daughter set out upon what became a farewell tour. Lee did not want it so. One of the reasons he hesitated to undertake the trip was the concern that "he could not go to Savannah without meeting more people than he wanted to." And when people gathered to see him at train stations along the route, Lee asked, "Why should they want to see me?" Certainly some part of Lee enjoyed the adulation, and defeated generals rarely received plaudits to the point of veneration that Lee received. But a shy man with a sick heart did not need so much enforced extroversion, and Lee knew it.[12]

They left Lexington on the packet boat for Richmond on the afternoon of March 24, 1870. They traveled through the night and then boarded a train for the city. They arrived on the afternoon of March 25 and registered at the Exchange and Ballard House, two hotels on Franklin Street connected by an enclosed "bridge" above the street. Lee and his daughter remained in Richmond three days. Agnes received and returned calls; her father consulted three physicians and rested as much as possible. The doctors made "hotel calls," and Lee declined as courteously as he could invitations from the Virginia Senate and old friends.[13]

But Lee could not very well refuse to see people who called upon him at his hotel. One such caller was George E. Pickett. Lee had encountered John S.

Mosby earlier; then Mosby encountered Pickett after visiting with Lee, and Pickett agreed to go to see the man who had relieved him from command on the condition that Mosby go too. No one knows what happened during the meeting, which was probably strained at best. But when Pickett was leaving with Mosby, he referred to Lee as "that old man" and said that Lee had "had my division massacred at Gettysburg." Mosby responded, "But he made you immortal." Pickett, who had become a broken, pitiable person during the course of the war, probably never understood either Lee or Mosby.[14]

The Lees left Richmond by train on March 28 and arrived in Warrenton, North Carolina, the same evening. They stayed with the John White family at Ingleside and went to visit Annie's grave the next morning bearing white hyacinths. Lee termed the pilgrimage "mournful, yet soothing to my feelings." Of course the women who had placed a monument at the grave were on hand, and dinner followed the visit, and Lee wrote that he and Agnes had encountered "all the citizens of Warrenton."

A letter from Agnes perhaps best describes the journey from Warrenton to Savannah (March 29–April 1). "I wish you could travel with papa," she wrote Mary Lee, "to see the affection and feeling shown toward him everywhere." Agnes told her mother that they had spent the night in a "sleeping-car," but remained "wakeful" from the novelty. "At Raleigh and another place the people crowded to the depot and called 'Lee! Lee!' and cheered vociferously, but we were locked up and 'mum.'" Then the news spread that Lee was aboard the train roaring south, and the attention increased:

Everywhere along the road where meals were provided the landlords invited us in and when we would not get out, sent coffee and lunches. Even [United States] soldiers on the train sent in fruit, and I think we were expected to die of eating. At Charlotte and Salisbury there were other crowds and bands. . . . Namesakes appeared on the way, of all sizes. Old ladies stretched their heads into the windows at way stations, and then drew back and said "He is mightily like his pictures." We reached Augusta Wednesday night [March 30]. The mayor and council met us, having heard a few minutes before that papa was on the train. We were whirled off to the [Planter's] hotel, and papa decided to spend Thursday [March 31] there. They had a reception the whole of the morning. Crowds came. Wounded soldiers, servants, and working-men even. The sweetest little children—namesakes—dressed to their eyes, with bouquets of japonica—or tiny cards in their little fat hands—with their names.

Within the crowd at Augusta was a thirteen-year-old boy who persisted until he stood next to Lee and could stare up into the general's face. The boy was Woodrow Wilson.

Robert Lee was considerably less impressed with the crowds, bands, lunches, and "little fat hands" than his daughter. He had made this trip in search of warm weather and quiet rest, and he had not yet found either one. To Mary Lee he announced, "I have had a tedious journey upon the whole, and have more than ever regretted that I undertook it."[15]

They reached Savannah on April 1 and a large crowd awaited them there.

In time Lee's escort of friends and former subordinates extricated him from his admirers, took him to the home of former Quartermaster General Andrew Lawton, and from there to Andrew Lowe's home, where he stayed while in the city.

Lee remained in Savannah for some time—twelve days. His pace slowed, and though he endured many calls and visits, he should have been able to rest. Lee told his wife on April 11, "I feel stronger than when I came. The warmer weather has also dispelled some of the rheumatic pains in my back, but I perceive no change in the stricture in my chest. If I attempt to walk beyond a very slow gait the pain is always there."[16]

Agnes fell ill in Savannah and so they delayed the trip to Florida. Lee wrote his wife, "You know she [Agnes] is like her papa—always wanting [lacking] something." Although he was writing about Agnes's health, this was a very important observation to make about himself.

At last on April 12 father and daughter boarded the steamer *Nick King* for Palatka, Florida, a town up the St. Johns River. They did visit Cumberland Island, where Agnes decorated her paternal grandfather's grave with fresh flowers and Lee paid "my tribute of respect" for what he presumed would be the last time. They steamed up the St. Johns to Palatka, spent a night with friends, and picked oranges from trees, then stopped for an evening at Jacksonville, and returned to Savannah on April 16. There they remained for another nine days, until on April 25 Lee and his daughter commenced a circuitous journey homeward up the eastern coast.[17]

They went by train first to Charleston, staying at 60 Montague Street with W. Jefferson Bennett, who had two sons at Washington College. The arrival was quiet; but the bands, receptions, and visits soon began. Lee came closer to a speech than he did anywhere else on his tour on the afternoon of April 27 before some massed firemen and a band. He thanked those assembled and blamed illness for his incapacity to say more.

On April 28, the Lees traveled north to Wilmington, North Carolina, which they entered aboard a special train escorted by cadets from Cape Fear Academy. A dinner in Lee's honor and many callers occupied the visitors until they reboarded the train on April 30 for Portsmouth, Virginia. There a cannon boomed in salute, and crowds of people cheered Lee's walk from the train to the ferry for Norfolk. Walter Taylor was among the greeters and accompanied Lee and his daughter to Norfolk. Throughout the passage across the Elizabeth River, a cannon fired and fireworks exploded to hail Lee's presence.

Another throng cheered Lee's arrival at Norfolk and a "rebel yell" rang in the air. Taylor took charge, shepherded Lee and Agnes to a waiting carriage, and escorted them to the home of Dr. William Selden, who was both host and resident physician for Lee's visit. A glittering dinner party and another large reception followed; then on May 5 Lee and Agnes took a steamer up the James to Brandon plantation, where they had some rest amid visits and calls. Next they moved further up the James to Shirley on May 10. At Lee's mother's childhood home, someone remembered that Lee still liked for people to tickle his hands. "We regarded him with the greatest veneration. We had heard of God, but here was General Lee."[18]

On May 12 they left Shirley by boat for Richmond and from there traveled by train to White House on the Pamunkey. By design Mary Lee coordinated a visit to Rooney and Tabb's home with her husband's arrival, warning that "He looks fatter, but I do not like his complexion, and he still seems stiff." Lee was once more able to play with his grandson/namesake, and Robert Junior took his father to see Romancoke, which the elder Lee pronounced crude and then tried to cover his shock with jests. With Rob, Lee visited White Marsh in Gloucester County, home of Rebecca and Prosser Tabb, who were his cousins by birth and marriage respectively. They remained two nights, and then Lee returned to White House where Markie Williams was also in residence.[19]

Lee traveled to Richmond on May 23 to see the physicians who had examined him before his trip to Warrenton and Savannah. He also purchased some silver-plated forks and spoons that he sent to Romancoke for Rob to civilize his life somewhat. A third chore in Richmond involved Edward V. Valentine, a young artist who measured Lee on May 25 for a projected bust. Valentine planned to come to Lexington to create the model and asked Lee about a convenient time. Lee replied that he would have more time in the fall, but wanted Valentine to come soon. At the time, Valentine ascribed Lee's haste to his thoughts about the general "uncertainty of life."

Lee, still with Agnes, arrived home in Lexington on May 26, after a little more than two months on the road. His health was no better; but given Lee's itinerary, the receptions, dinners, and other social obligations of his journey, he was fortunate to be alive.

Valentine came in early June to make his model for the bust; he worked and Lee sat in a vacant store on the ground floor of the hotel on Main Street. Valentine managed to secure from Lee a pair of his old boots—size 4 1/2C—as a souvenir of the occasion. Lee also agreed to have photographs taken for Valentine to use in completing his work. As the sculptor was thanking Lee and saying goodbye in the parlor, Lee said abruptly, "I feel that I have an incurable disease coming on me—old age. I would like to go to some quiet place in the country and rest."[20]

Lee was only sixty-three; his West Point classmate Joseph E. Johnston lived to become eighty-four and Jefferson Davis died at eighty-one. But then Lee's father died at sixty-two; his mother at fifty-six; and his paternal grandparents at fifty-nine and fifty-eight. Now Lee not only moved like an old man; he had finally begun to look old. Still, he did not go to any quiet spot in the country to rest. Instead, he set out upon more travels during the summer of 1870.

First he rode a train to Baltimore and endured "the hottest day I ever experienced" and the "hottest position I ever occupied." He wrote Mary Lee, "I never recollect having suffered so much." The purpose of Lee's trip was an examination and consultation by Dr. Thomas H. Buckler, who spent two hours thumping and quizzing a naked Lee before telling him that he had a "rheumatic constitution" and prescribing lemon juice. Buckler, who possessed impressive credentials and considerable renown, also advised Lee to guard against catching cold.

From Baltimore, Lee went to Goodwood to visit his cousin Charles Henry Carter and his daughter Annette Carter. Then he returned to Virginia and stopped in Alexandria for a series of visits. He spoke with his lawyer Francis L. Smith about trying to recover Arlington—"The prospect is not promising." He went to "the Hill," Seminary Hill, site of Virginia Theological Seminary (Episcopal), to see Samuel Cooper (former Adjutant General of the Confederate army), James M. Mason (former senator and unofficial Confederate ambassador to Great Britain), and Bishop John L. Johns. He spent time with first cousin Cassius Lee and said some candid things in a rare discussion of the war (for example, that with Jackson alive, he would have won at Gettysburg). On July 19, Lee left Alexandria and went to Ravensworth to visit his aunt Anna Maria Fitzhugh. He had planned to extend his travels to visit White House again, but he caught a summer cold and a prolonged heatwave sapped his strength. His pain returned and increased. He wrote Custis to tell him about the change of plans, to assure Custis he loved him, and to inform him, "I feel that my opportunities of enjoying your company are becoming daily more precarious."[21]

Lee returned home again on July 25 but did not remain long in Lexington. He went with James J. White to Hot Springs to try another water cure. White had become Lee's friend and confidant at Washington College. On a previous trip to White Sulphur Springs, White had shared a bed with Lee, but slept not a bit, recounting that he "would as soon have thought of sleeping with the Archangel Gabriel as with General Lee." At Hot Springs, Lee essentially endured both the social scene and the waters. "I hope that I am better, but am aware of no material change, except that I am weaker," he wrote Mary Lee, adding, "I am very anxious to get back. It is very wearying at these public places and the benefit hardly worth the cost." Lee left the spa on August 29 in order to attend a meeting of the Valley Railroad Company in Staunton on August 30. For reasons quite unclear he agreed at the meeting to accept the task of being president of a railroad not yet built. The railroad did seem a good idea, especially for Lexington and anyone living the Valley, and Lee's name would help raise the funds necessary to begin construction. But Lee had devoted much of his life of late to saying no to any and all such offers. In this case he made an exception and returned to Lexington as president of Washington College and the Valley Railroad. He did say in the course of admitting that prospects for his railroad were less than sanguine, "It seems to me that I have already led enough forlorn hopes."[22]

Back in Lexington, Lee prepared for another opening of the college and the commencement of classes. For almost six months he seemed to have been preparing for death; he sensed its approach in his failing strength, periodic pain, and aging appearance. He undertook his farewell tour, visited the graves of his daughter and father, spent time with his living children, called upon as many friends and relatives as possible, consulted physicians in vain to solve the riddle of his increasing debility, submitted to sitting for a sculpture and posing for photographs, and tried to heal himself with hot water. Maybe he agreed to become the president of the Valley Railroad Company in the wild hope that he would live to see rails and trains. At any rate Lee satisfied himself that he had done everything he possibly could to prolong life and prepare for death. So he watched another autumn begin; he saw the sleepy little town stir as students again came to the college and the Institute, and one more time he witnessed the energy and enthusiasm that marked the academic New Year. Lee felt better and wrote to his host in Baltimore, "My pains are less and my strength greater. In fact, I suppose I am as well as I shall be."[23]

Lee resumed his routine at his home and the college—breakfast, chapel, office, college affairs, dinner, nap, ride if possible, home in the evening. Meetings and social occasions blended into his schedule; on September 27, Lee attended a faculty meeting. The next day, he presided as senior warden over a vestry meeting at Grace Church.

Lee did not much want to leave home on this damp, chilly afternoon. As he left his house he kissed Mildred and commented, "I wish I did not have to go & listen to all that pow wow." Then he draped his military cape about himself and stepped out into the rain.

The vestry meeting began at 4:00 P.M. and ran late. Grace Church was in the early stages of a campaign to expand the church building, and the attempt to raise necessary funds provoked much discussion. Lee said little; he simply sat in the unheated church with his cape around his shoulders. Although he presided, he tended to allow discussion to go to completion in hopes of reaching consensus, and then to inject his own views. In the vestry as in his headquarters Lee worked to avoid conflict.

After more than three hours, past 7:00 P.M., the members were still seeking funds from contributions to raise the rector's salary. They were $55 short of the figure upon which they had agreed. At this juncture Lee spoke. "I will give that sum," he announced in a soft voice. Lee's last gift concluded the meeting; it was his last public statement.

He walked home in the rain, went first to his room to shed his cape, and then came into the dining room where Mary Lee had been waiting for half an hour. "You have kept us waiting a long time," she said. Lee took his place at the foot of the table, still standing, and seemed ready to say grace for the supper. But he could not speak, though he seemed to be trying, and after a moment he sat down in his chair. "Let me pour you out a cup of tea," his wife offered and then observed, "you look so tired." Lee tried again to speak, to answer; he could not. He sat up straight in his chair, as if coming to attention; but at the same time over his face spread, Mary Lee remembered, "an expression of resignation that was sublime."

Mary Lee with Custis and Agnes went to the stricken man; they called Mildred from the parlor where she was talking with two students and sent for Drs. Barton and Madison. While awaiting the physicians' arrival, the family helped Lee to his easy chair. Still he could only babble incoherently when he tried to speak and he appeared strangely passive, sadly resigned to whatever had afflicted him.

This attitude persisted after Barton and Madison had both arrived and begun examining their patient. The doctors had a bed brought into the dining room and placed in the bay window. They undressed Lee, who winced in apparent pain in the process, and put him to bed. Lee then "turned over & went quietly to sleep & slept long & tranquilly."

The family and physicians held out hope that he would respond to rest and recover. Mary Lee and Mildred, too, could never forget Lee's look, his ethereal expression—"that look always haunted me even when the physicians were so hopeful of his recovery" . . . "he had taken leave of earth tho perfectly conscious until the last 24 hours. . . ," recalled Mary Lee. Mildred remembered: "His beautiful sad eyes always gave me a look of love & recognition . . ." and "that solemn unutterable look. . . ."[24]

But most of all those who watched and waited remembered the quiet. Mildred said it best—"his lips never uttered a sound! The silence was awful!" Mary Lee recalled that her husband communicated "with a warm pressure of the hand yet rarely attempted to speak save in his dreams when his mind wandered to those dreadful battlefields." The physicians reported that Lee was "averse to speaking using preferably monosyllables."

The best diagnosis from long range is that Lee suffered a stroke—a rare stroke unaccompanied by paralysis. He suffered blockage of arteries serving his brain, most likely one or both frontal lobes, which produced a condition called abulia, "an absence of will." Also impaired by Lee's stroke was his cough reflex; he was unable to expectorate, and so some of the ordinarily healthful foods and drinks administered by family and advised by his physicians found their way into Lee's lungs and provoked pneumonia. The pneumonia eventually killed Lee—product of his inability to cough and of his conscientious family and friends, who fed and forced liquids in their efforts to heal him.[25]

Late nineteenth-century Americans were fascinated with death and especially the responses of dying people to the transition from life to death. Deathbed scenes and speeches were important, and witnesses strained to recall and record gestures, grimaces, groans, and every intelligible word of people in the course of dying. "Last words" were extremely important as the expression of the dying person's unique insight upon human experience, as evidence of his or her claims for salvation, and as the person's ultimate statement about his or her life and times.

But those who waited beside Lee's bed for some profound revelation seemed to wait in vain. Lee spoke an average of one word per day, according to those who remained with him for the first twelve days after his stroke. By the standards of the day, Lee may have lived an exemplary life; but he certainly was doing a poor job of dying. "The silence was awful!"

Robert Lee lay on his bed in his favorite space in an essentially undistinguished home rendered extraordinary because he had lived and now lay within it, suspended between life and death, for two long weeks. He was profoundly silent. The last recorded sentence of any consequence Robert E. Lee spoke was, "I will give that sum"—in one sense a mundane statement designed to invoke closure upon a three-hour vestry meeting, in another sense not a statement at all, but an act of offering, Lee once again giving something of himself to promote "the happiness & welfare" of others. Those who waited for words from Lee on his deathbed missed the point. Lee was not word; Lee was deed.

To understand Robert E. Lee it was often important to look beyond his words and watch what he did rather than listen to or read what he said. Lee's actions often modified his words, and sometimes the deeds contradicted the words. To Jefferson Davis, he often understated enormously the goals of his projected campaigns. Then, while Davis assumed that Lee invaded Pennsylvania only to draw an enemy army out of Virginia, Lee risked his army and his country in search of a decisive battle to win the war. Lee's words and attention to detail might vex and abuse members of his staff, especially as the war went badly for the Army of Northern Virginia. Yet on one of the most important evenings of the war, while Lee attempted to extricate his army from the trenches of Petersburg, Walter Taylor asked to be excused, and Lee at once assented. Lee wrote down a great deal of doom about Rooney when the little boy lost the ends of his fingers at age eight. But all the while Lee was moralizing on paper he was sitting all night at Rooney's bedside acting out his love. Lee spoke the sin-obsessed language of evangelical Christianity and likely believed many of its general tenets. But he acted out grace when he strode alone to kneel at the communion rail with an African American at St. Paul's Church, Richmond, in 1865.

Mildred Lee spoke for all of those who watched Lee's dying days and nights when she later asserted, "To me, he seems a Hero—& all other men small in comparison."[26]

Lee was indeed a hero—but even those closest to him could not know Lee whole, could not penetrate his reserve and understand the series of paradoxes that conditioned Lee's life. He seemed preoccupied with sin; yet he believed in redemption. He spent his life working with men and pursuing what society considered the most manly calling of all—that of a warrior; yet he lived for women—his real friends were female. He was a soldier who sought nothing so much as battle—"We must strike those people"—yet he avoided conflict in his relationships with people and in a very real sense thrust himself into the American Civil War in order to escape conflict. His students were "my boys," and Lee assumed the role of parent at Washington College; yet he reduced the many rules to one and so treated "boys" as responsible adults.

Mildred Lee was right—her father was a Hero (with a capital "H"). But Lee was as well Human (also with a capital "H"). Better than most people Lee knew that the human condition is flawed. Had the church not taught the doctrine of original sin, Lee would have invented it. Lee was born bound—to his father's debt and disgrace, to his mother's obsession with self-control and "correct" behavior, to an education absorbed in rules and rote; bound in young manhood to a profession in which advancement came with geological speed and more often than not resulted more from deeds undone than the other way around, to a marriage of propriety that compelled Lee to look elsewhere for friendship, to the presumption of racial superiority and the pretensions of a social elite, to children who seemed incapable of stepping beyond Lee's shadow and becoming themselves; bound in the prime of his life to a nascent nation ever in the throes of defining and defending itself at once, to an army always outnumbered and ill-supplied that required genius in command merely to survive; then bound to the shame of treason and the ignominy of defeat, to a tiny college about to fade into oblivion at worst or merited obscurity at best; and finally bound by cardiovascular disease to impotence in what should have been the pinnacle of his mature life.

Lee knew frustration full measure. He experienced far more than his share of failure. Better than most people, Lee was aware of the constraints, the bounds, which characterize the human condition.

But he was a hero. Lee was a hero because of his response to that human condition that constrained him. He all but defined self-control and obeyed rules meticulously; yet he did so in order to be independent, to be free. Lee spent himself, gave his life away, because he believed that evil was selfishness. "Dissimilar as are characters, intellects, & situations. The great duty of life is the same, the promotion of the happiness & welfare of our fellow men."[27]

Late in his life Lee wrote of his daughter Agnes, "You know she is like her papa—always wanting something." This was a rare insight—the sort of revelation about himself that Lee seldom shared. He was "always wanting something," always missing something. But more often than not, Lee transformed adversity into advantage. He lived his advice to his son Curtis when he wrote, "All is bright if you will think it so. All is happy if you will make it so. . . . Live in the world you inhabit. Look upon things as they are. Take them as you find them. Make the best of them. Turn them to your advantage."[28]

Lee was a tragic hero. Certainly he experienced ample sorrow and catastrophic loss during his life. But his was a comic vision of life. He appreciated absurdity in the human condition and refused to take himself or anyone else too seriously. When an admirer in Scotland sent to Lee in Lexington a "superb afghan" and a tea cozy, Lee opened the parcel, draped the afghan about his shoulders, donned the tea cozy as a helmet, and commenced to dance to the tune Mildred was playing on the piano. Yet as often happened, the person to whom Lee confessed his antic refused to understand. She repeated Lee's story to her sister and added, "Forgive *our hero,* exhibiting himself in such a costume, and acting in so childish a manner."[29]

So those who wrung their hands at Lee's dying silence despaired. Outside, rain came in torrents for several days after Lee's stroke, and flash floods interrupted the mail and access to Lexington after the rain abated. The pneumonia set in, and Lee began to sink steadily. On October 10, Mildred remembered that "a change came—he seemed to suffer more. . . ." On Tuesday,

October 11, "his face had an agonized expression. . . ." This was "another awful day—every one frightened & crying. . . ." That night the Reverend William Pendleton appeared, and Mary Lee, Custis, Agnes, and Mildred knelt around the bed. In all probability Pendleton read "A Prayer for a sick person, when there appeareth but small hope of recovery":

O Father of mercies, and God of all comfort, our only help in time of need; We fly unto thee for succour in behalf of this thy servant, here lying under thy hand in great weakness of body. Look graciously upon him, O Lord. . . .[30]

Mildred recalled:

Wednesday morning found us still watching—a lovely October day—the 12th 1870— at 9, he seemed to be struggling—I rushed out for the doctor (Madison). He came, looked at him, and without saying a word walked quietly away.[31]

Drs. Madison and Barton reported later in print:

It soon became evident from his rapid and feeble pulse, deepening unconsciousness and accelerated breathing, that his case was hopeless. Still the stimulants were perseveringly used up to daybreak, when he became unable to swallow. . . . From daylight his decline was rapid, but gentle. Soon after 9 o'clock A.M. he turned, with assistance, upon his right side, then closed his eyes and as tranquilly as the setting sun his noble spirit passed into the presence of his Maker.[32]

Robert E. Lee had died.

Apotheosis

I T WAS an extremely inconvenient time to die in Lexington, Virginia. The town had been all but incommunicado for several days before that sunny October 12, 1870. Very heavy rains, followed by flash floods, not only interrupted access in and out of Lexington; the North River overflowed its banks and washed away every one of undertaker C. M. Coombs's coffins. In order to bury Lee with appropriate propriety, two men, Harry Wallace and C. H. Chittum, searched downstream, "rescued" a coffin from an island in the river, and hauled it back into Lexington.[1]

Once in the coffin, Lee's physical remains lay in state in the Washington College chapel he had helped to design and construct. Students of the college, cadets from VMI, local residents, and anyone who could travel to Lexington filed past the open casket to see what was left of Lee a final time. On October 15, 1870, at 10:00 A.M. the procession formed in front of the President's House. An escort of honor, distinguished visitors, dignitaries, trustees, guard of honor, clergy, the hearse, pallbearers, Traveller, the attending physicians, and more moved through the town, Institute, and college to reach the chapel where Lee's body had been all along. The funeral service followed. Then the pallbearers placed the coffin in a vault under the chapel; those near enough heard the commitment; and it was over.[2]

Already, though, the process of apotheosis, the transformation of something or someone to the status of a god, had begun. It had begun even while Lee still lived and defeated Confederate Southerners needed to reaffirm that good people can lose wars, that might does not necessarily mean right, and that virtue exists independently of victory.

Lee, when he died, was already well on the way to becoming a Christ figure, and many people have since confused the two. Winfield Scott surely tempted Lee in Washington with field command of the United States Army; Satan tempted Jesus in the wilderness with bread, power, and fame. Lee poured forth his soul at Gettysburg; Jesus suffered in Gethsemane. But Jesus triumphed over Golgotha; Lee ennobled Appomattox.[3]

Apotheosis understood, however, is seldom enough. Disciples of Lee made his life into legend, myth, and image, and so rendered Lee both more and less than he was. Ironically, the process began with Lee's "last words." Lee after his stroke on September 28 was passive and silent; the Lee legend has words. "Tell Hill he *must* come up." " 'Strike the tent,' he said and spoke no more." Lee, in all probability never said these "last words"; but that really mattered very little.[4]

Beyond that moment at the supper table, after a three-hour-plus vestry meeting, following the news that he had kept the family waiting a long time, Lee was no longer in control. From some time after 9:00 A.M. on October 12, he was free.

ABBREVIATIONS

Battles and Leaders—Robert Underwood Johnson and Clarence Clough Buel, eds., *Battles and Leaders of the Civil War,* 4 vols. (New York, 1887)

Diary—Robert E. Lee Diary, MSS1L51B52, VHS

Duke—Manuscript Department, William R. Perkins Library, Duke University, Durham, North Carolina

GHS—Georgia Historical Society, Savannah, Georgia

MOC—Eleanor S. Brockenbrough Library, Museum of the Confederacy, Richmond, Virginia

O.R.—U.S. War Department, *War of the Rebellion, A Compilation of the Official Records of the Union Armies,* 70 vols. in 127 (Washington, DC, 1880–1901), series I unless otherwise indicated

SHSP—*Southern Historical Society Papers*

Stratford—Dupont Library, Stratford Hall, Stratford, Virginia

USMA—United States Military Academy Library and Archives, West Point, New York

U.Va.—University of Virginia Library, Charlottesville, Virginia

VHS—Virginia Historical Society, Richmond, Virginia

VSL—Virginia State Library, Richmond, Virginia

Wartime Papers—Clifford Dowdey and Louis H. Manarin, eds., *The Wartime Papers of R. E. Lee* (New York, 1961)

W & L—University Library, Washington and Lee University, Lexington, Virginia

Notes

Prologue: Advent

1. Henry Lee to C. C. Lee, Nassau, June 18, 1817, Robert E. Lee, "Life of General Henry Lee," *Memoirs of the War in the Southern Department of the United States,* ed. Robert E. Lee (New York, 1869), 71.
2. Biographies of Lee include Charles Royster, *Light-Horse Harry Lee and the Legacy of the American Revolution* (Cambridge, Engl. 1982), and Thomas Boyd, *Light-Horse Harry Lee* (New York, 1931). Works on the Lee family include Burton J. Hendrick, *The Lees of Virginia; Biography of a Family* (New York, 1935); Ethel Armes, *Stratford Hall: The Great House of the Lees* (Richmond, VA, 1936); and especially Paul C. Nagel, *The Lees of Virginia: Seven Generations of an American Family* (New York, 1990).
3. Nagel, *Lees,* 174–76; Douglas S. Freeman, *R. E. Lee: A Biography,* 4 vols. (New York, 1934–35), I, 7–9; Armes, *Stratford,* 268–78.
4. *Virginia Gazette,* June 26, 1793, quoted in Armes, *Stratford,* 271–78.
5. Armes, *Stratford,* 265 (portrait), 274–75; Nagel, *Lees,* 164–65; Boyd, *Light-Horse Harry,* 201–04; Royster, *Lee,* 64–66, and portraits that follow p. 144.
6. Nagel, *Lees,* 165–69; Royster, *Lee,* 77.
7. Nagel, *Lees,* 175, 34–35.
8. *Ibid.,* 175–76; Armes, *Stratford,* 278; W. Asbury Christian, *Richmond: Her Past and Present* (Richmond, VA, 1912), 35.
9. Samuel Appleton Storrow to My Dear Sister, 1821, in Hendrick, *Lees,* 380–82.
10. Armes, *Stratford,* 277, 280–81; Nagel, *Lees,* 176.
11. Nagel, *Lees,* 176–77.
12. The best way to appreciate Shirley is to visit the place. In addition, see Calder Loth, ed., *The Virginia Landmarks Register* (3rd ed., Charlottesville, VA, 1986), 85–86, and Emmie Ferguson Farrar, *Old Virginia Houses Along the James* (New York, 1957), 88–91.
13. Stratford, too, is well worth a visit. Also see Loth, ed., *Virginia Landmarks Register,* 480, and Emmie Ferguson Farrar and Emilee Hines, *Old Virginia Houses: The Northern Peninsulas* (New York, 1972), 62–74. About Harry Lee's homecoming and the tragedies on the steps, see Nagel, *Lees,* 164, 206–07.
14. Nagel, *Lees,* 164–65, 180–81, 194–95; Boyd, *Light-Horse Harry,* 277–83; Armes, *Stratford,* 283–85.
15. Boyd, *Light-Horse Harry,* 251–53.
16. *Ibid.;* the best, and gentlest, analysis of Henry Lee's politics is Royster, *Lee,* 117–68.
17. Nagel, *Lees,* 178; Boyd, *Light-Horse Harry,* 268–74.
18. Boyd, *Light-Horse Harry,* 280–83; Nagel, *Lees,* 178–80.
19. Armes, *Stratford,* 303–05.
20. Nagel, *Lees,* 203–04.
21. *Ibid.,* 179, 195–96; Freeman, *Lee,* I, 1–2, 11–12; Armes, *Stratford,* 306–08.

1. *"Robert Was Always Good"*

1. Thomas Boyd, *Light-Horse Harry Lee* (New York, 1931), 287.
2. *A Cursory Sketch of the Motives and Proceedings of the Party Which Sways the Affairs of the Union. . . .* (Philadelphia, 1809), 37.
3. Boyd, *Light-Horse Harry,* 293–300; Paul C. Nagel, *The Lees of Virginia: Seven Generations of an American Family* (New York, 1990), 181; Burton J. Hendrick, *The Lees of Virginia: Biography of a Family* (Boston, 1935), 389–90.
4. Hendrick, *Lees,* 389–90; Henry Lee to Madison, Spots. C. House, 19th Aug. 09; Robert A. Rutland, et al., eds., *The Papers of James Madison: Presidential Series,* (Charlottesville, VA, 1984), I, 334–35.
5. Ann Lee to Carter Berkeley, Stratford, November 26, 1809, in Ethel Armes, *Stratford Hall: The Great House of the Lees* (Richmond, VA, 1936), 323–24.
6. Nagel, *Lees,* 196–98, 204–05; Douglas S. Freeman, *R. E. Lee: A Biography,* 4 vols. (New York, 1934–35), I, 13–19.
7. Armes, *Stratford Hall,* 310 (photograph); Alonzo T. Dill and Mary Tyler Cheek, *A Visit to Stratford and the Story of the Lees* (Stratford, VA, 1986), 16–17.
8. Nagel, *Lees,* 197.
9. Boyd, *Light-Horse Harry,* 304; Henry Lee, *Memoirs of the War in the Southern Department of the United States,* ed., Robert E. Lee (New York,

1869); Charles Royster, *Light-Horse Harry Lee and the Legacy of the American Revolution* (Cambridge, Engl., 1981), 189–227.

10. Royster, *Lee,* 154–68; Boyd, *Light-Horse Harry,* 307–27.

11. Boyd, *Light-Horse Harry,* 330–33. Monroe was often benefactor to Lee and his family despite believing Lee "trouble." Monroe to Madison, Richmond, May 23, 1801, in Robert J. Brugger, et al., eds., *The Papers of James Madison: Secretary of State Series* (Charlottesville, VA, 1986), I, 222–25.

12. Lee's letters from the West Indies and quotations from his journal are in Armes, *Stratford,* 345–59. Robert E. Lee offered the letters to Carter in his edition of his father's *Memoirs of the War in the Southern Department of the United States,* 57–78.

13. C. C. Lee to R. E. Lee, Fine Creek, Powhatan County, July 25, 1866, Lee, *Memoirs,* ed., Lee, 56–57. Henry Lee to C. C. Lee, Nassau, February 9, 1817, in Lee, *Memoirs,* ed., Lee, 63–66.

14. Freeman, *Lee,* I, 29–31; Ann Lee to C. C. Lee, Alexandria, May 8, 1816, in Armes, *Stratford,*

354–55; Ann Lee to C. C. Lee, Alexandria, July 17, 1816, in Armes, *Stratford,* 356–57.

15. Nagel, *Lee,* 231–32.

16. *Ibid.,* 198; Ann Lee to C. C. Lee, Alexandria, May 8, 1816, in Armes, *Stratford,* 354–55; Ann Lee to C. C. Lee, Alexandria, July 17, 1816, in Armes, *Stratford,* 356–57.

17. Nagel, *Lees,* 204–06.

18. *Ibid.,* 183–84; Royster, *Lee,* 3–7; Boyd, *Light-Horse Harry,* 339–43.

19. William Barnwell to Henry Lee, Cumberland Sound, March 27, 1818; James Shaw to Henry Lee, Dungeness, Cumberland Island, March 26, 1818; James H. Causten to Ann Lee, Baltimore, April 11, 1818, George Bolling Lee Papers, VHS.

20. See Thomas L. Connelly, *The Marble Man: Robert E. Lee and His Image in American Society* (New York, 1977), 5–6; Freeman, *Lee,* I, 66–67, 159–69, IV, 415–18; A. L. Long, *Memoirs of Robert E. Lee* (Blue and Grey Press ed., Secaucus, NJ, 1983), 22–23.

21. Robert E. Lee, "Life of General Henry Lee," *Memoirs of the War in the Southern Department of the United States,* ed., Robert E. Lee, 53, 40.

2. *"How Can I Live Without Robert?"*

1. Paul C. Nagel, *The Lees of Virginia: Seven Generations of an American Family* (New York, 1990), follows 178.

2. *Ibid.,* 197–200; Douglas S. Freeman, *R. E. Lee: A Biography,* 4 vols. (New York, 1934–35), I, 33–34, 87–88.

3. Nagel, *Lees,* 199–200; *Historical Register of Harvard University, 1636–1936* (Cambridge, MA, 1937), 70–72.

4. Freeman, *Lee,* I, 33–36.

5. *Ibid.,* 20; Eleanor Lee Templeman, "Ravensworth," *Historical Society of Fairfax County, Virginia,* 7 (1960–61), 46–49; Jean Geddes, *Fairfax County Historical Highlights from 1607* (Middleburg, VA, 1967), 75–77.

6. Nagel, *Lees,* 234–35.

7. Freeman, *Lee,* I, 34–35.

8. Nagel, *Lees,* 203–213.

9. Henry Lee to William Berkley Lewis, Paris, July 26, 1833, Henry Lee Papers, VHS.

10. Nagel, *Lees,* 212–17.

11. W. B. Leary letter quoted in Freeman, *Lee,* I, 40.

12. Bertram Wyatt-Brown, *Southern Honor: Ethics and Behavior in the Old South* (New York, 1982), 91–96.

13. Cf. Freeman, *Lee,* I, 37–38.

14. Leonard D. White, *The Jeffersonians: A Study in Administrative History, 1801–1829* (New York, 1951), 255–56; Freeman, *Lee,* I, 38.

15. W. H. Fitzhugh to Calhoun, Ravensworth, February 7, 1824, Freeman, *Lee,* I, 39.

16. These letters are printed in Freeman, *Lee,* I, 40–43. Henry Lee was a friend of Garrett, who in turn was close to Calhoun. Calhoun to R. S. Garrett, Washington, June 6, 1824, in W. Edwin Hemphill, ed., *The Papers of John C. Calhoun* (Columbia, SC, 1976), IX, 138–40.

17. *Ibid.,* 43–45 and 44n.

18. *Ibid.,* 46–47.

19. Stephen E. Ambrose, *Duty, Honor, Country: A History of West Point* (Baltimore, 1966), 157–58.

20. Freeman, *Lee,* I, 47.

21. Ann Lee to C. C. Lee, Alexandria, July 17, 1816, in Ethel Armes, *Stratford Hall: The Great House of the Lees* (Richmond, VA, 1936), 356–57; on Southern evangelicalism, see Donald A. Mathews, *Religion in the Old South* (Chicago, 1977), especially xvi–xvii.

22. Essay on "moral training" in the rear of Lee diary kept during the 1850s. Diary.

3. The *"Marble Model"*

1. Douglas L. Freeman, *R. E. Lee: A Biography,* 4 vols. (New York, 1934–35), I, 48 and n.; Sidney Forman, *West Point: A History of the United States Military Academy* (New York, 1950), 3–7.

2. Freeman, *Lee,* I, 48–49; James L. Morrison, Jr., *"The Best School in the World": West Point, the Pre–Civil War Years, 1833–1866* (Kent, OH, 1986); Stephen E. Ambrose, *Duty, Honor, Country: A History of West Point* (Baltimore, 1966), especially 147–51; contemporary maps and views of West Point are in West Point Military Library, *The Centennial of the U.S. Military Academy at West Point, New York,* 2 vols. (Greenwood Reprinting, New York, 1969), I.

3. Freeman, *Lee,* I, 50; Morrison, *"Best School,"* 3–4; Ambrose, *Duty, Honor, Country,* 62–86; and R. Ernest Dupuy, *Where They Have Trod: The West Point Tradition in American Life* (New

York, 1960), which is a tribute/biography of Thayer.

4. Leonard D. White, *The Jeffersonians: A Study in Administrative History, 1801–1829* (New York, 1951), 255–56; Leonard D. White, *The Jacksonians: A Study in Administrative History, 1829–1861* (New York, 1954), 207–208; Freeman, *Lee,* I, 50–51; and R. Morrison, *"Best School,"* 64–66; West Point Library, *Centennial,* I, 506.

5. Captain F. W. Staden, "Uniform of Cadets, 1794–1902," in West Point Library, *Centennial,* I, 508–21; Ambrose, *Duty, Honor, Country,* 153–54; Freeman, *Lee,* I, 51–52.

6. Morrison, *"Best School,"* 77–78; Ambrose, *Duty, Honor, Country,* 154–55.

7. Freeman, *Lee,* I, 52–55; Ambrose, *Duty, Honor, Country,* 149–51; Morrison, *"Best School,"* 73–74, 78–85; White, *Jeffersonians,* 257–58.

8. USMA, manuscript records, National Archives; White, *The Jacksonians,* 211.
9. Ambrose, *Duty, Honor, Country,* 155–57, 162–64.
10. Freeman, *Lee,* I, 55–83.
11. Ambrose, *Duty, Honor, Country,* 158–59; Morrison, *"Best School,"* 70.
12. Morrison, *"Best School,"* 71–72; Freeman, *Lee,* I, 55–56.
13. Ambrose, *Duty, Honor, Country,* 148–49.
14. Freeman, *Lee,* I, 58–68; Morrison, *"Best School,"* 160–63.
15. Freeman, *Lee,* I, 68.
16. *Ibid.,* 68–81; Morrison, *"Best School,"* 160–63.
17. Freeman, *Lee,* I, 81–82; Morrison, *"Best School,"* 164–65.
18. Freeman, *Lee,* I, 84–85; George W. Cullum, *Biographical Register of the Officers and Graduates of the U.S. Military Academy . . . 1802 to 1890,* 3 vols. (3rd ed., Boston and New York, 1891), 419–20.
19. Morrison, *"Best School,"* 87–89.
20. Ambrose, *Duty, Honor, Country,* 87–90.
21. *Ibid.,* 80–81.
22. Freeman, *Lee,* I, 58–59.

23. Quoted in *ibid.,* 63.
24. Ambrose, *Duty, Honor, Country,* 89; Morrison, *"Best School,"* 57; White, *Jeffersonians,* 254; West Point Library, *Centennial,* I, 368.
25. Freeman, *Lee,* I, 64–67, 72–73.
26. *Ibid.,* 64.
27. *Ibid.,* 63.
28. Morrison, *"Best School,"* 164–65.
29. Freeman, *Lee,* I, 82–83; Ambrose, *Duty, Honor, Country,* 149.
30. Jefferson Davis to Joseph Emory Davis, West Point, January 12, 1825, in Haskell M. Monroe, Jr., and James T. McIntosh, eds., *The Papers of Jefferson Davis* (Baton Rouge, LA, 1971), I, 17–21 and notes.
31. Freeman, *Lee,* I, 82.
32. *Ibid.,* 84–85, 68. Freeman states that Lee was five feet, ten and a half inches tall. However, the sculptor Edward Virginius Valentine made a series of very detailed measurements of Lee on May 25, 1870, for a statue, and recorded Lee's height as five feet, eleven inches. Edward Virginius Valentine Papers, Valentine Museum, Richmond, Virginia.

4. *"As Bold as a Sheep"*

1. Paul C. Nagel, *The Lees of Virginia: Seven Generations of an American Family* (New York, 1990), 200.
2. See Douglas S. Freeman, *R. E. Lee: A Biography,* 4 vols. (New York, 1934–35), I, 87–91. Ann Lee to Dr. Carter Berkeley, Stratford, November 26, 1809, in Ethel Armes, *Stratford Hall: The Great House of the Lees* (Richmond, VA, 1936), 323–24.
3. Nagel, *Lees,* 200–01; Lee to Carter Lee, Arlington, September 22, 1830, Lee to Carter, Old Point, October 12, 1831, Robert E. Lee Papers, U.Va. Lee's letter books in the Lee Family Papers, MSS/L51C, VHS indicate that he invested in bank stock and later in bonds. Lee's letters make mention of property in slaves, but only a few. Lee's will—one copy of which is in the Robert E. Lee Papers, Library of Congress, Washington, DC, written in 1846—lists only one slave and her children with his property. The will lists stocks and bonds worth $38,750.
4. Lee to Gratiot, Georgetown, July 31, 1829, Record Group 77, Boxes 55 and 56, National Archives, Washington, DC; Freeman, *Lee,* I, 92; Nagel, *Lees,* 201.
5. Freeman, *Lee,* I, 99; Mary Custis to Lee, Arlington, September 20, 1829, Lee Family Papers, MSS/L51C, VHS.
6. Gratiot to Lee, Washington, August 8, 1829, Record Group 77, Boxes 55 and 56, National Archives, Washington, DC.
7. George W. Cullum, *Biographical Register of Officers and Graduates of the U.S. Military Academy,* 2 vols. (New York, 1868–79), I, 425.
8. Freeman, *Lee,* I, 94–95.
9. Margaret Sanborn, *Robert E. Lee,* 2 vols. (Philadelphia, 1966–67), I, 68–69.
10. Freeman, *Lee,* I, 95–96; A. Sydney Johnson, et al., *An Ecological Survey of the Coastal Region of Georgia,* National Park Service Scientific Monograph Series, no. 3 (Washington, DC, 1974).
11. Lee to Carter Lee, Cockspur, May 8, 1830, and November 16, 1830, Robert E. Lee Papers, U.Va.
12. Lee to Carter Lee, Cockspur, May 8, 1830, Robert E. Lee Papers, U.Va.; Freeman, *Lee,* I, 101; Sanborn, *Lee,* 72–73; Cullum, *Biographical Register,* I, 425.

13. Nagel, *Lees,* 212–21.
14. *Daily Savannah Republican,* March 19 and March 20, 1830.
15. Nagel, *Lees,* 244–45.
16. Rose Mortimer Ellzey MacDonald, *Mrs. Robert E. Lee* (Boston, 1939), 5–7; Sanborn, *Lee,* 104.
17. Quoted in Sara B. Bearss, "The Farmer of Arlington: George W. P. Custis and the Arlington Sheep Shearings," *Virginia Cavalcade,* 38 (Winter 1989), 124.
18. *Ibid.,* 124–33; Freeman, *Lee,* I, 129–31; Nagel, *Lees,* 234–35.
19. Lee to Carter Lee, Arlington, September 24, 1830, Robert E. Lee Papers, U.Va.; Freeman, *Lee* I, 104; Sanborn, *Lee,* 76–77.
20. Sanborn, *Lee,* 76–77; Bearss, "Farmer of Arlington," 132; MacDonald, *Mrs. Lee,* 29–31.
21. Lee to Carter Lee, Arlington, September 24, 1830, September 30, 1830, Robert E. Lee Papers, U.Va.
22. Lee to Carter Lee, Arlington, September 30, 1830, Savannah, November 16, 1830, Robert E. Lee Papers, U.Va; Lee to Gratiot, Cockspur Island, November 11, 1830, December 1, 1830, Record Group 77, Boxes 55 and 56, National Archives, Washington, DC.
23. Lee to Carter Lee, January 4, 1831, Robert E. Lee Papers, U.Va.
24. Lee to Carter Lee, February 27, 1831, Robert E. Lee Papers, U.Va.; Freeman, *Lee* I, 100–01.
25. Lee to Eliza Mackay, Cockspur, April 13, 1831, Robert E. Lee Papers, GHS; Freeman, *Lee,* I, 101–03.
26. Lee to Carter Lee, May 26, 1831, Robert E. Lee Papers, U.Va.; Lee to Talcott, Ravensworth, July 13, 1831, Lee Family Papers, MSS2L5156, VHS.
27. Anna Maria Sarah (Goldsborough) Fitzhugh to Mary Custis, n.p., Saturday [1831], George Bolling Lee Papers, MSS1L5114B, VHS; Bearss, "Farmer of Arlington," 132.
28. Lee to Carter Lee, June 15, 1831, Robert E. Lee Papers, U.Va.; Anna Maria Sarah (Goldsborough) Fitzhugh to Mary Custis, n.p., Saturday [1831], George Bolling Lee Papers, MSS1L5114B, VHS.
29. Freeman, *Lee,* I, 105 and n.
30. Lee to Talcott, Ravensworth, July 13, 1831, Rob-

ert Edward Lee Papers, MSS2L515B, VHS; Mac-Donald, *Mrs. Lee,* 31–35; Freeman, *Lee,* I, 105–06.
31. Lee to Talcott, Ravensworth, July 13, 1831,

Robert Edward Lee Papers, MSS2L515B, VHS.
32. *Ibid.;* Nagel, *Lees,* 235–38; Freeman, *Lee,* I, 107–10.

5. *"Happy as a Clam in High Water"*

1. Lee to Andrew Talcott, Arlington, July 13, 1831, typescript in Lee Papers, MOC; Richard P. Weinert, Jr., and Col. Robert Arthur, *Defender of the Chesapeake: The Story of Fort Monroe* (Shippensburg, PA, 1989), 89n.
2. Lee to Mary Lee, Old Point, April 17, 1832, in Norma B. Cuthbert, "To Molly: Five Early Letters from Robert E. Lee to His Wife," *Huntington Library Quarterly* (May 1952), 260.
3. Lee to Mary Lee, Old Point, April 24, 1832, Lee to Mary Lee, June 2 [1832]; Lee and Mary Lee to Mrs. M. F. Custis, [August 28–31, 1831], Lee Family Papers, MSS1L51C5, VHS; Lee to General Gratiot, Fortress Monroe, November 16, 1831, National Archives, Washington, DC.
4. See Henry Irving Tragle, *The Southampton Slave Revolt of 1831: A Compilation of Source Material* (Amherst, MA, 1971).
5. Lee and Mary Lee to Mrs. M. F. Custis, [August 28–31, 1831], Lee Family Papers, MSS1L51C5, VHS.
6. Douglas S. Freeman, *R. E. Lee: A Biography,* 4 vols. (New York, 1934–35), I, 112.
7. Lee to General Gratiot, Fortress Monroe, November 16, 1831, with enclosures, National Archives, Washington, DC.
8. Quoted in Weinert and Arthur, *Defender,* 73–74.
9. *Ibid.,* 72–73; Freeman, *Lee,* I, 119–21.
10. See George Green Shackelford, "From the Society's Collections: Lieutenant Lee Reports to Captain Talcott on Fort Calhoun's Construction at Rip Raps," *Virginia Magazine of History and Biography,* 60 (July 1952), 458–87.
11. Lee W. Cullum, *Biographical Register of the Officers and Graduates of the U.S. Military Academy,* 3 vols. (3rd ed., New York, 1891), 420.
12. Lee to General Gratiot, Fort Monroe, June 6, 1834, Lee Family Papers, MSS1L5156A28, Lee to Carter Lee, Fort Monroe, August 20, 1834, Robert E. Lee Papers, U.Va.
13. Lee and Mary Lee to Mrs. M. F. Custis, [August 28–31, 1831], Lee Family Papers, MSS1L51C5, VHS; Lee to Talcott, Arlington, July 13, 1831, typescript in Lee Papers, MOC.
14. Lee to Mary Lee, Fort Monroe, November 27, 1833, in Cuthbert, "To Molly," 267.
15. Lee to Mary Lee, St. Louis, August 5, 1837, Lee Family Papers, MSS1L51C19, VHS.
16. Lee to Talcott, Fort Monroe, April 10, 1834, Lee Family Papers, MSS1L5156A23, VHS.
17. Lee to Mary Lee, Old Point, April 17, 1833, and Lee to Mary Lee, Fort Monroe, November 27, 1833, in Cuthbert, "To Molly," 260, 268.

18. Lee and Mary Lee to Mrs. M. F. Custis, [August 28–31, 1831], Lee Family Papers, MSS1L51C5, VHS.
19. This understanding of the Arlington attraction is original in Thomas L. Connelly, *The Marble Man: Robert E. Lee and His Image in American Society* (New York, 1977), 166–67.
20. Weinert and Arthur, *Defender,* 89n; Lee to Mary Lee, Old Point, April 17, 1833, and Fort Monroe, June 6, 1832, in Cuthbert, "To Molly," 260, 264–65; Shackelford, "Lee Reports," 464 and n.
21. Lee to Mary Lee, Old Point, April 24, 1832, Lee Family Papers, MSS1L51C7, VHS.
22. *Ibid.,* and Lee to Mary Lee, Old Point, April 17, 1832, in Cuthbert, "To Molly," 262.
23. Quoted in Freeman, *Lee,* I, 371–73.
24. Lee to Mary Lee, Old Point, June 6, 1832, in Cuthbert, "To Molly," 264.
25. See Douglas Freeman, "Lee and the Ladies: Unpublished Letters of Robert E. Lee," *Scribner's Magazine,* LXXVIII (October 1925), 344–48; Lee to Andrew Talcott, Washington, February 21, 1833, Lee Family Papers, MSS1L5156A4, VHS.
26. Lee to Jack Mackay, February 3, 1834, quoted in Freeman, *Lee,* I, 117.
27. Lee to Mary Lee, Old Point, April 24, 1832, Lee Family Papers, MSS1L51C7, VHS.
28. Lee to Jack Mackay, Fort Monroe, June 26, 1834, and St. Louis, October 22, 1837, Letters of R. E. Lee (typescript), GHS; Lee to Andrew Talcott, Washington, February 10, 1835, in Shackelford, "Lee Reports," 479–80; Lee to Andrew Talcott, Fort Monroe, August 2, 1833, Lee Family Papers, MSS1L5156A5, VHS.
29. Letter quoted in Freeman, *Lee,* I, 113–14.
30. Lee to Andrew Talcott, Fort Monroe, July 3, 1833, in Shackelford, "Lee Reports," 469.
31. Lee to General Gratiot, Fort Monroe, July 6, 1833 (with enclosures and endorsement), National Archives, Washington, DC.
32. Lee to Andrew Talcott, Fort Monroe, August 3, 1833, Lee Family Papers, MSS1L5156A5, VHS.
33. Freeman, *Lee,* I, 124–25.
34. Lee to Carter Lee, Fort Monroe, August 20, 1834, Robert E. Lee Papers, U.Va.
35. Shackelford, "Lee Reports," 469–70, 462.
36. Lee to General Gratiot, Fort Calhoun, September 1, 1834, National Archives, Washington, DC.
37. Lee to Talcott, Fort Calhoun, November 1, 1834, in Shackelford, "Lee Reports," 475–76.

6. *"I Must Get Away from Here"*

1. See Paul C. Nagel, *The Lees of Virginia: Seven Generations of an American Family* (New York, 1990), 234–35, 242; Douglas S. Freeman, *R. E. Lee, A Biography,* 4 vols (New York, 1934–35), I, 129–31; and Rose Mortimer Ellzey Macdonald, *Mrs. Robert E. Lee* (Boston, 1939), 56–57.
2. Mary Custis to Mary Lee, Arlington, October 6, 1831, Custis Family Papers MSS2C9695A1, VHS.
3. Lee to Custis, Old Point, May 22, 1832, Robert E. Lee Papers, Duke.

4. Lee to Carter Lee, Washington, May 2, 1836, Robert E. Lee Papers, U.Va.
5. Lee to Mary Lee, Old Point, April 24, 1832, Family Papers, MSS1L51C7, VHS.
6. Notes, essays, in rear of Diary.
7. Robert and Mary Lee to Eliza Mackay Stiles, January 4, 1832, quoted in Freeman, *Lee,* I, 114.
8. Lee to Talcott, Washington, November 28, 1834, quoted in George Green Shackelford, ed., "From the Society's Collections: Lieutenant Lee Reports to Captain Talcott on Fort Calhoun's Construc-

tion on the Rip Raps," *Virginia Magazine of History and Biography,* 60 (July 1952), 472; A. L. Long, *Memoirs of Robert E. Lee* (Blue and Grey Press ed., Secaucus, NJ, 1983), 36–37; "those who can sleep. . . ." quoted in Freeman, *Lee,* I, 133; Lee request for "⅛ of a cask of good wine . . . also some brandy" in Lee to Mary Lee, Old Point, June 6, 1832, in Norma B. Cuthbert, "To Molly: Five Early Letters from Robert E. Lee to His Wife," *Huntington Library Quarterly* (May 1952), 265.

9. See Constance McLaughlin Green, *Washington: Village and Capital 1800–1878* (Princeton, NJ, 1962); Margaret Leech, *Reveille in Washington, 1860–1865* (New York, 1941); and Long, *Memoirs,* 36–37.

10. Lee to Talcott, Washington, February 21, 1833, Lee Family Papers, MSS1L5156A4, VHS.

11. Freeman, *Lee,* I, 131.

12. *Ibid.,* 168–69.

13. *Ibid.,* 159–69; Judith Hynson, "Lee Coat of Arms," typescript report prepared for Robert E. Lee Memorial Association, MOC.

14. H. Lee, *Observations on the Writings of Thomas Jefferson, With Particular Reference to the Attack They Contain on the Memory of the Late General Henry Lee* (2nd ed., ed., Charles Carter Lee, Philadelphia, 1839), 256.

15. Lee to Carter Lee, Arlington, May 17, 1835, Robert E. Lee Papers, U.Va.

16. Robert E. Lee Headquarters Papers, VHS.

17. Lee wrote, for example, in the rear of a diary he kept during the 1850s, "Education consists very much in the suppression of coarse animal emotions & the escalation of the higher faculties & feelings." Diary. And he referred to the slave experience of African Americans as "the painful discipline . . . necessary for their instruction . . . [which] will prepare & lead them to better things," in a letter quoted in Freeman, *Lee,* I, 371–73.

18. These examples are from Letters Sent, Engineer Department, M113, National Archives, Washington, DC.

19. Lee to Talcott, Washington, February 13, 1836, Talcott Papers, MSS1T1434B178, VHS.

20. Lee to Carter Lee, Washington, February 24, 1835, Robert E. Lee Papers, U.Va.; Lee to Charles Gratiot, Washington, March 18, 1835, National Archives, Washington, DC.

21. Lee to Charles Gratiot, Washington, March 18, 1835, National Archives, Washington, DC; Long, *Memoirs,* 35.

22. Lee to Carter Lee, Arlington, May 17, 1835, Robert E. Lee Papers, U.Va.

23. Lee to George Cullum, Turtle Island, Michigan, July 31, 1835, Lee Family Papers, MSS1L5156A30, VHS.

24. *Ibid.*

25. For the story of this letter and Lee biographer Douglas S. Freeman (whose sense of humor in this instance was less than that of his subject), see John L Gignilliat, "A Historian's Dilemma: A Posthumous Footnote for *Freeman's R. E. Lee,*" *Journal of Southern History XLIII* (May 1977), 217–36.

26. Lee to Mary Lee, Detroit, August 21, 1835, in Cuthbert, "To Molly," 271.

27. Mary Lee's birthdate is taken from a photograph of the Custis Family Bible in Mary P. Coulling, *The Lee Girls* (Winston-Salem, NC, 1987), plate 2 following p. 114. Lee to Mary Lee, South Bend of Lake Michigan, September 2, 1835, in Cuthbert, "To Molly," 274; Lee to Talcott, Washington, October 7, 1835, Talcott Papers, MSS1T14B159, VHS.

28. Lee to Talcott, Washington, October 12, 1835, Talcott Papers, MSS1T1434B162; Lee to Talcott, Washington, October 21, 1835, Talcott Papers, MSS1T1434B165, VHS; Lee to Talcott, Washington, November 9, 1835, in Shackelford, "From the Society's Collections," 480; Lee to Talcott, Washington, November 18, 1835, Talcott Papers, MSS1T1434B171; and Lee to Talcott, Washington, November 25, 1835, Talcott Papers, MSS1T1434B172, VHS.

29. Lee to Talcott, n.p., February 1836, Talcott Papers, MSS1T1434B177, VHS; Lee to Talcott, n.p., June 22, 1836, in Shackelford, "From the Society's Collections," 483.

30. Lee to Carter Lee, Warrenton Springs, August 2, 1836, Robert E. Lee Papers, U.Va.

31. William Henry Fitzhugh (Rooney) Lee was born May 30, 1837 (Custis Bible photograph in Coulling, *Lee Girls*).

32. Freeman, *Lee,* I, 135; Lee's anxiety about promotion appears in Lee to Talcott, n.p., February 1836, Talcott Papers, MSS1T1434B177, VHS.

33. Lee to Talcott, Washington, February 2, 1837, Talcott Papers, MSS1T1434B186, VHS.

34. Freeman, *Lee,* I, 137–39.

35. Lee to Talcott, Washington, June 29, 1837, Talcott Papers, MSS1T1434B190, VHS.

7. *"They Wanted a Skillful Engineer . . . and Sent Me"*

1. Rose Mortimer Ellzey MacDonald, *Mrs. Robert E. Lee* (Boston, 1939), 61; Mary P. Coulling, *The Lee Girls* (Winston-Salem, NC, 1987), photograph of Custis Family Bible 2 following p. 114; Lee to Jack Mackay, St. Louis, October 22, 1837, Lee Papers, GHS.

2. Lee Report, St. Louis, December 6, 1837, printed in *Executive Documents,* 25th Congress, 2d Session, vol. I, no. 139; Stella M. Drumm, "Robert E. Lee and the Improvement of the Mississippi River," *Missouri Historical Society Collections,* 6 (February 1929), 158–59; Douglas S. Freeman, *R. E. Lee: A Biography,* 4 vols. (New York, 1934–35), I, 145–46.

3. Freeman, *Lee,* I, 140; Ezra J. Warner, *Generals in Blue: Lives of the Union Commanders* (Baton Rouge, LA, 1964), 318–19; A. L. Long, *Memoirs of Robert E. Lee* (Blue and Grey Press ed., Secaucus, NJ, 1983), 40–44.

4. Long, *Memoirs,* 41; Drumm, "Lee and the Mississippi River," 159; Lee to Andrew Talcott, St. Louis, August 25, 1837, Talcott Papers, MSS1T1434B191, VHS.

5. Lee to Mary Lee, St. Louis, August 5, 1837, Lee Family Papers, MSS1L51C19, VHS.

6. *Ibid.;* Lee to Andrew Talcott, St. Louis, August 15, 1837, Talcott Papers, MSS1T1434B191, VHS.

7. Lee to Mary Lee, St. Louis, August 21, 1837, Lee Papers, U.Va.

8. *Ibid.;* Lee to Carter Lee, St. Louis, October 8, 1837, Lee Papers, U.Va.; Lee to Mary Lee, Des Moines Rapids, September 10, 1837, Lee Family Papers, MSS1L51C20, VHS.

9. Lee to Andrew Talcott, St. Louis, October 11, 1837, Talcott Papers, MSS1T1434B192, VHS.

10. Lee to Mary Lee, Des Moines Rapids, September 10, 1837, Lee Family Papers, MSS1L51C20, VHS.

11. Lee to Carter Lee, St. Louis, October 8, 1837, Lee Papers, U.Va.; Lee to Jack Mackay, St. Louis, October 22, 1837, Lee Papers, GHS.
12. Lee Report, St. Louis, December 6, 1837, printed in *Executive Documents,* 25th Congress, 2d Session, vol. I, no. 139.
13. Lee to Mary Lee, Des Moines Rapids, September 10, 1837, Lee Family Papers, MSS1L51C20; Lee to Andrew Talcott, St. Louis, October 11, 1837, Talcott Papers, VHS; Lee to Carter Lee, St. Louis, October 8, 1837, Lee Papers, U.Va.
14. Lee to Carter Lee, St. Louis, October 8, 1837, Lee Papers, U.Va.; Long, *Memoirs,* 42; Freeman, *Lee,* I, 147; Missouri Historical Society, *Glimpses of the Past,* III (January–February 1936), "Letters of Robert E. Lee to Henry Kayser, 1838–1846."
15. Long, *Memoirs,* 42; Drumm, "Lee and the Mississippi River," 158–59; James Neal Primm, *Lion of the Valley: St. Louis, Missouri* (Boulder, CO, 1981), 156.
16. Lee Report, St. Louis, December 6, 1837, printed in *Executive Documents,* 25th Congress, 2d Session, vol. I, no. 139; Freeman, *Lee,* I 127, 147; Lee Report, St. Louis, October 6, 1840, printed in *Executive Documents,* 26th Congress, 2d Session, vol. I, no. 2.
17. Contract, December 13, 1837, Lee Papers, Missouri Historical Society, St. Louis, Missouri; Freeman, *Lee,* I, 147–48; Lee to Henry Kayser, Arlington, February 1, 1838, in "Lee to Kayser Letters," 4–6.
18. Lee to Mary Lee, Des Moines Rapids, September 10, 1837, Lee Family Papers, MSS1L51C20, VHS; Lee to Jack Mackay, St. Louis, October 22, 1837, Lee Papers, GHS.
19. Freeman, *Lee,* I, 148; Lee to Henry Kayser, Arlington, February 1, 1838, March 9, 1838, and Baltimore, April 2, 1838, "Lee to Kayser Letters," 4–9; MacDonald, *Mrs. Lee,* 68–69; Roy Meredith, *The Face of Robert E. Lee in Life and Legend* (New York, 1947), 17–19.
20. Mary Lee letter quoted in MacDonald, *Mrs. Lee,* 68–71; Freeman, *Lee,* I, 149.
21. Ruth Musser and John C. Krantz, Jr., "The Friendship of General Robert E. Lee and Dr. Wm. Beaumont," *Bulletin of the Institute of the History of Medicine,* VI (May 1929), 167–79; Beverly Orndorf, "Stomach 'Window' Made History," Richmond *Times-Dispatch,* July 30, 1989, G2.
22. Mrs. Max W. Myer, "Sarah Beaumont: Her Life and Loves," Missouri Historical Society *Bulletin,* XVII (October 1960), 16–25; Freeman, *Lee,* I, 80.
23. Mary Lee letters quoted in MacDonald, *Mrs. Lee,* 75–76; Mary and Robert Lee to George Washington Parke Custis, St. Louis, August 25, 1837[8], Lee Papers, U.Va.
24. Lee to Jack Mackay, St. Louis, June 27, 1838, Lee Papers, GHS.
25. Lee Report, St. Louis, October 24, 1838, printed in *Executive Documents,* 25th Congress, 3rd Session, vol. I, no. 1.
26. George W. Cullum, *Biographical Register of Officers and Graduates of the U.S. Military Academy,* 2 vols. (New York, 1868–79), I, 420.
27. Lee to Carter Lee, St. Louis, December 24, 1838, Lee Papers, U.Va.
28. Freeman, *Lee,* I, 157–58; Lee to Andrew Talcott, St. Louis, January 1, 1839, Talcott Papers, MSS1T1434B196, VHS.
29. Freeman, *Lee,* I, 159–69; Peter Temin, *The Jacksonian Economy* (New York, 1969); Lee to Horace Bliss, St. Louis, March 29, 1839, Lee Family Papers, MSS1L51C734, VHS.
30. Lee to Horace Bliss, St. Louis, March 29, 1839, Lee Family Papers, MSS1L51C734, VHS; John Fletcher Darby, *Personal Recollections* (St. Louis, 1880), 227–30.
31. Long, *Memoirs,* 43; Hyde, *Encyclopedia of the History of St. Louis,* 4 vols. (New York, 1899), 1054–56.
32. Lee Report, St. Louis, October 21, 1839, printed in *Executive Documents,* 26th Congress, 1st Session, vol. I, no. 1.
33. Mary Lee letter quoted in MacDonald, *Mrs. Lee,* 78.
34. Lee to Andrew Talcott, Arlington, May 18, 1839, Talcott Papers, MSS1T1434B198, VHS; Lee to Mary Lee, Louisville, June 5, 1839, quoted in J. William Jones, *Personal Reminiscences of General Robert E. Lee* (United States Historical Society ed., Baton Rouge, LA, 1989), 369.
35. Lee to Mary Lee, June 5, 1839, quoted in Jones, *Personal Reminiscences,* 369.
36. Lee Report, St. Louis, October 21, 1839, printed in *Executive Documents,* 26th Congress, 1st Session, vol. I, no. 1; Freeman, *Lee,* I, 174; Primm, *Lion,* 156.
37. Inventory, September 18, 1839, Lee Papers, Missouri Historical Society, St. Louis, Missouri; Lee to Jack Mackay, St. Louis, November 17, 1839, Lee Papers, GHS.
38. MacDonald, *Mrs. Lee,* 79.
39. Freeman, *Lee,* I, 178.
40. Paul C. Nagel, *The Lees of Virginia: Seven Generations of an American Family* (New York, 1990), 226–29.
41. Lee to Carter Lee, Arlington, January 30, 1840, February 23, 1840, and August 22, 1840, Lee Papers, U.Va.; Nagel, *Lee Family,* 229.
42. Freeman, *Lee,* I, 178–79; Lee to Mary Lee, White Sulphur Springs, August 4, 1840, Lee Family Papers, MSS1L51C26, VHS.
43. Lee to Tasy Beaumont, Arlington, January 21, 1840, Robert Edward Lee Papers, MSS2L515A40, and Lee to Bettie and Mattie Mason, St. Louis, August 31, 1840, Lee Family Papers, MSS1L51C734, VHS.
44. Inventory, January 1, 1840, Lee Papers, Missouri Historical Society, St. Louis, Missouri; Lee Report, St. Louis, October 21, 1840, printed in *Executive Documents,* 26th Congress, 1st Session, vol. I, no. 1; Primm, *Lion,* 156–57; Drumm, "Lee and the Mississippi River," 170–71.
45. Mark Twain, *Life on the Mississippi* (New York, 1874 and 1875), 470.
46. Lee to Jack Mackay, St. Louis, October 22, 1837, Lee Papers, GHS.

8. *"You Are Right in My Interest in the Pretty Women"*

1. Douglas S. Freeman, *R. E. Lee: A Biography,* 4 vols. (New York, 1934–35), I, 184–87; Federal Writers Project, *New York City Guide* (New York, 1970), 469.
2. George W. Cullum, *Biographical Register of the Officers and Graduates of the U.S. Military Academy,* 2 vols. (New York, 1869–79), I, 420.
3. Lee's reports to Totten, as well as his design of a new barracks for West Point, are in his letter-books at the Virginia Historical Society (Lee Family Papers, MSS1L51C735). See also Freeman, *Lee,* I, 184–202.
4. Robert E. Lee [Jr.], *Recollections and Letters of General Robert E. Lee* (Garden City, NY, 1904),

6–7; Mary P. Coulling, *The Lee Girls* (Winston-Salem, NC 1987), 16–17.

5. Cf. Freeman, *Lee,* I, 184–202, a chapter covering these years entitled "Five Drab Years End in Opportunity." Cf. also Thomas L. Connelly, *The Marble Man: Robert E. Lee and His Image in American Society* (New York, 1977), 163–93.

6. Lee to Fred. A. Smith, St. Louis, August 12, 1839, Lee Family Papers, MSS1L51C734, VHS.

7. James L. Morrison, Jr., *"The Best School in the World": West Point, the Pre–Civil War Years, 1833–1866* (Kent OH, 1986), 3–4, 37–60; Stephen E. Ambrose, *Duty, Honor, Country: A History of West Point* (Baltimore, 1966), 62–86.

8. Freeman, *Lee,* I, 186; Coulling, *Lee Girls,* photograph of Custis Family Bible, plate 2 following p. 114.

9. Lee to Mary Lee, Fort Hamilton, April 18, 1841, Robert E. Lee Papers, U.Va.; *New York City Guide,* 436–65.

10. Lee to Mary Lee, St. Louis, October 16, 1837, quoted in J. William Jones, *Personal Reminiscences of General Robert E. Lee* (United States Historical Society ed., Baton Rouge, LA, 1989), 368.

11. Quoted in Paul C. Nagel, *The Lees of Virginia: Seven Generations of an American Family* (New York, 1990), 242.

12. Coulling, *Lee Girls,* photograph of Custis Family Bible, plate 2 following p. 114; Rose Mortimer Ellzey MacDonald, *Mrs. Robert E. Lee* (Boston, 1939), 125–26, 151, 164; Lee's letters to Martha Custis Williams during 1844 printed in Avery Craven, ed., *"To Markie": The Letters of Robert E. Lee to Martha Custis Williams* (Cambridge, MA, 1933), 3–6.

13. Lee to Mary Lee, St. Louis, October 16, 1837, quoted in Jones, *Reminiscences,* 368–69; Lee to Mary Lee, Fort Hamilton, May 19, 1846, Lee Family Papers MSS1L51C48; and Lee to Mary Lee, Fort Hamilton, March 7, 1846, Lee Family Papers, MSS1L51C43, VHS.

14. Lee to Mary Custis ("Mother"), Fort Hamilton, May 13, [n.d.], George Bolling Lee Papers, MSS1L5114C6, VHS.

15. Coulling, *Lee Girls,* 17; Lee's will, one copy of which is in the Virginia Historical Society (MSS2L515A18).

16. Lee to Custis Lee, Fort Hamilton, November 30, 1845, Lee Family Papers, MSS1L51C35, VHS; Rooney Lee and Lee to Custis Lee, Fort Hamilton, December 18, 1845, Robert E. Lee Papers, U.Va.

17. Harper Lee, *To Kill a Mockingbird* (Popular Library, New York, 1962), 284.

18. Lee to Tasy (Sarah Beaumont Keim), Fort Hamilton, March 11, 1843, Robert Edward Lee Papers, MSS2L515A170, VHS.

19. Lee to Kayser, Fort Hamilton, June 16, 1845, printed in Missouri Historical Society, *Glimpses of the Past,* III (January–February 1936), "Letters of Robert E. Lee to Henry Kayser, 1838–1846," 38.

20. Lee to Markie (Martha Custis Williams), Fort Hamilton, September 2, 1844, in Craven, ed., *"To Markie,"* 4; Lee to Markie, Fort Hamilton, September 17, 1845, in Craven, ed., *"To Markie,"* 13; Craven, ed., *"To Markie,"* v–vii; National Park Service, *Arlington House* (Washington, DC, 1985), 41.

21. See Connelly, *Marble Man,* 172–76.

22. Twint quoted in A. L. Long, *Memoirs of Robert E. Lee* (Blue and Grey Press ed., Secaucus, NJ, 1983), 66–67. See Edgar Allan Poe, "Desultory Notes on Cats," in *The Unabridged Edgar Allan Poe* (Philadelphia, 1983), 984: "Cats were first invented in the Garden of Eden. According to the Rabbins, Eve had a pet cat, called Pusey; and from that circumstance arose a sect of cat-worshippers among the Eastern nations, called Puseyites, a sect which it is said, is still in existence somewhere."

23. Lee to Carter Lee, Arlington, February 14, 1843; Robert E. Lee Papers; Lee to Carter Lee, Fort Hamilton, July 13, 1846, Robert E. Lee Papers, U.Va.

24. Letters from the Secretary of War, May 18, 1842, and December 13, 1842, printed in *Executive Documents,* 27th Congress, 2d Session, vol. IV, no. 226; 27th Congress, 3d Session, vol. 1, no. 4; and "Changes in the Pay of the Army" in *Executive Documents,* 28th Congress, 1st Session, vol. V, no. 219.

25. Morrison, *"Best School,"* 20.

26. Freeman, *Lee,* I, 188; Lee to George A. Smith, Arlington, January 2, 1845, and September 18, 1845, Lee Family Papers, MSS1L51C734, and Lee to Mary Lee, San Antonio, September 13, 1856, Lee Family Papers, MSS1L51C168, VHS.

27. Lee to Mary Lee, Steamboat off Port Lavaca, Texas, August [September] 13, 1846, Lee Family Papers, MSS1L51C50, VHS.

28. Lee to Carter Lee, Washington, February 24, 1835, Robert E. Lee Papers, U.Va.

29. Records of Lee's investments and investing are in his letter books (Lee Family Papers, MSS1L51C734 and 735) at the Virginia Historical Society, his correspondence with Henry Kayser at the Missouri Historical Society, St. Louis. A letter to Anna Fitzhugh, Fort Hamilton, March 5, 1842, Lee Papers, Duke, is interesting in regards to investment strategy. One copy of Lee's will is in the Virginia Historical Society (MSS2L515A18).

30. This correspondence is in Lee's letter books (Lee Family Papers, MSS1L51C734 and 735) at the Virginia Historical Society, and in Lee's correspondence with Henry Kayser at the Missouri Historical Society.

31. Robert E. Lee microfilm reel from Records of the Adjutant General's Office, National Archives, Washington, DC; Lee to General N. Townson, Fort Hamilton, February 7 and February 9, 1846, and Lee to General R. Jones, Fort Hamilton, February 16, 1846, in Lee Letter book (MSS1L51C735), VHS.

32. Nagel, *Lees of Virginia,* 245; Lee to Carter Lee, Arlington, February 14, 1843, Robert E. Lee Papers, U.Va.

33. Lee to Henry Kayser, Fort Hamilton, December 19, 1845, in *Glimpses,* 41.

34. Lee to Mary Custis, Fort Hamilton, April 13 [n.d.], George Bolling Lee Papers, MSS1L5114C6, VHS.

35. Lee to Jack Mackay, Washington, March 18, 1845, typescript in GHS.

36. Mary Drake and William S. McFeely, eds., *Ulysses S. Grant: Memoirs and Selected Letters* (Library of America ed., New York, 1990), 33; on Scott, see the *Dictionary of American Biography.*

37. Freeman, *Lee,* I, 192.

38. Lee to Joseph Totten, Fort Hamilton, June 17, 1845, Lee Family Papers, MSS1L5C734, VHS.

39. Lee to Jack Mackay, Fort Hamilton, June 21, 1845, typescript in GHS.

40. Freeman, *Lee,* I, 202; the best military study of the Mexican War is still K. Jack Bauer, *The Mexican War, 1846–1848* (New York, 1974); the best work on the war is Otis A. Singletary, *The Mexican War* (Chicago, 1960).

41. Lee to Mary Lee, steamboat off Port Lavaca,

Texas, August [September ?] 13, 1846, Lee Family Papers, MSS1L51C50, VHS.

42. Lee to Rooney Lee, Fort Hamilton, March 31, 1846, Lee Family Papers, MSS1L51C45, VHS.

9. *"I Have Done No Good"*

1. Lee to Mary Lee, Steamboat from New Orleans to Lavaca, Texas, August [September] 13, 1846, Lee Family Papers, MSS1L51C50, VHS.
2. K. Jack Bauer, *The Mexican War, 1846–1848* (New York, 1974), 145–51.
3. *Ibid.,* 66–80; Robert W. Johannsen, *To the Halls of Montezuma: The Mexican War in the American Imagination* (New York, 1985), 7–16.
4. Roy Meredith, *The Face of Robert E. Lee: In Life and in Legend* (New York, 1947), 22–23.
5. Lee to Mary Lee, Steamboat from New Orleans to Lavaca, Texas, August [September] 13, 1846, Lee Family Papers, MSS1L51C50, VHS; Bauer, *Mexican War,* 146–48; T. Harry Williams in his edited volume, *With Beauregard in Mexico: The Mexican War Reminiscences of P. G. T. Beauregard* (Baton Rouge, LA, 1956), notes (27n): "Nearly all of the young regular officers who wrote about the Mexican War spilled pots of ink detailing the deficiencies of the volunteers." Lieutenant George B. McClellan wrote in his diary that "500 resolute men" could defeat the 1,700 volunteers in his column, "and all, from the General down to the dirtiest rascal of the filthy crew, would have been scared out of their wits (if they ever had any)." William Starr Myers, ed., *The Mexican War Diary of George B. McClellan* (Princeton, NJ, 1917), 36–37.
6. Douglas S. Freeman, *R. E. Lee: A Biography,* 4 vols. (New York, 1934–35), I, 205; Bauer, *Mexican War,* 147.
7. Williams, ed., *With Beauregard,* 9; Johannsen, *To the Halls,* 12–16.
8. Bauer, *Mexican War,* 146–49; Lee to Mary Lee, Rio Grande, October 11, 1846, quoted in Fitzhugh Lee, *General Lee* (New York, 1904), 34.
9. Bauer, *Mexican War,* 148–49; Lee to Mary Lee, Camp Near Monclova, November 11, 1846, Lee Family Papers, MSS1L51C59, VHS.
10. Lee to Mary Lee, Camp Near Monclova, November 11, 1846, Lee Family Papers, MSS1L51C59, VHS.
11. Bauer, *Mexican War,* 150–51, 201–08; George W. Hughes, *Memoir,* published in *Senate Executive Documents,* 31st Congress, 1st Session, vol. I, no. 32, 33–34.
12. Lee to Mary Lee, Camp Near Alamos River, October 19, 1846, Lee Family Papers, MSS1L51C57; and Lee to Custis and William [Rooney], Camp Near Saltillo, December 24, 1846, Lee Family Papers, MSS1L51C66, VHS.
13. Lee to Mary Lee, Camp Near Alamos River, October 19, 1846, Lee Family Papers, MSS1L51C57; Lee to Mary Lee, Camp Near Monclova, November 4, 1846, Lee Family Papers, MSS1L51C58, VHS.
14. Lee to Mary Lee, Camp Near Monclova, November 11, 1846, Lee Family Papers, MSS1L51C59, VHS.
15. Lee to Mary Lee, Camp Near Monclova, November 4, 1846, Lee Family Papers, MSS1L51C58, VHS. Other officers were not as impressed with Mexican food. Captain George W. Hughes, for example, wrote in his *Memoir* (published in *Senate Executive Documents,* 31st Congress, 1st Session, vol. I, no. 5. 32, 42), "Mexican cookery is, to my taste, *detestable;* but many Americans, less fastidious perhaps, affect to like it. Everything is rendered as hot as fire by *red pepper,* which enters in enormous quantities into each dish as an essential ingredient."
16. Lee to Mary Lee, Camp Near Parras, December 6, 1846, Lee Family Papers, MSS1L51C64, VHS.
17. Lee to Custis and William [Rooney] Lee, Camp Near Saltillo, December 24, 1846, Lee Family Papers, MSS1L51C66, VHS.
18. Lee to Mary Lee, Camp Near Saltillo, December 25, 1846, Lee Family Papers, MSS1L51C67, VHS.
19. Freeman, *Lee,* I, 217; A. L. Long, *Memoirs of Robert E. Lee* (Blue and Grey Press ed., Secaucus, NJ, 1983), 49–51; J. William Jones, *Personal Reminiscences of General Robert E. Lee* (United States Historical Society ed., Baton Rouge, LA, 1989), 288–90.
20. Freeman, *Lee,* I, 217–18; Lee to Mary Lee, Camp near Saltillo, December 25, 1846, Lee Family Papers, MSS1L51C67, VHS; Lee to My Dear Boys, Ship *Massachusetts,* Off Lobos, February 27, 1847, printed in Jones, *Personal Reminiscences,* 371–73.
21. Winfield Scott, *Memoirs of Lieut.-General Scott* (New York, 1864), 423; Freeman, *Lee,* I, 218–23.
22. Lee to My Dear Boys, Ship *Massachusetts,* Off Lobos, February 27, 1847, in Jones, *Personal Reminiscences,* 371–73.
23. Lee to Mary Custis, Ship *Massachusetts,* Off Lobos Island, February 22, 1847, Lee Family Papers, MSS1L51C, VHS.
24. Lee to My Dear Boys, Ship *Massachusetts,* Off Lobos, February 27, 1847, in Jones, *Personal Reminiscences,* 371–73.
25. *Ibid.;* Lee to Mary Custis, Ship *Massachusetts,* Off Lobos Island, February 22, 1847, Lee Family Papers, MSS1L51C, VHS.
26. Bauer, *Mexican War,* 210–18.
27. *Ibid.,* 244–48; Freeman, *Lee,* I, 222–28.
28. Williams, ed., *With Beauregard,* 26–27.
29. Bauer, *Mexican War,* 249–50; Freeman, *Lee,* I, 229–31.
30. Lee letter printed in Fitzhugh Lee, *General Lee,* 36–37.
31. Quoted in J. William Jones, *Life and Letters of Robert Edward Lee, Soldier and Man* (Washington, DC, 1906), 45–46; Freeman, *Lee,* I, 230–32.
32. Bauer, *Mexican War,* 250–53; Freeman, *Lee,* I, 232–34.
33. Bauer, *Mexican War,* 252; Lee to Smith Lee, March 27, 1847, in Fitzhugh Lee, *General Lee,* 37.
34. Lee letter in Fitzhugh Lee, *General Lee,* 36–37; Lee to Smith Lee, March 27, 1847, in Fitzhugh Lee, *General Lee,* 37; Lee to Mary Lee, Vera Cruz, April 12, 1847, George Bolling Lee Papers, MSS1L5114C17, VHS.
35. Mary Drake and William S. McFeely, eds., *Ulysses S. Grant: Memoirs and Selected Letters* (Library of America ed., New York, 1990), 65.
36. Lee to Mary Lee, Vera Cruz, April 12, 1847, George Bolling Lee Papers, MSS1L5114C17, VHS.
37. Bauer, *Mexican War,* 259–60; Hunt's story is in Long, *Memoirs,* 68–70.

10. *"The Gallant, Indefatigable Captain Lee"*

1. Fitzwalter told this story to A. L. Long, who included it in his *Memoirs of Robert E. Lee* (Blue and Grey Press ed., Secaucus, NJ, 1983), 53.
2. K. Jack Bauer, *The Mexican War, 1846–1848* (New York, 1974), 263–64. For good maps, see Vincent J. Esposito, ed., *The West Point Atlas of American Wars*, 2 vols. (New York, 1959), I, map 15C.
3. Lee letter, Perote, April 25, 1847, quoted in Fitzhugh Lee, *General Lee* (New York, 1904), 38.
4. Bauer, *Mexican War*, 264–68; Scott's Report of Cerro Gordo printed in *Senate Executive Documents*, 30th Congress, 1st Session, vol. I, 261–64.
5. Lee letter, Perote, April 25, 1847, quoted in Fitzhugh Lee, *Lee*, 39; Bauer, *Mexican War*, 267–68.
6. T. Harry Williams, ed., *With Beauregard in Mexico: The Mexican War Reminiscences of P. G. T. Beauregard* (Baton Rouge, LA, 1956), 40.
7. William Starr Myers, *The Mexican War Diary of George B. McClellan* (Princeton, NJ, 1917), 70–71; Lee to Mary Lee, Vera Cruz, April 12, 1847, George Bolling Lee Papers, MSS1L5114C17, VHS.
8. Scott's Report of Cerro Gordo printed in *Senate Executive Documents*, 30th Congress, 1st Session, vol. I, 263; Douglas S. Freeman, *R. E. Lee: A Biography*, 4 vols. (New York, 1934–35), I, 248; George W. Cullum, *Biographical Register of the Officers and Graduates of the U.S. Military Academy*, 2 vols. (New York, 1869–79), I, 420.
9. Lee to Custis Lee, Perote, April 25, 1847, in Fitzhugh Lee, *Lee*, 40–41.
10. Bauer, *Mexican War*, 268–74.
11. Freeman, *Lee*, I, 250–51.
12. *Ibid.*; Bauer, *Mexican War*, 272.
13. Bauer, *Mexican War*, 288–91.
14. Williams, ed., *With Beauregard*, 47–48; Lee to Major J. L. Smith, Tacubaya, August 21, 1847, Lee Family Papers, MSS1L51C735, VHS; Freeman, *Lee*, I, 256–58; Bauer, *Mexican War*, 291.
15. Lee to Major J. L. Smith, Tacubaya, August 21, 1847, Lee Family Papers, MSS1L51C735, VHS; Freeman, *Lee* I, 258–72; Bauer, *Mexican War*, 291–301.
16. Scott's Report of Contreras and Churubusco, printed in *Senate Executive Documents*, 30th Congress, 1st Session, vol. I, 306, 315; "Pillow Talk," printed in *Senate Executive Documents*, 30th Congress, 1st Session, vol. VIII, 73; Cullum, *Biographical Register*, I, 420.
17. Bauer, *Mexican War*, 306–03; Freeman, *Lee*, I, 272–73.
18. Freeman, *Lee*, I, 272–73; Lee to Major J. L. Smith, Tacubaya, August 21, 1847, Lee Family Papers, MSS1L51C735, VHS; "Pillow Talk," printed in *Senate Executive Documents*, 30th Congress, 1st Session, vol. VIII, 55, 461.
19. Bauer, *Mexican War*, 308–11; Lee to Major J. L. Smith, City of Mexico, September 15, 1847, Lee Family Papers, MSS1L51C735, VHS.
20. Bauer, *Mexican War*, 311–13; Williams, ed., *With Beauregard*, 68–74.
21. Lee to Major J. L. Smith, City of Mexico, September 15, 1847, Lee Family Papers, MSS1L51C735, VHS; "Pillow Talk," printed in *Senate Executive Documents*, 30th Congress, 1st Session, vol. VIII, 143–44.
22. Scott's Report of the Battle for Mexico City, printed in *Senate Executive Documents*, 30th Congress, 1st Session, vol. I, 375–425; "Pillow Talk," printed in *Senate Executive Documents*, 30th Congress, 1st Session, vol. VIII, 529; Bauer, *Mexican War*, 316–18; Freeman, *Lee* I, 281–83; Lee to Major J. L. Smith, City of Mexico, September 15, 1847, Lee Family Papers, MSS1L51X735, VHS; Cullum, *Biographical Register*, I, 421.
23. Bauer, *Mexican War*, 358–74; see also Robert W. Johannsen, *To the Halls of Montezuma: The Mexican War in the American Imagination* (New York, 1985), 270–301.
24. Lee to Mary Lee, Mexico City, February 13, 1848, Lee Family Papers, MSS1L51C76, VHS.
25. Lee to Carter Lee, Mexico City, February 13, 1848, Robert E. Lee Papers, U.Va.
26. Lee to Mary Lee, Mexico City, February 8, 1848, Lee Family Papers, MSS1L51C74, VHS.
27. Lee to Anna Fitzhugh, Mexico, April 12, 1848, Lee Family Papers, MSS1L51C80, and Lee to John Mackay, City of Mexico, October 2, 1847, Robert Edward Lee Papers, MSS2L515A62, VHS.
28. Lee to Carter Lee, Mexico, February 13, 1848, Robert E. Lee Papers, U.Va.
29. Lee to Jack Mackay, City of Mexico, October 2, 1848, Robert Edward Lee Papers, MSS2L515A62, VHS.
30. Bauer, *Mexican War*, 371–74.
31. Lee to Carter Lee, City of Mexico, March 18, 1848, Robert E. Lee Papers, U.Va.; "Pillow Talk," printed in *Senate Executive Documents*, 30th Congress, 1st Session, vol. VIII.
32. "Pillow Talk," printed in *Senate Executive Documents*, 30th Congress, 1st Session, vol. I 55, 75–80, 143–46, and Hitchcock to *New York Sun*, October 26, 1847.
33. Lee to Carter Lee, Mexico City, March 18, 1848, Robert E. Lee Papers, U.Va.; Bauer, *Mexican War*, 373–74.
34. Lee to Parke Custis, Mexico City, April 8, 1848, Lee Family Papers, MSS1L51C79, VHS; Lee to Carter Lee, Mexico City, March 18, 1848, U.Va.
35. Long, *Memoirs*, 64.
36. Lee to Mary Lee, Mexico City, February 13, 1848, Lee Family Papers, MSS1L51C76; Lee to Agnes Lee, Mexico City, February 12, 1848, Lee Family Papers, MSS1L51C51–75, VHS; Lee to Annie Lee, Mexico City, February 29, 1848, Lee Papers, W & L.
37. Scott's words quoted in Freeman, *Lee* I, 294; E. D. Keyes, *Fifty Years' Observation of Men and Events* (New York, 1884), 206.
38. For this emphasis, see Grady McWhiney and Perry D. Jamieson, *Attack and Die: Civil War Military Tactics and the Southern Heritage* (University Press, AL, 1982), 27–47.
39. Winfield Scott, *Memoirs* (New York, 1864), 416.
40. Robert E. Lee, Jr., *Recollections and Letters of General Robert E. Lee* (Garden City, NY, 1904), 3–4.

11. *"I Am Fond of Independence"*

1. Lee to Smith Lee, Arlington, June 30, 1848, in Fitzhugh Lee, *General Lee* (New York, 1904), 49–50; Douglas S. Freeman, *R. E. Lee: A Biography*, 4 vols. (New York, 1934–35), I, 302–03.
2. The best source of information on Arlington

House is the house itself, as restored and kept by the National Park Service. Helpful, too, are the "handout" sheet offered to visitors and handbook (number 133), *Arlington House: A Guide to Arlington House, the Robert E. Lee Memorial* (Washington, DC, 1985).

3. *Ibid.* Seventh U.S. Census (1850), manuscript returns; Inventory of Personal Property at Arlington, January 1, 1858, Robert E. Lee Papers, Box 15, W & L.

4. Robert E. Lee, Jr., *Recollections and Letters of General Robert E. Lee* (Garden City, NY, 1904), 5–6.

5. Mary Custis to Custis letter printed in Rose Mortimer Ellzey MacDonald, *Mrs. Robert E. Lee* (Boston, 1939), 104–06.

6. Lee, Jr., *Lee,* 9; Mary P. Coulling, "Nicknames, Cats, and Catsup Bottles: The Family Life of the R. W. Lees," *W & L The Alumni Magazine of Washington and Lee* (Winter 1989), 10–14.

7. Freeman, *Lee,* I, 303.

8. *Ibid.,* 303–04; George W. Cullum, *Biographical Register of the Officers and Graduates of the U.S. Military Academy,* 2 vols. (New York, 1869–79), I, 421; Lee to Markie, Arlington, April 1, 1849, in Avery Craven, ed., *"To Markie": The Letters of Robert E. Lee to Martha Custis Williams* (Cambridge, MA, 1933), 22, places him at Arlington on that date.

9. Lee to Mary Lee, Off Cedar Key, February 13, 1849, Lee Family Papers, MSS1L51C87; Lee to R. Jones, Baltimore, January 7, 1850, Lee Papers, VHS.

10. Freeman, *Lee,* I, 309; Mary P. Coulling, *The Lee Girls* (Winston-Salem, NC, 1987), 26.

11. Lee to Mary Lee, Sollers' Point, June 23, 1849, Lee Family Papers, MSS1L51C93, VHS.

12. Reports on the work are printed in *Senate Executive Documents,* 31st Congress, 1st Session, vol. I, 217; 31st Congress, 2nd Session, vol. I, 355; 32nd Congress, 1st Session, vol. I, 351.

13. Lee to Mary Lee, Baltimore, August 7, 1849, Lee Family Papers, MSS1L51C96, VHS.

14. Lee to Mary Lee, Newport, August 15, 1849, Lee Family Papers, MSS1L51C97, VHS.

15. Lee to Mary Lee, Newport, August 24, 1849, Lee Family Papers, MSS1L51C99, VHS.

16. Lee to Mary Lee, Newport, August 25, 1849, Lee Family Papers, MSS1L51C100; Lee to Mary Lee, West Point, August 31, 1849, Lee Family Papers, MSS1L51C101, VHS.

17. *Senate Executive Documents,* 31st Congress, 1st Session, vol. I, 217; MacDonald, *Mrs. Lee,* 102–03; Lee, Jr., *Lee,* 11.

18. Lee to Davis, Baltimore, February 2, 1850, Lee Papers, VHS.

19. Freeman, *Lee,* I, 306–07; Davis statement in A. L. Long, *Memoirs of Robert E. Lee* (Blue and Grey Press ed., Secaucus, NJ, 1983), 72–73.

20. Lee to R. Jones, Baltimore, January 7, 1850, Lee Family Papers, MSS1L51C734; Lee to Scott, Baltimore, February 5, 1850, Lee Family Papers, MSS1L51C734, VHS.

21. Lee to Mary Lee, Baltimore, January 2, 1851, Lee Family Papers, MSS1L51C107, VHS.

22. Coulling, *Lee Girls,* 37; Lee to Markie, Baltimore, May 10, 1851, in Craven, ed., *"To Markie,"* 24–27; Paul C. Nagel, *The Lees of Virginia: Seven Generations of an American Family* (New York, 1990), 259.

23. Lee to Custis Lee, Baltimore, April 13, 1851, Family Papers, MSS1L51C109, VHS.

24. Freeman, *Lee,* I, 310–11; Emory M. Thomas, *Bold Dragoon: The Life of J. E. B. Stuart* (New York, 1986), 24–25 and note.

25. Lee to Custis Lee, Baltimore, June 22, 1851, USMA.

26. Freeman, *Lee,* I, 311; Thomas, *Bold Dragoon,* 25.

27. *The Book of Common Prayer* (New York, 1850), 12.

28. Lee to Custis Lee, Baltimore, March 28, 1852, Robert Edward Lee Papers, MSS2L515A75, VHS.

29. Lee to Mary Custis, Baltimore, March 17, 1852, Lee Family Papers, MSS1L51C734, VHS.

30. Lee to Joseph Totten, Fort Carroll, May 28, 1852, Lee Family Papers, MSS1L5K735 Lee to Totten, Fort Carroll, July 1, 1852, Lee Family Papers, MSS1L51C735; Lee to Totten, Baltimore, July 25, 1852, Lee Family Papers, MSS1L51C734, VHS.

31. Lee to Dennis Mahan, Arlington, August 16, 1852, Lee Family Papers, MSS1L51C734, VHS.

12. *"The Climate Is as Harsh to Me as My Duties"*

1. Douglas S. Freeman, *R. E. Lee: A Biography,* 4 vols. (New York, 1934–35), I, 319; George W. Cullum, *Biographical Register of the Offices and Graduates of the U.S. Military Academy,* 2 vols. (New York, 1869–79), I, 420.

2. James L. Morrison, Jr., *"The Best School in the World": West Point, the Pre–Civil War Years, 1833–1866* (Kent, OH, 1986), 113–51; Stephen E. Ambrose, *Duty, Honor, Country: A History of West Point* (Baltimore, 1966), 166.

3. Lee to Joseph Totten, West Point, March 15, 1853, Superintendent's Letter Book, USMA; Freeman, *Lee,* I. 329.

4. Freeman, *Lee,* I, 347–48; Morrison, *"Best School,"* 114–25.

5. Lee to Joseph Totten, West Point, January 9, 1854, Superintendent's Letter Book, USMA; Freeman, *Lee,* I, 332.

6. Lee to Joseph Totten, West Point, October 9, 1852, October 8, 1853, October 7, 1854; March 4, 1853, Superintendent's Letter Book, USMA; Freeman, *Lee* I, 326–27; Ambrose, *Duty, Honor, Country,* 141–42.

7. Rosters of academic and military staff members and the corps of cadets in *Senate Executive Documents,* 33rd Congress, 2nd Session, vol. II, 117–58; Lee to Anna Whistler, West Point, September 28, 1852, Superintendent's Letter Book, USMA; on Whistler, see Stanley Weintraub, *Whistler: A Biography* (New York, 1974), and Gordon Fleming, *The Young Whistler, 1834–66* (London, 1978).

8. Fleming, *Young Whistler,* 98.

9. *Ibid.,* 99. Lee to Anna Whistler, West Point, May 26, 1853, and August 31, 1853, Superintendent's Letter Book, USMA.

10. Lee to Joseph Totten, West Point, March 10, 1854. Superintendent's Letter Book, USMA.

11. Weintraub, *Whistler,* 23–24; Fleming insists that Whistler self-destructed on purpose (*Young Whistler,* 102–07).

12. Lee to Markie, West Point, June 29, 1854, in Avery Craven, ed., *"To Markie": The Letters of Robert E. Lee to Martha Custis Williams* (Cambridge, MA, 1933), 49; Lee to Joseph Totten, West Point, July 8, 1854, Superintendent's Letter Book, USMA.

13. Freeman, *Lee,* I, 332–34; Lee to Joseph Totten, West Point, December 28, 1853, and September 1, 1854, Superintendent's Letter Book, USMA.

14. Robert E. Lee, Jr., *Recollections and Letters of General Robert E. Lee* (Garden City, NY, 1904), 12–13.
15. Lee to Markie, West Point, September 16, 1853, in Craven, ed., *"To Markie,"* 35–37.
16. Jefferson Davis, "Robert E. Lee," *North American Review,* 150 (January 1890), 57; Lee to Joseph Totten, West Point, January 29, 1855, Superintendent's Letter Book, USMA.
17. Mary Custis Lee de Butts, ed., *Growing Up in the 1850s: The Journal of Agnes Lee* (Chapel Hill, NC, 1984), 27, 30, 32.
18. Lee to Anna Fitzhugh, West Point, April 28, 1854, Lee Family Papers, MSS1L51C137, VHS.
19. Lee to Markie, West Point, June 29, 1854, in Craven, ed. *"To Markie,"* 48.
20. Lee to Anna Fitzhugh, West Point, April 3, 1854, Lee Family Papers, MSS1L51C132, VHS.
21. Morrison, *"Best School,"* Freeman, *Lee,* I, 352–58.
22. Freeman, *Lee,* I, 352–58; Ambrose, *Duty, Honor, Country,* 99–102; Morrison, *"Best School,"* 47–49.
23. Lee Investment Statement, Robert E. Lee Papers, W & L; Lee will, Robert Edward Lee Papers, MSS2L515A18, VHS; *Senate Executive Documents,* 33rd Congress, 2nd Session, vol. II, 136.
24. Freeman, *Lee,* I, 346.
25. Mary P. Coulling, *The Lee Girls* (Winston-Salem, NC, 1987), 34–35.
26. de Butts, ed., *Agnes Lee,* 13; Lee to Markie, West Point, June 23, 1853, in Craven, ed. *"To Markie,"* 31.
27. Lee to Mary Lee, West Point, April 27, 1853, Lee Family Papers, MSS1L51C117, and May 2, 1853, Lee Family Papers, MSS1L51C118, VHS. For a sample of Mary Custis's saintly outlook, see her letter to Custis Lee, Arlington, December 5, 1861, Lee Family Papers, MSS1L51C110, VHS.
28. de Butts, ed., *Agnes Lee,* 14, 17–18; Lee to Mary Lee, West Point, May 18, 1853, Lee Family Papers, MSS1L51C125, and May 10, 1853, Lee Family Papers, MSS1L51C122, VHS.
29. de Butts, ed., *Agnes Lee,* 18–19; *The Book of Common Prayer* (New York, 1850), 205–06.
30. Notes—essays in Diary; see also Emory M. Thomas, "God and General Lee," *Anglican and Episcopal History,* LX (March 1991), 15–24, which concludes:

Though evangelically idyllic,
Pious and Virginiaphilic,
Not God; he was Lee
No Puritan Lee,
The Paul he resembled was Tillich.

31. Lee, Jr., *Lee,* 12; de Butts, ed., *Agnes Lee,* 31, 28, 30, 45; Morrison, *"Best School,"* 55.
32. de Butts, ed., *Agnes Lee,* 25, 40–41; Freeman, *Lee,* I, 349–50.
33. Freeman, *Lee,* I, 352–58; Lee to Bonaparte, West Point, March 12, 1853, Robert E. Lee Papers, W & L.
34. Lee to Markie, West Point, March 14, 1855, in Craven, ed., *"To Markie,"* 52–53.
35. Cullum, *Biographical Register,* 421; de Butts, ed., *Agnes Lee,* 52–59.
36. *Senate Executive Documents,* 33rd Congress, 2nd Session, vol. II, 133.
37. *Senate Executive Documents,* 33rd Congress, 1st Session, vol. II, 200; Lee to Mrs. A. A. Draper, West Point, December 21, 1852, Mrs. A. A. Draper Papers, USMA.

13. *"The Question Which I Have Staved Off for 20 Years"*

1. Lee to Andrew Talcott, Washington, June 29, 1837, Talcott Papers, MSS1T1434B190, VHS.
2. Lee to Markie, West Point, March 14, 1855, in Avery Craven, ed., *"To Markie": The Letters of Robert E. Lee to Martha Custis Williams* (Cambridge, MA, 1933), 53.
3. George W. Cullum, *Biographical Register of the Officers and Graduates of the U.S. Military Academy,* 2 vols. (New York, 1869–79), I, 421; Lee to Carter Lee, Louisville, May 10, 1855, U Va.; on Johnston, see Charles P. Roland, *Albert Sidney Johnston, Soldier of Three Republics* (Austin, TX, 1964); Mary Lee to John R. Peters, West Point, February 2, 1855, Lee Papers, MSS1L514B67, VHS.
4. Diary.
5. Lee to Mary Lee, Jefferson Barracks, July 1, 1855, Lee Family Papers, MSS1L51C141; July 9, 1855, Lee Papers, MSS1L5113A80; September 9, 1855, Lee Family Papers, MSS1L51C147, VHS; Lee to G. W. P. Custis, West Point, March 2, 1855, Lee Family Papers, MSS1L51C126–50, VHS.
6. Diary.
7. Lee to G. W. P. Custis, West Point, March 2, 1855, Lee Family Papers, MSS1L51C126–50; Lee to Mary Lee, Fort Mason, March 28, 1856, Lee Family Papers, MSS1L51C152, VHS.
8. Lee to William F. Wickham, Arlington, January 2, 1856; Lee to Francis Nelson, White House, February 15, 1856; Lee to William Overton Winston, Hanover Court House, February 18, 1856, Lee Family Papers, MSS1L51C734, VHS.
9. Diary.
10. Lee to Agnes Lee, Camp Cooper, August 4, 1856, Lee Papers, MSS2L515A77; Lee to Mary Lee, Camp Cooper, April 12, 1856, Lee Family Papers, MSS1L51C154, VHS; Lee to Eliza Mackay Stiles, Indian Territory, May 24, 1856, Lee Papers, GHS; Diary; Carl Coke Rister, *Robert E. Lee in Texas* (Norman, OK, 1946), 3–4, 17–18.
11. Rister, *Lee in Texas,* 25–36; Lee to Mary Lee, Camp Cooper, April 12, 1856, Lee Family Papers, MSS1L51C154, VHS.
12. Lee to Mary Lee, Camp Cooper, April 12, 1856, Lee Family Papers, MSS1L51C154; Lee to Eliza Mackay Stiles, Camp on the Clear Fork of the Brazos, May 24, 1856, Lee Papers, GHS.
13. Rister, *Lee in Texas,* 40–52; Diary; Douglas S. Freeman, *R. E. Lee: A Biography,* 4 vols. (New York, 1934–35), I, 366–68; Lee to Mary Lee, Camp Cooper, August 4, 1856, Lee Family Papers, MSS1L51C151; Lee's Report of Don Carlos Buell, Camp Cooper, July 24, 1856, Lee Family Papers, MSS1L51C735, VHS.
14. Lee to William Overton Winston, Camp Cooper, July 24, 1856, Robert Edward Lee Papers, MSS2L515A172; Lee to Mary Lee, Camp Cooper, August 4, 1856, Lee Family Papers, MSS1L51C161; Lee to Mary Lee, Ringgold Barracks, October 13(?), 1856, Lee Family Papers, MSS1L51C169, VHS.
15. Henry Adams, *The Education of Henry Adams: An Autobiography* (Boston, 1918), 57–58.
16. Mary Custis to Custis Lee, Arlington, December 5, 1851, Lee Family Papers, MSS1L51C110, VHS.
17. Lee to Mary Lee, Camp Cooper, August 4, 1856, Lee Family Papers, MSS1L51C161; Lee to Mary Lee, San Antonio, September 13, 1856, Lee Family Papers, MSS1L51C168; Lee to Mary Lee, Jefferson Barracks, September 9, 1855, Lee Family Papers, MSS1L51C147; Lee to Rooney Lee,

Ringgold Barracks, November 1, 1856, Lee Family Papers, MSS1L51C734; Lee to Mary Lee, Fort Brown, December 20, 1856, Lee Family Papers, MSS1L51C180, VHS.
18. Lee to Eliza Mackay Stiles, Camp Cooper, August 14, 1856, Lee Papers, GHS; Rister, *Lee in Texas,* 61–76; Diary.
19. Diary.
20. Lee to Mary Lee, Camp Cooper, May 18, 1857, Lee Family Papers, MSS1L51C203, VHS; Lee to Nephew, Arlington, September 6, 1858, Robert E. Lee Papers, Stratford; Lee to Custis Lee, Baltimore, March 28, 1852, Robert Edward Lee Papers, MSS2L515A75; Lee to Mary Lee, Baltimore, August 15, 1849, Lee Family Papers, MSS1L51C97, VHS; Lee to Agnes Lee, August 11, 1855, quoted in Freeman, *Lee,* I, 361–62.
21. Mary Lee to Lee, Arlington, July 24, 1857, Lee Family Papers, MSS1L51C213; Lee to Winfield Scott, San Antonio, August 11, 1857, Lee Family Papers, MSS1L51C734, VHS; Scott to John B. Floyd, Washington, May 8, 1857, in Edward S. Ellis, *The Camp Fires of General Lee* (Philadelphia, 1886), 71.
22. Lee to Mary Lee, San Antonio, July 27, 1857, Lee Family Papers, MSS1L51C219, VHS.
23. Lee to Mary Lee, Fort Brown, January 31, 1857, Lee Family Papers, MSS1L51C186, VHS.

24. Diary.
25. Mary Lee to Lee, Berkley Springs, August 4 [1857], Lee Family Papers, MSS1L51C222, VHS.
26. Lee to Mary Lee, San Antonio, August 22, 1857, Lee Family Papers, MSS1L51C225, VHS; Paul C. Nagel, *The Lees of Virginia: Seven Generations of an American Family* (New York, 1990), 260; Lee to Charlotte Wickham, San Antonio, October 10, 1857, Lee Family Papers, MSS1L51C734, VHS.
27. See Kenneth M. Stampp, *America in 1857: A Nation on the Brink* (New York, 1990); Lee to Edward Childe, Fort Brown, January 9, 1857, Robert E. Lee Papers, Stratford.
28. Lee to Mary Lee, Fort Brown, December 27, 1856, Lee Family Papers, MSS1L51C181.
29. Contract with James Eveleth, Washington, August 1, 1852, Lee Family Papers, MSS1L51C734, VHS; Lee to Mary Lee, Fort Brown, December 27, 1856, Lee Family Papers, MSS1L51C181.
30. Freeman, *Lee,* I, 377; Rose Mortimer Ellzey MacDonald, *Mrs. Robert E. Lee* (Boston, 1939), 123–25; Diary.
31. Diary; Lee to Albert Sidney Johnston, San Antonio, October 25, 1857, Mrs. Mason Barret Collection, Howard-Tilton Library, Tulane University, New Orleans, Louisiana.

14. *"How Hard It Is to Get Contentment"*

1. Robert E. Lee, Jr., *Recollections and Letters of General Robert E. Lee* (Garden City, NY, 1904), 20–21; Thomas L. Connelly, *The Marble Man: Robert E. Lee and His Image in American Society* (New York, 1977), 218–19.
2. Douglas S. Freeman, *R. E. Lee: A Biography,* 4 vols. (New York, 1934–35), I, 379–80; Lee to Anna Fitzhugh, Arlington, November 22, 1857, Lee Papers, Duke; and Paul C. Nagel, *The Lees of Virginia: Seven Generations of an American Family* (New York, 1990), 260–61.
3. Lee to Custis Lee, Arlington, March 12, 1858, and January 17, 1858, Lee Papers, Duke; Freeman, *Lee,* I, 382–83.
4. Diary; Freeman, *Lee,* I, 380n.
5. Lee to Custis Lee, Arlington, March 17, 1858, Lee Papers, Duke.
6. Lee to Edward C. Turner, Arlington, February 13, 1858, U.Va.; Lee to Anna Fitzhugh, Arlington, November 22, 1857, Lee Papers, Duke; Freeman, *Lee* I, 379–81; Lee to Custis Lee, Arlington, March 17, 1858, Lee Papers, Duke.
7. Mary Lee to W. G. Webster, Arlington, February 17, 1858, MOC; Lee to Custis Lee, Arlington, January 17, 1858, Lee Papers, Duke.
8. Lee to Rooney Lee, Arlington, May 30, 1858, George Bolling Lee Papers, MSS1L5114C26; Lee to William O. Winston, Alexandria, July 8, 1858, Winston Papers, MSS2W7336C3, VHS; Freeman, *Lee,* I, 390.
9. *New York Tribune,* June 24, 1859.
10. Lee to Custis Lee, Arlington, July 2, 1859, in J. William Jones, *Life and Letters of Robert Edward Lee, Soldier and Man* (Washington, DC, 1906), 102; *New York Tribune,* June 28, 1859.
11. Lee to Rooney Lee, Arlington, February 24, 1858, George Bolling Lee Papers, MSS1L5114C25, VHS; Lee to Rooney Lee, San Antonio, March 12, 1860, George Bolling Lee Papers, MSS1L5114C32, VHS.
12. Freeman, *Lee,* I, 386–90.
13. Diary; Richard Eppes Diary, Eppes Papers, VHS.
14. Diary; Lee to Rooney Lee, Arlington, New

Year; 1860, George Bolling Lee Papers, MSS1L5114C31, VHS; Freeman, *Lee,* I, 403.
15. Stuart to My Dear Mama, January 31, 1860, Stuart Papers, VHS, printed as " 'The Greatest Service I Rendered the State'; J. E. B. Stuart's Account of the Capture of John Brown," *Virginia Magazine of History and Biography,* 94 (July 1986), 345–57; Freeman, *Lee,* I, 394–97.
16. Freeman, *Lee,* I, 394–97; Stephen B. Oates, *To Purge This Land with Blood: A Biography of John Brown* (New York, 1970), 298–300.
17. Israel Green, "The Capture of John Brown," *North American Review* (December 1885), 564–65; Freeman, *Lee,* I, 397–400; Oates, *Brown,* 300–02; Stuart to My Dear Mama, January 31, 1860, Stuart Papers, VHS.
18. Freeman, *Lee* I, 396n; cf. Craig M. Simpson, *A Good Southerner: The Life of Henry A. Wise of Virginia* (Chapel Hill, NC, 1985), 203–18.
19. Oates, *Brown,* 334–36.
20. Emory M. Thomas, *The Confederate Nation, 1861–1865* (New York, 1979), 1–4.
21. Freeman, *Lee,* I, 403; Emory M. Thomas, *Travels to Hallowed Ground: A Historian's Journey to the American Civil War* (Columbia, SC, 1987), 12–18.
22. Diary; Freeman, *Lee,* I, 403–04.
23. Lee, Jr., *Lee,* 306.
24. Lee to Anne Lee, San Antonio, August 27, 1860, Lee Family Papers, MSS1L51C260; Lee to Rooney Lee, Ringgold Barracks, April 2, 1860, George Bolling Lee Papers, MSS1L5114C330, VHS; Freeman, *Lee,* I, 409–10.
25. Freeman, *Lee,* I, 405–09; Diary; Lee to Rooney Lee, San Antonio, May 19, 1860, George Bolling Lee Papers, MSS1L5114C34, VHS.
26. Lee to Mary Lee, Fort Brown, April 25, 1860, Lee Family Papers, MSS1L51C250, VHS; Lee to Custis Lee, San Antonio, July 4, 1860, Robert E. Lee Papers, Library of Congress, Washington, DC; Lee to Agnes Lee, San Antonio, June 8, 1860, Lee Family Papers, MSS1L51C253, VHS; Lee to Mary Lee, San Antonio, June 18, 1860, Lee Family Papers, MSS1L51C255, VHS.

27. Lee to Agnes Lee, San Antonio, June 8, 1860, Lee Family Papers, MSS1L51C253, VHS.
28. Lee to Rooney Lee, San Antonio, December 3, 1860, George Bolling Lee Papers, MSS1L5114C340, VHS; Lee to Annette Carter, Fort Mason, January 16, 1861, Robert E. Lee Papers, W & L; Avery Craven, ed., *"To Markie": The Letters of Robert E. Lee to Martha Custis Williams* (Cambridge, MA, 1933), 56n; Lee to Markie, Fort Mason, January 22, 1861, in Craven, *"To Markie,"* 58.
29. Lee to Custis Lee, Fort Mason, January 30, 1861, Lee Papers, Duke: Lee to Mary Lee, Fort Mason, January 23, 1861, Lee Family Papers, MSS1L51C271, VHS; Lee letter of January 23, 1861 (probably to Custis Lee), printed in Freeman, *Lee,* I, 420–21.
30. Diary; Mrs. Caroline Baldwin Darron, "Recollections of the Twiggs Surrender," in *Battles and Leaders,* I, 36 and n.
31. Diary; E. D. Keyes, *Fifty Years' Observation of Men and Events* (New York, 1884), 205–07; Freeman, *Lee,* I, 431–32.
32. Freeman, *Lee,* I, 434; Walker to Lee, March 15,

1861, in *O.R.,* series IV, vol. I, 165–66; Lee to Lorenzo Thomas, Arlington, March 30, 1861, National Archives, Robert E. Lee microfilm.
33. Lee to Reverdy Johnson, Lexington, February 25, 1868, in Lee, Jr., *Lee,* 27–28; Freeman, *Lee,* I, 439; Joseph E. Johnston, *Narrative of Military Operations* (New York, 1874), 10.
34. Rose Mortimer Ellzey MacDonald, *Mrs. Robert E. Lee* (Boston, 1939), 144; *Wartime Papers,* 8–10; Freeman, *Lee,* I, 440–45.
35. Freeman, *Lee,* I, 445–47, 463–64; *Wartime Papers,* 10; James I, Robertson, Jr., ed., *Proceedings of the Advisory Council of the State of Virginia* (Richmond, VA, 1977), 1–2; Freeman, *Lee,* John Letcher of Virginia: The Story of Virginia's Civil War Governor* (University Press, AL, 1966), 119.
36. Lee to sister [Ann Marshall], Arlington, April 20, 1861, printed in Freeman, *Lee,* I, 443; This context requires reference to Bertram Wyatt-Brown, *Southern Honor: Ethics and Behavior in the Old South* (New York, 1982), and Bertram Wyatt-Brown, *Yankee Saints and Southern Sinners* (Baton Rouge, LA, 1985), 183–213.

15. *"Can Anybody Say They Know His Brother?"*

1. George H. Reese, ed., *Proceedings of the Virginia State Convention of 1861,* 4 vols. (Richmond, VA, 1965), IV, 256–57; Douglas S. Freeman, *R. E. Lee: A Biography,* 4 vols. (New York, 1934–35), I, 464–65; Richmond *Dispatch,* April 23, 1861.
2. Richmond *Examiner,* March 19, 1861; the editorial "Gli Animali Parlanti" is also in Frederick S. Daniel, *The Richmond Examiner During the War* (New York, 1868), 7–18. See also Emory M. Thomas, *The Confederate State of Richmond; A Biography of the Capital* (Austin, TX, 1971), 7–8, and Virginius Dabney, *Pistols and Pointed Pens: The Dueling Editors of Old Virginia* (Chapel Hill, NC, 1987), 38–60.
3. Calder Loth, ed., *The Virginia Landmarks Register* (3rd ed.), Charlottesville, NC, 1986), 390–91; Reese, ed., *Proceedings,* 368–70.
4. Walter Taylor, *General Lee: His Campaigns in Virginia, 1861–1865* (Morningside ed., Dayton, OH, 1975), 21–22; A. L. Long, *Memoirs of Robert E. Lee* (Blue and Grey Press ed., Secaucus, NJ, 1983), 98, 112 13.
5. See chapter 14, n. 00 and note; Long, *Memoirs,* 112.
6. Reese, ed., *Proceedings,* IV, 371–72.
7. Freeman, *Lee,* I, 470; Alexander H. Stephens, *A Constitutional View of the Late War Between the States,* 2 vols. (Chicago, 1868–70), II, 385.
8. Lee to John Letcher, Richmond, June 15, 1861, *Wartime Papers,* 50–52; William H. Richardson to John Letcher, Richmond, April 17, 1861, in Reese, ed., *Proceedings,* IV, 90–92; Lee A. Wallace, Jr., *A Guide to Virginia Military Organizations, 1861–1865* (Richmond, VA, 1964), 9–12.
9. Lee to John Letcher, Richmond, June 15, 1861, *Wartime Papers,* 50–52; Letcher Proclamation, Richmond, May 3, 1861, *O.R.,* II, 797–98; Freeman, *Lee* I, 492–94.
10. Freeman, *Lee,* I, 484–88; see Douglas S. Freeman, *Lee's Lieutenants: A Study in Command,* 3 vols. (New York, 1942–44), III, xvi–xxvi.
11. Freeman, *Lee,* I, 489, 639; James I. Robertson, Jr., ed., *Proceedings of the Advisory Council of the State of Virginia, April 21–June 19, 1861* (Richmond, VA, 1977), 50 and 53n; C. Vann Woodward, ed., *Mary Chestnut's Civil War* (New Haven, 1981), 14n., 16; Freeman, *Lee's Lieutenants,* I, 720n; Taylor, *General Lee,* 21.

12. Lee to Mary Lee, Richmond, May 16, 1861, *Wartime Papers,* 31; Lee to Mary Lee, Manassas, May 28, 1861, *ibid.,* 39–40; Lee to Mary Lee, Richmond, June 9, 1861, *ibid.,* 45–46; Freeman, *Lee,* I, 511; Lee to Mary Lee, Richmond, June 11, 1861, *Wartime Papers,* 47–48; Lee to Mary Lee, Richmond, June 24, 1861, *ibid.,* 53–54; Lee to Mary Lee, Richmond, May 25, 1861, *ibid.,* 36–37.
13. Mary Lee to General Sanford, May 30, 1861, typescript in Lee Papers, MOC; Irvin McDowell to Mary Lee, Arlington, May 30, 1861, Lee Papers, MOC.
14. Lee to Mary Lee, Richmond, June 11, 1861, *Wartime Papers,* 47–48.
15. Lee to Jefferson Davis, telegram, Richmond, May 7, 1861, *ibid.,* 21.
16. Taylor, *General Lee,* 25.
17. William Kauffman Scarborough, ed., *The Diary of Edmund Ruffin,* 3 vols. (Baton Rouge, LA, 1972–89), II, 26–27, 99; Robertson, ed., *Advisory Council,* 49n
18. Ruffin to Jefferson Davis, telegram, Richmond, May 16, 1861, *O.R.,* LI, part 2, 92; Bledsoe to Jefferson Davis, U.Va., May 10, 1861, in Lynda Lasswell Crist and Mary Seaton Dix, eds., *The Papers of Jefferson Davis,* vol. 7 (Baton Rouge, LA, 1992), 160–62 and n.
19. Walter Taylor, *Four Years with General Lee* (New York, 1878), 11.
20. D. G. Duncan to Leroy Pope Walker, Richmond, April 26, 1861, *O.R.,* L1, part 2, 39; D. G. Duncan to Leroy Pope Walker, Richmond, May 5, 1861, *O.R.,* L1, part 2, 65–66; D. G. Duncan to Leroy Pope Walker, Richmond, May 7, 1861, *O.R.,* L1, part 2, 71.
21. Emory M. Thomas, *The Confederate Nation, 1861–1865* (New York 1979), 98–101; Thomas, *Richmond,* 32–34, 41–42.
22. Richmond *Whig,* June 7, 1861.
23. Thomas, *Richmond,* 41–42; John Letcher to Lee, Richmond, May 7, 1861, *O.R.,* II, 813, gave Lee command of all troops from any states if they were in Virginia; Letcher Proclamation incorporated in Lee's General Orders No. 25, June 8, 1861, *O.R.,* II, 911–12; Lee to Mary Lee, Richmond, June 9, 1861, *Wartime Papers,* 45–46.
24. The standard biography of Davis is now William

C. Davis, *Jefferson Davis: The Man and His Hour* (New York, 1991).

25. T. Harry Williams, *P. G. T. Beauregard: Napoleon in Gray* (Baton Rouge, LA, 1955), 65–66, 74–75; Freeman, *Lee's Lieutenants,* I, 42–43.
26. The standard campaign study of First Manassas/Bull Run is William C. Davis, *Battle at Bull Run: A History of the First Major Campaign of the Civil War* (Garden City, NY, 1977).

27. Lee to Custis Lee, Valley Mountain, September 3, 1861, *Wartime Papers,* 69–70.
28. For the background events of Lee's sojourn into western Virginia (and for his actions there), see Jack Zinn, *R. E. Lee's Cheat Mountain Campaign* (Parsons, WV, 1974); Freeman, *Lee,* I, 541–42.
29. Freeman, *Lee,* I, 539.
30. Taylor, *General Lee,* 25.
31. Woodward, ed., *Mary Chesnut,* 116.

16. *"Never Fought a Battle . . . Pious Horror of Guerrillas . . . Extreme Tenderness of Blood"*

1. Jack Zinn, *R. E. Lee's Cheat Mountain Campaign* (Parson, WV, 1974), 91–95; Douglas S. Freeman, *R. E. Lee: A Biography,* 4 vols. (New York, 1934–35), I, 557; John H. Worsham, *One of Jackson's Foot Cavalry* (Jackson, TN, 1961), 17; Eva Margaret Carnes, "George W. (Bishop) Peterkin at Valley Mountain," *Randolph County Historical Society Magazine of History and Biography,* 12 (April 1961), 97–98.
2. Lee to Annie and Agnes Lee, Valley Mountain, August 29, 1861, *Wartime Papers,* 67; Lee to Mary Lee, Valley Mountain, August 9, 1861, *ibid.,* 63; Lee to Custis Lee, Valley Mountain, September 3, 1861, *ibid.,* 69–70.
3. Lee to Custis Lee, Valley Mountain, September 3, 1861, *ibid.,* 69–70; Lee to Mary Lee, Valley Mountain, September 1, 1861, *ibid.,* 68–69; Walter Taylor, *Four Years with General Lee* (New York, 1878), 17.
4. Robert E. Lee, Jr., *Recollections and Letters of General Robert E. Lee* (Garden City, NY, 1904), 40–41; Walter Taylor, *General Lee: His Campaigns in Virginia, 1861–1865* (Morningside ed., Dayton, OH, 1975), 31, 35–36.
5. Ezra J. Warner, *Generals in Gray: Lives of the Confederate Commanders* (Baton Rouge, LA, 1959), 193–94; William L. Wessels, *Born to Be a Soldier: The Military Career of William Wing Loring of St. Augustine, Florida* (Fort Worth, FL, 1971).
6. Zinn, *Cheat Mountain,* 36–39; Lee to Mary Lee, Valley Mountain, August 9, 1861, *Wartime Papers,* 63–64.
7. Allan Nevins, *The War for the Union,* Vol. I, *The Improvised War, 1861–1862* (New York, 1959), 226–46. The standard biography of Rosecrans (called Rosencrantz by many Confederates) is William M. Lamers, *The Edge of Glory: A Biography of William S. Rosecrans, U.S.A.* (New York, 1961).
8. Lee to Samuel Cooper, Valley Mountain, August 13, 1861, Robert Edward Lee Papers, 1861, MSS3L515B249, VHS.
9. *Ibid.;* Zinn, *Cheat Mountain,* 14–31, 112–14.
10. Edward A. Pollard, *The First Year of the War* (Richmond, VA, 1862), 160–62; Warner, *Generals in Gray,* 89–90; Craig M. Simpson, *A Good Southerner: The Life of Henry A. Wise of Virginia* (Chapel Hill, NC, 1985), 254–62.
11. The confirmed list of full generals is in *O.R.,* V, 828–29; Zinn, *Cheat Mountain,* 72–81, Freeman, *Lee,* I, 541–42, 552–53; Cooper to Lee, Richmond, September 4, 1861, Robert Edward Lee Papers, 1861, MSS3L515B37–58, VHS.
12. A. L. Long, *Memoirs of Robert E. Lee* (Blue and Grey Press ed., Secaucus, NJ, 1983), 120–21.
13. Zinn, *Cheat Mountain,* 43–45, 82–84; Long, *Memoirs,* 122–23; Warner, *Generals in Gray,* 266–67.
14. Garnett Andrews, "A Battle Planned Not Fought," *Confederate Veteran,* V (June 1887), 294; Taylor, *Four Years,* 22–26; Zinn, *Cheat Mountain,* 112–16.
15. Zinn, *Cheat Mountain,* 156; Taylor, *Four Years,* 28–29.
16. Rust to Loring, Camp Bartow, September 13, 1861, *O.R.,* V, 191–92; Zinn, *Cheat Mountain,* 146–54, 171–78; Freeman, *Lee,* I, 566–68.
17. Lee's letters are printed in Lee, Jr., *Recollections,* 44–47.
18. Special Order, September 14, 1861, *O.R.,* V, 192–93.
19. Lee to Mary Lee, Valley Mountain, September 17, 1861, *Wartime Papers,* 73–74; Zinn, *Cheat Mountain,* 186–92.
20. Zinn, *Cheat Mountain,* 201–02; Freeman, *Lee,* I, 583–87; Taylor, *Four Years,* 32–33.
21. T. C. Morton, "Anecdotes of General R. E. Lee," *SHSP,* XI, 519; Lee to Mary Lee, Camp on Sewell's Mountain, September 26, 1861, *Wartime Papers,* 78.
22. Wise to Lee, Dogwood Gap Camp, September 11, 1861, Lee Papers, VHS; Freeman, *Lee,* I, 591–92; Cooper to Lee, Richmond, September 12, 1861, Robert Edward Lee Papers, 1861, MSS3L515B37–38, VHS.
23. Lee to Floyd, Sewell Mountain, September 25, 1861, *O.R.,* LI, part 2, 312; Freeman, *Lee,* I, 583–87; Benjamin to Wise, Richmond, September 20, 1861, *O.R.,* V, 148–49; Taylor, *General Lee,* 34.
24. Freeman, *Lee,* I, 595–97; Taylor, *Four Years,* 34 and n., 35; Davis speech quoted in Lee, Jr., *Recollections,* 53.
25. Lee to Mary Lee, Sewell's Mountain, October 7, 1861, *Wartime Papers,* 79–80; Lee to Mary Lee, Valley Mountain, September 9, 1861, *ibid.,* 70–71; *Richmond Enquirer,* September 6, 1861, and October 7, 1861; *Richmond Whig,* September 17, 1861; *Richmond Examiner,* September 14, 1861.
26. Pollard, *First Year,* 168, 354n.
27. Dr. J. R. Buist letter printed in *National Intelligencer,* November 22, 1861, and cited in Zinn, *Cheat Mountain,* 201; Freeman, *Lee,* I, 602–03, 644–45; Zinn, *Cheat Mountain,* 88, 202; John Preston Sheffey to Josephine, Camp Arbuckle, October 12, 1861, in Joan Tracy Armstrong, ed., "The Civil War Letters of Captain John Preston Sheffey," typescript in possession of Marshall Steck Collins, Marion, Virginia.
28. Zinn, *Cheat Mountain,* 76, 89.

17. *"Low-Country Gentlemen Curse Lee"*

1. See Emory M. Thomas, *The Confederate Nation, 1861–1865* (New York, 1979), 120–36.
2. Richmond *Dispatch*, November 1, 1861; Douglas S. Freeman, *R. E. Lee: A Biography*, 4 vols. (New York, 1934–35), I, 605.
3. Daniel Ammen, "DuPont and the Port Royal Expedition," *Battles and Leaders*, I, 671–91; Special Orders No. 206, Richmond, November 5, 1861, *Wartime Papers*, 84.
4. Lee to Benjamin, Coosawhatchie, November 9, 1861, *Wartime Papers*, 85; Lee to Mildred Lee, Charleston, November 15, 1861, *ibid.*, 86.
5. Robert E. Lee, Jr., *Recollections and Letters of General Robert E. Lee* (Garden City, NY, 1904), 53; Davis to Joseph E. Brown, Richmond, November 6, 1861, and calendered in Lynda Laswell Crist and Mary Seaton Dix, eds., *The Papers of Jefferson Davis*, Vol. 7 (Baton Rouge, LA, 1992), 397; Frederick Maurice, ed., *An Aide-de-Camp of Lee . . . Charles Marshall. . . .* (Boston, 1927), 59.
6. Lee to Cooper, Savannah, November 21, 1861, *Wartime Papers*, 87–88; Lee to Annie and Agnes Lee, Savannah, November 22, 1861, *ibid.*, 89.
7. See Lee to Joseph R. Anderson, Coosawhatchie, January 28, 1862, *ibid.*, 108–09.
8. Lee to Annie Lee, Coosawhatchie, December 8, 1861, *ibid.*, 91; Lee to Custis Lee, Coosawhatchie, December 29, 1861, *ibid.*, 98; Lee to Mary Lee, Savannah, February 8, 1862, *ibid.*, 111–12; Lee to Annie Lee, Savannah, March 2, 1862, *ibid.*, 121–22.
9. Lee to Francis Pickens, Coosawhatchie, December 27, 1861, *O.R.*, VI, 357.
10. Lee to Governor Brown, Savannah, February 10, 1862, *O.R.*, VI, 379.
11. Lee to Cooper, Savannah, February 18, 1862, *Wartime Papers*, 115; Lee to Ripley, Savannah, February 19, 1862, *ibid.*, 116.
12. C. Vann Woodward, ed., *Mary Chesnut's Civil War* (New Haven, 1981), 246; William Kauffman Searborough, ed., *The Diary of Edmund Ruffin*, 3 vols. (Baton Rouge, LA, 1972–89), II, 177; Robert K. Krick, "The Army of Northern Virginia in September 1862: Its Circumstances, Its Opportunities, and Why It Should Not Have Been at Sharpsburg," in Gary W. Gallagher, ed., *Antietam: Essays on the 1862 Maryland Campaign* (Kent, OH, 1989), 49–50; Pickens to Davis, Columbia, January 7, 1862, *O.R.*, VI, 366.
13. Walter Taylor, *General Lee: His Campaigns in Virginia, 1861–1865* (Morningside ed., Dayton, OH, 1975), 40–41; A. L. Long, *Memoirs of Robert*

E. Lee (Blue and Grey Press ed., Secaucus, NJ, 1983), 134–35; Charleston *Mercury*, December 12, 13, and 25, 1861.
14. Lee to Benjamin, Coosawhatchie, December 20, 1861, *Wartime Papers*, 92.
15. See Thomas, *Confederate Nation*, 120–28.
16. Lee to Mary Lee, Coosawhatchie, December 25, 1861, *Wartime Papers*, 96.
17. Lee to Mary Lee, Coosawhatchie, January 4, 1862, Robert E. Lee Papers, Duke; Lee to Custis Lee, Coosawhatchie, January 19, 1862, Robert E. Lee Papers, Duke.
18. Lee to Annie and Agnes Lee, Savannah, November 22, 1861, *Wartime Papers*, 88–89; Lee to Mary Lee, Coosawhatchie, December 25, 1861, *ibid.*, 96.
19. Long, *Memoirs*, 22–23; Lee to Mary Lee, Coosawhatchie, January 18, 1862, *Wartime Papers*, 103–04; Lee to Custis Lee, Coosawhatchie, January 19, 1862, Robert E. Lee Papers, Duke. Some question exists about the possibility of an earlier visit during the period when Lee was on duty at Cockspur Island. See John Morgan Dederer, "Robert E. Lee's First Visit to His Father's Grave: Reevaluating Well-Known Historical Documents," *Virginia Magazine of History and Biography*, 102 (January 1994), 73–88.
20. Lee to Annie Lee, Savannah, March 2, 1862, *Wartime Papers*, 121–22.
21. See Emory M. Thomas, *Travels to Hallowed Ground* (Columbia, SC, 1987), 61–65.
22. Davis to Lee, Richmond, March 2, 1862, telegram, *O.R.*, VI, 400; Lee to Davis, Savannah, March 2, 1862, telegram, *Wartime Papers*, 123.
23. Charleston *Mercury*, March 5, 1862; "Hermes" was John W. Bagby, editor of the *Southern Literary Messenger*.
24. *Ibid.*; Freeman, *Lee*, II, 4–6; General Orders No. 14, Richmond, March 13, 1862, *Wartime Papers*, 127.
25. Lee to Mary Lee, Richmond, March 13, 1862, *Wartime Papers*, 127–28; Lee to Carter Lee, Richmond, March 14, 1861[2], Robert E. Lee Papers, W & L.
26. See Thomas, *Confederate Nation*, 138–44.
27. Lee to Mary Lee, Richmond, March 14, 1862, *Wartime Papers*, 128.
28. Lee to Mary Lee, Richmond, April 30, 1862, *ibid.*, 15; Lee to Mary Lee, Richmond, March 15, 1862, *ibid.*, 129; Lee, Jr., *Recollections*, 70; Lee to Mary Lee, Richmond, March 22, 1862, *Wartime Papers*, 134.

18. *"Lee Is Audacity Personified"*

1. Lee to Mary Lee, Richmond, March 22, 1862, *Wartime Papers*, 134.
2. Studies of McClellan's Peninsula Campaign include Stephen W. Sears, *To the Gates of Richmond: The Peninsula Campaign* (New York, 1992); Clifford Dowdey, *The Seven Days: The Emergence of Lee* (Boston, 1964); and the extensive attention in Douglas S. Freeman, *R. E. Lee: A Biography*, 4 vols. (New York, 1934–35), II, 1–249.
3. Frederick Maurice, ed., *An Aide-de-Camp of Lee . . . Charles Marshall. . . .* (Boston, 1927), 30–43; Emory M. Thomas, *The Confederate Nation, 1861–1865* (New York, 1979), 152–55; and Albert B. Moore, *Conscription*

and Conflict in the Confederacy (New York, 1924).
4. The standard work on the *Virginia* and the *Monitor* is William C. Davis, *Duel Between the First Ironclads* (Garden City, NY, 1975). The important work is William N. Still, Jr., *Iron Afloat: The Story of the Confederate Armorclads* (Nashville, TN, 1971).
5. Thomas, *Confederate Nation*, 145 ff.
6. Douglas S. Freeman, *Lee's Lieutenants: A Study in Command*, 3 vols. (New York, 1942–44), I, 148–53; Joseph E. Johnston, *Narrative of Military Operations*, ed. Frank E. Vandiver (Bloomington, IN, 1959), 112–14; Magruder to Lee, Yorktown, April 5, 1862, *O.R.*, XI, 3, 425; Magruder to Lee,

Yorktown, April 15, 1862, *O.R.*, XI, 3, 442; Magruder to George Wythe Randolph, Baylor's House, James River, April 5, 1862, *O.R.*, II, 2, 532.
7. Special Orders No. 6, Richmond, April 12, 1862, *Wartime Papers*, 145; Freeman, *Lee*, II, 2–4; Freeman, *Lee's Lieutenants*, I, 137–47.
8. Freeman, *Lee's Lieutenants*, I, 148–51; Johnston, *Narrative*, 112–16.
9. Thomas, *Confederate Nation*, 123–28.
10. Lee to Magruder, Richmond, March 29, 1862, *Wartime Papers*, 140.
11. Lee to Pemberton, telegram, Richmond, April 21, 1862, *ibid.*, 145.
12. Lee to Henry Heth, Richmond, April 18, 1862, *ibid.*, 146–47; Lee to Humphrey Marshall, Richmond, April 18, 1862, *ibid.*, 147.
13. Lee to Pemberton, Richmond, April 20, 1862, *ibid.*, 150.
14. Lee to Jackson, Richmond, April 21, 1862, *ibid.*,
15. Lee to Mary Lee, Richmond, April 22, 1862, *ibid.*, 153–54.
16. *Ibid.*
17. Lee to Johnston, Richmond, April 21, 1862, *ibid.*, 152–53; Freeman, *Lee's Lieutenants*, I, 145.
18. Lee to Huger, Richmond, April 30, 1862, *Wartime Papers*, 162; Lee to Mallory, Richmond, April 8, 1862, *ibid.*, 143; Lee to Johnston, Richmond, April 30, 1862, *ibid.*, 161; Lee to Johnston, Richmond, May 2, 1862, *ibid.*, 164; Dowdey, *Seven Days*, 65–68; Sears, *Gates of Richmond*, 92–94; Alfred L. Rives to Judah Benjamin, Richmond, March 12, 1862, *O.R.*, IX, 61–62; Thomas, *Confederate Nation*, 159–60.
19. Lee to Mary Lee, Richmond, May 13, 1862, *Wartime Papers*, 172.
20. Freeman, *Lee*, II, 252–53; Lee to Mary Lee, Coosawhatchie, December 25, 1861, *Wartime Papers*, 96.
21. Emory M. Thomas, *The Confederate State of Richmond: A Biography of the Capital* (Austin, TX, 1971), 92–94; Thomas, *Confederate Nation*, 159.
22. Walter F. McCaleb, ed., *Memoirs, with Special Reference to Secession and the Civil War*, by John H. Reagan (New York, 1906), 139; Freeman, *Lee*, II, 48.
23. Sears, *Gates of Richmond*, 92–94; Freeman, *Lee's Lieutenants*, I, 209–11.
24. Lee to Johnston, Richmond, May 18, 1862, *Wartime Papers*, 176 (italics added); Lee to Johnston,

Richmond, May 21, 1862, *ibid.*, 176–77; Freeman, *Lee*, II, 60–61.
25. Lee to Jackson, Richmond, May 16, 1862, *Wartime Papers*, 175; Sears, *Gates of Richmond*, 110–12.
26. Freeman, *Lee*, II, 67–74; Dowdey, *Seven Days*, 84–127; Sears, *Gates of Richmond*, 118–44; Edward Porter Alexander, *Fighting for the Confederacy: The Personal Recollections of General Edward Porter Alexander*, ed. Gary W. Gallagher (Chapel Hill, NC, 1989), 88.
27. Freeman, *Lee*, II, 74; Alexander, *Fighting*, 88; Dowdey, *Seven Days*, 127.
28. Special Orders No. 22, Richmond, June 1, 1862, *Wartime Papers*, 181–82; Maurice, ed., *Marshall*, 79–80; Walter H. Taylor, *General Lee: His Campaigns in Virginia, 1861–1865* (Morningside ed., Dayton, OH, 1975), 57; Lee to Walter H. Stevens, Headquarters, Dabb's House, June 3, 1862, *Wartime Papers*, 182–83.
29. Freeman, *Lee*, II, 86–87; Lee to Davis, Headquarters near Richmond, June 5, 1862, *Wartime Papers*, 184.
30. Lee to Chass, Dabb's, June 22, 1862, *Wartime Papers*, 197.
31. R. H. Gray to his father, Camp near Richmond, July 10, 1862, Lee Papers (24072), VSL.
32. Alexander, *Fighting*, 91, 568n.
33. See Freeman, *Lee*, I, 294–300.
34. Lee to Mary Lee, June 10, 1862, *Wartime Papers*, 189.
35. Thomas, *Confederate Nation*, 156–58; Russell F. Weigley, *The American Way of War: A History of United States Military Strategy and Policy* (New York, 1973).
36. Freeman, *Lee*, I, 641–43, II, 13, 77; H. Douglas Pitts, "Dabbs House: A Historical Treasure," typescript at VHS; A. L. Long, *Memoirs of Robert E. Lee* (Blue and Grey Press ed., Secaucus, NJ, 1983), 166; Taylor, *General Lee*, 55; Alexander, *Fighting*, 89.
37. Maurice, ed., *Marshall*, 77–78 and n.; Freeman, *Lee*, II, 88–89.
38. Lee to Davis, Dabb's, June 5, 1862, *Wartime Papers*, 183–84; see also Lee to Josiah Gorgas, Headquarters, June 5, 1862, *ibid.*, 185.
39. McClellan to Wife, June 15, 1862, quoted in Sears, *Gates of Richmond*, 159.
40. Lee to Davis, Headquarters, June 10, 1862, *Wartime Papers*, 188.

19. *"The Federal Army Should Have Been Destroyed"*

1. Douglas S. Freeman, *R. E. Lee: A Biography*, 4 vols. (New York, 1934–35), II, 252–54; Rose Mortimer Ellzey MacDonald, *Mrs. Robert E. Lee* (Boston, 1939), 161–63.
2. Freeman, *Lee*, II, 253–54; Report of Colonel Robert O. Taylor, June 1, 1862, *O.R.*, XI, 1, 738; Report of J. H. Simpson, June 16, 1862, *O.R.*, XI, 1, 1051; Memorandom of J. H. Simpson, *O.R.* XI, part 1, 1060.
3. Lee to Mary Lee, Richmond, June 10, 1862, *Wartime Papers*, 189; Lee to Chass, Dabb's, June 22, 1862, *Wartime Papers*, 197.
4. It is possible that Lee visited Mary Lee at White House on his way to Richmond from South Carolina; a few days remain unaccounted. But Lee's letter of March 14, 1862, to his wife does not indicate that he had recently visited with her. Lee to Mary Lee, Richmond, March 14, 1862, *Wartime Papers*, 127–28; Lee to Mary Lee, Dabb's, June 10, 1862, *ibid.*, 190; Lee to Mary Lee, June 25, 1862, *ibid.*, 201;

Lee to Mary Lee, Dabb's Farm, July 9, 1862, *ibid.*, 230.
5. Emory M. Thomas, *Bold Dragoon: The Life of J. E. B. Stuart* (New York, 1986), 109–24; Lee to Stuart, Dabb's, June 11, 1862, *Wartime Papers*, 192; Douglas S. Freeman, *Lee's Lieutenants: A Study in Command*, 3 vols. (New York, 1942–44), I, 275–302.
6. For Jackson's campaign, see Robert G. Tanner, *Stonewall in the Valley: Thomas J. "Stonewall" Jackson's Shenandoah Valley Campaign, Spring 1862* (Garden City, NY, 1976), and Freeman, *Lee's Lieutenants*, I, 303–488. Jackson to Lee, Near Mount Meridian, June 13, 1862, *Wartime Papers*, 193; A. L. Long, *Memoirs of Robert E. Lee* (Blue and Grey Press ed., Secaucus, NJ, 1983), 166.
7. Lee to Jackson, Headquarters, Near Richmond, June 16, 1862, *Wartime Papers*, 194; Daniel H. Hill, "Lee Attacks North of the Chickahominy," in *Battles and Leaders*, II, 347.

8. Frank E. Vandiver, *Mighty Stonewall* (New York, 1957), 293–94.
9. Biographies of Lee's principal subordinates at this juncture include Vandiver, *ibid.;* Hal Bridges, *Lee's Maverick General: Daniel Harvey Hill* (New York, 1961); James I. Robertson, Jr., *General A. P. Hill: The Story of a Confederate Warrior* (New York, 1987); and William G. Piston, *Lee's Tarnished Lieutenant: James Longstreet and His Place in Southern History* (Athens, GA, 1987).
10. Stephen W. Sears, *To the Gates of Richmond: The Peninsula Campaign* (New York, 1992), 155–56, 374–78, 385–91.
11. Frederick Maurice, ed., *An Aide-de-Camp of Lee . . . Charles Marshall. . . .* (Boston, 1927), 84–85; James Longstreet, *From Manassas to Appomattox: Memoirs of the Civil War in America* (Philadelphia, 1896), 121–22; Walter H. Taylor, *General Lee: His Campaigns in Virginia, 1861–1865* (Morningside ed., Dayton, OH 1975), 60–62.
12. Maurice, ed., *Marshall,* 86; General Orders No. 75, Headquarters, Department of Northern Virginia, June 24, 1862, *Wartime Papers,* 198–200.
13. Lee to Davis, Headquarters, June 24 [25], 1862, *ibid.,* 200; Sears, *Gates of Richmond,* 184–89; Freeman, *Lee,* II, 118–20; Lee to Davis, HQ, June 26, 1862, *Wartime Papers,* 201; Lee to Huger, HQ, June 26, 1862, *ibid.,* 201–202.
14. T. C. DeLeon, *Four Years in Rebel Capitals* (Mobile, AL, 1890), 204; Lee to Davis, Headquarters, June 24 [25], 1862, *Wartime Papers,* 200.
15. Lee to Davis, Headquarters, Dabb's House, June 26, 1862, *Wartime Papers,* 201; General Orders No. 75, Headquarters, Department of Northern Virginia, June 24, 1862, *ibid.,* 198–99; Report on Seven Days, Headquarters, Army of Northern Virginia, March 6, 1863, *ibid.,* 211–14; Taylor, *General Lee,* 65–66; Chilton to Davis, Headquarters, June 26, 1862, *Wartime Papers,* 202.
16. Freeman, *Lee,* II, 122–35; Clifford Dowdey, *The Seven Days: The Emergence of Lee* (Boston, 1964), 172–92; General Orders No. 75, Headquarters, Department of Northern Virginia, June 24, 1862, *Wartime Papers,* 198–99; Maurice, ed., *Marshall,* 91; Joseph L. Brent, *Memoirs of the War* (New Orleans, 1940), 160–62.
17. Sears, *Gates of Richmond,* 199–203; Vandiver, *Mighty Stonewall,* 300–02.
18. Freeman, *Lee,* II, 129–35; Constance Cary Harrison, *Recollections Grave and Gay* (New York, 1911), 72–73; Sears, *Gates to Richmond,* 208.
19. Maurice, ed., *Marshall,* 89–96; Freeman, *Lee,* II, 136–38; Sears, *Gates to Richmond,* 219.
20. Maurice, ed., *Marshall,* 99; Sears, *Gates to Richmond,* 217–35; Freeman, *Lee,* II, 138–52.
21. Taylor, *General Lee,* 68; Maurice, ed., *Marshall,* 99; Freeman, *Lee,* II, 155–56 and n.; Sears, *Gates to Richmond,* 235–48; Dowdey, *Seven Days,* 235–45.
22. Freeman, *Lee,* II, 159–65; D. R. Jones Report, July 28, 1862, *O.R.,* XI, 2, 690; Stuart Report, July 14, 1862, *O.R.,* XI, 2, 515–17; Sears, *Gates to Richmond,* 258–59.
23. Lee to Davis, Headquarters, Williamsburg Road, June 29, 1862, *Wartime Papers,* 205–06; Freeman, *Lee,* II, 165.
24. Freeman, *Lee,* II, 166–78; Sears, *Gates to Richmond,* 260–63; Magruder Report, *O.R.,* XI, 2, 662–63; Brent, *Memoirs,* 192.
25. Lee to Magruder, Headquarters, Army of Northern Virginia, June 29, 1862, *Wartime Papers,* 205; Sears, *Gates to Richmond,* 269–74.
26. Freeman, *Lee's Lieutenants,* I, 561–64; Freeman, *Lee,* II, 572–82; Vandiver, *Mighty Stonewall,* 315–17.
27. Freeman, *Lee,* II, 179–99; Dowdey, *Seven Days,* 282–315; Sears, *Gates to Richmond,* 277–307; Freeman, *Lee's Lieutenants,* I, 565–87; John Goode, *Recollections of a Lifetime* (Washington, DC, 1906), 58, cited in Freeman, *Lee,* II, 202.
28. Daniel H. Hill, "McClellan's Change of Base and Malvern Hill," in *Battles and Leaders,* II, 391; Hill's Report, July 3, 1863, *O.R.,* XI, 2, 628; Longstreet, *Memoirs,* 143; Freeman, *Lee,* II, 200–04.
29. Lee's order, prepared by Chilton, is in *O.R.,* XI, 2, 677; Freeman, *Lee,* II, 205–10.
30. Lee's attack orders are in *O.R.,* XI, 2, 677–78; Freeman, *Lee,* II, 210–11.
31. Sears, *Gates to Richmond,* 322–36; Freeman, *Lee's Lieutenants,* I, 599–604; Dowdey, *Seven Days,* 338–46; Freeman, *Lee,* II, 210–19; Hill, "McClellan's Change of Base and Malvern Hill," 394.
32. John Lamb, conversation with Freeman, cited in *Lee,* II, 218–19 and note.
33. General Orders No. 75, Headquarters in the Field, July 7, 1862, *Wartime Papers,* 210; Lee to Mary Lee, Dabb's Farm, July 9, 1862, *ibid.,* 230; Lee's Report, March 6, 1863, *ibid.,* 221.
34. Robert E. Lee, Jr., *Recollections and Letters of General Robert E. Lee* (Garden City, NY, 1904), 73–74.

20. *"We Cannot Afford to Be Idle"*

1. Douglas S. Freeman, *R. E. Lee: A Biography,* 4 vols. (New York, 1934–35), II, 249–50.
2. *Ibid.,* II, 347–48, 239–40; Captain Justus Scheibert, *Seven Months in the Rebel States During the North American War, 1863,* trans. Joseph C. Hayes, ed. William Stanley Hoole (Tuscaloosa, AL, 1958), 120. Justus Scheibert, *Der Bergkrieg in den nordamerikanischen Staaten* (Berlin, 1874), 39.
3. Freeman, *Lee,* II, 245–48; Douglas S. Freeman, *Lee's Lieutenants: A Study in Command,* 3 vols. (New York, 1942–44) I, 670–75.
4. *O.R.,* XI, part 2, 487; *O.R.,* XI, part 3, 640; *O.R.,* XI, part 2, 486; *O.R.,* XI, part 3, 630; *O.R.,* XI, part 2, 488; *O.R.,* XIII, 855, 860.
5. Freeman, *Lee,* II, 245–48.
6. *Ibid.,* 257; see Freeman, *Lee's Lieutenants,* I, 605–75, for a discussion of Lee's reorganization and assessment of his subordinates.
7. One example of Lee's effort to gain greater control of his army was his protest to Secretary of War George Wythe Randolph over transfers, furloughs, and details authorized by the War Department but not approved by Lee—"unless the applications pass through the headquarters of this army I am unable to judge of their propriety." Lee to Randolph, Headquarters, July 12, 1862, *Wartime Papers,* 231.
8. Lee to Davis, Headquarters, July 26, 1862, *ibid.,* 238.
9. Smith to Johnston, White Sulphur Springs, July 13, 1862, *O.R.,* LI, part 2, 593–94.
10. See Craig L. Symonds, *Joseph E. Johnston: A Civil War Biography* (New York, 1992), 199.
11. Lee to Davis, Headquarters, August 14, 1862, *Wartime Papers,* 254; on the Lee-Davis bond, see William C. Davis, *Jefferson Davis: The Man and His Hour* (New York, 1991), 426–28.

12. Stephen W. Sears, *George B. McClellan: The Young Napoleon* (New York, 1988), 223–47.

13. John Hennessy, *Return to Bull Run: The Campaign and Battle of Second Manassas* (New York, 1993), 3–21; *O.R.,* XII, part 3, 473–74.

14. Hennessy, *Return to Bull Run,* 22; Frederick S. Daniel, ed., *The Richmond Examiner During the War* (New York, 1868), 56; Lee to Mildred Lee, Headquarters, July 28, 1862, *Wartime Papers,* 240.

15. *O.R.,* XII, part 915; Freeman, *Lee* II, 261–64; Lee to Jackson, Headquarters, July 27, 1862, *Wartime Papers,* 239; *O.R.,* series II, IV, 329–30, 836.

16. Cf. Alan T. Nolan, *Lee Considered: General Robert E. Lee and Civil War History* (Chapel Hill, NC, 1991), 107–11.

17. Lee to Davis, New Market, August 7, 1862, *Wartime Papers,* 246–47; Sears, *McClellan,* 243–45; Freeman, *Lee,* II, 269–71.

18. Lee to Randolph, Headquarters, July 28, 1862, *Wartime Papers,* 240–41; Lee to D. H. Hill, Headquarters, August 2, 1862, *ibid.,* 242; Lee to D. H. Hill, Headquarters, August 3, 1862, *ibid.,* 244; Lee to D. H. Hill, Headquarters, August 4, 1862, *ibid.,* 244; Lee to D. H. Hill, Headquarters, August 7, 1862, *ibid.,* 246; Hall Bridges, *Lee's Maverick General: Daniel Harvey Hill* (New York, 1961), 149–51.

19. Robert K. Krick, *Stonewall Jackson at Cedar Mountain* (Chapel Hill, NC, 1990), 367–76; Lee to Jackson, Headquarters, August 12, 1862, *Wartime Papers,* 251; Lee to Smith, August 14, 1862, *ibid.,* 254–55; Lee to Davis, Gordonsville, August 16, 1862, *ibid.,* 256–57; Walter H. Taylor to Sister, August 17, 1862, Taylor Papers, microfilm in VSL.

20. Sears, *McClellan,* 246–47; Lee to Davis, Headquarters, East of Orange Court House, August 17, 1862, *Wartime Papers,* 258–59; Freeman, *Lee's Lieutenants,* II, 54–55.

21. Lee to Mary Lee, Headquarters, Orange Court House, August 17, 1862, *Wartime Papers,* 258; Vincent J. Esposito, ed., *The West Point Atlas of American Wars,* 2 vols. (New York, 1959), I, map 57.

22. Special Orders No. 185, August 19, 1862, *Wartime Papers,* 259–60; Esposito, ed., *Atlas,* map 57; Lee to Davis, Headquarters, Rappahannock River, August 23, 1862, *Wartime Papers,* 261–62; Lee to Davis, Jefferson, August 24, 1862, *ibid.,* 263.

23. Freeman, *Lee,* II, 299–303; Freeman, *Lee's Lieutenants,* II, 82–83; Frank E. Vandiver, *Mighty Stonewall* (New York, 1957), 352; Hennessy, *Return to Bull Run,* 91–93.

24. Esposito, ed., *Atlas,* map 58; Emory M. Thomas, *Bold Dragoon: The Life of J. E. B. Stuart* (New York, 1986), 152–53; Vandiver, *Mighty Stonewall,* 358–62; Freeman, *Lee,* II, 319–20; Freeman, *Lee's Lieutenants,* II, 96–107; Hennessy, *Return to Bull Run,* 95–127.

25. Esposito, ed., *Atlas,* maps 60–61; Freeman, *Lee,* II, 312–16; Hennessy, *Return to Bull Run,* 150–58.

26. A. L. Long, *Memoirs of Robert E. Lee* (Blue and Grey Press ed., Secaucus, NJ, 1983), 191–95.

27. Esposito, ed., *Atlas,* map 62; Hennessy, *Return to Bull Run,* 191–230, 279–81, 306–19; James Longstreet, "Our March Against Pope," in *Battles and Leaders,* II, 519–21.

28. Hennessy, *Return to Bull Run,* 362–424.

29. Robert E. Lee, Jr., *Recollections and Letters of General Robert E. Lee* (Garden City, NY, 1904), 76–77.

30. Lee to Davis, Telegram, Groveton, August 30,

1862, 10 o'clock P.M., *Wartime Papers,* 268; Lee to Davis, Near Groveton, August 30, 1862, *ibid.,* 267; Esposito, ed., *Atlas,* map 64; Hennessy, *Return to Bull Run,* 456–62.

31. Esposito, ed., *Atlas,* map 64; Walter H. Taylor, *General Lee: His Campaigns in Virginia, 1861–1865* (Morningside ed., Dayton, OH, 1975), 115–16; Frederick Maurice, ed., *An Aide-de-Camp of Lee... Charles Marshall....* (Boston, 1927), 141; Lee, Jr., *Recollections,* 416.

32. Freeman, *Lee,* II, 340; H. W. Thomas, *History of the Doles Cooke Brigade* (Atlanta, 1903), 469; Taylor, *General Lee,* 115.

33. Hennessy, *Return to Bull Run,* 451–55, 471–72; Lee to Davis, Dranesville, September 3, 1862, *Wartime Papers,* 293.

34. "To the People of Maryland," Near Fredericktown, September 8, 1862, *Wartime Papers,* 299; Lee to Davis, Leesburg, September 4, 1862, *ibid.,* 294; General Orders No. 102, *O.R.,* XIX, part 2, 592; Lee to Davis, Two Miles from Fredericktown, September 7, 1862, *Wartime Papers,* 298; Lee to Davis, Fredericktown, September 8, 1862, *ibid.,* 301.

35. Lee to Davis, Leesburg, September 4, 1862, *ibid.,* 294; Lee to Davis, Leesburg, September 5, 1862, *ibid.,* 295; Lee to Davis, Telegram, 13 miles from Fredericktown, Maryland, September 6, 1862, *ibid.,* 296; Lee to Davis, two miles from Fredericktown, September 7, 1862, *ibid.,* 297; Davis to Lee, Richmond, September 7, 1862, *O.R.,* XIX, part 2, 598–99.

36. Lee to Davis, Near Fredericktown, September 9, 1862, *Wartime Papers,* 303.

37. Special Orders No. 191, September 9, 1862, *ibid.,* 301–03; Dennis E. Frye, "Drama Between the Rivers: Harpers Ferry in the 1862 Maryland Campaign," in Gary W. Gallagher, ed., *Antietam: Essays on the 1862 Maryland Campaign* (Kent, OH, 1989), 14–34; Freeman, *Lee,* II, 359–65.

38. Stephen W. Sears, *Landscape Turned Red: The Battle of Antietam* (New York, 1983), 112–17; Taylor, *General Lee,* 125; Maurice, ed., *Marshall,* 160–62; Long, *Memoirs,* 213; a second standard campaign study of Antietam, in addition to Sears, is James V. Murfin, *The Gleam of Bayonets: The Battle of Antietam and the Maryland Campaign of 1862* (New York, 1965), and see also Jay Luvaas and Colonel Harold W. Nelson, *The U.S. Army War College Guide to the Battle of Antietam* (Carlisle, PA, 1987).

39. Leighton Parks, "What a Boy Saw of the Civil War," *Century Magazine,* 70 (June 1905), 258ff, cited in Freeman, *Lee,* II, 355.

40. Robert K. Krick, "The Army of Northern Virginia in September 1862: Its Circumstances, Its Opportunities, and Why It Should Not Have Been at Sharpsburg," in Gallagher, ed., *Antietam,* 39–44. The quotation from Shepherdstown is from Mary Bedinger Mitchell on page 43 in Krick's essay. Lee to Davis, Hagerstown, September 13, 1862, *Wartime Papers,* 307; Lee to Davis, Fredericktown, September 7, 1862, *O.R.* XIX, part 2, 597–98.

41. John B. Hood, *Advance and Retreat,* new ed. with intro. by Richard N. Current (Bloomington, IN, 1959), 38–39; James I. Robertson, Jr., *General A. P. Hill: The Story of a Confederate Warrior* (New York, 1987), 130–34; Special Orders No. 193, September 14, 1862, *O.R.,* XIX, part 2, 609.

42. Sears, *Landscape Turned Red,* 124–62; Murfin, *The Gleam of Bayonets,* 159–208.

43. W. H. Morgan, *Personal Reminiscences of the War of 1861–65...* (Lynchburg, VA, 1911), 141,

cited in Freeman, *Lee,* II, 378. The best case against giving battle is Krick's in "The Army of Northern Virginia."
44. See Esposito, ed., *Atlas,* maps 66–67.
45. Lee to Davis, Sharpsburg, September 16, 1862, *Wartime Papers,* 309–10.
46. Freeman, *Lee,* II, 387–404; Freeman, *Lee's Lieutenants,* II, 203–25; Sears, *Landscape Turned Red,* 180–297; Murfin, *The Gleam of Bayonets,* 209–88.
47. Sears, *Landscape Turned Red,* 294–96; Murfin, *The Gleam of Bayonets,* 374–77; Luvaas and

Nelson, *War College Guide to Antietam,* 301–02.
48. Esposito, ed., *Atlas,* map 69; Murfin, *The Gleam of Bayonets,* 325–27; Sears, *Landscape Turned Red,* 303–17.
49. Freeman, *Lee,* II, 414.
50. James Longstreet, "The Invasion of Maryland," in *Battles and Leaders,* II, 671; Long, *Memoirs,* 221–22.
51. Long, *Memoirs,* 222. In fact the soldier survived the battle and did not face charges.
52. Lee, Jr., *Recollections,* 78.

21. *"It Is Well That War Is So Terrible"*

1. Emory M. Thomas, *The Confederate Nation, 1861–1865* (New York, 1979), 179–80; William Kauffman Scarborough, *The Diary of Edmund Ruffin,* 3 vols. (Baton Rouge, LA, 1972–89), II, 445–46; Lord Granville to Russell, September 29, 1862, quoted in Frank E. Vandiver, *Basic History of the Confederacy* (Princeton, NJ, 1962), 146–48; see also D. P. Crook, *The North, the South, and the Powers, 1861–1865* (New York, 1974), 242.
2. Quoted in Frederick S. Daniel, ed., *The Richmond Examiner During the War* (New York, 1868), 60.
3. Walter Herren Taylor to Sister, September 21, 1862, and Taylor to Sister, September 28, 1862, Walter Herren Taylor Papers, microfilm in VSL; Lee Report in *Wartime Papers,* 323.
4. Lee to Annie and Agnes Lee, Washington's Run, September 30, 1862, MSS1L51C387, Lee Family Papers, VHS; Mary P. Coulling, *The Lee Girls* (Winston-Salem, NC, 1987), 104.
5. See Robert K. Krick, "The Army of Northern Virginia in September 1862: Its Circumstances, Its Opportunities, and Why It Should Not Have Been at Sharpsburg," in Gary W. Gallagher, ed., *Antietam: Essays on the 1862 Maryland Campaign* (Kent, OH, 1989), 39–44; Douglas S. Freeman, *R. E. Lee: A Biography,* 4 vols. (New York, 1934–35), II, 415–20.
6. Vincent J. Esposito, ed., *The West Point Atlas of American Wars,* 2 vols. (New York, 1959), I, map 70; Lee to Randolph, Headquarters, November 10, 1862, *Wartime Papers,* 332; Lee to Custis, Camp, Culpeper Court House, November 10, 1862, *ibid.,* 333.
7. Coulling, *Lee Girls,* 106–08; Rose Mortimer Ellzey MacDonald, *Mrs. Robert E. Lee* (Boston, 1939), 165–67; Lee to Mary Lee, Camp near Washington's Run, September 29, 1862, Lee Family Papers, MSS151C385, VHS.
8. Coulling, *Lee Girls,* 108–11; Agnes to Mildred, Jones Springs, October 20, 1862, Lee Family Papers, VHS.
9. Walter H. Taylor, *Four Years with General Lee* (New York, 1878), 76; letter to daughter Mary quoted in Robert E. Lee, Jr., *Recollections and Letters of General Robert E. Lee* (Garden City, NY, 1904), 80.
10. Lee to Chass, Camp near Winchester, October 19, 1862, George Bolling Lee Papers, MSS1L5114C53, VHS; Lee to Chass, Fredericksburg, December 10, 1862, *Wartime Papers,* 357.
11. Coulling, *Lee Girls,* 90–91; Lee to Markie, Camp on Washington's Run, October 2, 1862, Robert Edward Lee Papers, MSS2L515A35, VHS.
12. Gary Gallagher, ed., *Fighting for the Confederacy: The Personal Recollections of General Edward Porter Alexander* (Chapel Hill, NC, 1989), 156–58.
13. *O.R.,* XIX, part 2, 660, 774, 713; *O.R.,* XXI,

1056; Lee to Wilcox, Camp, November 12, 1862, Robert Edward Lee Papers MSS2L515A12; Lee to Randolph, telegram, October 18, 1862, Lee Headquarters Papers, MSS3L515A, VHS.
14. Emory M. Thomas, *Bold Dragoon: The Life of J. E. B. Stuart* (New York, 1986), 173–80; Freeman, *Lee,* II, 426–27.
15. Edward J. Stackpole, *Drama on the Rappahannock: The Fredericksburg Campaign* (Harrisburg, PA, 1957), 50–63; see also William Marvel, *Burnside* (Chapel Hill, NC, 1991).
16. James Longstreet, "The Battle of Fredericksburg," in *Battles and Leaders,* III, 70; *O.R.,* XXI, 83–84, 101–02; Lee to Jackson, Camp near Culpeper Court House, November 19, 1862, *Wartime Papers,* 341; Lee to Davis, telegram, November 20, 1862, *ibid.,* 341.
17. Lee to Randolph, Culpeper, November 17, 1862, *ibid.,* 337–38.
18. Esposito, ed., *Atlas,* maps 71–72; Stackpole, *Fredericksburg,* 99–113; Freeman, *Lee,* II, 433–42; A. L. Long, *Memoirs of Robert E. Lee* (Blue and Grey Press ed., Secaucus, NJ, 1983), 240; Douglas Southall Freeman, *Lee's Lieutenants: A Study in Command,* 3 vols. (New York, 1942–44), II, 325–38.
19. Stackpole, *Fredericksburg,* 174; Freeman, *Lee,* II, 443; Gallagher, ed., *Alexander,* 167–68.
20. Freeman, *Lee,* II, 441–51; Esposito, ed., *Atlas,* map 72; Heros von Borcke, *Memoirs of the Confederate War for Independence,* 2 vols. (Morningside ed., Dayton, OH, 1985), II, 108–10; G. Moxley Sorrel, *Recollections of a Confederate Staff Officer* (Jackson, TN, 1958), 138.
21. Stackpole, *Fredericksburg,* 172–216; Freeman, *Lee's Lieutenants,* II, 359–68; Freeman, *Lee,* II, 451–74.
22. John Esten Cooke, *A Life of Gen. Robert E. Lee* (New York, 1871), 184.
23. Longstreet, "Fredericksburg," in *Battles and Leaders,* III, 79–81; Gallagher, ed., *Alexander,* 169.
24. Stackpole, *Fredericksburg,* 172–216; Freeman, *Lee's Lieutenants,* II, 349–51, 369–73.
25. James Longstreet, *From Manassas to Appomattox: Memoirs of the Civil War in America,* ed. James I. Robertson, Jr. (Bloomington, IN, 1960), 316–17; Esposito, ed., *Atlas,* map 73; Stackpole, *Fredericksburg,* 279–81.
26. Lee to Mary Lee, Camp, Fredericksburg, December 16, 1862, *Wartime Papers,* 364–65.
27. Stackpole, *Fredericksburg,* 243–50.
28. Lee to Smith, Camp near Fredericksburg, January 4, 1863, *Wartime Papers,* 384.
29. Lee to Mary Lee, Camp, Fredericksburg, December 25, 1862, *ibid.,* 380.
30. Deed of Emancipation, December 29, 1862, Lee Papers, MOC; Lee to Custis, Camp, November 28, 1862, Lee Papers, Duke; Lee to Mary Lee,

Camp, Fredericksburg, January 8, 1863, Lee Family Papers, MSS1L51C427, VHS.
31. Lee to Mary Lee, Camp, Fredericksburg, December 21, 1862, *Wartime Papers*, 379.
32. Lee to Mary Lee, Camp, February 8, 1863, *ibid.*, 402.

33. Edward A. Pollard, *The First Year of the War*, corrected and improved ed. (Richmond, VA, 1863), 357–59.
34. Lee to Mary Lee, Camp, Fredericksburg, December 21, 1862, *Wartime Papers*, 378–79.

22. *"From Such a Scene . . . Men . . . Rose to the Dignity of Gods"*

1. Lee to Mary Lee, Camp, Fredericksburg, March 19, 1863, *Wartime Papers*, 415; *Southern Literary Messenger*, (January 1863), 34–35; J. Cutler Andrews, *The South Reports the Civil War* (Princeton, NJ, 1970), 50–51, 194n.
2. Lee to Mary Lee, Camp, Fredericksburg, January 21, 1863, Lee Family Papers, MSS1L51C429, VHS.
3. Lee to Agnes Lee, Camp, Fredericksburg, February 6, 1863, *Wartime Papers*, 400; Lee to Mary Lee, Camp, February 8, 1863, *ibid.*, 401; Lee to Davis, Headquarters, January 23, 1863, *ibid.*, 394; Lee to Seddon, Headquarters, January 29, 1863, 397; Lee to Agnes Lee, Camp, Fredericksburg, February 20, 1863, *ibid.*, 407; Lee to Mary Lee, Camp, Fredericksburg, February 23, 1863, *ibid.*, 407–08; Lee to Custis Lee, Camp, Fredericksburg, February 28, 1863, *ibid.*, 411; Lee to Mary Lee, HQ, Fredericksburg, March 27, 1863, *ibid.*, 419.
4. Mary P. Coulling, *The Lee Girls* (Winston-Salem, NC, 1987), 114–15; Wickham Memoir quoted in *ibid.*, 115; John C. Stiles, "One of War's Mysteries," *Confederate Veteran*, 29 (June 1921), 225, 238; G. A. Williams, "Light on a War Mystery," *Confederate Veteran*, 29 (July 1921), 263–64.
5. Lee to Seddon, Headquarters, March 27, 1863, *Wartime Papers*, 418–19; Douglas S. Freeman, *R. E. Lee: A Biography*, 4 vols. (New York, 1934–35), II, 494–95; *O.R.*, XXI, 1088; *O.R.*, LI, part 2, 674–75.
6. Lee to Seddon, Headquarters, January 10, 1863, *Wartime Papers*, 389; Lee to Custis Lee, Headquarters, February 28, 1863, *ibid.*, 411–12.
7. Lee to Agnes Lee, Camp, Fredericksburg, February 6, 1863, *Wartime Papers*, 400; Walter H. Taylor, *Four Years with General Lee* (New York, 1878), 77.
8. Lee to Custis Lee, Camp, February 12, 1863, Lee Papers, Duke.
9. Lee to Mary Lee, Camp, February 8, 1863, *Wartime Papers*, 401.
10. Lee to Mary Lee, Camp, Fredericksburg, March 6, 1863, Lee Family Papers, MSS1L51C436, VHS; Lee to Mary Lee, Camp, Fredericksburg, March 9, 1863, *Wartime Papers*, 413.
11. *O.R.*, LI, part 2, 683; *O.R.*, XXV, part 2, 664; Lee to Mary Lee, Camp, March 19, 1863, *Wartime Papers*, 414; Lee to Mary Lee, Headquarters, Fredericksburg, March 27, 1863, *ibid.*, 419.
12. Lee to Mary Lee, Near Fredericksburg, April 5, 1863, *Wartime Papers*, 427–28.
13. Lee to Mary Lee, Fredericksburg, April 12, 1863, *ibid.*, 432; Lee to Agnes Lee, Near Fredericksburg, April 11, 1863, *ibid.*, 431–32; Lee to Mary Lee, Camp, Fredericksburg, April 19, 1863, *ibid.*, 438; Lee to Mary Lee, Camp, Fredericksburg, April 24, 1863, *ibid.*, 440.
14. Samuel Merrifield Bemiss to his children, Camp, Near Fredericksburg, April 10, 1863, Bemiss Family Papers, MSS1B4255D23, VHS; Lee to Agnes Lee, Near Fredericksburg, April 11, 1863, *Wartime Papers*, 431–32; Lee to Mary Lee, Camp, Rappahannock, October 24, 1863, *ibid.*, 616; Lee to Mary Lee, Baltimore, July 2, 1870, quoted in Robert E. Lee, Jr., *Recollections and*

Letters of General Robert E. Lee (Garden City, NY, 1904), 413.
15. Lewellys F. Barker, "General Lee's Malady and the Probable Causes of His Death," in Freeman, *Lee*, IV, 524–25; Marvin P. Rozear, et al., "R. E. Lee's Stroke," *Virginia Magazine of History and Biography*, 98 (April 1990), 291–308.
16. Lee to Mary Lee, Camp, Fredericksburg, January 29, 1863, *Wartime Papers*, 396; the standard biography of Hooker is still Walter H. Herbert, *Fighting Joe Hooker* (Indianapolis, 1944).
17. Lee to Agnes Lee, Camp, Fredericksburg, February 6, 1863, *Wartime Papers*, 400; Emory M. Thomas, *Bold Dragoon: The Life of J. E. B. Stuart* (New York, 1986), 204–07.
18. Lee to Mary Lee, Camp, Fredericksburg, April 19, 1863, *Wartime Papers*, 437–38.
19. Bryan Steel Wills, "In Charge: Command Relationships in the Suffolk Campaign, 1863," M.A. thesis, University of Georgia, 1985; Douglas Southall Freeman, *Lee's Lieutenants: A Study in Command*, 3 vols. (New York, 1942–44), II, 467–94; Lee to Longstreet, Headquarters, April 27, 1863, *Wartime Papers*, 441.
20. Ernest B. Furguson, *Chancellorsville, 1863: The Souls of the Brave* (New York, 1992), 88; cf. Freeman, *Lee*, II, 506–07.
21. See Vincent J. Esposito, ed., *The West Point Atlas of American Wars*, 2 vols. (New York, 1959), I, maps 84–85.
22. Lee to Cooper, telegram, Fredericksburg, April 29, 1863, *Wartime Papers*, 441–42; Lee to Davis, telegram, Fredericksburg, April 29, 1863, *ibid.*, 442; Lee to Cooper, Fredericksburg, April 29, 1863, *ibid.*, 443; Lee to McLaws, Headquarters, April 29, 1863, P.M., *ibid.*, 444; Lee to Anderson, Headquarters, April 29, 1863, 6¾ P.M., *ibid.*, 445.
23. Esposito, ed., *Atlas*, I, map 84; Lee to War Department, telegram [April 30, 1863], 12 o'clock, *Wartime Papers*, 449.
24. Esposito, ed., *Atlas*, I, map 85; Thomas, *Bold Dragoon*, 208–09.
25. Furguson, *Chancellorsville*, 119–32; *O.R.*, XXV, part 2, 328.
26. Freeman, *Lee*, II, 518–24; Furguson, *Chancellorsville*, 138–43; Frank E. Vandiver, *Mighty Stonewall* (New York, 1957), 463–68; Gary W. Gallagher, ed., *Fighting for the Confederacy: The Personal Recollections of General Edward Porter Alexander* (Chapel Hill, NC, 1989), 199–200; A. L. Long, *Memoirs of Robert E. Lee* (Blue and Grey Press ed., Secaucus, NJ, 1983), 252–55; Frederick Maurice, ed., *An Aide-de-Camp of Lee . . . Charles Marshall. . . .* (Boston, 1927), 163–70; Jay Luvaas and Harold W. Nelson, eds., *The U.S. Army War College Guide to the Battles of Chancellorsville and Fredericksburg* (Carlisle, PA, 1988), 171–72.
27. Esposito, ed., *Atlas*, I, maps, 86–87; Furguson, *Chancellorsville*, 147–49.
28. Lee to Davis, Headquarters, Near Chancellorsville, May 2, 1863, *Wartime Papers*, 450–51.
29. Esposito, ed., *Atlas*, I, map 87–88; Vandiver, *Mighty Stonewall*, 468–77; Freeman, *Lee*, II, 525–32.

30. John Esten Cooke, *A Life of Gen. Robert E. Lee* (New York, 1871), 238–39; Jed Hotchkiss, *Confederate Military History*, III, 387; Lee to Stuart, May 3, 1863, 3 A.M., *Wartime Papers*, 451; Lee to Stuart, May 3, 1863, 3:30 A.M., *ibid.*, 451–52.
31. Gallagher, ed., *Alexander*, 205–10.
32. Furgurson, *Chancellorsville*, 240–41.
33. *O.R.*, XXV, part 2, 377–79.

34. Lee to Davis, telegram, Milford, May 3, 1863, *Wartime Papers*, 452.
35. Esposito, ed., *Atlas*, I, maps 89–91; Freeman, *Lee's Lieutenants*, II, 603–35.
36. Maurice, ed., *Marshall*, 172–73; Cooke, *Lee*, 244–45; Furgurson, *Chancellorsville*, 249–50; Freeman, *Lee*, II, 541–42; Walter H. Taylor, *General Lee: His Campaigns in Virginia, 1861–1865* (Morningside ed., Dayton, OH, 1975), 169.

23. "*Too Bad! Too Bad! OH! TOO BAD!*"

1. Frank E. Vandiver, *Mighty Stonewall* (New York, 1957), 468, 487–92; Douglas S. Freeman, *R. E. Lee: A Biography*, 4 vols. (New York, 1934–35), II, 524; G. F. R. Henderson, *Stonewall Jackson and the American Civil War*, 2 vols. (New York, 1898), II, 433; *O.R.*, XXV, part 2, 769.
2. Lee to Seddon, telegram, Headquarters, Fredericksburg, May 10, 1863, *Wartime Papers*, 483; General Orders No. 61, May 11, 1863, *ibid.*; Lee to Custis Lee, Camp, May 11, 1863, *ibid.*, 484; Henderson, *Stonewall Jackson*, II, 477.
3. Lee to Davis, telegram, Headquarters, Guiney's, May 5, 1863, *Wartime Papers*, 455; *SHSP*, VIII, 230; Freeman, *Lee*, II, 535.
4. Freeman, *Lee*, III, 19; Craig L. Symonds, *Joseph E. Johnston: A Civil War Biography* (New York, 1992), 204–14; Emory M. Thomas, *The Confederate Nation, 1861–1865* (New York, 1979), 218–19.
5. Thomas Lawrence Connelly and Archer Jones, *The Politics of Command: Factions and Ideas in Confederate Strategy* (Baton Rouge, LA, 1973), 49–66; William Garrett Piston, *Lee's Tarnished Lieutenant: James Longstreet and His Place in Southern History* (Athens, GA, 1987), 42–43; Frederick Maurice, ed., *An Aide-de-Camp of Lee . . . Charles Marshall. . . .* (Boston, 1927), 182–94; Lee to Davis, Headquarters, June 2, 1863, *O.R.*, XXV, part 2, 849; A. L. Long, *Memoirs of Robert E. Lee* (Blue and Grey Press ed., Secaucus, NJ, 1983), 267–69; Walter H. Taylor, *Four Years with General Lee* (New York, 1878), 90–91; Walter H. Taylor, *General Lee: His Campaigns in Virginia, 1861–1865* (Morningside ed., Dayton, OH, 1975), 179–80.
6. Lee to Davis, Headquarters, June 10, 1863, *Wartime Papers*, 307–09.
7. Lee to Davis, Camp, Fredericksburg, May 20, 1863, *ibid.*, 488; William Miller Owen, *In Camp and Battle with the Washington Artillery* (Boston, 1885; 2nd ed., New Orleans, 1964), 157; Brian Steel Wills, "In Charge: Command Relationships in the Suffolk Campaign, 1863," M.A. thesis, University of Georgia, 1985; cf. Piston, *Tarnished Lieutenant*, 36–41.
8. Lee to Davis, Camp, Fredericksburg, May 20, 1863, *Wartime Papers*, 488; Percy G. Hamlin, "*Old Bald Head" (General R. S. Ewell): The Portrait of a Soldier* (Strasburg, VA, 1940).
9. Lee to Davis, Camp, Fredericksburg, May 20, 1863, *Wartime Papers*, 488; James I. Robertson, Jr., *General A. P. Hill: The Story of a Confederate Warrior* (New York, 1987), 11–12, 192–94.
10. Lee to Davis, Camp, Fredericksburg, May 20, 1863, *Wartime Papers*, 488; Douglas Southall Freeman, *Lee's Lieutenants*, 3 vols. (New York, 1942–44), II, 689–714; Freeman, *Lee* III, 8–17; Piston, *Tarnished Lieutenant*, 38–42; James Longstreet, *From Manassas to Appomattox*, ed. James I. Robertson, Jr. (Bloomington, IN, 1960), 332.
11. Lee to Seddon, Headquarters, May 30, 1863, *Wartime Papers*, 497–98; Lee to Seddon, Head-

quarters, May 20, 1863, *ibid.*, 489; Lee to Davis, Headquarters, Culpeper, June 7, 1863, *ibid.*, 502–03; *O.R.*, XXVII, part 2, 347.
12. H. B. McClellan, *The Life and Campaigns of Major-General J. E. B. Stuart* (Boston and New York, 1885), 261–62; Emory M. Thomas, *Bold Dragoon: The Life of J. E. B. Stuart* (New York, 1986), 219–20 and note; Heros von Borcke, *Memoirs of the Confederate War for Independence*, 2 vols. (Morningside ed., Dayton, OH, 1985), II, 267; Freeman, *Lee's Lieutenants*, III, 3–5; John Esten Cooke, *Wearing of the Gray*, ed. Phillip Van Doren Stern (Bloomington, IN, 1959), 305–06; Lee to Mary Lee, Culpeper, June 9, 1863, *Wartime Papers*, 507.
13. Thomas, *Bold Dragoon*, 220–25; Stephen Z. Starr, *The Union Cavalry in the Civil War*, 3 vols. (Baton Rouge, LA, 1979–85), I, 366–73, 376–77, 380–87; Freeman, *Lee's Lieutenants*, III, 9–14; McClellan, *Stuart*, 264–92; Stuart's Report, *O.R.*, XXVII, part 2, 679–85; W. W. Blackford, *War Years with Jeb Stuart* (New York, 1945), 213–16.
14. *O.R.*, LI, part 2, 722; *O.R.*, XXVII, part 3, 876; Thomas, *Bold Dragoon*, 225–31.
15. Freeman, *Lee's Lieutenants*, III, 12n; Robert E. Lee, Jr., *Recollections and Letters of General Robert E. Lee* (Garden City, NY, 1904), 96–97; Thomas, *Bold Dragoon*, 230–34.
16. Lee to Davis, Headquarters, June 15, 1863, 7 A.M., *Wartime Papers*, 514; Lee to Longstreet, Headquarters, June 15, 1863, 8½ P.M., *ibid.*, 516; Lee to A. P. Hill, Headquarters, June 16, 1863, *ibid.*, 517; Lee to Davis, Headquarters, June 18, 1863, *ibid.*, 519; Vincent J. Esposito, ed., *The West Point Atlas of American Wars*, 2 vols. (New York, 1959), map 93; *O.R.*, XXVII, part 3, 900; General Orders No. 73, Chambersburg, June 27, 1863, *Wartime Papers*, 533–34; Lee to Davis, Headquarters, June 23, 1863, *ibid.*, 529–30.
17. Freeman, *Lee*, III, 52; Lee to Davis, Opposite Williamsport, June 25, 1863, *Wartime Papers*, 530; Lee to Davis, Headquarters, June 23, 1863, *ibid.*, 529–30; Lee to Davis, Williamsport, June 25, 1863, *ibid.*, 532–33; William C. Davis, *Jefferson Davis: The Man and His Hour* (New York, 1991), 505.
18. The Trimble material is in *SHSP*, XXVI, 119–21.
19. Thomas, *Bold Dragoon*, 234–46.
20. Lee to Ewell, Chambersburg, June 28, 1863, 7½ A.M., *Wartime Papers*, 534–35; Esposito, ed., *Atlas*, map 94.
21. Freeman Cleaves, *Meade of Gettysburg* (reprint, Norman, OK, 1991), 124–26; Esposito, ed., *Atlas*, map 94; Edwin B. Coddington, *The Gettysburg Campaign: A Study in Command* (New York, 1968), 242–51.
22. Freeman, *Lee*, III, 60–62 and n.; Maurice, ed., *Marshall*, 218–19; James Longstreet, "Lee's Invasion of Pennsylvania," in *Battles and Leaders*, III, 249–50; Longstreet, *Manassas to Appomattox*, 383n.; George Cary Eggleston, *A Rebel's Recollections* (Bloomington, IN 1959), 145–46.
23. Maurice, ed., *Marshall*, 217–24; Longstreet,

Manassas to Appomattox, 351–52; Taylor, *Four Years,* 92–93.

24. Esposito, ed., *Atlas,* maps 95–96; the standard study of Gettysburg remains Edwin B. Coddington, *The Gettysburg Campaign: A Study in Command* (New York, 1968). Also important are Richard A. Sauers, comp., *The Gettysburg Campaign, June 3–August 1, 1863: A Comprehensive, Selectively Annotated Bibliography* (Westport, CN, 1982), William A. Frasinito, *Gettysburg: A Journey in Time* (New York, 1975), and Jay Luvaas and Harold W. Nelson, eds., *The U.S. Army War College Guide to the Battle of Gettysburg* (Carlisle, PA 1986). For July 1, 1863, see Warren W. Hassler, Jr., *Crisis at the Crossroads: The First Day at Gettysburg* (Montgomery, AL, 1970), and Gary W. Gallagher, ed., *The First Day at Gettysburg* (Kent, OH, 1992).

25. Freeman, *Lee,* III, 69–72; the Lee quotation is from *SHSP,* IV, 158.

26. See Esposito, ed., *Atlas,* map 98, and Craig L. Symonds, *Gettysburg: A Battlefield Atlas* (Baltimore, 1992).

27. Taylor, *General Lee,* 190.

28. Maurice, ed., *Marshall,* 232–33; James Longstreet, "Lee's Right Wing at Gettysburg," in *Battles and Leaders,* III, 339.

29. The Trimble-Ewell exchange is in *SHSP,* XL, 273; Freeman, *Lee,* III, 77–78.

30. Maurice, ed., *Marshall,* 232–35; *O.R.,* XXVII, part 2, 446; Longstreet, *Manassas to Appomattox,* 359–61; Taylor, *General Lee,* 193–95; Freeman, *Lee,* III, 83–84; Long, *Memoirs,* 281.

31. *SHSP,* V; Freeman, *Lee,* III, 85–90; Harry W. Pfanz, *Gettysburg: The Second Day* (Chapel Hill, NC, 1987), 104–111; Long, *Memoirs,* 281–82; Maurice, ed., *Marshall,* 233–34, and Trimble in *SHSP,* XXVI, 125.

32. The interpretation here depends much upon Robert K. Krick, "If Longstreet . . . Says So, It Is Most Likely Not True: James Longstreet and the Second Day at Gettysburg," in Gary W. Gal-

lagher, ed., *The Second Day at Gettysburg* (Kent, OH, 1993); cf. Piston, *Tarnished Lieutenant,* 55–58; Longstreet, *Manassas to Appomattox,* 358.

33. Esposito, ed., *Atlas,* map 98; Pfanz, *Second Day,* 149–424; Coddington, *Gettysburg,* 385–441.

34. Arthur James Lyon Fremantle, *The Freemantle Diary,* ed. Walter Lord (New York, 1954), 208.

35. Thomas, *Bold Dragoon,* 246; John W. Thomason, Jr., *Jeb Stuart* (New York, 1980); 440; McClellan, *Stuart,* 332; Lee's Report, *Wartime Papers,* 580.

36. Longstreet in *Annals of the War* (Philadelphia, 1879), 429, cited in Freeman, *Lee,* III, 107; Lee's Report, *Wartime Papers,* 579.

37. Longstreet, "Right Wing," 343.

38. Freeman, *Lee,* III, 108–14; George R. Stewart, *Pickett's Charge: A Microhistory of the Final Attack at Gettysburg, July 3, 1863* (Boston, 1959), 82–124; Coddington, *Gettysburg,* 455–76.

39. Gary W. Gallagher, ed., *Fighting for the Confederacy: The Personal Recollections of General Edward Porter Alexander* (Chapel Hill, NC, 1989), 255–59.

40. Freeman, *Lee,* III, 120–28; Stewart, *Pickett's Charge,* 162–245; Coddington, *Gettysburg,* 501–19; Symonds, *Gettysburg Atlas,* 70–73; Luvaas and Nelson, eds., *War College Guide to Gettysburg,* 174.

41. Gallagher, ed., *Alexander,* 265–67; Freemantle, *Diary,* 214–15; Freeman, *Lee,* III, 128–33.

42. John D. Imboden, "The Confederate Retreat from Gettysburg," in *Battles and Leaders,* III, 420–22.

43. Maurice, ed., *Marshall,* 233; Blackford, *War Years,* 228–33.

44. Taylor, *Four Years,* 107–09; Long, *Memoirs,* 289–90; Gallagher, ed., *Alexander,* 280–83; Longstreet, *Manassas to Appomattox,* 397–401.

45. William Faulkner, *Intruder in the Dust* (New York, 1948), 194–95.

46. Freeman, *Lee's Lieutenants,* III, 20–26; *O.R.,* XXVII, part 3, 879.

24. *"I Was Influenced by the Bribe"*

1. Lee's Report, *Wartime Papers,* 580–82; John D. Imboden, "The Confederate Retreat from Gettysburg," in *Battles and Leaders,* III, 423–24.

2. Jay Luvaas and Harold W. Nelson, eds. *The U.S. Army War College Guide to the Battle of Gettysburg* (Carlisle, PA, 1986), 231; Douglas Southall Freeman, *Lee's Lieutenants: A Study in Command,* 3 vols. (New Yrok, 1942–44), III, 190; Vincent J. Esposito, ed., *The West Point Atlas of American Wars,* 2 vols. (New York, 1959), map 99; Lee to Davis, Headquarters, July 29, 1863, *Wartime Papers,* 563; Douglas S. Freeman, *R. E. Lee: A Biography,* 4 vols. (New York, 1934–35), III, 135–36.

3. Imboden, "Retreat," 424.

4. Gary W. Gallagher, ed., *Fighting for the Confederacy: The Personal Recollections of General Edward Porter Alexander* (Chapel Hill, NC, 1989), 270–71; James Longstreet, *From Manassas to Appomattox,* ed. James I. Robertson, Jr. (Bloomington, In, 1960), 429; John Esten Cooke, *Robert E. Lee* (New York, 1899), 333–34.

5. Arthur James Lyon Fremantle, *The Freemantle Diary,* ed. Walter Lord (New York, 1954), 191, 229–30; Lee to Mary Lee, Williamsport, July 7, 1863, *Wartime Papers,* 542; Robert E. Lee, J., *Recollections and Letters of General Robert E. Lee* (Garden City, NY, 1904), 98–100.

6. Lee to Mary Lee, Camp Near Hagerstown, July 12, 1863, *Wartime Papers,* 547; Esposito, ed.,

Atlas I, map 117; Freeman, *Lee,* III, 144–45; Lee to Davis, Headquarters, July 29, 1863, *Wartime Papers,* 564.

7. See Thomas L. Connelly, "Vicksburg: Strategic Point or Propaganda Device?", *Military Affairs,* XXXIV (1970), 49–53.

8. Richmond *Examiner,* July 17, 1863; Charleston *Mercury,* July 16, July 30, 1863; Rome [Georgia] *Tri-Weekly Courier,* August 18, 1863.

9. Wigfall to Clay, quoted in Alvy L. King, *Louis T. Wigfall: Southern Fire-eater* (Baton Rouge, LA, 1970), 170.

10. Lee to Mary Lee, Camp Near Hagerstown, July 17, 1863, *Wartime Papers,* 547; Lee to Mary Lee, Bunker Hill, July 15, 1863, *ibid.,* 551; Frederick Maurice, ed., *An Aide-de-Camp of Lee . . . Charles Marshall. . . .* (Boston, 1927), 250–52.

11. Lee to Davis, Camp, Culpeper, July 31, 1863, *Wartime Papers,* 565.

12. Lee to Davis, Camp, Orange, August 8, 1863, *ibid.,* 589–90.

13. *O.R.,* XXIX, part 2, 640.

14. Lee, Jr, *Recollections and Letters,* 105–06.

15. *O.R.,* XXIX, part 2, 641; *O.R.,* LI, part 2, 754; Lee to Davis, Headquarters, August 17, 1863, *Wartime Papers,* 591; *O.R.,* XXIX, part 2, 806–07; Freeman, *Lee's Lieutenants,* III, 318–19.

16. *O.R.,* LI, part 2, 759; Lee to Mary Lee, Camp, Orange, September 4, 1863, *Wartime Papers,* 595; Lee to James Longstreet, Richmond, August 31,

1863, *ibid.*, 594; Lee to Davis, Richmond, September 6, 1863, *ibid.*, 596.
17. *O.R.*, XXIX, part 2, 702, 709; Lee to Davis, Richmond, September 6, 1863, *Wartime Papers*, 596.
18. Lee to Davis, September 23, 1863, *Wartime Papers*, 602–03; Esposito, ed., *Atlas*, I, maps 117–18; Freeman, *Lee*, III, 162–69; Lee to Davis, Camp, Orange C.H., September 30, 1863, *Wartime Papers*, 606.
19. Lee to Mary Lee, Camp, Orange C.H., September 4, 1863, *Wartime Papers*, 595; Freeman, *Lee*, III, 170; *O.R.*, XXIX, part 2, 781; Lee to Mary Lee, Rappahannock River, October 19, 1863, *Wartime Papers*, 611.
20. Lee's Report, *O.R.*, XXIX, part 1, 410–11; Freeman, *Lee*, III, 180–83.
21. *O.R.*, XXIX, part 1, 242, 433; James I. Robertson, Jr., *General A. P. Hill: The Study of a Confederate Warrior* (New York, 1987), 226–40; Emory M. Thomas, *Bold Dragoon: The Life of J. E. B. Stuart* (New York, 1986), 263–69.
22. Lee to Davis, Bristoe Station, October 17, 1863, *Wartime Papers*, 609; Hill's Report, *O.R.*, XXIX, part 1, 428; Freeman, *Lee's Lieutenants*, III, 239–47; A. L. Long, *Memoirs of Robert E. Lee* (Blue and Grey Press ed., Secaucus, NJ, 1983), 311.
23. Lee to Samuel Cooper, Headquarters, October 23, 1863, *Wartime Papers*, 613; Freeman, *Lee*, III, 183–93.
24. Esposito, ed., *Atlas*, I, map 119; Freeman, *Lee*, III, 194–203; Freeman, *Lee's Lieutenants*, III, 269–79; Walter H. Taylor, *Four Years with General Lee* (New York, 1878), 120–21.
25. Cooke, *Lee*, 369; Jay Luvaas and Wilbur S. Nye, "The Campaign that History Forgot: Mine Run," *Civil War Times Illustrated*, VIII (1969), vii, 11–36; Hill's Report, *O.R.* XXIX, part 1, 896; Lee's Report, *Wartime Papers*, 635; Charles S. Venable, "General Lee in the Wilderness Campaign," in *Battles and Letters*, IV, 240.
26. Lee to Davis, Headquarters, December 3, 1863, *Wartime Papers*, 641; Davis to Lee, Richmond, December 5, 1863, *O.R.*, XXIX, part 2, 861; Lee to Davis, Headquarters, Rapidan, December 7, 1863, *Wartime Papers*, 642.

27. Lee to Stuart, Camp, December 9, 1863, *Wartime Papers*, 642–43; *O.R.*, XXXI, part 3, 835–36; C. Vann Woodward, ed., *Mary Chestnut's Civil War* (New Haven, 1981), 507.
28. Freeman, *Lee*, III, 208 and n.; Lee to Mary Lee, Camp, Rappahannock, October 28, 1863, *Wartime Papers*, 615; Lee to Mildred Lee, Camp, Rappahannock, October 31, 1863, Lee Family Papers, MSS1L51C484, VHS.
29. Lee had last seen his wife in May 1863. Lee to Mary Lee, Camp, Fredericksburg, May 20, 1863, *Wartime Papers*, 486; Freeman, *Lee*, III, 209.
30. Lee to Mary Lee, Camp, Fredericksburg, March 9, 1863, *Wartime Papers*, 413; Lee to Mary Lee, Camp, Fredericksburg, May 23, 1863, *ibid.*, 491; Lee to Mary Lee, Camp, December 5, 1863, Lee Family Papers, MSS1L51C 494, VHS.
31. Lee to Mary Lee, Orange, Xmas night, 1863, *Wartime Papers*, 644; see also anon., *Fort-La-Fayette Life, 1863–64* (London, 1865).
32. Mary P. Coulling, *The Lee Girls* (Winston-Salem, NC, 1987), 128–33; Lee, Jr., *Recollections and Letters*, 119.
33. Lee to Mary Lee, Camp, Rapidan, December 4, 1863, *Wartime Papers*, 632.
34. Freeman, *Lee*, III, 214; Lee to Custis Lee, Camp, Orange, August 18, 1863, *Wartime Papers*, 592.
35. Richmond *Examiner*, December 31, 1863.
36. Lee to Mrs. Taylor, Camp, Fredericksburg, May 29, 1863, Lee Headquarters Papers, MSS3L515A, VHS.
37. Lee to Mrs. Taylor, Camp, Orange, August 13, 1863, Lee Headquarter Papers, MSS3L515A, VHS.
38. Long, *Memoirs*, 306.
39. Lucy Minnegerode and Lou Haxall to Lee, n.p., n.d., Robinson Family Papers, MSS1R5685C50, VHS.
40. Lee to Robinson, December 8, 1863, Robinson Family Papers, MSS1R5685C51; Lee to Lou & Lucy, Richmond, December 14, 1863, Robinson Family Papers, MSS1R5685C52, VHS.
41. Lee to Mary Lee, Camp, December 22, 1863, *Wartime Papers*, 643–44; Freeman, *Lee*, III, 216.

25. *"We Must Never Let Them Pass Us Again"*

1. *The Virginia Landmarks Register*, 3rd ed. ed. Calder Loth (Charlottesville, VA, 1986), 388; Mary Wingfield Scott, *Houses of Old Richmond* (New York, 1941), 224–27; Lee to Mary Lee, Camp December 22, 1863, *Wartime Papers*, 644; C. Vann Woodward, ed., *Mary Chestnut's Civil War* (New Haven, 1981), 573–74.
2. Lee to Mary Lee, Orange C.H., April 27, 1864, Lee Family Papers, MSS1L51C515, VHS; Lee to Mary Lee, Camp, December 22, 1863, *Wartime Papers*, 644.
3. Woodward, ed., *Mary Chestnut's Civil War*, 569.
4. Douglas S. Freeman, *R. E. Lee: A Biography*, 4 vols. (New York, 1934–35), III, 245–53; Lee to Northrop, Headquarters, January 5, 1864, *Wartime Papers*, 647–48; Lee to Lawton, Headquarters, January 20, 1864, *ibid.*, 656–57; Lee to Seddon, Headquarters, January 22, 1864, *ibid.*, 659–60; Lee to Mary Lee, Camp, January 24, 1864, *ibid.*, 661.
5. Scott, *Houses of Old Richmond*, 224; Lee to Mary Lee, Camp, Orange Court House, May 2, 1864; *Wartime Papers*, 717; the sock correspondence is in *ibid.*, 649–717; and Lee to Mary Lee, Camp, April 21, 1864, Lee Family Papers, MSS1L51C513; Lee to Mary Lee, Camp, April 22, 1864, Lee Family Papers,

MSS1L51C515, VHS; the incident in 1862 opens chapter 18.
6. *O.R.*, series II, V, 706; *O.R.*, series II, VII, 119. Lee to Mary Lee, Camp, Orange C H., March 29, 1864, *Wartime Papers*, 687.
7. Lee to Mary Lee, Camp, Orange C. H., February 14, 1864, *Wartime Papers*, 671; Mary P. Coulling, *The Lee Girls* (Winston-Salem, NC, 1987), 135–36; Lee to Mary Lee, Camp, March 24, 1864, *Wartime Papers*, 681; Lee to Mary Lee, Camp, April 23, 1864, *ibid.*, 705; Lee to Mary Lee, Camp, July 7, 1864, *ibid.*, 816; Lee to Mildred Lee, Camp, Petersburg, July 5, 1864, *ibid.*, 814.
8. Lee to Custis Lee, Camp, Orange C.H., March 29, 1864, *ibid.*, 685–86; Lee to Custis Lee, Camp, April 9, 1864, *ibid.*, 695–96.
9. The point made here is also the thesis of Gary W. Gallagher in "The Army of Northern Virginia in May 1864: A Crisis of High Command," *Civil War History*, 36 (June 1990), 101–18; convenient sources of the order of battle at Chancellorsville and the Wilderness are Ernest B. Furgurson, *Chancellorsville, 1863: The Souls of the Brave* (New York, 1992), 359–62, and Robert Garth Scott, *Into the Wilderness with the Army of the Potomac* (Bloomington, In, 1985), 194–202. Information about Lee's subordinate generals is in

Ezra J. Warner, *Generals in Gray: Lives of the Confederate Commanders* (Baton Rouge, LA, 1959). Lee's letter to Ewell is in *O.R.*, XXXIII, 1095–96.

10. See Douglas Southall Freeman, *Lee's Lieutenants: A Study of Command*, 3 vols. (New York, 1942–44), III, 339–41; Emory M. Thomas, *Bold Dragoon: The Life of J. E. B. Stuart* (New York, 1986), 257–82; and Gallagher, "Crisis of High Command," 106–107.

11. *O.R.*, XXXIII, 1290; Vincent J. Esposito, ed., *The West Point Atlas of American Wars*, 2 vols. (New York, 1959), I, map 120; Grady McWhiney and Perry D. Jamieson, *Attack and Die; Civil War Military Tactics and the Southern Heritage* (University Press, AL, 1982), 19.

12. Lee to Davis, Headquarters, Orange, February 3, 1864, *Wartime Papers*, 666–67.

13. Lee to Longstreet, Headquarters, February 17, 1864, John Walter Fairfax Papers, MSS1F1613A 9–10, VHS; Freeman, *Lee*, III, 263; Ulysses S. Grant, *Memoirs and Selected Letters*, ed. Mary Drake and William S. McFeely (New York, 1990), 469–74.

14. Lee to Walter H. Taylor, Richmond, December 12, 1863, Lee Papers, Stratford Hall; Lee to Davis, Headquarters, March 25, 1864, *Wartime Papers*, 682–83.

15. Freeman, *Lee*, III, 218–19 and n.; Virgil Carrington Jones, *Eight Hours Before Richmond* (New York, 1957); "Total War and Apricot Jam," in Emory M. Thomas, *Travels to Hallowed Ground: A Historian's Journey to the American Civil War* (Columbia, SC, 1987), 83–99; Lee to Seddon, Headquarters, March 6, 1864, *Wartime Papers*, 678–79.

16. Lee to Braxton Bragg, telegram, Orange Court House, May 4, 1864, *Wartime Papers*, 718.

17. For the Wilderness Campaign, see Edward Steere, *The Wilderness Campaign* (Harrisburg, PA, 1960), Scott, *Into the Wilderness*, Clifford Dowdey, *Lee's Last Campaign* (Boston, 1960), Earl Scherick Miers, *The Last Campaign: Grant Saves the Union* (Philadelphia, 1972), Noah Andre Trudeau, *Bloody Roads South: The Wilderness of Cold Harbor* (Boston, 1990), and appropriate portions of Freeman, *Lee* and *Lee's Lieutenants*.

18. Charles S. Venable, "General Lee in the Wilderness Campaign," in *Battles and Leaders*, IV, 241; Freeman, *Lee*, III, 269–84; Esposito, ed., *Atlas*, I, maps 121–23.

19. James I. Robertson, Jr., *General A. P. Hill: The Story of a Confederate Warrior* (New York, 1987), 259–64.

20. Gary W. Gallagher, ed., *Fighting for the Confederacy: The Personal Recollections of General Edward Porter Alexander* (Chapel Hill, NC, 1989), 357–60.

21. *Ibid.*, 358; Venable, "Lee in the Wilderness," 241; Walter H. Taylor, *General Lee: His Campaigns in Virginia, 1861–1863* (Morningside ed., Dayton,

OH, 1975), 234; Charles S. Venable, "Campaign from the Wilderness to Petersburg," *SHSP*, XIV, 525–26.

22. Freeman, *Lee*, III, 293–95; Gallagher, ed., *Alexander*, 360–65; G. Moxley Sorrel, *Recollections of a Confederate Staff Officer* 2nd ed., New York, 1917), 238–39.

23. Gallagher, ed., *Alexander*, 365; Freeman, *Lee*, III, 297–303.

24. John B. Gordon, *Reminiscences of the Civil War* (New York, 1903), 268–69; Freeman, *Lee*, III, 298–303, 302n.

25. Robertson, *Hill*, 268; *O.R.*, XXXVI, part 1, 1041, 1071; Freeman, *Lee*, III, 304–11; Venable, "Wilderness to Petersburg," 532.

26. Venable, "Lee to the Wilderness," 242; Gallagher, ed., *Alexander*, 370–72; Freeman, *Lee*, III, 311–13.

27. Esposito, ed., *Atlas*, I, maps 126–27; Thomas, *Stuart*, 288–89.

28. Venable, "Wilderness to Petersburg," 528–29; Taylor, *General Lee*, 240; Gallagher, ed., *Alexander*, 373; Freeman, *Lee*, III, 313–14.

29. Freeman, *Lee*, III, 315–28; William D. Matter, *If It Takes All Summer: The Battle of Spotsylvania* (Chapel Hill, NC, 1988), 191–268; A. L. Long, *Memoirs of Robert E. Lee* (Blue and Grey Press ed., Secaucus, NJ, 1983), 341; Robert Stiles, *Four Years Under Marse Robert* (Morningside ed., Dayton, OH, 1977; Sorrel, *Recollections*, 246; Venable, "Lee in the Wilderness," 243.

30. Thomas, *Stuart*, 290–97; Lee to Mary Lee, Spotsylvania Court House, May 16, 1864, *Wartime Papers*, 731; General Orders No. 44, May 20, 1864, *ibid.*, 736.

31. Esposito, ed., *Atlas*, I, maps 131–34; Lee to Davis, telegram, Spotsylvania Court House, May 15, 1864, *Wartime Papers*, 730; Lee to Seddon, telegram, Spotsylvania Court House, May 18, 1864, *ibid.*, 734.

32. Freeman, *Lee's Lieutenants*, III, 498–99, 510; Venable, "Wilderness to Petersburg," 535; Freeman, *Lee*, III, 356–57; Esposito, ed., *Atlas*, I, map 135.

33. Esposito, ed., *Atlas*, I, 134–36; Venable, "Lee in the Wilderness," 244; Taylor, *General Lee*, 246; Lee to Beauregard, telegram, Atlee's, 7½ P.M., May 30, 1864, and Lee to Davis, telegram, Atlee's, 7½ P.M., May 30, 1864, Telegraph Book, Lee Headquarters Papers, VHS; *O.R.*, XXXVI, part 3, 817–18; Lee to Hill, Headquarters, June 1864, *Wartime Papers*, 759–60.

34. Trudeau, *Bloody Roads South*, 264–99; Gallagher, ed., *Alexander*, 404–07; Freeman, *Lee*, III, 386–91; Grant, *Memoirs*, 579–88.

35. Gallagher, *Alexander*, 408–14; Esposito, ed., *Atlas*, I, map 137; McWhiney and Jamieson, *Attack and Die*, 19.

36. J. R. Montgomery letter, MOC.

37. Cf. Long, *Memoirs*, 341.

38. Freeman, *Lee*, III, 331.

26. *"I Go to Petersburg"*

1. Charles S. Venable, "The Campaign from the Wilderness to Petersburg," *SHSP*, XIV, 535n., 536; Lee to Davis, Headquarters, near Gaines' Mill, June 3, 1864, 1 P.M., *Wartime Papers*, 763; Shelby Foote makes much of the casualties and the protocol for the truce at Cold Harbor in *The Civil War: A Narrative*, 3 vols. (New York, 1968–75), III, 290–96.

2. The correspondence between Grant and Lee relating to a truce is in *O.R.*, XXXVI, part 3, 600, 638–39, 666–67.

3. Douglas Southall Freeman, *R. E. Lee: A Biography*, 4 vols. (New York, 1934–35), III, 393–98.

4. Lee to Davis, Headquarters, June 11, 1864, *Wartime Papers*, 774–75; Lee to Davis, Headquarters on the field, June 6, 1864, 7½ A.M., *ibid.*, 767;

Freeman, *Lee,* III, 396; Jubal Anderson Early, *War Memoirs,* ed. Frank E. Vandiver (Bloomington, In. 1960), 364; Lee to Davis, Headquarters, June 14, 1864, 3¾ P.M., *Wartime Papers,* 778–79.

5. Freeman, *Lee,* III, 405–07; Early, *Memoirs,* 371–81; Venable, "Wilderness to Petersburg," 538.

6. Lee to Jackson, Richmond, May 16, 1862, *Wartime Papers,* 174; Lee to Davis, Headquarters, near Fredericksburg, January 13, 1863, *ibid.,* 391; Lee to Davis, Headquarters, June 11, 1864, *ibid.,* 778; Lee to Davis, June 14, 1864, 12:50 P.M., *ibid.,* 777.

7. Ulysses S. Grant, *Memoirs and Selected Letters,* ed. Mary Drake and William S. McFeely (New York, 1990), 590–602; Vincent J. Esposito, ed., *West Point Atlas of American Wars,* 2 vols. (New York, 1959) I, map 137; Noah Andre Trudeau, *The Last Citadel: Petersburg, Virginia, June 1864–April 1865* (Boston, 1991), 24–25.

8. T. Harry Williams, *P. G. T. Beauregard: Napoleon in Gray* (Baton Rouge, LA, 1955), 225–27.

9. Lee to Bragg, telegram, Mechanicsville, June 9, 1864, 4:45 P.M., *Wartime Papers,* 772; Beauregard to Lee, telegram, Petersburg, June 15, 1864, 11:15 P.M., *O.R.,* XL, part 2, 657; Lee to Beauregard, Drewry's Bluff, June 16, 1864, 3 P.M., *Wartime Papers,* 785; Lee to Bragg, Headquarters, June 9, 1864, 2½ P.M., *ibid.,* 770–71.

10. Lee to Mary Lee, June 12, 1864, *Wartime Papers,* 775; Lee to Cooper, Headquarters, June 12, 1864, *ibid.,* 776; Lee to Seddon, Headquarters, June 13, 1864, 10 P.M., *ibid.,* 776–77; Beauregard to Bragg material in *O.R.,* XL, part 2, 647–48.

11. This correspondence is in *O.R.,* XL, part 2, 652–56.

12. Lee to Bragg, Headquarters, June 15, 1864, 12:20 P.M., *Wartime Papers,* 781.

13. *O.R.,* XL, part 2, 677, 659.

14. Lee to Davis, Drewry's Bluff, June 16, 1864, 7:31 P.M., *Wartime Papers,* 786.

15. *O.R.,* XL, part 2, 660–67.

16. Lee to Davis, Headquarters, June 18, 1864, *Wartime Papers,* 791–92.

17. Esposito, ed., *Atlas,* I, map 138; Williams, *Beauregard,* 227–35.

18. Trudeau, *Last Citadel,* 4–6; Robert E. Lee, Jr., *Recollections and Letters of General Robert E. Lee* (Garden City, NY, 1904), 133; Freeman, *Lee,* III, 457.

19. Freeman, *Lee,* III, 448.

20. James I. Robertson. Jr., *General A. P. Hill: The Story of a Confederate Warrior* (New York, 1987), 284–87.

21. Richard J. Sommers, *Richmond Redeemed: The Siege at Petersburg* (New York, 1981), 1–3.

22. Quoted in J. William Jones, *Personal Reminiscences of General Robert E. Lee* (United States Historical Society ed., Richmond, VA, 1989), 40.

27. *"Ah! But He Is a Queer Old Genius"*

1. Walter Herren Taylor to Betty (Elizabeth Selden) Saunders, Camp at Violet Bank, July 22, 1864, Walter Herren Taylor Papers, microfilm (28114, reel 2) at VSL.

2. Gary W. Gallagher, ed., *Fighting for the Confederacy: The Personal Recollections of General Edward Porter Alexander* (Chapel Hill, NC, 1989), 456 and n. 67; Noah Andre Trudeau, *The Last Citadel: Petersburg, Virginia, June 1864–April 1865* (Boston, 1991), 102–27.

3. Douglas Southall Freeman, *R. E. Lee: A Biography,* 4 vols. (New York, 1934–35), III, 467–68; Vincent J. Esposito, ed., *West Point Atlas of American Wars,* 2 vols. (New York, 1959), I, map 139; *O.R.,* XL, part 1, 167.

4. J. Roderick Heller, III, and Carolyn Ayres Heller, eds., *The Confederacy Is on Her Way Up the Spout: Letters to South Carolina, 1861 1864* (Athens, GA, 1992), 123; Gallagher, ed., *Alexander,* 462; Phoebe Yates Pember, *A Southern Woman's Story: Life in Confederate Richmond* (Mockingbird Books, St. Simon's Island, GA, 1974), 62.

5. Lee to Grant, Headquarters, October 19, 1864, Lee Papers, USMA, is the source of the Lee quotation.

6. Lee to Mary Lee, Camp, July 10, 1864, *Wartime Papers,* 818; Lee to Davis, Petersburg, July 23, 1864, *ibid.,* 824; Lee to Custis Lee, Camp, July 24, 1864, *ibid.,* 825.

7. Lee to Davis, Headquarters, June 26, 1864, *ibid.,* 807.

8. Lee to Davis, telegram, Headquarters near Petersburg, July 12, 1864, *ibid.,* 821; Lee to Davis, Camp, July 12, 1864, 9½ P.M., *ibid.,* 821.

9. The report is in *O.R.,* XLII, part 1, 958.

10. For the events chronicled, see E. B. Long, with Barbara Long, *The Civil War Day by Day: An Almanac, 1861–1865* (Garden City, NY, 1971), and appropriate volumes of *O.R.*

11. Lee to Mary Lee, Camp, July 31, 1864, *Wartime Papers,* 827–28.

12. Walter H. Taylor, *General Lee: His Campaigns in Virginia, 1861–1865* (Morningside ed., Dayton, OH, 1975), 258.

13. Lee to Mary Lee, Camp, August 7, 1864, *Wartime Papers,* 829; Freeman, *Lee,* III, 479; *O.R.,* XLIII, part 1, 996.

14. Lee to Davis, Headquarters, August 9, 1864, *Wartime Papers,* 830.

15. Lee to Pickett, telegram, Petersburg, August 9, 1864, *ibid.;* Lee to Davis, Headquarters, August 12, 1864, *ibid.,* 833–34.

16. Freeman, *Lee,* III, 480–83; Robert E. Lee, Jr., *Recollections and Letters of General Robert E. Lee* (Garden City, NY, 1904), 137; Lee to Davis, telegram, Chaffin's Bluff, August 16, 1864, 10:35 A.M., *Wartime Papers,* 838; Lee to Seddon, telegram, Chaffin's Bluff, August 16, 1864, 4 P.M., *ibid.,* 838.

17. Taylor to Wilcox, telegram, August 18, 1864, *Wartime Papers,* 839; Gallagher, ed., *Alexander,* 473–74; Freeman, *Lee,* III, 485–90.

18. Lee to Davis, Headquarters, September 2, 1864, *Wartime Papers,* 847.

19. *O.R.,* XLII, part 1, 842.

20. Lee to Mary Lee, Camp, Petersburg, September 18, 1864, *Wartime Papers,* 855; Lee to Richard H. Anderson, telegram, Headquarters, September 23, 1864, *ibid.,* 856.

21. Freeman, *Lee,* III, 499–504; Gallagher, ed., *Alexander,* 478–79.

22. Lee to Seddon, telegram, Headquarters, Chaffin's Bluff, October 7, 1864, *Wartime Papers,* 861.

23. Lee to Seddon, telegram, Chaffin's Bluff, October 13, 1864, *ibid.,* 863; *O.R.,* XLII, part 1, 734.

24. *O.R.,* XLII, part 1, 871.

25. Lee to Seddon, telegram, Chaffin's Bluff, October 21, 1864, *Wartime Papers,* 864–65.

26. Lee to Mary Lee, Chaffin's Bluff, October 25, 1864, *ibid.,* 865.

27. *O.R.,* XLII, Part 1, 871–72; for this action see especially Richard J. Sommers, *Richmond Re-*

deemed: The Siege of Petersburg (Garden City, NY, 1981).

28. Walter H. Taylor, *Four Years with General Lee* (New York, 1878), 141.

29. Lee to Davis, Petersburg, November 2, 1864, *Wartime Papers*, 868.

30. Lee to Mary Lee, Petersburg, November 12, 1864, Lee Family Papers, MSS1L51C550, VHS.

31. Lee to Hampton, [November 21, 1864,] *Wartime Papers*, 871.

32. Lee to Mary Lee, Petersburg, November 25, 1864, *ibid.*, 871–72.

33. Freeman, *Lee*, III, 521–24.

34. Lee to Mary Lee, Petersburg, December 30, 1864, *Wartime Papers*, 880.

35. Lee to Mary Lee, January 8, 1865, Lee Papers, VHS.

36. Lee to Hunter, Headquarters, January 11, 1865, Lee Papers, MOC.

37. Lee to Farmers East of the Blue Ridge, Headquarters, January 12, 1865, *Wartime Papers*, 883.

38. Lee to Longstreet, Headquarters, January 19, John Walter Fairfax Papers, MSS1F1613A2, VHS.

39. Lee to Seddon, Headquarters, January 27, 1865, *Wartime Papers*, 286–87.

40. Lee to Davis, Headquarters, January 30, 1865, Lee Papers, USMA.

41. Freeman, *Lee*, III, 525–37.

42. Lee to Hetty Cary Pegram, Petersburg, February 11, 1865, Robert Edward Lee Papers, MSS2L515A21, VHS.

43. Freeman, *Lee*, III, 533–34, 6; Lee to Breckinridge, Headquarters, February 24, 1865, *Wartime Papers*, 910; Taylor, *Four Years*, 145–46.

44. Lee to Cooper, February 25, 1865, Headquarters Papers, VHS.

45. Lee to Grant, Headquarters, March 2, 1865, *Wartime Papers*, 911–12; Lee to Davis, Petersburg, March 2, 1865, *ibid.*, 911.

46. George T. Lee, "Reminiscences of General Robert E. Lee, 1865–68," typescript, Lee Papers, W & L.

47. Lee to Breckinridge, Headquarters, March 14, 1865, Headquarters Papers, VHS.

48. Freeman, *Lee*, III, 541.

49. *Ibid.*, IV, 14–55.

50. Lee to Breckinridge, Headquarters, April 2, 1865, *Wartime Papers*, 924.

51. Even Lee's enemies, even after Appomattox, honored Lee's mystique. "To tell the truth, we none of us realize even yet that he has actually surrendered. I had a sort of impression that we should fight him all our lives. He was like a ghost to children, something that haunted us so long that we could not realize that he and his army were really out of existence to us. It will take me some months to be conscious of this fact." *War Diary and Letters of Stephen Minot Weld, 1861–1865* (2nd ed., Boston, 1979), 396.

52. Taylor to Betty Saunders, Camp, Violet Bank, July 25, 1864, Walter Herren Taylor Papers, microfilm (28114, reel 2) at VSL.

53. *Ibid.*, August 1, 1864.

54. Taylor quotations in A. L. Long, *Memoirs of Robert E. Lee* (Blue and Grey Press ed., Secaucus, NJ, 1983), 399–400.

55. Gallagher, ed., *Alexander*, 481–82.

56. Long, *Memoirs*, 388.

57. *Ibid.*, 400–01.

58. Lee, "Reminiscences of General Robert E. Lee," Lee Papers, WEL.

59. Gallagher, ed., *Alexander*, 489.

60. Ulysses S. Grant, *Memoirs and Selected Letters*, ed. Mary Drake and William S. McFeely (New York, 1990), 598.

61. Walter H. Taylor, *General Lee: His Campaigns in Virginia, 1861–1865* (Morningside ed., Dayton, OH, 1975), 273; Long, *Memoirs*, 397; Freeman, *Lee*, IV, 521; Freeman, *Lee*, III, 531.

62. Long, *Memoirs*, 387–88; J. William Jones, *Personal Reminiscences of General Robert E. Lee* (U.S. Historical Society ed., Richmond, VA, 1989), 164.

63. Mrs. Burton Harrison, *Recollections Grave and Gay* (Richmond, VA, 1911), 150.

64. Taylor, *General Lee*, 276–78.

29. "I Would Rather Die a Thousand Deaths"

1. James I, Robertson, Jr., *General A. P. Hill: The Story of a Confederate Warrior* (New York, 1987), 315–18; *SHSP*, XII (1884), 184; *Confederate Veteran*, XXVII (1919), 342; William H. Palmer to Walter H. Taylor, Blacksburg, Virginia, June 25, 1905, Lee Papers, Stratford Hall.

2. Walter H. Taylor, *General Lee: His Campaigns in Virginia, 1861–1865* (Morningside ed., Dayton, Oh, 1975), 276–78; Emory M. Thomas, *The Confederate State of Richmond: A Biography of the Capital* (Austin, TX, 1971), 194–98; Rembert W. Patrick, *The Fall of Richmond* (Baton Rouge, LA, 1960).

3. Douglas Southall Freeman, *R. E. Lee: A Biography*, 4 vols. (New York, 1934–35), IV, 57–59. Douglas Southall Freeman, *Lee's Lieutenants: A Study in Command*, 3 vols. (New York, 1942–44), II, 680–87; Vincent J. Esposito, ed., *West Point Atlas of American Wars*, 2 vols. (New York, 1959), I, map 144; Taylor, *General Lee*, 275–76.

4. Taylor, *General Lee*, 279; Freeman, *Lee*, IV, 59–63.

5. Freeman, *Lee*, IV, 66–67, 509–513; Lee to Davis, Near Appomattox Court House, April 12, 1865, *Wartime Papers*, 935–36.

6. Freeman, *Lee*, IV, 71–78; Gary W. Gallagher, ed., *Fighting for the Confederacy: The Personal Recollections of General Edward Porter Alexan-der* (Chapel Hill, NC, 1989), 520–21; Lee to Davis, Near Appomattox Court House, April 12, 1865, *Wartime Papers*, 936.

7. Esposito, ed., *Atlas*, I, maps 143–44; Freeman, *Lee's Lieutenants*. III, 694–97; Freeman, *Lee*, IV, 82; *O.R.*, XLVI, part 1, 1295.

8. James Longstreet, *From Manassas to Appomattox: Memoirs of the Civil War in America*, ed. James I. Robertson, Jr. (Bloomington, IN, 1960), 614–15; Freeman, *Lee's Lieutenants*, III, 698–711; Freeman, *Lee*, IV, 86–93.

9. Freeman, *Lee*, IV, 93–100; Lee to Davis, Near Appomattox Court House, April 12, 1865, *Wartime Papers*, 936–37; A. L. Long, *Memoirs of Robert E. Lee* (Blue and Grey Press ed., Secaucus, NJ, 1983), 413.

10. Gallagher, ed., *Alexander*, 527; Long, *Memoirs*, 415; Freeman, *Lee*, IV, 103n.

11. Long, *Memoirs*, 418; *O.R.*, XLVI, part 3, 619; Longstreet, *Memoirs*, 619.

12. Long, *Memoirs*, 418.

13. Freeman, *Lee*, IV, 106–08.

14. Gallagher, ed., *Alexander*, 527–28; Long, *Memoirs*, 418.

15. Susan P. Lee, *Memoirs of William Nelson Pendleton* (Philadelphia, 1893), 402; Gallagher, ed., *Alexander*, 528; Long, *Memoirs*, 416–17.

16. This may have occurred on April 9. The best ac-

count is William H. Palmer to Walter H. Taylor, White Sulphur Springs, June 24, 1911, Lee Papers, Stratford Hall; see also Freeman, *Lee,* IV, 111–12.

17. Freeman, *Lee,* IV, 112; Gallagher, ed., *Alexander,* 528–29; Long, *Memoirs,* 419; Taylor, *General Lee,* 284.

18. Freeman, *Lee,* IV, 1145–19; Long, *Memoirs,* 420; John Esten Cooke, *A Life of Gen. Robert E. Lee* (New York, 1875), 459; *O.R.,* XLVI, part 1, 1266, 1303.

19. Long, *Memoirs,* 421; Lee to Davis, Near Appomattox Court House, April 12, 1865, *Wartime Papers,* 937; Freeman, *Lee,* IV, 118–21.

20. William H. Palmer to Walter H. Taylor, Blacksburg, Virginia, June 25, 1905, Lee Papers, Stratford Hall; *Confederate Veteran,* XXVII (1919), 342; Freeman, *Lee,* IV, 121; Cooke, *Lee,* 461.

21. Gallagher, ed., *Alexander,* 530–33; a slightly different version of Lee's response appears in Edward Porter Alexander, *Military Memoirs of a*

Confederate (Morningside ed., Dayton, OH, 1977), 605.

22. Freeman, *Lee,* IV, 124–25; *O.R.,* XLVI, part 3, 664.

23. Gallagher, ed., *Alexander,* 535–37; Taylor, *General Lee,* 288–90; Freeman, *Lee,* IV, 126–30.

24. *O.R.,* XLVI, part 3, 665; Freeman, *Lee,* IV, 129–30, 513–15.

25. Gallagher, ed., *Alexander,* 537–38.

26. Taylor, *General Lee,* 290; *O.R.,* XLVI, part 3, 665; Freeman, *Lee,* IV, 131–35; Ulysses S. Grant, *Memoirs and Selected Letters,* ed. Mary Drake and William S. McFeely, (Library of America ed., New York, 1990), 735; William S. McFeely, *Grant: A Biography* (New York, 1981), 219.

27. Grant, *Memoirs,* 735–41; Freeman, *Lee,* IV, 136–43; George A. Forsyth, "The Closing Scene at Appomattox Court House," *Harper's Magazine,* (April 1898), 708–10.

28. *SHSP,* XXXVIII, 12; Freeman, *Lee,* IV, 144–48.

29. Susan Leigh Blackford, *Memoirs of Life In and Out of the Army in Virginia,* 2 vols. (Lynchburg, VA, 1894–96), II, iv; Freeman, *Lee,* IV, 145.

29. *"After Four Years of Arduous Service"*

1. Copies of General Orders No. 9 are in MOC; the text is most available in *Wartime Papers,* 934–35; Charles Marshall, "General Lee's Farewell Address to His Army," in *Battles and Leaders,* IV 747; Douglas Southall Freeman, *R. E. Lee: A Biography,* 4 vols. (New York, 1934–35), IV, 149–50.

2. *Wartime Papers,* 934–35; Freeman, *Lee,* IV, 157–58 and notes.

3. Lee to Davis, Near Appomattox Court House, April 12, 1865, *Wartime Papers,* 935–38.

4. Lee to Davis, Richmond, April 20, 1865, *ibid.,* 938–39.

5. Joshua L. Chamberlain, *Passing of the Armies* (New York, 1915); Freeman, *Lee,* IV, 157–64; Walter H. Taylor, *General Lee: His Campaigns in Virginia, 1861–1865* (Morningside ed., Dayton, OH, 1975), 296–97.

6. Robert E. Lee, Jr., *Recollections and Letters of General Robert E. Lee* (Garden City, NY, 1904), 155–60.

7. *New York Herald,* April 29, 1865; Charles Bracelen Flood, *Lee: The Last Years* (Boston, 1981), 49–50; Lee, Jr., *Recollections and Letters,* 159, 170.

8. Freeman, *Lee,* IV, 197.

9. A good study of postwar rancor and Grant as pacifier is Brooks D. Simpson, *Let Us Have Peace: Ulysses S. Grant and the Politics of War and Reconstruction, 1861–1868* (Chapel Hill, NC, 1991).

10. Freeman, *Lee,* IV, 202; Lee to Grant, Richmond, June 13, 1865, in Lee, Jr., *Recollections and Letters,* 164; Lee to Johnson, Richmond, June 13, 1865, in *ibid.,* 164–65.

11. Lee to Beauregard, October 3, 1865, in J. William Jones, *Life and Letters of Robert Edward Lee, Soldier and Man* (Washington, DC, 1906), 390.

12. For desertion policy, see chapter 24; Lee to Mary Lee, Orange County, April 21, 1864, Lee Family Papers, MSS1L51C513, VHS.

13. Simpson, *Let Us Have Peace,* 106–09.

14. Lee, Jr., *Recollections and Letters,* 166–69.

15. T. L. Broun, "Negro Communed at St. Paul's Church," *Confederate Veteran,* XIII (1905), 360.

16. Lee to Markie, Richmond, May 2, 1865, printed in Avery Craven, ed. *"To Markie": The Letters of Robert E. Lee to Martha Custis Williams* (Cambridge, MA, 1933), 60–61; Lee to Markie, Richmond, June 20, 1865, *ibid.,* 62–63.

17. Joseph H. Crute, Jr., *The Derwent Letters* (Powhatan, VA, 1985), 13–14.

18. *Ibid.,* 15; Lee to Rooney Lee, Near Cartersville, July 29, 1865, George Bolling Lee Papers, MSS1L5114C62, VHS.

19. Crute, *Derwent Letters,* 15.

20. Lee to Walter Taylor, Near Cartersville, July 31, 1865, Stratford Hall; Lee to Carter Lee, Near Cartersville, August 18, 1865, W & L.

21. Lee to Rob, Near Cartersville, July 22, 1865, in Lee, Jr., *Recollections and Letters,* 175–76; Lee to Rob, Near Cartersville, August 21, 1865, in *ibid.,* 176–77; Mildred Lee to Lucy Blain, Derwent, August 14, 1865, W & L; Lee to Fitz Lee, Near Cartersville, July 29, 1865, George Bolling Lee Papers, MSS1L5114C62, VHS.

22. Lee to Rob, Near Cartersville, August 21, 1865, in Lee, Jr., *Recollections and Letters,* 177; Mary Lee quoted in Rose Mortimer Ellzey MacDonald, *Mrs. Robert E. Lee* (Boston, 1939), 200; Ollinger Crenshaw, *General Lee's College: The Rise and Growth of Washington and Lee University* (New York, 1969), 145–47, 325–28.

23. Brockenbrough to Lee, on board packet *Jefferson,* August 10, 1865, W & L; Pendleton to Lee, Lexington, August 5, 1865, W & L; Freeman, *Lee,* IV, 215.

24. Pendleton to Lee, Lexington, August 5, 1865, W & L; Lee, Jr., *Recollections and Letters,* 179–80; John H. Cocke to Mrs. A. Moore, Oakland, January 3, 1905, "A Ride with Gen. R. E. Lee," W & L.

25. Lee to Trustees, Powhatan Co., August 24, 1865, W & L; Lee, Jr., *Recollections and Letters,* 183.

26. Crute, *Derwent Letters,* 36–37.

27. *Ibid.;* Lee to Mary Lee, Lexington, September 19, 1865, in Lee, Jr., *Recollections and Letters,* 184–85; Freeman, *Lee,* IV, 226–29; Crenshaw, *General Lee's College,* 69–78, 89; Eighth U.S. Census (1860).

28. Lee, Jr., *Recollections and Letters,* 185–86; Lee to Mary Lee, Rockbridge Baths, September 25, 1865, in *ibid.,* 186–87; Lee to Mary Lee, Lexington, October 3, 1865, Lee Family Papers, MSS1L51C597, VHS.

29. Crenshaw, *General Lee's College,* 149; *New York Herald,* "Inauguration of General Lee," in Franklin L. Riley, ed., *General Robert E. Lee After Appomattox* (New York, 1930), 12–15.

30. Lee to Mary Lee, October 3, 1865, in Lee, Jr., *Recollections and Letters,* 187; Report to Trustees, June, 1865, W & L.
31. Freeman, *Lee,* IV, 230–48.
32. Petition to Senate and House of Delegates of Virginia, December 4, 1865, W & L.
33. Lee to Anna Fitzhugh, Lexington, December 14, 1865, George Bolling Lee Papers, MSS1L5114C66, VHS.
34. Crenshaw, *General Lee's College,* 175–81.
35. R. R. Harrison to Lee, Richmond, November 8, 1865, W & L; Lee to Rooney Lee, Lexington, November 13, 1865, George Bolling Lee Papers, MSS1L5144C64, VHS; Rooney Lee to Lee, White House, November 21, 1865, W & L; Lee to

Rooney Lee, Lexington, November 28, 1865, George Bolling Lee Papers, MSS1L5114C65, VHS.
36. Lee to Markie, Lexington, December 20, 1865, in Craven, ed., *"To Markie,"* 66–67; Lee to Rob Lee, Lexington, October 19, 1865, Lee Family Papers, MSS1L51C601, VHS.
37. Report to Trustees, June 1866, W & L; Lee, Jr., *Recollections and Letters,* 190–203; Lee to Mary Lee, Lexington, October 27, 1865, Lee Family Papers, MSS1L51C605, VHS.
38. Lee to Smith Lee, Lexington, January 4, 1866, Lee Papers, VSL.
39. Lee, Jr., *Recollections and Letters,* 204.

30. *"I Am Considered Now Such a Monster"*

1. *New York Herald* correspondent, "Inauguration of General Lee, as President of Washington College," in Franklin L. Riley, ed., *General Robert E. Lee After Appomattox* (New York, 1930), 14.
2. Elmer Otis Parker, "Why Was Lee Not Pardoned?", *Prologue,* 2 (Winter 1970), 181; Charles Braceland Flood, *Lee: The Last Years* (Boston, 1981), 276 and n.; Lee to Rooney Lee, Near Cartersville, Cumberland County, Virginia, July 29, 1865, in Robert E. Lee Jr., *Recollections and Letters of General Robert E. Lee* (Garden City, NY, 1904), 178; *New York Times,* July 23, 1975; August 6, 1975.
3. Douglas Southall Freeman, *R. E. Lee: A Biography* 4 vols. (New York, 1934–35), IV, 250–51; Mrs. Margaret J. Preston, "General Lee After the War," *Century Magazine,* 38 (1889), 274; Lee to Markie, Lexington, April 7, 1866 in Avery Craven, ed., *"To Markie": The Letters of Robert E. Lee to Martha Custis Williams* (Cambridge, MA, 1933), 68.
4. Flood, *Last Years,* 119–24; *Report of the Joint Committee on Reconstruction,* 39th Congress, 1st Session (Washington, DC, 1866), 129–36.
5. Mary Lee to Emily Mason, Lexington, February, 1866, Lee Papers; Mary Lee to Emily Mason, Lexington, April 20, 1866, Lee Papers; Mary Lee to Emily Mason, Lexington, May 20, 1866, Lee Papers, MOC.
6. Mary Lee to Emily Mason, May 20, 1866, Lee Papers, MOC; Freeman, *Lee,* IV, 230–31; Mary Lee to Emily Mason, Lexington, February 18, 1866, Lee Papers, MOC; Allen W. Moger, "Letters to General Lee After the War," *Virginia Magazine of History and Biography,* 64 (January 1956), 30–69; Flood, *Last Years,* 141–42; William P. Neale to Lee, Bethany, Brook Co., W.Va., January 29, 1866, Lee Papers; A. L. Masurier and J. W. Verlander to Lee, Richmond, August 28, 1866, Lee Papers; A. L. Masurier to Lee, Richmond, September 5, 1866, Lee Papers, W & L.
7. J. C. Davis to Lee, Greenway, January 20, 1866, Lee Papers, W & L.
8. Lee to Jubal Early, Lexington, October 15, 1866, typescript from Early Papers, Library of Congress, in Lee Papers, W & L; Lee to Mrs. Jackson, Lexington, January 25, 1866, typescript, MOC.
9. Lee to S. Maupin, Lexington, October 17, 1866, Lee Papers; Lee to Churchill J. Gibson, Lexington, January 24, 1866, Lee Papers, W & L.
10. Thomas H. Williamson to Mrs. William Eoff, Lexington, October 12, 1866, Lee Papers, W & L.
11. Robert Ould to Lee, Richmond, January 31, 1867, Lee Papers, W & L; Lee to Ould, Lexington, February 4, 1867, quoted in Freeman, *Lee,* IV, 310–11.
12. Lee to Ould, Lexington, March 29, 1867, Robert

Edward Lee Papers, MSS2L515A1; Lee to R. I. Moses, Lexington, April 13, 1867, Lee Family Papers, MSS1L51C738; Lee to Dabney H. Maury, Lexington, May 23, 1867, Lee Family Papers, MSS1L51C738, VHS.
13. Mary Lee to Emily Mason, Lexington, February 22, 1867, Lee Papers, MOC.
14. Freeman, *Lee,* IV, 316–17; Lee to J. S. Sharp, Lexington, April 13, 1867, Lee Papers, W & L.
15. Lee to Jno. W. Jordon, Lexington, November 20, 1868, Lee Papers, Letter Book II, 209; Lee Notice, Letter Book II, 208, W & L.
16. Freeman, *Lee,* IV, 320–32; Lee to Markie, Lexington, October 4, 1867, in Craven, ed., *"To Markie,"* 76; Lee to Rooney Lee, Lexington, September 20, 1867, in Lee, Jr., *Recollections and Letters,* 283.
17. Freeman, *Lee,* IV, 333–37; Lee to Rooney Lee, Lexington, October 25, 1867, in Lee, Jr., *Recollections and Letters,* 284–85; Lee to Mary Lee, Exchange Hotel, Richmond, November 26, 1867, in *ibid.,* 286–87; Flood, *Last Years,* 170–71; E. C. Gordon, "Recollections of General Robert E. Lee's Administration as President of Washington College," in Riley, *After Appomattox,* 96–97.
18. Lee to Mary Lee, Petersburg, November 29, 1867, Lee Family Papers, MSS1L51C648, VHS; Lee to Rooney Lee, Lexington, December 21, 1867, in Lee, Jr., *Recollections and Letters,* 293; Freeman, *Lee,* IV, 339–43.
19. Lee to Markie, Lexington, January 1, 1868, in Craven, ed., *"To Markie,"* 78.
20. Freeman, *Lee,* IV, 345–48; Flood, *Last Years,* 176–77; Olinger Crenshaw, *General Lee's College: The Rise and Growth of Washington and Lee University* (New York, 1969), 153–54; extract from the affidavit of Erastus C. Johnston, Lexington, February 5, 1868, Lee Papers, W & L.
21. Freeman, *Lee,* IV, 347–48; Notes on students, Lee Papers, W & L; Lee to George Sergeant, Lexington, February 15, 1868, Lee Papers, Letter Book II, 42, W & L.
22. Crenshaw, *General Lee's College,* 150–53; *New York Independent,* March 12, April 2, and April 16, 1868; Freeman, *Lee,* IV, 351–57.
23. Lee to Winchester Hall, Lexington, April 29, 1868, Lee Papers, Letter Book II, 115, W & L; Lee to J. G. Parkhurst, Lexington, April 29, 1868, Lee Papers, Letter Book II, 116; the *Tribune* letter is printed in Walter Greigh Preston, *Lee: West Point and Lexington* (Yellow Springs, OH, 1934), 86–87.
24. D. Gardiner Tyler, statement in Riley, *After Appomattox,* 129–30; Lee to J. B. Strickland, 4 P.M., May 10, 1868, Lee Papers, Letter Book II, 119–20, W & L; Freeman, *Lee,* IV, 358–60.
25. Freeman, *Lee,* IV, 360–89; Lee to Reverdy John-

son, Lexington, February 25, 1868, Lee Family Papers, MSS1L51C738, VHS; the Smith Island correspondence is in the Lee Papers, W & L, and at VHS, MSS1L51C738 and MSS1L5114D27; Lee to Mrs. E. Neal, Lexington, January 29, 1869, Lee Papers, Letter Book II, 231, W & L.

26. Lee, et al., to William S. Rosecrans, White Sulphur Springs, W. Va., August 26, 1868, Lee Family Papers, MSS1L51C738, VHS, printed in Freeman, *Lee*, IV, 375–77.

27. Lee to Annette Carter, Lexington, March 28, 1868, Lee Papers, W & L.

28. Flood, *Last Year*, 208–10; Freeman, *Lee*, IV, 401–02, 520–21.

29. Christina Bond, "Recollections of General Robert E. Lee," *South Atlantic Quarterly*, XXIV (1925) 333–48.

30. Lee to Hon. D. McConaughy, Lexington, August 9, 1869, Lee Papers, W & L.

31. *"We Have But One Rule Here"*

1. Pendleton to Lee, Lexington, January 20, 1868, Lee Papers; Lee to J. M. Platt, Lexington, December 12, 1867, Lee Papers, Letter Book II, 18; Lee to J. M. Platt, Lexington, February 13, 1868, Lee Papers, Letter Book II, 44–45; J. M. Platt to Lee, St. Louis, February 20, 1868, Lee Papers; Lee to J. M. Platt, Lexington, February 27, 1868, Lee Papers, Letter Book II, 58–59; W. G. Clarke to Lee, St. Louis, March 10, 1868, Lee Papers; Lee to J. M. Platt, Lexington, March 13, 1868, Lee Papers, Letter Book II, 71–72; Notes on Students in connection with the Johnston incident, Lee Papers; all W & L.

2. Richard P. Rogers to sister, Lexington, November 30, 1867, Lee Papers, W & L; M. W. Humphreys, "Reminiscences of General Lee as President of Washington College," in Franklin L. Riley, ed., *General Robert E. Lee After Appomattox* (New York, 1930), 32–34.

3. E. E. Starkey to Lee, Louisville, July 6, 1867, Lee Papers, W & L.

4. Lee to Douglas Frazer, Lexington, March 2, 1868, Lee Papers, Letter Book II, 61–62, W & L.

5. "Brief Statements by 'Lee Alumni,'" in Riley, ed., *After Appomattox*, 106–41; John B. Collyar, "A College Boy's Observations of General Lee," in *ibid.*, 65–74.

6. Humphreys, "Reminiscences," 38.

7. C. A. Graves, "General Lee at Lexington," in Riley, ed., *After Appomattox*, 24–25.

8. Edward S. Joynes, "General Robert E. Lee as College President," in Riley, ed., *After Appomattox*, 17; Humphreys, "Reminiscences," 36–38; Graves, "Lee at Lexington," 28.

9. Collyar, "College Boy's Observation," 66.

10. The Lee quotation (italics in original) is from Edward V. Valentine, "Reminiscences of General Lee," in Riley, ed., *After Appomattox*, 155; see

also Emory M. Thomas, "God and General Lee," *Anglican and Episcopal History*, LX (March 1991), 15–24.

11. Walter Creigh Preston, *Lee: West Point and Lexington* (Yellow Springs, OH, 1934), 77–78.

12. J. C. Whitlock to Lee, Newstead, Kentucky, November 23, 1867, Lee Papers, W & L.

13. J. W. Ewing, "An Incident in the Life of General R. E. Lee," in Riley, ed., *After Appomattox*, 70; Graves, "Lee at Lexington," 24–25.

14. Lee to Professor S. Maupin, Lexington, May 15, 1867, Lee Family Papers, MSS1L51C738, VHS.

15. Lee to Professor J. B. Minor, Lexington, January 17, 1867, Lee Family Papers, MSS1L51C738, VHS.

16. Ollinger Crenshaw, *General Lee's College: The Rise and Growth of Washington and Lee University* (New York, 1969), 166–68; Humphreys, "Reminiscences," 38; Graves, "Lee at Lexington," 23–24.

17. Preston, *West Point and Lexington*, 56–57.

18. Douglas Southall Freeman, *R. E. Lee: A Biography*, 4 vols. (New York, 1934–35), IV, 420–32; Crenshaw, *General Lee's College*, 160–66; Preston, *West Point and Lexington*, 61–70; Report to Trustees, June 22, 1869, Lee Papers, W & L; Lee to Board of Trustees, Lexington, March 30, 1869, Lee Papers, Letter Book II; 237–38, W & L.

19. Robert E. Lee, Jr., *Recollections and Letters of General Robert E. Lee* (Garden City, NY, 1904), 218–34; Freeman, *Lee*, IV, 235–36, 261, 418–19.

20. Henry Lee, *Memoirs of the War in the Southern Department of the United States*, 3rd ed. by Robert E. Lee (New York, 1869), 53; Lee, Jr., *Recollections and Letters*, 398.

21. Crenshaw, *General Lee's College*, 117, 157–58; Humphreys, "Reminiscences," 39.

32. *"I Will Give That Sum"*

1. Douglas Southall Freeman, *R. E. Lee: A Biography*, 4 vols. (New York, 1934–35), IV, 408–09, 391; Charles Bracelen Flood, *Lee: The Last Years* (Boston, 1981), 211–12; Robert E. Lee, Jr., *Recollections and Letters of General Robert E. Lee* (New York, 1904), 357–58; Royster Lyle, Jr., and Sally Munger Mann, *The Architecture of Historic Lexington* (Charlottesville, VA, 1977), 162–65.

2. Portion of Lee letter in Lee, Jr., *Recollections and Letters*, 360; Lee to Mary Lee, Alexandria, July 25, 1869, in *ibid.*, 361–62; Lee, Jr., *Recollections and Letters*, 363.

3. Lee to Mary Lee, White House, New Kent, August 1, 1869, in *ibid.*, 363–64; Lee, Jr., *Recollections and Letters*, 364, 368; Lee to unnamed correspondent, White House, August 1, 1869, in *ibid.*, 364–65.

4. Flood, *Last Years*, 287, 217–22; Edouard Brunner to author, Washington, DC, May 22, 1989.

5. Lee, Jr., *Recollections and Letters*, 371; Lee to

Markie, Lexington, November 27, 1869, in Avery Craven, ed., *"To Markie": The Letters of Robert E. Lee to Martha Custis Williams* (Cambridge, MA, 1934), 87.

6. Lee to Mildred Lee, Lexington, January 8, 1870, in Lee, Jr., *Recollections and Letters*, 380–81.

7. Lee to Mary Lee, White House, August 10, 1869, in *ibid.*, 363; Lee to Markie, Lexington, April 14, 1868, Craven, ed., *"To Markie,"* 81.

8. Lee to Annette Carter, Lexington, June 2, 1870, Annette Carter File in Lee Papers, W & L; Lee to Mary Lee, Alexandria, July 15, 1870, in Lee, Jr., *Recollections and Letters*, 414.

9. Lee to Caroline C. Stuart, Lexington, July 4, 1868, "Driver Letters," Lee Papers, W & L.

10. Lee to Charlotte Haxall, Lexington, November 2, 1868, Lee Family Papers, MSS1L51C659, VHS.

11. Lee to Mildred Lee, Lexington, February 2, 1870, Lee Family Papers, MSS1L51C680, VHS; Lee to Robert Carter, Lexington, February 16, 1870,

typescript at Shirley Plantation; Lee to Genl Corse, Francis S. Smith, et al., Lexington, March 18, 1870, Lee Papers, W & L.

12. William Preston Johnston memorandum, March 18, 1870, William Preston Johnston Papers, Howard-Tilton Memorial Library, Tulane University, Box 54, folder 10; Lee to Mildred Lee, Lexington, March 21, 1870, in Lee, Jr., *Recollections and Letters*, 384; Lee, Jr., *Recollections and Letters*, 388.

13. Freeman, *Lee*, IV, 444; Lee to Mary Lee, Richmond, March 29, 1870, in Lee, Jr., *Recollections and Letters*, 288–89.

14. John S. Mosby, *Memoirs of John S. Mosby*, ed. Charles W. Russell (Boston, 1917), 380–81; Lesley Gordon-Burr, "Assumed a Darker Hue: Major General George E. Pickett, May, 1863–May, 1864," M.A. thesis, University of Georgia, 1991.

15. Freeman, *Lee*, IV, 446–49; Lee to Mary Lee, Savannah, April 2, 1870, in Lee, Jr., *Recollections and Letters*, 390–91; Agnes to Mary Lee, Savannah, April 3, 1870, in *ibid.*, 391–94.

16. Freeman, *Lee*, IV, 449–53; Lee to Mary Lee, Savannah, April 11, 1870, Lee Family Papers, MSS1L51C687, VHS.

17. Lee to Mary Lee, Savannah, April 17 (?), 1870, in Lee, Jr., *Recollections and Letters*, 395; Lee to Mary Lee, Savannah, April 18, 1870, in *ibid.*, 397–400; Freeman, *Lee*, IV, 449–53.

18. Freeman, *Lee*, IV, 453–59; Lee to Mary Lee, "Brandon," May 7, 1870, in Lee, Jr., *Recollections and Letters*, 401–02; Lee, Jr., *Recollections and Letters*, 405.

19. Freeman, *Lee*, IV, 460–63; Mary Lee to Mildred, White House, May 9, 13, 1870, in Lee, Jr., *Recollections and Letters*, 405; Lee, Jr., *Recollections and Letters*, 405–10.

20. Lee to Mildred Lee, Richmond, May 23, 1870, in Lee, Jr., *Recollections and Letters*, 411; Edward V. Valentine, "Reminiscences of General Lee," *The Outlook*, 84 (December 1906), 964–68; Elizabeth Gray Valentine, *Dawn to Twilight: The*

Works of Edward V. Valentine (Richmond, VA, 1929); Freeman, *Lee*, IV, 464–67.

21. Lee to Mary Lee, Baltimore, July 2, 1870, in Lee, Jr., *Recollections and Letters*, 412–13; Freeman, *Lee*, IV, 473–77; Lee to Mary Lee, Alexandria, July 15, 1870, in Lee, Jr., *Recollections and Letters*, 414; Lee to Mary Lee, Ravensworth, July 20, 1870, in *ibid.*, 417–19; Lee to Custis Lee, Ravensworth, July 22, 1870, Lee Papers, W & L.

22. Freeman, *Lee*, IV, 478–80; Valentine, "Reminiscences," 968; Lee to Mary Lee, Hot Springs, August 19, 1870, in Lee, Jr., *Recollections and Letters*, 425–26; Lee to Mary Lee, Hot Springs, August 23, 1870, in *ibid.*, 428; "forlorn hopes" quoted in Robert W. Winston, *Robert E. Lee* (New York, 1934), 407.

23. Lee to S. H. Tagart, Lexington, September 28, 1870, Lee Papers, W & L.

24. Mildred Lee, "My Recollections of My Father's Death," typescript in Lee Papers, W & L, original at VHS; William Preston Johnston, "Personal Reminiscences of General Robert E. Lee," quoted in Lee, Jr., *Recollections and Letters*, 434–39; Mary Lee to Robert Chilton, Lexington, December 12, 1870, Lee Papers, MOC.

25. Marvin P. Rozear, et al., "R. E. Lee's Stroke," *Virginia Magazine of History and Biography* 98 (April 1990), 291–308.

26. Mildred Lee, "Recollections."

27. Diary.

28. Lee to Mary Lee, Savannah, April 17, 1870, in Lee, Jr., *Recollections and Letters*, 395; Lee to Mr. Boo [Custis], March 28, 1852, Lee Papers, VHS.

29. Ollinger Crenshaw, *General Lee's College: The Rise and Growth of Washington and Lee University* (New York, 1969), 155–56.

30. *The Book of Common Prayer* (New York, 1850), 212–13.

31. Mildred Lee, "Recollections."

32. R. L. Madison and H. T. Barton, letter, October 21, 1870, in *Richmond and Louisville Medical Journal*, IX and X (1870), 516–23.

Apotheosis

1. "General Lee's Coffin," Lee Papers, W & L.

2. "Funeral Obsequies," broadside, Lee Papers, W & L; Douglas Southall Freeman, *R. E. Lee: A Biography*, 4 vols. (New York, 1934–35), IV, 526–28.

3. Emory M. Thomas, "God and General Lee," *An-glican and Episcopal History*, LII (March 1991), 15–24.

4. Marvin P. Rozear, et al., "R. E. Lee's Stroke," *Virginia Magazine of History and Biography*, 98 (April 1990), 291–308.

Bibliography

Listed here are essentially the materials cited in the Notes. For more extensive bibliographies of Robert E. Lee, see William Hollis and Marshall Fishwick, *A Preliminary Checklist of Writings About R. E. Lee* (Charlottesville, VA, 1951) as well as other biographies of Lee.

Manuscript Materials

The most important single collection of Lee and Lee Family Papers is at the Virginia Historical Society in Richmond, Virginia. Also in Richmond are Lee manuscripts at the Virginia State Library and the Eleanor S. Brockenbrough Library at the Museum of the Confederacy. As might be expected, Washington and Lee University in Lexington, Virginia, has a significant Lee collection, too.

Lee manuscript materials are also scattered in many repositories throughout the United States, and some remain in private hands. Letters by and about Lee, hitherto unknown, surface every few years even now, a century and a quarter after his death. Below are the collections of manuscripts consulted for this work.

Armstrong, Joan Tracy, ed. "The Civil War Letters of Captain John Preston Sheffey": typescript, Marshall Steck Collins, Marion, Virginia
Robert E. Lee Papers: Perkins Library, Duke University, Durham, North Carolina
Robert E. Lee Papers: Georgia Historical Society, Savannah, Georgia
Confederate Soldiers Reminiscences, Vol. XII. Georgia State Archives, Atlanta, Georgia
Robert E. Lee Papers: Henry E. Huntington Library, San Marino, California
Robert E. Lee Papers: Library of Congress, Washington, DC
Robert E. Lee Microfilm: National Archives, Washington, DC
Records of the Adjutant General's Office: National Archives, Washington, DC
Record Group 77, Boxes 55 & 56: National Archives, Washington, DC
Lee Papers: Missouri Historical Society, St. Louis, Missouri
Lee Papers: Eleanor S. Brockenbrough Library, Museum of the Confederacy, Richmond, Virginia
J. R. Montgomery Letter: Museum of the Confederacy, Richmond, Virginia
Robert E. Lee Papers: Jessie Ball dePont Library, Stratford Hall, Stratford, Virginia
William Preston Johnston Papers: Howard-Tilton Library, Tulane University, New Orleans, Louisiana
Mrs. Mason Barret Collection: Howard-Tilton Library, Tulane University, New Orleans, Louisiana
Robert E. Lee Papers: United States Military Academy Library and Archives, West Point, New York
Mrs. A. A. Draper Papers: United States Military Academy Library and Archives, West Point, New York
Superintendents Letter Books: United States Military Academy Library and Archives, West Point, New York
Robert E. Lee Papers: University of Virginia Library, Charlottesville, Virginia

Edward Virginius Valentine Papers: Valentine Museum, Richmond, Virginia
Bemiss Family Papers: Virginia Historical Society, Richmond, Virginia
(H. Douglas Pitts) "Dabb's House: A Historical Treasure": Virginia Historical Society, Rich-
    mond, Virginia
Richard Eppes Diary, Eppes Papers: Virginia Historical Society, Richmond, Virginia
George Bolling Lee Papers: Virginia Historical Society, Richmond, Virginia
Henry Lee Papers: Virginia Historical Society, Richmond, Virginia
Lee Family Papers: Virginia Historical Society, Richmond, Virginia
Robert E. Lee Diary: Virginia Historical Society, Richmond, Virginia
Robert E. Lee Headquarters Papers: Virginia Historical Society, Richmond, Virginia
Robert Edward Lee Papers: Virginia Historical Society, Richmond, Virginia
J. E. B. Stuart Papers: Virginia Historical Society, Richmond, Virginia
Talcott Papers: Virginia Historical Society, Richmond, Virginia
Robert Edward Lee Papers: Virginia State Library, Richmond, Virginia
Walter Herren Taylor Papers (microfilm): Virginia State Library, Richmond, Virginia
Robert E. Lee Papers: Washington & Lee University, Lexington, Virginia

NEWSPAPERS AND PERIODICALS

Charleston *Mercury*
Confederate Veteran
Daily Savannah Republican
National Intelligencer
New York Herald
New York Independent
New York Times

New York Tribune
Richmond Times-Dispatch
Richmond and Louisville
    Medical Journal
Richmond *Dispatch*
Richmond *Enquirer*
Richmond *Examiner*

Richmond *Whig*
Rome [Georgia]
    Tri-Weekly Courier
Southern Illustrated News
Southern Literary Messenger
Virginia Gazette

OTHER PRINTED MATERIALS

Atlas to Accompany the Official Record of the Union and Confederate Armies. Arno Press ed., New
    York, 1978.
The Centennial of the United States Military Academy at West Point, New York, 2 vols. Greenwood
    Reprinting, New York, 1969.
Cullum, George W., *Biographical Register of the Officers and Graduates of the U.S. Military
    Academy . . . 1802 to 1890,* 3 vols. 3rd ed., Boston and New York, 1891.
Dill, Alonzo T., and Mary Tyler Cheek, *A Visit to Stratford and the Story of the Lees,* Stratford,
    VA, 1986.
Esposito, Vincent J., ed., *The West Point Atlas of American Wars.* 2 vols., New York, 1959.
Loth, Calder, ed., *The Virginia Landmarks Register.* 3rd ed., Charlottesville, VA, 1986.
Poe, Edgar Allan, "Desultory Notes on Cats," *The Unabridged Edward Allan Poe.* Philadelphia,
    1983.
Sauers, Richard A., comp., *The Gettysburg Campaign, June 3–August 1, 1863: A Comprehensive,
    Selectively Annotated Bibliography.* Westport, CN, 1982.
Symonds, Craig L., *Gettysburg: A Battlefield Atlas.* Baltimore, 1992.
Wallace, Lee A., Jr., *A Guide to Virginia Military Organizations, 1861–1865.* Richmond, VA,
    1964.

PRINTED PRIMARY SOURCES

Fortunately for the student of Robert E. Lee, a good proportion of his papers, public and private,
are in print. Many Lee materials, however, remain only in manuscript. And so significant and so
enigmatic was Lee that he all but cries out for published volumes of his papers bringing together
the accurate texts of scattered works currently in and out of print as well as important manuscripts. Here are the printed primary sources used for this biography.

Adams, Henry, *The Education of Henry Adams: An Autobiography.* Boston, 1918.
Alexander, Edward Porter, ed. Gary W. Gallagher, *Fighting for the Confederacy: The Personal
    Recollections of General Edward Porter Alexander.* Chapel Hill, NC, 1989.
Alexander, Edward Porter, *Military Memoirs of a Confederate.* Morningside Bookshop ed., Day-
    ton, OH, 1977.

Ammen, Daniel, "DuPont and the Port Royal Expedition," in Johnson and Buel, eds., *Battles and Leaders of the Civil War*, I, 671–90.

Andrews, Garnett, "A Battle Planned Not Fought," *Confederate Veteran*, V (June 1887).

Arlington House: A Guide to Arlington House: The Robert E. Lee Memorial. Washington, DC, 1985.

Blackford, Susan Leigh, *Memoirs of Life in and out of the Army in Virginia.* 2 vols., Lynchburg, VA, 1894–96.

Blackford, W. W., *War Years with Jeb Stuart.* New York, 1945.

Bond, Christina, "Recollections of General Robert E. Lee," *South Atlantic Quarterly*, XXIV (1925), 333–48.

Brent, Joseph L., *Memoirs of the War.* New Orleans, 1940.

"Brief Statements by 'Lee Alumni,' " in Riley, ed., *General Robert E. Lee After Appomattox.*

Broun, T. L., "Negro Communed at St. Paul's Church," *Confederate Veteran*, XIII (1905), 360.

Brugger, Robert J., et al., eds., *The Papers of James Madison: Secretary of State Series*, 2 vols. Charlottesville, VA, 1986– .

Chamberlain, Joshua L., *Passing of the Armies.* New York, 1915.

"Changes in the Pay of the Army," *Senate Executive Documents*, 28th Congress, 1st Session, vol. V.

Christ, Lynda Lasswell, and Mary Seaton Dix, eds., *The Papers of Jefferson Davis.* Vol. 7, Baton Rouge, LA, 1992.

Collyar, John B., "A College Boy's Observations of General Lee," in Riley, ed., *General Robert E. Lee After Appomattox.*

Cooke, John Esten, *A Life of Gen. Robert E. Lee.* New York, 1871.

———, *Wearing of the Gray*, ed. Phillip Van Doren Stern. Bloomington, IN, 1959.

Craven, Avery, ed., *"To Markie": The Letters of Robert E. Lee to Martha Custis Williams.* Cambridge, MA, 1933.

Crute, Joseph H., Jr., *The Derwent Letters.* Powhatan, VA, 1985.

A Cursory Sketch of the Motives & Proceedings of the Party Which Sways the Affairs of the Union. . . . Philadelphia, 1809.

Cuthbert, Norma R., "To Molly: Five Early Letters from Robert E. Lee to His Wife," *Huntington Library Quarterly* (May 1952).

Daniel, Frederick S., *The Richmond Examiner During the War.* New York, 1868.

Darby, John Fletcher, *Personal Recollections.* St. Louis, 1880.

Darrow, Caroline Baldwin (Mrs.), "Recollections of the Twiggs Surrender," in Johnson and Buel, eds., *Battles and Leaders of the Civil War*, I, 33–39.

Davis, Jefferson, "Robert E. Lee," *North American Review* (January 1890).

deButts, Mary Custis Lee, ed., *Growing Up in the 1850s: The Journal of Agnes Lee.* Chapel Hill, NC, 1984.

DeLeon, T. C., *Four Years in Rebel Capitals.* Mobile, AL, 1890.

Dowdey, Clifford, and Louis H. Manarin, eds., *The Wartime Papers of R. E. Lee.* Boston, 1961.

Early, Jubal Anderson, *War Memoirs*, ed. Frank E. Vandiver. Bloomington, IN, 1960.

Eggleston, George Cary, *A Rebel's Recollections.* Bloomington, IN, 1959.

Eighth U.S. Census (1860).

Ellis, Edward S., *The Camp Fires of General Lee.* Philadelphia, 1886.

Ewing, J. W., "An Incident in the Life of R. E. Lee," in Riley, ed., *General Robert E. Lee After Appomattox.*

Forsyth, George A., "The Closing Scene at Appomattox Court House," *Harper's Magazine* (April 1898).

Fremantle, Arthur James Lyon, *The Frematle Diary*, ed. Walter Lord. New York, 1954.

Goode, John, *Recollections of a Lifetime.* Washington, DC, 1906.

Gordon, E. C., "Recollections of General Robert E. Lee's Administration As President of Washington College," in Riley, ed., *General Robert E. Lee After Appomattox.*

Gordon, John B., *Reminiscences of the Civil War.* New York, 1903.

Grant, Ulysses S., *Memoirs and Selected Letters*, eds., Mary Drake McFeely and William S. McFeely. New York, 1990.

Graves, C. A., "General Lee at Lexington," in Franklin L. Riley, ed., *General Robert E. Lee After Appomattox.*

" 'The Greatest Service I Rendered the State': J. E. B. Stuart's Account of the Capture of John Brown," *Virginia Magazine of History and Biography*, 94 (July 1986).

Green, Israel, "The Capture of John Brown," *North American Review* (December 1885).

Harrison, Constance Cary, *Recollections Grave and Gay*. New York, 1911.

Heller, J. Roderick, III, and Carolyn Ayres Heller, eds., *The Confederacy Is on Her Way Up the Spout: Letters to South Carolina, 1861–1864*. Athens, GA, 1992.

Hemphill, W. Edwin, et al eds., *The Papers of John C. Calhoun. 21 vols. to date* Columbia, SC, 1976.

Hill, Daniel H., "Lee Attacks North of the Chickahominy," in Johnson and Buel, eds., *Battles and Leaders of the Civil War,* II, 347–62.

———, "McClellan's Change of Base and Malvern Hill," in Johnson and Buel, eds., *Battles and Leaders of the Civil War,* II, 383–95.

Historical Register of Harvard University 1836–1936. Cambridge, MA, 1937.

Hood, John B., *Advance and Retreat,* new ed., intro. by Richard N. Current. Bloomington, IN, 1959.

Hughes, George W., *"Memoir"* in *Senate Executive Documents,* 31st Congress, 1st Session.

Humphreys, M. W., "Reminiscences of General Lee as President of Washington College," in Riley, ed., *General Robert E. Lee After Appomattox.*

Imboden, John D., "The Confederate Retreat From Gettysburg," in Johnson and Buel, eds., *Battles and Leaders of the Civil War,* III, 420–28.

Johnson, Robert Underwood, and Clarence Clough Buel, eds., *Battles and Leaders of the Civil War.* 4 vols., New York, 1887.

Johnston, Joseph E., ed. Frank E. Vandiver, *Narrative of Military Operations.* New York, 1874.

Jones, J. William, *Life and Letters of Robert Edward Lee, Soldier and Man.* Washington, DC, 1906.

———, *Personal Reminiscences of General Robert E. Lee.* United States Historical Society ed., Richmond, VA, 1989.

Joynes, Edward S., "General Robert E. Lee as College President," in Riley, ed., *General Robert E. Lee After Appomattox.*

Keyes, E. D., *Fifty Years Observation of Men and Events.* New York, 1884.

Lee, Fitzhugh, *General Lee.* New York, 1904.

Lee, H., *Observations on the Writings of Thomas Jefferson, With Particular Reference to the Attack They Contain on the Memory of the Late General Henry Lee,* 2nd ed., ed. Charles Carter Lee. Philadelphia, 1839.

Lee, Henry, *Memoirs of the War in the Southern Department of the United States,* ed. Robert E. Lee. New York, 1869.

Lee Reports. *Senate Executive Documents,* 25th Congress, 2nd Session, vol. I; 3rd Session, vol. I; and 26th Congress, 1st Session, vol. I.

Lee, Robert E., Jr., *Recollections and Letters of General Robert E. Lee.* New York, 1905.

Lee, Susan P., *Memoirs of William Nelson Pendleton.* Philadelphia, 1893.

Letters from the Secretary of War. *Senate Executive Documents,* 27th Congress, 2nd Session, vol. IV, and 3rd Session, vol. I.

Long, A. L., *Memoirs of Robert E. Lee.* Blue and Grey Press ed., Secaucus, NJ, 1983.

Longstreet, James, "The Battle of Fredericksburg," in Johnson and Buel, eds., *Battles and Leaders of the Civil War,* III, 70–85.

———, *From Manassas to Appomattox: Memoirs of the Civil War in America.* Philadelphia, 1896.

———, "The Invasion of Maryland," in Johnson and Buel, eds., *Battles and Leaders of the Civil War,* II, 663–74.

———, "Lee's Invasion of Pennsylvania," in Johnson and Buel, eds., *Battles and Leaders of the Civil War,* III, 244–50.

———, "Lee's Right Wing at Gettysburg," in Johnson and Buel, eds., *Battles and Leaders of the Civil War,* III, 339–53.

———, "Our March Against Pope," in Johnson and Buel, eds., *Battles and Leaders of the Civil War,* II, 512–26.

Marshall, Charles, "General Lee's Farewell Address to His Army," in Johnson and Buel, eds., *Battles and Leaders of the Civil War,* IV, 747.

Maurice, Frederick, ed., *An Aide-de-Camp of Lee . . . Charles Marshall. . . .* Boston, 1927.

McCaleb, Walter F., ed. John H. Reagan, *Memoirs with Special Reference to Secession and the Civil War.* New York, 1906.

McClellan, H. B., *The Life and Campaigns of Major-General J. E. B. Stuart.* Boston and New York, 1885.

Missouri Historical Society, *Glimpses of the Past,* III (January–February 1936), "Letters of Robert E. Lee to Henry Kayser 1838–1846."

Moger, Allen W., "Letters to General Lee After the War," *Virginia Magazine of History and Biography,* 64 (January 1956).

Monroe, Haskell M., Jr., and James T. McIntosh, eds., *The Papers of Jefferson Davis.* Baton Rouge, LA, 1971.

Morgan, W. H., *Personal Reminiscences of the War of 1861–65.* . . . Lynchburg, VA, 1911.

Mosby, John S., *Memoirs of John S. Mosby,* ed. Charles W. Russell. Boston, 1917.

Myers, William Starr, ed., *The Mexican War Diary of George B. McClellan.* Princeton, NJ, 1917.

New York Herald, "Inauguration of General Lee," in Riley, ed., *General Robert E. Lee After Appomattox.*

Owen, William Miller, *In Camp and Battle with the Washington Artillery.* Boston, 1885; 2nd ed., New Orleans, 1964.

Parks, Leighton, "What a Boy Saw of the Civil War," *Century Magazine,* 70 (June 1905).

Pember, Phoebe Yates, *A Southern Woman's Story: Life in Confederate Richmond.* Mockingbird Books ed., St. Simons Island, GA, 1974.

Pollard, Edward A., *The First Year of the War.* Richmond, VA, 1862, and corrected and improved ed., Richmond, VA, 1863.

Preston, Margaret J. (Mrs.), "General Lee After the War," *Century Magazine,* 38 (June 1889).

Reese, George H., ed., *Proceedings of Virginia State Convention of 1861.* 4 vols., Richmond, VA, 1965.

Report of the Joint Committee on Reconstruction. 39th Congress, 1st Session. Washington, DC, 1866.

Riley, Franklin L., ed., *General Robert E. Lee After Appomattox.* New York, 1930.

Robertson, James I., Jr., ed., *Proceedings of the Advisory Council of the State of Virginia, April 21–June 19, 1861.* Richmond, VA, 1977.

Rutland, Robert A., et al., eds. *The Papers of James Madison: Presidential Series.* 2 vols. Charlottesville, VA, 1984.

Scarborough, William Kauffman, ed., *The Diary of Edmund Ruffin,* 3 vols., Baton Rouge, LA, 1972–89.

Scheibert, Captain Justus, *Seven Months in the Rebel States During the North American War, 1863,* trans. Joseph C. Hayes and ed. William Stanley Hoole. Tuscaloosa, AL, 1958.

———, *Der Bergerkrieg in den nordamerikanischen Staaten.* Berlin, 1874.

Scott, Winfield, *Memoirs of Lieut.-General Scott.* New York, 1864.

Scott's Report of the Battle of Mexico City. *Senate Executive Documents,* 30th Congress, 1st Session, vol. I.

Scott's Report of Cerro Gordo. *Senate Executive Documents,* 30th Congress, 1st Session, vol. I.

Scott's Report of Contreras and Churubuco. *Senate Executive Documents,* 30th Congress, 1st Session, vol. I.

["Pillow Talk"]. *Senate Executive Documents,* 30th Congress, 1st Session, vol. VIII. Seventh U.S. Census (1850).

Somel, G. Moxley, *Recollections of a Confederate Staff Officer.* Jackson, TN, 1958.

Stephens, Alexander H., *A Constitutional View of the Late War Between the States.* 2 vols., Chicago, 1868–70.

Stiles, John C., "One of War's Mysteries," *Confederate Veteran,* 29 (June 1921).

Stiles, Robert, *Four Years Under Marse Robert.* Morningside Bookshop ed., Dayton, OH, 1977.

Shackelford, George Green, ed., "From the Society's Collections: Lieutenant Lee Reports to Captain Talcott on Fort Calhoun's Construction at Rip Raps," *Virginia Magazine of History and Biography,* 60 (July 1952).

Taylor, Walter, *Four Years with General Lee.* New York, 1878.

———, *General Lee: His Campaigns in Virginia 1861–1865.* Morningside ed., Dayton, OH, 1975.

Thomas, H. W., *History of the Doles Cooke Brigade.* Atlanta, GA, 1903.

Tragle, Henry Irving, *The Southhampton Slave Revolt of 1831: A Compilation of Source Material.* Amherst, MA, 1971.

Twain, Mark, *Life on the Mississippi.* New York, 1874 and 1875.

U.S. War Department, *War of the Rebellion, A Compilation of the Official Records of the Union and Confederate Armies.* 70 vols. in 127, Washington, DC, 1880–1901.

Valentine, Edward V., "Reminiscences of General Lee," in Riley, ed., *General Robert E. Lee After Appomattox.*

———, "Reminiscences of General Lee," *The Outlook,* 84 (December 1906).

Valentine, Elizabeth Gray, *Dawn to Twilight: The Works of Edward V. Valentine.* Richmond, VA, 1929.

Venable, Charles S., "Campaign from the Wilderness to Petersburg," *Southern Historical Society Papers,* XIV (1886).

———, "General Lee in the Wilderness Campaign," in Johnson and Buel, eds., *Battles and Leaders of the Civil War,* IV, 240–46.

von Borcke, Heros, *Memoirs of the Confederate War for Independence.* 2 vols., Morningside ed., Dayton, OH, 1985.

War Diary and Letters of Stephen Minot Weld, 1861–1865. 2nd ed., Boston, 1979.

Williams, G. A., "Light on a War Mystery," *Confederate Veteran,* 29 (July 1921).

Williams, T. Harry, ed., *With Beauregard in Mexico: The Mexican War Reminiscences of P. G. T. Beauregard.* Baton Rouge, LA, 1956.

Woodward, C. Vann, ed., *Mary Chestnut's Civil War.* New Haven, 1981.

Worsham, John H., *One of Jackson's Foot Calvary.* Jackson, TN, 1961.

SECONDARY WORKS: BOOKS

Writings directly about Robert E. Lee divide broadly into two classes. The first, best exemplified by Douglas Southall Freeman's majestic four volumes of *R. E. Lee: A Biography,* present Lee as a secular saint cum military genius. The second species, the best of which is Thomas L. Connelly's *The Marble Man: Robert E. Lee and His Image in American Society,* the worst, Alan T. Nolan, *Lee Considered: General Robert E. Lee and Civil War History,* is revisionist. Connelly and others pose serious questions about Lee's character and command. This biography most likely qualifies historiographically as "post revisionism."

Below are the secondary sources used for this work that touch on Lee and related topics.

Ambrose, Stephen E., *Duty, Honor, Country: A History of West Point.* Baltimore, 1966.

Andrews, J. Cutler, *The South Reports the Civil War.* Princeton, NJ, 1970.

Armes, Ethel, *Stratford Hall: The Great House of the Lees.* Richmond, VA, 1936.

Bauer, K. Jack, *The Mexican War, 1846–1848.* New York, 1974.

Boney, Francis N., *John Letcher of Virginia: The Story of Virginia's Civil War Governor.* University Press, AL, 1966.

Boyd, Thomas, *Light-Horse Harry Lee.* New York, 1931.

Bridges, Hal, *Lee's Maverick General: Daniel Harvey Hill.* New York, 1961.

Christian, W. Asbury, *Richmond: Her Past and Present.* Richmond, VA, 1912.

Cleaves, Freeman, *Meade of Gettysburg.* Reprint, Norman, OK, 1991.

Coddington, Edwin, B., *The Gettysburg Campaign: A Study in Command.* New York, 1968.

Connelly, Thomas, L., *The Marble Man: Robert E. Lee and His Image in American Society.* New York, 1977.

———, and Barbara Bellows, *God and General Longstreet: The Lost Cause and the Southern Mind.* Baton Rouge, LA, 1982.

———, and Archer Jones, *The Politics of Command: Factions and Ideas in Confederate Strategy.* Baton Rouge, LA, 1973.

Coulling, Mary P., *The Lee Girls.* Winston-Salem, NC, 1987.

Crenshaw, Ollinger, *General Lee's College: The Rise and Growth of Washington and Lee University.* New York, 1969.

Crooke, D. P., *The North, the South, and the Powers, 1861–1865.* New York, 1974.

Dabney, Virginius, *Pistols and Pointed Pens: The Dueling Editors and Old Virginia.* Chapel Hill, NC, 1987.

Davis, William C., *Battle of Bull Run: A History of the First Major Campaign of the Civil War.* Garden City, NY, 1977.

———, *Duel Between the Ironclads.* Garden City, NY, 1975.

———, *Jefferson Davis: The Man and His Hour.* New York, 1991.

Dowdey, Clifford, *Lee's Last Campaign.* Boston, 1960.

———, *The Seven Days: The Emergence of Lee.* Boston, 1964.

Dupuy, R. Ernest, *Where They Have Trod: The West Point Tradition in American Life.* New York, 1960.

Farrar, Emmie Ferguson, *Old Virginia Houses Along the James.* New York, 1957.

Farrar, Emmie Ferguson, and Emilee Hines, *Old Virginia Houses: The Northern Peninsulas.* New York, 1972.

Fleming, Gordon, *The Young Whistler, 1834–66.* London, 1978.

Flood, Charles Bracelen, *Lee: The Last Years.* Boston, 1981.

Foote, Shelby, *The Civil War: A Narrative.* 3 vols., New York, 1968–75.

Forman, Sidney, *West Point: A History of the United States Military Academy.* New York, 1950.

Frassanito, William A., *Gettysburg: A Journey in Time.* New York, 1975.

Freeman, Douglas S., *Lee's Lieutenants: A Study in Command.* 3 vols., New York, 1942–44.

Freeman, Douglas S., *R. E. Lee: A Biography.* 4 vols., New York, 1934–35.

Furgurson, Ernest B., *Chancellorsville, 1863: The Souls of the Brave.* New York, 1992.

Gallagher, Gary W., ed., *The First Day at Gettysburg.* Kent, OH, 1992.

Geddes, Jean, *Fairfax County Historical Highlights from 1607.* Middleburg, VA, 1967.

Gordon-Burr, Lesley, "Assumed a Darker Hue: Major General George E. Pickett, May 1863–May 1864," M.A. thesis, University of Georgia, 1991.

Green, Constance McLaughlin, *Washington: Village and Capital 1800–1878.* Princeton, NJ, 1962.

Hamlin, Percy G., *"Old Bald Head" (General R. S. Ewell): The Portrait of a Soldier* Strasburg, VA, 1940.

Hassler, Warren, W., Jr., *Crisis at the Crossroads: The First Day at Gettysburg.* Montgomery, AL, 1970.

Henderson, G. F. R., *Stonewall Jackson and the American Civil War.* 2 vols., New York, 1898.

Hendrick, Burton J., *The Lees of Virginia: Biography of a Family.* New York, 1935.

Hennessy, John, *Return to Bull Run: The Campaign and Battle of Second Manassas.* New York, 1993.

Herbert, Walter H., *Fighting Joe Hooker.* Indianapolis, IN, 1944.

Johannsen, Robert W., *To the Halls of Montezuma: The Mexican War in the American Imagination.* New York, 1985.

Johnson, A. Sidney, et al., *An Ecological Survey of the Coastal Region of Georgia.* National Park Service Scientific Monograph, series no. 3, Washington, DC, 1974.

Jones, Virgil Carrington, *Eight Hours Before Richmond.* New York, 1957.

King, Alvy L., *Louis T. Wigfall: Southern Fire-eater.* Baton Rouge, LA, 1970.

Krick, Robert K., *Stonewall Jackson at Cedar Mountain.* Chapel Hill, NC, 1990.

Lamers, William M., *The Edge of Glory: A Biography of William S. Rosecrans, U.S.A.* New York, 1961.

Leech, Margaret, *Reveille in Washington, 1860–1865.* New York, 1941.

Luvaas, Jay, and Col. Harold W. Nelson, *The US Army War College Guide to the Battle of Antietam.* Carlisle, PA, 1987.

———, eds., *The US Army War College Guide to the Battles of Chancellorsville and Fredericksburg.* Carlisle, PA, 1988.

———, eds., *The US Army War College Guide to the Battle of Gettysburg.* Carlisle, PA, 1986.

Lyle, Royster, Jr., and Sally Munger Mann, *The Architecture of Historic Lexington.* Charlottesville, VA, 1977.

MacDonald, Rose Mortimer Ellzey, *Mrs. Robert E. Lee.* Boston, 1939.

Marvel, William, *Burnside.* Chapel Hill, NC, 1991.

Matter, William D., *If It Takes All Summer: The Battle of Spotsylvania.* Chapel Hill, NC, 1988.

Mathews, Donald A., *Religion in the Old South.* Chicago, 1977.

McFeely, William S., *Grant: A Biography.* New York, 1981.

McWhiney, Grady, and Perry D. Jamieson, *Attack and Die: Civil War Military Tactics and the Southern Heritage.* University Press, AL, 1982.

Meredith, Roy, *The Face of Robert E. Lee in Life and Legend.* New York, 1947.

Miers, Earl Scherick, *The Last Campaign: Grant Saves the Union.* Philadelphia, 1972.

Moore, Albert B., *Conscription and Conflict in the Confederacy.* New York, 1924.

Moorison, James L., Jr., *"The Best School in the World": West Point, the Pre–Civil War Years 1833–1866.* Kent, OH, 1986.

Murfin, James V., *The Gleam of Bayonets: The Battle of Antietam and the Maryland Campaign of 1862.* New York, 1965.

Nagel, Paul C., *The Lees of Virginia: Seven Generations of an American Family.* New York, 1990.

Nevins, Allan, *The War for the Union.* Vol. I, *The Improvised War, 1861–1862.* New York, 1959.

Nolan, Alan T., *Lee Considered: General Robert E. Lee and Civil War History.* Chapel Hill, NC, 1991.

Oates, Stephen B., *To Purge This Land with Blood: A Biography of John Brown.* New York, 1970.

Patrick, Rembert W., *The Fall of Richmond.* Baton Rouge, LA, 1960.

Pfanz, Harry W., *Gettysburg: The Second Day*. Chapel Hill, NC, 1987.
Piston, William G., *Lee's Tarnished Lieutenant: James Longstreet and His Place in Southern History*. Athens, GA, 1987.
Preston, Walter Creigh, *Lee: West Point and Lexington*. Yellow Spring, OH, 1934.
Primm, James Neal, *Lion of the Valley: St. Louis, Missouri*. Boulder, CO, 1981.
Rister, Carl Coke, *Robert E. Lee in Texas*. Norman, OK, 1946.
Robertson, James I., Jr., *General A. P. Hill: The Story of a Confederate Warrior*. New York, 1987.
Roland, Charles P., *Albert Sidney Johnston, Soldier of Three Republics*. Austin, TX, 1964.
Royster, Charles, *Light-Horse Harry Lee and the Legacy of the American Revolution*. Cambridge, Engl., 1982.
Sanborn, Margaret, *Robert E. Lee*. 2 vols., Philadelphia, 1966–67.
Scott, Mary Wingfield, *Houses of Old Richmond*. New York, 1941.
Scott, Robert Garth, *Into the Wilderness with the Army of the Potomac*. Bloomington, IN, 1985.
Sears, Stephen W., *George B. McClellan: The Young Napoleon*. New York, 1988.
———, *Landscape Turned Red: The Battle of Antietam*. New York, 1983.
———, *To the Gates of Richmond: The Peninsula Campaign*. New York, 1992.
Simpson, Brooks D., *Let Us Have Peace: Ulysses S. Grant and the Politics of War and Reconstruction, 1861–1868*. Chapel Hill, NC, 1991.
Simpson, Craig M., *A Good Southerner: The Life of Henry A. Wise of Virginia*. Chapel Hill, NC, 1985.
Singletary, Otis A., *The Mexican War*. Chicago, 1960.
Sommers, Richard J., *Richmond Redeemed: The Siege at Petersburg*. New York, 1981.
Stackpole, Edward J., *Drama on the Rappahannock: The Frederickburg Campaign*. Harrisburg, PA, 1957.
Stampp, Kenneth M., *America in 1857: A Nation on the Brink*. New York, 1990.
Starr, Stephen Z., *The Union Calvary in the Civil War*. 3 vols., Baton Rouge, LA, 1979, 1981, and 1985.
Steere, Edward, *The Wilderness Campaign*. Harrisburg, PA, 1960.
Stewart, George R., *Pickett's Charge: A Microhistory of the Final Attack at Gettysburg, July 3, 1983*. Boston, 1959.
Still, William N., Jr., *Iron Afloat: The Story of the Confederate Armorclads*. Nashville, TN, 1971.
Symonds, Craig L., *Joseph E. Johnston: A Civil War Biography*. New York, 1992.
Tanner, Robert G., *Stonewall in the Valley: Thomas J. "Stonewall" Jackson's Shenandoah Valley Campaign, Spring, 1862*. Garden City, NY, 1976.
Temin, Peter, *The Jacksonian Economy*. New York, 1969.
Thomas, Emory M., *Bold Dragoon: The Life of J. E. B. Stuart*. New York, 1986.
———, *The Confederate Nation, 1861–1865*. New York, 1979.
———, *The Confederate State of Richmond: A Biography of the Capital*. Austin, TX, 1971.
———, *Travels of Hallowed Ground: A Historian's Journey to the American Civil War*. Columbia, SC, 1987.
Thomason, John W., Jr., *Jeb Stuart*. New York, 1930.
Trudeau, Noah Andre, *Bloody Roads South: The Wilderness to Cold Harbor*. Boston, 1990.
———, *The Last Citadel: Petersburg, Virginia, June 1864–April 1865*. Boston, 1991.
Vandiver, Frank E., *Basic History of the Confederacy*. Princeton, NJ, 1962.
———, *Mighty Stonewall*. New York, 1957.
Warner, Ezra J., *Generals in Blue: Lives of the Union Commanders*. Baton Rouge, LA, 1964.
———, *Generals in Gray: Lives of the Confederate Commanders*. Baton Rouge, LA, 1959.
Weigley, Russell F., *The American Way of War: A History of United States Military Strategy and Policy*. New York, 1973.
Weinert, Richard P., Jr., and Col. Robert Arthur, *Defender of the Chesapeake: The Story of Fort Monroe*. Shippensburg, PA, 1989.
Weintraub, Stanley, *Whistler: A Biography*. New York, 1974.
Wessels, William L., *Born to Be a Soldier: The Military Career of William Wing Loring of St. Augustine, Florida*. Fort Worth, FL, 1971.
White, Leonard, D., *The Jacksonians: A Study in Administrative History, 1829–1861*. New York, 1954.
———, *The Jeffersonians: A Study in Administrative History, 1801–1829*. New York, 1951.
Wills, Bryan Steel, "In Charge: Command Relationships in the Suffolk Campaign, 1863," M.A. thesis, University of Georgia, 1985.

Winston, Robert W., *Robert E. Lee.* New York, 1934.
Wyatt-Brown, Bertram, *Southern Honor: Ethics and Behavior in the Old South.* New York, 1982.
————, *Yankee Saints and Southern Sinners.* Baton Rouge, LA, 1985.
Zinn, Jack, *R. E. Lee's Cheat Mountain Campaign.* Parson, WV, 1974.

SECONDARY WORKS: ARTICLES AND ESSAYS

Bearss, Sara B., "The Farmer of Arlington: George W. P. Custis and the Arlington Sheep Shearings," *Virginia Cavalcade,* 38 (Winter 1989).
Carnes, Eva Margaret, "George W. (Bishop) Peterkin at Valley Mountain," *Randolph County Historical Society Magazine of History and Biography,* 12 (April 1961).
Connelly, Thomas L., "Vicksburg: Strategic Point or Propaganda Device," *Military Affairs,* XXXIV (1970).
Coulling, Mary P., "Nicknames, Cats, and Catsup Bottles: The Family Life of R. E. Lee," *W & L: The Alumni Magazine of Washington and Lee* (Winter 1989).
Drumm, Stella M., "Robert E. Lee and the Improvement of the Mississippi River," *Missouri Historical Society Collections,* 6 (February 1929).
Freeman, Douglas, "Lee & the Ladies: Unpublished Letters of Robert E. Lee," *Scribner's Magazine,* LXXVIII (October 1952).
Frye, Dennis E., "Drama Between the Rivers: Harpers Ferry in the 1862 Maryland Campaign," in Gallagher, ed., *Antietam: Essays on the 1862 Maryland Campaign.*
Gallagher, Gary W., "The Army of Northern Virginia in May 1864: A Crisis of High Command," *Civil War History,* 36 (June 1990).
————, ed. *Antietam: Essays on the 1862 Maryland Campaign.* Kent, OH, 1989.
————, ed. *The Second Day at Gettysburg.* Kent, OH, 1993.
Gignilliat, John L., "A Historian's Dilemma: A Posthumous Footnote for Freeman's *R. E. Lee,*" *Journal of Southern History,* XLIII (May 1977).
Krick, Robert K., "The Army of Northern Virginia in September 1862: Its Circumstances, Its Opportunities, and Why It Should Not Have Been at Sharpsburg," in Gallagher, ed., *Antietam: Essays on the 1862 Maryland Campaign.*
————, "If Longstreet . . . Says So, It Is Most Likely Not True: James Longstreet and the Second Day at Gettysburg," in Gallagher, ed., *The Second Day at Gettysburg.*
Luvaas, Jay, and Wilbur S. Nye, "The Campaign That History Forgot: Mine Run," *Civil War Times Illustrated,* VIII (1969).
Musser, Ruth, and John C. Krantz, Jr., "The Friendship of General Robert E. Lee and Dr. Wm. Beaumont," *Bulletin of the Institute of the History of Medicine,* VI (May 1938).
Myers, Mrs. Max W., "Sarah Beaumont: Her Life and Loves," *Missouri Historical Society Bulletin,* XVII (October 1960).
Parker, Elmer Otis, "Why Was Lee Not Pardoned?", *Prologue,* 2 (Winter 1970).
Rozear, Marvin P., et al., "R. E. Lee's Stroke," *Virginia Magazine of History and Biography,* 98 (April 1990).
Templeman, Eleanor Lee, "Ravensworth," *Historical Society of Fairfax County, Virginia,* 7 (1960–61).
Thomas, Emory M., "God and General Lee," *Anglican and Episcopal History,* LX (March 1991).

Index